AF599347

THE PALM COLLECTION AT THE JARDÍN BOTÁNICO CULIACÁN

THE PALM COLLECTION AT THE JARDÍN BOTÁNICO CULIACÁN

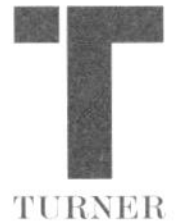

CONTENTS

FOREWORD

Agustín Coppel Luken

It is with great pleasure that I present this book that came about at the initiative of my son, Julián Coppel Gómez. With this publication we celebrate the recognition that the Jardín Botánico Culiacán (Botanical Garden of Culiacán) has obtained for its outstanding work in the National Palm Collection, as well as to make visible the effort of all the people involved in such a meaningful project.

I cannot recall an exact date which marks the origin of what has been accomplished today, because it would entail the moment in which the mother of Carlos Murillo Depraect established the first plant nursery in the city, or when he acquired the first palm of his collection; I wonder how far back we would need to go. The most interesting part is to think of the many years of hard work and dedication put in by so many of us; that is why this book aims to be, in a sense, the compilation of it all.

The National Palm Collection captivates me, I compare its creation with the act of collecting art, which always implies an exciting process: a search for that specific object or, in this case, that palm tree which is the single most attractive one, the rarest, the most exotic; the work of tracking it down, moving it, nurturing it, reproducing and nursing it for its survival and for the enjoyment of others that share a passion for the same kind of living things. As Antoine de Saint-Exupéry says in *The Little Prince*, it is the time and the work that you dedicate to something what makes it special; I want to express with this, that the collection, in addition to having a scientific nature, also has an emotional one. Because one cannot go and buy the National Palm Collection, one has to build it.

And indeed, this project has represented a difficult task, because the state of Sinaloa is not known for being a land of great palm diversity, which means that the majority of them have been brought from different territories; some from other parts of the world and many from national regions. My personal favorite is the *Chamaedorea tuerckheimii*, which you can find in the jungle, but, on many occasions, it remains unnoticed because of its small size and the fact that it grows in the understory of rainforest. What I like about this diminutive palm is that, apart from its very original and beautiful shape, it has all the characteristics of a larger palm only on a smaller scale. Due to its coveted beauty, this species has decreased in number over the last few years. For this reason it is difficult to find specimens in common spaces, they only exist in hard to reach areas, or in specialized collections, like the Jardín Botánico Culiacán.

Mexico is the country that has the highest number of species of the *Chamaedorea* genus and most of them grow in the wild, however, many of these species can already be found at the nursery of the Jardín Botánico Culiacán, which gives me great satisfaction because it means that each day we get closer to our goal of having the largest collection of palms in the country.

We understand that this endeavor implies an enormous responsibility, given that palm trees are living organisms and that we have to take care of them every single day of this year, the next year, the one that follows and so on; because the older the botanical garden gets, the more experience and recognition it will acquire. The latter also involves an increase in the number of visitors, which is why we are interested in promoting not only the beauty of the collection, but also its scientific and ecological background. For this purpose, we included the glossary at the end of the book, a section that will likely go unnoticed to scientists or people involved in the topic, but will be of great help for the non-professionals, allowing them to delve into the topic and make them fall in love with it.

To summarize, one of the goals of producing this book is that the visitors, both local and international, who approach the National Palm Collection, recognize the project, benefit from it and appreciate it. It is an effort to contribute to the research of such an important plant family, and at the same time, it is a review of the stage in which the collection finds itself at this point.

Finally, I would like to bring to mind the vision and endearment that Carlos Murillo Depraect dedicated to his collection. His learning about palms was born of passion; he studied botany out of sheer enjoyment. At some point, he invited me to collaborate and little by little, together we made the Jardín Botánico Culiacán grow.

I would like to thank Carlos Murillo Michel for his contributions, his appreciation and care towards the garden, a project that for him means not only a valuable and beautiful place, but a legacy from his father. Also, in recent years, Erika Pagaza Calderón, has been a cornerstone in the development of this space, she and her team of botanists have given shape to the garden with the biological research center, without which, the garden could not honor its name, because a botanical garden is only that which complies with purposes of scientific research, education and conservation.

Giving thanks always involves long lists of participants and it is impossible to mention everyone; my purpose is not to make the beginning of this fascinating book tiresome, however, I cannot fail to mention the invaluable support of Bárbara Apodaca, América Ávalos, Ernesto Beltrán, Carlos Gandarilla, Cuauhtémoc Niebla, Juan Rovalo, and Óscar Vélez.

In the same way, I want to thank the essential collaborations of Clementina Equihua Zamora, an eminent biologist specialized in plant ecology, and Scott Zona, a world-renowned botanist specialized in palms, with whom it has been an honor to work, even from afar. Likewise, I thank Miguel Ángel García Bielma who has played a fundamental role in collecting numerous specimens for the collection. Without any of the aforementioned, this great book would not have been possible.

THE JARDÍN BOTÁNICO CULIACÁN

Carlos Murillo Michel

Director of the Jardín Botánico Culiacán

Human beings are completely dependent upon plants. Aside from being one of our main sources of food, plants also purify the air, are used in the manufacture of countless objects essential to human survival, and provide ingredients for medicines used to cure diseases. Today, with the fast growth of the global population and of economic activity, the pressure on these resources has intensified to the point of driving many species to the verge of extinction. In particular, the negative effects of climate change on natural resources threaten the well-being, stability, and security of all human beings. It is urgently important, therefore, that people be educated about the responsible and sustainable use of plants, in order to mitigate climate change and conserve the environment.

The Jardín Botánico Culiacán was originally established and continues to grow as an agent of change in fostering harmonious relations between human beings and nature.

It was my father, Carlos Murillo Depraect, who founded the Jardín Botánico Culiacán. As a visionary individual of great wisdom, he cultivated a range of interests, from his work in construction (he was a civil engineer by profession), to the study of painting, to his great passion for astronomy. He owned countless books on this last subject and enjoyed taking photographs of constellations, galaxies, and planetary systems, which he shared in the form of slides through lectures on astronomy and at informal gatherings with friends. Surprisingly enough, even this interest did not equal his passion for botany and gardening, the hobbies to which he devoted the greater part of his attention.

He had inherited a love of plants from his mother, who started her first greenhouse at her home in downtown Culiacán back in the 1940s. There she cultivated and sold a variety of local species. My father's interest in botany came as no surprise, after growing up in such an environment. He started his first botanical collection in a garden in Culiacán that belonged to my maternal grandparents, where he undertook to gather and reproduce the species he found most interesting. At first, his choice of plants was mainly determined by their ornamental qualities, but he gradually became more involved with the scientific aspects of his collection. Thus, he managed to combine his skills and knowledge to create something different, something that brought together these two different aspects of nature.

For many years, the collection was just a hobby for my father: as a civil engineer, he had a career in the construction business. Fortunately, he was sometimes able to combine his love of plants with his professional activity, using specimens from his collection for the planter boxes of the buildings he constructed. As time went by, his fondness for plants also became widely known, so he received numerous commissions involving landscaping and the rehabilitation of public space. It was thanks to such projects that he began to conceive the idea of creating a space for the conservation of Culiacán's botanical heritage, a place where people could not only enjoy the beauty of nature but also learn about how important it is to care for and protect the environment. The public space projects commissioned by the state government taught him how a botanical garden of this kind should work, so he knew precisely what he wanted and how it would be administered.

In the 1980s, on returning to Culiacán after three months in Paris, my father met with Antonio Toledo Corro, the governor of the state of Sinaloa, at a club near the site now occupied by the botanical garden. There, he proposed the idea of purchasing the lot and turning it into a sanctuary, a green space, a botanical garden to be stocked initially with donations from his own collections.

Toledo Corro was thrilled by the idea, and in 1986 work began on the 75-acre lot, which, on the governor's initiative, was declared a protected green area by the state congress. The first infrastructure to be installed included some of the paths, the entrance area, and the restrooms. On December 29th, 1986, two days before the governor left office, the Jardín Botánico Culiacán was officially inaugurated. From then on, my father began moving his private collection to the new space, gradually establishing the various collections and different areas that make up the garden today. This continued for ten years: the space was opened to the public, with free admission, and managed by a public/private administration that—truth be told—was sadly inadequate, owing both to insufficient funding and to a lack enthusiasm on the part of the staff.

In 1990 my father met the Coppel brothers, who contacted him to plant the trees and do the landscaping for their Los Álamos real estate development. Months later, once the project had been completed, Agustín Coppel Luken paid a visit to my father at the botanical garden. Agustín recounts how my father gave him a tour of the place, passionately explaining each one of the species they came across. He was very impressed, not only by the garden itself, which he thought had great potential, but also by how knowledgeable and up-to-date my father was. He decided to find a way to put all of that knowledge to good use.

From the beginning, my father was very clear about the funding required for the garden and he proposed to Agustín the creation of the Sociedad Botánica y Zoológica de Sinaloa (Botanic and Zoological Society of Sinaloa), a nonprofit organization that would manage the garden, while at the same time promoting the general care and protection of green areas and fostering botanical research. All this was to be undertaken in a serious, formal manner, under the responsibility of highly qualified professionals.

In 1996, through the support of Agustín Coppel and of others who had been members of the board of the botanical garden and ecological park for years, the nonprofit organization as constituted today was finally established. Since that date, the Sociedad has been lending its support to the garden and to the efforts of its director. Through this organization, the Jardín Botánico Culiacán has been able to increase its funding, create a more efficient management—with less red tape and greater financial security—, and garner increased support from the state and municipal governments, helping it reach its full potential.

The Jardín Botánico Culiacán was established just over thirty years ago and it remains a testament to the vision and tenacity of its founder. The space has become a museum of living plants, where a large variety of species is displayed and preserved. Indeed, the research staff is working hard to create the National Palm Collection, which as of today already contains over 60 of 100 palm species that are found in Mexico.

This collection also originated with my father, for palms happened to be his favorite plants. He collected them with special enthusiasm, which is why the botanical garden possesses such a wide variety of species of this important botanical family. It is said that my father was also responsible for introducing the royal palm (*Roystonea regia*) into the landscape of Culiacán, as well as several other trees and plants that have become iconic in the city.

Engineer Murillo Depraect considered the creation of the Jardín Botánico Culiacán his greatest achievement. Even when it was going through difficult times, he was unable to part with it. He used to walk through the park every morning and give instructions to the gardeners. Although the development of the project has been, and remains, an ongoing struggle, we are proud to see how it has grown and how important it has become, in terms of both science and its impact on society.

This book is a result of the commitment of the Jardín Botánico Culiacán to fostering a greater understanding of the riches of our plant heritage. We hope it will contribute to the preservation, care, and safeguarding of these natural resources so indispensable to human beings.

AN INTRODUCTION TO THE PALM FAMILY

Scott Zona and Clementina Equihua

Ph.D. in Botany
Botanist, researcher, educator, and writer

Ph.D. in Biology
Botanist and science writer

Wherever civilizations arose in palm-rich regions of the world, human beings have turned to palms to solve problems of food, shelter, materials, and medicine. In some cases, humans came to depend completely on palms for their basic needs. In ancient Mesopotamia, the date palm (*Phoenix dactylifera*) was domesticated for its fruit. As a useful food crop, it was carried throughout the Middle East, North Africa, and the Mediterranean region. In India, *Phoenix sylvestris*, probably an ancestor of the date palm, fulfilled the human desire for two basic substances: sugar and alcohol. In Southeast Asia, the palmyra palm (*Borassus flabellifer*) and sugar palm (*Arenga pinnata*) also satisfied these needs, while in the Philippines, the nipa palm (*Nypa fruticans*) supplied the same commodities. The region's abundant rattans (the *Calamus* species and its relatives) provided durable materials for baskets, furniture, and construction work. On the island of New Guinea, vast swamps of the sago palm (*Metroxylon sagu*) were the major source of starch for generations of humans, long before rice or other grains arrived on the scene. Farther east, the coconut (*Cocos nucifera*) provided a sealed, portable source of potable water that allowed the ancient Polynesians to sail across the vast Pacific Ocean. In tropical Africa, the African oil palm

(*Elaeis guineensis*) was the source of a vitamin-rich edible oil that underpinned regional diets, as well as a sugary sap that readily fermented into alcohol. Another widespread palm in the area, *Borassus aethiopum* or the African palmyra palm, was a source of sugar and alcohol. In the American tropics, an area exceptionally rich in native palms, they were used for thatch (species in the *Sabal, Geonoma,* and *Manicaria* genera), oil (species in *Attalea* and *Oenocarpus*), sugar and alcohol (species in *Acrocomia, Pseudophoenix,* and *Jubaea*), edible "hearts" (species in *Sabal* and *Euterpe*) and edible fruits (species in *Mauritia, Bactris,* and *Euterpe*). All over the world, palms fueled human development, and in some inhospitable areas they made possible the very existence of civilization.

The importance of palms to human civilization can be seen in palm iconography, which goes back thousands of years. There is an unbroken iconographic link from the palms depicted on the pharaonic tombs, where they symbolized an everlasting paradise in the afterlife, to the palm-shaded beaches depicted in travel advertisements, where they symbolize paradise in this life, in the form of a holiday by the sea. Palms were stamped onto Punic coins in the fifth century BCE and were depicted inside eighth century Buddhist temples in Java. Among Christians, the palm became a symbol of both peace and victory, a symbol still to be seen in Christian churches on Palm Sunday.

Global civilization in the twenty-first century embraces palms, although our relationship with the plant might best be described as "complicated." We enjoy the convenience and flavor of packaged cookies, candies, and snacks, but the palm oil with which many of these are made is environmentally problematic. The African oil palm (*Elaeis guineensis*) is the source of both palm oil (from the fruit) and palm kernel oil (from the seeds). It is by far the most productive oil crop for tropical climates and, as a long-lived perennial crop (rather than an annual crop, like soybeans), it requires less input from farmers: it is planted only once, with fewer applications of pesticides and fertilizers. But palm oil has a dark side. Oil palm plantations are replacing forest in some of the most biologically diverse areas of the world (for example, in Peru, Indonesia, and Malaysia, and extending into Mexico as well). The plants and animals that live in those forests cannot live on oil palm plantations. Charismatic animals such as the orangutan of Borneo are losing out to them and have become a rallying cry for conservationists. Nevertheless, the demand for palm oil continues to rise.

The gentler side of our relationship with palms is our love of them as ornamental landscape plants. Exotic palms were the height of fashion in nineteenth century Europe, as conservatories, greenhouses, and even parlors were packed with a surprisingly wide array of species. Nurseries supplied palms collected in the tropics and collectors eagerly purchased the newest, rarest imports. Some species were even named in nursery catalogues, rather than in the scientific literature of the day. Nowadays, palms have seen a new surge in popularity, but the foci of this modern mania are in the warmer areas of the world, where palms can be grown outside in landscape settings. Thailand, Singapore, Queensland in Australia, and the US states of Hawaii, California, Texas, and Florida are now places with large and active communities of palm collectors. Some things never change: collectors continue to demand rare new species, whether as novelties or as status symbols. Unfortunately, overcollecting for the nursery trade has had a negative impact on the wild populations of some palms.

Palm use in all forms will surely increase with the passage of time. As lovers of these beautiful plants, what we have to do, besides enjoying them when we see them in gardens and in the wild, is to contribute to the legal trade. As with any other merchandise, we can promote and consume plants that have been produced and obtained legally. We encourage plant collectors to get information on the origin of the plants or other products that they are buying. Modern consumers read the labels and buy what least impacts the planet. This is also a good practice for palm consumers of any kind.

Palms and humans are bound to each other in both material and abstract ways that show no signs of diminishing. Palms are as important to our twenty-first century material culture as they were to the ancient Aztecs, and as ornamental features of gardens and resorts they are more important than ever.

The palm collection here at the Jardín Botánico Culiacán is now one of the largest collections of palm species in Mexico. Visitors will be able to see and learn about palms from all over the world, as well as about palms native to Mexico.

THE NATIONAL PALM COLLECTION: PRESERVATION AT THE JARDÍN BOTÁNICO CULIACÁN

Erika Pagaza Calderón

Master of Science
Scientific Director and Curator of the Jardín Botánico Culiacán

The central objective of the Jardín Botánico Culiacán is to promote awareness in the community of how an ethical understanding of and relationship with nature can be maintained. To this end, the botanical garden has sought to become an integral part of society: a multifaceted entity in which different disciplines, such as art, architecture, and botany can converge, offering visitors a memorable sensory experience that at the same time provokes reflection.

In order to achieve this goal, our educational department has developed various outreach programs for children and teenagers, the sectors of the population that visit the space most often. Our aim is to promote respect and care for the environment among young people, while conveying the importance of plants as one of the principal sources of human wellbeing.

Another purpose of the project and indeed one of the most important tasks of the botanical garden is the preservation of species in the face of an ongoing decrease in plant diversity. In order to achieve this, the Jardín Botánico Culiacán has created a program called "Trees of the Future Network" which consists of planting trees today so that future generations may enjoy them, even if those actually planting them will never be able to see them in their fully developed state.

The Jardín Botánico Culiacán also functions as a biological research center, where different plant species are identified and their specific characteristics, modes of reproduction, physiology, growth, development, and adaptations to the environment are studied, as well as their geographical distribution. We also work with endangered species, doing what we can to further their preservation.

The various species are planted in the garden in accord with qualitative, rather than quantitative, criteria. In other words, we seek to ensure that each species is cultivated in its ideal location, where it can help to create a landscape with identity, value, and a sustainable perspective.

With the help of our center for research and conservation, we have reproduced more than fifty native species, creating what I have called a "heritage landscape": a collection of the most important species in Sinaloa, which will eventually be donated to the city so that they can become an integral part of its urban landscape.

The botanical garden's central focus, the National Palm Collection, is also part of this effort: its aim is to conserve and cultivate specimens of every species of palm that currently exists in Mexico and so to ensure that those now in danger of extinction will never in fact disappear.

Although this project was only fully established in 2016, the original idea was conceived more than fifteen years ago, when biologist and researcher Javier Caballero Nieto met Carlos Murillo Depraect, the founder of the Jardín Botánico Culiacán. During that encounter, the two men shared their love of palms and imagined the possibility of gathering together, in a single space, specimens of all the palm species to be found in Mexico.

In 2007, following the death of Murillo Depraect, Dr. Caballero who was then the director of the botanical garden of the Universidad Nacional Autónoma de México (UNAM, National Autonomous University of Mexico) took up the idea again, proposing the project at a meeting of the Asociación Mexicana de Jardines Botánicos (Mexican Association of Botanical Gardens) as one of the improvements to be undertaken at the Jardín Botánico Culiacán.

A team was formed that included a number of well-known and enthusiastic scientists, such as Hermilo Quero Rico (a pioneer in the study of Mexican palms) and Miguel Ángel García Bielma (also a specialist in the area). Working with their field assistants, both of these scientists undertook an intensive search for palm species in even the remotest parts of Mexico. Rescues were performed in eight states of southern Mexico, as specimens of endangered species were transported across the country, to the city of Culiacán, where they were documented, replanted, and acclimatized, so that their conservation and reproduction could be ensured.

This arduous and painstaking work continues today, as part of an ongoing process: every day, more and more species from Mexico and other parts of the world are included in the collection; conservationists are working hard to find the best methods for their cultivation, reproduction, and dispersion, in order to ensure the survival of the species; and expeditions to different parts of Mexico are constantly being organized, so that all species native to the country may be added to the collection. We are confident that, within a few years, the National Palm Collection, will contribute to the reintroduction and reproduction of these species in their original habitats, and so to the restoration of the areas in which they used to grow, as part of a larger recovery of Mexico's natural heritage.

Palms are currently one of the botanical families with the greatest potential for use and consumption by human beings. Many species have great economic, cultural, and ecological value, as the source of many different materials. One of the most remarkable features of these plants is their resilience: they have an enormous capacity for adaptation, even when they have been burnt, cut down, or damaged by hurricanes. When we visit the Palmetum, it is important to understand the properties of the different species, apart from their beauty, and to imagine them in their natural habitats, which range from rain forests to deserts.

Although the National Palm Collection remains a challenge for the Jardín Botánico Culiacán, it is also its greatest pride. We are able to share with a wider public one of the most beautiful and important botanical collections ever documented in the history of our country. In 2017 the Asociación Mexicana de Jardines Botánicos recognized our collection as being the most representative in the country, containing as it does more than 60 of the over 100 species currently found in Mexico.

Through its many activities, the Jardín Botánico Culiacán reaffirms its stance in favor of sustainable development and public awareness. It is a public space that owes its existence to a collaboration between government (both state and municipal) and the private sector, in the form of the Sociedad Botánica y Zoológica de Sinaloa. Of course, it also thrives on the love, patience, and enthusiasm of the scientists, gardeners, and volunteers who contribute on a daily basis to its growth and operation.

THE PALMETUM AT THE JARDÍN BOTÁNICO CULIACÁN

Miguel Ángel García Bielma

Master of Science
Botanic collector and Mexican palm specialist

The Jardín Botánico Culiacán's National Palm Collection is the largest and most important of its kind in Mexico, with more than 100 species of the botanical family *Arecaceae*: palms. Some of its specimens come from different parts of the world and, of course, others are endemic to Mexico. The Palmetum is home to the world's largest species of palm tree (*Corypha umbraculifera*) and the smallest (*Chamaedorea tenella*); one from Africa (*Elaeis guineensis*), and also, one of the only two native European species (*Chamaerops humilis*); one that has large thorns and another that seems to be covered in velvet. The sheer diversity of shapes and textures on display is extraordinary.

Humans have a time-honored and cultural connection to this group of plants: palms are a source of food, their fibers are worked to produce basketry and handcrafts such as hats; and their foliage is used for housing construction, flower arrangements and traditional ceremonies. Furthermore, palm oil is a mainstay for the economy of many communities and regions. Even though they are highly appreciated as ornamental and shade-giving plants, they face several threats that could lead to their extinction.

This collection began with ornamental plants but has since evolved to include palm trees not only for exhibition but also for reproduction. A seed bank has also been set up since numbers have dwindled drastically in their original ecosystems such as tropical forests, which provide a habitat for more than half of the species of palm trees.

In their natural state, palm trees perform an important ecological function. A third of them grow in low-humidity environments, where the fauna depends on their flowers, fruits and foliage for sustenance, and they also provide shelter from the scorching sun. Many species also grow in humid zones. In the tropical regions, they are source of nourishment for animals such as birds, bats, mice, and monkeys, and they also prevent soil erosion, nurse other plants, and generate microenvironments.

However, changes to natural regions and increasing urbanization have had a negative impact on the population of palm trees in their normal habitat. The cutting and burning of forests for livestock and agricultural activities, compounded by the trafficking of exotic species, are common threats to the survival of several species, including palm trees.

Even more worrying is that the vast majority of palm trees' biological diversity has been wiped out, signifying an irreparable genetic loss. This underscores the importance of collections such as the one held in the Jardín Botánico Culiacán that provide a shelter for this botanical family. This will benefit future research and projects that could mitigate this threat, not only in Mexico but also throughout South America, Asia, and Africa, where they are also at risk. This work means Mexico is playing a leading role on the world stage. The Palmetum has undoubtedly become a remarkable collection, not only for the area of Culiacán, but more widely for the state of Sinaloa and Mexico as a whole. It can make an impact—through specific actions—by protecting species facing the greatest risk of extinction. Apart from promoting their production for ornamental purposes, the Jardín Botánico Culiacán also participates in training researchers who nurture and preserve these plants.

The importance of palm trees is undeniable as a species that has evolved alongside humanity. Its future is intertwined with ours.

WHAT IS A PALM?

Scott Zona and Clementina Equihua

Ph.D. in Botany
Botanist, researcher, educator, and writer

Ph.D. in Biology
Botanist and science writer

Palms comprise a family of flowering plants known to botanists as the *Arecaceae* or *Palmae*. They are related to grasses, gingers, bananas, and bromeliads, as well as, very distantly, to agaves, dracaenas, and orchids. Cycads and tree-ferns, which have a palm-like growth habit, are not flowering plants and, consequently, are not related to palms at all. Palms comprise an ancient lineage of plants, the extant members of which are classified into 181 genera and around 2,500 species.

Palms, like other plants, are known by their popular names, but each one also has a scientific name and fits into a meticulous system of classification. The taxonomic classification of the coconut palm, *Cocos nucifera*, is shown here:

Domain: *Eukaryota*
- Kingdom: *Plantae*
  - Division: *Spermatophytina*
    - Class: Magnoliopsida
      - Order: Arecales
        - Family: *Arecaceae*
          - Genus: *Cocos*
            - Species: *Cocos nucifera*

There are many unique features found only in palms. Palm roots are unique among angiosperms in having cell walls in which the cellulose fibrils are randomly oriented. Also, the stems of palms have no secondary thickening, meaning that the stems do not add to their circumference once they reach maturity. While this feature is not unique to palms, it is uncommon elsewhere in the plant kingdom. Stems in climbing palms (rattans) can be extraordinarily long. The longest single stem in the plant kingdom belongs to an Asian rattan, *Calamus manan*, for which a length of 554 feet has been recorded. By comparison, the tallest tree in the world, the sequoia of California (*Sequoia sempervirens*), is only 377 feet tall. If the rattan were a self-supporting tree, it would be much taller than a sequoia.

The leaves of palms are their most distinctive feature: they are large and plicate (folded like an accordion), with bases that clasp and encircle the stem. The largest leaf in the plant kingdom is the leaf of an African palm, *Raphia regalis*, which has been recorded at 82 feet long. The development of a palm's leaf blade is unique. The embryonic leaf blade undergoes differential growth, with some areas growing faster than others. This growth causes the plicate folds in the blade. Later, the leaf develops splits owing to programmed cell death. These splits allow the segment of the leaf to be separate at maturity, as for example the segments of a coconut palm leaf. The process of folding and then splitting is unique to palms, being found in no other family of plants.

The flowers of palms are small and not very distinctive: they usually have three sepals, three petals, six stamens, and a gynoecium (pistil) of three united carpels. In this respect, they are similar to the flowers of agaves and lilies, which are usually larger and showier than palm flowers. What palm flowers lack in size, however, they can make up for in quantity. Some palms have flower clusters bearing millions of individual flowers.

The fruits and seeds of palms are relatively large. In fact, the largest, heaviest seed in the plant kingdom is that of the double-coconut or *coco de mer* palm (*Lodoicea maldivica*). Its seed can take five to seven years to mature and weighs just under 40 pounds. Most palm seeds, of course, are smaller and less massive, but they are still, in general, larger than those of near relatives (grasses, bananas, gingers, bromeliads, etc.). One lineage within the palms, that of the coconut and its relatives, have seeds with an oily storage tissue (the endosperm). These palms are exploited for their oily seeds. All other palms have, as their storage product, complex polysaccharides called mannans, which are indigestible to humans and most animals, although some seed-eating insects can digest mannans.

A frequently asked question is: Are palms trees? Palm stems typically do not branch above ground (although there are some exceptions) and never increase in diameter with age. Moreover, they are not wood producers. Palms do not generally form large, shade-giving canopies like oak trees or mango trees. The structure and anatomy of their stems is very different from those of pines, oaks, or other trees. And a palm has far fewer leaves than even a small oak tree. On the other hand, palms are often tall and co-occur with trees in the upper stratum of a forest. Their stems are hard and woody and can be used for construction. Birds, bats, and other animals build nests or take refuge in tall palms as they do in trees. They visit the flowers and eat the fruits of tall palms, just as they do other trees.

So are palms trees? The answer depends on the context of the question and of the species. Obviously, small palms and liana palms are not trees. Tall palms may be trees in the ecological sense, but not in terms of landscape design, as having arborescent shapes. But if tall palms are not trees, what are they? They are palms.

The different forms, colors, and textures of palm leaves, the flowers in attractive clusters, and the beautiful fruits that range from green to cream, yellow, red, purple, or black, are some of the unmistakable characteristics of palms, true princes of the plant kingdom.

I

MATURE PALMS

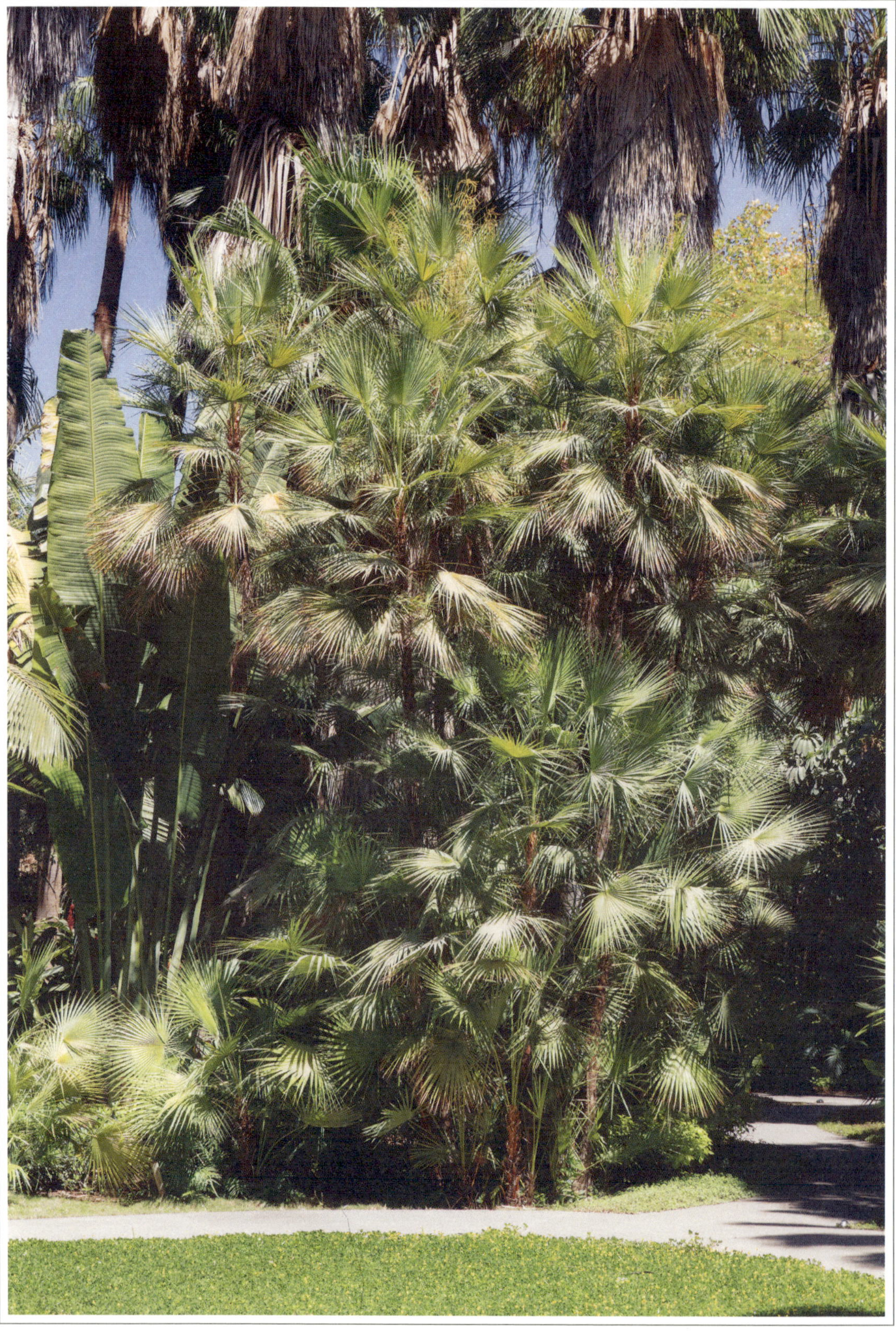

1

EVERGLADES PALM

Acoelorrhaphe wrightii (Griseb. & H.Wendl.) H.Wendl. ex Becc.

Status: Assessment of global conservation status required
Distribution: The Bahamas, Florida, Cuba, the Yucatán Peninsula, and the Caribbean coast of Central America

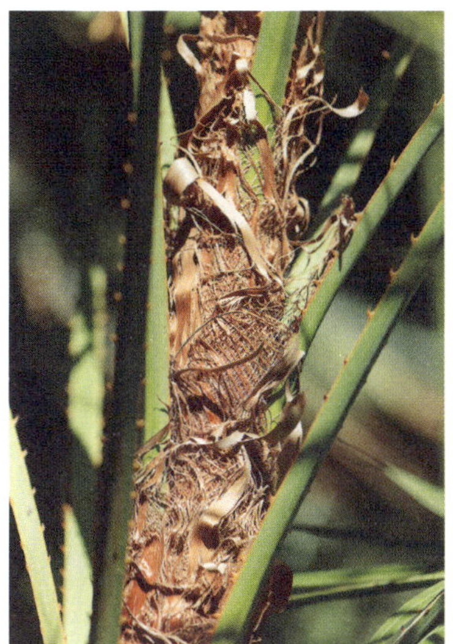
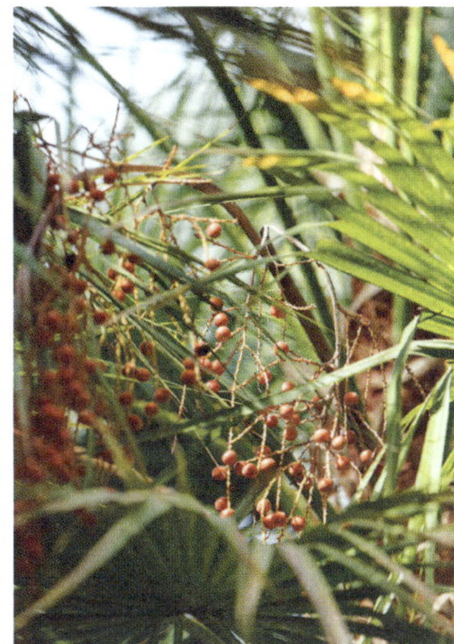
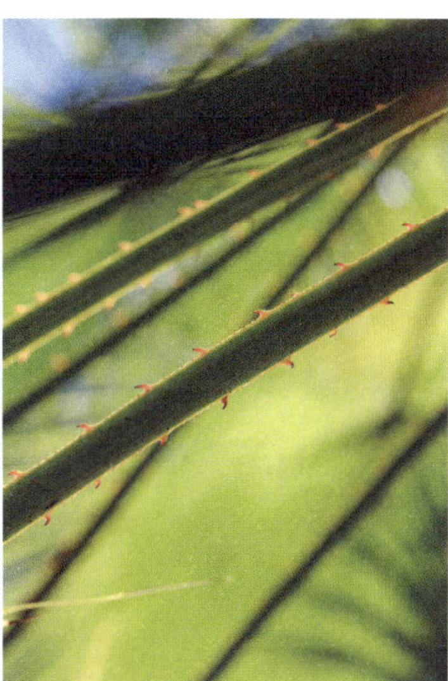

1. Leaf bases. 2. Unripe fruits. 3. Teeth on the leaf-stalks.

This species, which may reach up to 26 feet tall, is widespread in low, seasonally flooded areas, and when close to the sea tolerates some salinity. This palm produces large clumps of slender stems, each bearing a few fan-shaped leaves. The leaf-stalks are armed with large curved teeth. The palm produces an annual crop of small purple-black fruits, which are eaten by birds. Although the plants grow in flooded zones, the seeds germinate only when the flood waters recede: they cannot germinate underwater. It is a popular plant for gardening purposes (in public parks and private gardens) and in some areas of the Yucatán Peninsula it is used as an urban plant. The stems are used for building rustic houses and the leaves for making brooms.

The first specimen at the Jardín Botánico Culiacán was cultivated by Carlos Murillo Depraect. It was one of his favorites, so he always took special care of it. Biologists observed furrowed wood turtles (*Rhinoclemmys areolata*) eating fruits of this palm when collecting specimens for the garden in 2016.

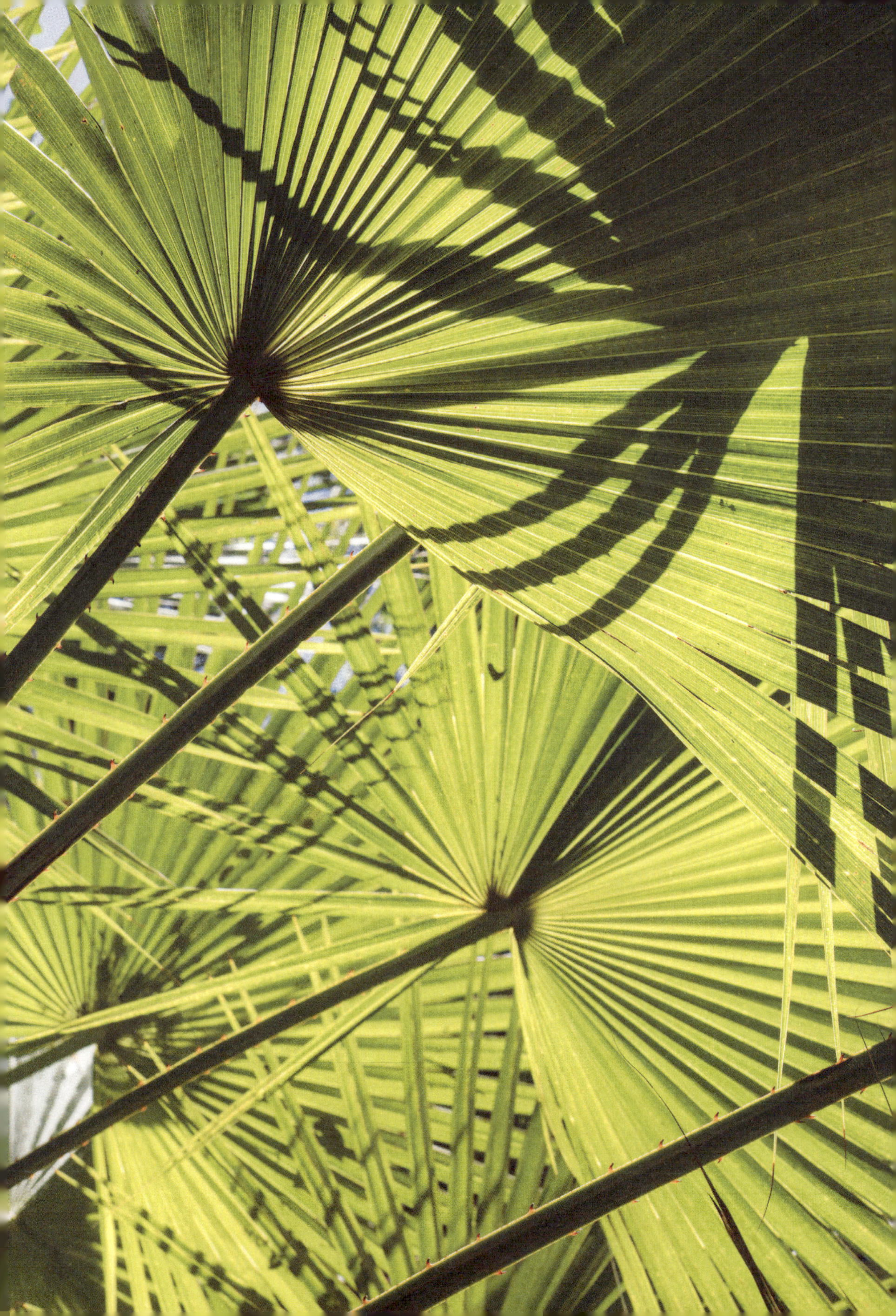

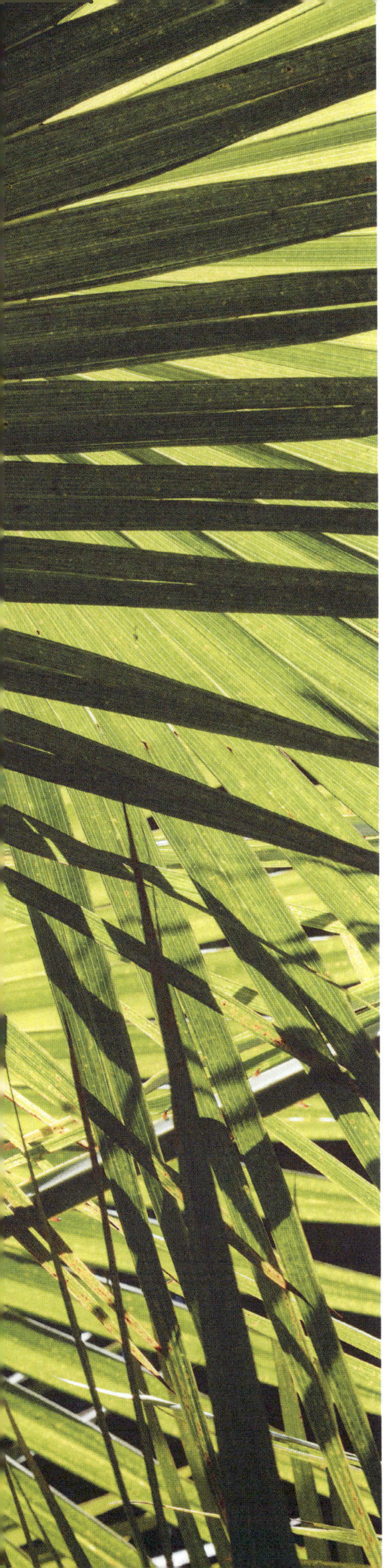

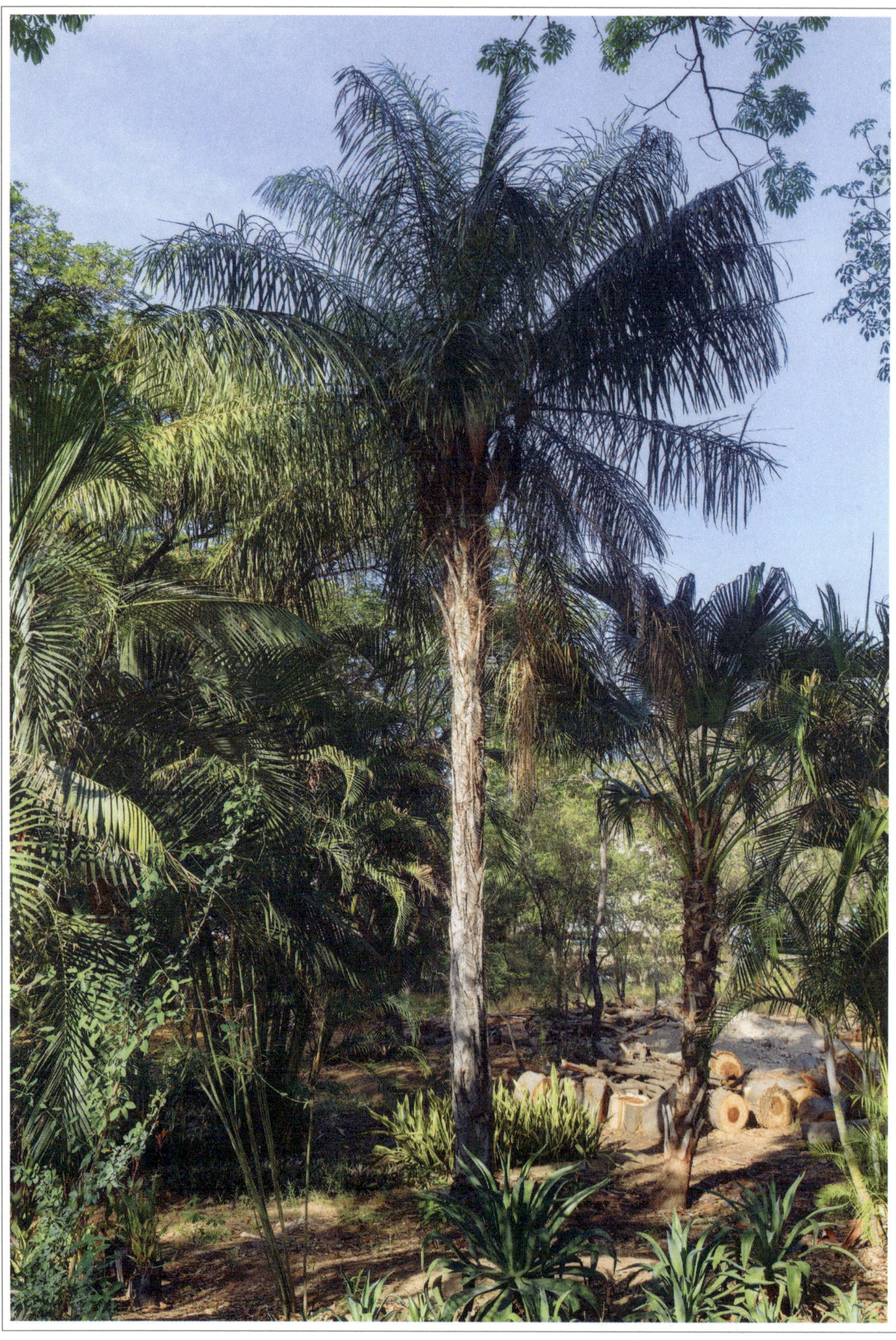

2

MACAW PALM

Acrocomia aculeata (Jacq.) Lodd. ex Mart.

Status: Assessment of global conservation status required
Distribution: Widespread throughout southern Mexico, the Caribbean, and Central and South America

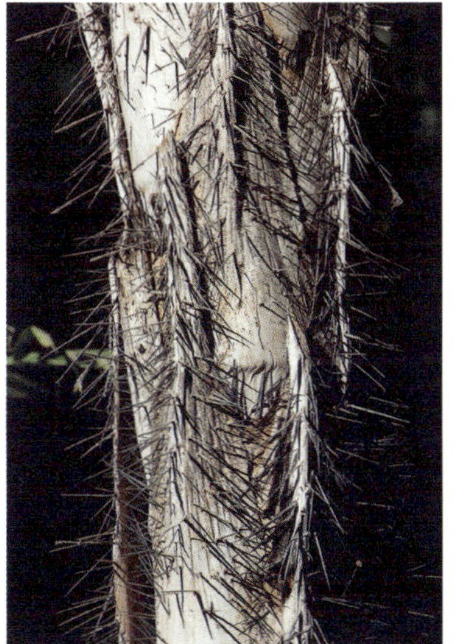
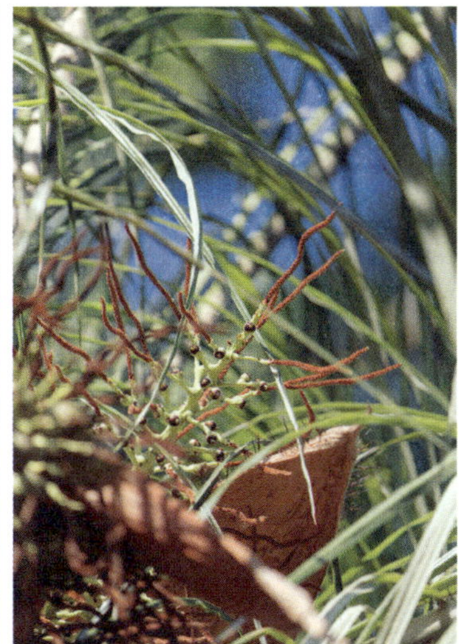
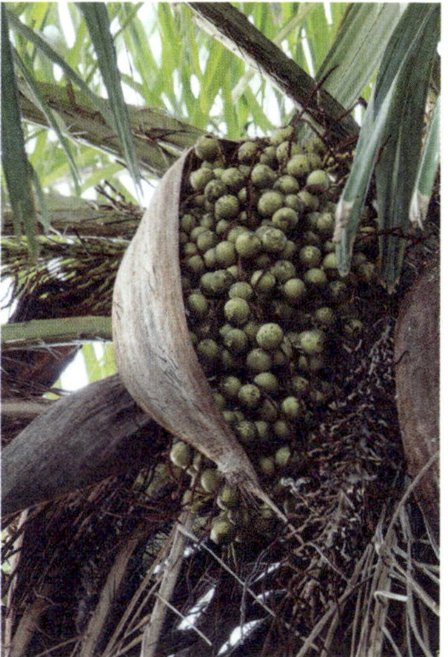

1. Spines on the leaf bases. 2. Juvenile fruits. 3. Unripe fruits.

This is a sturdy, spiny palm generally measuring from 40 to 50 feet in height, with some specimens reaching up to 66 feet. There is some evidence from DNA studies that more than one species may be masquerading under the same name. Despite its prickly black spines, it is a useful palm: the fruits are edible (they were highly prized by prehispanic cultures) and the sap from the palm is extracted and fermented into an alcoholic beverage known in the region as *vino de coyol* or *vino de taberna*. In order for the sap to be extracted, the tree is cut down and the stem is laid on its side. A hollow depression is carved into the stem, just below the leaves, near the terminal bud. For several days—or even up to a few weeks—the sap accumulates in the depression and can be repeatedly collected. Without refrigeration, the sap ferments very quickly. Some people believe that chewing the seeds can cure certain intestinal disorders, but there is no scientific evidence for this.

This palm is one of the most difficult plants for the staff at the Jardín Botánico Culiacán to prune, because the spines can cause painful puncture wounds.

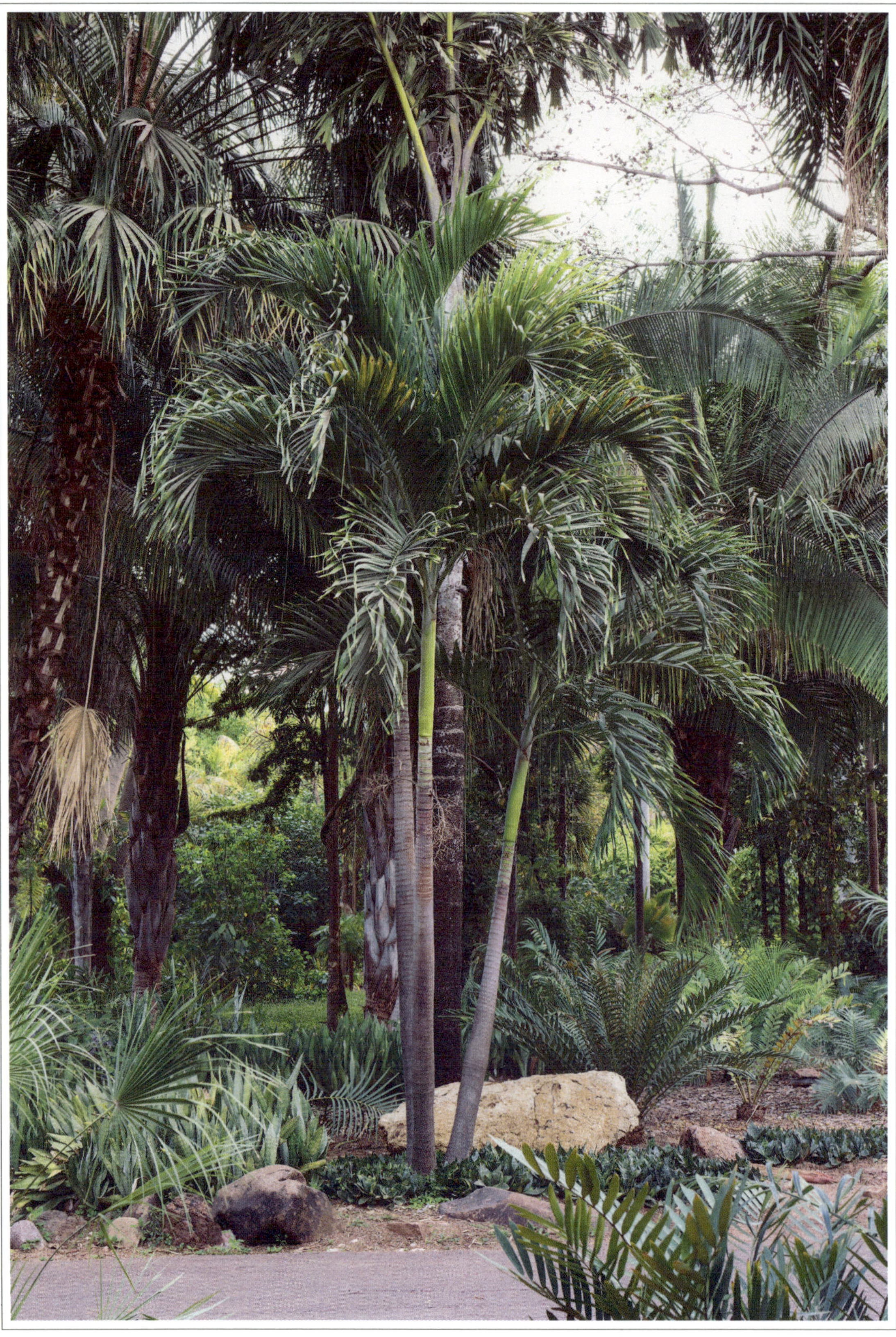

3

CHRISTMAS PALM, MANILA PALM

Adonidia merrillii (Becc.) Becc.

Status: Designated as Near Threatened on the IUCN Red List
Distribution: Palawan and its offshore islands (the Philippines)

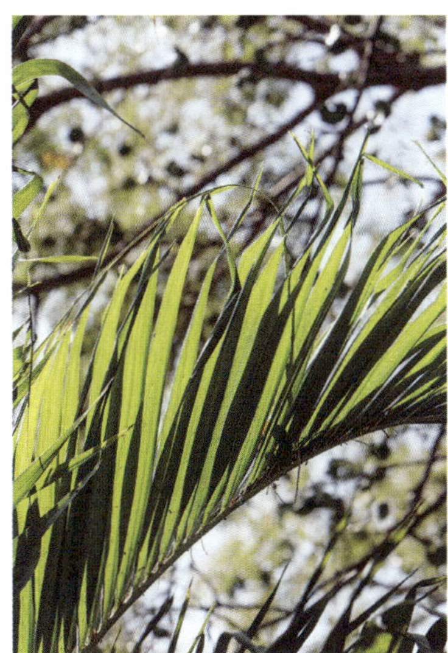

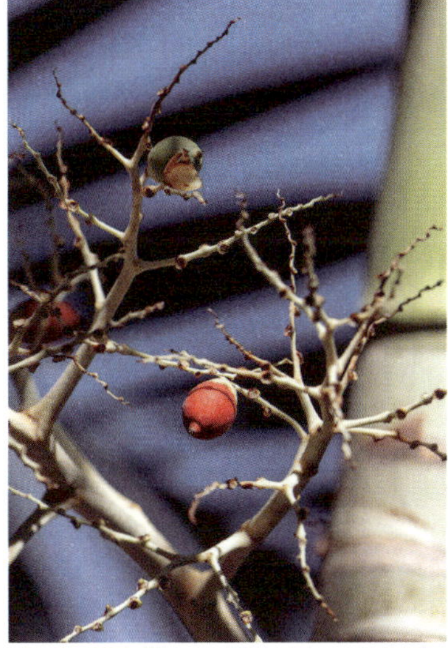

1. Leaf detail. 2. Ripe fruit.

This popular palm is native to karst limestone outcrops on Palawan and its offshore islands in the Philippines. It grows quickly from seed and may reach up to seven or 26 feet in height. *Adonidia merrillii* was cultivated as an ornamental street tree in Manila in the early twentieth century, even before it was named by botanists. It is still widely grown in warm areas of the world. This species is sometimes called the Christmas palm because it produces clusters of attractive red fruits around Christmas time. The IUCN Red List designates this palm as Near Threatened, but plants sold in nurseries are propagated from seeds of palms in cultivation.

In Culiacán, this palm was introduced by the late Carlos Murillo Depraect, who cultivated it for the houses he designed and built. Some of those specimens still survive in the houses.

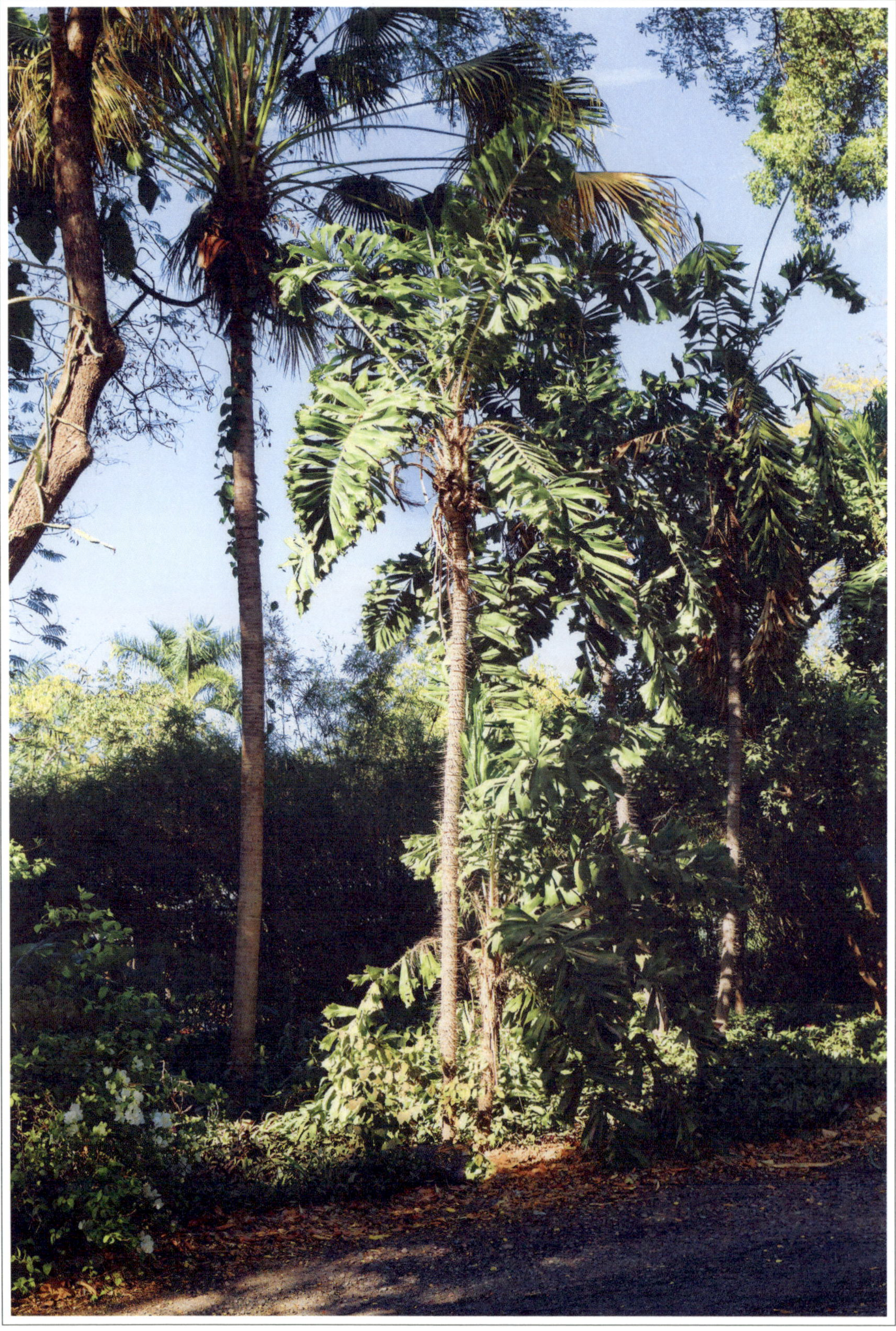

4
MARAY, COYURE

Aiphanes horrida (Jacq.) Burret

Status: Assessment of global conservation status required
Distribution: Northern South America

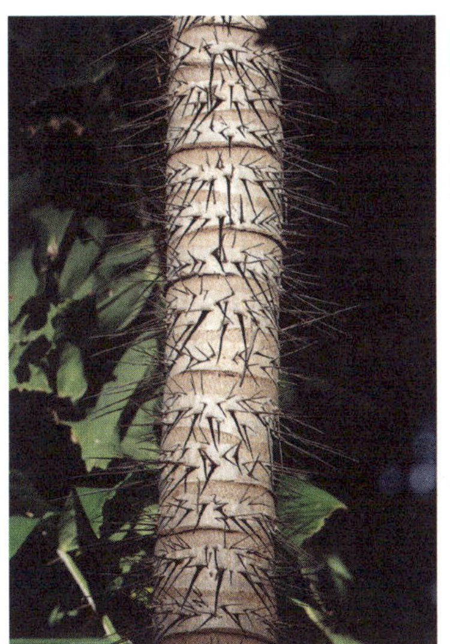
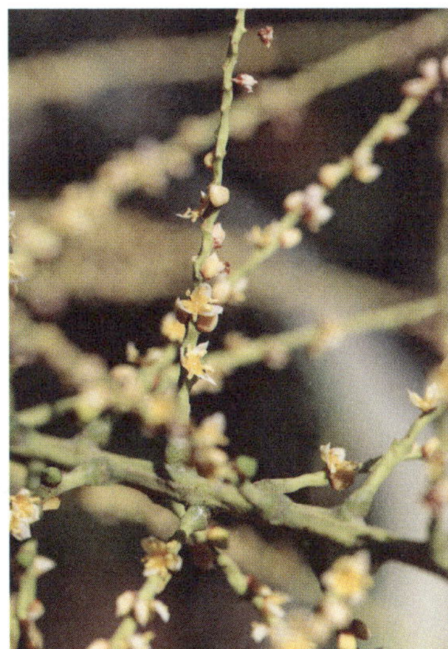
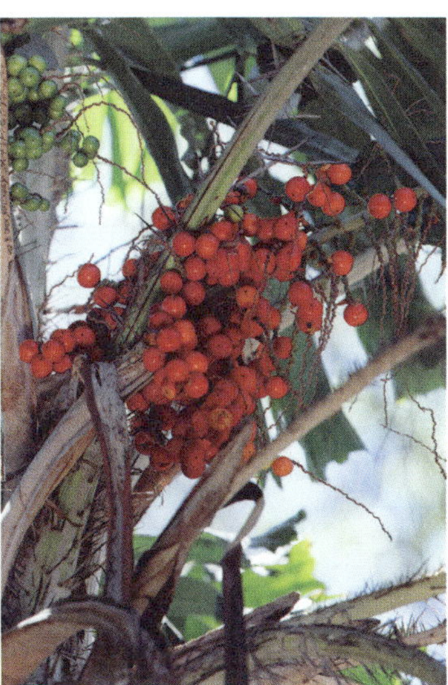

1. Spiny stem. 2. Flowers. 3. Ripe fruits.

This is a solitary, medium-sized palm, which grows up to 35 feet. It is popular for cultivation, despite the fearsome spines that clothe the trunk and leaves. If you can overlook the sharp spines, however, you will see that there is much to admire about this palm. The undulating leaflets are wedge-shaped and arranged in irregular groups, giving the palm a truly exotic appearance. The long, pendulous clusters of small white flowers end in juicy, bright red fruits, which are high in beta-carotene. In Colombia, the fruits are eaten, although the palm is not commercially cultivated for its fruit.

This palm was planted at the Jardín Botánico Culiacán fifteen years ago and it has grown very well since then. The gardeners have wanted to transplant it but, owing to its slender, spiny stem (four to six inches in diameter), they have not been able to do so.

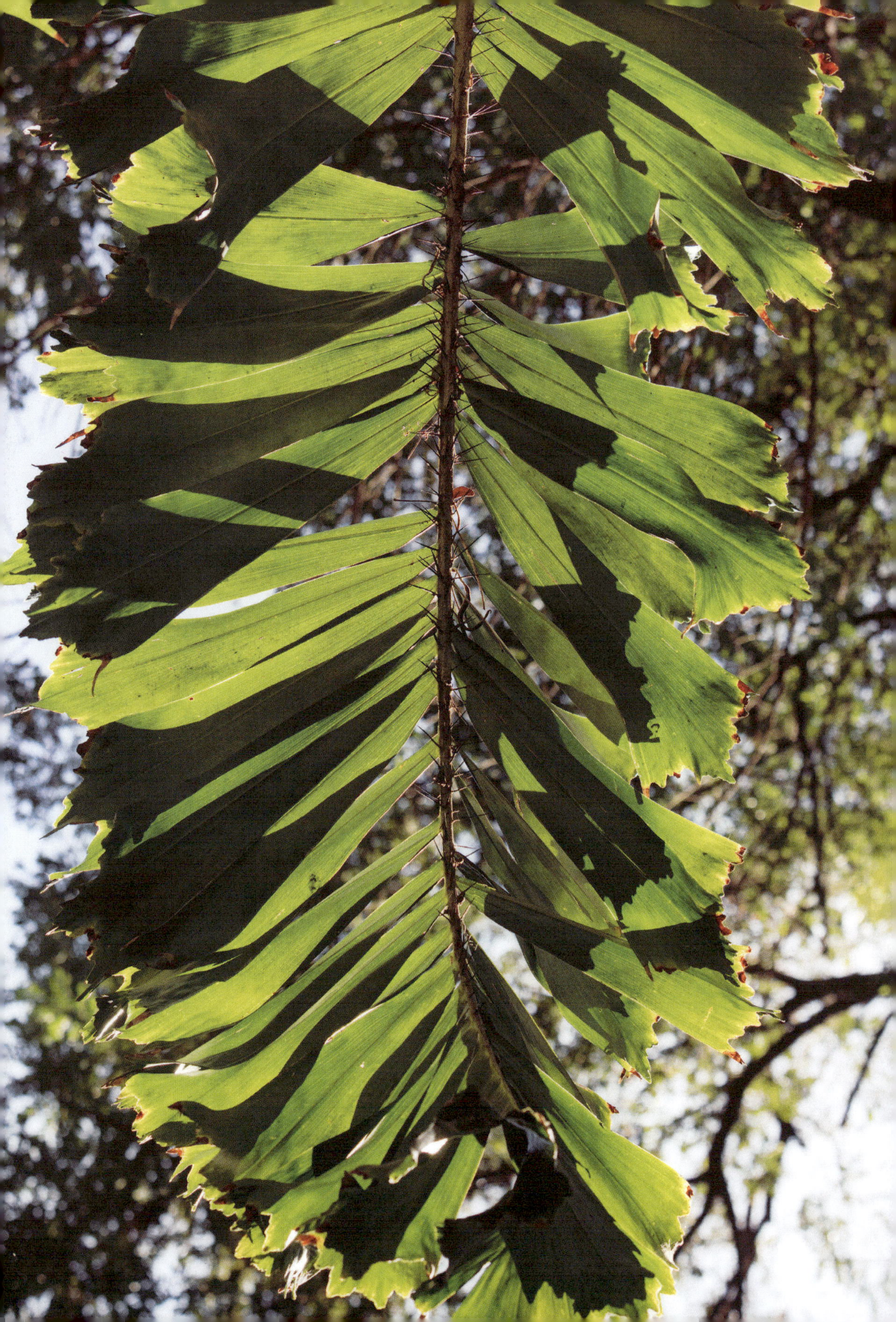

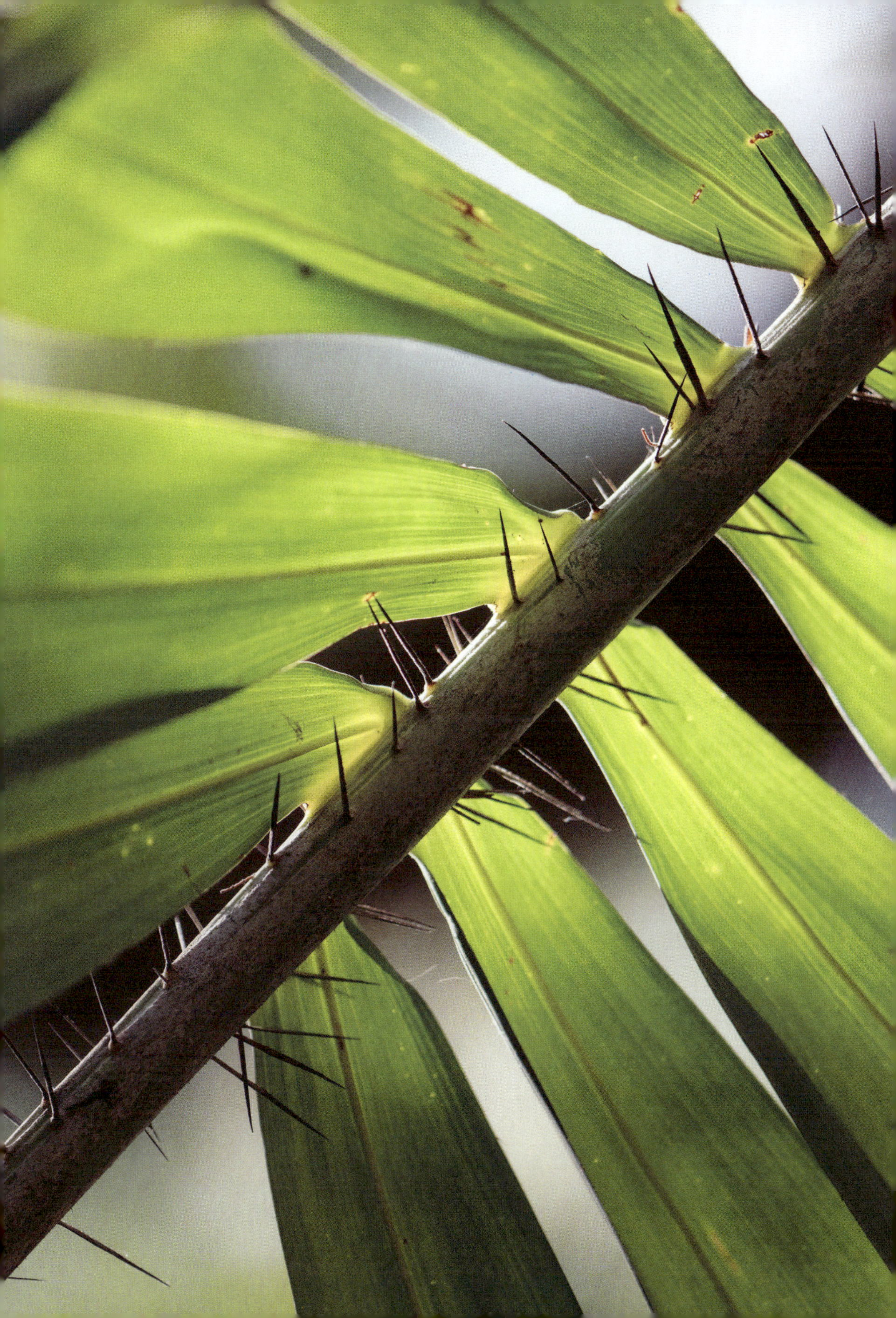

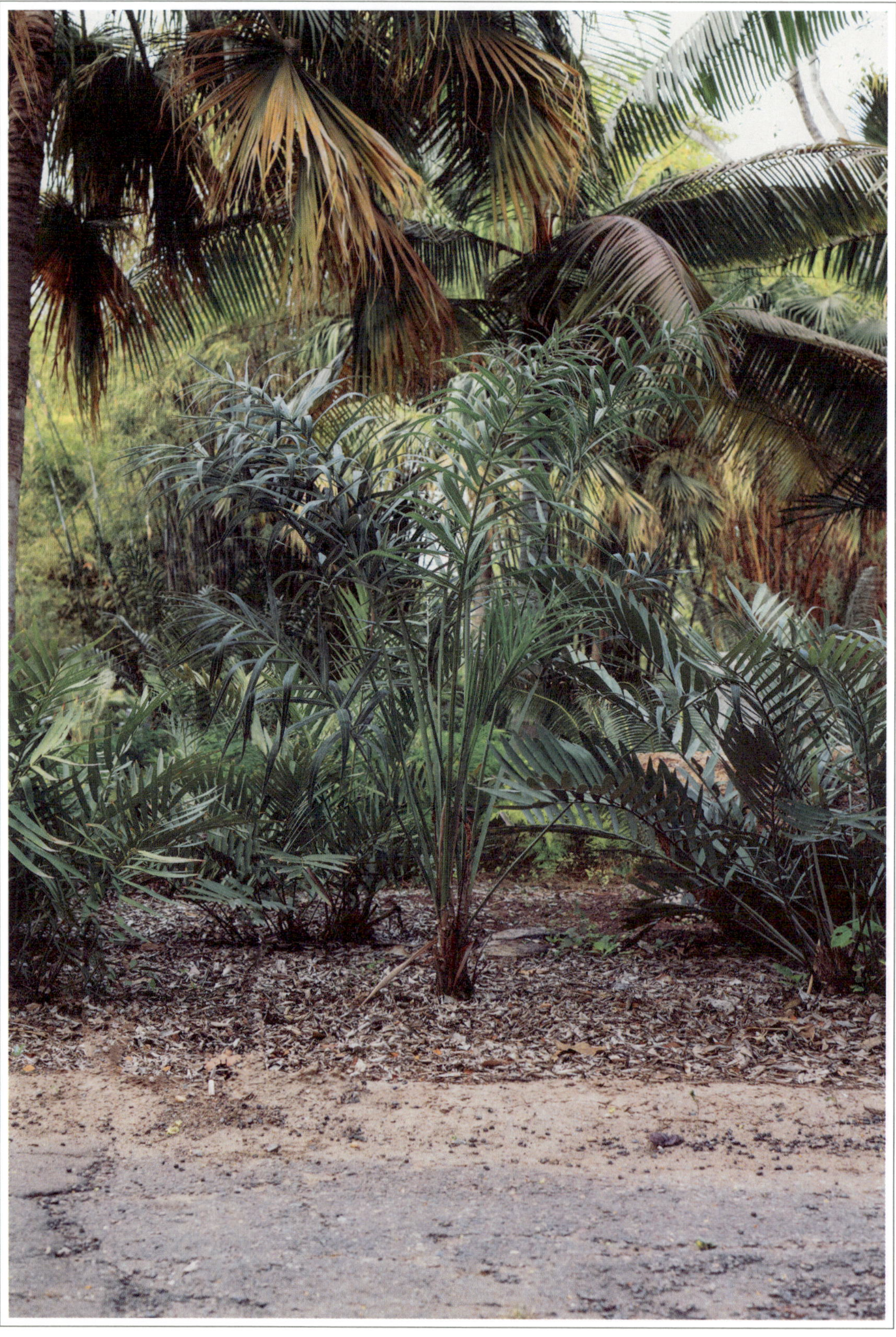

5

SEASHORE PALM, RESTINGA PALM

Allagoptera arenaria (Gomes) Kuntze

Status: Assessment of global conservation status required
Distribution: Along the coastline of southern Brazil

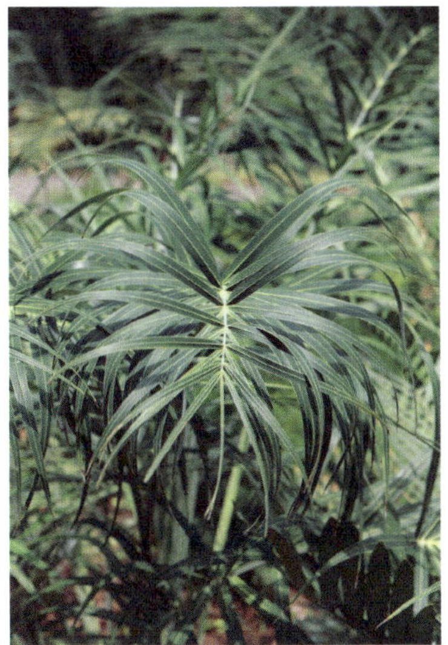

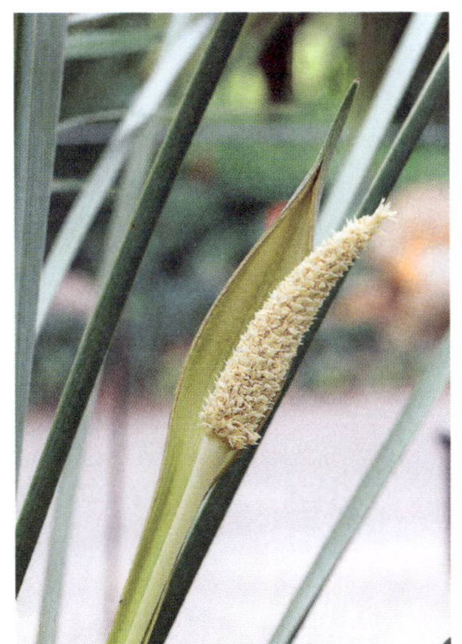

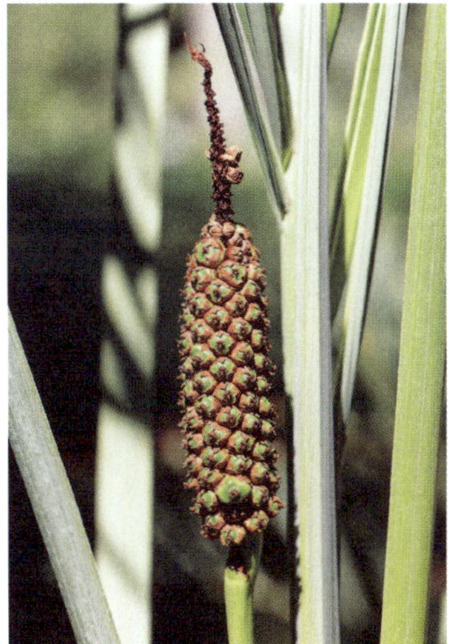

1. Leaf detail. 2. Inflorescence. 3. Unripe fruits.

This shrubby palm grows up to 6.5 feet in height in sandy soils (*arenaria* means "sandy") along the coastline of southern Brazil. It forms large colonies on sand dunes just feet from the ocean, demonstrating a remarkable tolerance to salt spray and even occasional flooding. The stems of this palm ramify dichotomously (i.e. into two equal branches), which is unusual in palms and is thought to be an adaptation to the unstable habitat of shifting sand dunes. The flower clusters are erect and unbranched, which is also unusual for palms; in fruit, they resemble ears of maize or cycad cones. The fruits are edible and popularly sold as snacks on Brazilian beaches. The species is a valuable ornamental palm, but the seedlings grow slowly.

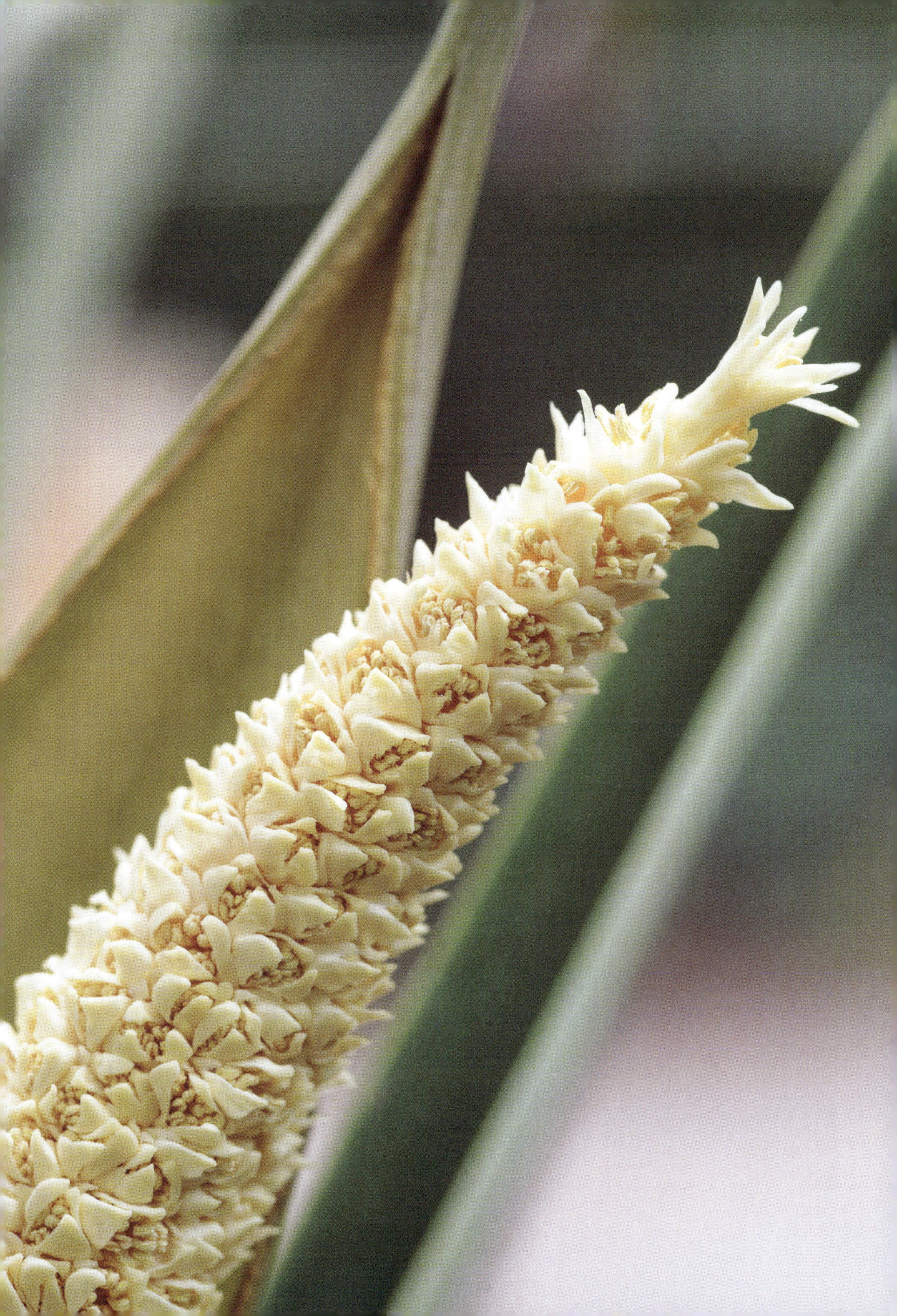

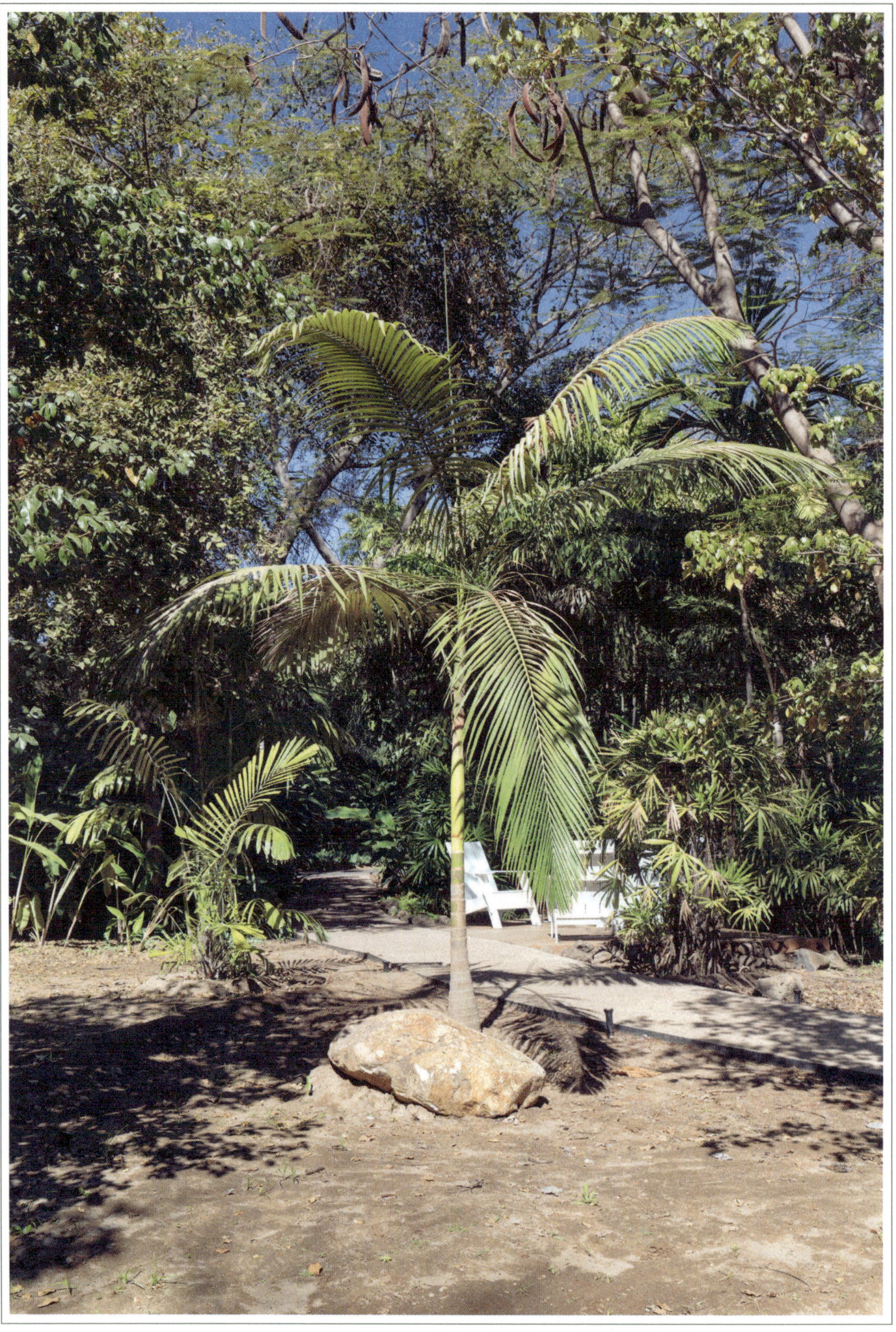

6

ALEXANDRA PALM

Archontophoenix alexandrae (F.Muell.) H.Wendl. & Drude

Status: Assessment of global conservation status required
Distribution: Queensland (Australia)

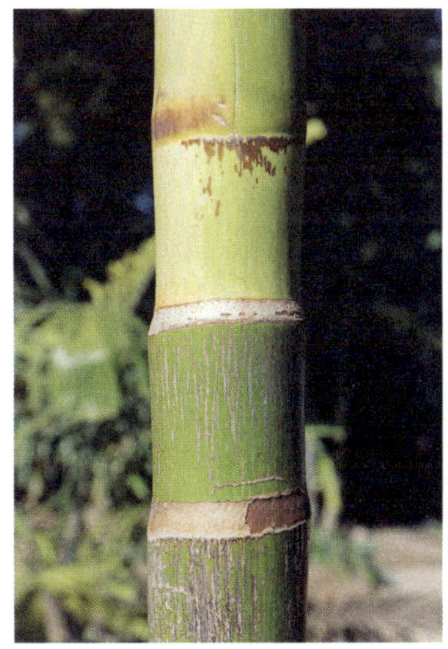

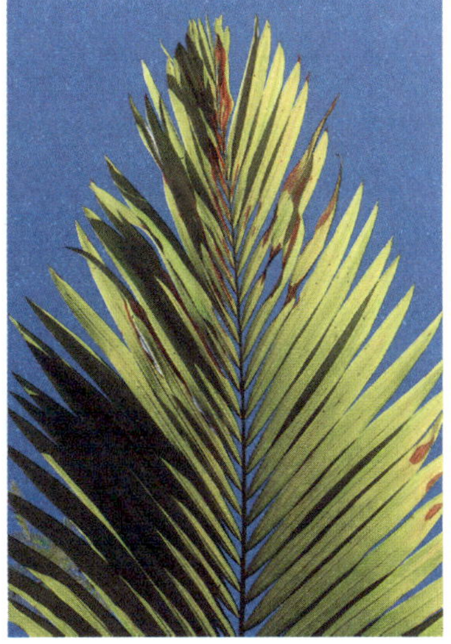

1. Leaf detail. 2. Bamboo-like trunk.

The Alexandra palm grows up to 80 feet tall. It is native to Queensland in Australia, but is now cultivated around the world as an ornamental plant. Its native habitat is rainforest and swamp forest, but the palm is adaptable to a variety of garden conditions. The pendulous clusters of small white flowers become laden with shiny red fruits that are irresistible to birds, which spread the seeds. An unanticipated consequence of birds feeding on the fruits is that this palm has become a naturalized weed in some parts of the world, such as Samoa and Hawaii.

Archontophoenix alexandrae is a species that can be seen in cultivation in gardens in Culiacán and other parts of the state of Sinaloa, though it remains difficult and expensive to acquire.

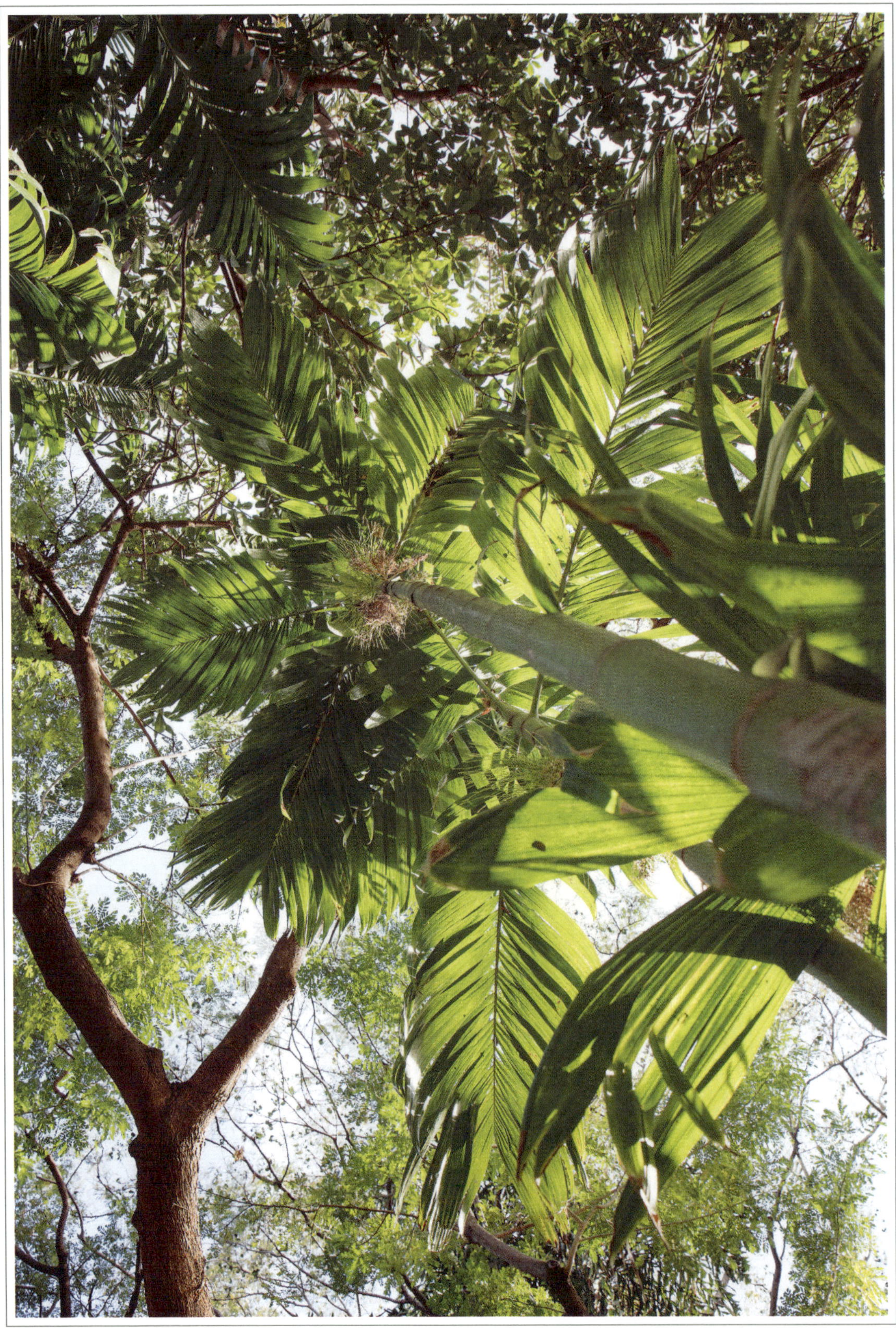

7

WILD ARECA PALM

Areca triandra Roxb.ex Buch.-Ham.

Status: Assessment of global conservation status required
Distribution: Southeast Asia

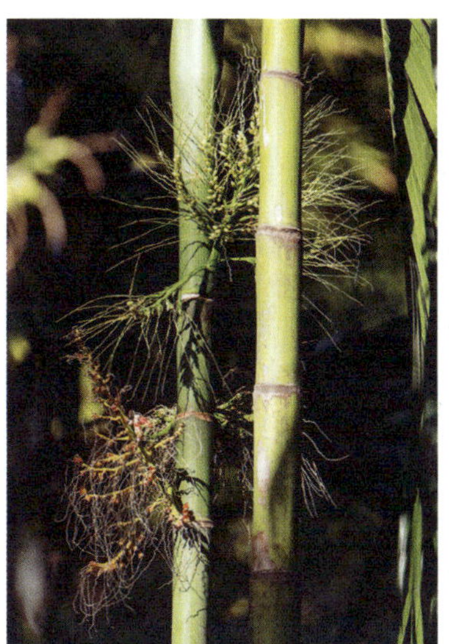
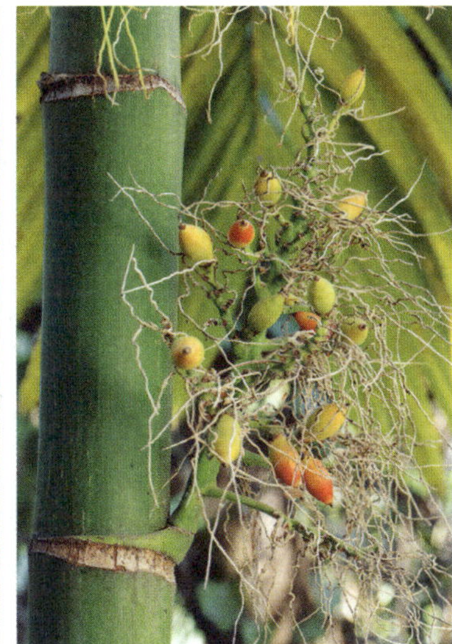
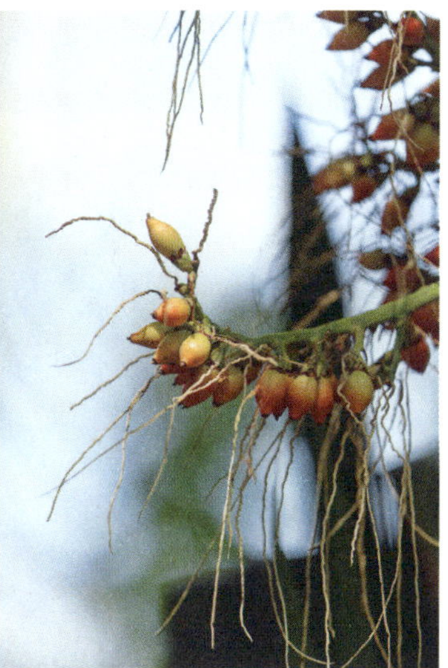

1. Stems. 2. Infrutescence with ripe fruits. 3. Fruits.

This species forms neat clusters of bamboo-like stems up to 16 feet tall and abundant light-green leaves. Airy inflorescences emerge below the leaf crown and bear small green flowers. The flowers may not be noticed, but their fragrance definitely will. They produce a strong lemon-scented perfume, perceptible from several feet away. Very few palms are grown for their fragrant flowers, but *Areca triandra* is one that earns a place in every garden of sweet-smelling plants. The species has been found to escape from cultivation and been naturalized in some parts of the world. Ornamental plants require high levels of humidity to produce abundant green foliage.

There are few specimens of this areca palm in the Jardín Botánico Culiacán: Carlos Murillo Depraect cultivated the adult ones in the 1980s and they are now more than thirty years old.

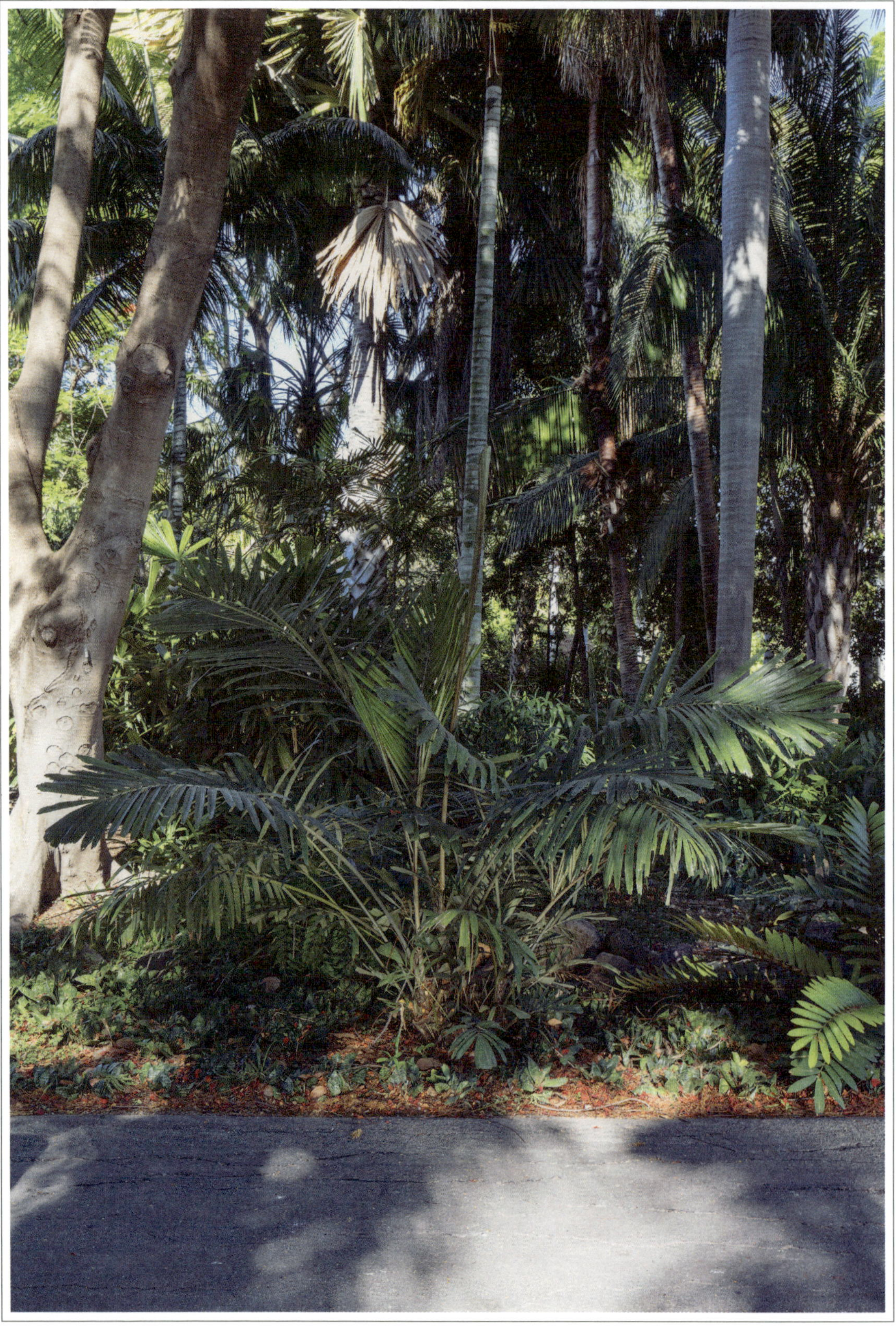

8

AUSTRALIAN SUGAR PALM

Arenga australasica (H. Wendl. & Drude) S. T. Blake ex H. E. Moore

Status: Assessment of global conservation status required
Distribution: Northern Australia

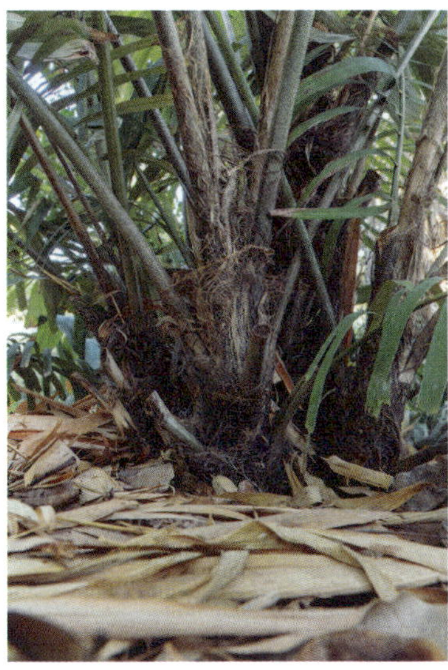

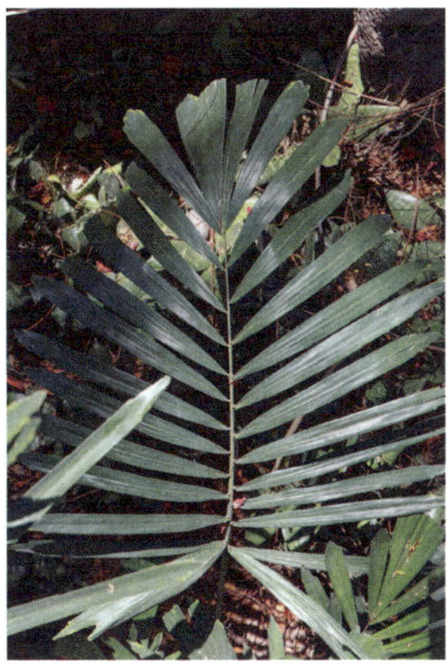

1. Stems. 2. Leaf.

This species looks very much like a larger version of its close relative *Arenga microcarpa*. The stems can grow up to 65 feet tall and the leaves can be as much as 13 feet long. Like other species of *Arenga*, this species produces successive flower stalks in a basipetal sequence (i.e. starting at the top of the stem and proceeding to the base). Its fruit is a deep bright purple, with oxalate crystals in the pulp, which is why they are very irritating to the skin when handled. After flowering and fruiting, the stems die, but other stems in the cluster continue to grow. Over time, the plant can form an immense clump of stems of different ages and lengths.

The Jardín Botánico Culiacán obtained a specimen in 2004 that is growing very slowly. Until it produces fruit, it will be the only specimen in the collection.

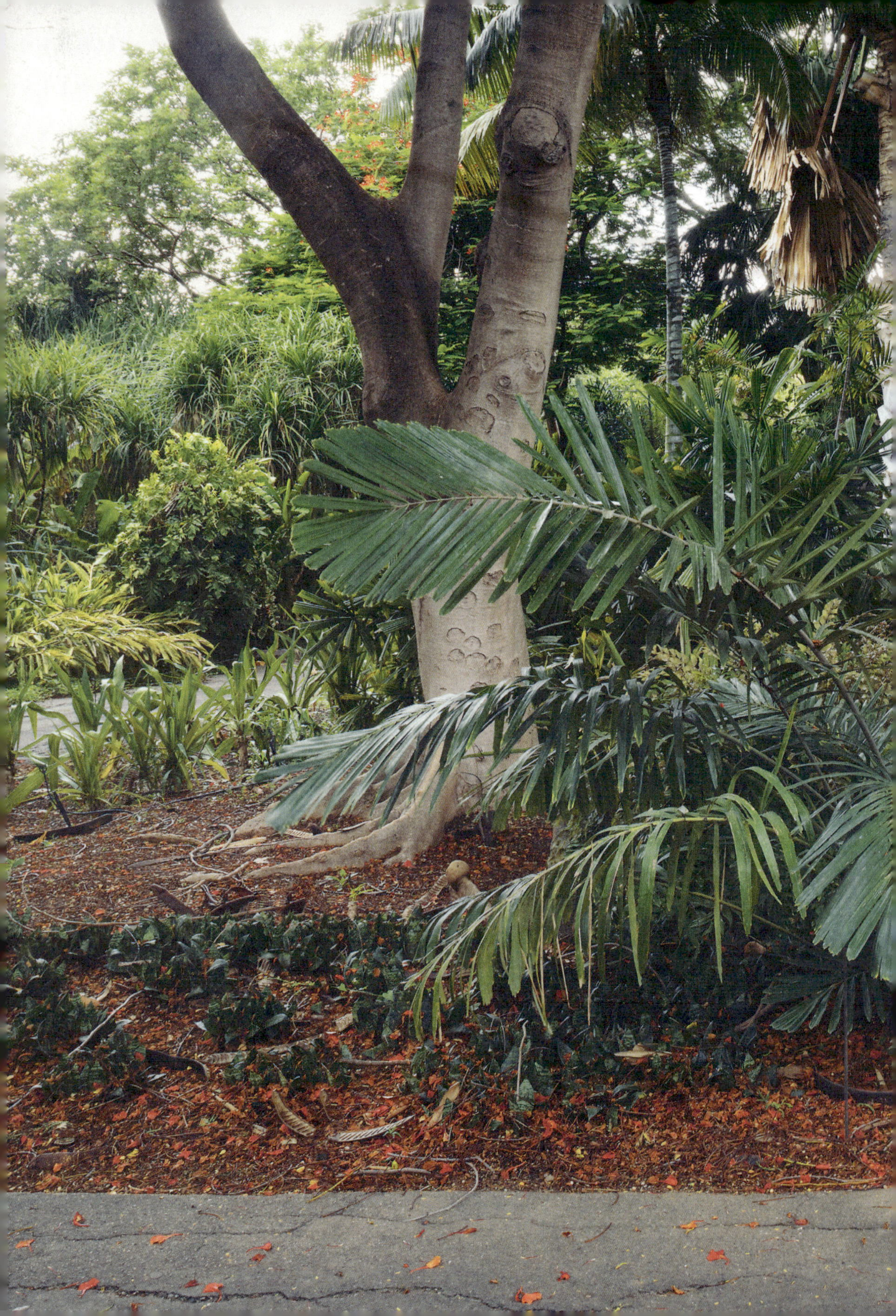

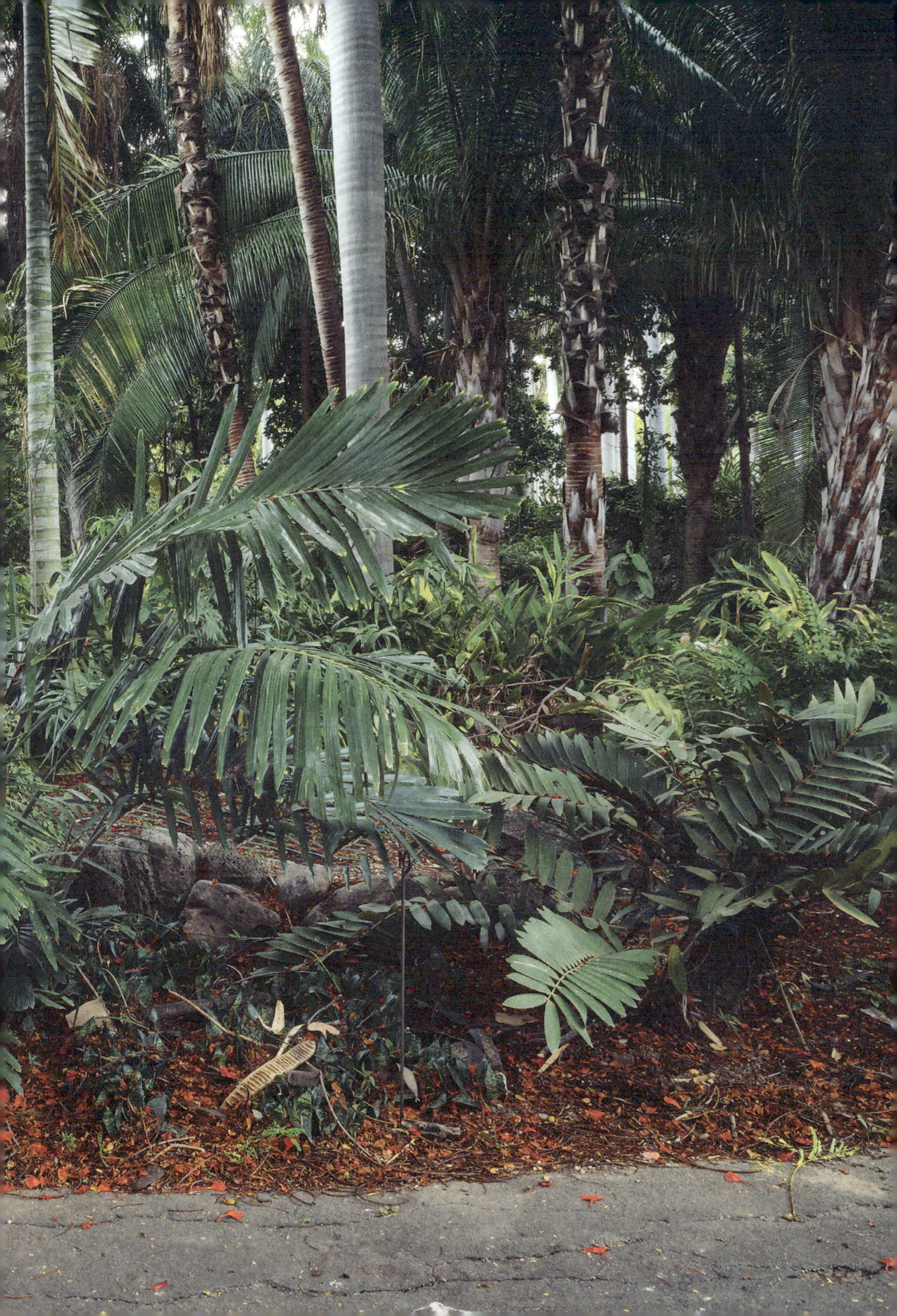

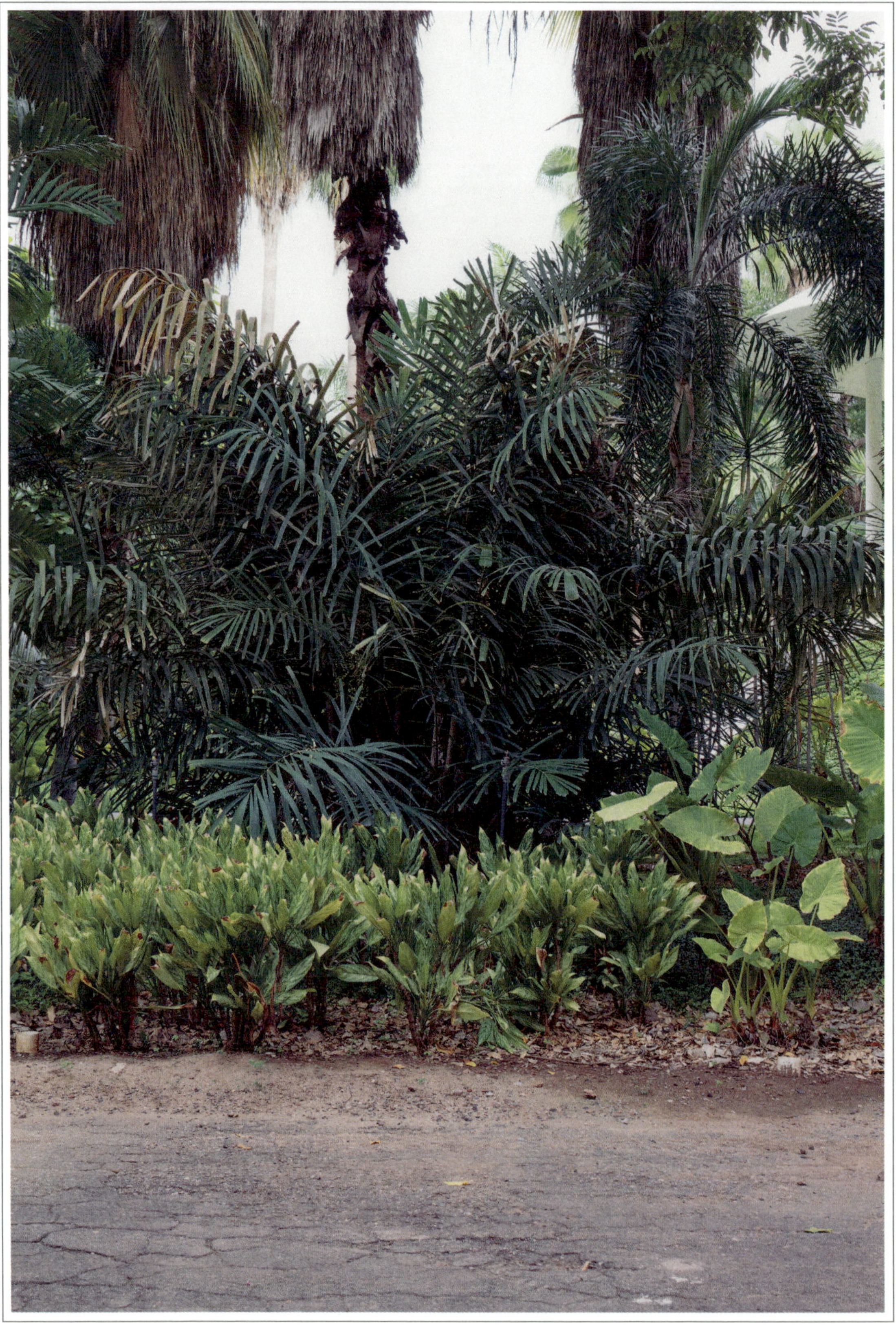

9
WILD SAGO PALM

Arenga microcarpa Becc.

Status: Assessment of global conservation status required
Distribution: Maluku Islands, New Guinea, and northern Australia

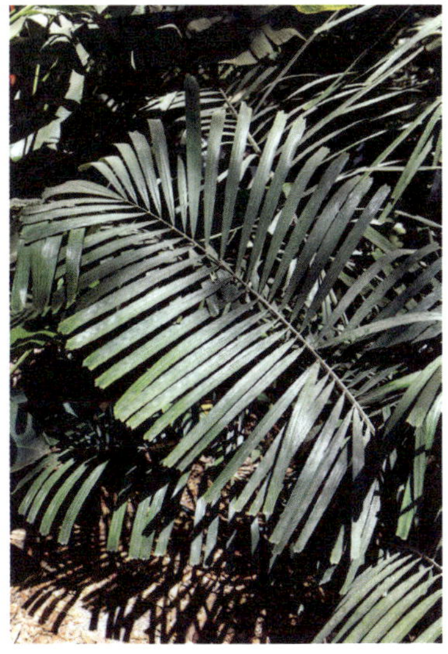

1. Leaf.

This species, which grows up to 25 feet tall, forms tight clusters of sturdy stems bearing long feather-shaped leaves (up to 10 feet in length) with silvery undersides. The palm occurs naturally in northern Australia and throughout the island of New Guinea, in tropical rain forests and swampy habitats. The genus *Arenga* has a peculiar flowering habit: at maturity each stem produces a terminal flower stalk, followed successively by other flower stalks lower on the stem. Flowering occurs over the course of many months. While the topmost terminal stalk is producing fruits, the lower stalks may be just emerging. When flowering and fruiting have finished, the individual stem dies. The dirty-yellow flowers are followed by fleshy fruits that turn from green to white to red and are toxic when handled. The trunks of *Arenga microcarpa* can be ground up to make sago flour. The indigenous peoples of the palm's native region use the leaves to make skirts for dancing.

This is a relatively new species at the Jardín Botánico Culiacán, the specimens arrived in 2015. Two of them were donated to the Jardín Botánico Benjamin Francis Johnston in Los Mochis (Benjamin Francis Johnston Botanical Garden), making *Arenga microcarpa* a symbol of collaboration between the two botanical gardens.

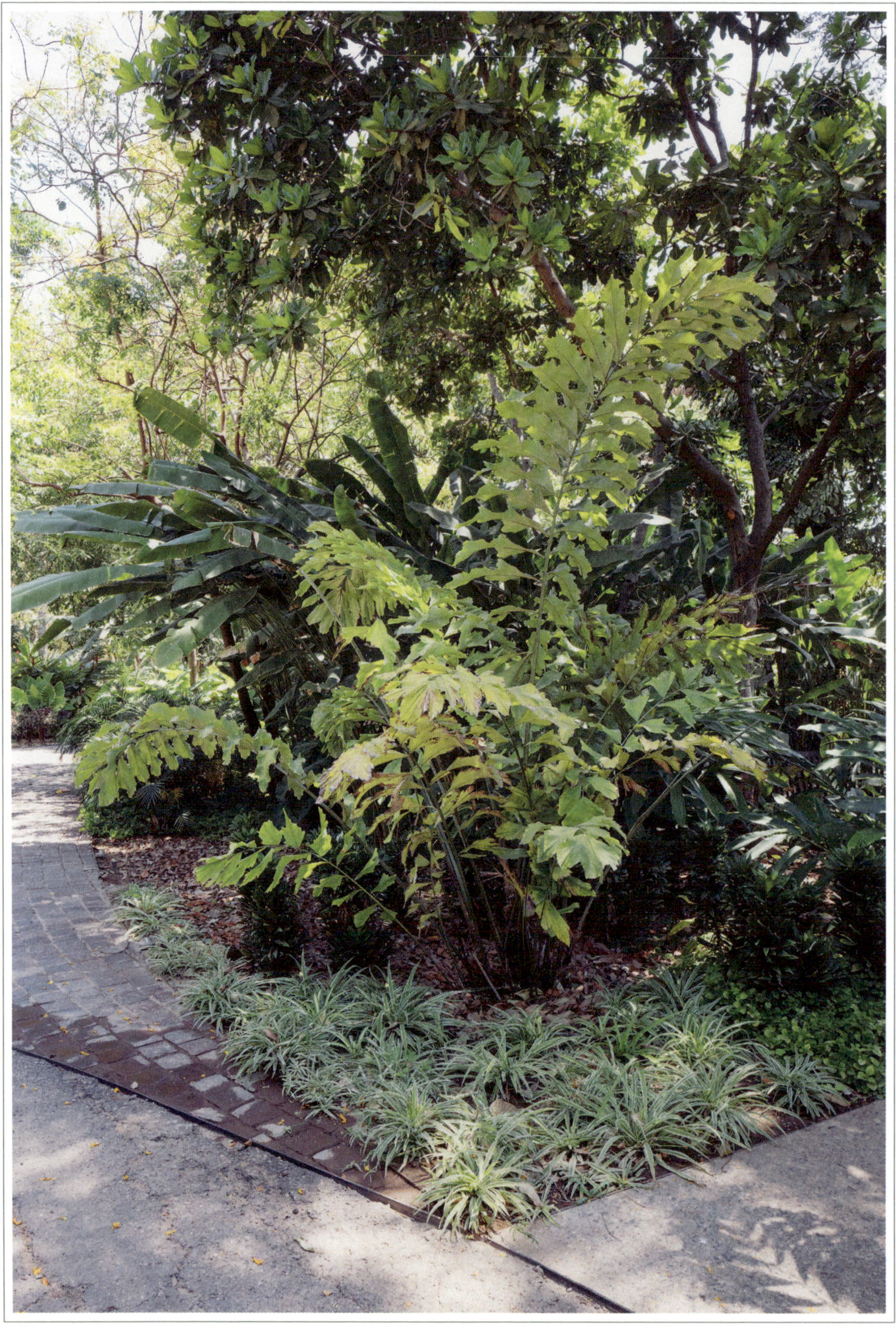

10

AREN GELORA

Arenga undulatifolia Becc.

Status: Assessment of global conservation status required
Distribution: Borneo, Sulawesi (Indonesia), and the Philippines

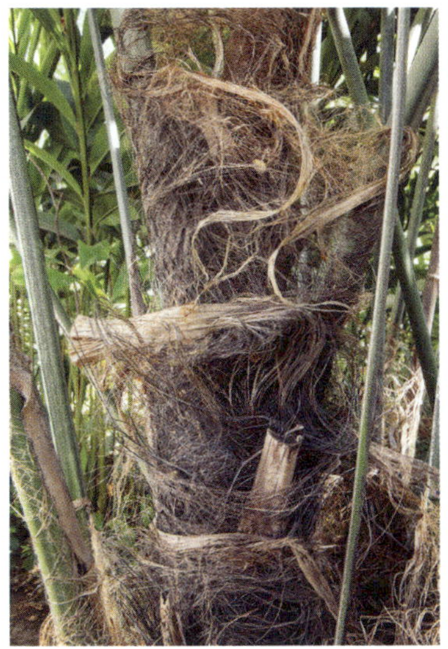
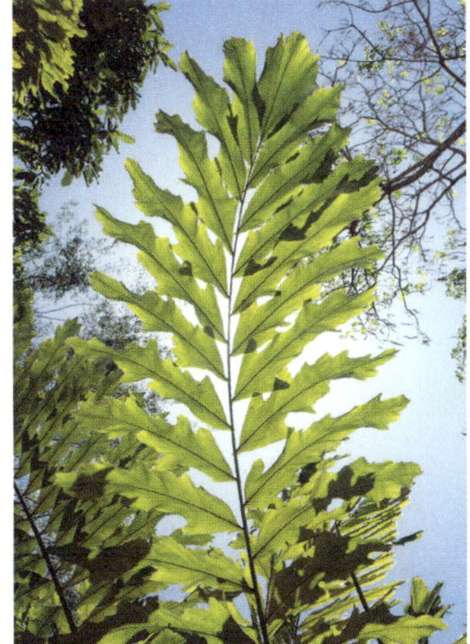
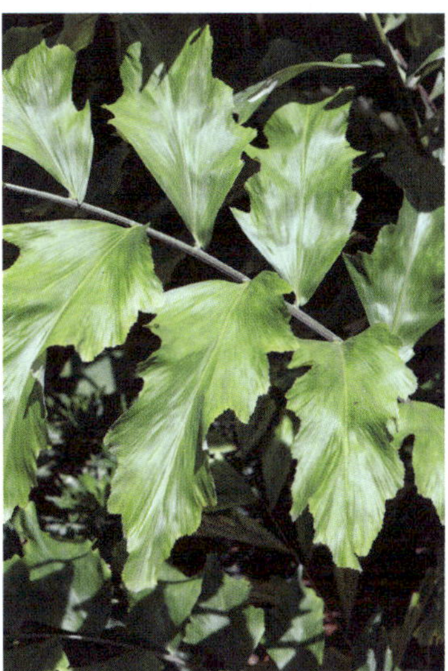

1. Leaf bases. 2. Leaf. 3. Leaf detail.

This palm produces multiple stems up to 35 feet tall, bearing several very large spreading leaves. Its scientific name highlights one of the most attractive aspects of the palm: the wavy or undulating margins of the leaflets. The result is a palm that is wider than it is tall. Like other species of *Arenga*, each stem will produce successive flower stalks from the top to the base and then die. Other stems in the cluster will continue to grow. *Arenga undulatifolia* produces round red fruits, very attractive visually, but toxic to humans. Asian palm civets (*Paradoxurus hermaphroditus*) eat the fruits and disperse the seeds throughout the forest. This is the same civet that plays a role in producing one of the most expensive coffees in the world.

Since 2011, the Jardín Botánico Culiacán has acquired several palms of the species from a collection in Yucatán. In 2015 new specimens of *Arenga undulatifolia* were placed in the Palmetum, surrounding *Encounter*, an art installation created by the American artist James Turrell.

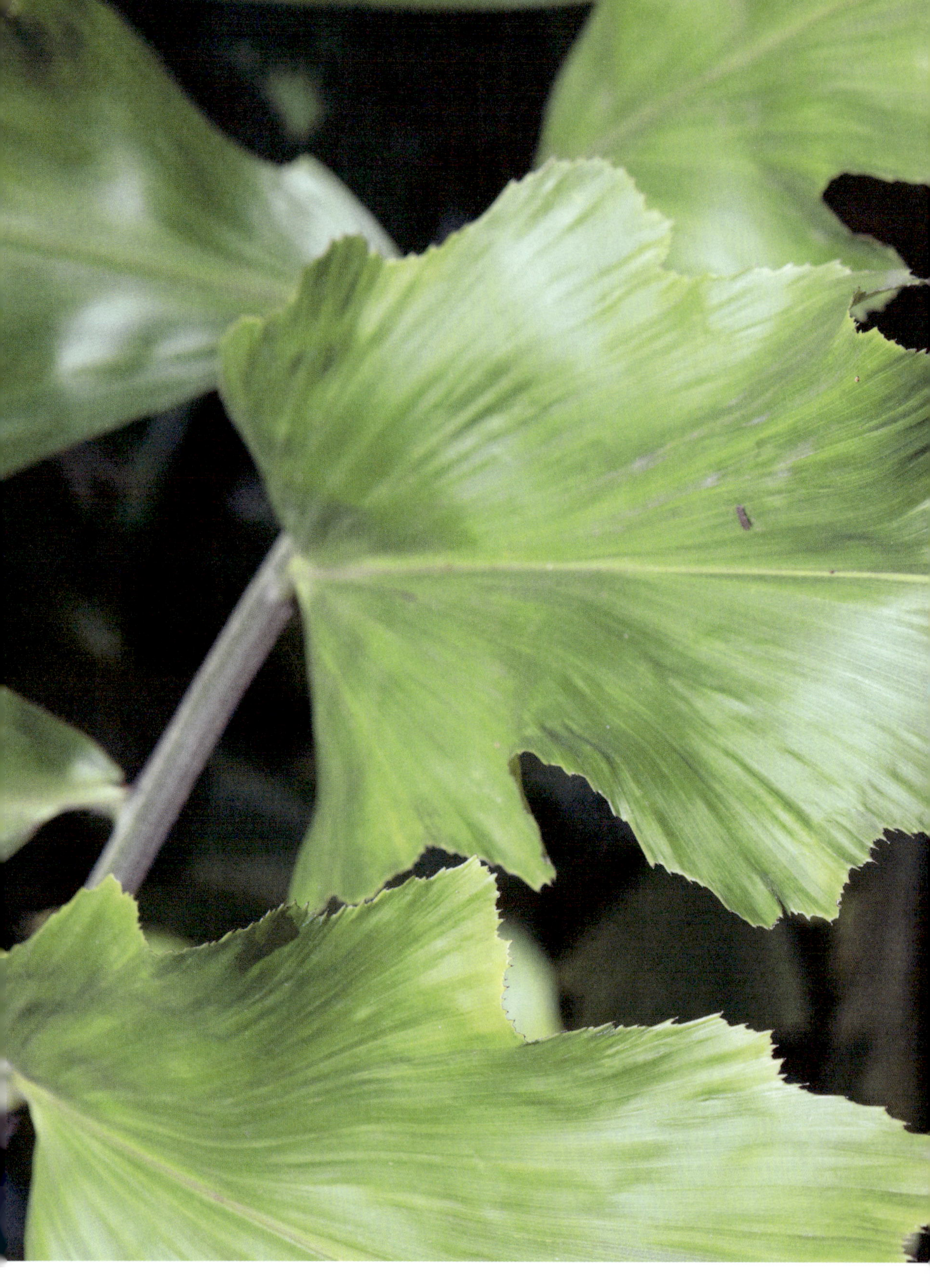

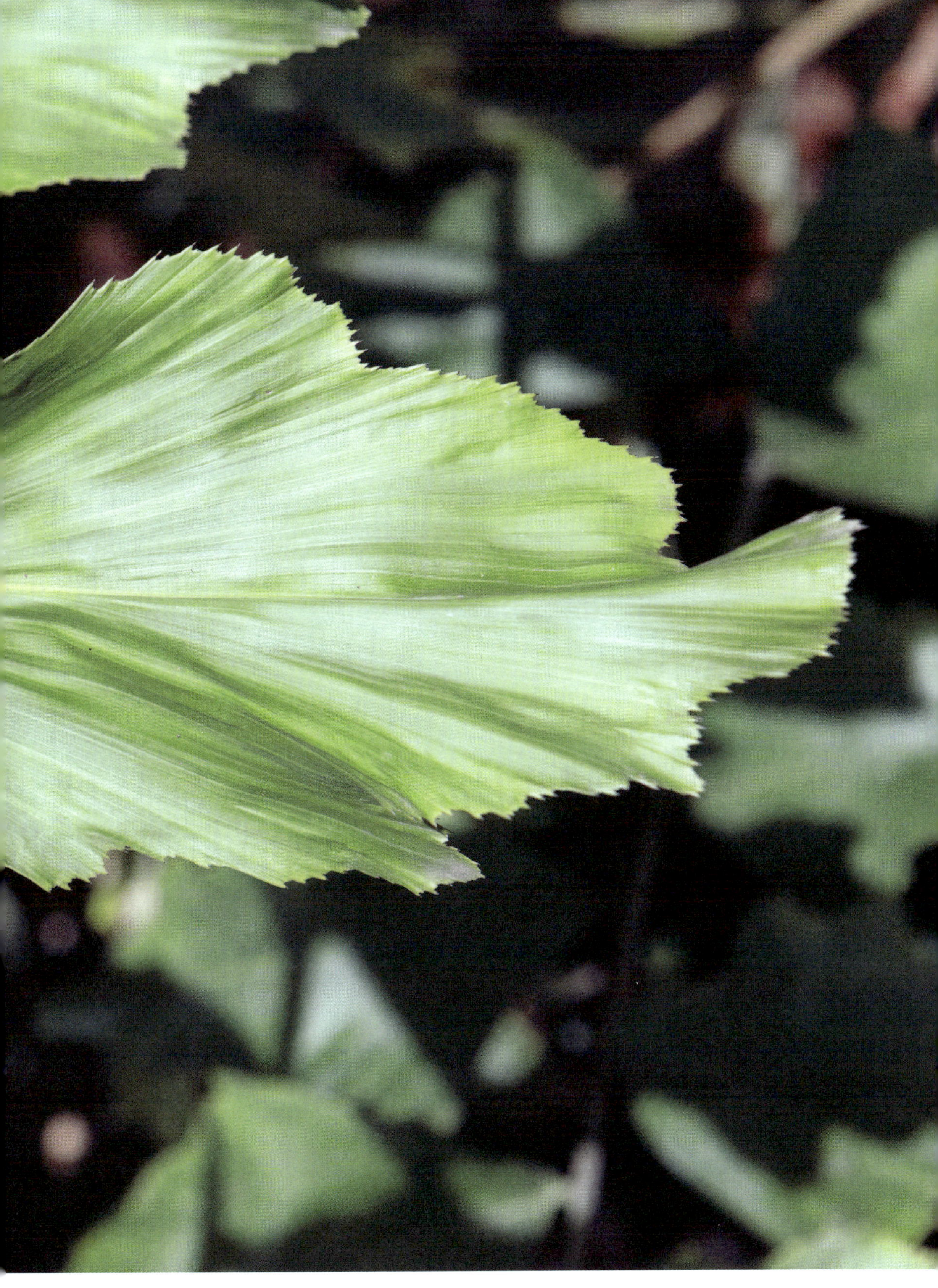

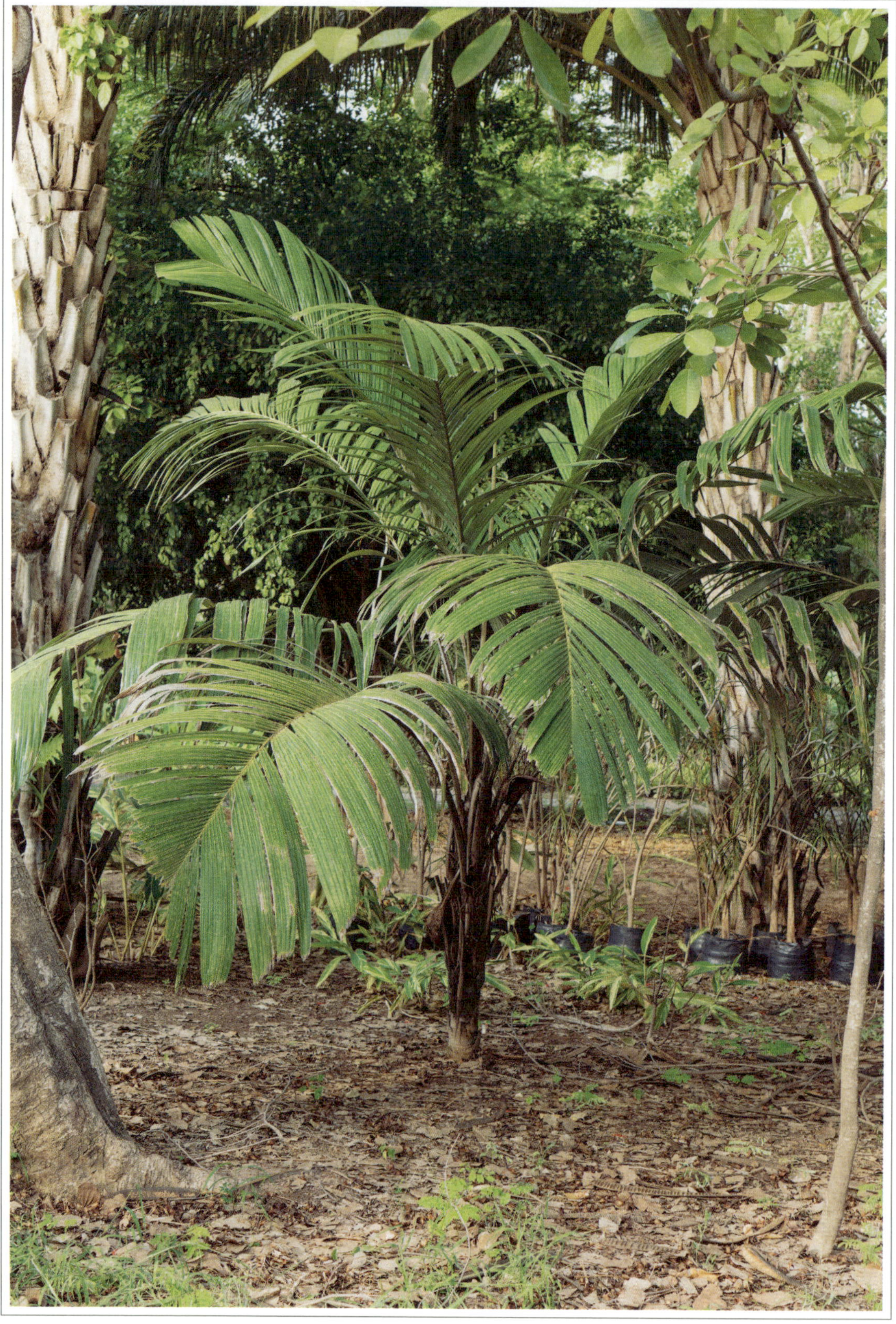

11

MEXICAN STARNUT PALM

Astrocaryum mexicanum Liebm. ex Mart.

Status: Assessment of global conservation status required
Distribution: From Mexico to Honduras

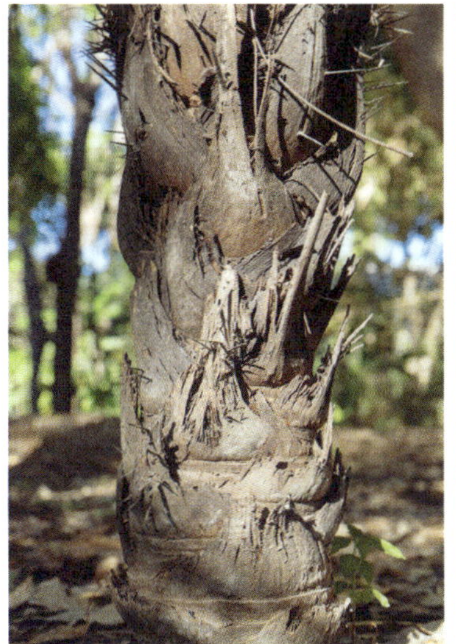

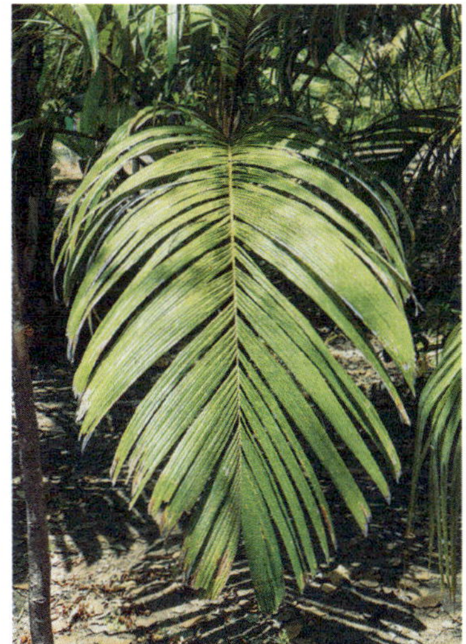

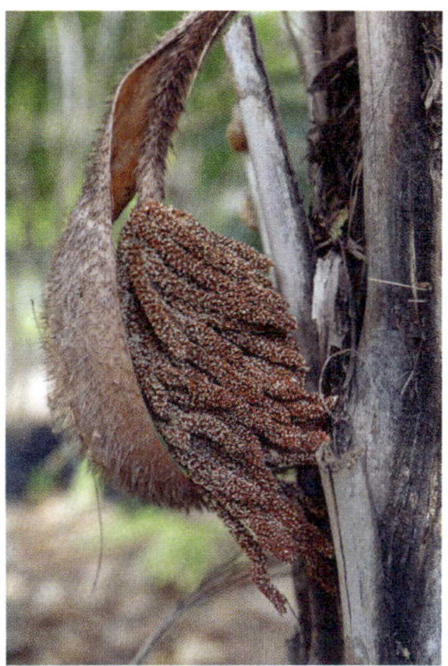

1. Trunk. 2. Leaf. 3. Flowers and spiny bract.

This palm is native to rainforests, from the Mexican state of Veracruz all the way to Honduras. Growing up to 20 feet tall, it is a plant found abundantly in the understory of rainforests. Its trunk, as well as its leaves, bracts, and fruits, are covered with spines. The flowers of *Astrocaryum mexicanum* are produced in clusters, technically called inflorescences, which may contain up to 10,000 male flowers and 60 female flowers. Pollen transportation is performed by beetles, which are attracted to the heat produced by the flowers (up to 45°F higher than the ambient air temperature). The fruits of the palm are small nuts, two inches in diameter, consumed by birds and fishes. The palm is useful to human beings: the young flowers and fruits are edible and the powdered seeds can be mixed with corn to make tortillas. The leaves can be used for roofing and the leaf stalks for hoes.

The species has been studied since the 1970s by Prof. José Sarukhán and his team from the Universidad Nacional Autónoma de México (UNAM) in an attempt to understand various aspects of its natural history and ecology. Tropical ecology in Mexico has flourished through the study of this species, thanks to which the age of a stretch of forest where it grows can now be estimated.

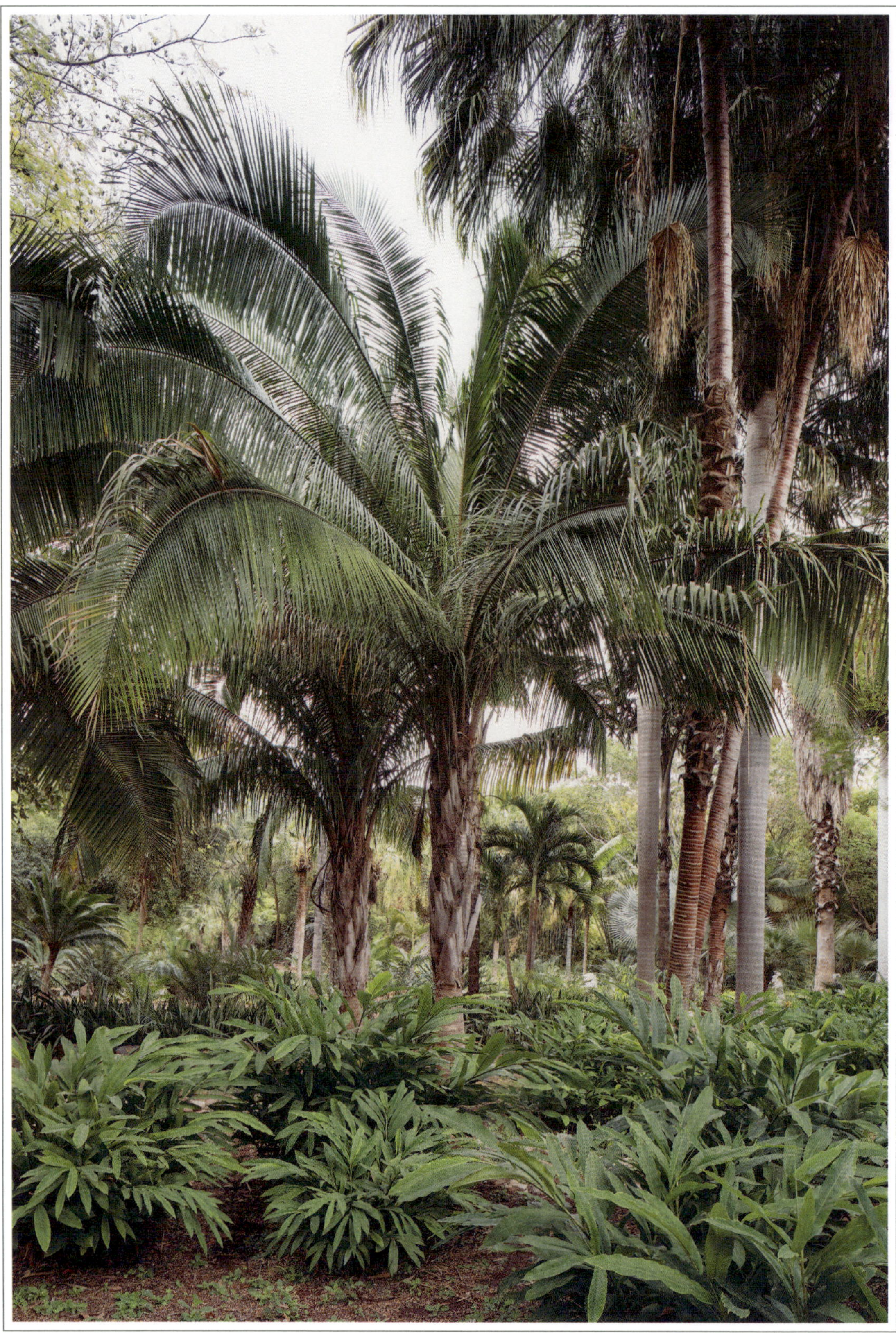

12

COHUNE PALM

Attalea cohune Mart.

Status: Assessment of global conservation status required
Distribution: Southern Mexico, including the Yucatán Peninsula, parts of Central America, and Colombia

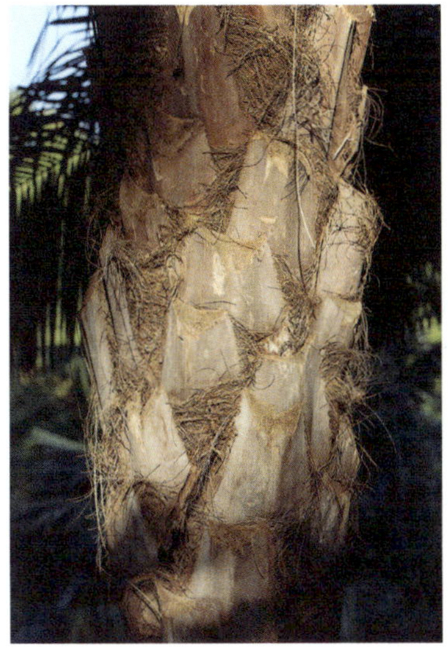

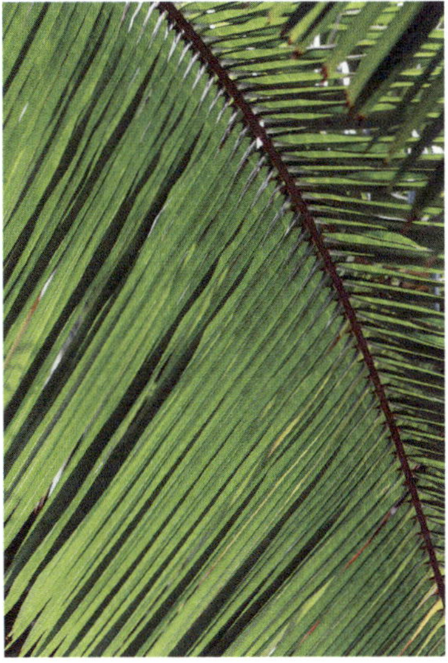

1. Trunk with retained leaf bases. 2. Leaf detail.

This massive palm, around 80 feet tall, with leaves 35 feet long, is found in southern Mexico, parts of Central America, and Colombia. The species often occurs in almost pure stands called *palmares*. It is slow growing and has a long juvenile stage. A seedling stem will spend many years underground, growing deeper and deeper, until eventually it turns and grows upward. After several years, the trunk begins to emerge from the ground and the palm begins to flower and fruit. The male and female flowers, born of the same inflorescence, are surrounded in bud by a woody, boat-shaped bract that protects them. The full-grown fruits, which resemble small coconuts, are greenish-brown and have a single hard nut enclosing several oily seeds. This palm was an extremely important palm for the ancient Mayans, who planted it near their settlements. Since ancient times the leaves have been used for roofing thatch, while the fruit is consumed and an edible oil is extracted from the seeds. A high-quality charcoal can be manufactured from the spent nuts. The fruits were formerly used to feed domesticated animals and to attract peccaries for hunting, but are used today for ceremonial purposes. In the past, the terminal bud was tapped for its sweet sap, which was fermented into an alcoholic beverage. This magnificent palm is being substituted by the coconut palm all along its distribution range, and the only country that has listed it as endangered is Colombia.

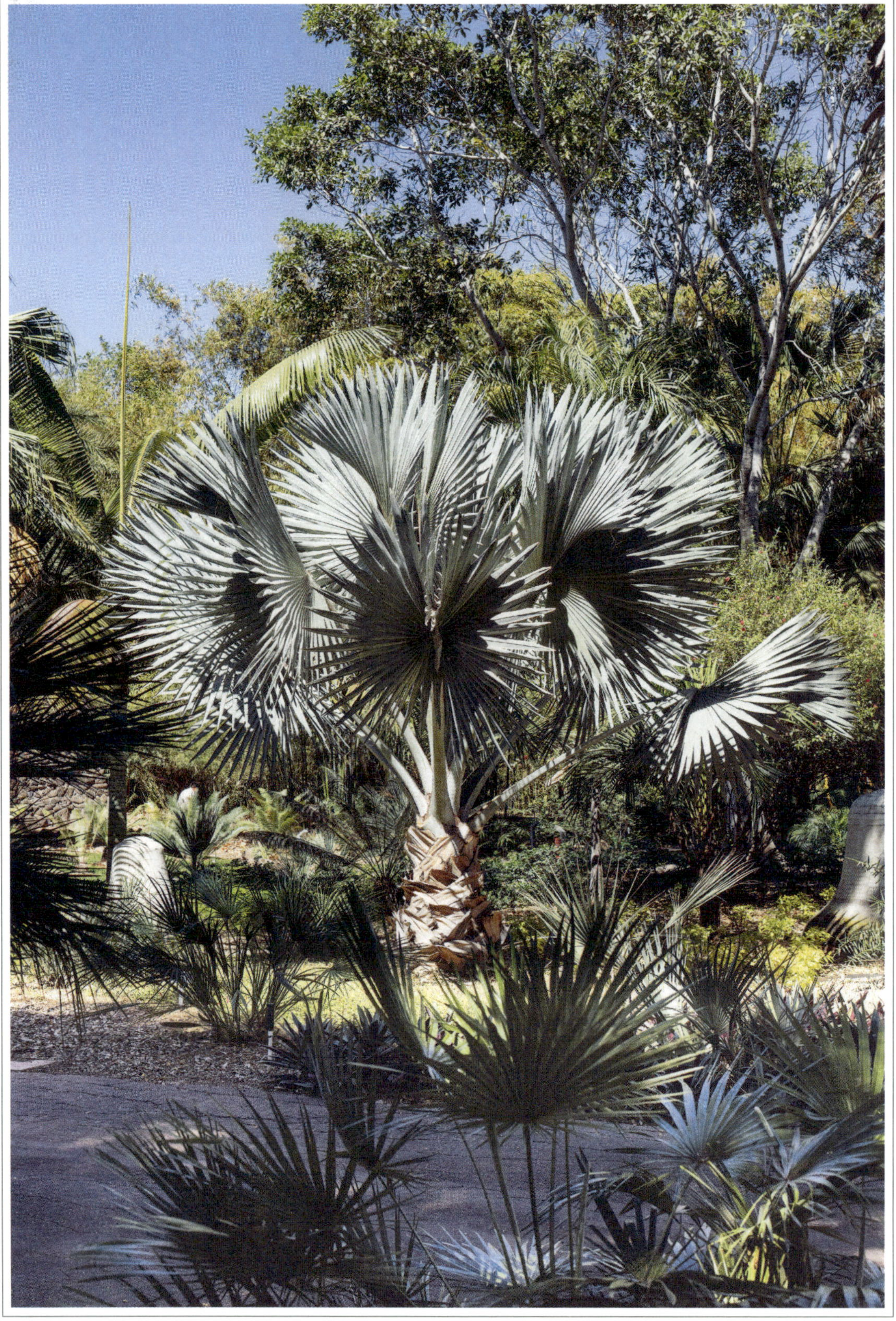

13
BISMARCK PALM

Bismarckia nobilis Hildebr. & H. Wendl.

Status: Designated as Least Concern on the IUCN Red List, but populations are declining
Distribution: Endemic to Madagascar

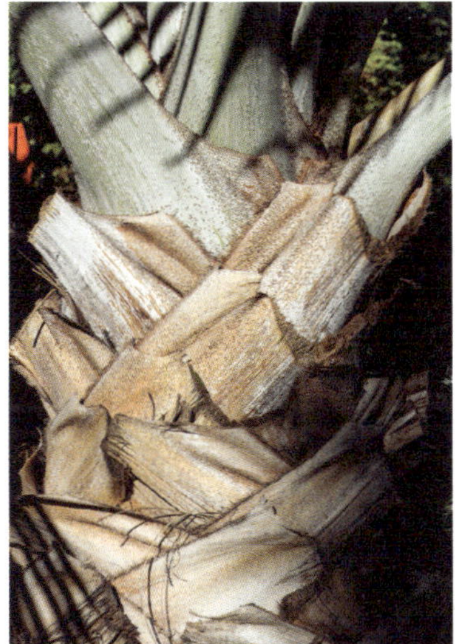

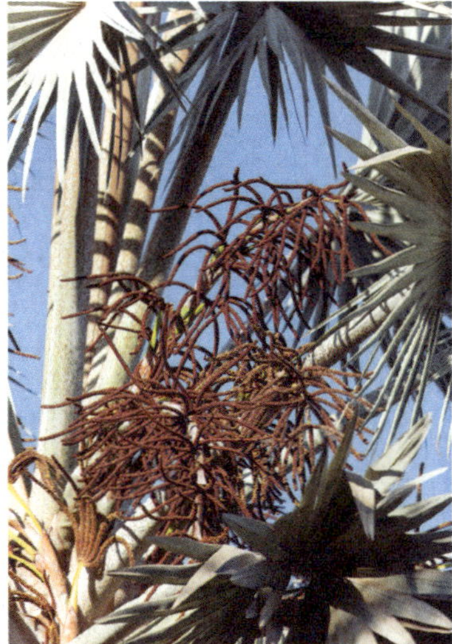

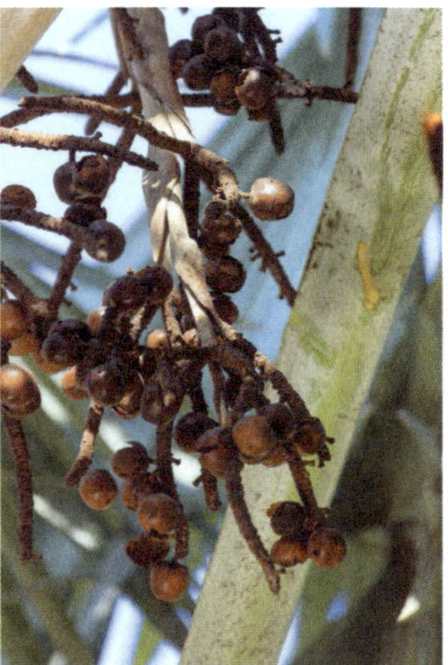

1. Trunk with retained leaf bases. 2. Inflorescence. 3. Fruits.

The Bismarck palm is found only in Madagascar, where it grows in open plains and seasonally flooded grasslands. The trunk is solitary, up to 80 feet tall, and the leaves are stiff and silvery green. The pale color of the leaves, which varies in intensity from palm to palm, is caused by a layer of wax on the surface. Like a lip-balm with sunscreen, the wax protects the leaves from drying out and from overexposure to the sun. The brown, spongy fruits are produced in abundance and only have one seed each. In Madagascar, the trunks are used for construction, while the leaves are sometimes used for roofing thatch and basketry. The local people attribute some medicinal properties to infusions made from this palm, but there is no scientific evidence for their efficacy. This striking palm is a popular landscape plant around the world. Much of its natural habitat is being transformed by agricultural expansion and fires, but it remains the only tree left in the landscape of Madagascar.

Carlos Murillo Depraect, the founder of the Jardín Botánico Culiacán, originally planted the seeds of this species of *Bismarckia* on his property in the town of Bachigualato, before transplanting the palms years later near the southern entrance of the garden.

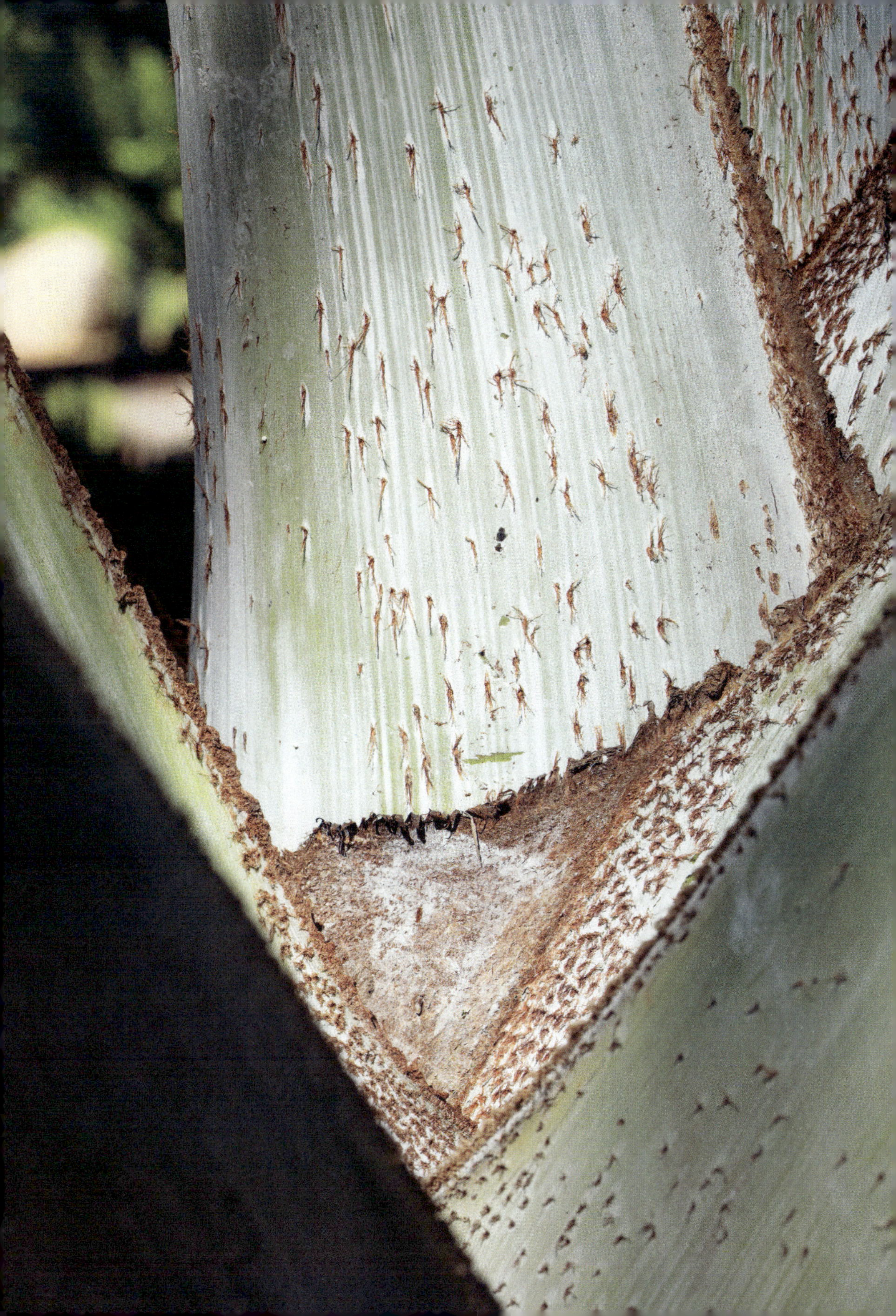

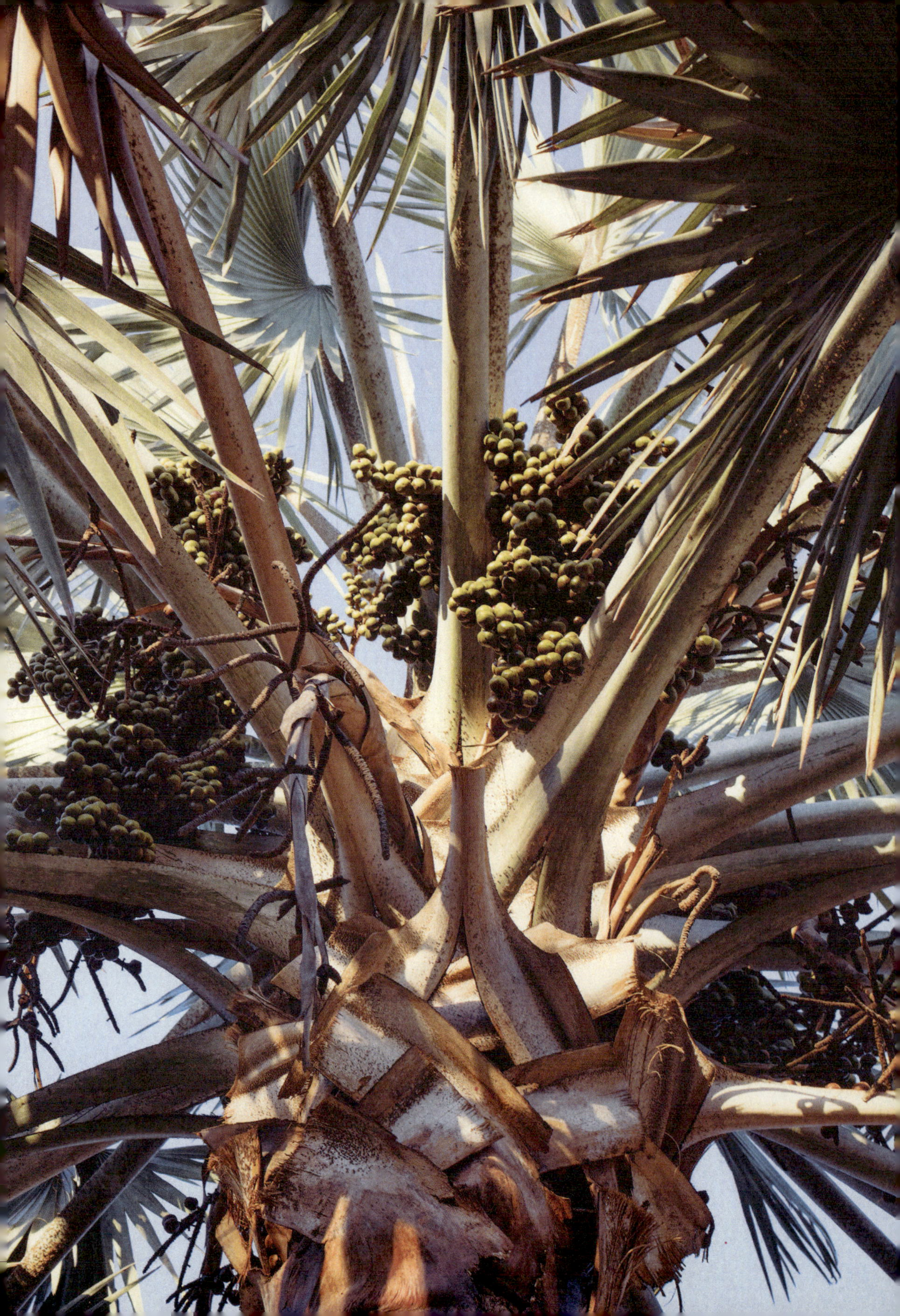

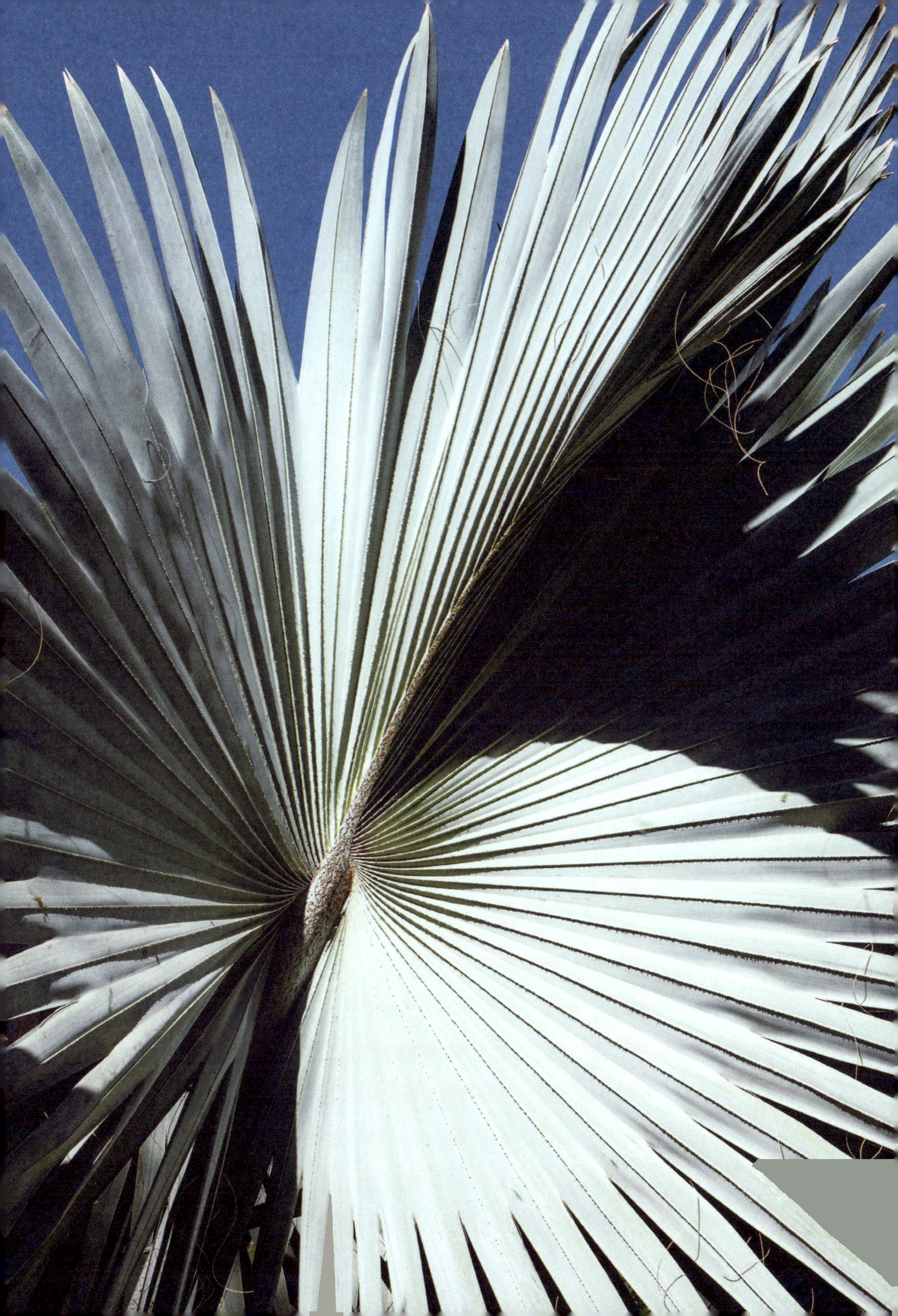

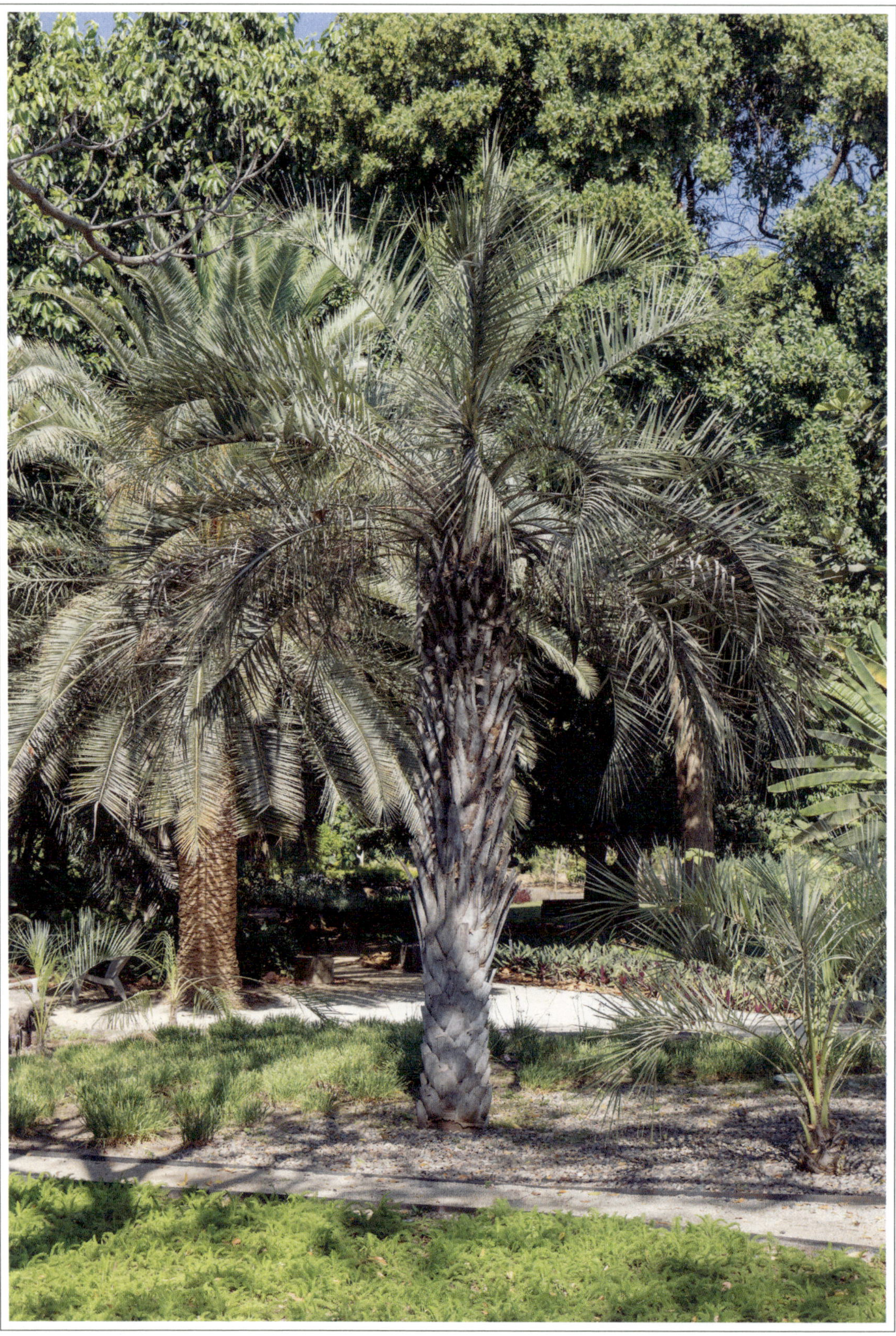

14

JELLY PALM

Butia odorata Barb. Rodr. ex Noblick

Status: Assessment of global conservation status required
Distribution: Southern Brazil and Uruguay bordering on Brazil

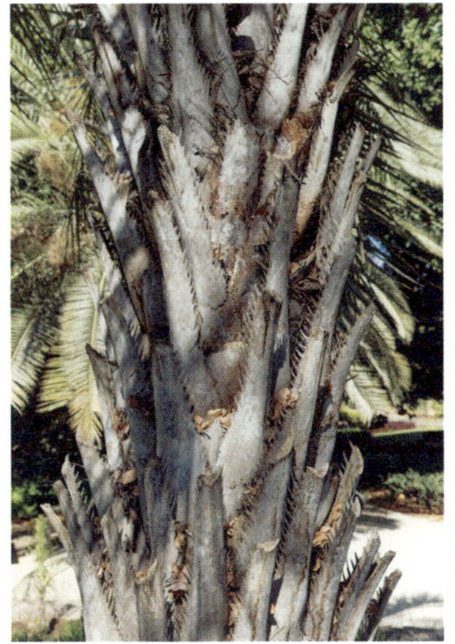

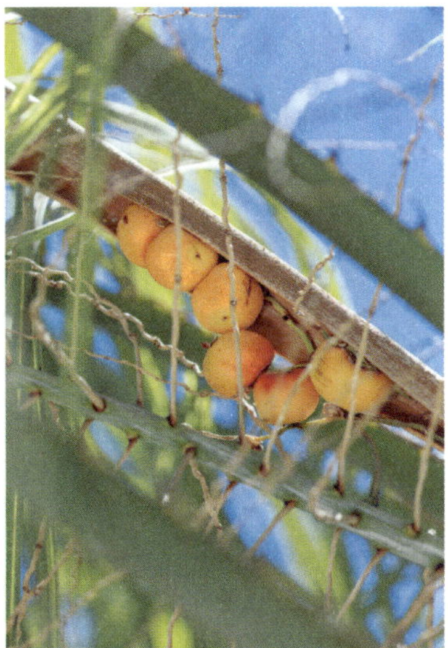

1. Trunk with retained leaf bases. 2. Ripe fruits.

A striking little palm, just over 16 feet tall, this species is originally from dry tropical forests and seasonally dry grasslands. Brazilian scientists call areas where *Butia odorata* is the most common species *butiazais*. It is a slow-growing palm, which can live for up to two hundred years. It has been cultivated in warm temperate and subtropical gardens for many decades, although for much of this period it was confused with the more delicate and tropical *Butia capitata*. Botanists cleared up the confusion in the early twenty-first century, and we now have the correct name for this popular ornamental palm, with its arching silvery leaves and edible fruits. Its flowers, which are pollinated by flies, wasps, and other insects, vary in color from yellow to pink to purple. The common name of the jelly palm comes from the usual way of consuming the fruits, which are used to flavor jelly.

The Jardín Botánico Culiacán has one specimen of *Butia odorata* (formerly confused with *Butia capitata*).

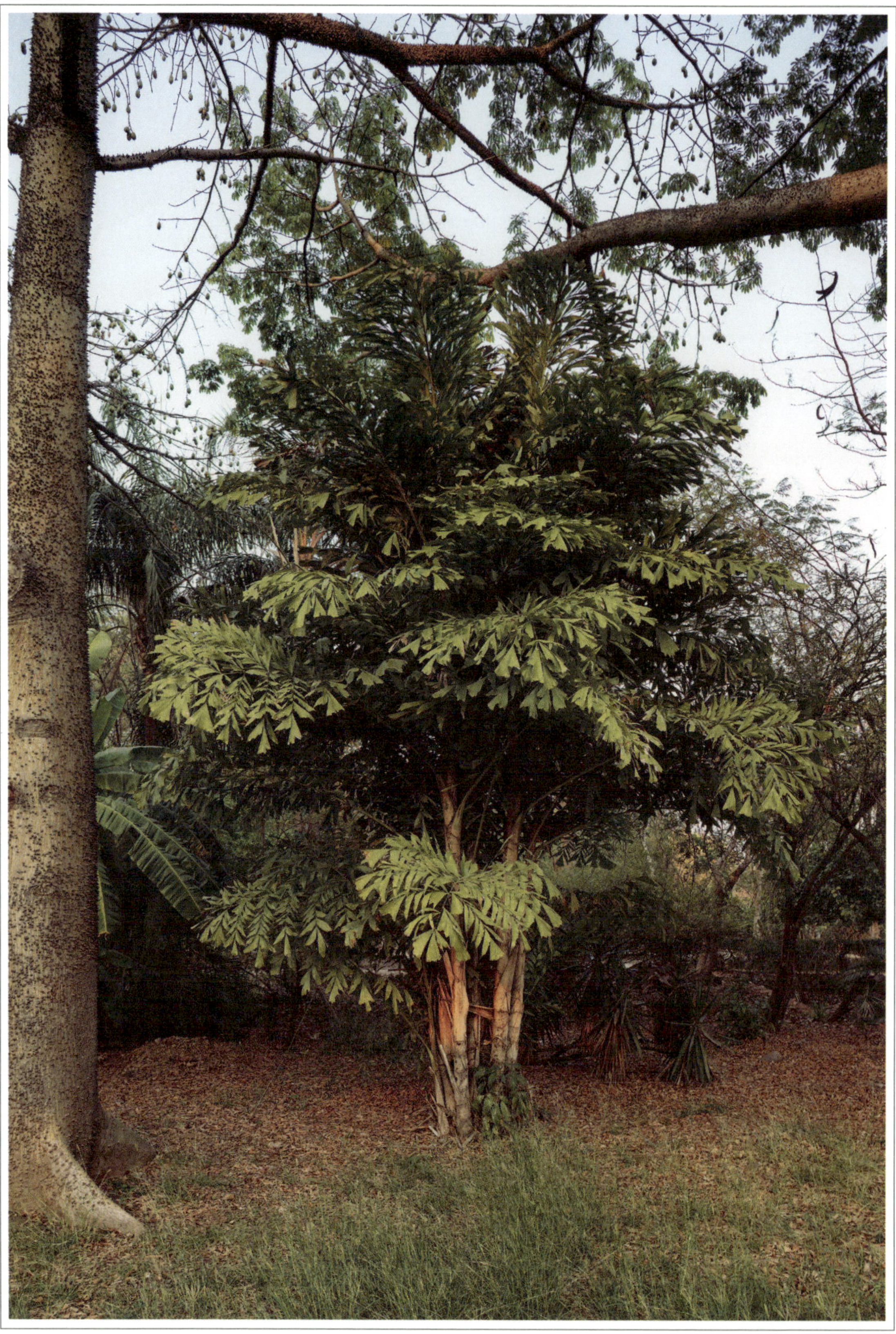

15
CLUSTERING FISHTAIL PALM

Caryota mitis Lour

Status: Assessment of global conservation status required
Distribution: Southern China, Southeast Asia, and the Philippines

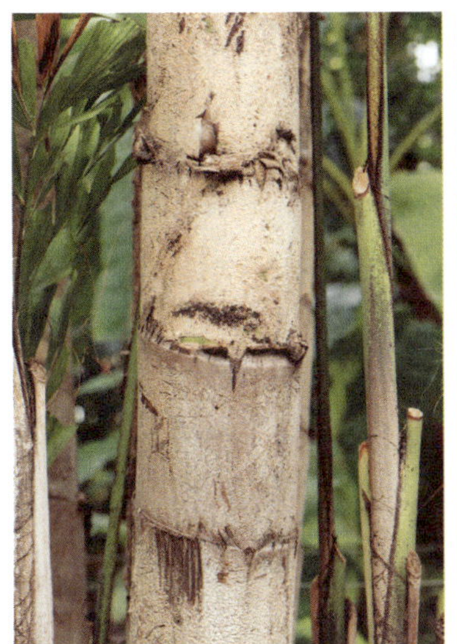
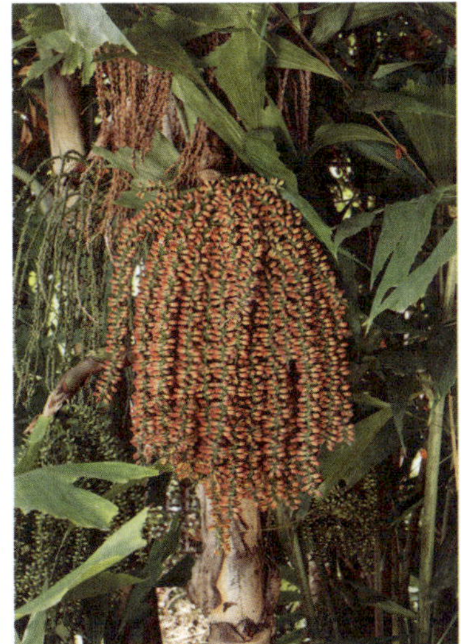
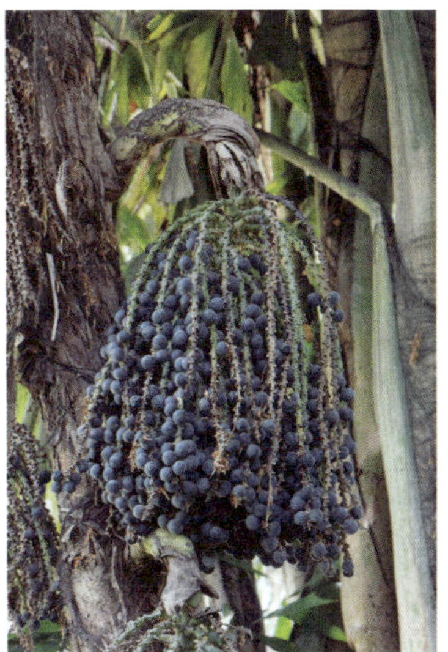

1. Stem. 2. Flower buds. 3. Ripe fruits.

Caryota mitis has multiple stems that grow up to 16 feet tall. Its leaves are divided into seemingly irregular segments that look like fishtails. Like other *Caryota* species, certain individual stems produce flowers and fruits and then die, while other stems continue to live. This species, native to tropical rainforests, is a popular garden plant, because it is fast-growing and forms a dense cluster of stems. All species of *Caryota* have a fleshy fruit that may contain one, two, or three seeds. The fruits should not be handled: they contain irritating, needle-shaped crystals of calcium oxalate that can cause severe dermatitis. In their native ecosystems, birds and other animals can consume the fruits without harm. Humans use the stems to make spears or to use as water pipes.

This species is part of the original collection donated by Carlos Murillo Depraect in the 1980s to establish the Jardín Botánico Culiacán.

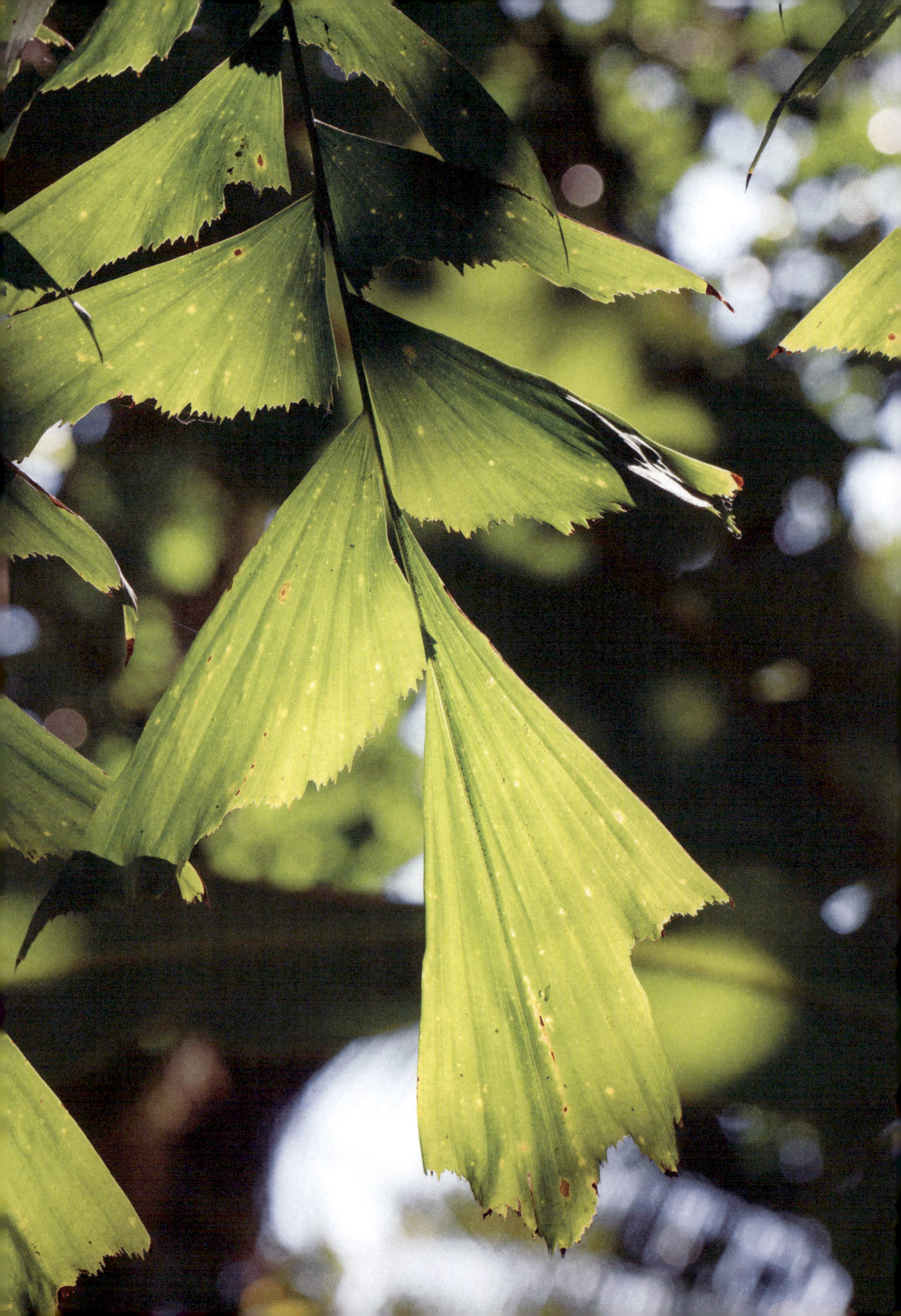

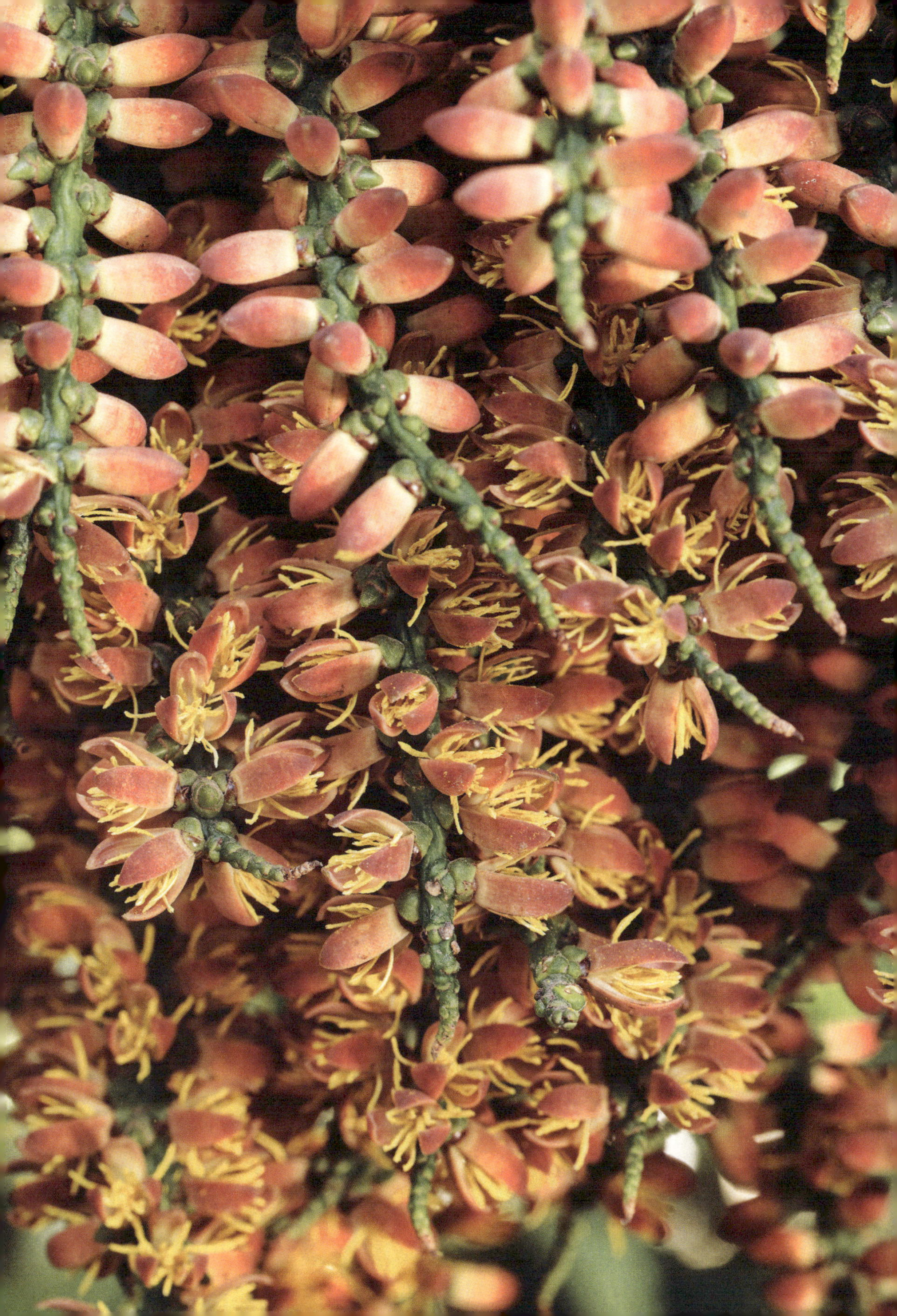

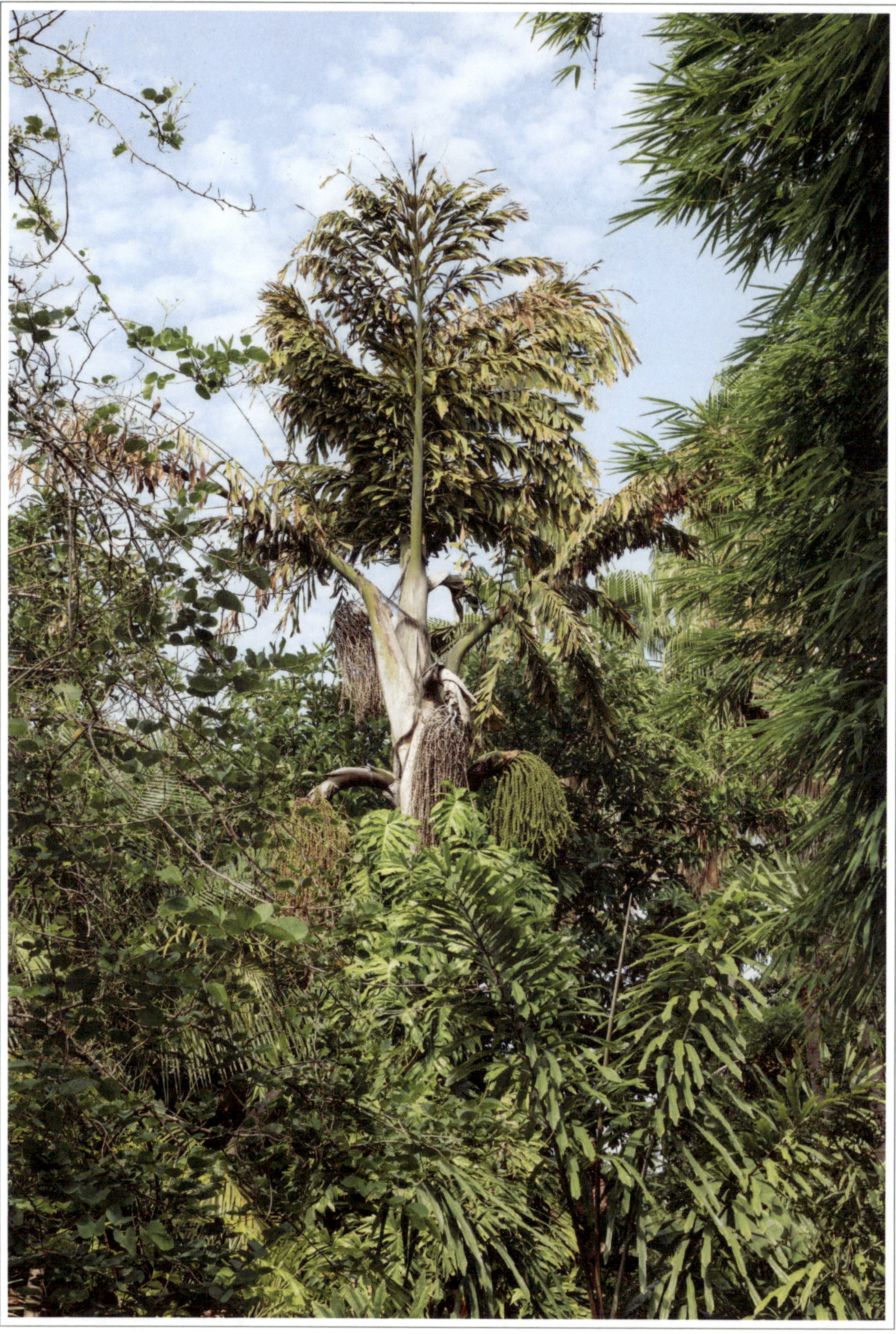

16

GIANT FISHTAIL PALM, BORNEO FISHTAIL PALM

Caryota no Becc.

Status: Designated as Least Concern on the IUCN Red List
Distribution: Borneo

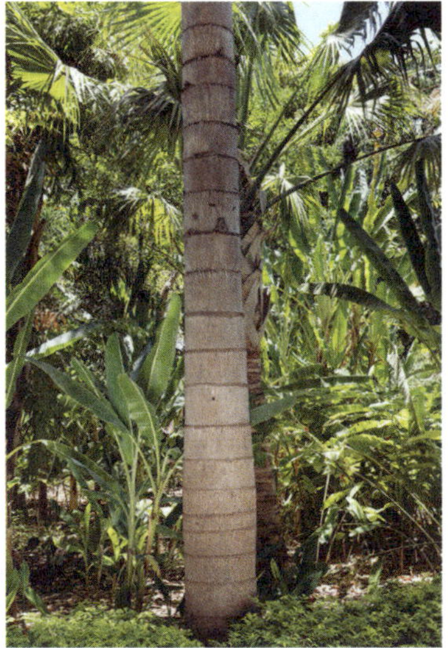
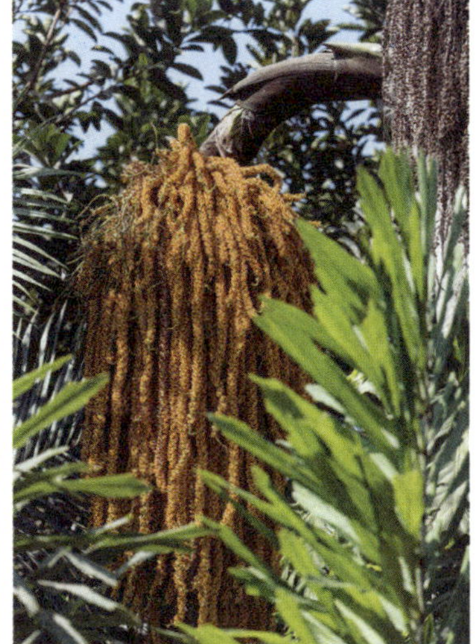
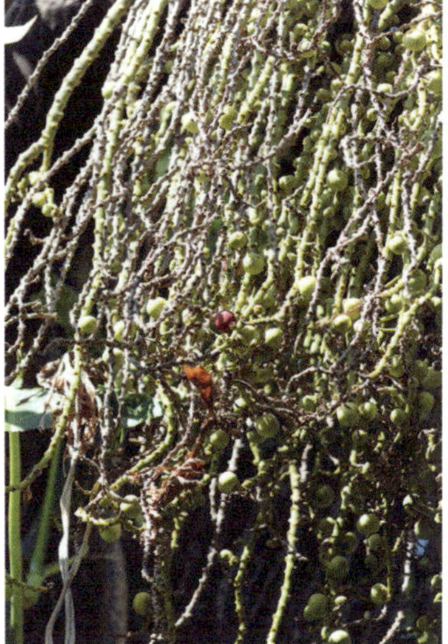

1. Trunk. 2. Inflorescence. 3. Unripe fruits.

Caryota no is a large, robust, single-stemmed species that grows up to 65 feet tall. Like all species in the genus *Caryota*, it has remarkably large, divided leaves. This is the only genus in the palm family with bipinnate leaves. If you compare a *Caryota* leaf to a leaf from a coconut palm, the difference is obvious. The coconut leaf has a long, central rachis that bears leaflets. In *Caryota*, the central rachis has secondary rachises, which bear the leaflets. As with all *Caryota* species, the leaflets of this palm resemble fishtails. After the palm flowers and produces fruits, it dies. The reproductive process can last many months. The fruits are round and ripen from green to purple to black. The terminal bud, called a "no," can be eaten. The soft inner core of the trunk is ground and washed to extract a kind of sago flour that is used for thickening soups and purées or for making desserts. The trunk is also used to obtain fibers for string or for weaving baskets.

The first *Caryota no* specimens at the Jardín Botánico Culiacán flowered and died after thirty years. New specimens are growing, ensuring that the species will continue to be represented at the garden.

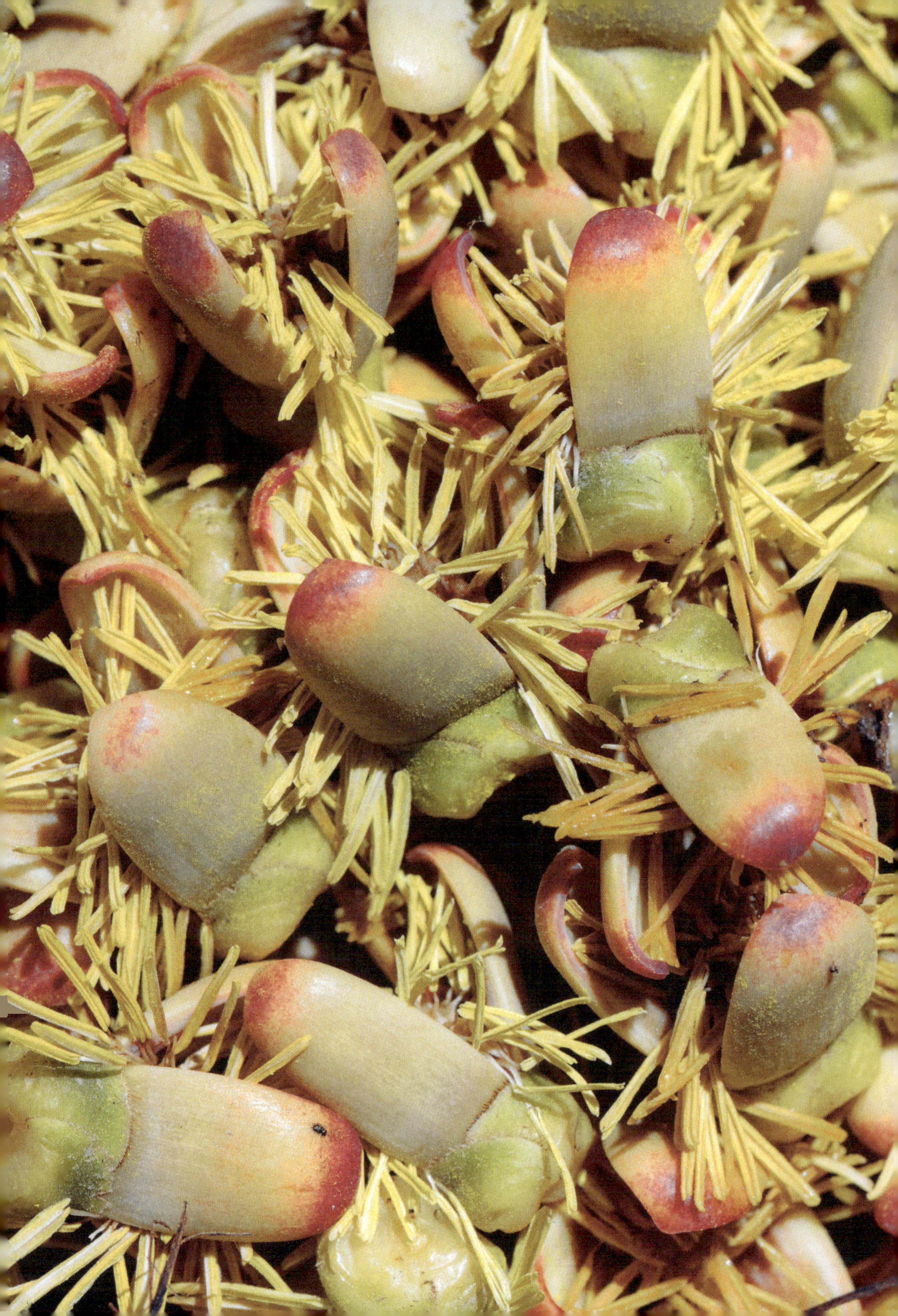

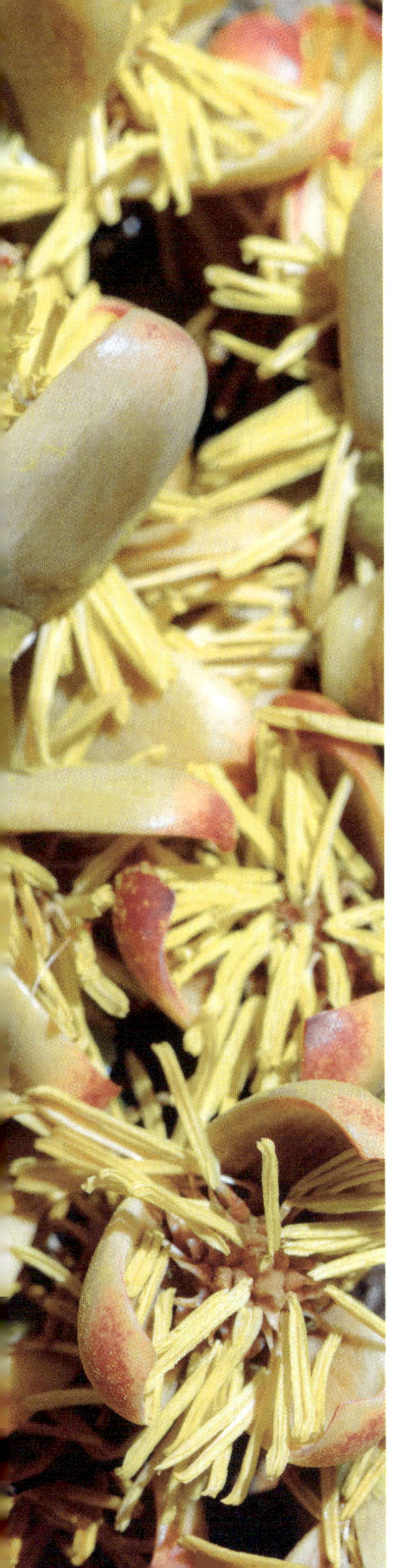

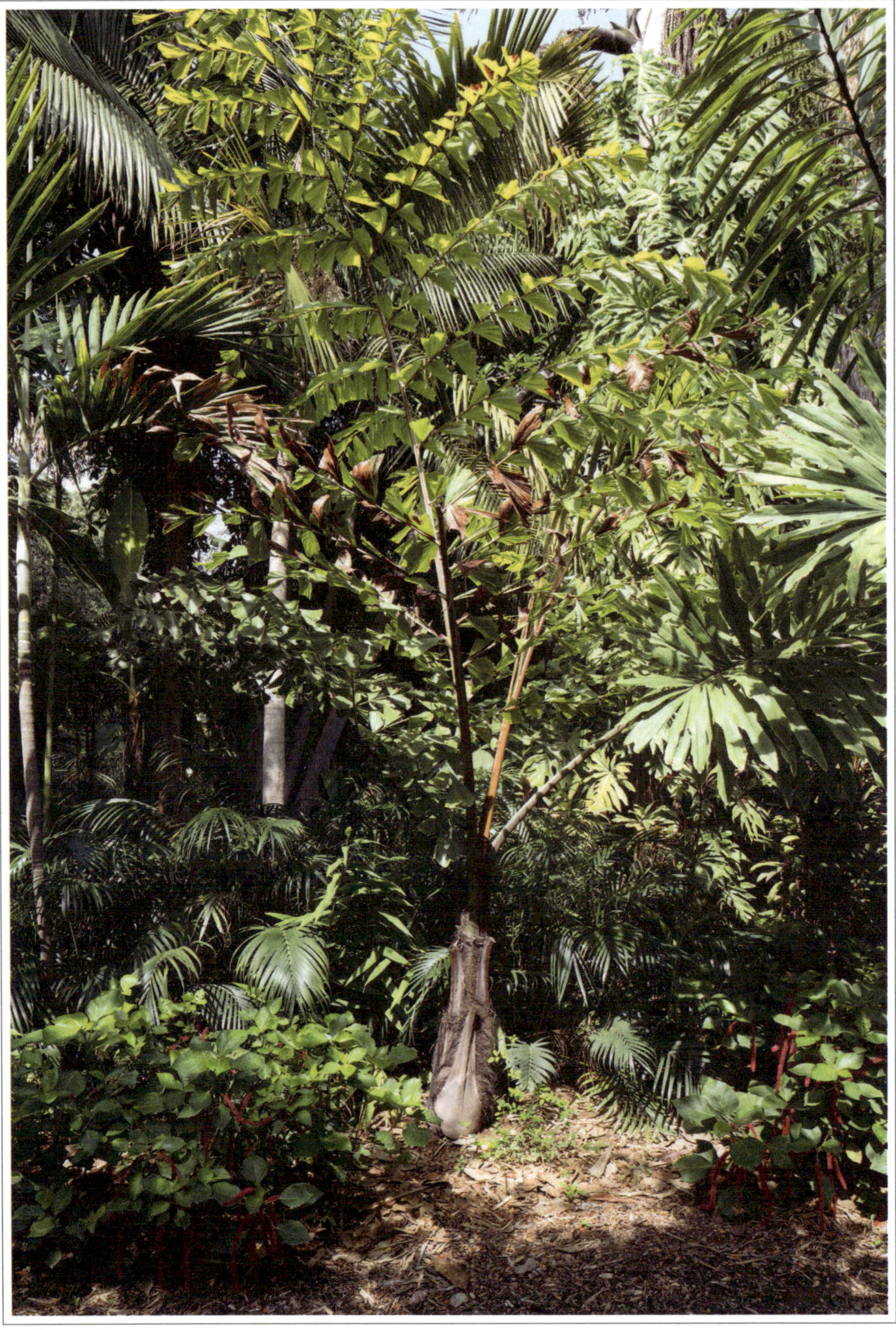

17

GIANT FISHTAIL PALM

Caryota obtusa Griff.

Status: Assessment of global conservation status required
Distribution: Northeastern India, Bangladesh, Thailand, and Laos

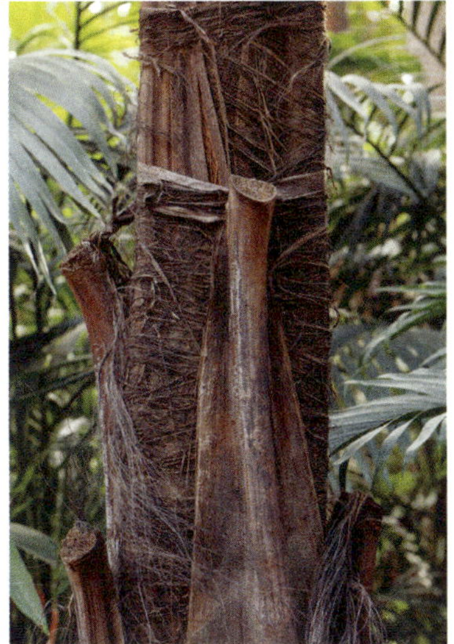

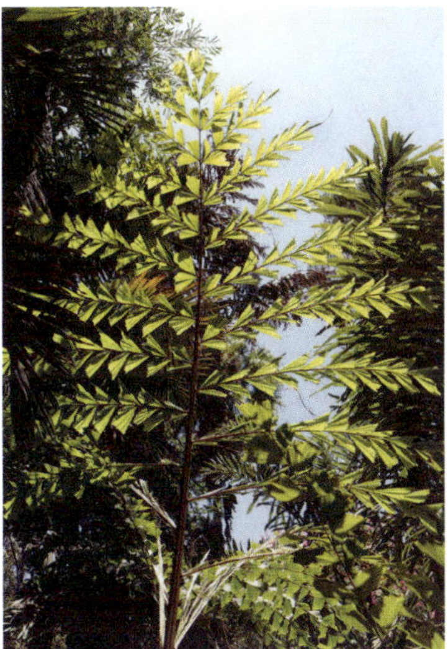

1. Trunk with leaf bases. 2. Leaf.

Caryota obtusa is one of the largest species in the genus. The stem is immense, reaching from 100 to 130 feet in height, and often slightly bottle-shaped or swollen in the middle. This giant palm occurs in rainforests and seasonally wet forests, but it can stand temperatures as low as 27°F. As in all *Caryota* species, the enormous spreading leaves are bipinnate and borne in a layered crown (see *Caryota cumingii*), with leaflets in the form of a fishtail. The giant fishtail palm dies after completing one life cycle, although the process of producing flowers and fruits can go on for many months. The inflorescences are very large—up to 20 feet long—and the dark red fruits should not be handled, as their flesh can cause dermatitis. In the palm's native forest habitat, some species of birds and mammals can eat the fruits without ill effects. Unfortunately, the fruits are also very attractive to animals native to Sinaloa, so the staff of the botanical gardens needs constantly to keep an eye open to prevent local animals from poisoning themselves.

The Jardín Botánico Culiacán acquired its specimens of *Caryota obtusa* in 2013.

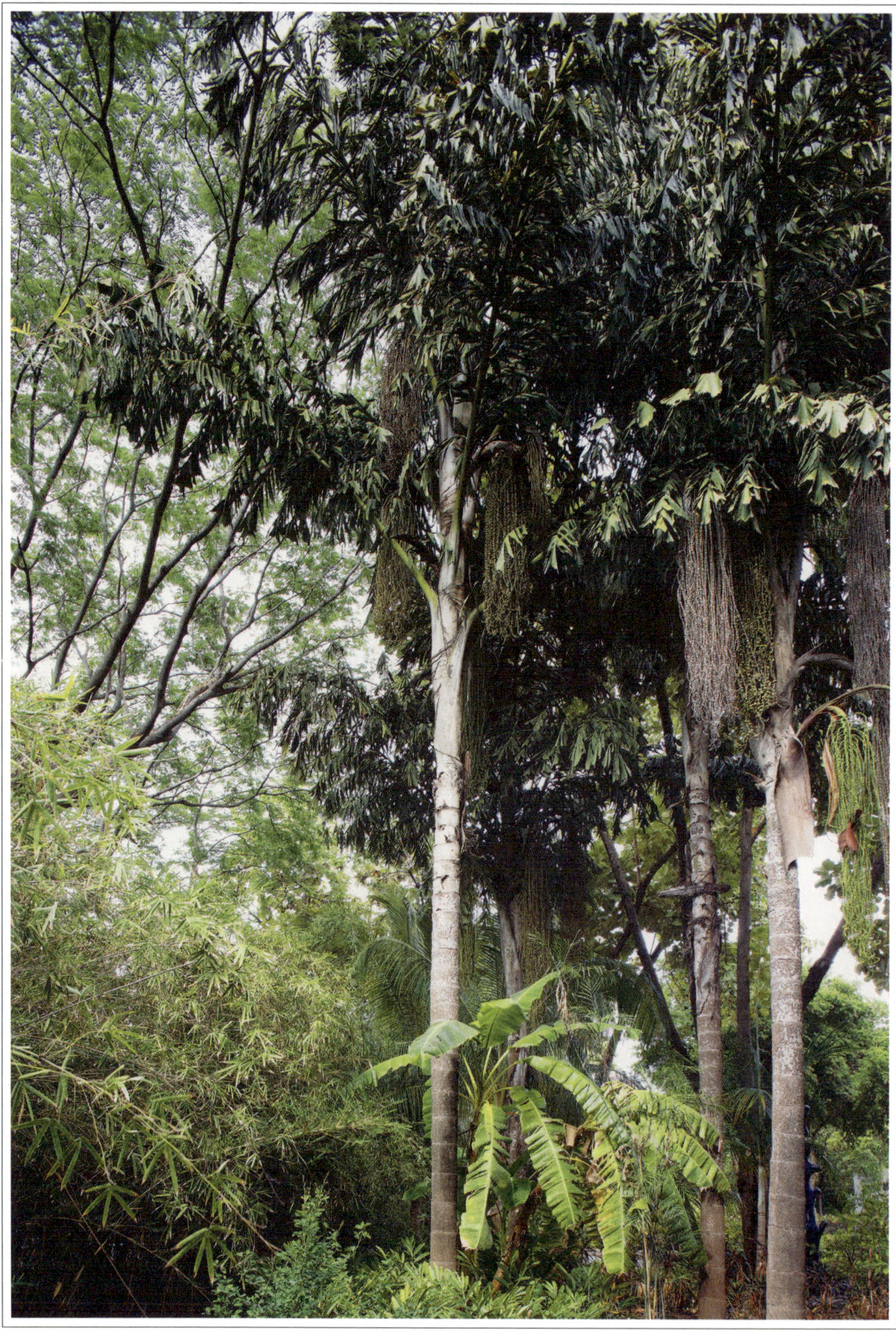

18

TODDY PALM, JAGGERY PALM, FISHTAIL WINE PALM, TODDY FISHTAIL PALM

Caryota urens L.

Status: Assessment of global conservation status required
Distribution: Southern Asia, Southeast Asia, and southern China

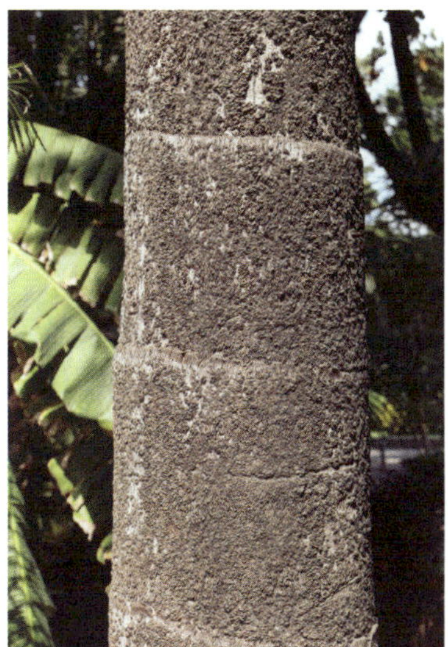
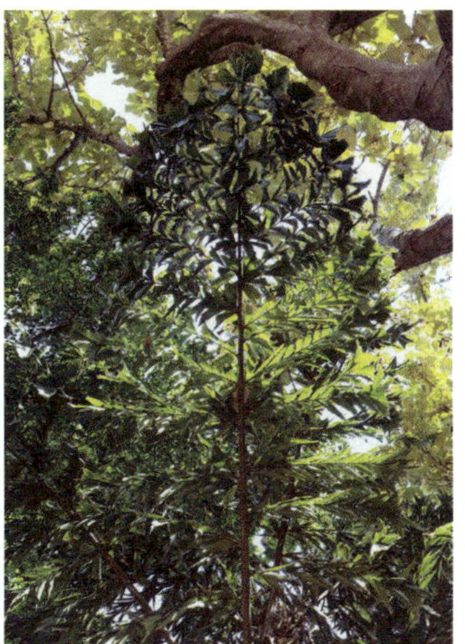
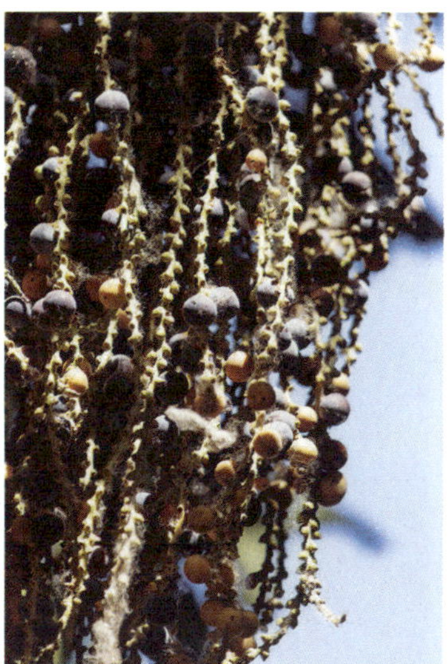

1. Trunk. 2. Leaf. 3. Fruits.

This single-stem species of *Caryota* is widespread in tropical rainforests across its distribution range, where it grows up to around 35 feet in height. Its trunk is silvery-gray. It is one of the most useful species of *Caryota*, and its wide distribution may be the result of human activity, which moves this valuable species across the region. The palm is one of several species that is used to produce sugar and alcohol. In *Caryota urens*, the flower stalk, which can be as much as 10 feet long, is tapped for its sap. The tip of the newly emergent flower stalk is cut and a recipient is attached. The sap collected from the cut stalk is fermented to make wine or boiled down into sugar. Each day, a little more of the tip is cut off in order to maintain the flow. Over several weeks, a single palm can produce many liters of sap. The fibers of the leaves are used to make string, brooms, and brushes.

The abundance of specimens of *Caryota urens* in the Jardín Botánico Culiacán since 1991 has served as a backup for the conservation of the species.

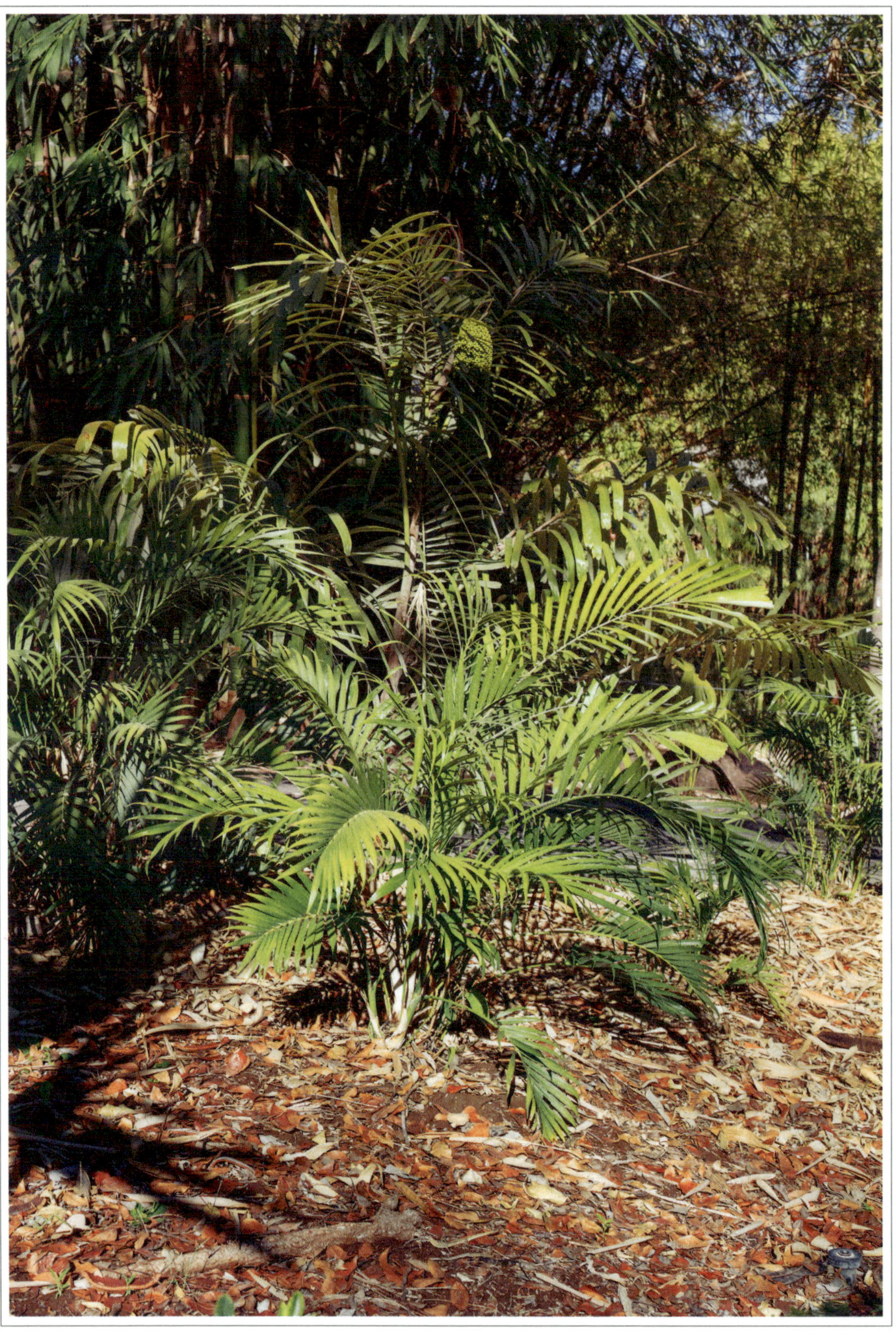

19

RIVER PALM, CASCADE PALM, CAT PALM

Chamaedorea cataractarum Mart.

Status: Designated as Threatened on the Mexican list of endangered species (NOM-059-SEMARNAT-2010)
Distribution: Southern Mexico

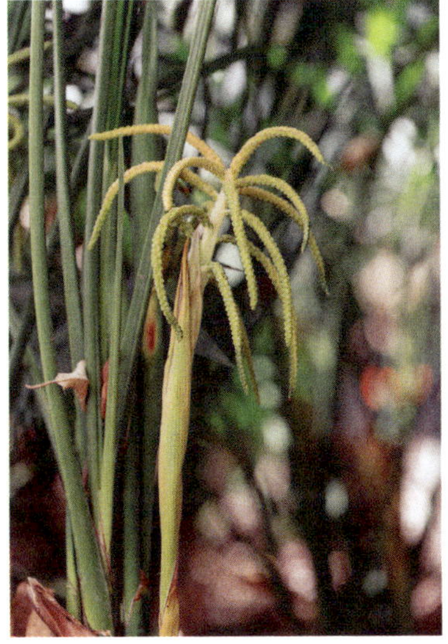

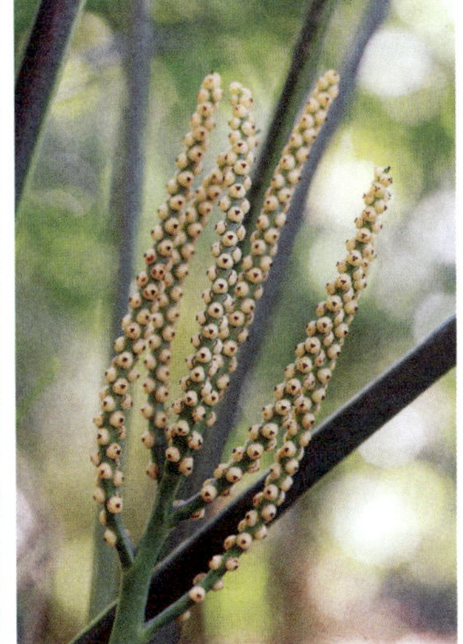

1. Male inflorescence. 2. Female inflorescence.

Chamaedorea cataractarum is a small, shrubby palm that produces a dense cluster of stems, each one up to 6.5 feet long. The species is endemic to southern Mexico, specifically Chiapas, Tabasco, and Oaxaca, but it has become widespread in cultivation. *Chamaedorea cataractarum* is what botanists call a rheophyte. Rheophytes typically grow on the banks of montane rivers and streams and have adaptations that allow them to resist the force of moving water. For example, many rheophytes have flexible stems and narrow leaves. This species has several adaptations to its unusual habitat: the leaves can bend without breaking, while the stem branches dichotomously and puts out roots wherever it comes into contact with soil. The shiny black fruits on orange stalks attract fruit-eating birds, which disperse the seeds. The fibers surrounding the seed expand after soaking in water for thirty to forty hours and form short hooks. Botanists believe these hooks allow the seeds to attach themselves to the river bank, where they can germinate and grow. In gardens, the species does not require fast-moving water and grows easily to form attractive, many-stemmed specimens.

The specimen at the Jardín Botánico Culiacán comes from the state of Chiapas in Mexico. When the specimen was collected, in the early 1990s, botanists had to visit an area controlled by the Zapatistas, which was by then very dangerous. Dense fog in the area also added to the difficulties of the trip.

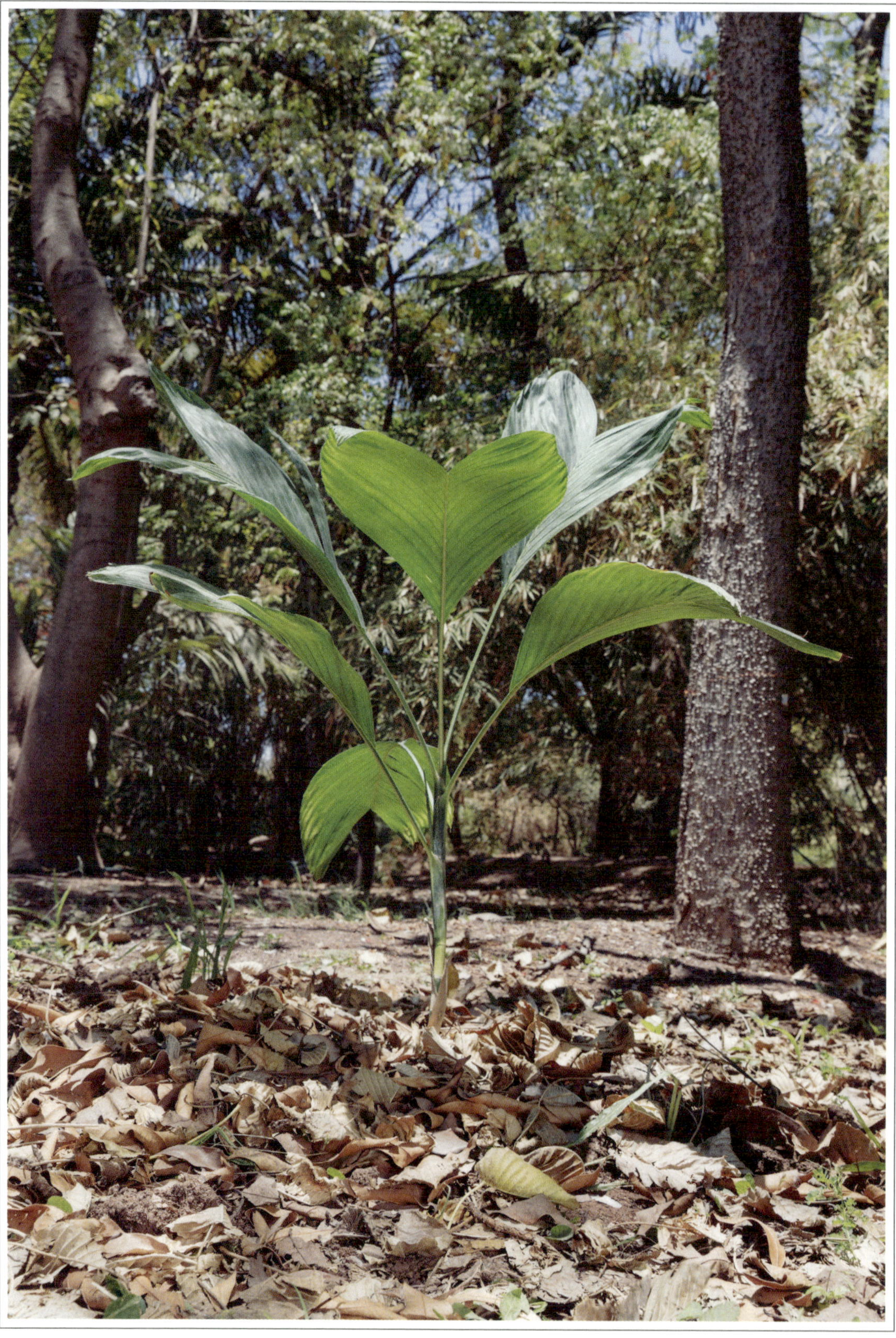

20

TUNA TAIL PALM, ERNEST AUGUST'S PALM, UNDERSTORY FISHTAIL PALM

Chamaedorea ernesti-augustii H. Wendl.

Status: Designated as Threatened on the Mexican list of endangered species (NOM-059-SEMARNAT-2010)
Distribution: Southern Mexico, Belize, Guatemala, and Honduras

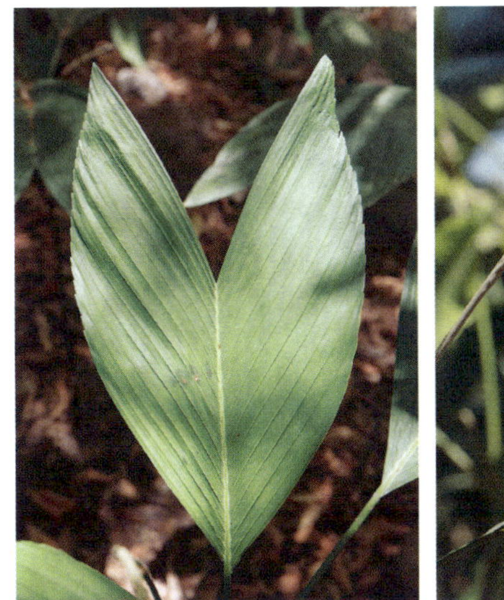
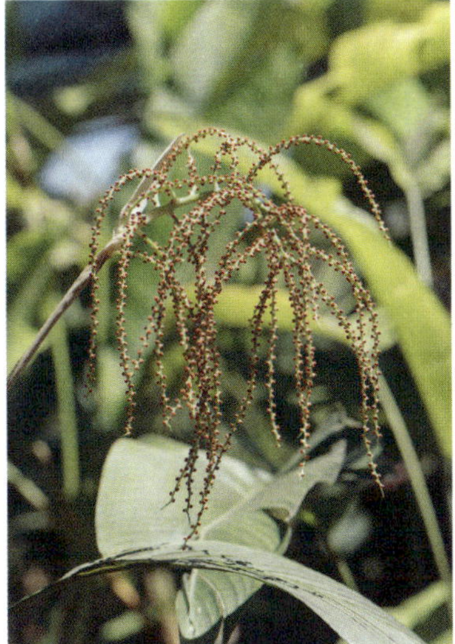
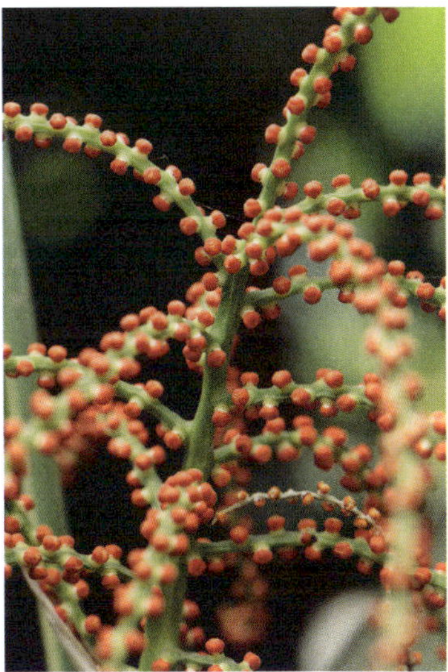

1. Leaf. 2. Male inflorescence. 3. Detail of the male inflorescence.

This *Chamaedorea* is a small, solitary palm, which grows up to 6.5 feet tall, with broad, undivided leaves that resemble the elaborate tail fin of a large, green fish. It grows in lowland rainforests and is widely regarded as one of the most beautiful species in the genus. As in all species of *Chamaedorea*, male and female flowers are born on separate plants. The male flower stalks are branched and green. The female stalks are unbranched, erect, and turn bright orange when bearing the small black fruits. This popular species of palm is grown in conservatories and gardens around the world.

The first specimens came to the Jardín Botánico Culiacán in 2014, purchased from nurseries that used them for cut leaves. A couple of years later, in 2016, the garden acquired more specimens. Today *Chamaedorea ernesti-augustii* is one of the best represented species in the palm collection. This is of great significance, for it is a threatened species that needs to be reproduced in cultivation to avoid extinction.

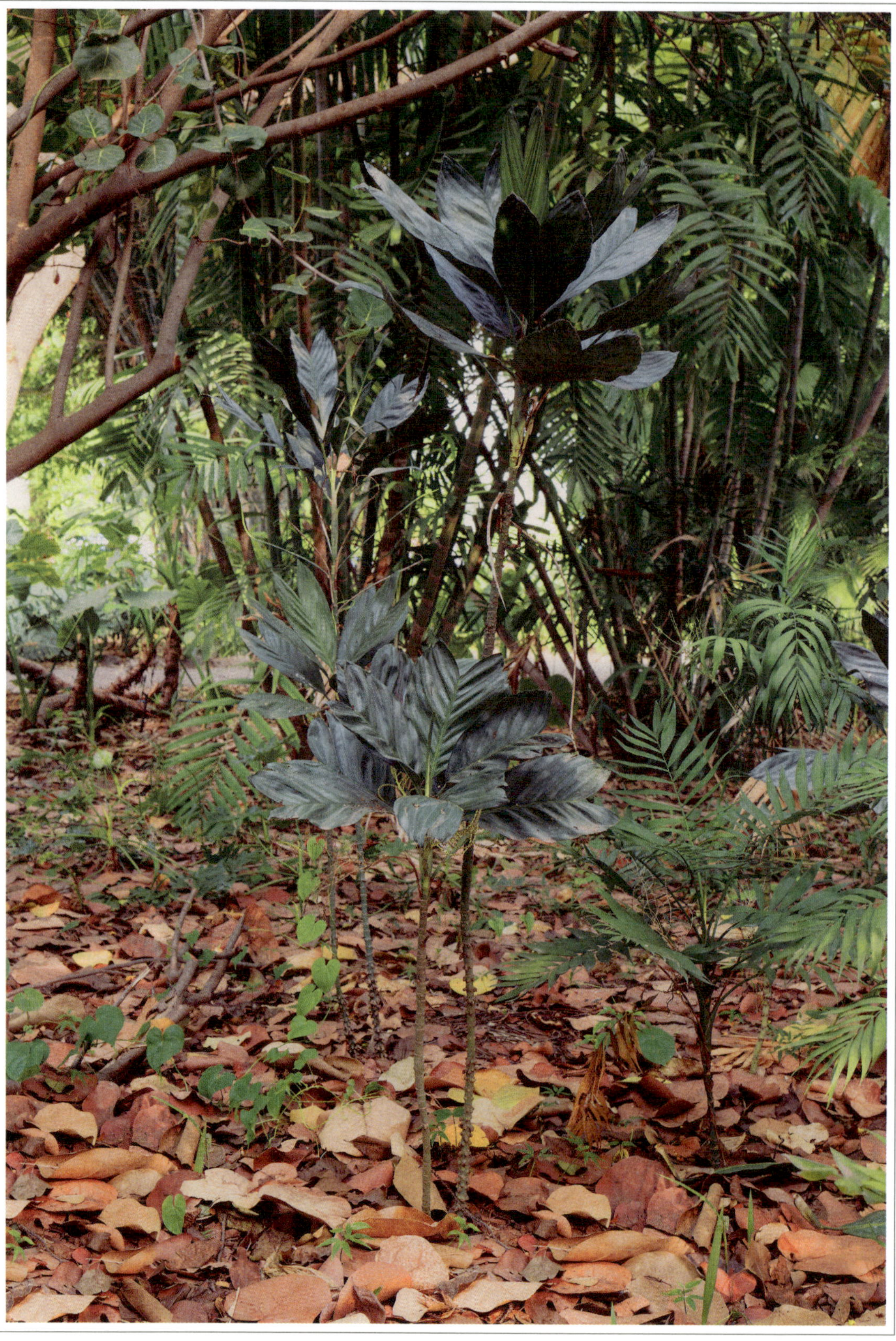

21

METALLIC PALM

Chamaedorea metallica O.F. Cook ex H.E. Moore

Status: Designated as Endangered on the Mexican list of endangered species (NOM-059-SEMARNAT-2010)
Distribution: Endemic to Veracruz, Mexico

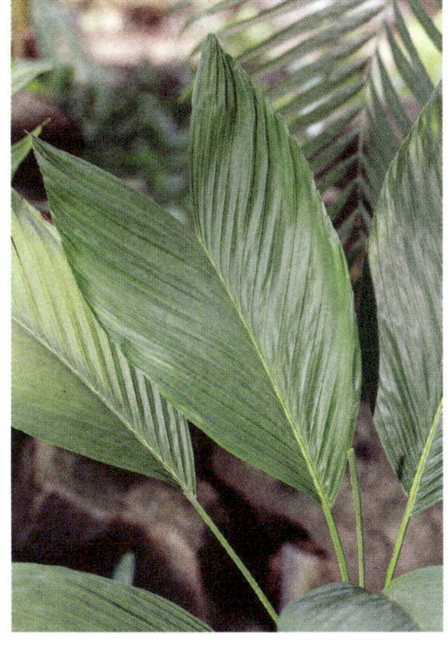
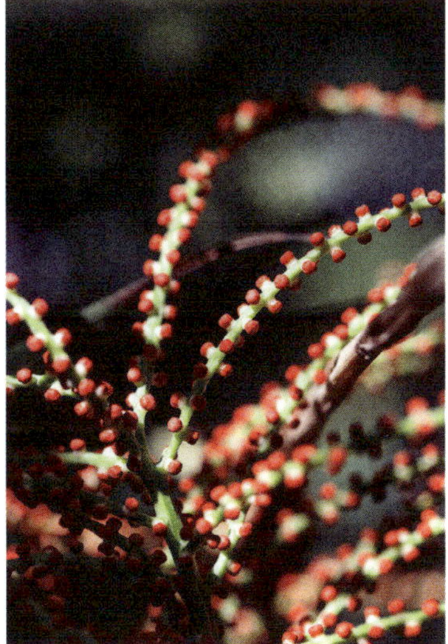

1. Leaf. 2. Detail of the male inflorescence.

This small, 10-feet-tall palm was first discovered in the state of Veracruz in 1905, but not named until 1966. *Chamaedorea metallica* is found only in Veracruz and has never been identified elsewhere in Mexico. The inspiration for the scientific name of the palm is easy to see: the leaves are of a dark, dull, metallic green—almost black in the best individuals. There is individual variation in leaf shape as well: most clones have undivided leaves, but some can have regularly or irregularly divided leaves. There are admirers of either form, but most nurseries grow and sell the undivided variety, which is extremely popular. The palm is small and solitary, but three or more plants are often placed together in a single pot to make a fuller, more appealing product. Both male and female flower stalks are upright and orange, but the female stalk is unbranched and bears small black fruits. The palm is slow-growing but durable, and tolerant of interior environments.

The first two specimens of *Chamaedorea metallica* acquired by the Jardín Botánico Culiacán arrived more than thirty years ago, in the 1980s, and are now in the rainforest exhibit. Today the collection has more than 20 specimens, many of them genuine treasures rescued from nurseries.

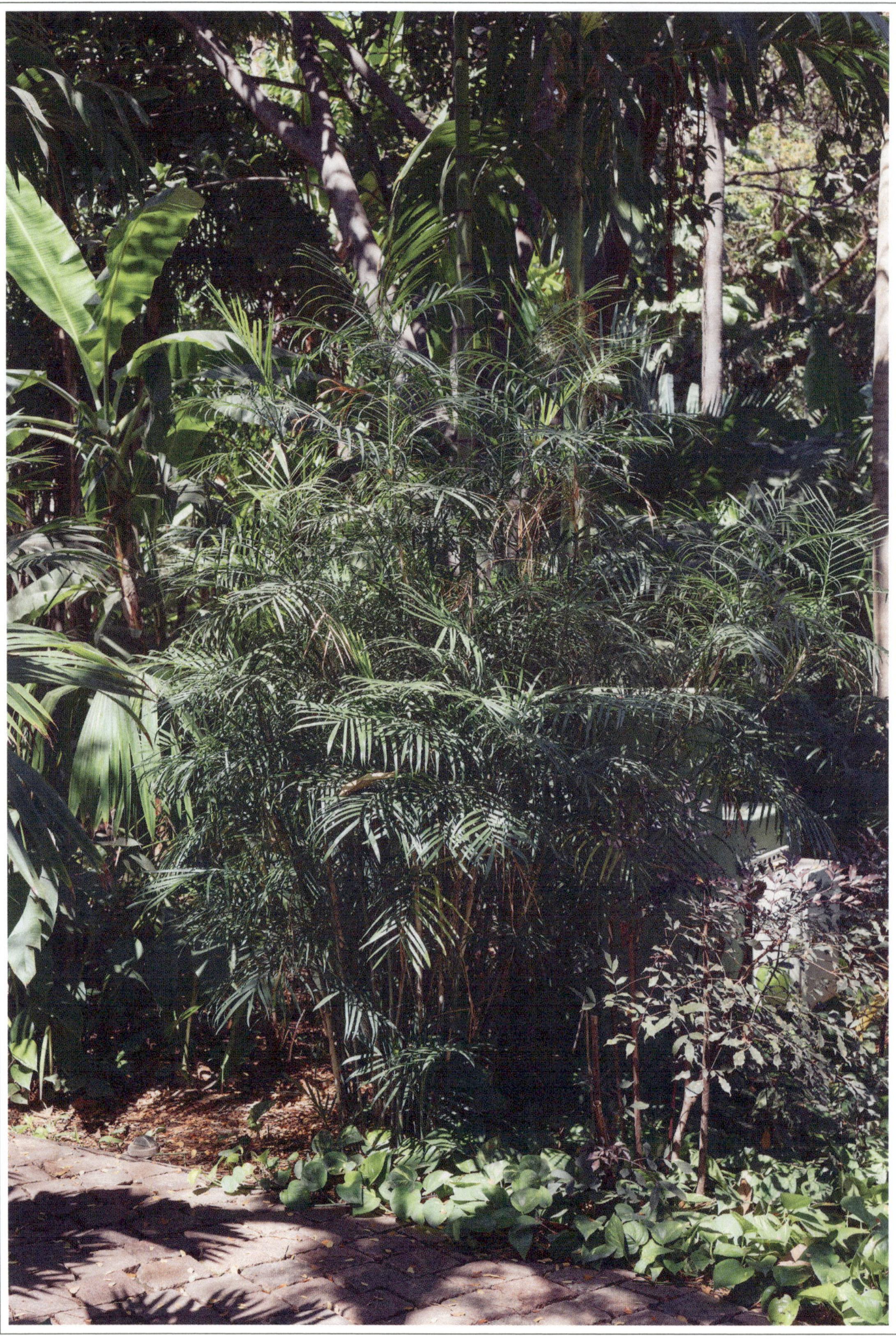

22

SEIFRIZ'S CHAMAEDOREA, BAMBOO PALM, REED PALM, BAMBUSINA

Chamaedorea seifrizii Burret

Status: Assessment of global conservation status required
Distribution: Southern Mexico, Belize, Guatemala, and Honduras

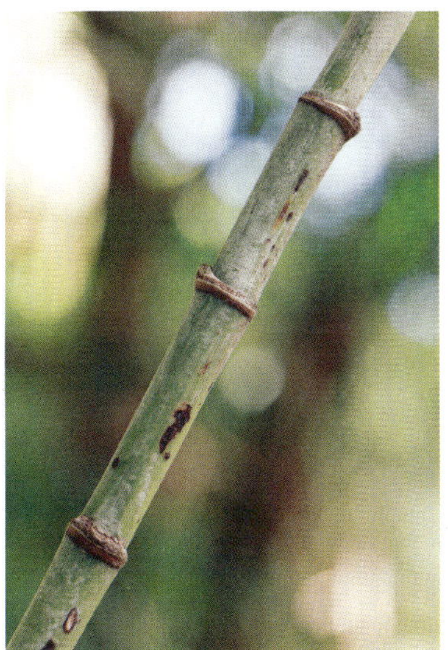
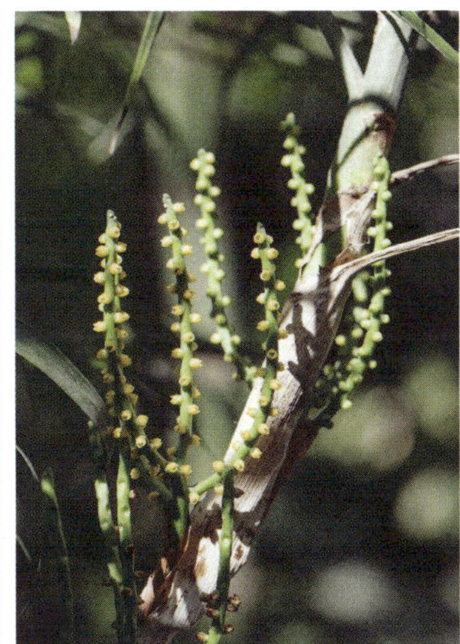
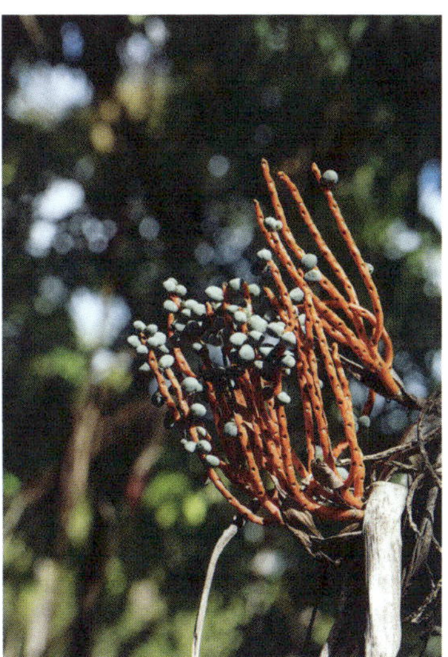

1. Stem. 2. Female inflorescence. 3. Ripe fruits.

One glance at the bambusina and you can see how it got its common name: the clustered, slender stems, two to 13 feet tall, are ringed or articulated just like bamboo. Some cultivated varieties have leaves in which the terminal leaflets are much wider than the other leaflets. This palm was first discovered growing around the ruins of Chichén Itzá, where it had possibly been established by the ancient Maya for ornamental or religious use. It occurs in seasonally dry woodlands, often near watercourses. This is one of the most common *Chamaedorea* species in cultivation. Millions of plants of this species are grown commercially in greenhouses in Europe, North America, and Asia, and are sold as houseplants or interiorscape plants all over the world.

There are many specimens of *Chamaedorea seifrizii* at the Jardín Botánico Culiacán, since it is so easily grown: more than 50 plants in different parts of the Palmetum. Most of these palms were acquired by the botanical garden around 1999, more than twenty years ago now, from the Bachigualato nursery, property of the late Carlos Murillo Depraect.

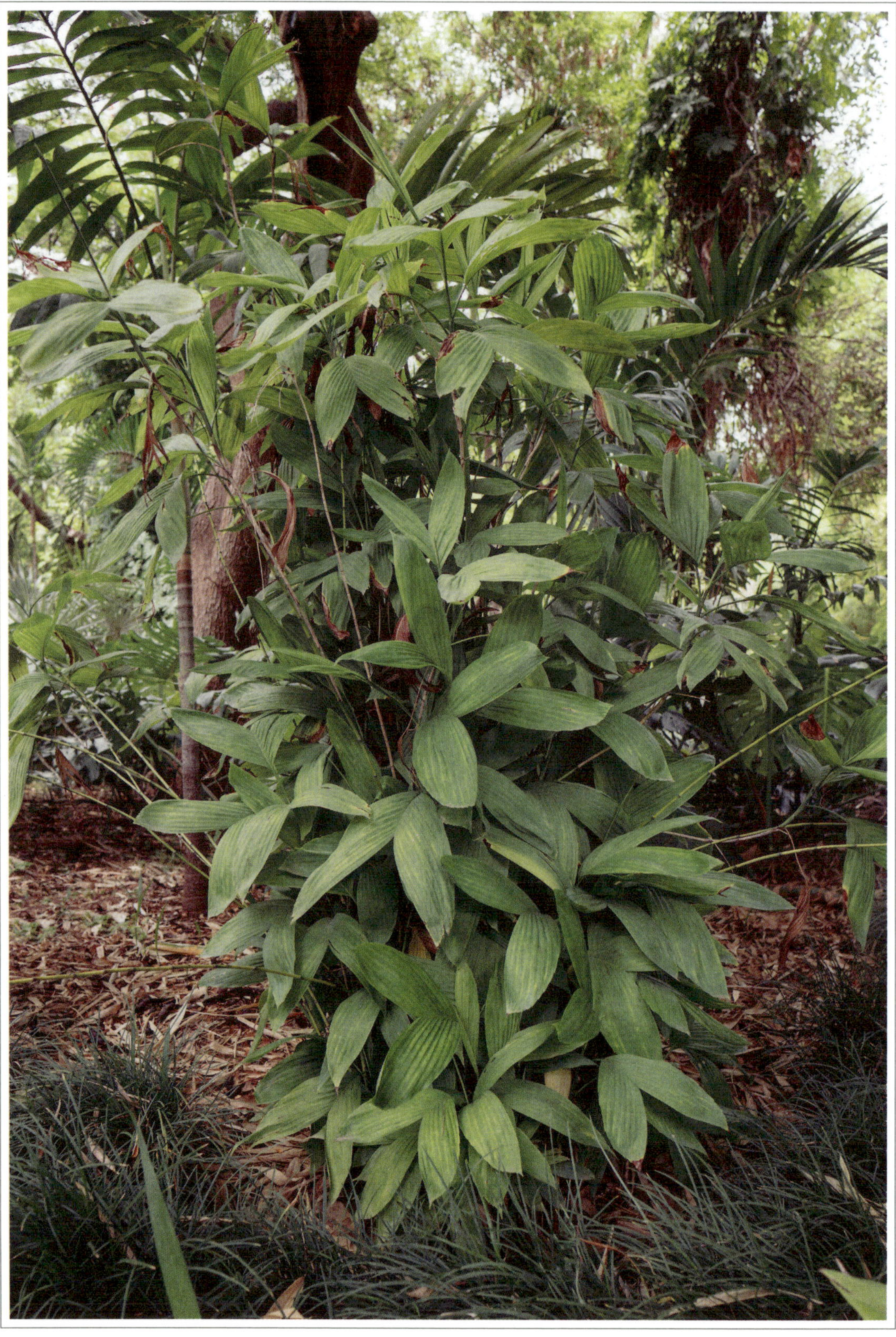

23

STOLON PALM

Chamaedorea stolonifera H. Wendl. ex Hook.f.

Status: Designated as Threatened on the Mexican list of endangered species (NOM-059-SEMARNAT-2010)
Distribution: Endemic to southern Mexico

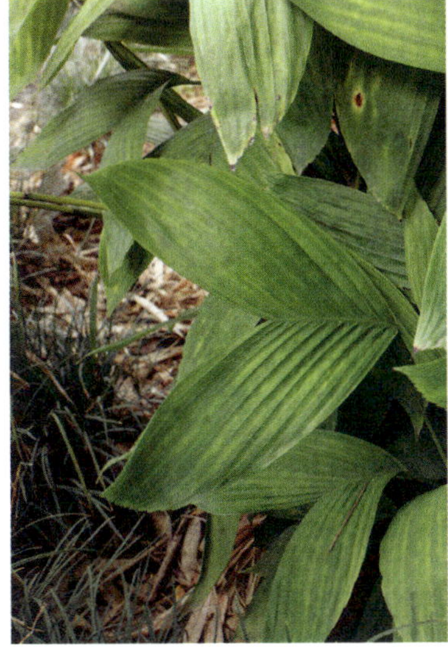

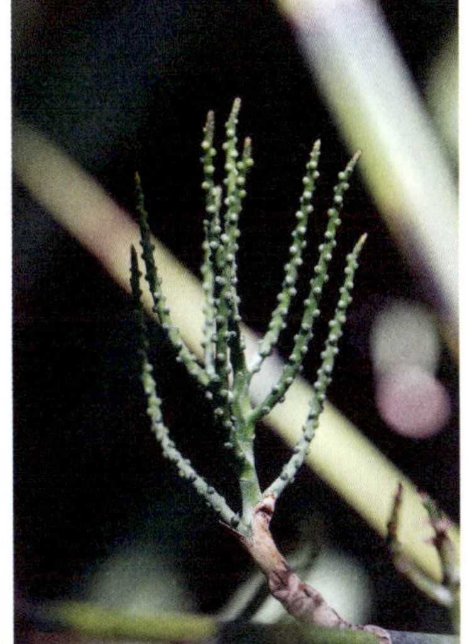

1. Leaf. 2. Male inflorescence.

The scientific name *stolonifera* means "producing stolons," which are the horizontal underground stems by which the small palm colonizes an area. This palm occurs in wet forests growing over limestone in the state of Chiapas. Abundant slender stems, up to 6.5 feet tall and about the diameter of a pencil, are produced in clusters on the stolons. Also, if a stem bends over and touches the soil, it will send out roots and begin to grow as a new plant. The leaves are small, undivided, and V-shaped. Because the palm is found in only one area, it could quickly become endangered, if more land is cleared for agriculture or if the palm begins to be exploited for the nursery trade.

The Jardín Botánico Culiacán has several specimens of *Chamaedorea stolonifera* that probably were added to the collection around 1999. In 2017 the garden received back a plant that Carlos Murillo Depraect had given as a present to a friend. After the friend died, his family decided the garden was the best place to ensure the survival of the palm.

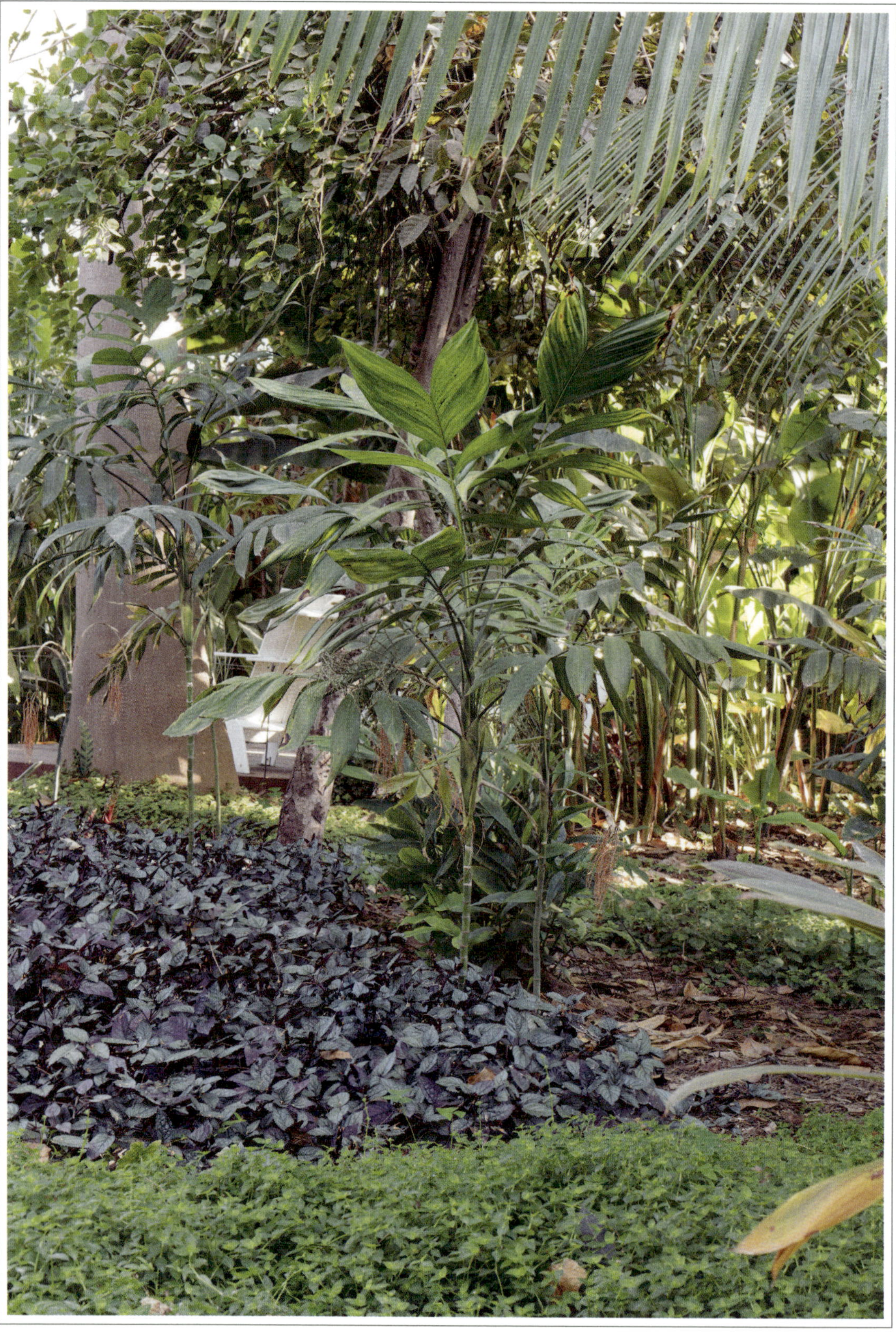

24
PACAYA PALM

Chamaedorea tepejilote Liebm.

Status: Assessment of global conservation status required
Distribution: From Mexico to Colombia

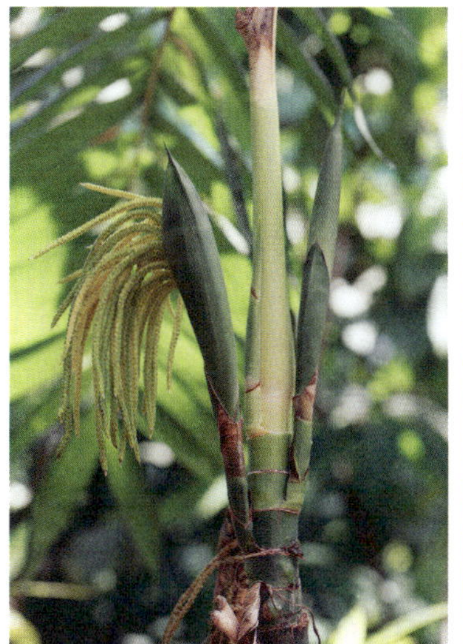
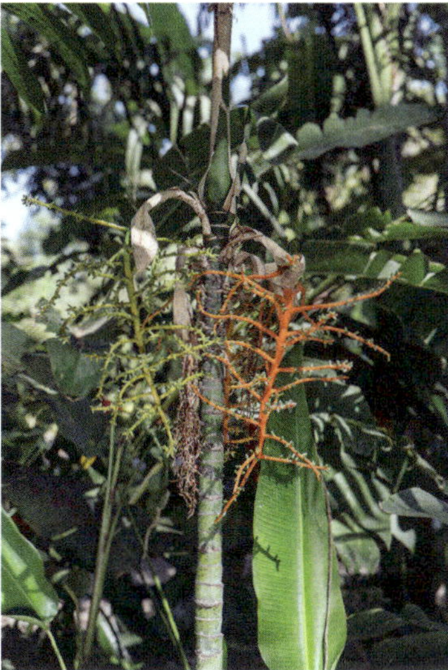
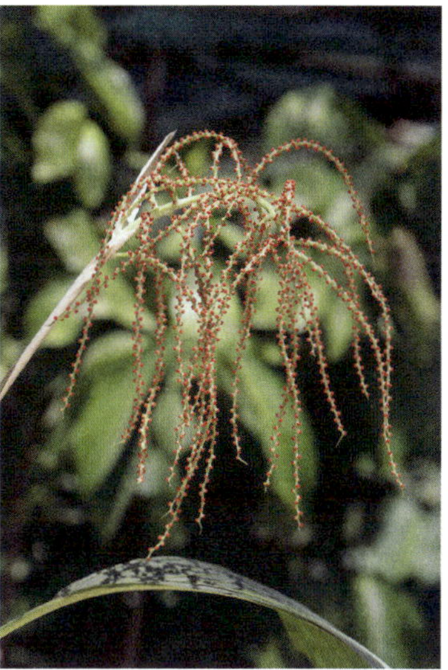

1. Male inflorescence. 2. Female inflorescence. 3. Male inflorescence.

This palm is common in the understory of tropical forests from Mexico to Colombia. It is a slender palm with one or several stems that may reach up to 16 feet in height. The flowers are small and greenish-yellow and grow in clusters. Several kinds of insects visit the flowers, especially beetles, but pollination is by the wind. Many indigenous peoples eat the immature flower clusters, which are called *pacaya*. In Guatemala, *pacaya* preserved in brine is an exported commodity. *Chamaedorea tepejilote* is used in other ways as well: the leaves are used for decoration in churches, and the palm is cultivated as a popular houseplant.

There are around 60 healthy specimens of *Chamaedorea tepejilote* at the Jardín Botánico Culiacán. The species was brought from Chiapas in 2014 and adapted perfectly to the climatic conditions of Culiacán.

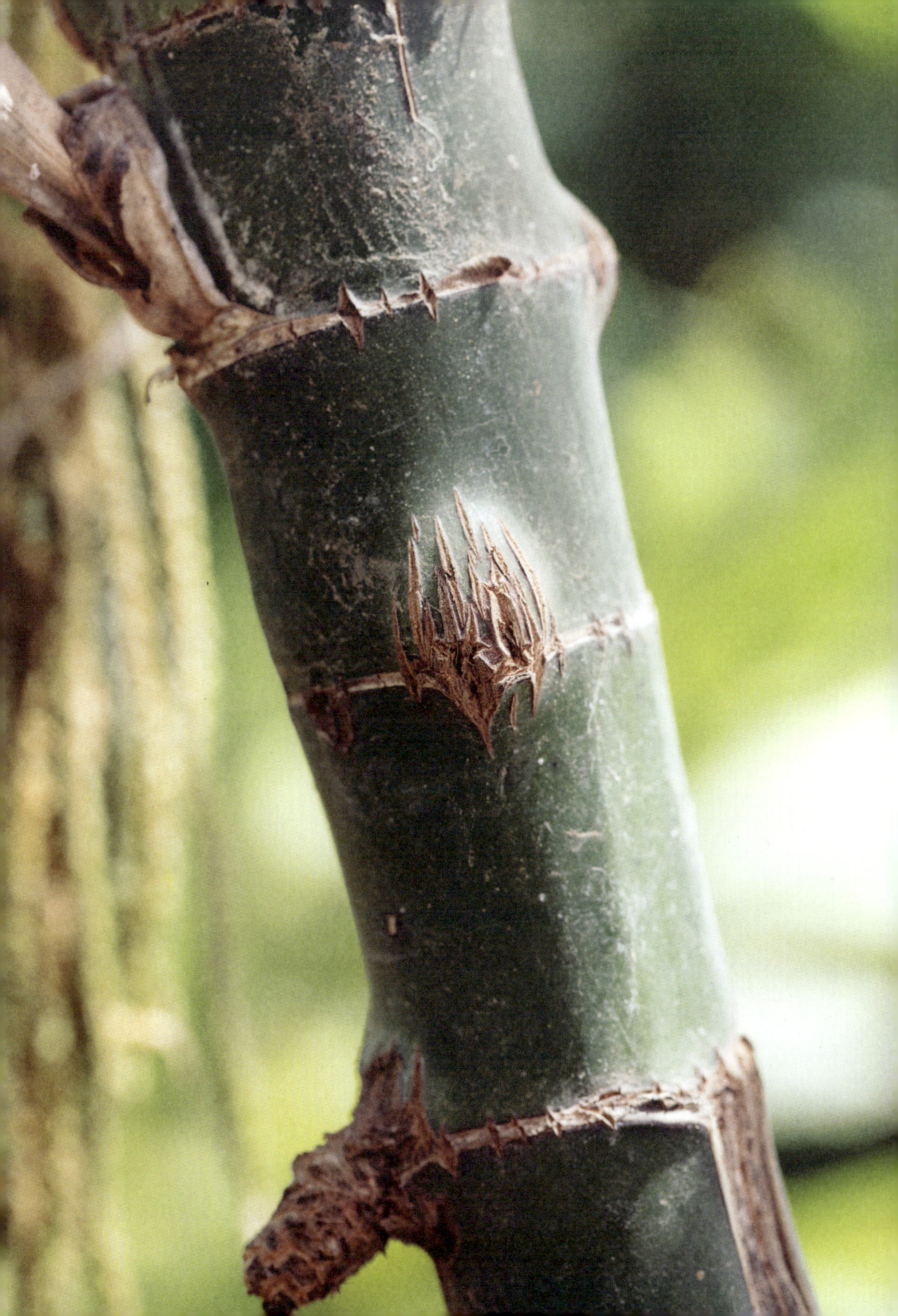

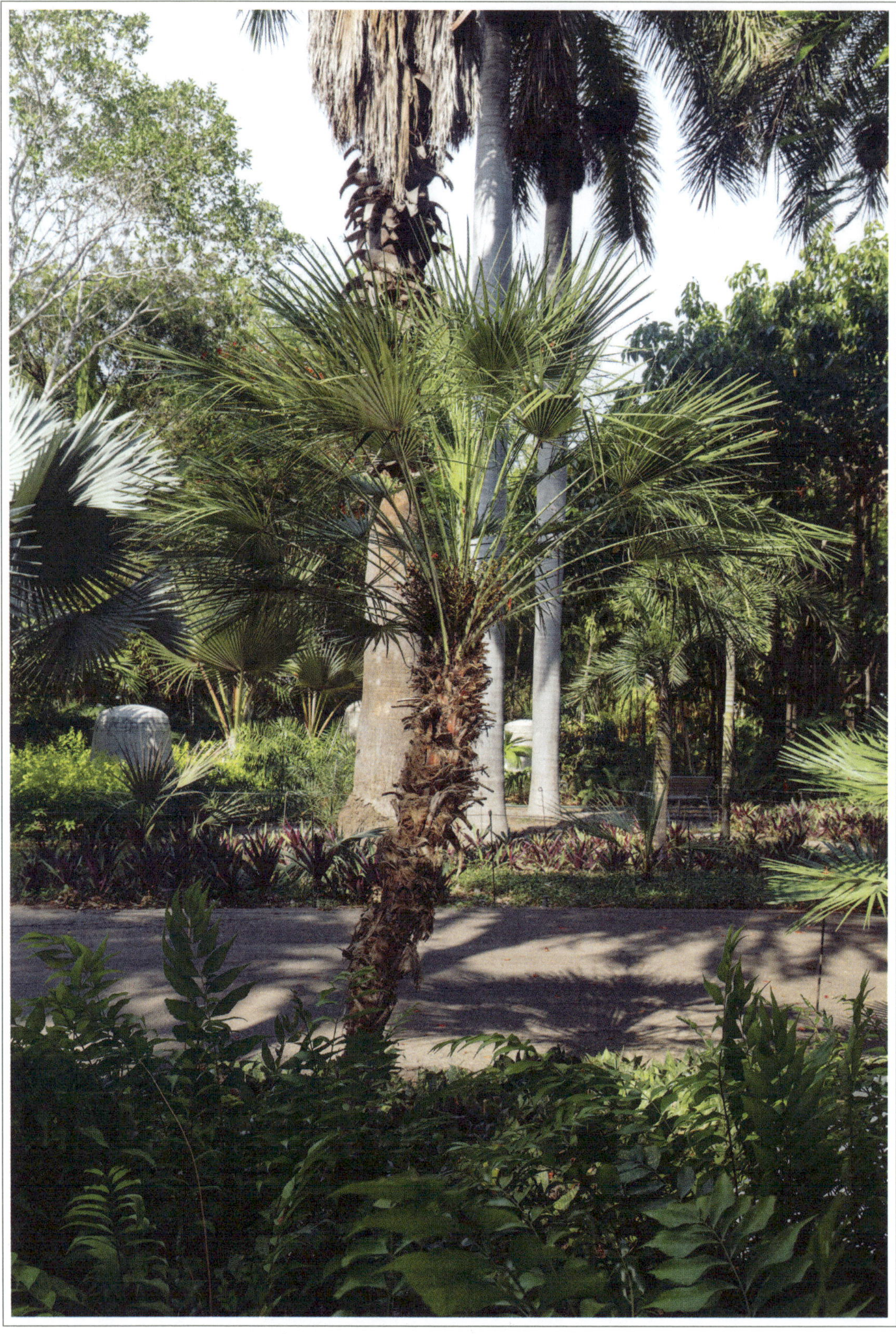

25

EUROPEAN FAN PALM, DWARF PALM

Chamaerops humilis L.

Status: Designated as Least Concern on the IUCN Red List
Distribution: Southern Europe and North Africa

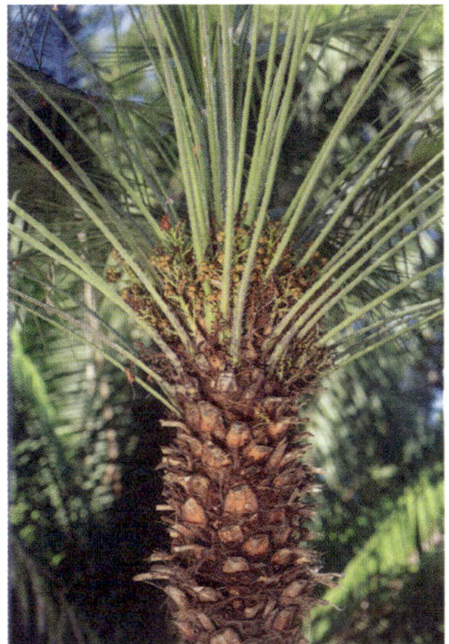

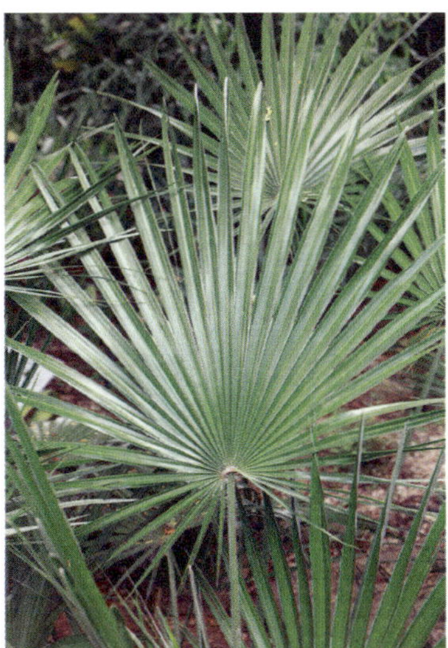

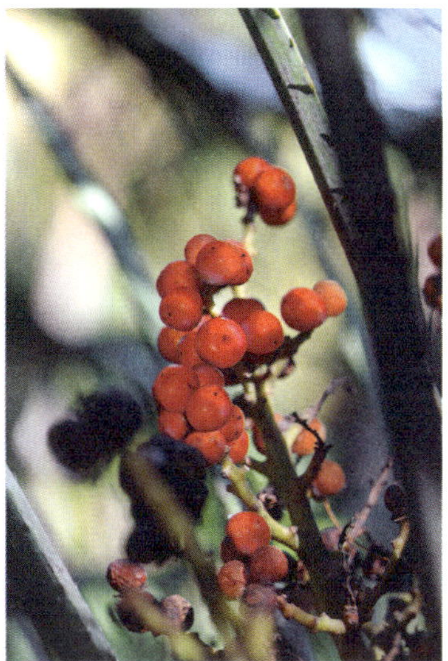

1. Detail of the stem and the leaf crown. 2. Leaf. 3. Ripe fruits.

Chamaerops humilis and *Phoenix theophrasti* are the only two species of palms native to Europe. The European fan palm, also called the dwarf palm, occurs naturally in seasonally dry habitats, so it is a durable, drought-tolerant palm suitable for cultivation. In some areas of the Iberian Peninsula it can grow at more than 3,280 feet above sea level. It produces solitary or clustered stems, up to 6.5 feet tall, and stiff, fan-shaped leaves, armed with needles. It also tolerates the cold better than most palms, so it is popular with gardeners. One of the most unusual features of this palm is that it attracts its pollinators—small weevils—by means of scent glands on its leaves. When the palm is flowering, the leaf below the flower cluster emits a jasmine-like fragrance from glands between the leaf segments. This is the only known case of a flowering plant attracting its pollinators with a perfume produced by the leaves.

The oldest specimen at the Jardín Botánico Culiacán is twenty-five years old, but, because it is very slow-growing, it is only 10 feet tall.

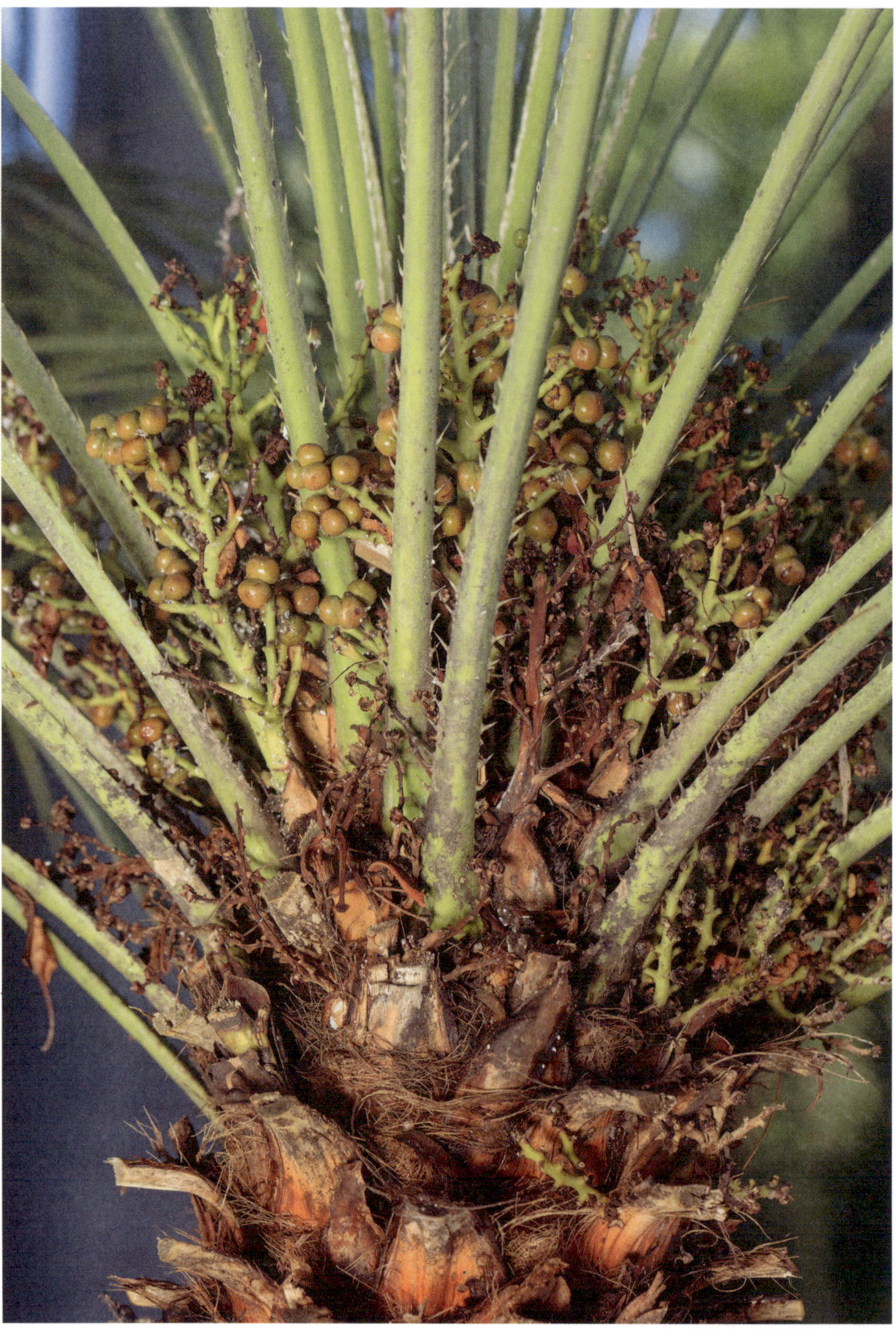

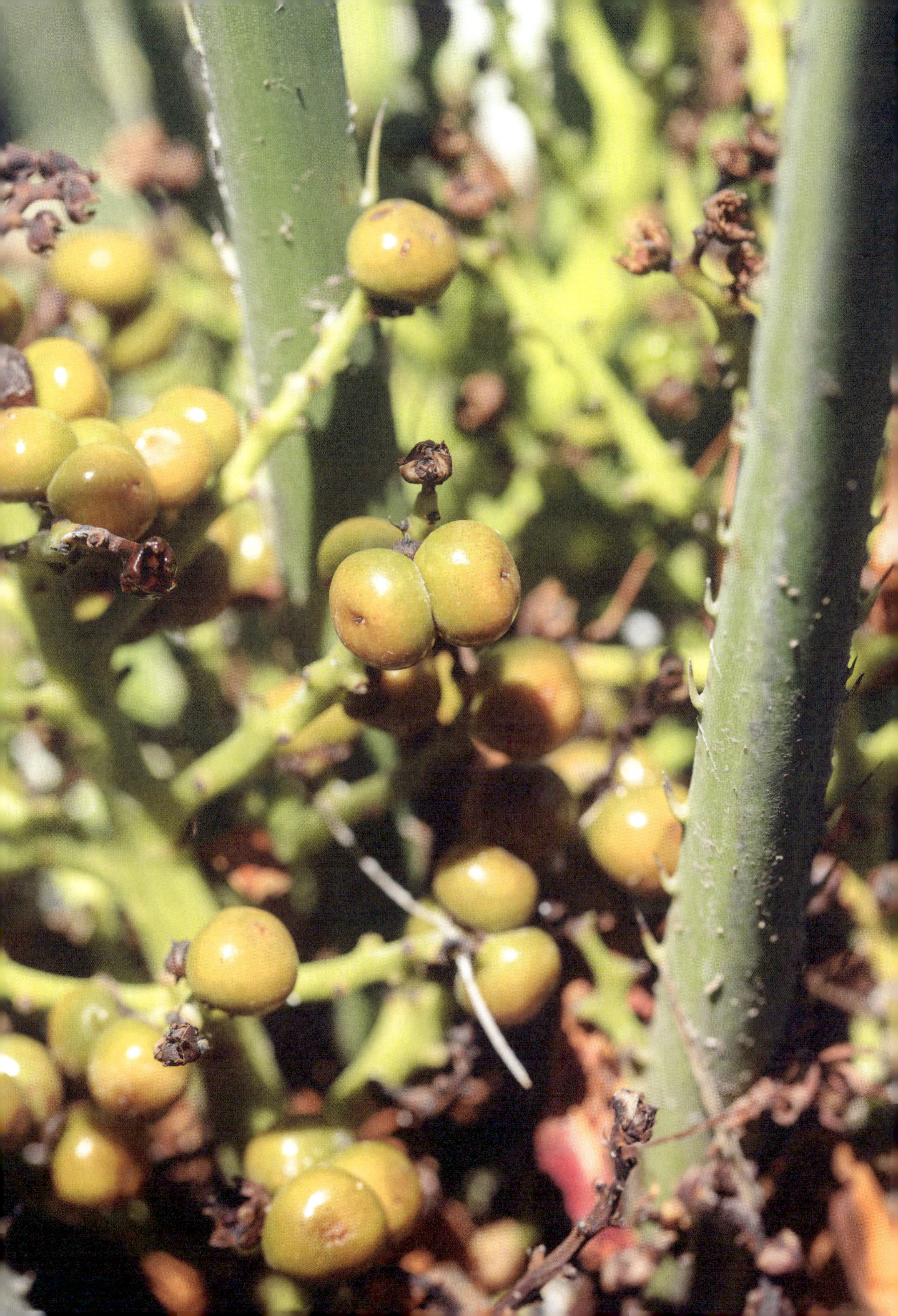

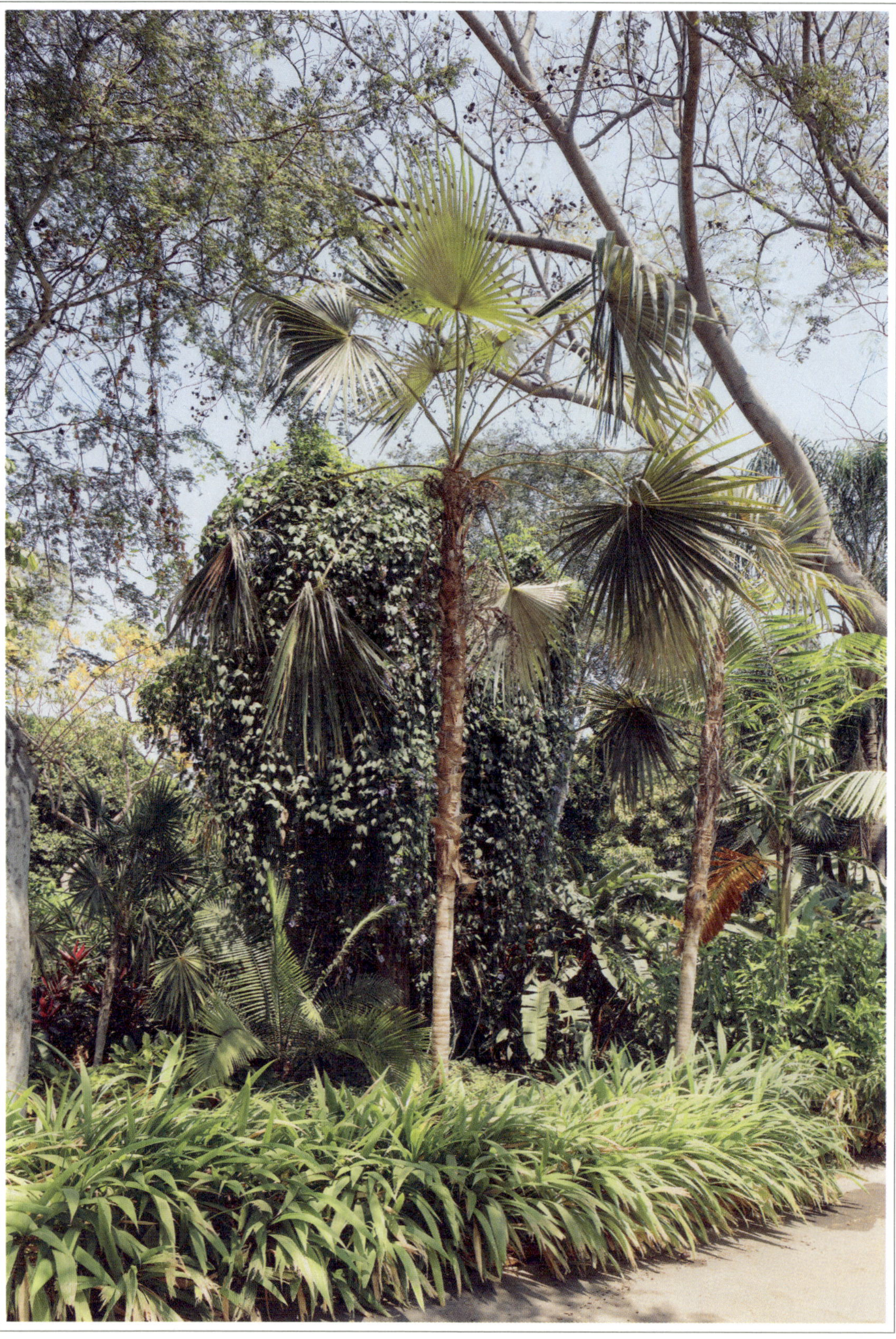

26

SILVER PALM

Coccothrinax argentea (Lodd. ex Schult. & Schult.f.) Sarg. ex Becc.

Status: Assessment of global conservation status required
Distribution: Island of Hispaniola (Haiti and the Dominican Republic)

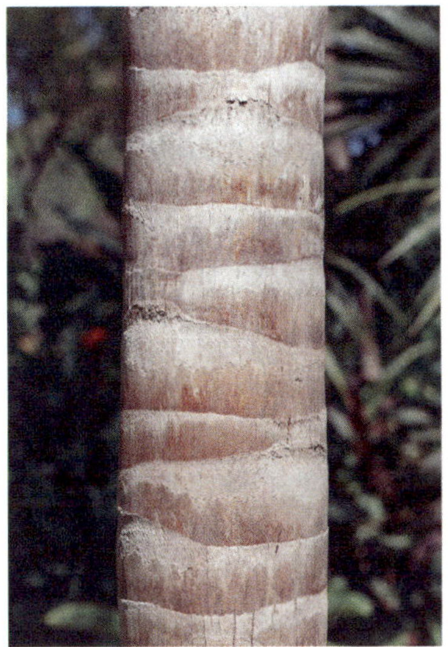

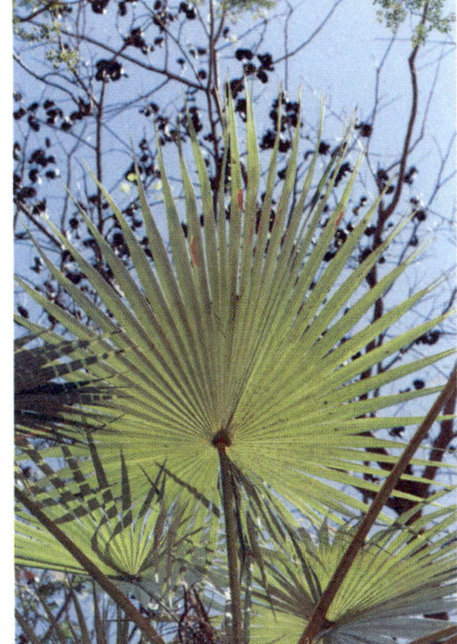

1. Stem. 2. Leaf.

This graceful fan palm has a solitary trunk up to 35 feet tall and a crown of a few leaves, which are silvery (*argentea* in Latin) on the undersides. In its native habitat, the palm grows on limestone in low, semi-deciduous forests. It bears masses of small white flowers that are pollinated by insects, as well as by the wind. The flowers are followed by small black fruits, which are consumed by birds.

The Jardín Botánico Culiacán used to have a specimen of *Coccothrinax argentea* that was one of its oldest and tallest palms. Unfortunately, it was lost in 2006, owing to the effects of Hurricane Lane, a category-3 storm that made landfall in the state of Sinaloa on September 16th of that year.

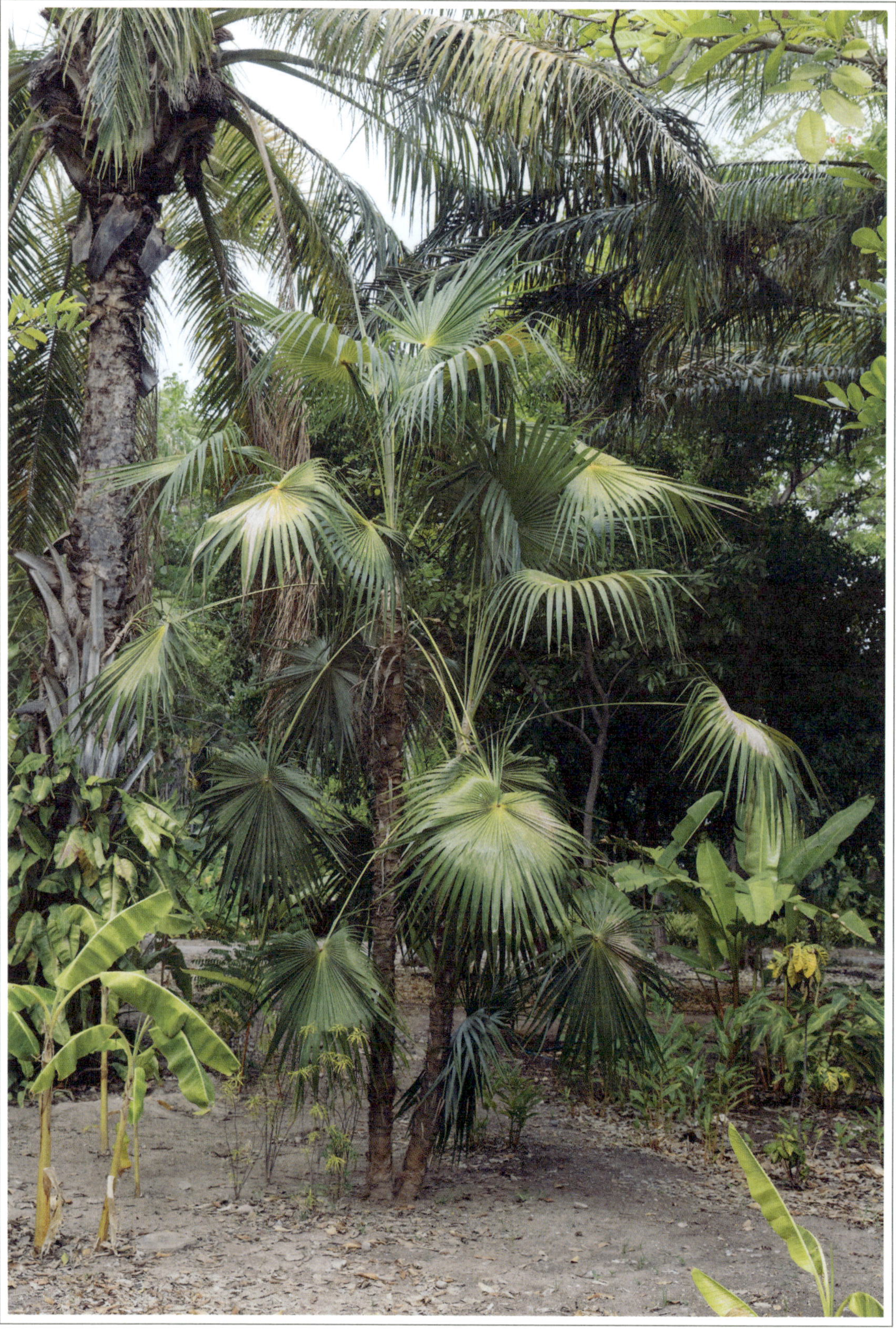

27

TYRE PALM, BARBADOS PALM

Coccothrinax barbadensis (Lodd. ex Mart.) Becc.

Status: Assessment of global conservation status required
Distribution: Several islands of the Lesser Antilles

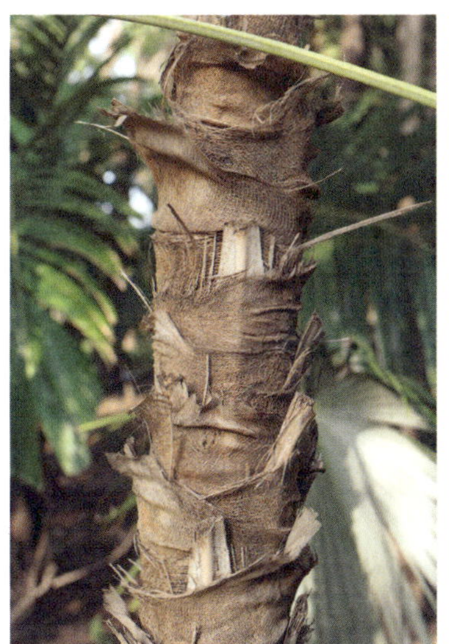
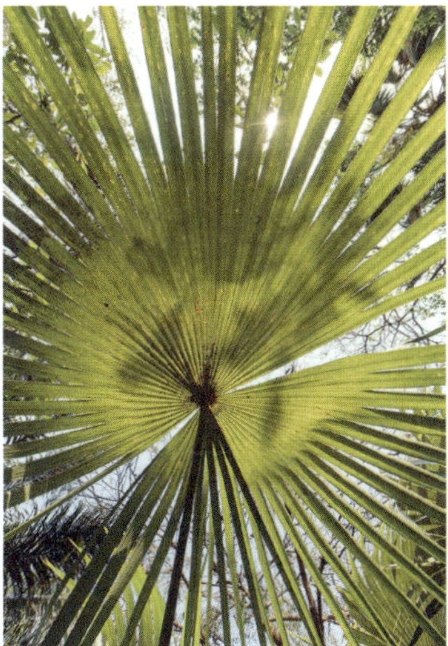
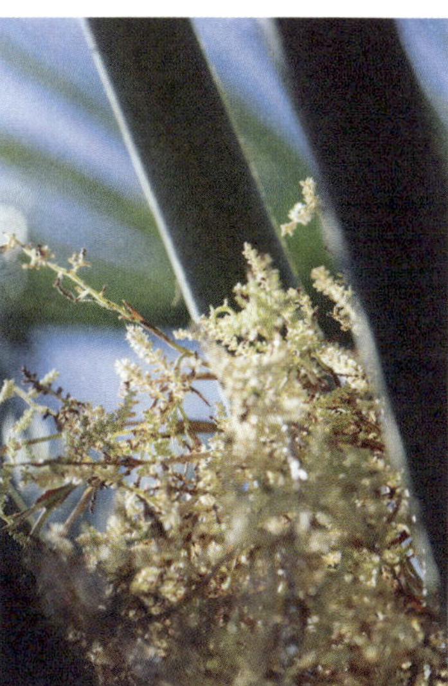

1. Trunk with leaf bases. 2. Leaf. 3. Flowers.

The species name means "of Barbados," but this palm is not only from Barbados. *Coccothrinax barbadensis* has a single trunk that grows to about 16 feet tall. Morphologically it is very similar to *Coccothrinax argentea*, the differences pertaining to the fruit. It occurs in low dry forests, but the wild populations on some islands, such as Antigua, have been diminished by deforestation or the burning of forests to create land for cattle grazing. In Antigua, a healthy population was found in a cemetery, where the plants are protected from the cattle. The young leaves are used to make brooms. Excessive harvesting of the leaves can weaken the palms, and in some areas populations are in decline because of over-harvesting.

This palm joined the collection of the Jardín Botánico Culiacán thanks to an exchange arranged by Carlos Murillo Depraect, who has been a member of the International Palm Society for over twenty years.

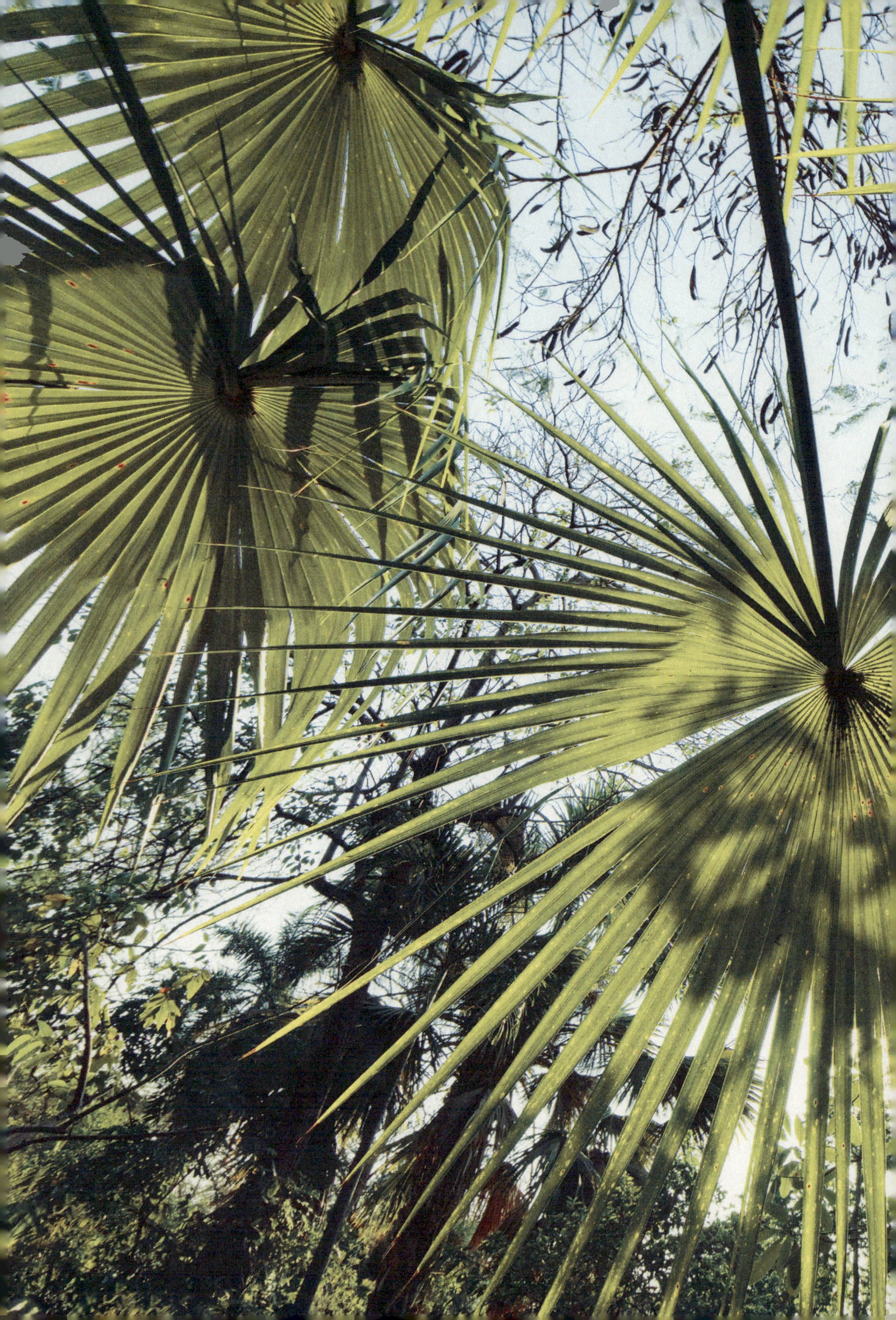

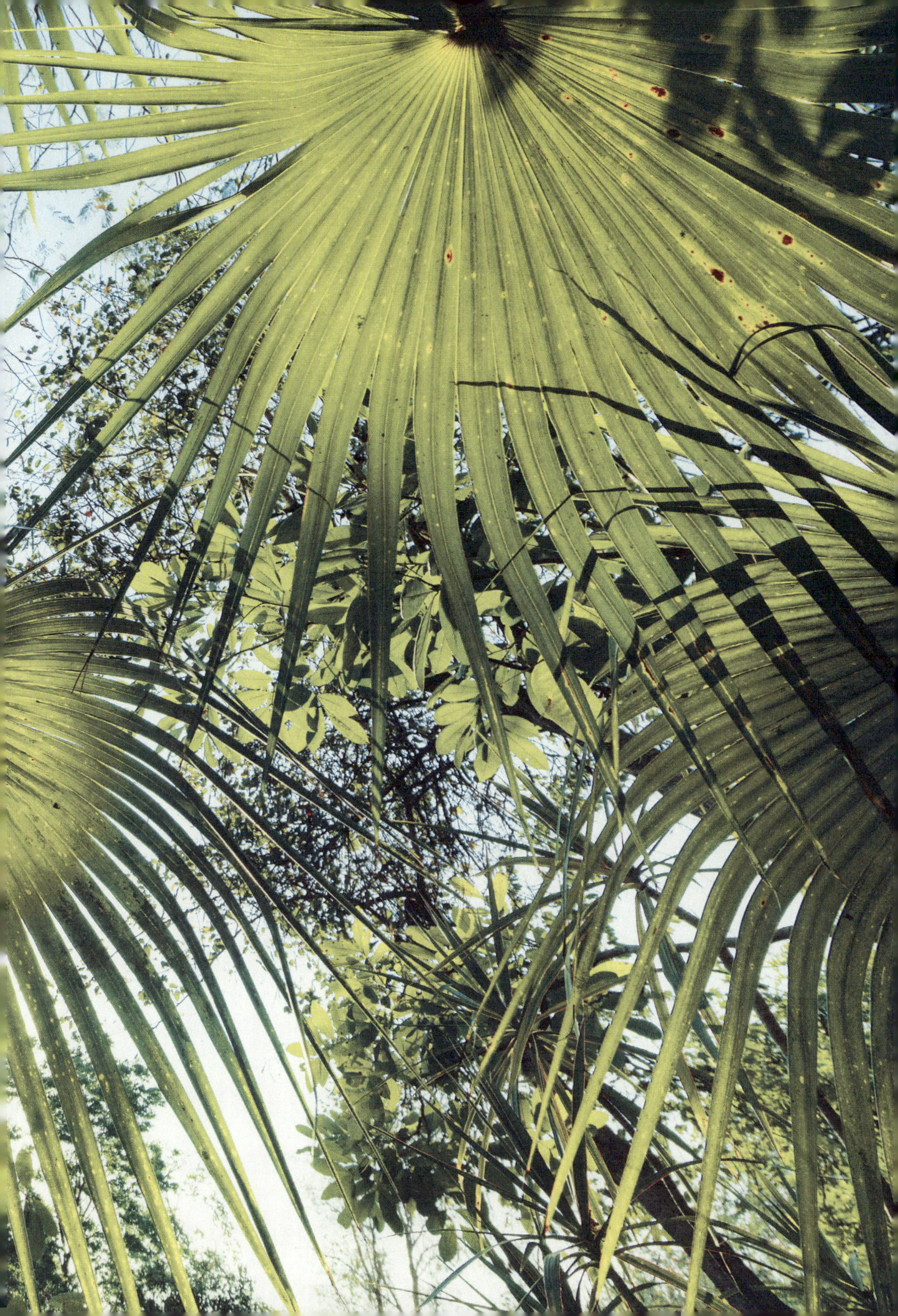

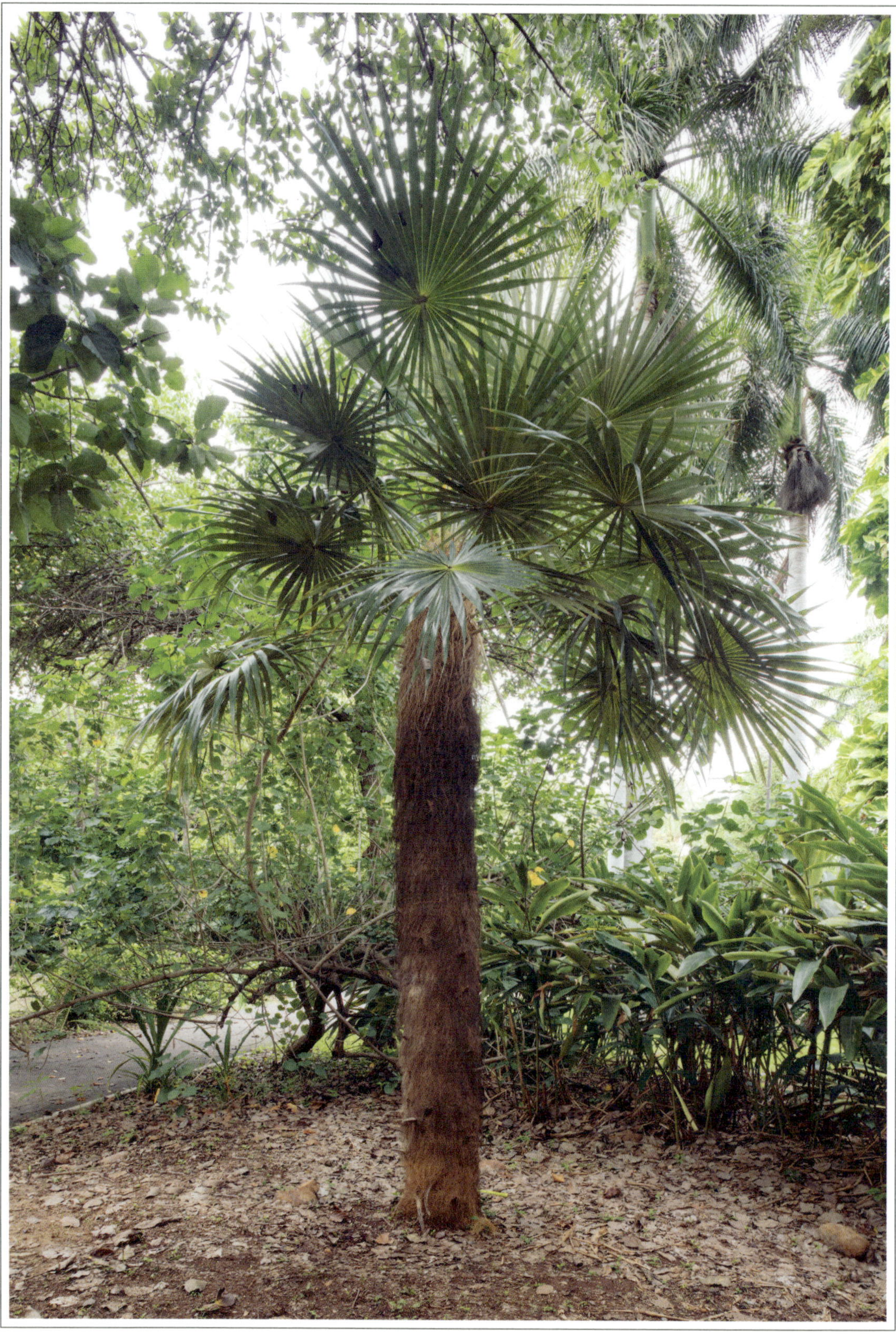

28

OLD MAN PALM

Coccothrinax crinita (Griseb. & H. Wendl. ex C. H. Wright) Becc.

Status: Designated as Critically Endangered on the Red List of Cuban flora (2016)
Distribution: Endemic to western Cuba

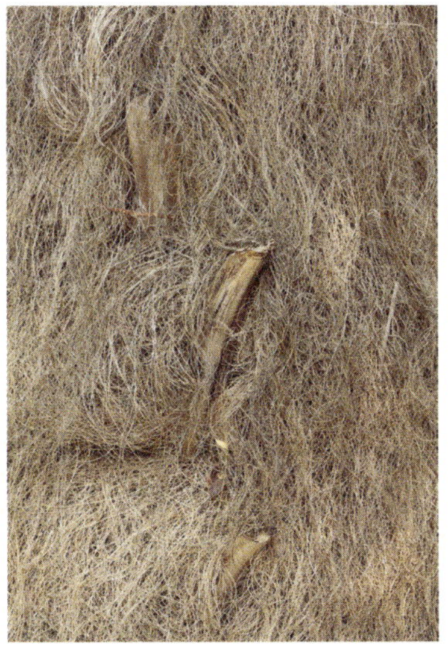

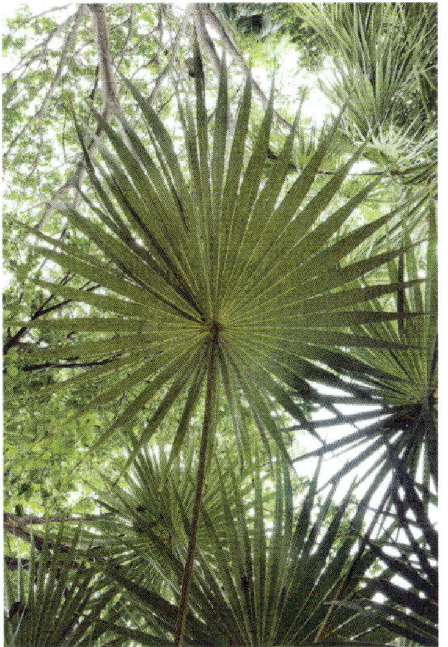

1. Fibers on the leaf base. 2. Leaf.

This attractive fan palm is critically endangered in a small, fragmented area of western Cuba, where invasive species of exotic trees and shrubs are altering the habitat. The palm, which grows up to 35 feet tall on hills with serpentine soils, is slow-growing and tolerant to drought. It is prized by growers for the long fibers hanging from the leaf bases, which can be used for making mats, brushes, and scrubbers. The long fibers account for the common name of the palm in Spanish, which means "bearded palm." In the Latin name of the species, the word *crinata* means "having a mane of horsehair," also because of how the long fibers look. Owing to habitat loss, exploitation of the palm is now forbidden. The Cuban government has initiated a conservation program that includes restoring the habitat by removing invasive trees and planting hundreds of nursery-grown seedlings into the wild. Specimens of *Coccothrinax crinita* were discovered in Sancti Spíritus in 2016, over a hundred years after it was thought to be extinct in that province. Some botanists believe, however, that plants from this region belong to a different subspecies.

For many years the species was represented at the Jardín Botánico Culiacán by only one specimen. It was only in 2017 that personnel succeeded in growing more specimens from seed.

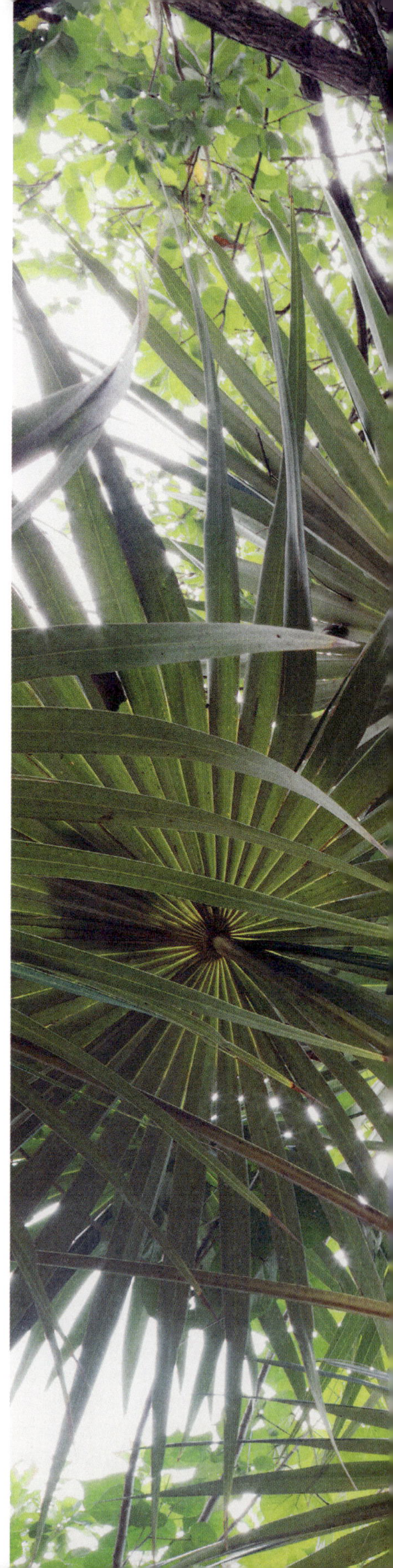

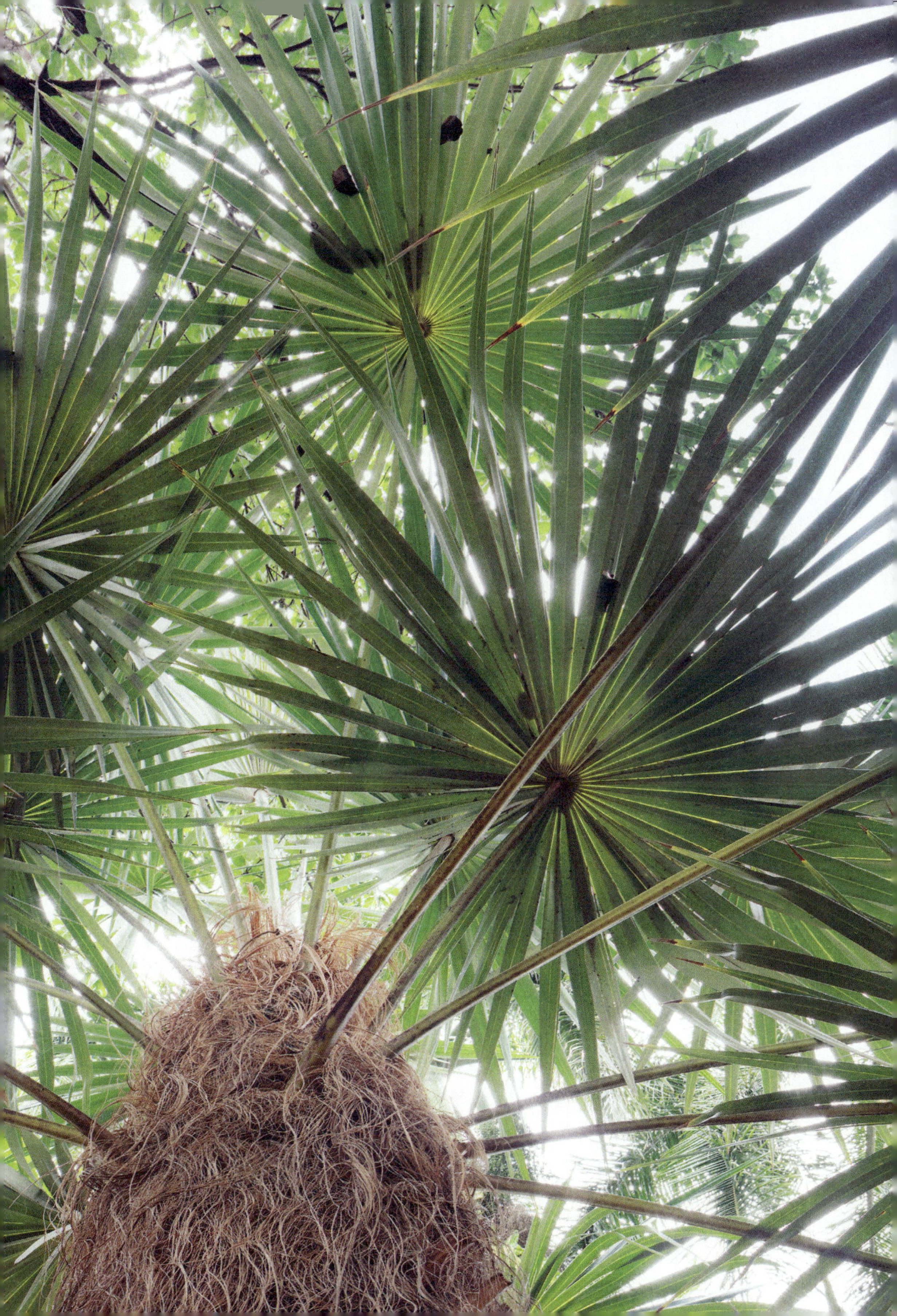

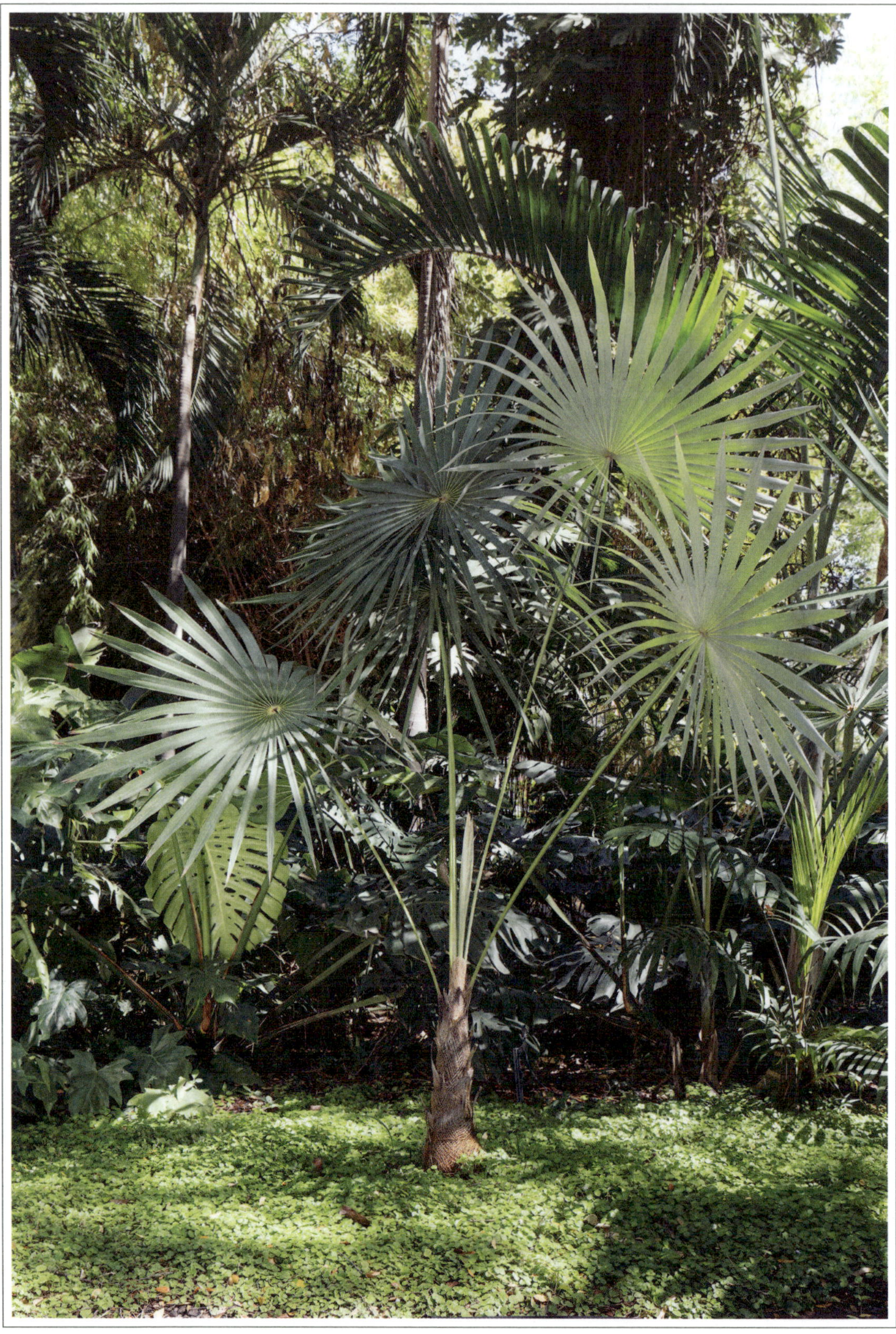

29

MIRAGUANO SILVER THATCH PALM, MIRAGUAMA PALM

Coccothrinax miraguama (Kunth) Becc.

Status: Assessment of global conservation status required
Distribution: Central Cuba

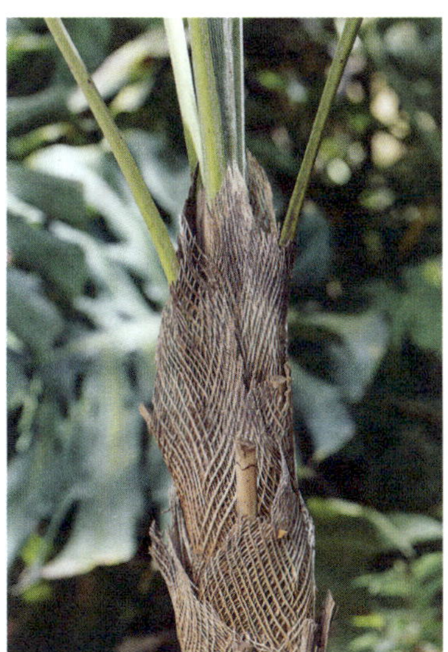
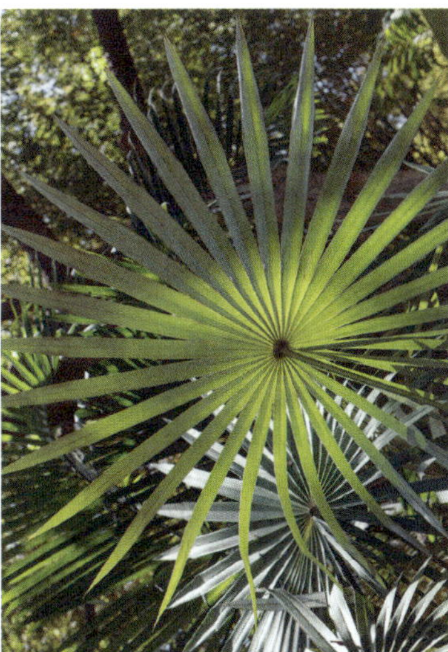
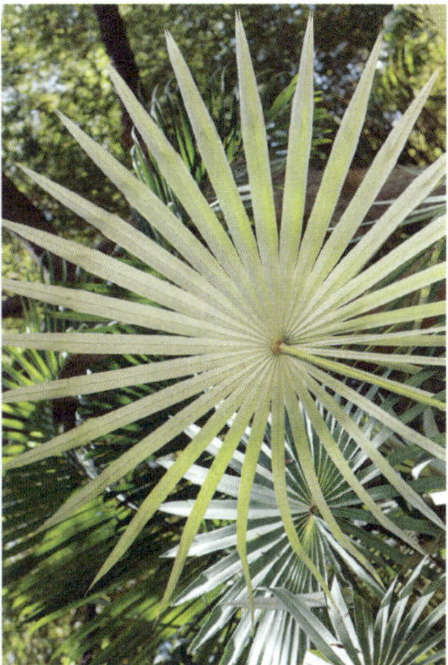

1. Trunk with leaf bases. 2. Superior side of the leaf. 3. Silvery inferior side of the leaf.

Cuba is home to 47 of the 62 species and subspecies that make up the genus *Coccothrinax*. *Coccothrinax miraguama* is widespread on a variety of soil types in woodlands and savannas. This species, which can eventually grow to 35 feet in height, is admired for its compact crown of stiff, almost circular leaves. The trunk is covered by symmetrical fibers that look almost human-made, but they disappear as the plant grows older. Its white or cream-colored flowers produce abundant fruits that change from purple to shiny black when ripe. Its slow growth rate is a cause of great frustration to gardeners. In cultivation, it can hybridize with other species, so seeds collected from gardens may not yield the actual species. In Cuba, the fibers of the leaf base are used to make brooms.

The specimens growing at the Jardín Botánico Culiacán are from a nursery in Yucatán, not from Cuba, and became part of the collection in 2010.

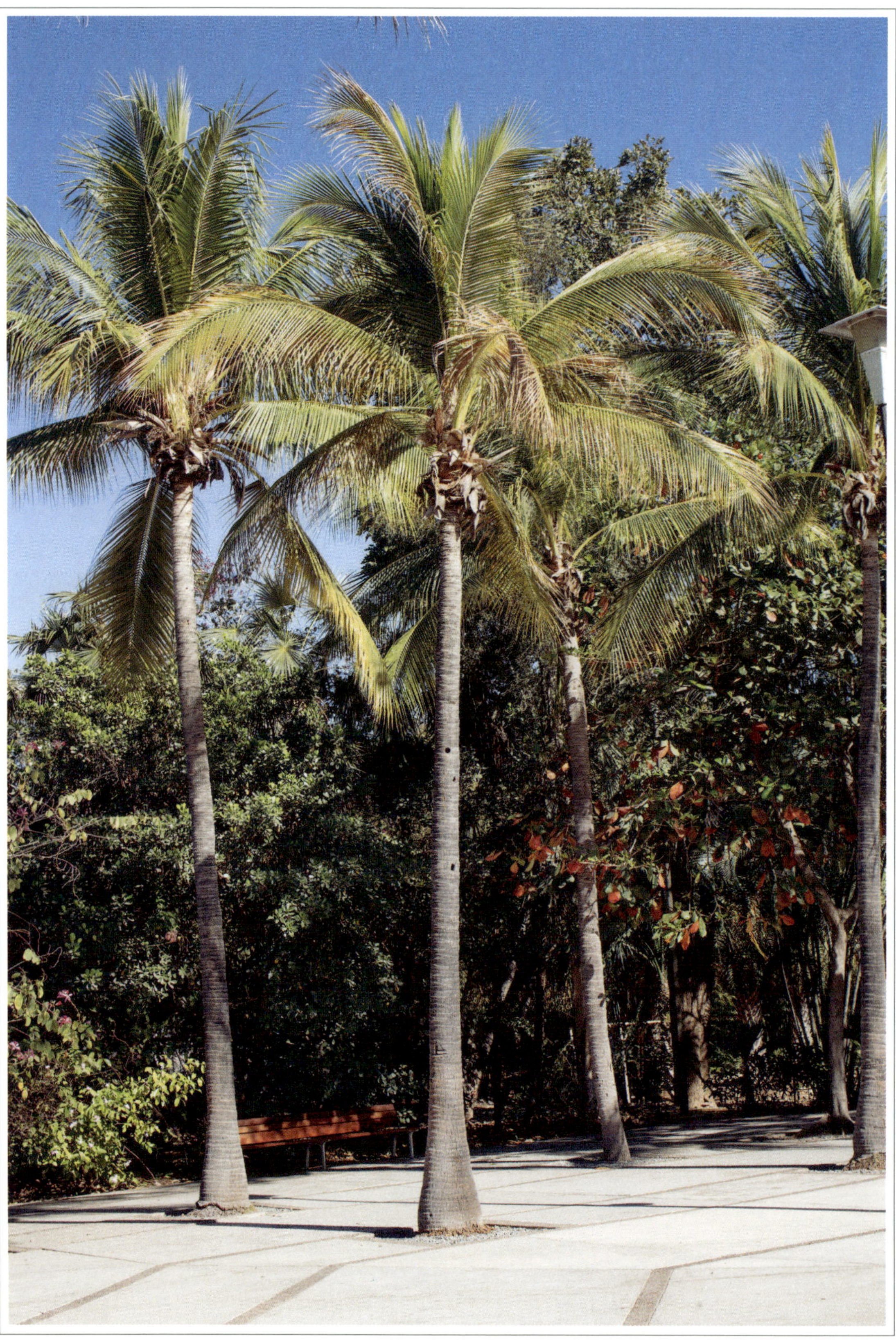

30
COCONUT PALM

Cocos nucifera L.

Status: Very common all over the world
Distribution: Cultivated worldwide

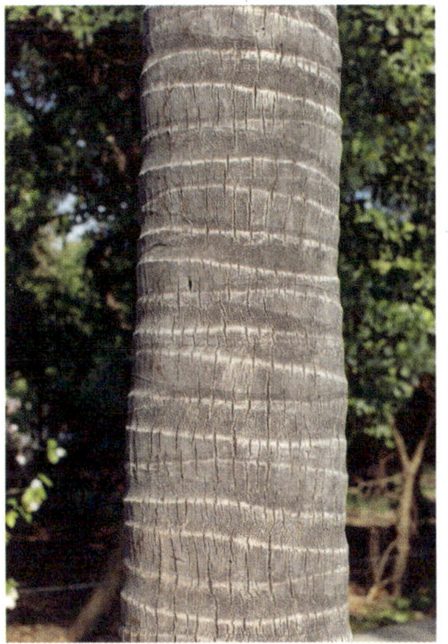
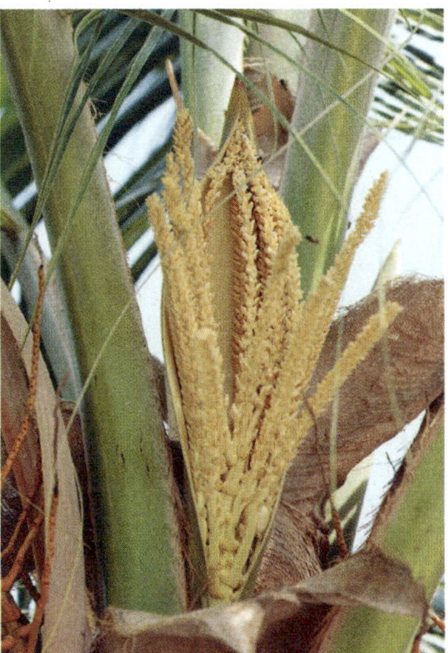
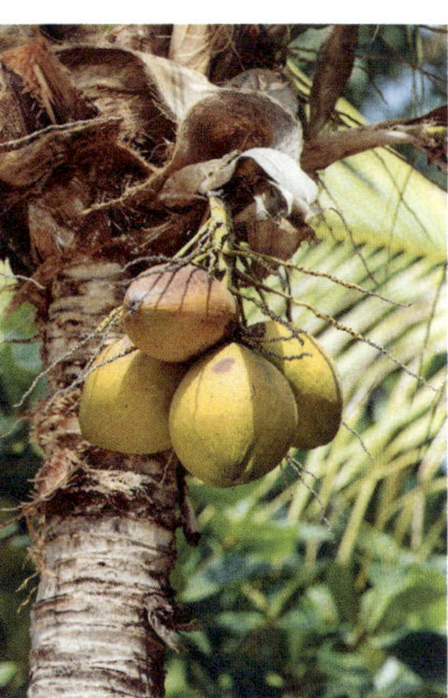

1.Trunk. 2.Flowers. 3.Fruits.

The coconut palm is a domesticated species that does not occur in the wild. It was domesticated in Southeast Asia in prehistory. Cultivated varieties of this palm can be of the dwarf variety or may reach up to 100 feet in height. The coconut palm has hundreds of uses, including those as roofing thatch, charcoal, beverages, fibers, and oil. The most important commercial uses of the palm are for the dried seed, called copra, and the oil extracted from this seed. In recent years, coconut water has become a popular beverage: it is now widely sold throughout the industrialized world and its oils are used in gastronomy. The species is found all over the tropical world, because its fruit (the coconut) disperses very well, floating in the sea: the seed remains viable for as long as the fruit is floating. The coconut palm was introduced to western Mexico from the Philippines and to eastern Mexico from the Caribbean, and so western and eastern varieties are genetically different. These differences are related to important ones in disease and pest susceptibility, productivity, and other agronomic factors. Unfortunately, there are numerous pests and diseases that threaten the coconut industry in most parts of the world.

At the Jardín Botánico Culiacán woodpeckers favor the coconut palms over all other trees.

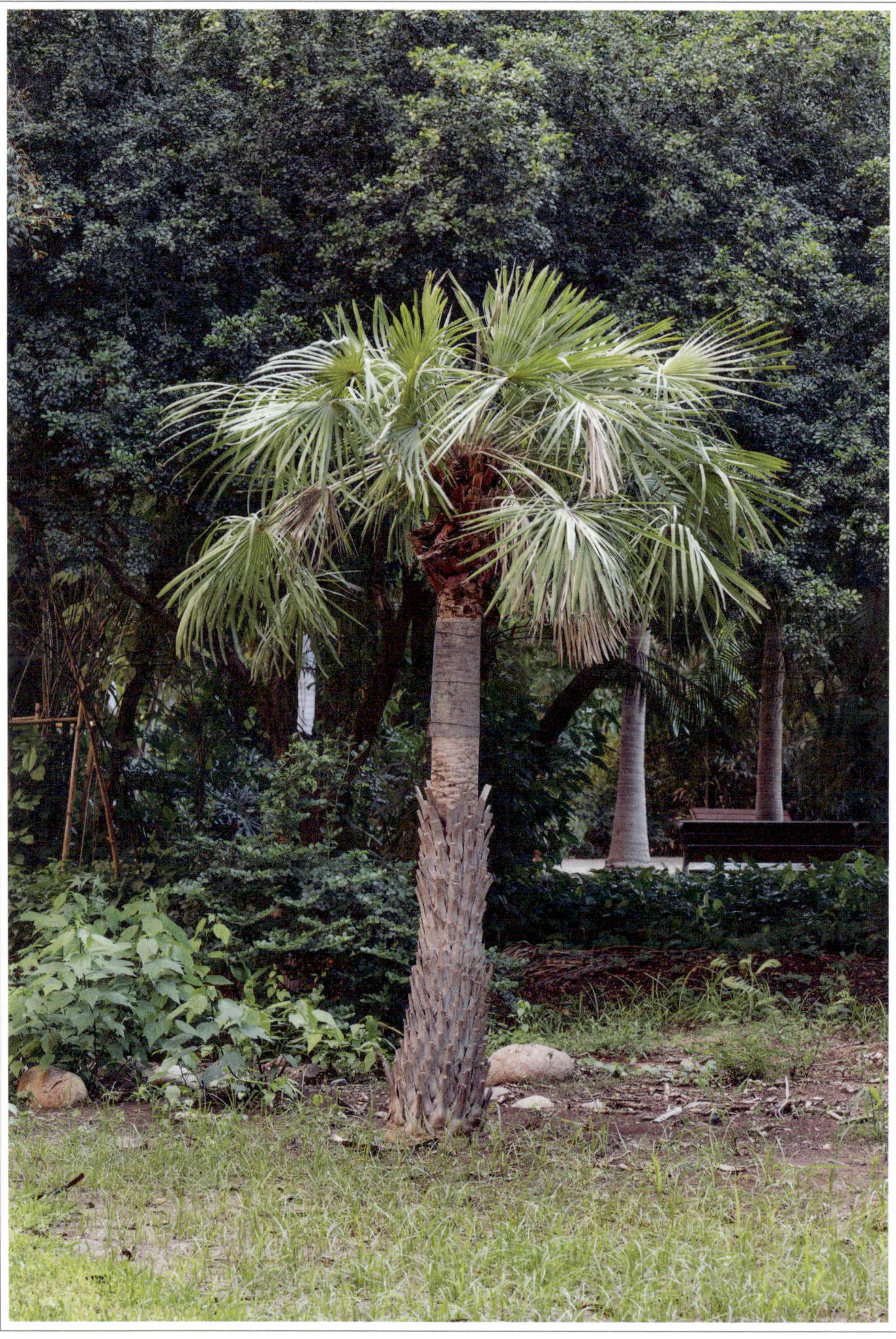

31
CARANDAY WAX PALM

Copernicia alba Morong

Status: Assessment of global conservation status required
Distribution: South America (Brazil, Bolivia, Paraguay, and Argentina)

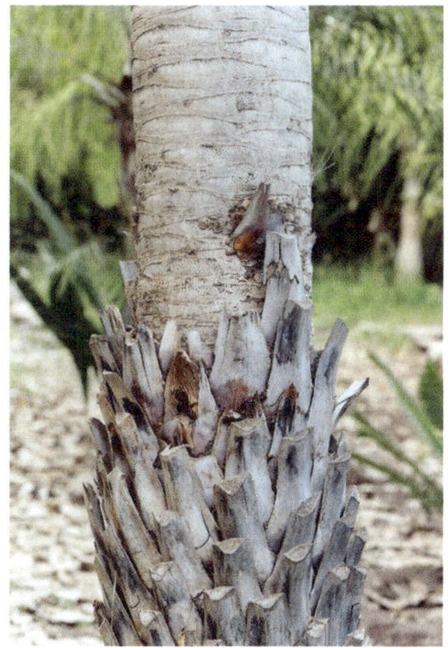
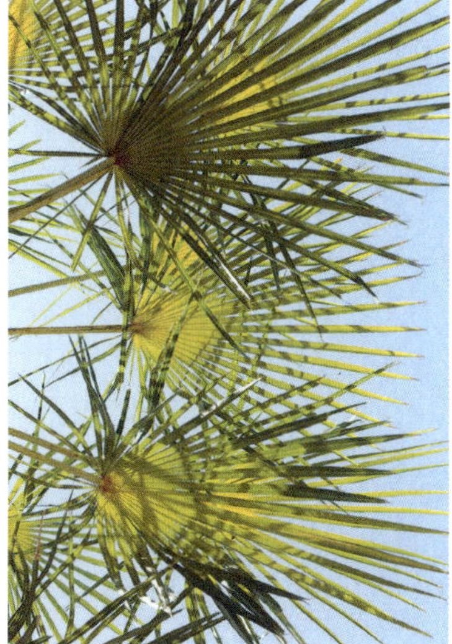

1. Trunk with retained leaf bases. 2. Leaf.

This solitary palm, which grows up to 65 (or sometimes even 100) feet tall, with its stiff, waxy, fan-shaped leaves, is one of three species of *Copernicia* native to South America: the other 26 species occur in Cuba and the island of Hispaniola. *Copernicia alba* occurs in nearly pure stands on periodically flooded savannas. Wax is sometimes harvested from the leaves. (For another source of wax from a palm, see *Copernicia prunifera*.) Parrots, the maned wolf, peccaries, and rheas eat the fruits, helping the dispersal of the plant. The stems are used for constructing fences and corrals and the leaf fibers for weaving hats, baskets, and rope. The genus was named for the Polish astronomer Nicolaus Copernicus (1473–1543), who established the idea that the Earth revolves around the Sun, overthrowing the prevailing belief that the Sun revolved around the Earth.

Copernicia palms arrived at the Jardín Botánico Culiacán more than thirty years ago, in the 1980s. The young plants have birdhouses to prevent woodpeckers from making holes in the delicate trunks.

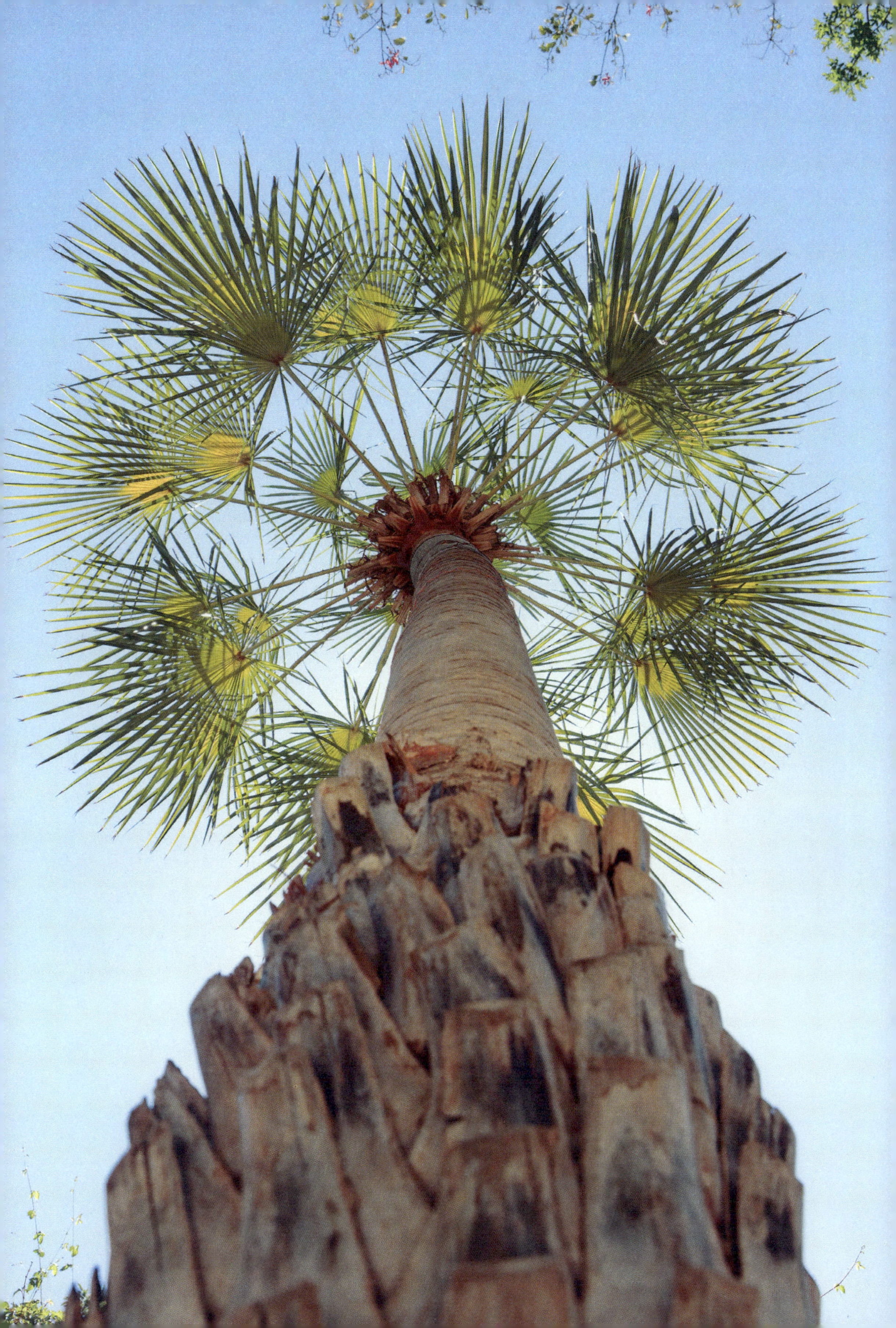

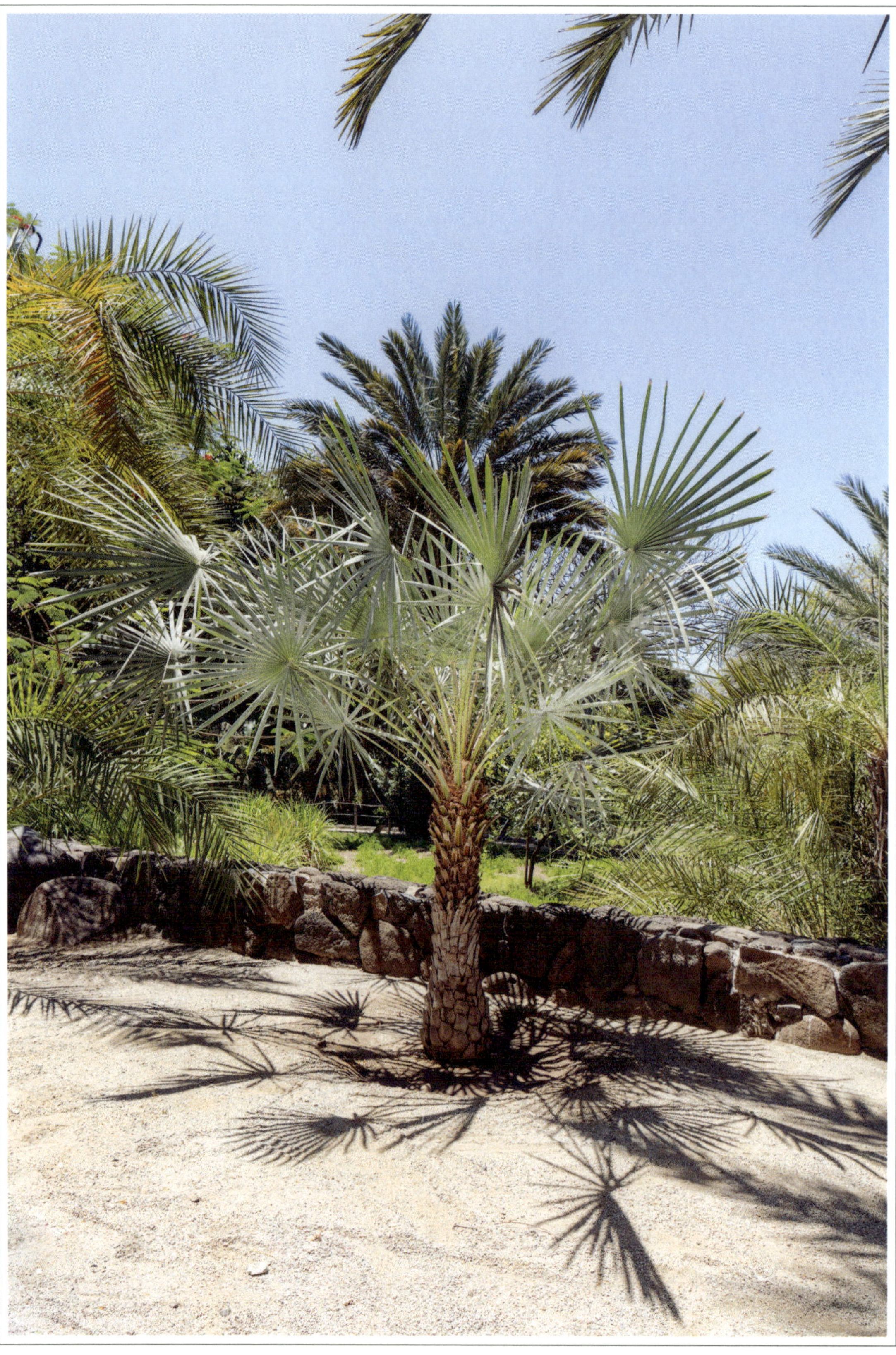

32

CARNAUBA WAX PALM

Copernicia prunifera (Mill.) H.E. Moore

Status: Assessment of global conservation status required
Distribution: South America

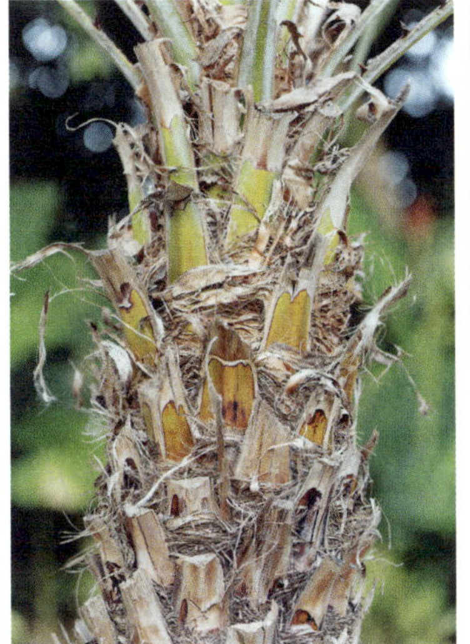

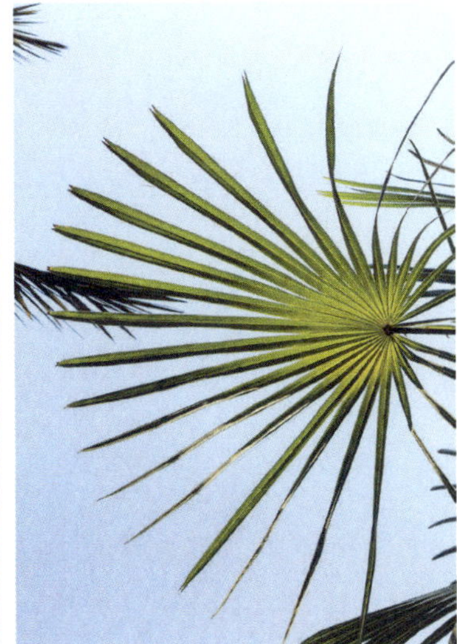

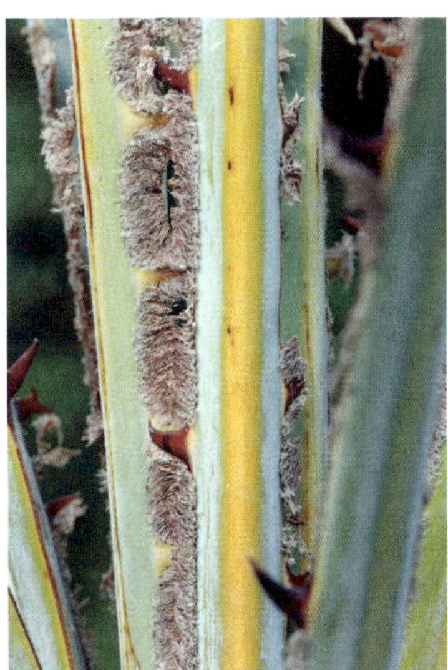

1. Trunk with retained leaf bases. 2. Leaf. 3. Detail of the leaf stems.

This attractive palm grows up to 35–50 feet tall and has a crown of heavily-armed, gray-green leaves. Its silhouette is recognizable by the slender trunk (around 10 inches in diameter) and its rounded crown, with stiff, fan shaped leaves. It is well-known for the carnauba wax it produces on the surfaces of its leaves. You may be carrying products with you now that have carnauba wax among their ingredients. The wax is used in lipstick and lip balm, eyeliner, and shoe polish, as well as in other polishes for wood, floors, automobiles, surfboards, and musical instruments. It is also used as a coating for paper, candies, and pills. The wax is harvested by cutting the leaves from the palm, allowing them to dry, and then brushing or beating them to dislodge the wax. Carnauba wax is very hard and has a high melting point, two attributes that make it ideal for a number of modern industrial uses. The fruits of the palm are edible.

The Jardín Botánico Culiacán has had a specimen since 2010, but it is a very slow-growing plant.

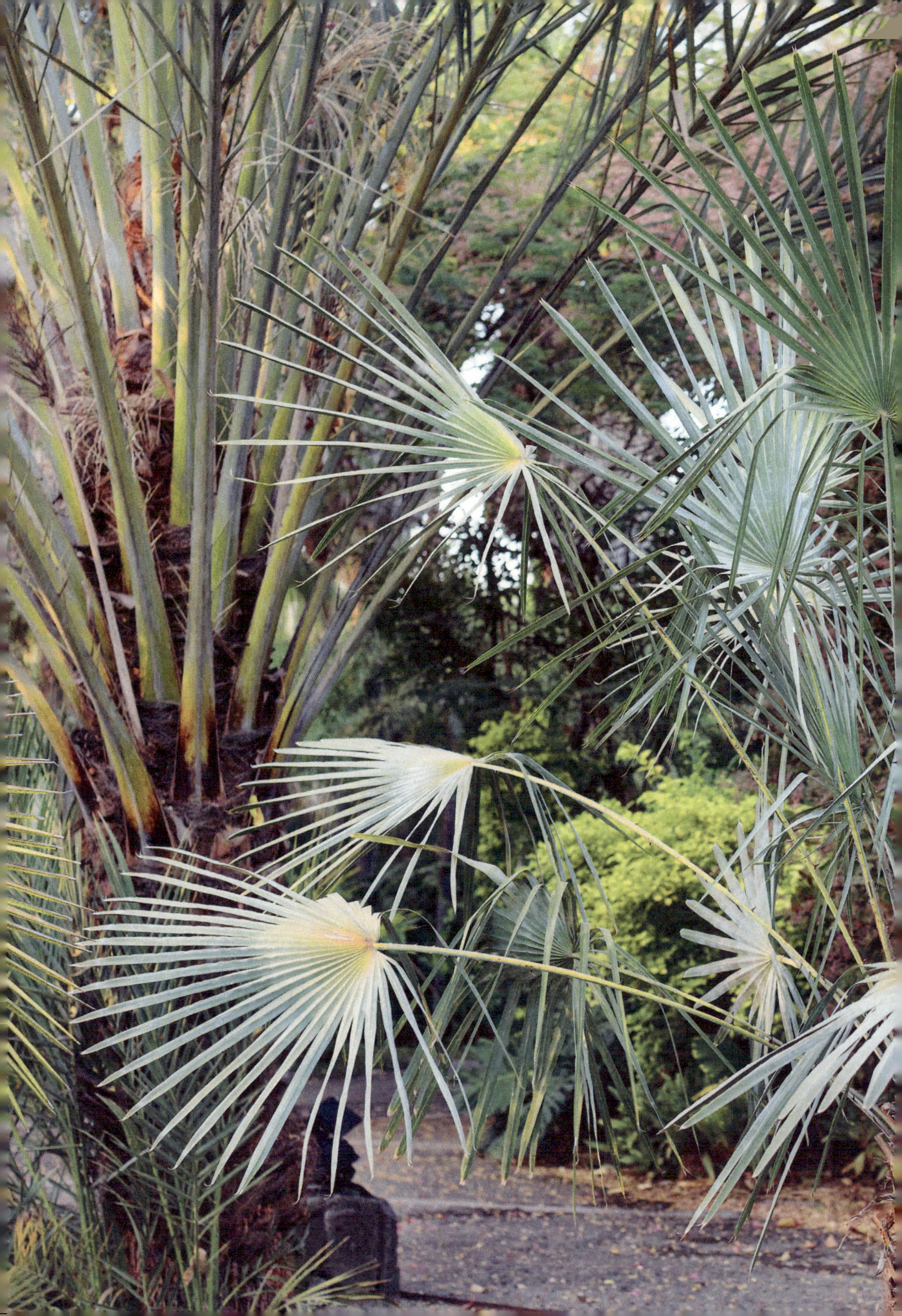

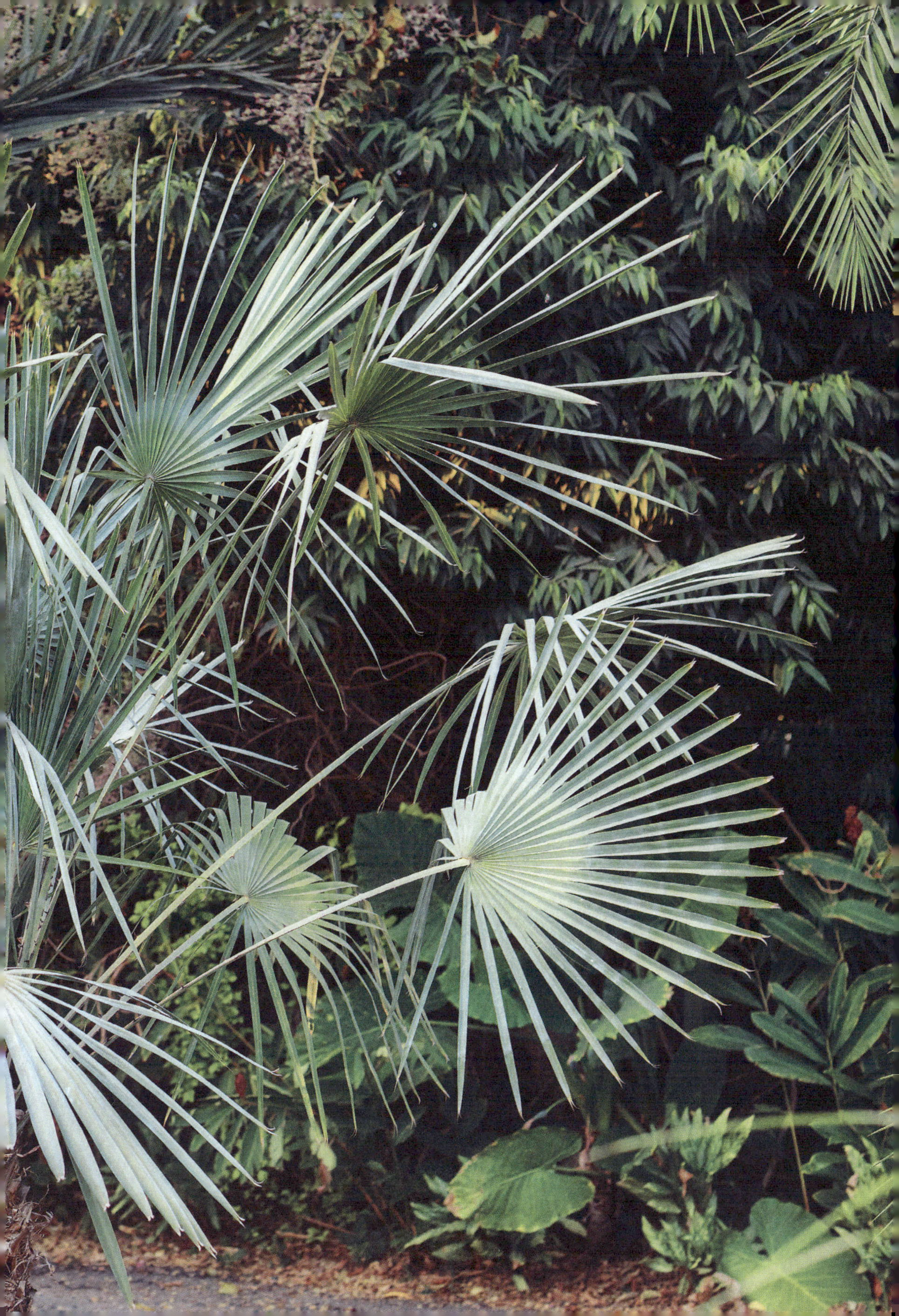

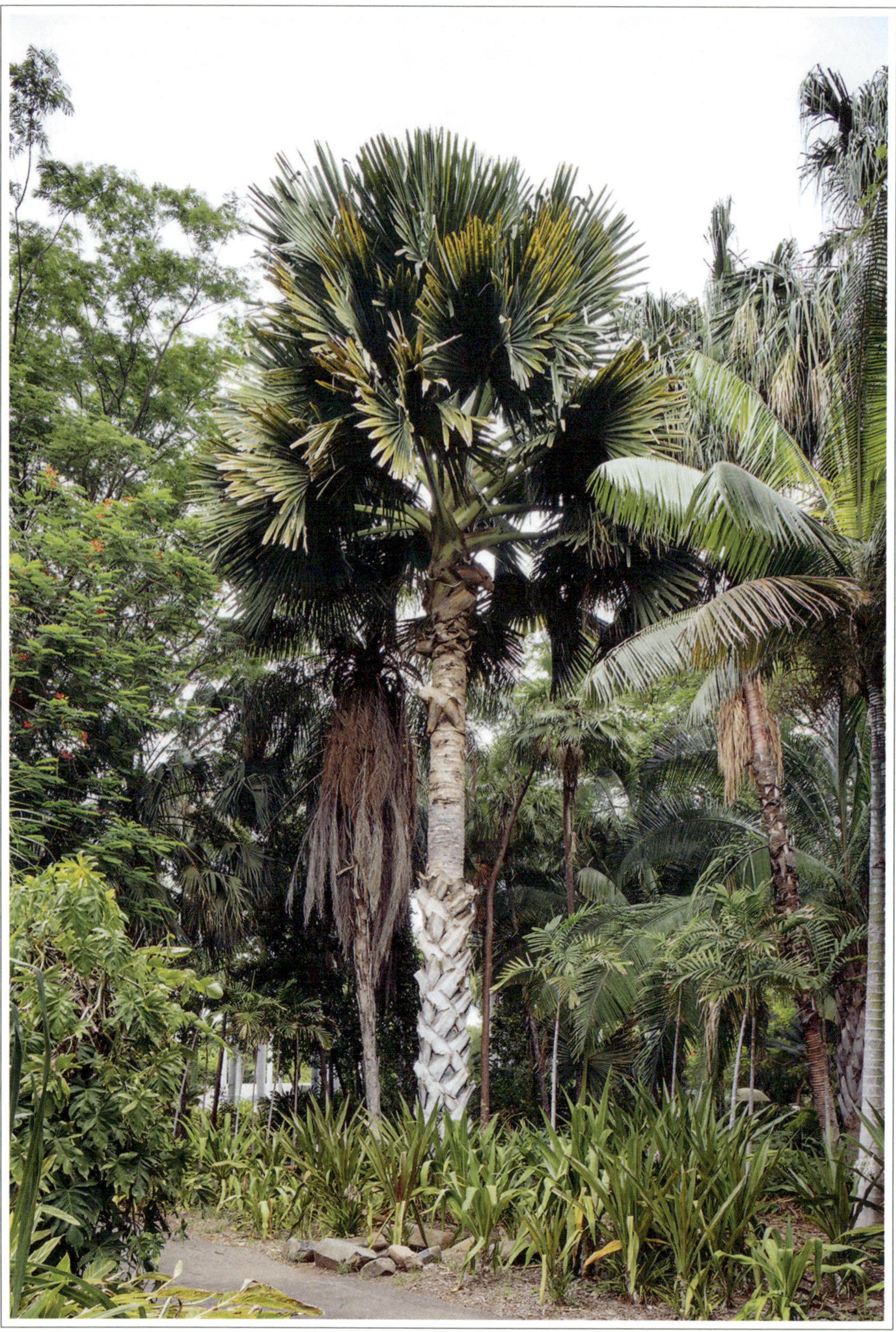

33
TALIPOT PALM

Corypha umbraculifera L.

Status: Assessment of global conservation status required
Distribution: India and Southeast Asia

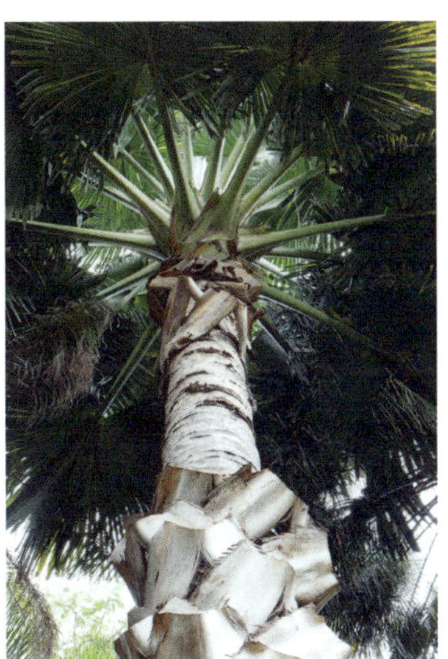
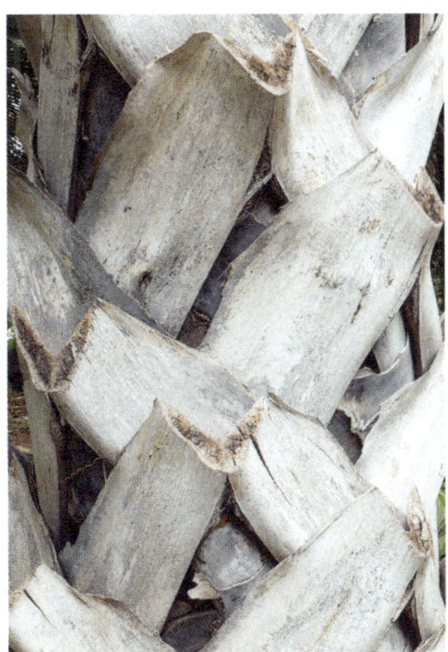
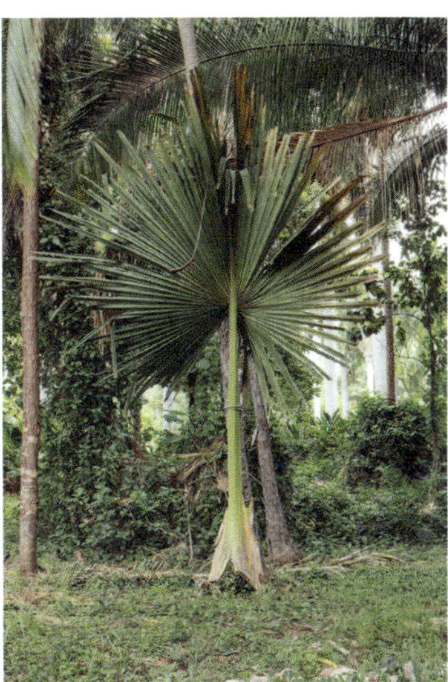

1. Trunk and crown. 2. Retained leaf bases. 3. Leaf.

This amazing species is a compendium of superlatives: it grows up to 100 feet tall and has the largest fan-shaped leaves in the plant kingdom, which may reach as much as 35 feet long. It also has the largest flower stalk bearing the most flowers: from three to 15 million flowers on a single flower stalk. The life cycle of this palm is equally amazing: when the palm reaches maturity (twenty to thirty years or more), it produces its record-holding flower stalk out of the top of the palm, and once the flowers and fruits have matured, the palm dies, like the agave. Unlike many agaves, however, it does not produce small plants around the base of the dying mother plant. Cutting off the flower stalk will not prevent the inevitable death of the palm. This species is native to India and Southeast Asia, but its original distribution is unknown, because it tends to be found close to human settlements. Humans have undoubtedly expanded the distribution of the palm, which is widely cultivated, especially in India and Sri Lanka, the leaves are used for roofing.

At the Jardín Botánico Culiacán the talipot palm is referred to as the "queen palm" because of its huge size.

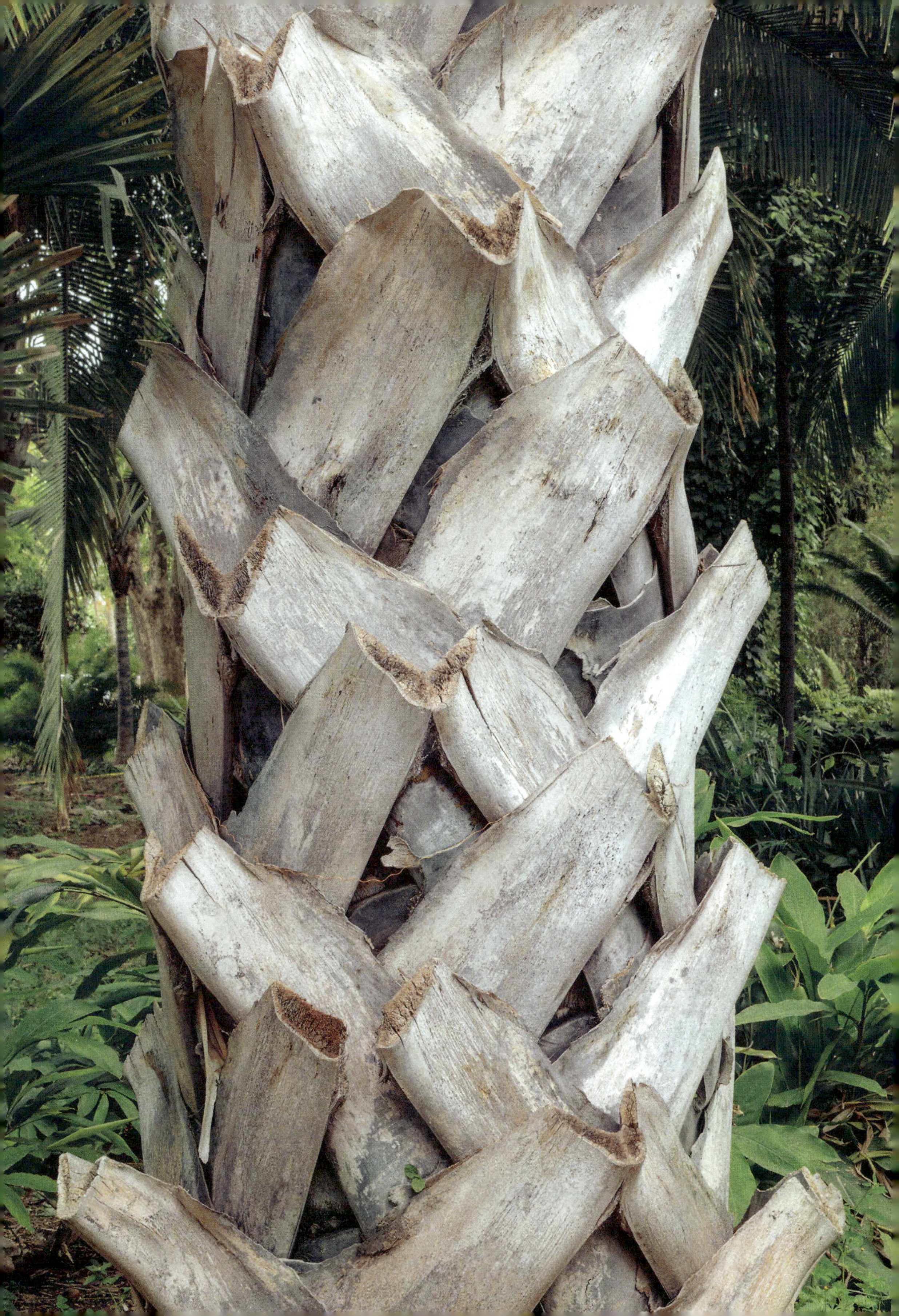

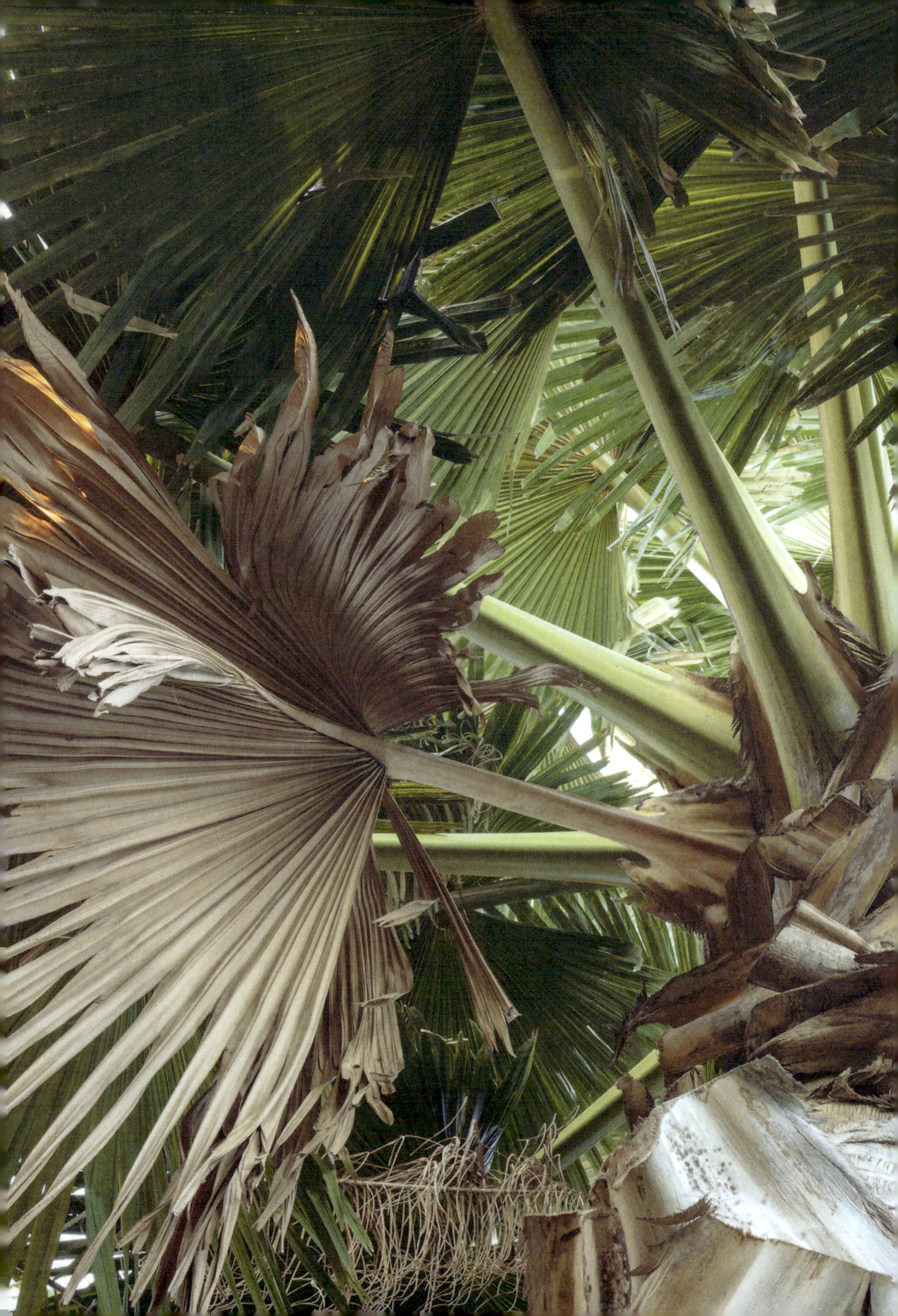

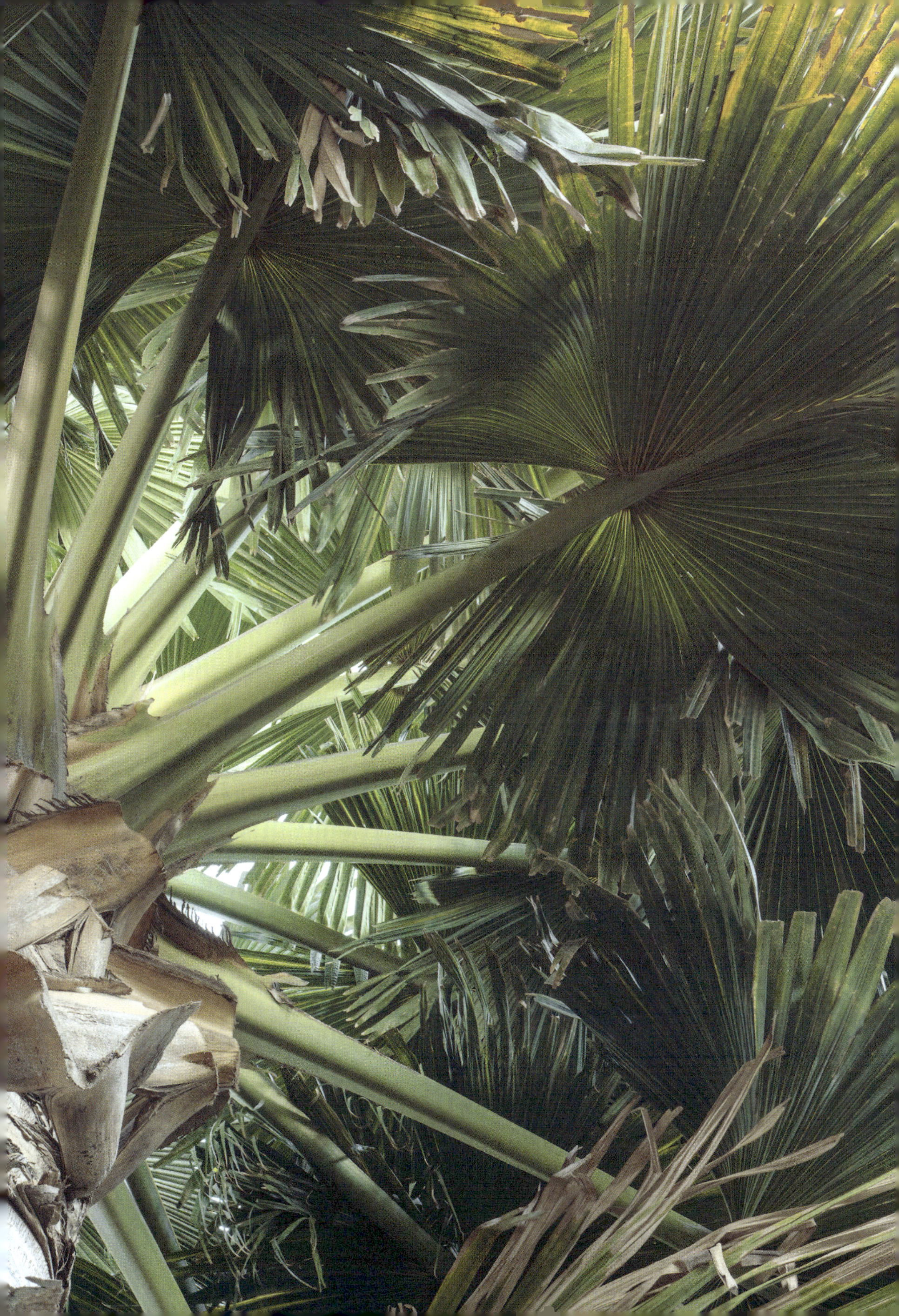

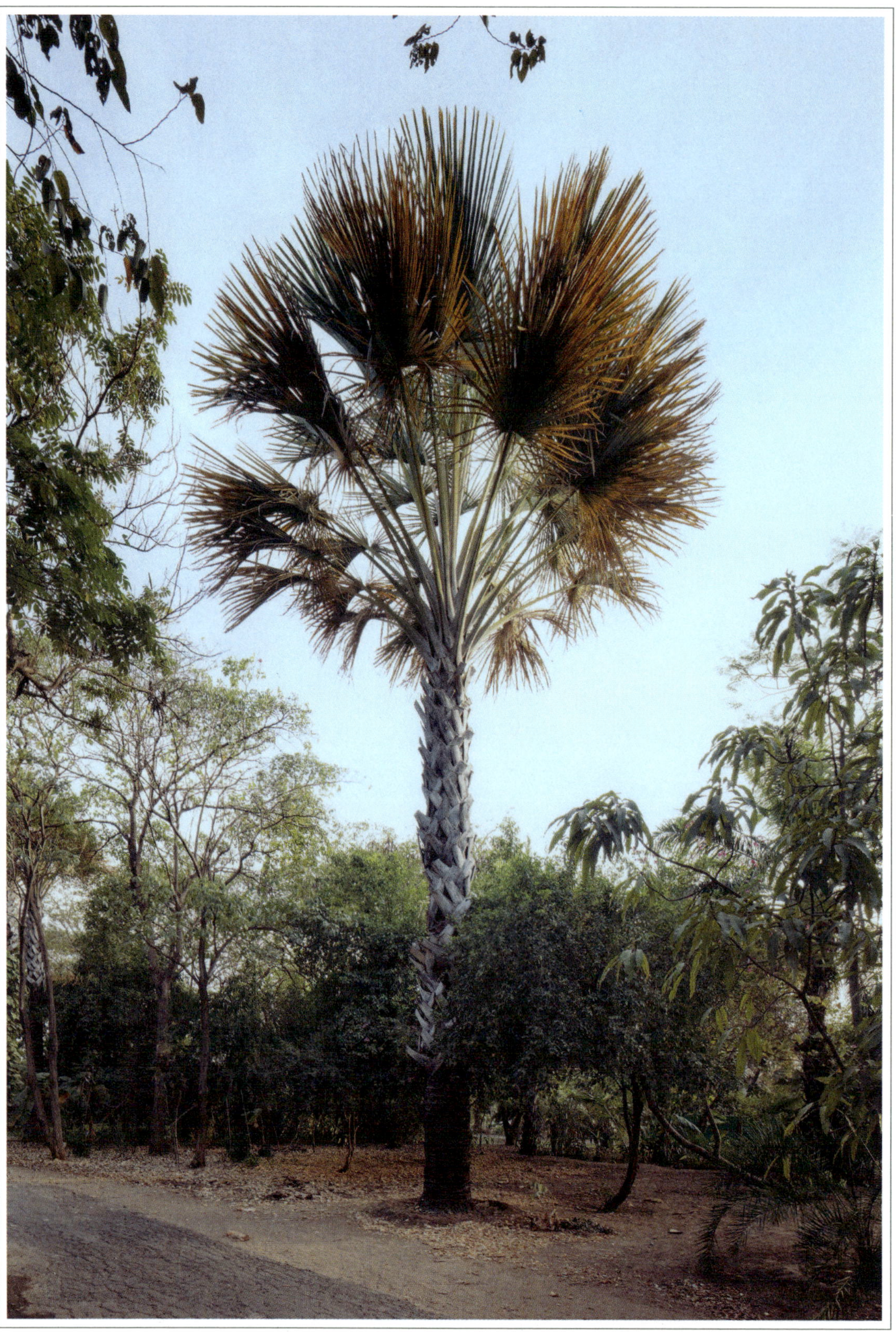

34
KENNEDY PALM, GEBANG PALM

Corypha utan Lam.

Status: Designated as Least Concern on the IUCN Red List
Distribution: India, Southeast Asia, and northern Australia

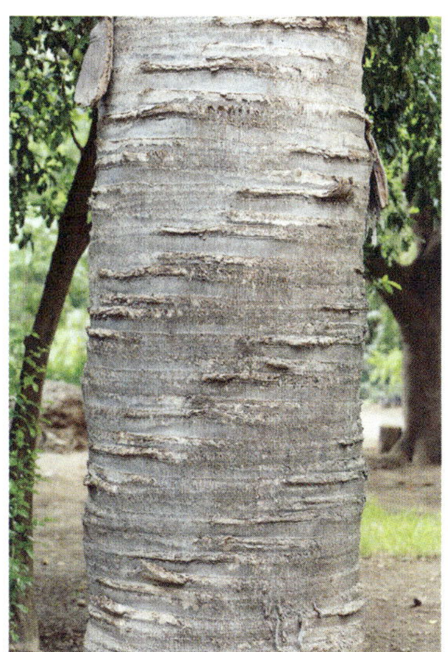
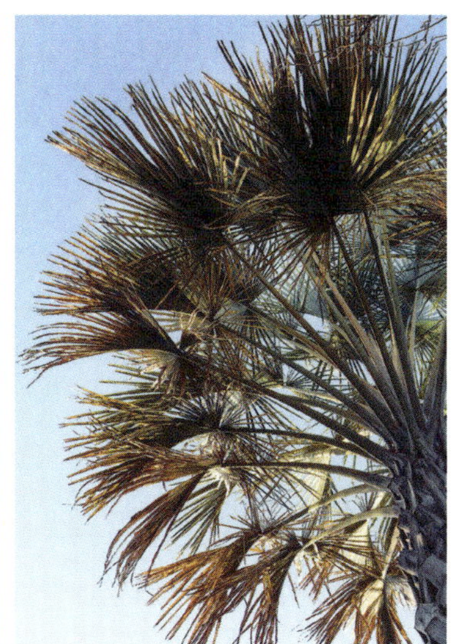
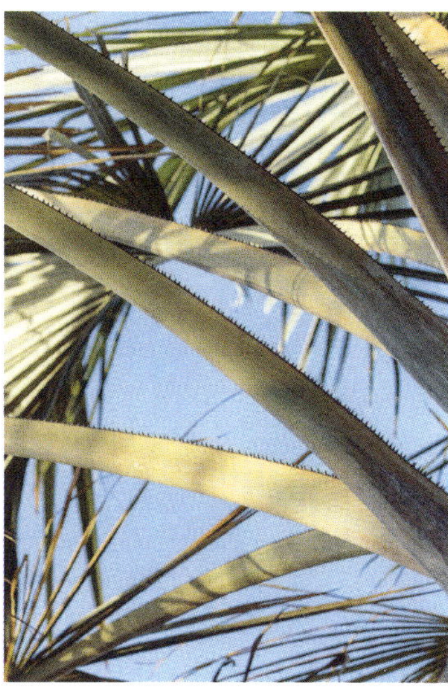

1. Trunk. 2. Leaf crown. 3. Detail of the leaf stems.

Corypha utan usually occurs in large groups of palms, in wet areas, such as seasonal streams and swamps. Like its relative, *Corypha umbraculifera*, this large palm has solitary stems and enormous fan-shaped leaves. It can be as tall or even taller than *Corypha umbraculifera*, up to 65 feet. It also produces a terminal flower stalk of flowers and fruits and then it dies. The leaf stalks are armed with ferocious teeth. Like other species of *Corypha*, the Gebang palm is widely used in its native regions: the leaves are used for making roofs, as well as for medicinal purposes. A liquor is produced from the fermented sap of the flower stalk. Many animals (mainly bats and reptiles) eat the fruits, and the seeds are used for making beads.

Carlos Murillo Depraect planted many specimens of *Corypha utan* palms, forming a passage or corridor, more than twenty years ago, in the 1990s. Its spectacular height is a testimony to its majesty.

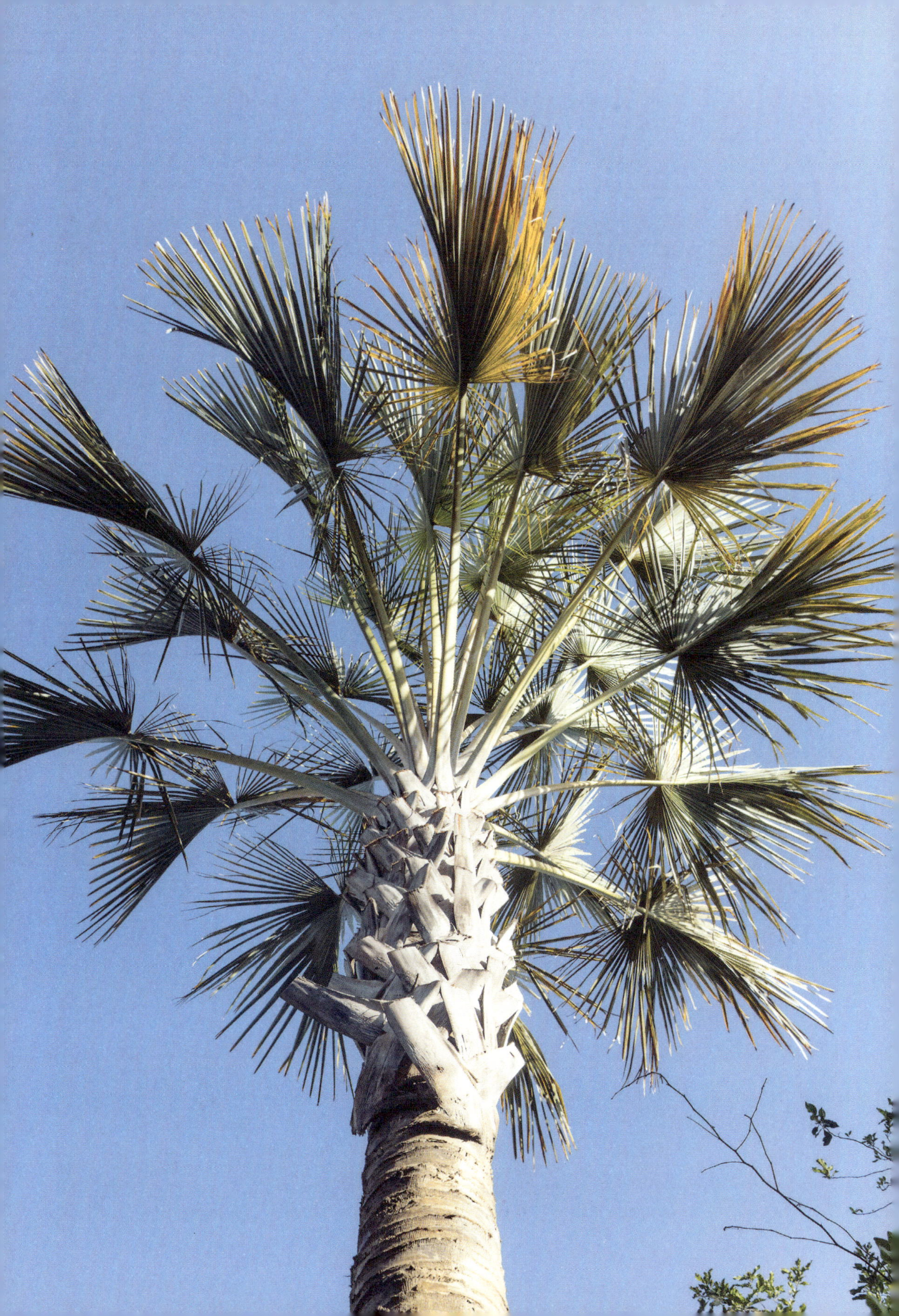

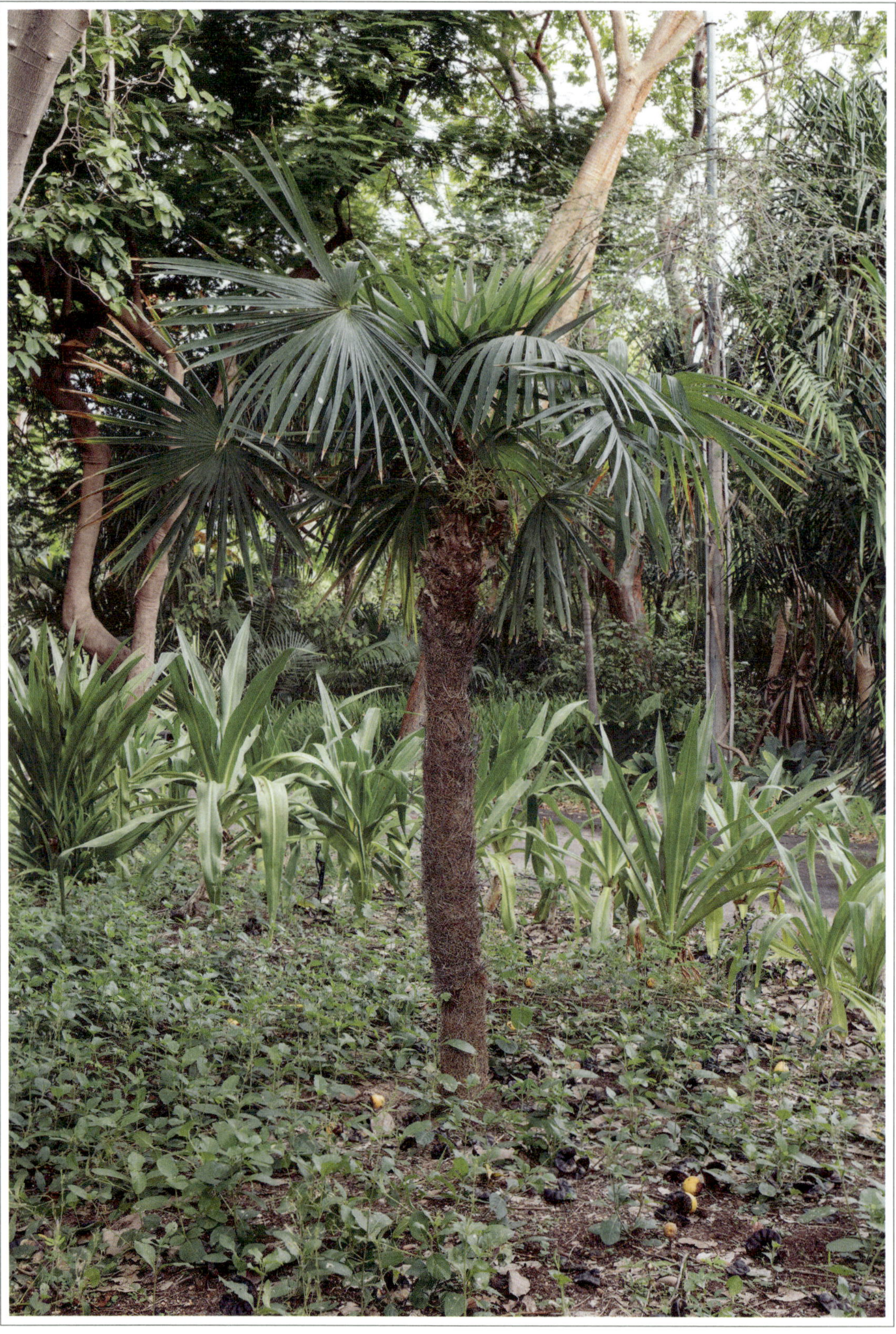

35

DWARF ROOTSPINE PALM

Cryosophila nana (Kunth) Blume

Status: Designated as Near Threatened on the IUCN Red List and as Threatened on the Mexican list of endangered species (NOM-059-SEMARNAT-2010)
Distribution: Endemic to western Mexico

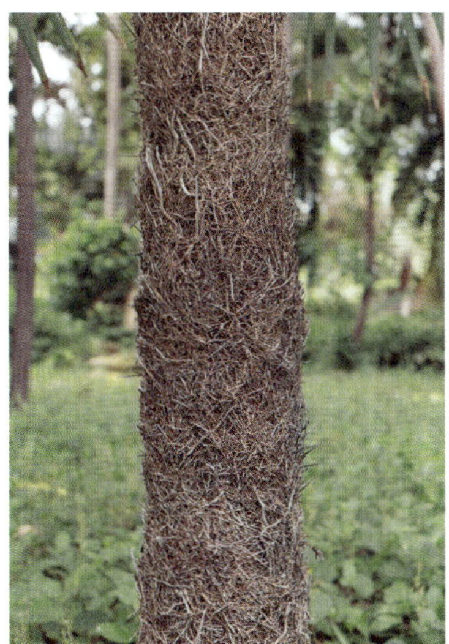
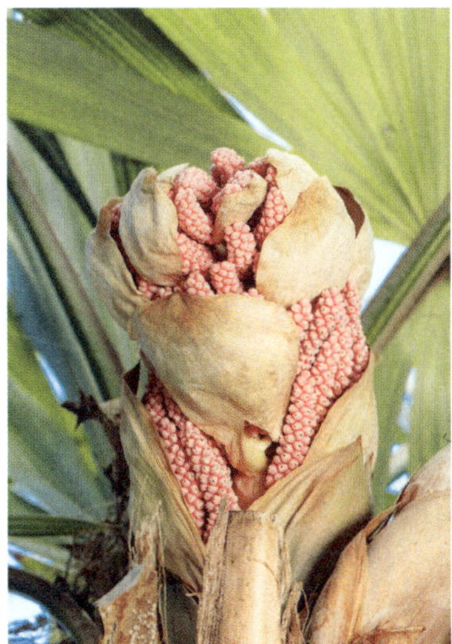
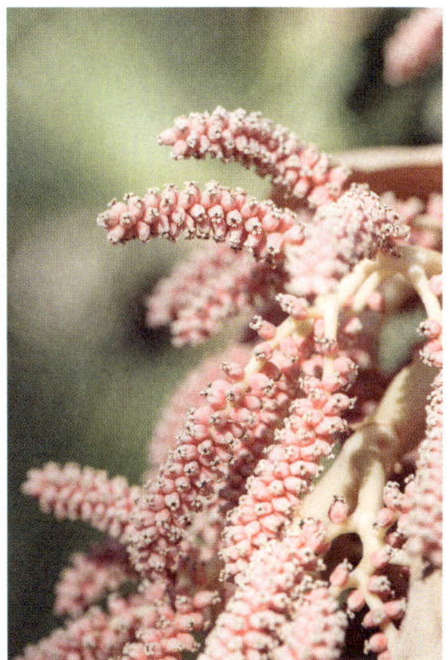

1. Trunk with spiny roots. 2. Inflorescence. 3. Flowers.

This small palm grows up to 16 feet tall in wet ravines and riverside forests. Palms of the genus *Cryosophila* are known as root-spine palms. If you look carefully at the base of the trunk, you will see it is armed with long spines. These spines are actually roots growing from the stem for a certain distance, which then cease to grow and become hard. Biologists suppose that the root-spine is a defense against certain kinds of herbivores. The trunk of the palm narrows towards the crown and ends in an abundance of deeply segmented leaves, which are neither grouped nor regularly arranged. Each leaf is split in the middle, as the leaves of all *Cryosophila* are, and green on the underside. The species has become very scarce because it is heavily exploited for its leaves, which are used for roofing and brooms.

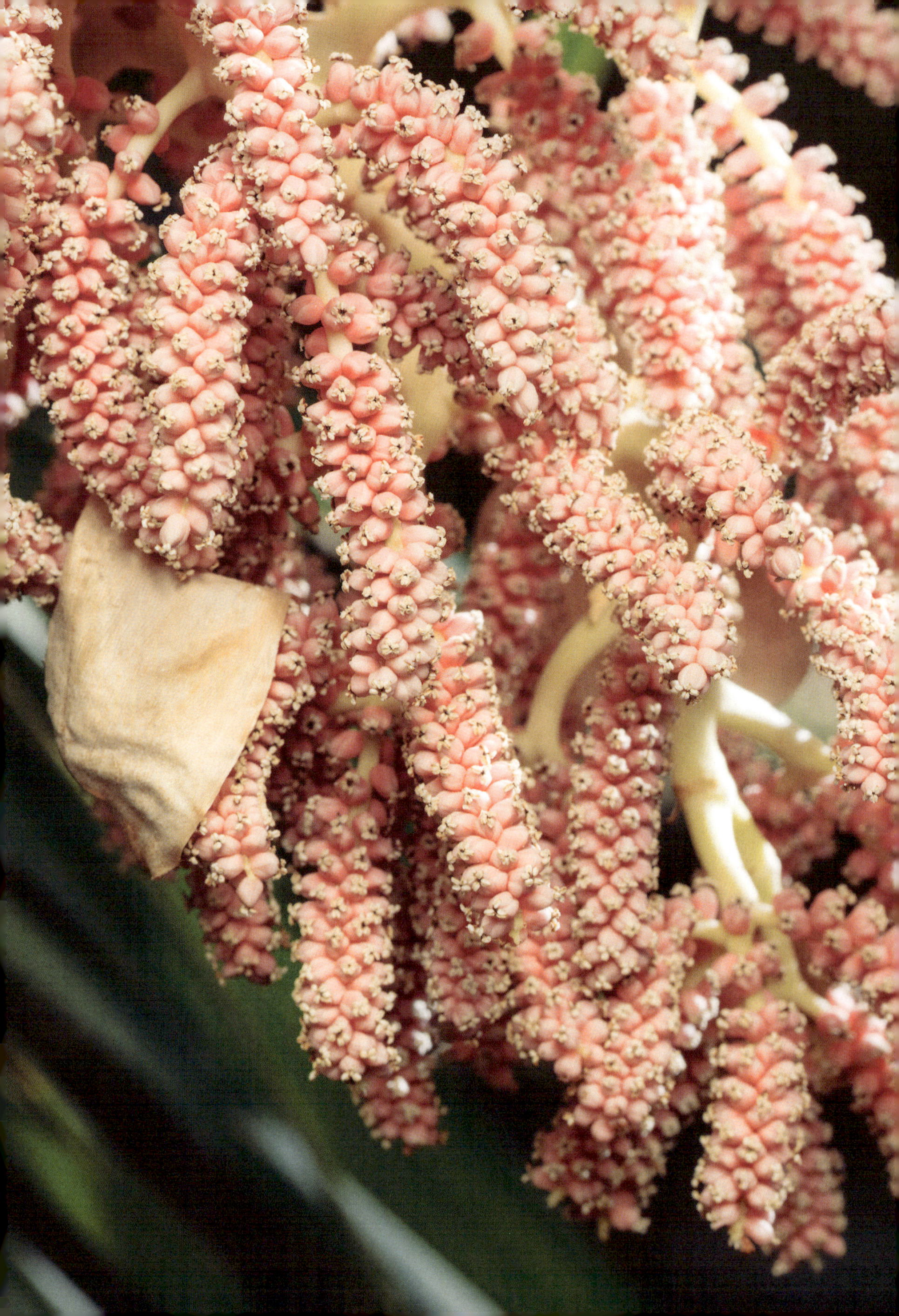

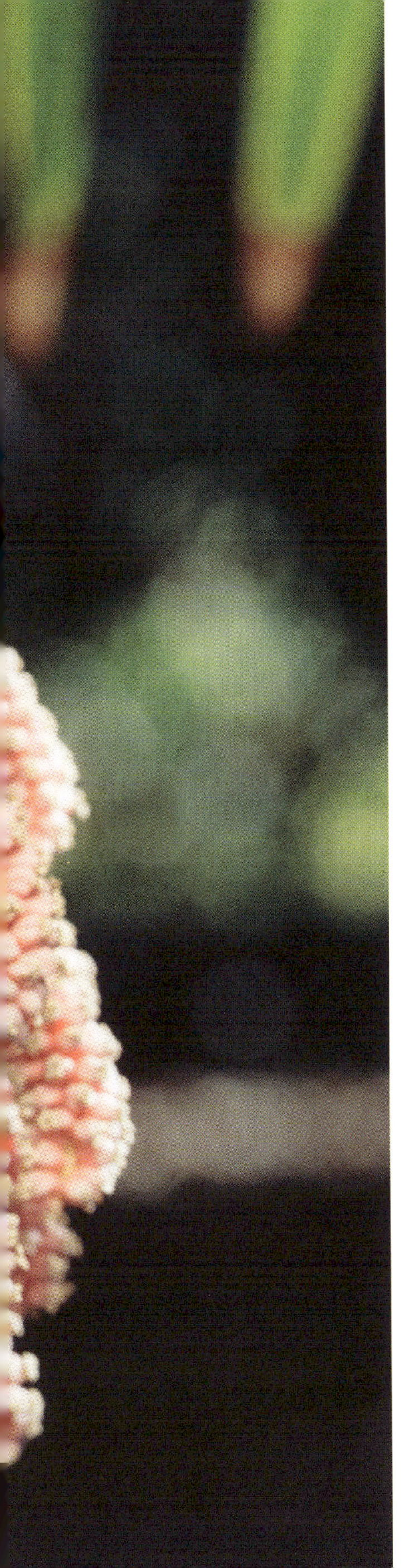

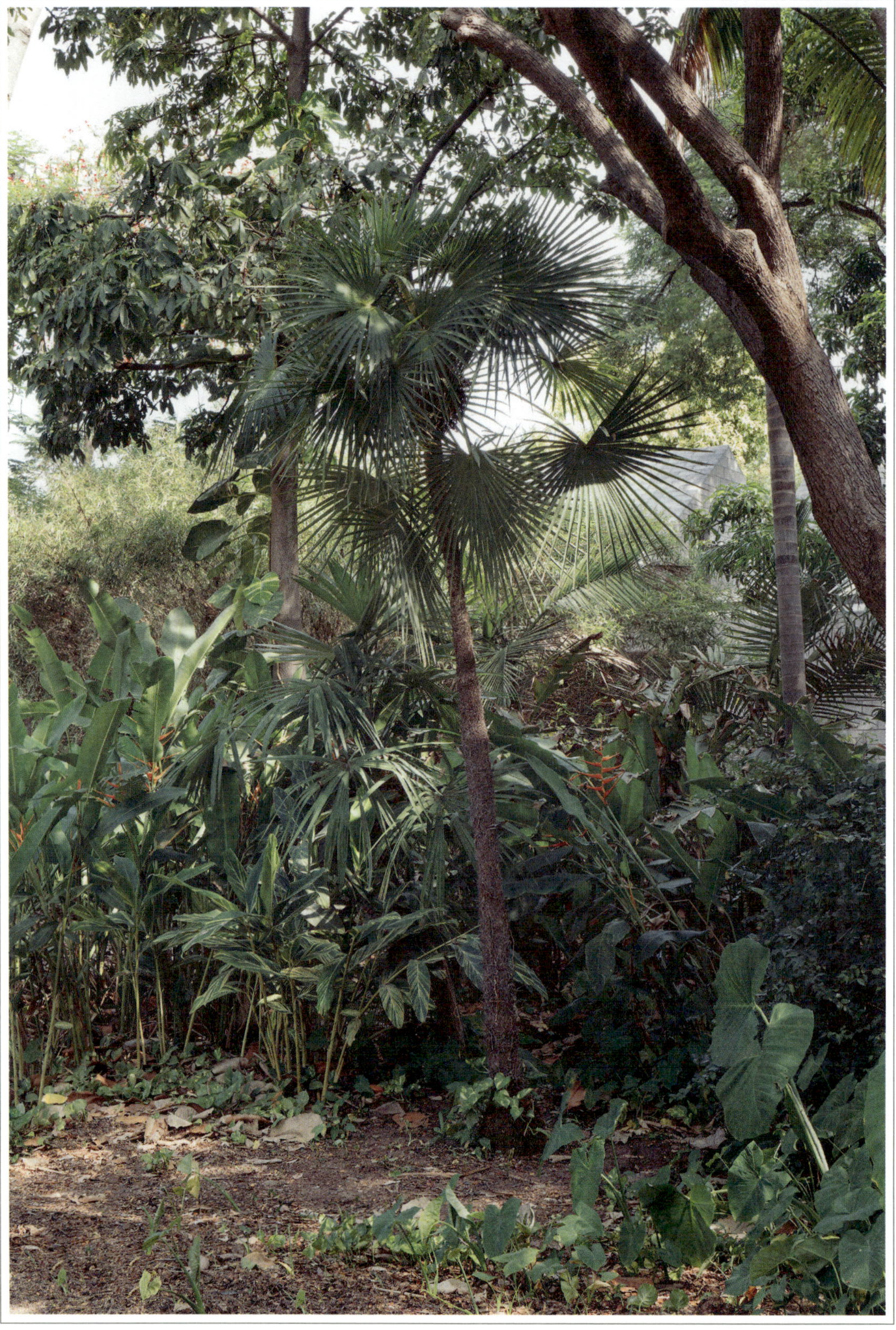

36

GUARA PALM, GUÁGUARA PALM, BROOM PALM, ROOTSPINE PALM, SILVER STAR PALM

Cryosophila warscewiczii (H. Wendl.) Bartlett

Status: Assessment of global conservation status required
Distribution: Nicaragua, Costa Rica, and Panama

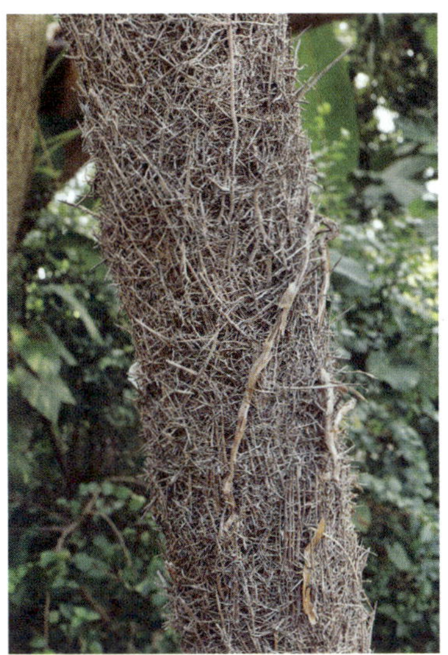
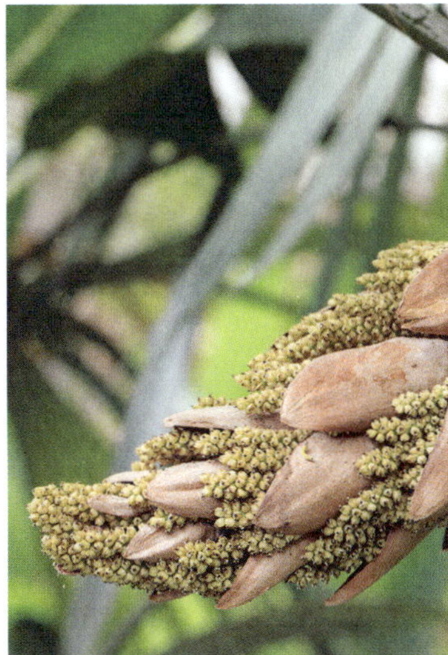
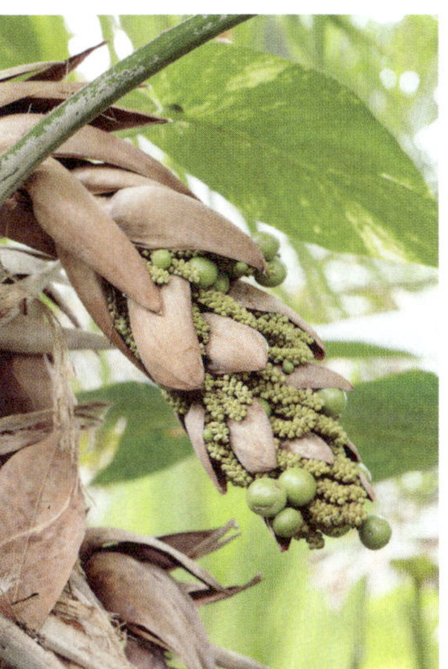

1. Trunk. 2. Inflorescence. 3. Unripe fruits.

This medium-sized palm, which grows to 35 feet tall, occurs in the understory of rainforests, under the tallest trees. *Cryosophila warscewiczii* is a fan palm with almost circular leaves, deeply divided in the middle, like those of all *Cryosophila* species, and leaf segments that are grouped in fives, sixes, or sevens. The underside of the leaf has conspicuous white hairs. The trunk of this palm is completely covered with fine spines, all the way to the base. Bats eat the oval fruits, dispersing the seeds in the forest, and use the leaves to make tents as refuges. Among humans, the leaves are widely used for brooms and roofs. In Costa Rica, both the heart of palm and its young inflorescence and fruits are sometimes harvested as food. The species was named (with a slight change of spelling) after Józef Warszewicz (1812–1866), a Polish botanist who collected plants throughout Central America.

Carlos Murillo Depraect, the founder of the Jardín Botánico Culiacán, cultivated palms of this species for more than thirty years. Some of the adult specimens were transplanted to build the Palmetum, and they are still healthy plants.

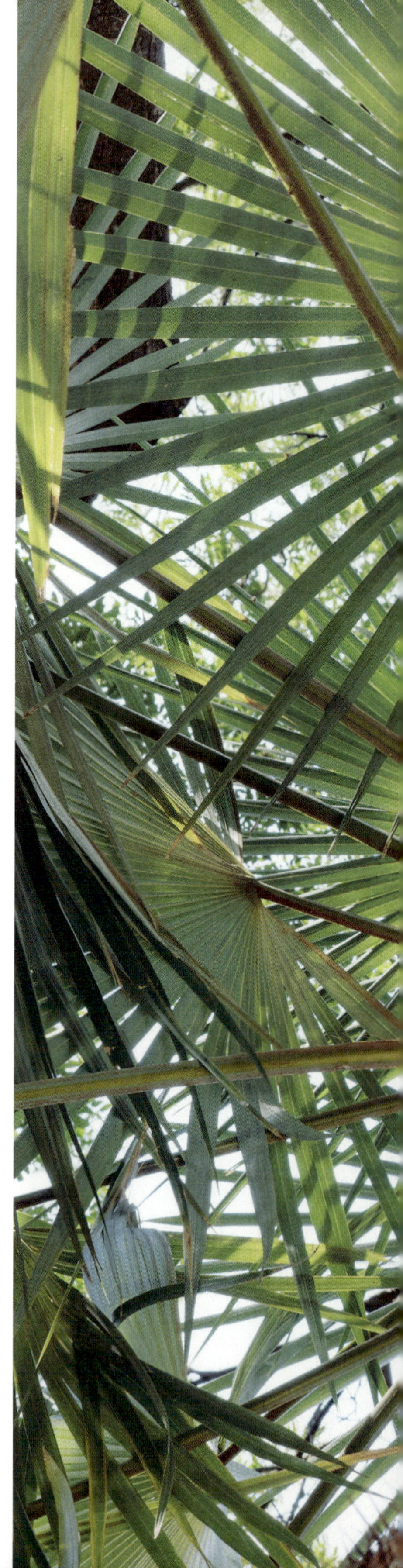

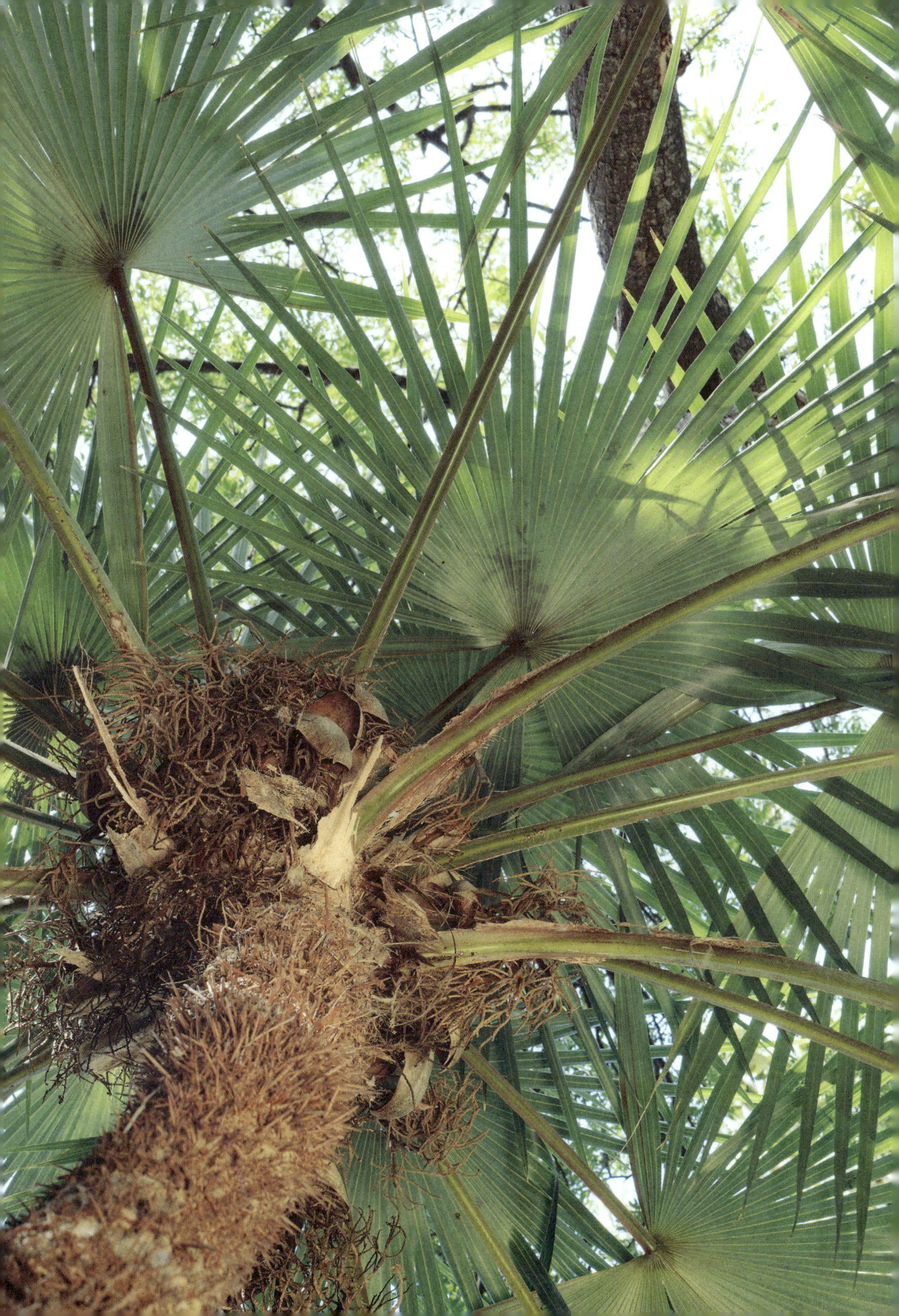

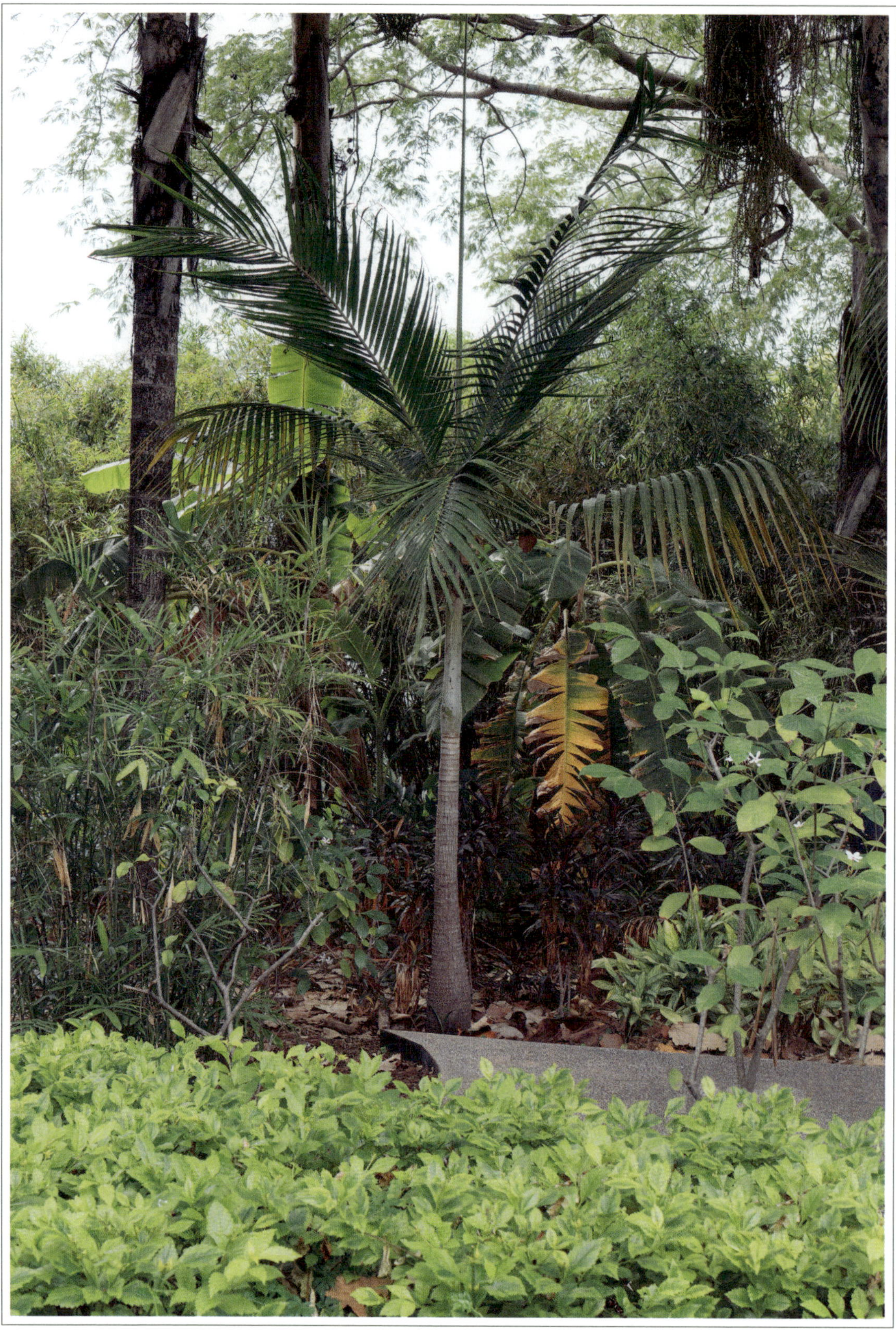

37
HURRICANE PALM, PRINCESS PALM

Dictyosperma album (Bory) Scheff.

Status: Designated as Critically Endangered on the IUCN Red List
Distribution: Mascarene Islands

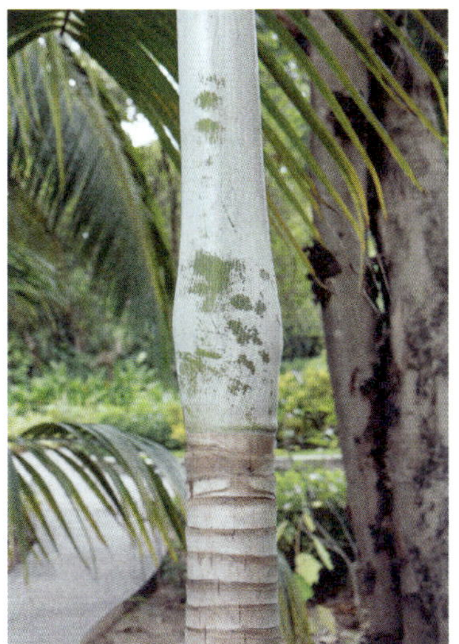
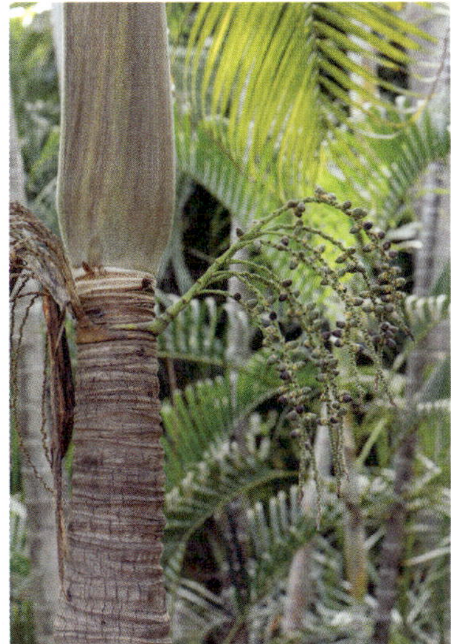
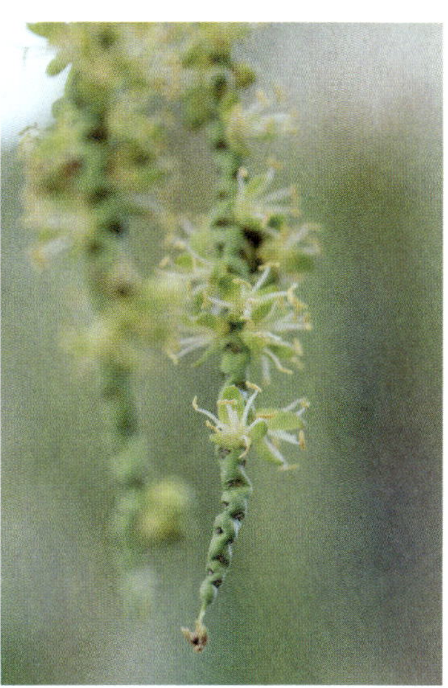

1. Trunk with leaf bases. 2. Inflorescence. 3. Male flowers.

This single-stemmed palm, which grows to a height of 40 feet, is found only in the Mascarene Islands, a small group of islands in the western Indian Ocean, east of Madagascar. It is found in tropical forests and coastal areas, including sometimes in flooded areas. It tolerates salty conditions and strong winds (the source of its common name). The leaves are long, shiny, and feather-like. The flowers, which have a strong fragrance, grow in long inflorescences that resemble horsetails, emerging between the trunk and the crown. The fruits are purple or violet when ripe and are eaten by crabs. Like other Mascarene palms (see *Hyophorbe* spp. & *Latania* spp.), *Dictyosperma album* is critically endangered in what remains of its native habitat. The Mascarene Islands have suffered extensive habitat destruction owing to agriculture, timber extraction, the introduction of animals, and invasive weeds; like most island organisms, *Dictyosperma* has declined in the face of these threats. Fewer than fifty individuals now remain in the wild. Ironically, the palm is widespread in gardens in the tropics, even in the Mascarene Islands, where it is grown both as an ornamental plant and as a source of edible palm heart. The few wild remaining individuals are not regenerating naturally, even though they are protected in a fenced reserve that is kept free of weeds.

The Jardín Botánico Culiacán has few specimens of this species. Two of them belong to the original palm collection assembled by Carlos Murillo Depraect.

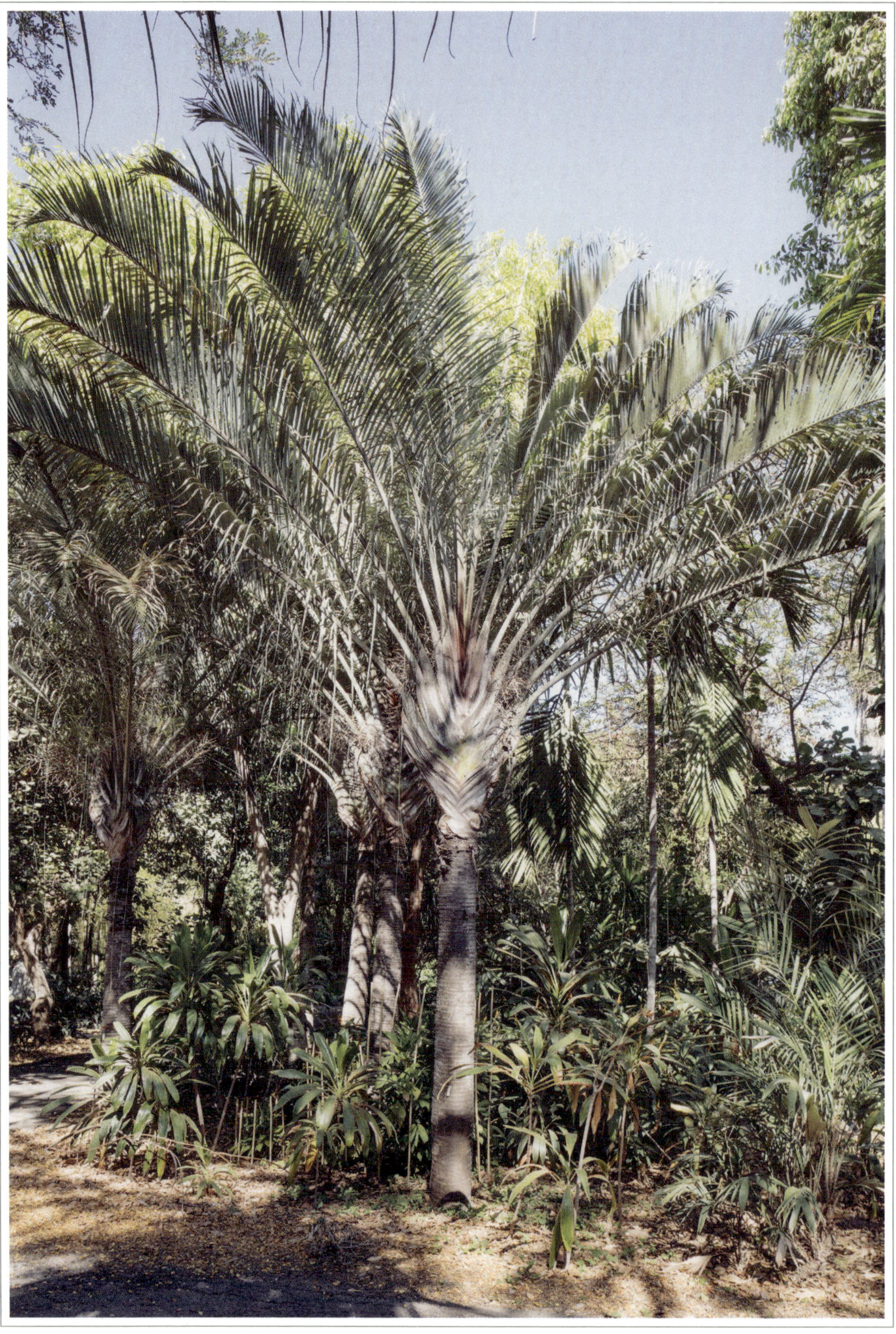

38

TRIANGLE PALM

Dypsis decaryi (Jum.) Beentje & J. Dransf.

Status: Designated as Vulnerable on the IUCN Red List
Distribution: Southern Madagascar

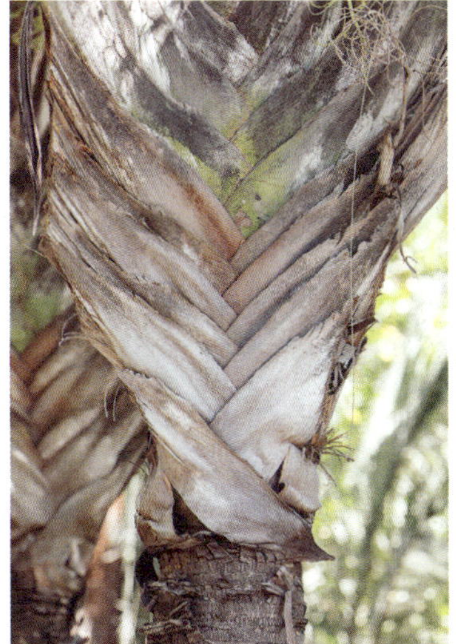
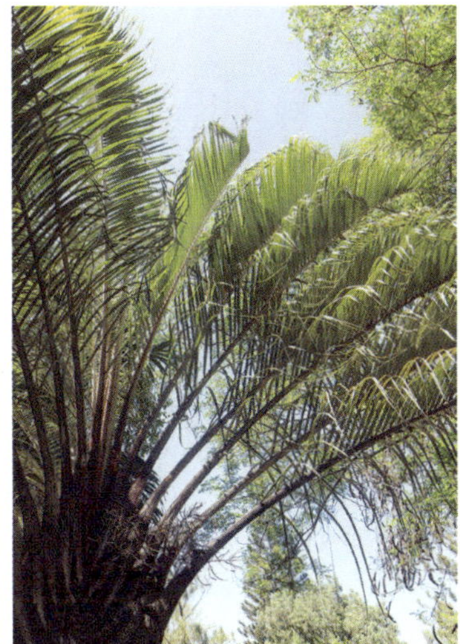
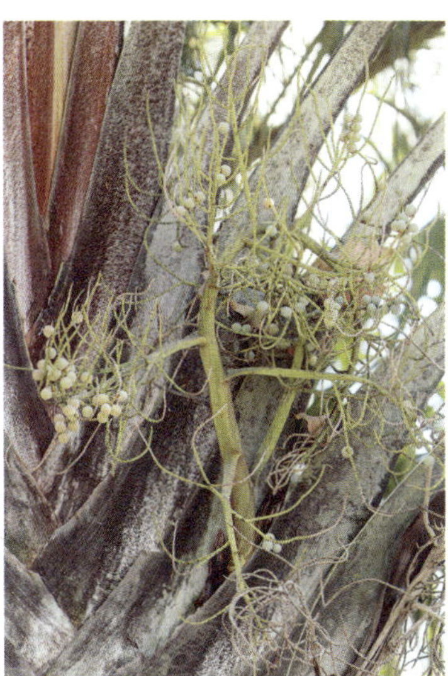

1. Trunk with leaf bases. 2. Leaf crown. 3. Unripe fruits.

It is easy to see how the triangle palm got its common name: its silvery green leaves are arranged in three ranks. First introduced to horticulture about fifty years ago, this species is now extraordinarily popular all around the world. This fast-growing solitary palm can quickly reach a height of 13 feet or more. It has beautiful, gray-green, pinnate leaves. In the wild, lemurs and parrots eat its fruits. Humans also eat the fruits and make a fermented beverage with them, while using the leaves for making roofs. The triangle palm will be vulnerable to extinction if its natural habitat, the contact zone between rainforest and xeric scrub in southernmost Madagascar, is destroyed.

When Carlos Murillo Depraect brought specimens of this palm to the Jardín Botánico Culiacán, the gardeners were amused by its shape. It seems to be a very resistant plant, because today it remains very healthy, and has never suffered from pests or diseases.

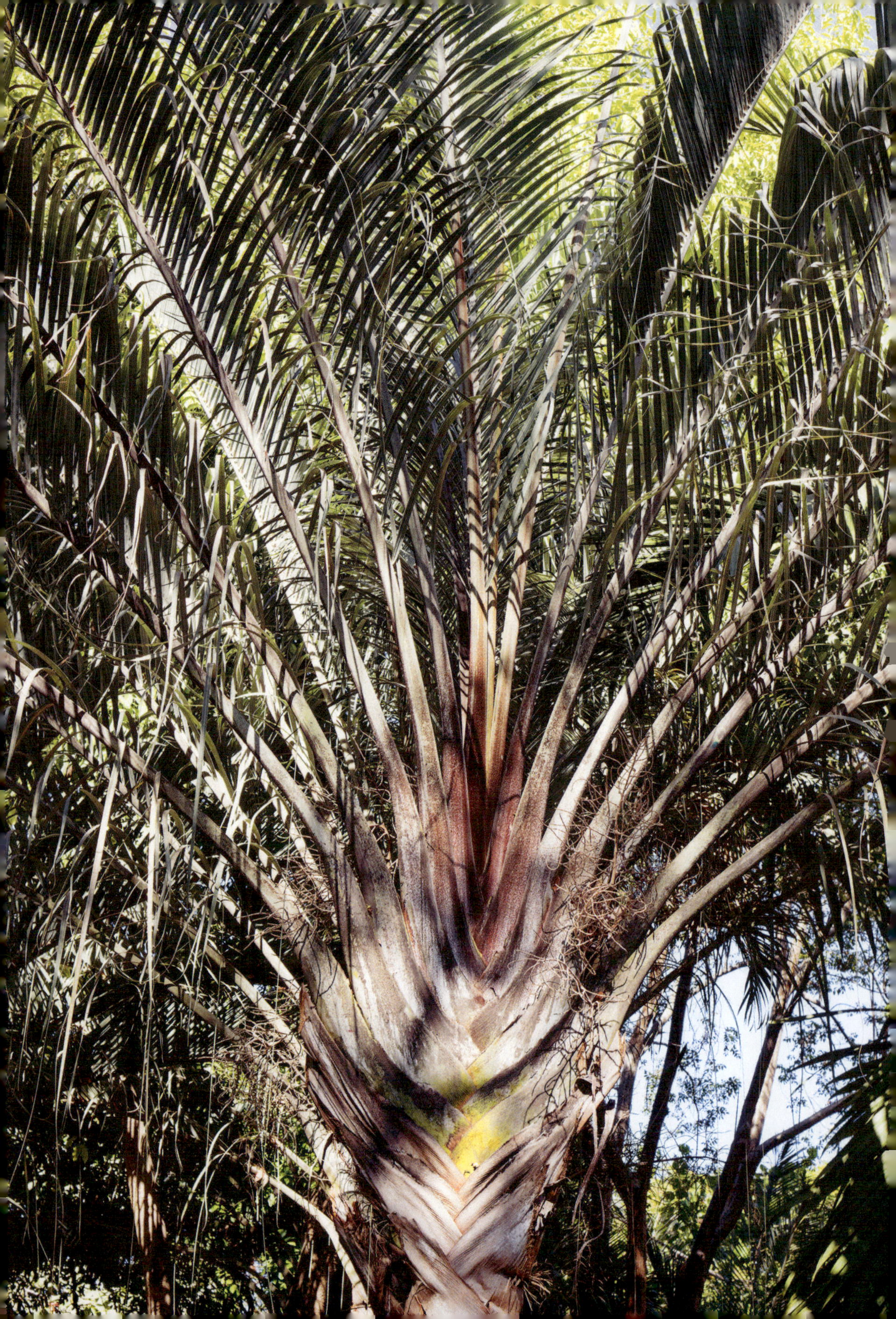

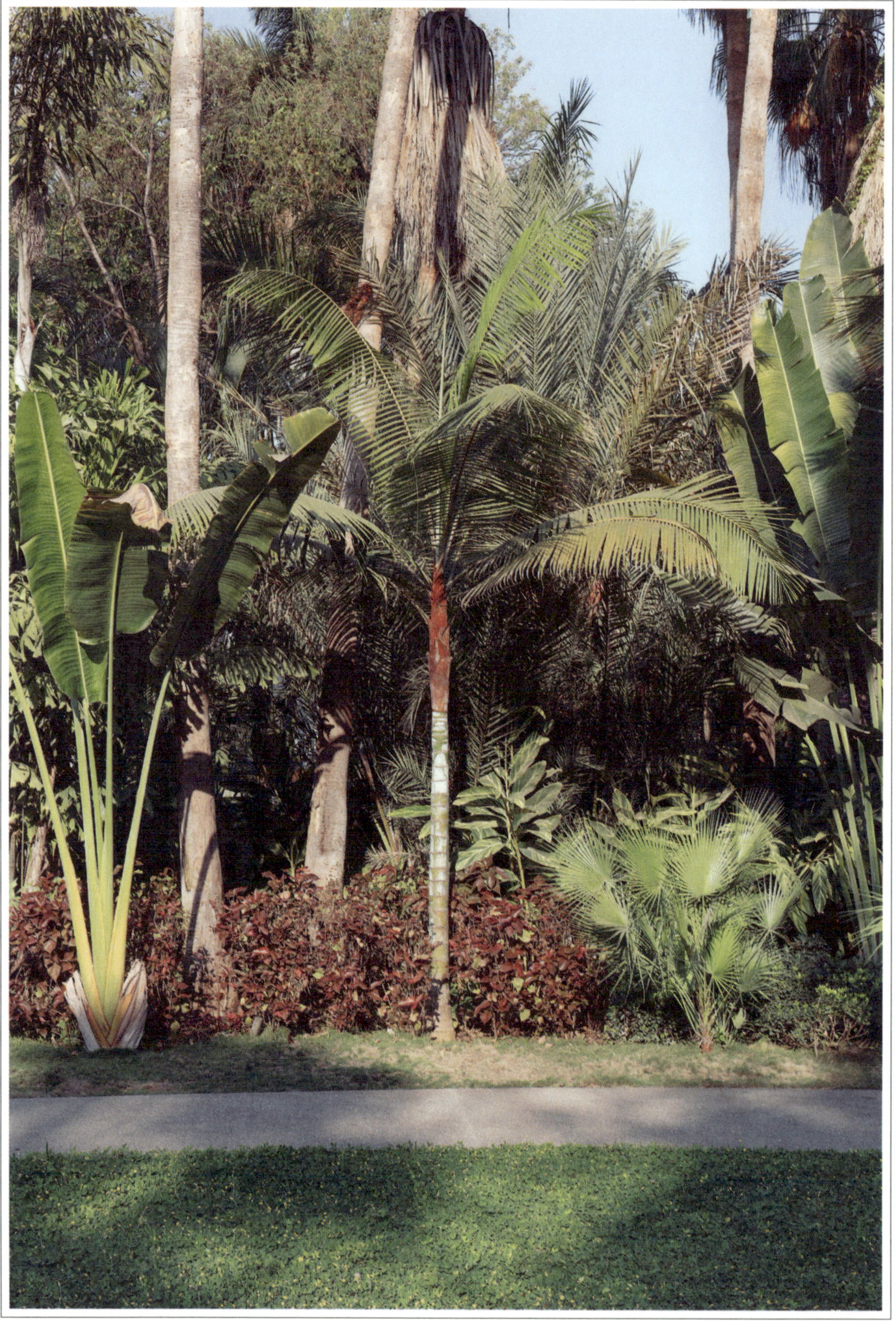

39

REDNECK PALM, TEDDY BEAR PALM

Dypsis lastelliana (Baill.) Beentje & J. Dransf.

Status: Designated as Least Concern on the IUCN Red List
Distribution: Endemic to Madagascar

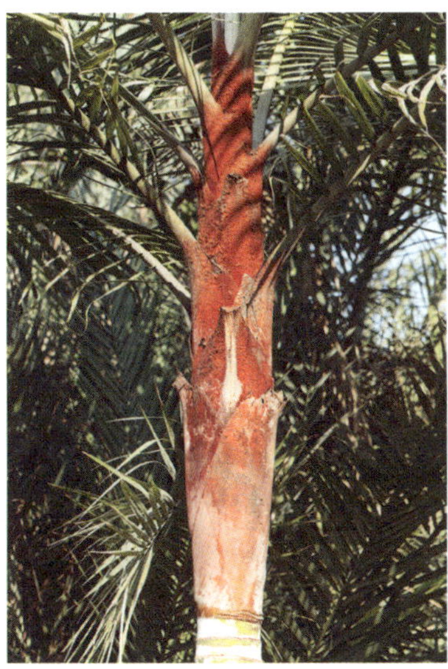

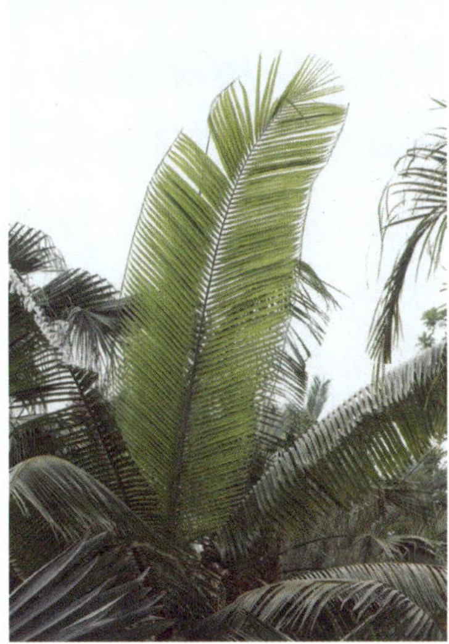

1. Leaf bases. 2. Leaf.

The genus *Dypsis* is remarkably variable in size and shape, ranging from knee-high shrubs in the shady understory to massive palms overtopping the forest canopy. It is a highly diverse genus of over 160 species from Madagascar, other Indian Ocean islands, and the adjacent African mainland. *Dypsis lastelliana* is a medium-sized solitary forest palm that grows from about four to 50 feet tall. Its most noteworthy features are the reddish-brown fuzz that covers the leaf bases and the whitish rings on the trunk. The long leaves are used for roofing, especially for churches and as a welcome sign in many villages. The fuzz is also used for making mattresses and even as a salt substitute in cooking. The palm heart is said to be bitter and inedible: it may contain cyanide, as does that of *Dypsis lutescens*.

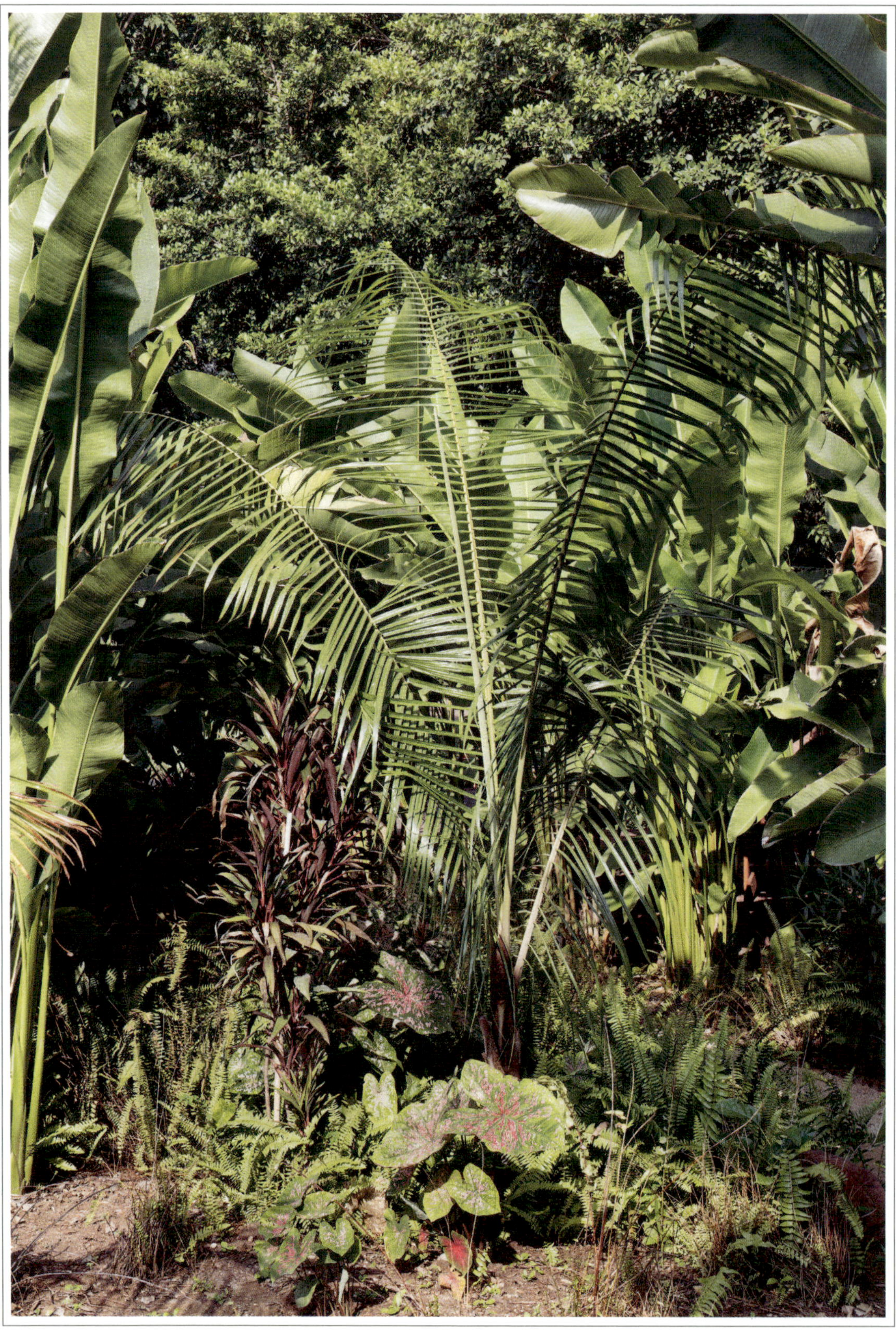

40

TEDDY BEAR PALM

Dypsis leptocheilos (Hodel) Beentje & J. Dransf.

Status: Designated as Critically Endangered on the IUCN Red List
Distribution: Madagascar

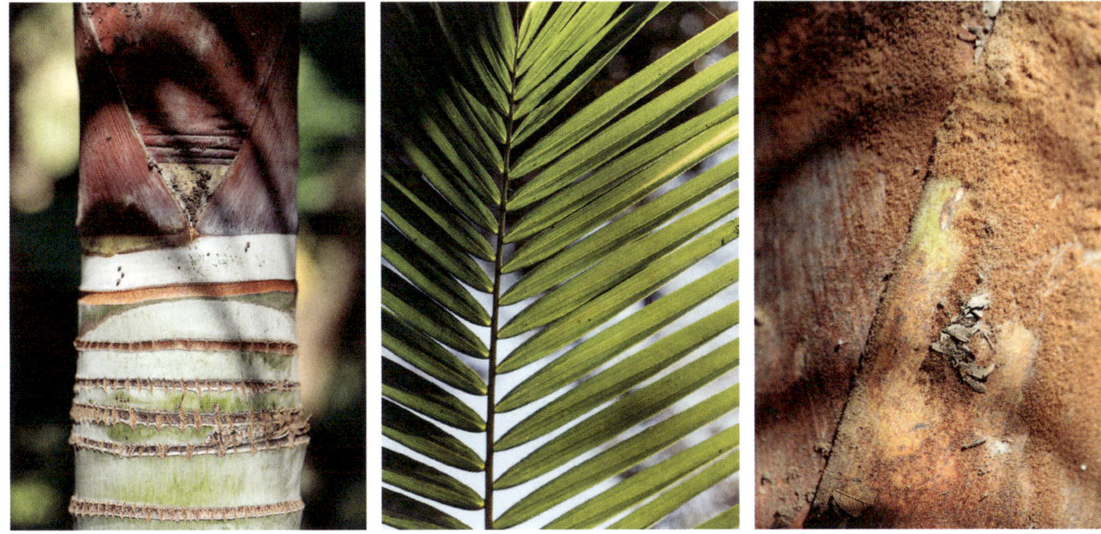

1. Trunk with leaf bases. 2. Detail of the leaf. 3. Detail of the "fur" on the leaf bases.

The story of *Dypsis leptocheilos* is another one of a palm originally found in cultivation and only later discovered in the wild. It is a solitary palm that grows up to 35 feet tall, with long graceful pinnate leaves. The species was first described from an individual in a botanical garden in Tahiti, but botanists eventually found it growing in two small areas in Madagascar. In its native habitat—freshwater swamps and seasonal rivers—it is critically endangered by habitat loss. The species gets its common name, the teddy bear palm, from the reddish brown "fur" on the leaf bases, which is the same color as that commonly seen on teddy bears. The fruits are brownish and spherical. The species is popular in cultivation because, in spite of its tropical origins, it is more cold-hardy and more drought-tolerant than most other species of *Dypsis*. It is not an edible plant, as its heart contains cyanide, a potent and fast-acting poison.

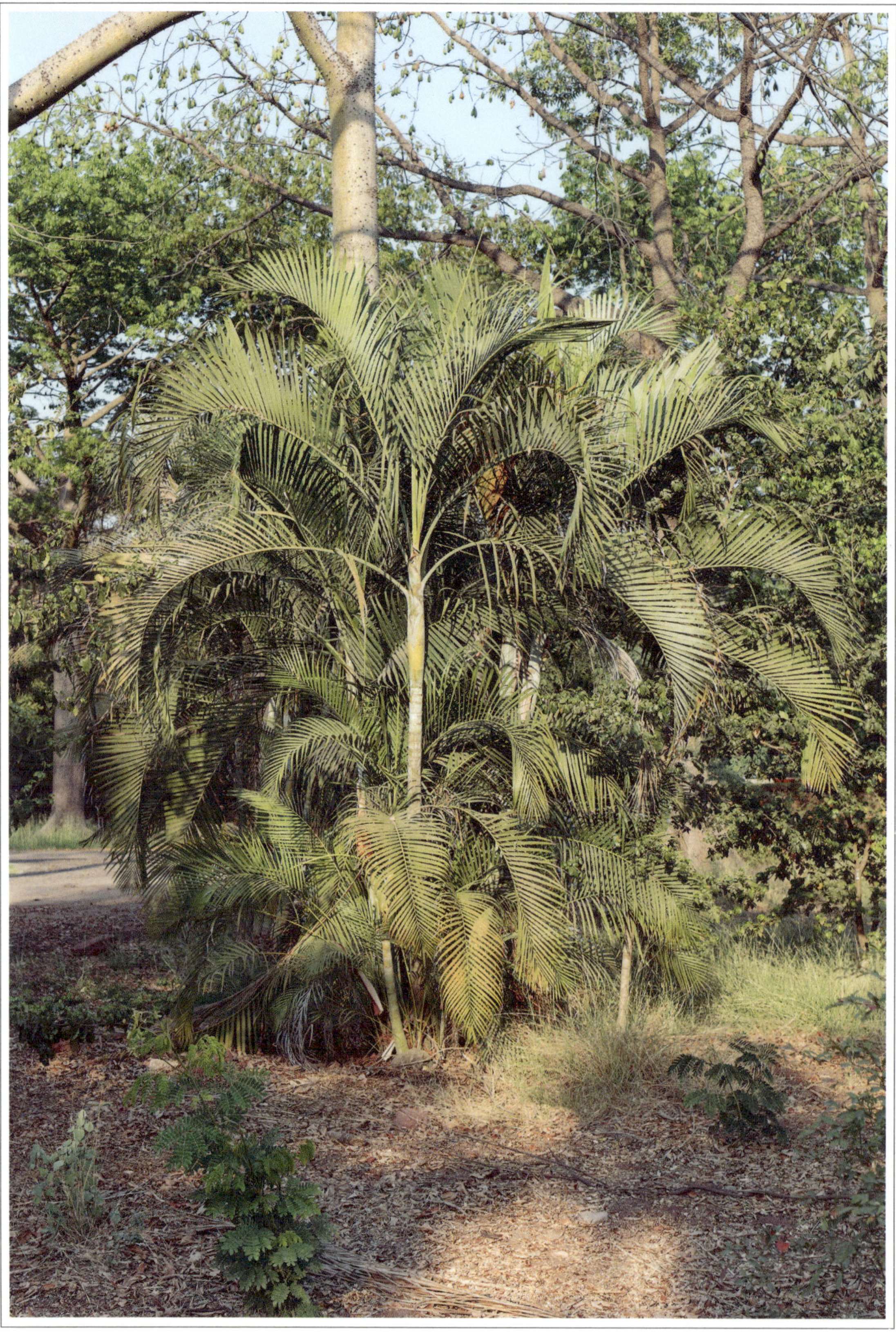

41

ARECA PALM

Dypsis lutescens (H. Wendl.) Beentje & J. Dransf.

Status: Designated as Near Threatened on the IUCN Red List
Distribution: Madagascar

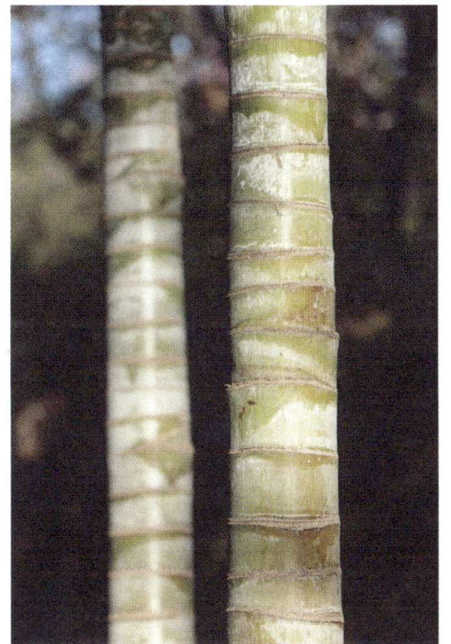
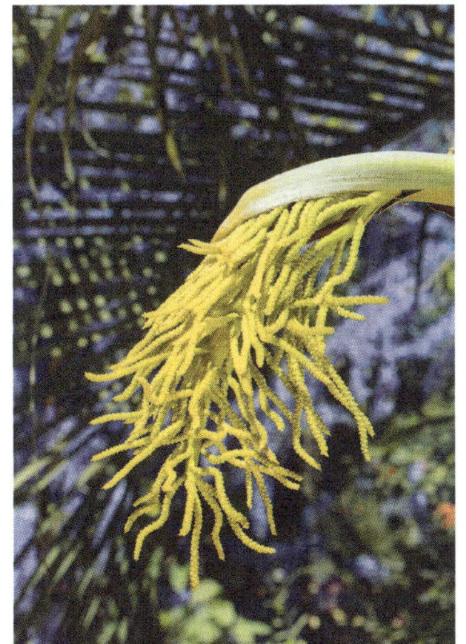
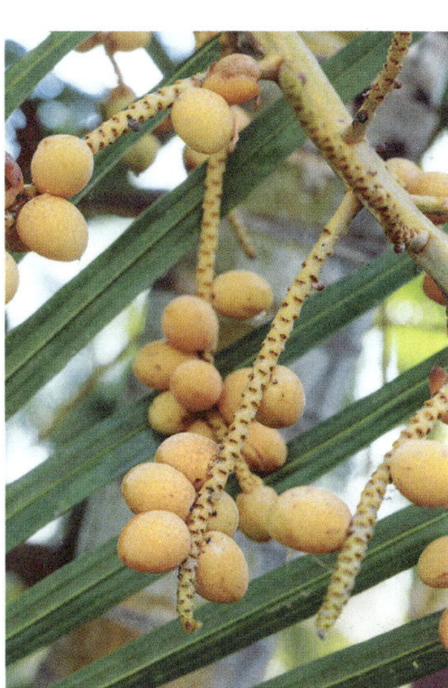

1. Stems. 2. Juvenile inflorescence. 3. Fruits.

Although threatened by rainforest destruction across some parts of its range in Madagascar, *Dypsis lutescens* is perhaps one of the most commonly cultivated ornamental palms in the world. Millions of plants are produced by nurseries, and in tropical and subtropical regions this palm is widely used in landscape design as a hedge or screen to generate privacy. The tight clusters of green ringed stems, up to 13 feet tall, resemble bamboo. One of its common names, the areca palm, is misleading, as *Dypsis lutescens* has nothing to do with the genus *Areca*, which is genus of palms from Southeast Asia. The species name, *lutescens*, means "yellowish" and refers to the naturally yellow leaf stalks, flower stalks, and fruits. The palm heart is inedible, as it contains cyanide, a natural toxin that rarely occurs in palms.

Plants of this species first arrived at the Jardín Botánico Culiacán twenty years ago. The staff clearly knows how to care for them, because the garden now has more than eighty specimens.

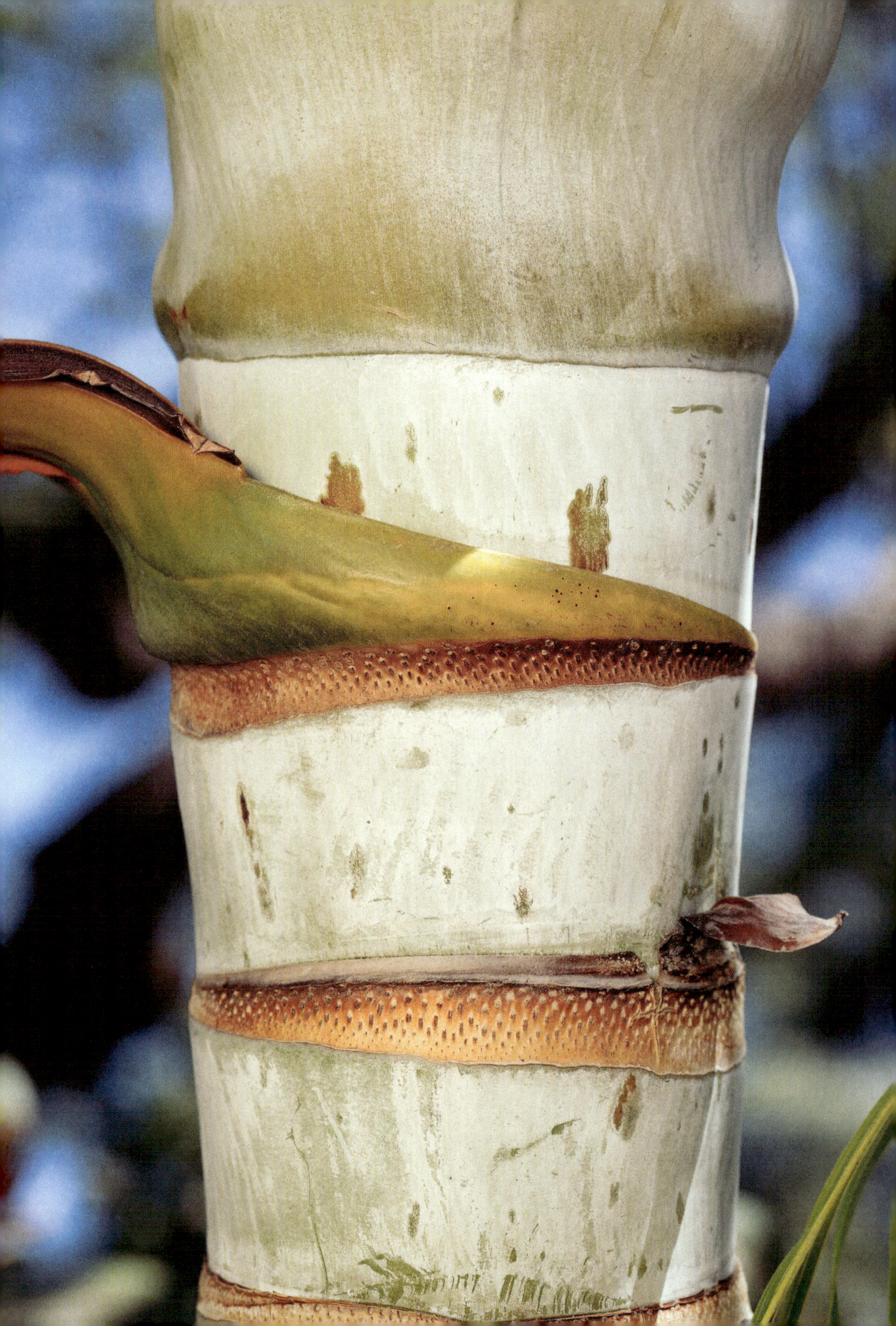

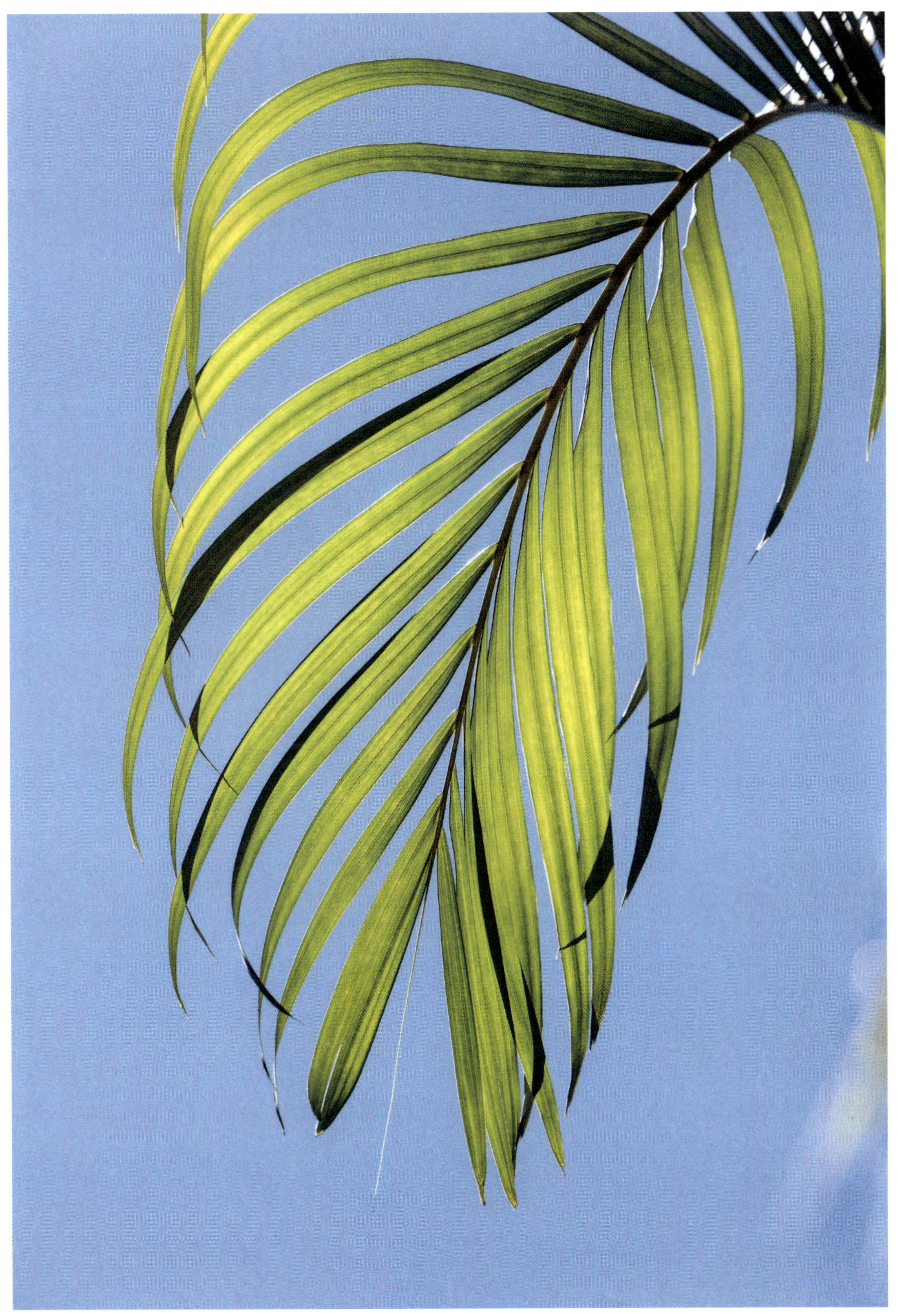

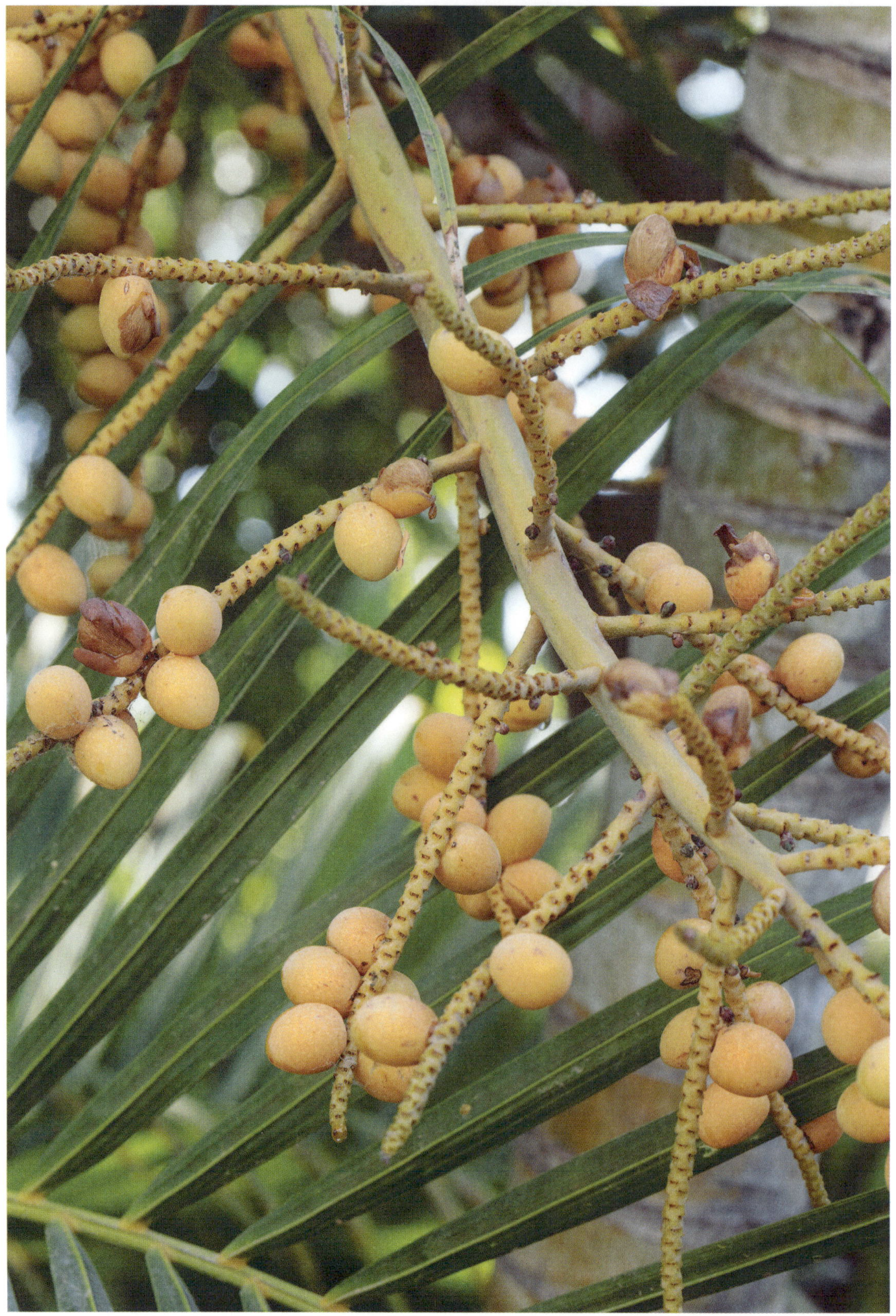

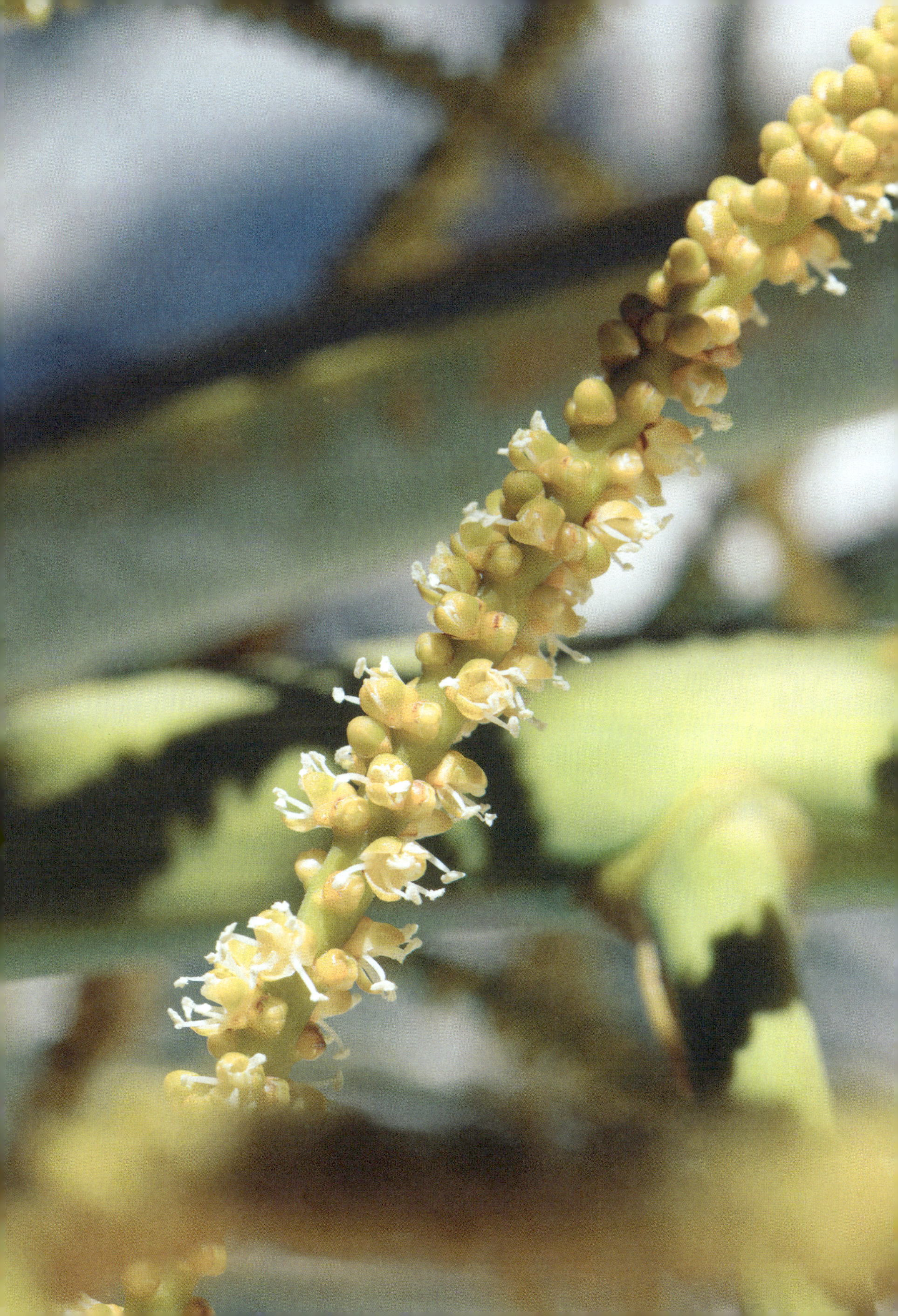

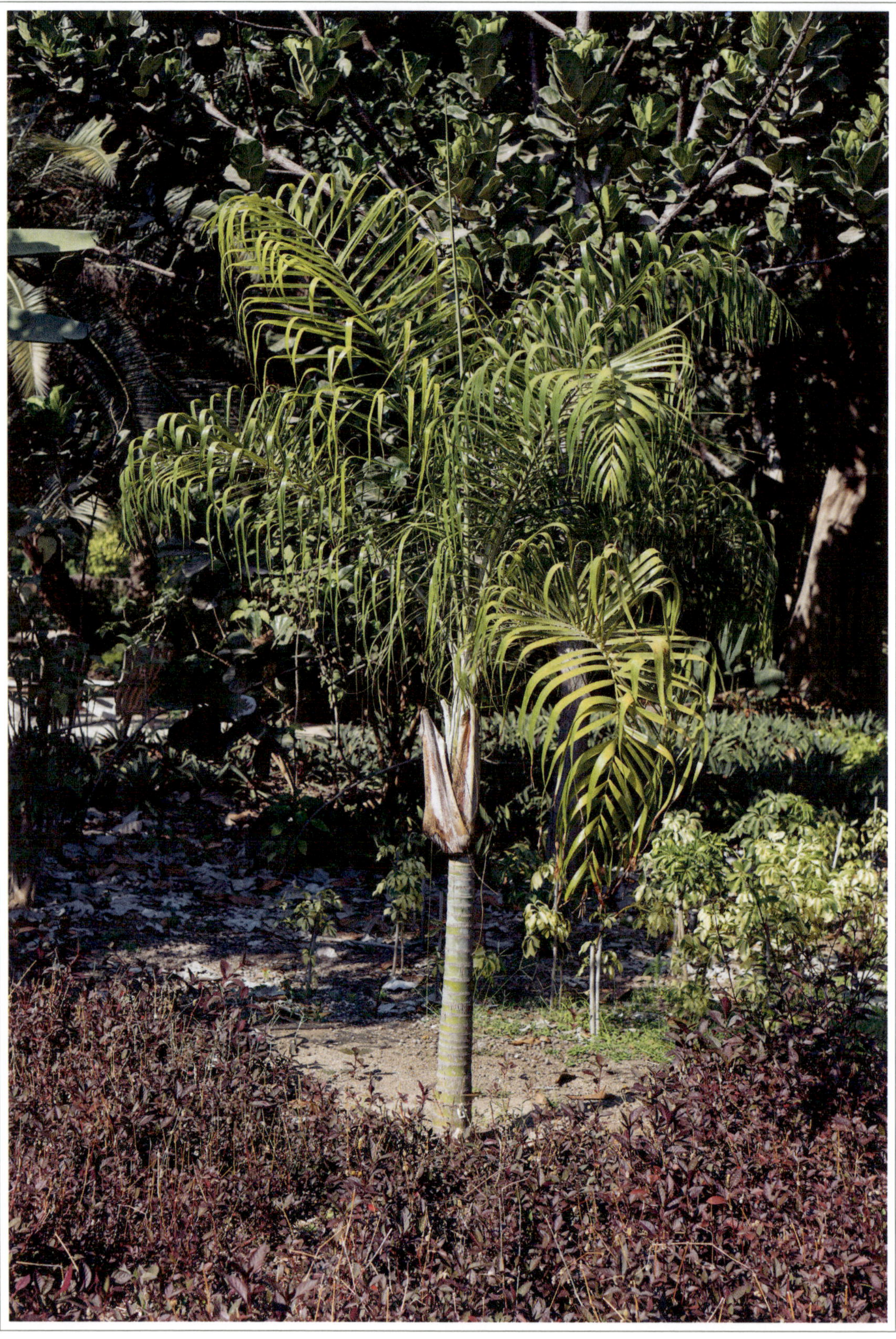

42
MADAGASCAR PALM

Dypsis madagascariensis (Becc.) Beentje & J. Dransf.

Status: Designated as Least Concern on the IUCN Red List
Distribution: Madagascar

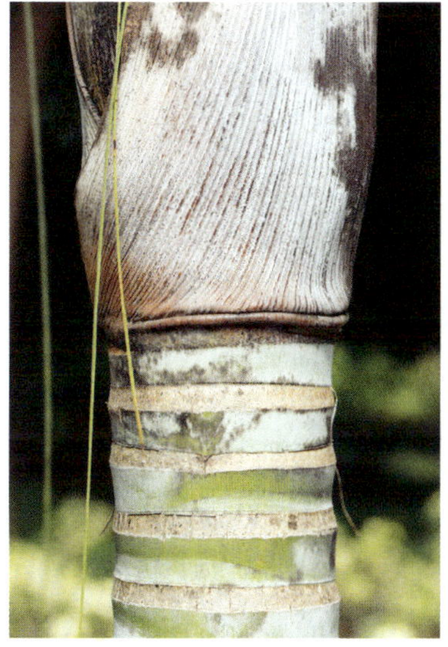
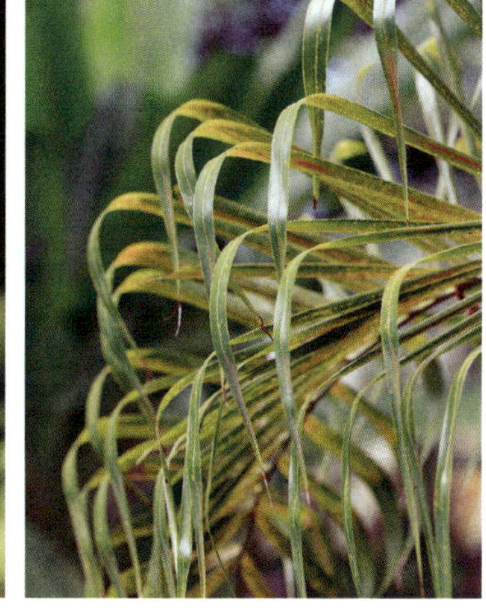

1. Trunk with leaf bases. 2. Detail of the leaf.

Unsurprisingly, the Madagascar palm is from Madagascar, where it grows in parts of the rainforests and semi-deciduous forests in the northwestern part of the island. It is a beautiful species, with solitary or clustering stems up to 35 feet in length and long, feather-like leaves. Although widespread in cultivation, its natural habitat is fragmented. The black lemur (*Eulemur macaco*), one of Madagascar's threatened primates, eats the round fruits of this palm and disperses the seeds, but just as the palm is threatened by habitat destruction and fragmentation, so is the black lemur. Recent research shows that many of Madagascar's native palms depend on lemurs for their dispersal, while the lemurs rely on palms for food. One cannot exist without the other. The challenge is to conserve both, so that both may survive.

The specimen of this palm at the Jardín Botánico Culiacán has been very much pampered since its arrival, because the gardeners did not know much about its needs, but they did know it came from a highly endangered habitat. The staff at the garden regularly checks its growth, hoping to be able to use the specimen one day to reintroduce the species into its original habitat.

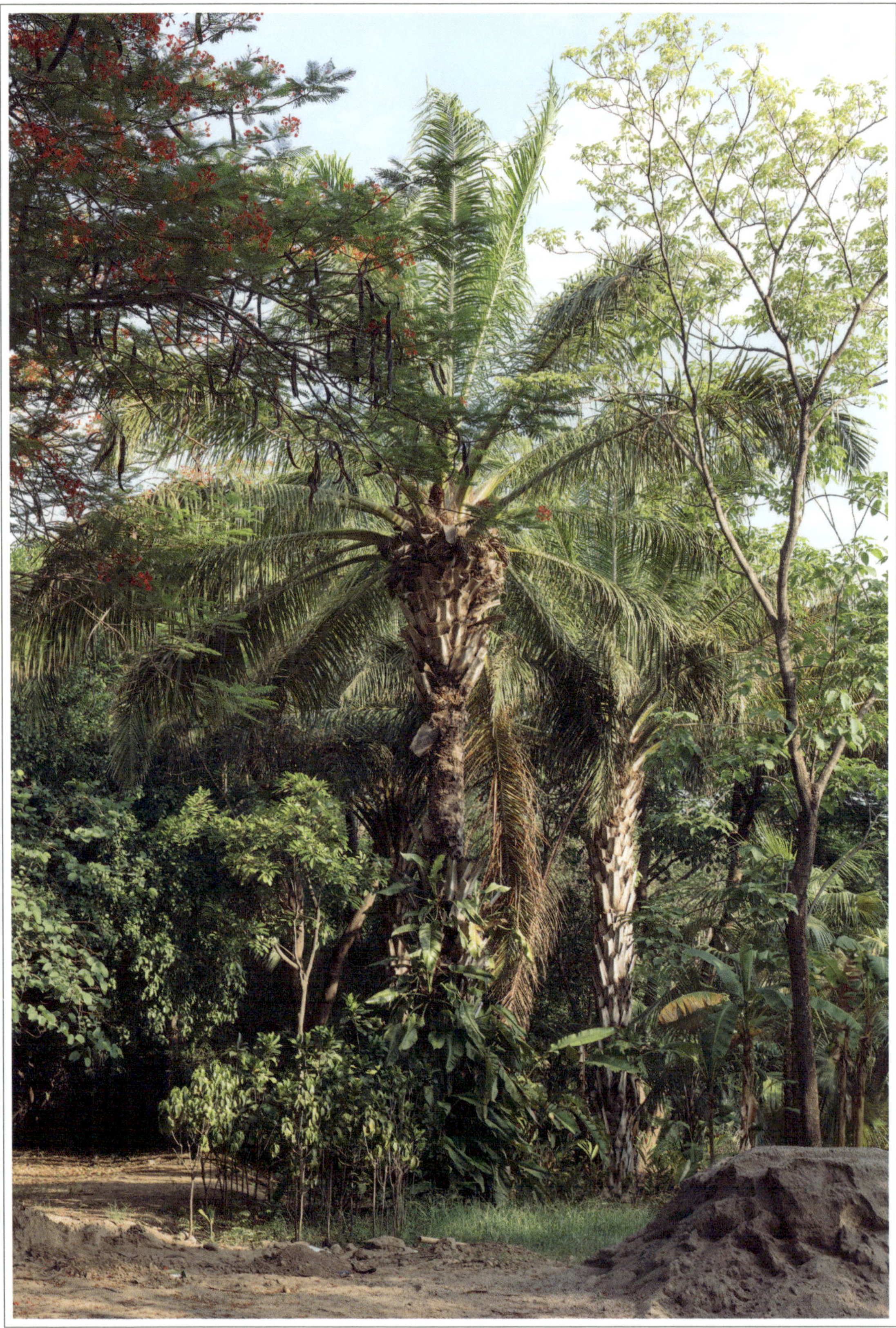

43
AFRICAN OIL PALM

Elaeis guineensis Jacq.

Status: Designated as Least Concern on the IUCN Red List
Distribution: West Africa

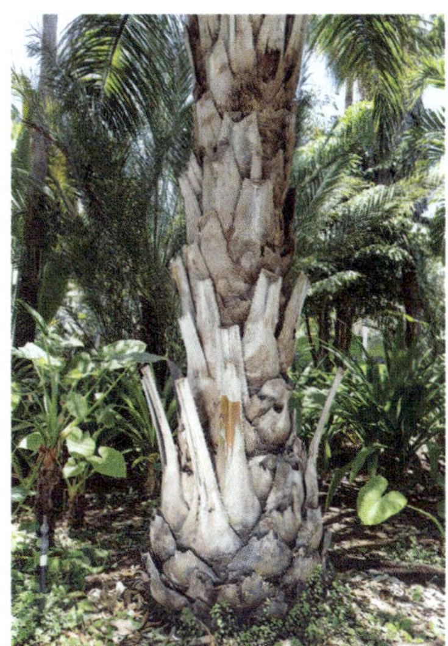
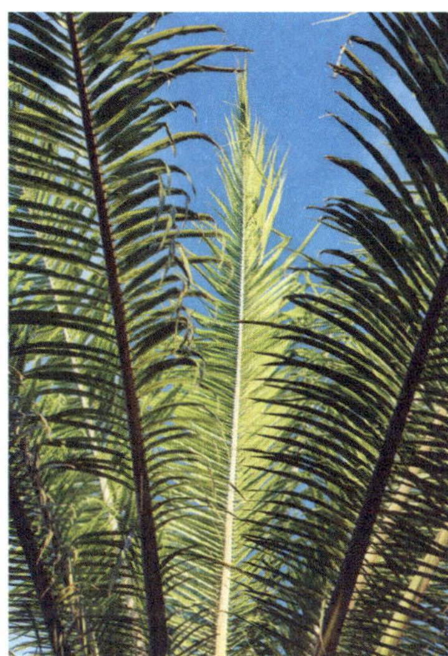
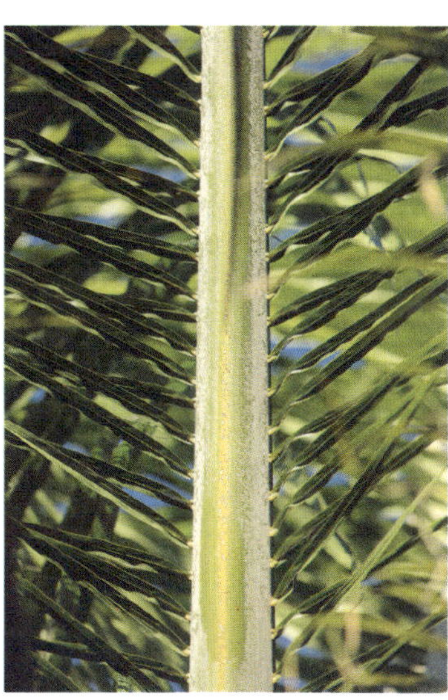

1. Trunk with leaf bases. 2. Leaves. 3. Detail of the leaf.

Originating in tropical west Africa, the African oil palm is a beautiful plant, but it has an ugly side. The palm is solitary, growing to 65 feet tall, and has a dense crown of long pinnate leaves, which bear spines on their bases. This large palm is the world's most important tropical oil crop. Millions of acres of tropical forests all over the world have been converted into plantations of African oil palm owing to demand for the oil derived from its fruits and seeds. Palm oil is used in foods, cosmetics, and biodiesel. Alarmed by the rapid spread of the crop, conservationists are urging the industry to grow the African oil palm more sustainably, without destroying more virgin forests, as its cultivation is transforming tropical ecosystems all over the world. The destruction of rainforest for the sake of the African oil palm is the main reason that the orangutan is endangered in Borneo. Because of campaigns to "save the orangutan," palm oil is gaining a bad reputation among informed consumers, but worldwide demand continues to rise. Consumers need to be aware of this problem and to start demanding products that use oil from sustainably cultivated palms.

The specimen of this palm, one of the founding plants of the Jardín Botánico Culiacán, is located at the main entrance. It was planted in 1986 near the cannonball tree (*Couroupita guianensis*).

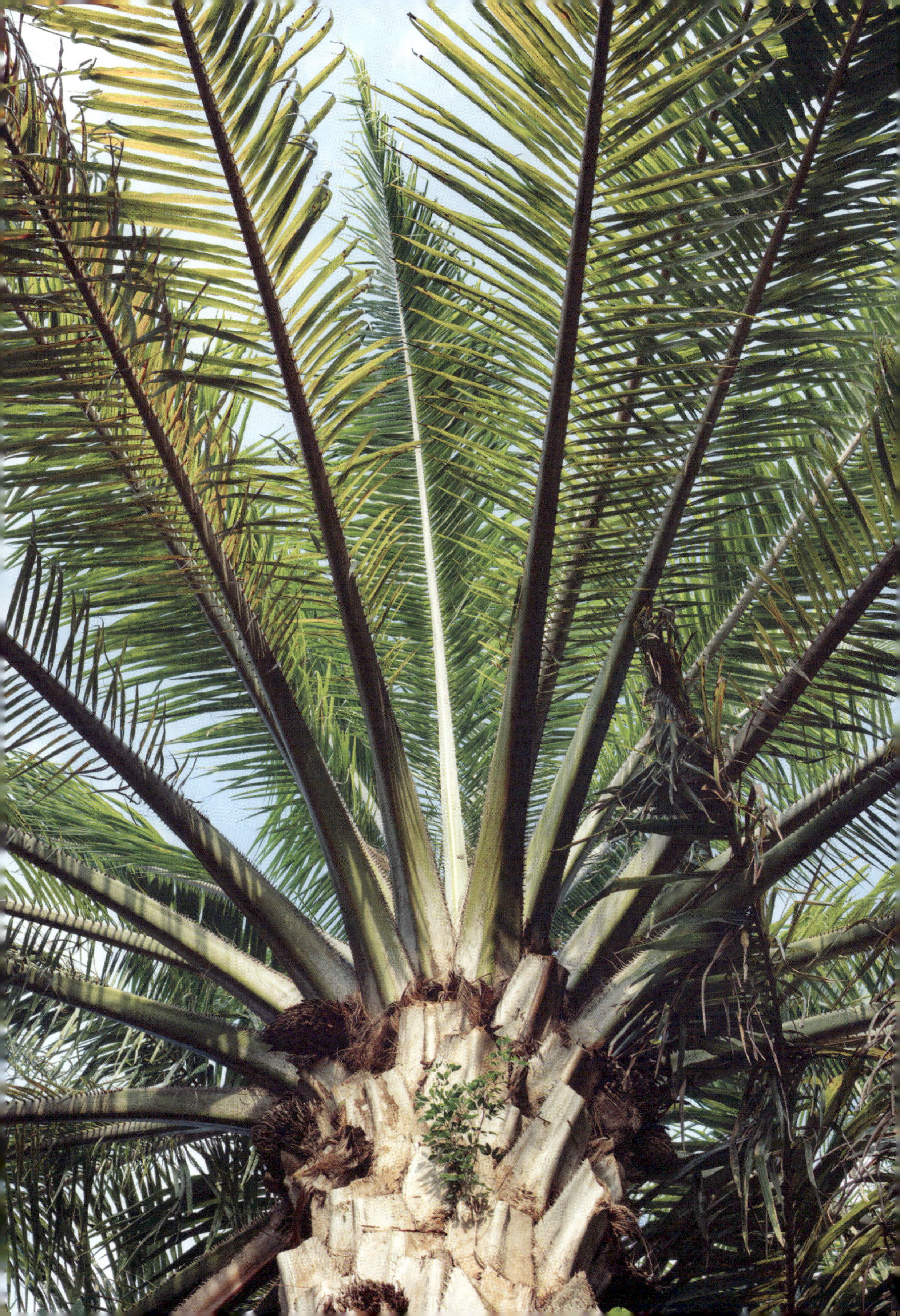

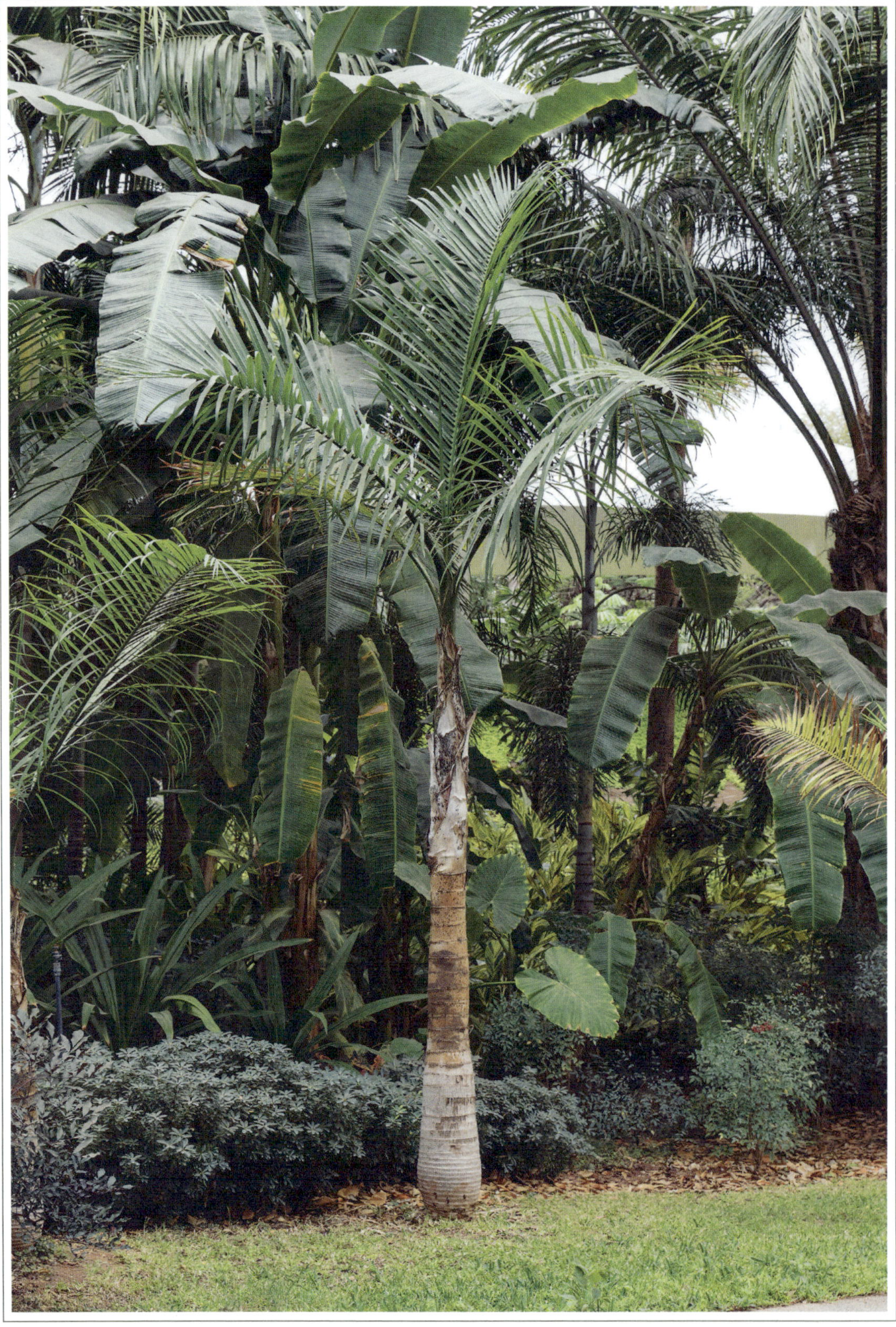

44
MOUNTAIN GAUSSIA

Gaussia gomez-pompae (H.J. Quero) H.J. Quero

Status: Designated as Threatened on the Mexican list of endangered species (NOM-059-SEMARNAT-2010)
Distribution: Endemic to southern Mexico (from Oaxaca to Tabasco)

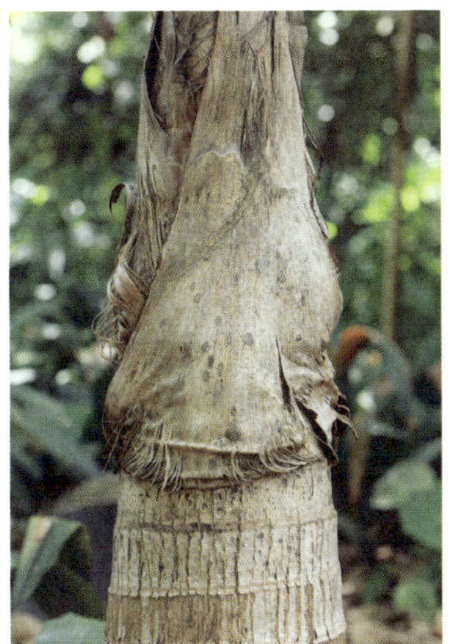

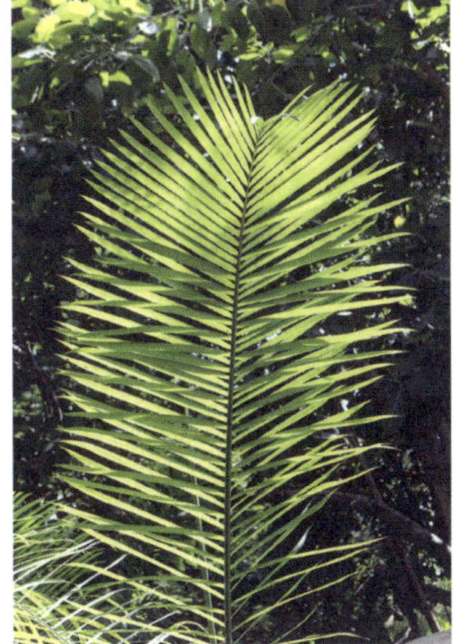

1. Trunk with leaf bases. 2. Leaves.

Gaussia gomez-pompae has a thick solitary water-storing stem that can reach a height of 35 feet or more. It occurs only in Oaxaca to Tabasco, where it grows on limestone hills. It bears a sparse crown of pinnate leaves, with the flower stalks borne well below the crown. The bright red, fleshy fruits are consumed by birds, which spread the seeds. The genus name *Gaussia* commemorates the German mathematician and physicist Johann Carl Friedrich Gauss (1777–1855), while the species name honors Mexican botanist and conservationist Dr. Arturo Gómez-Pompa.

Specimens of *Gaussia gomez-pompae* are relatively new to the Jardín Botánico Culiacán. They came from the Yucatán, donated by palm specialist Miguel Ángel García Bielma. Many of these palms are growing very well close to the auditorium.

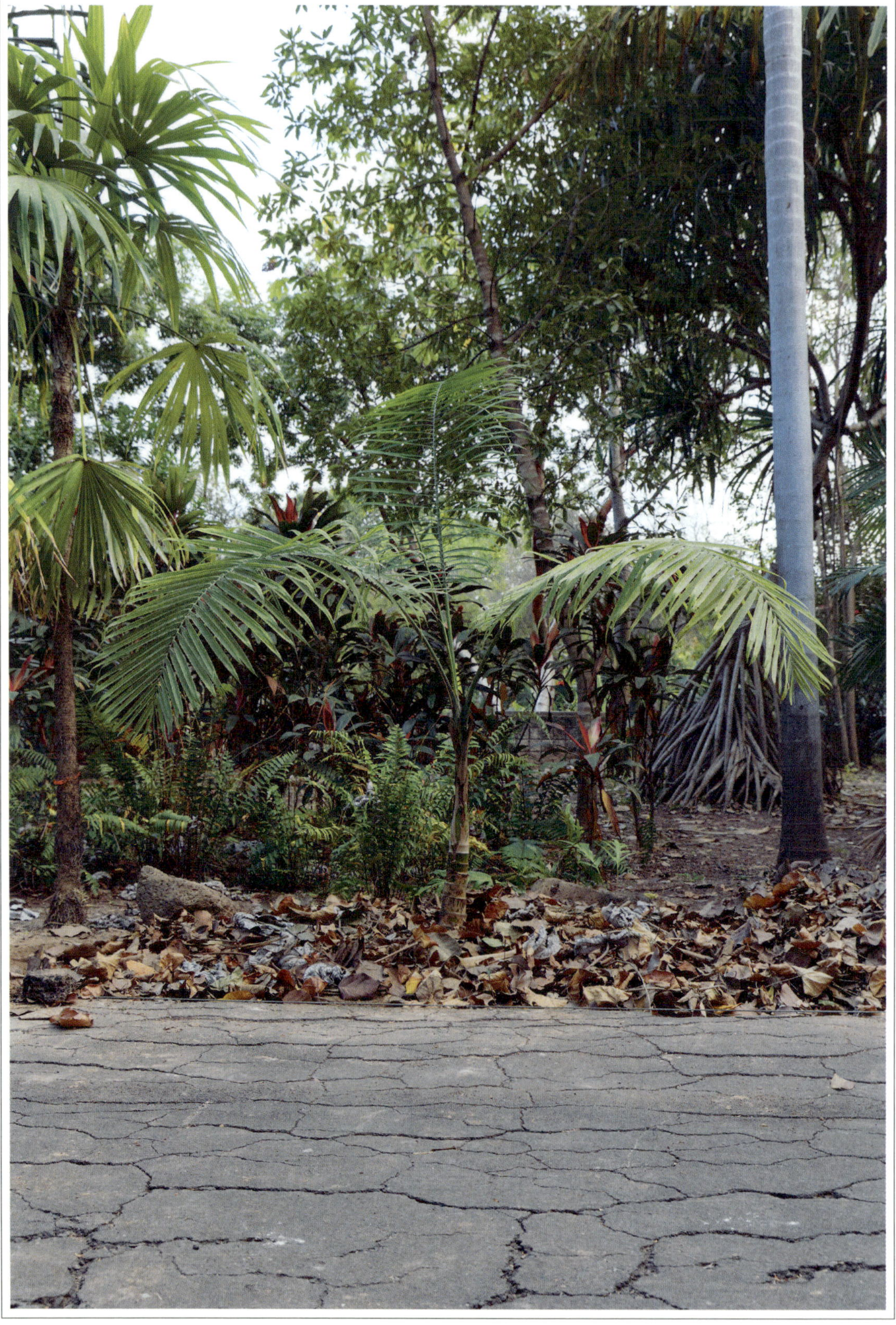

45

MAYA PALM

Gaussia maya (O.F. Cook) H.J. Quero & Read

Status: Designated as Threatened on the Mexican list of endangered species (NOM-059-SEMARNAT-2010)
Distribution: Southern Mexico, Belize, and Guatemala

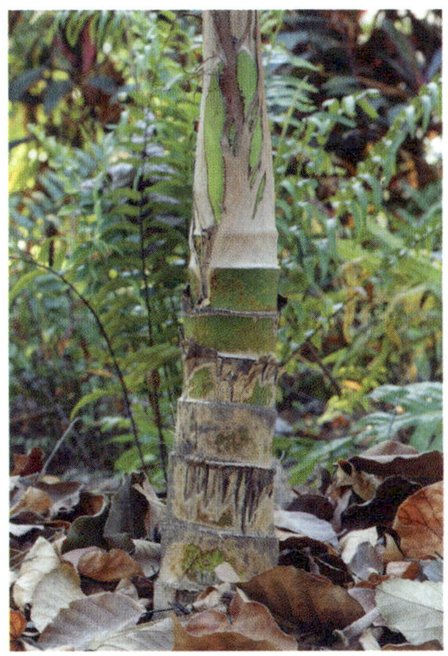
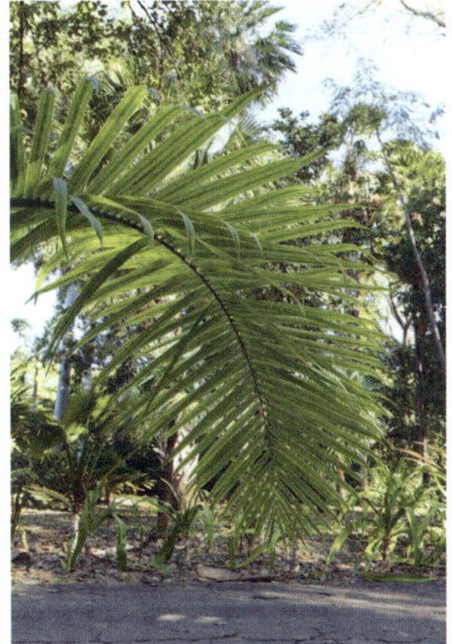

1. Trunk with leaf bases. 2. Leaf.

Gaussia is a genus of five species: two continental species, and three from the Greater Antilles. It has thick roots that tightly grip the limestone rocks on which it grows. The 35-feet-tall trunk is white, thick, and water-storing. *Gaussia maya* is the most widespread species, occurring in southern Mexico, Belize, and Guatemala. The species name honors the indigenous Maya people of the region. *Gaussia* has the unusual habit of dropping its leaflets and retaining its bare leaf rachis.

The first specimens came to the Jardín Botánico Culiacán in 2011, as donations from the Centro de Investigación Científica de Yucatán, and they are doing well. Later on, in 2016, Prof. Miguel Ángel García Bielma donated some specimens from Chiapas and Tabasco, sending them to the National Palm Collection, thus enriching the genetic diversity of the garden's collection.

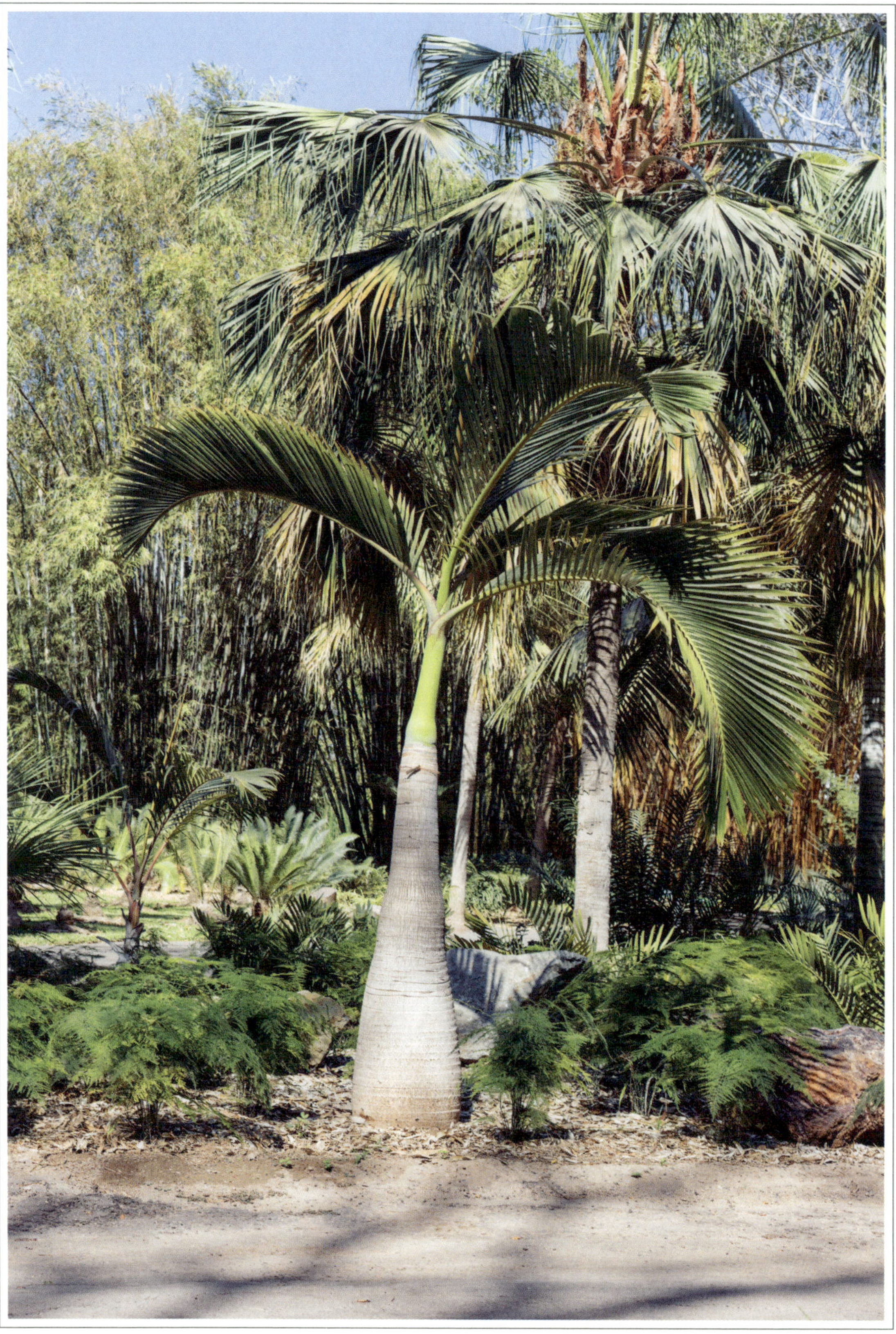

46

BOTTLE PALM

Hyophorbe lagenicaulis (L.H. Bailey) H.E. Moore

Status: Designated as Critically Endangered on the IUCN Red List
Distribution: Round Island (Mascarene Islands)

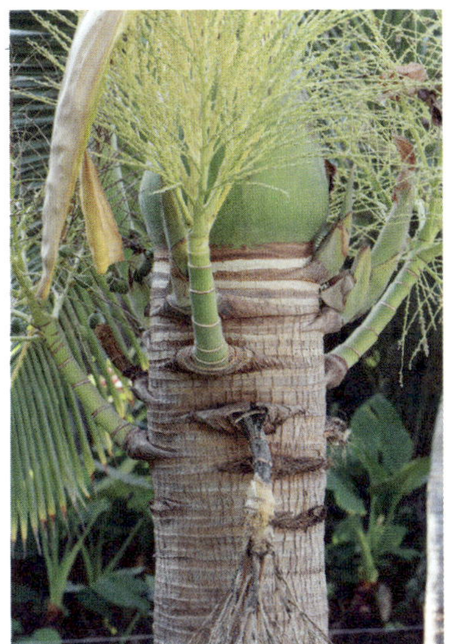

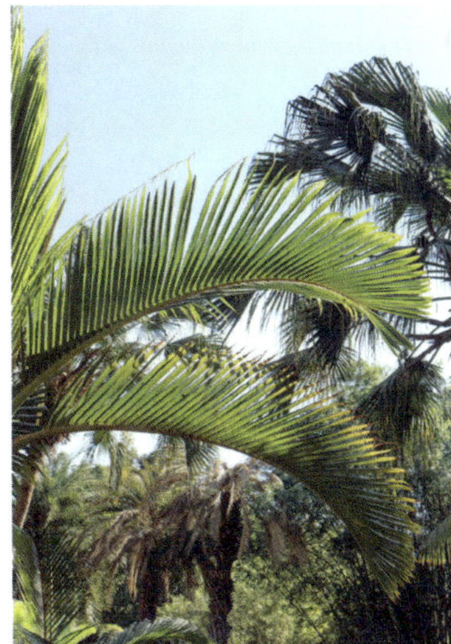

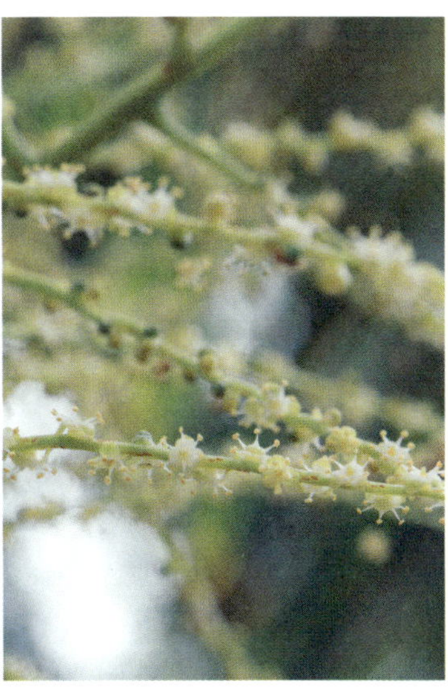

1. Trunk and inflorescences. 2. Leaves. 3. Flowers.

The bottle palm gets both its common name and its scientific name from the stout, bottle-like shape of the 13-feet-tall stem (from Lat. *lagena*, meaning "bottle," and *caulis*, meaning "stem"). Like most plants with enlarged, water-storing stems, this species originates in a seasonally dry area. It comes from Round Island, a tiny island off the coast of Mauritius, one of the Mascarene Islands, in the Indian Ocean, that was once famously home to the dodo bird. The bottle palm may have occurred on the main island of Mauritius, but like the dodo, it was wiped out by early settlers and their introduced animals. Following the removal of introduced goats and rabbits from Round Island in the 1970s and 1980s, the bottle palm population recovered, and conservationists recorded over 400 individuals (of various ages and sizes) during the last census. Because the bottle palm is still classified as Critically Endangered, it is the focus of intense conservation activity.

The first seeds acquired by the Jardín Botánico Culiacán came through an exchange with the International Palm Society. For Carlos Murillo Depraect, the palms that grew from these seeds were invaluable, so he asked his most trusted gardeners to help protect them, as specimens of *Hyophorbe lagenicaulis* are very rare and difficult to find.

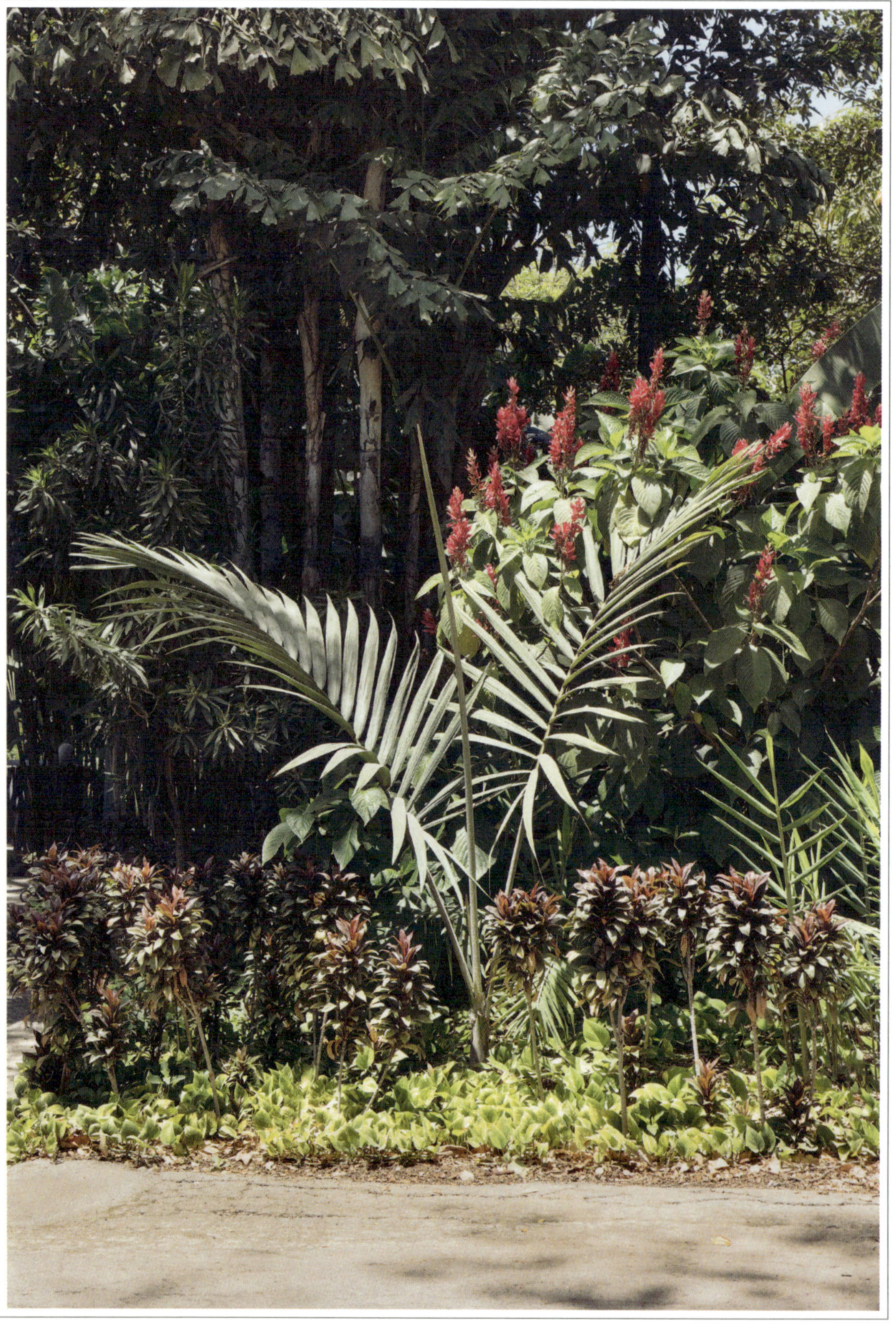

47

KENTIOPSIS PALM

Kentiopsis oliviformis (Brongn. & Gris) Brongn.

Status: Designated as Endangered on the IUCN Red List
Distribution: New Caledonia

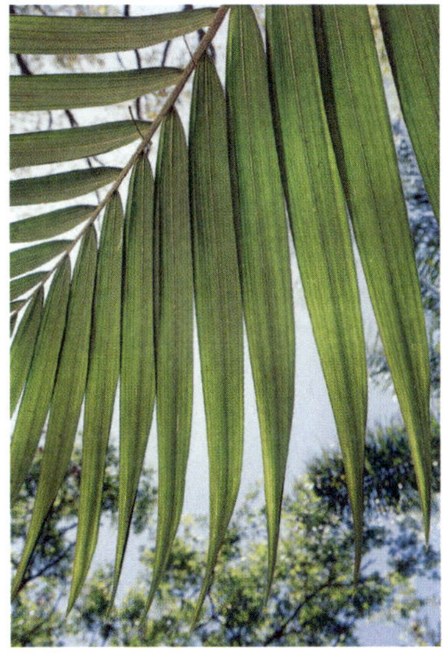

1. Leaf.

Kentiopsis oliviformis is one of four species in the genus, all of which are found only in tropical rainforests on the island of New Caledonia, in the southwestern Pacific Ocean. It grows in volcanic soil and can form 2.5 acres stands of this species alone. *Kentiopsis oliviformis* is a handsome species, with a solitary trunk up to 20 or even 100 feet tall, leaf bases patterned with gray and olive markings, and long, graceful, feather-like leaves. Its fruits are small, round, and red, resembling olives, which explains the scientific name of the species. In New Caledonia, the species occurs in moist forest, but in cultivation the species is tolerant of drier and more exposed conditions. The species is endangered in the wild. According to the IUCN, one of the reasons that populations of *Kentiopsis oliviformis* are decreasing is that introduced rats eat the seeds, and if any seeds survive to germinate, the seedlings are eaten by introduced deer. Island ecosystems are delicately balanced, and introduced animals can cause havoc. Moreover, there is pressure on the species from agricultural expansion, grazing, and harvesting of the palms to obtain the hearts, which are edible. The specimen in the Jardín Botánico Culiacán came from a nursery in El Rosario, Sinaloa.

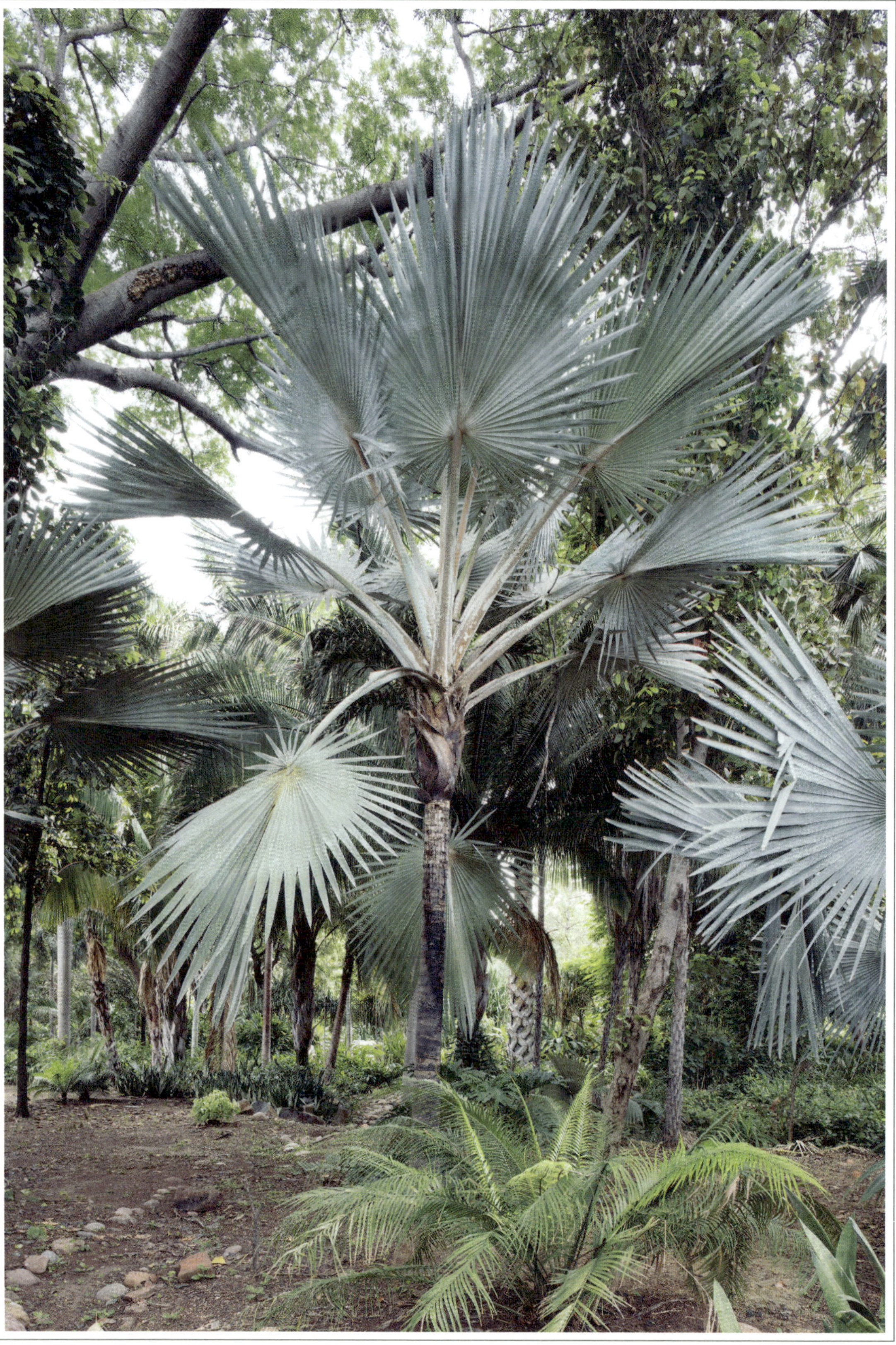

48

BLUE LATAN PALM

Latania loddigesii Mart.

Status: Designated as Endangered on the IUCN Red List
Distribution: Endemic to the Mascarene Islands

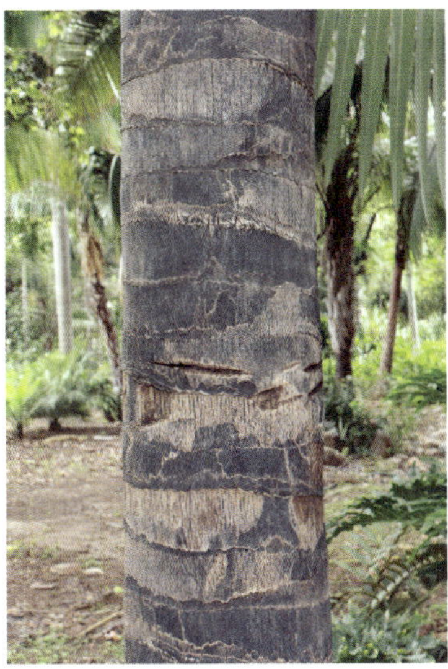
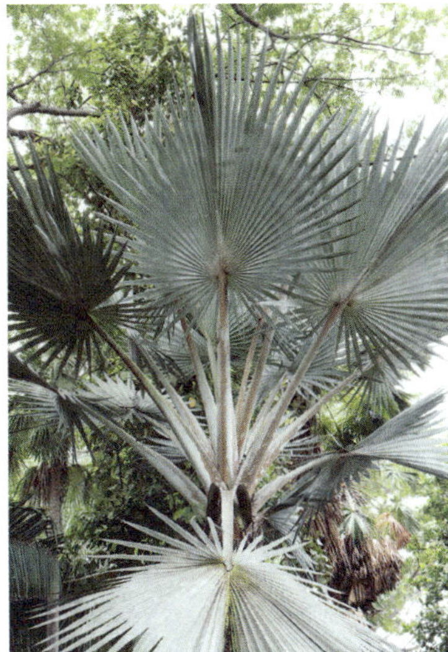
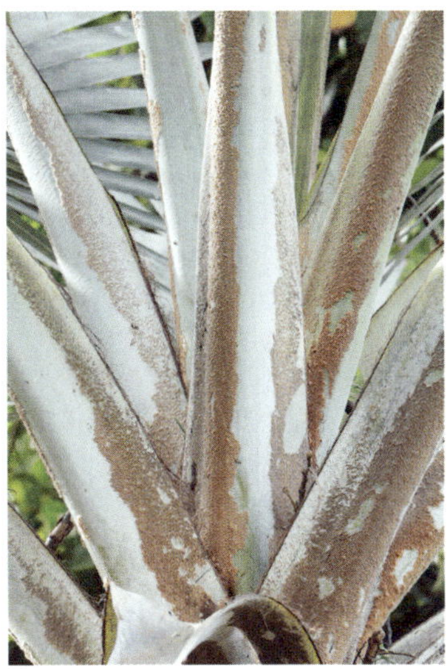

1. Trunk. 2. Crown leaf. 3. Leaf bases.

Latania loddigesii is a slow-growing palm that will eventually reach 35 feet in height. It is one of three species of *Latania*, all of which occur naturally only on the Mascarene Islands, in the western Indian Ocean. This species is confined to the island of Mauritius and its offshore islets, where it grows in fragments of the remaining original vegetation, on poor soils and in a dry climate. The large leaves get their silvery color from a superficial layer of wax, which suggests that the palm evolved in sunny, open habitats. Male and female flowers occur on separate palms, and both kinds of flowers are produced in long branched clusters. Each large fruit contains three seeds. Biologists believe that the seeds were an important food for the extinct broad-billed parrot (*Lophopsittacus mauritianus*), which cracked open and ate the seeds with its powerful beak. These small islands have suffered greatly from habitat destruction by agriculture, timber extraction, introduced animals, and invasive weeds, so it is not surprising that all three species of *Latania* are endangered. Nevertheless, *Latania loddigesii* is widely used in gardens around the world.

Carlos Murillo Depraect acquired three specimens of *Latania loddigesii* for the Jardín Botánico Culiacán in 1999. From these specimens, botanists at the garden are collaborating to reproduce the species.

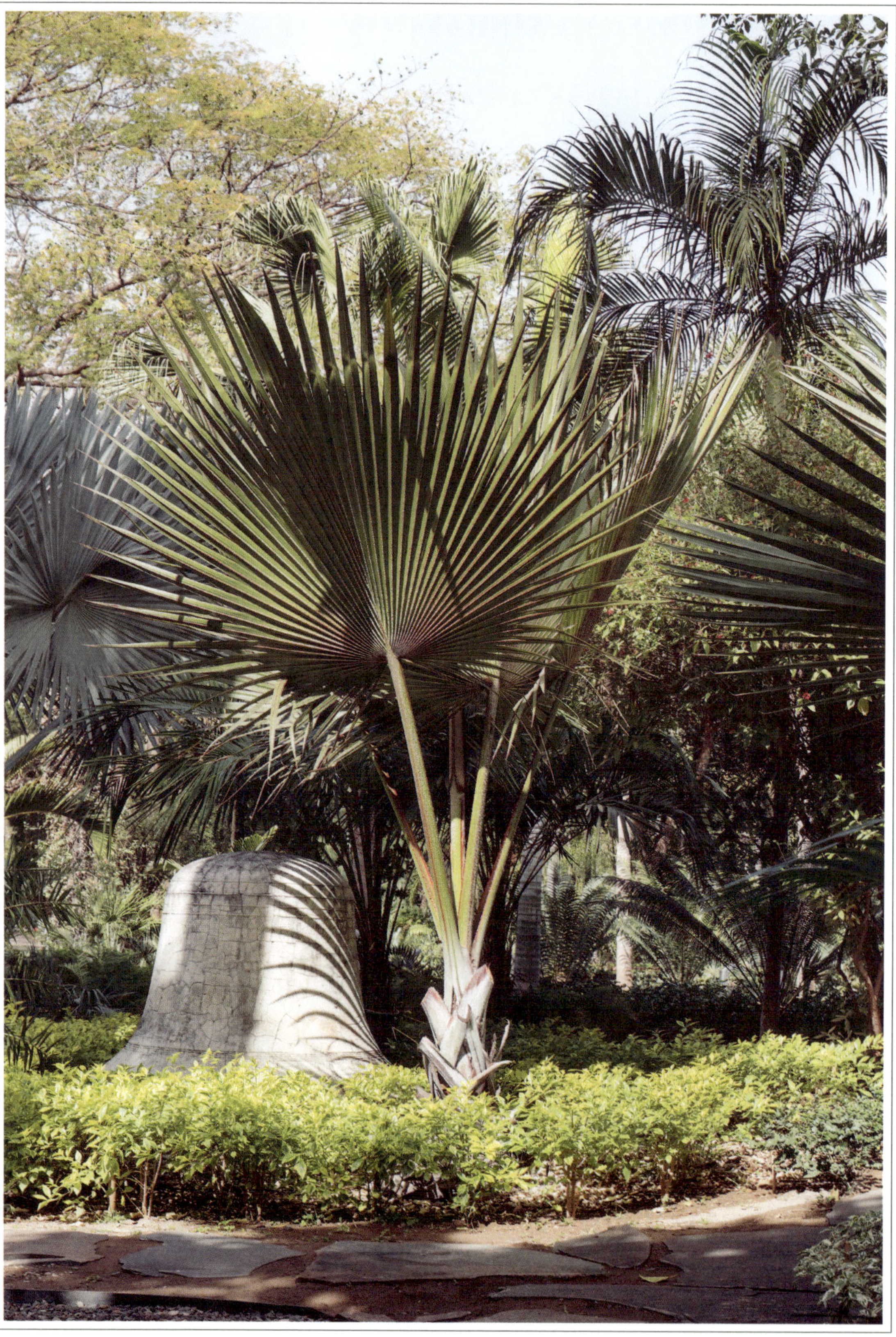

49

RED LATAN PALM

Latania lontaroides (Gaertn.) H.E. Moore.

Status: Designated as Endangered on the IUCN Red List
Distribution: Endemic to the Mascarene Islands

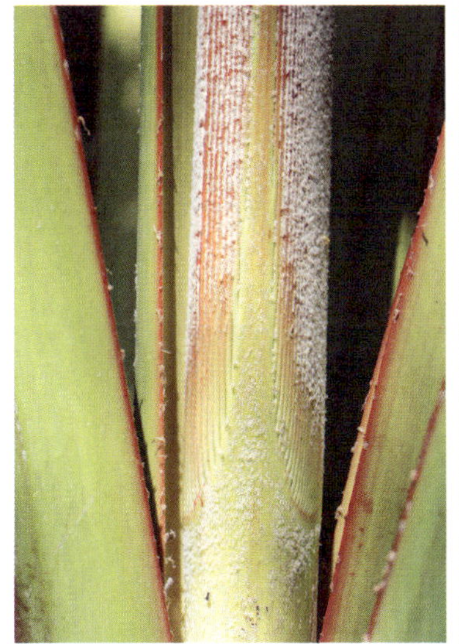

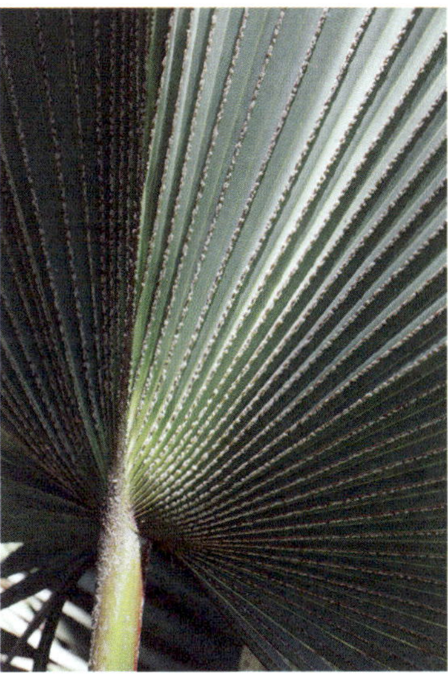

1. Detail of the petiole. 2. Leaf.

Latania lontaroides is a slow-growing palm that can reach up to 10 or sometimes even 50 feet tall. It is confined to the island of La Réunion, on dry to semi-dry coastlines, where fewer than 100 mature palms survive. Introduced rats eat the seeds, so the population is not regenerating, and rat eradication has not been possible. As a result, *Latania lontaroides* is endangered in the wild on the Mascarene Islands, but fortunately the species survives in cultivation. The dark brown flowers of *Latania lontaroides* are borne in clusters and are pollinated by bees. The fruits are also brown. The common name of the palm is derived from the red coloration of the leaves of the seedlings. Leaves from adult plants are large (around 10 feet long) and green. Many palm growers have acquired colorful seedlings, only to be disappointed when the palms mature and produce only green leaves.

The four specimens of *Latania lontaroides* were donated to the Jardín Botánico Culiacán in 2008, arriving via Acapulco, Guerrero.

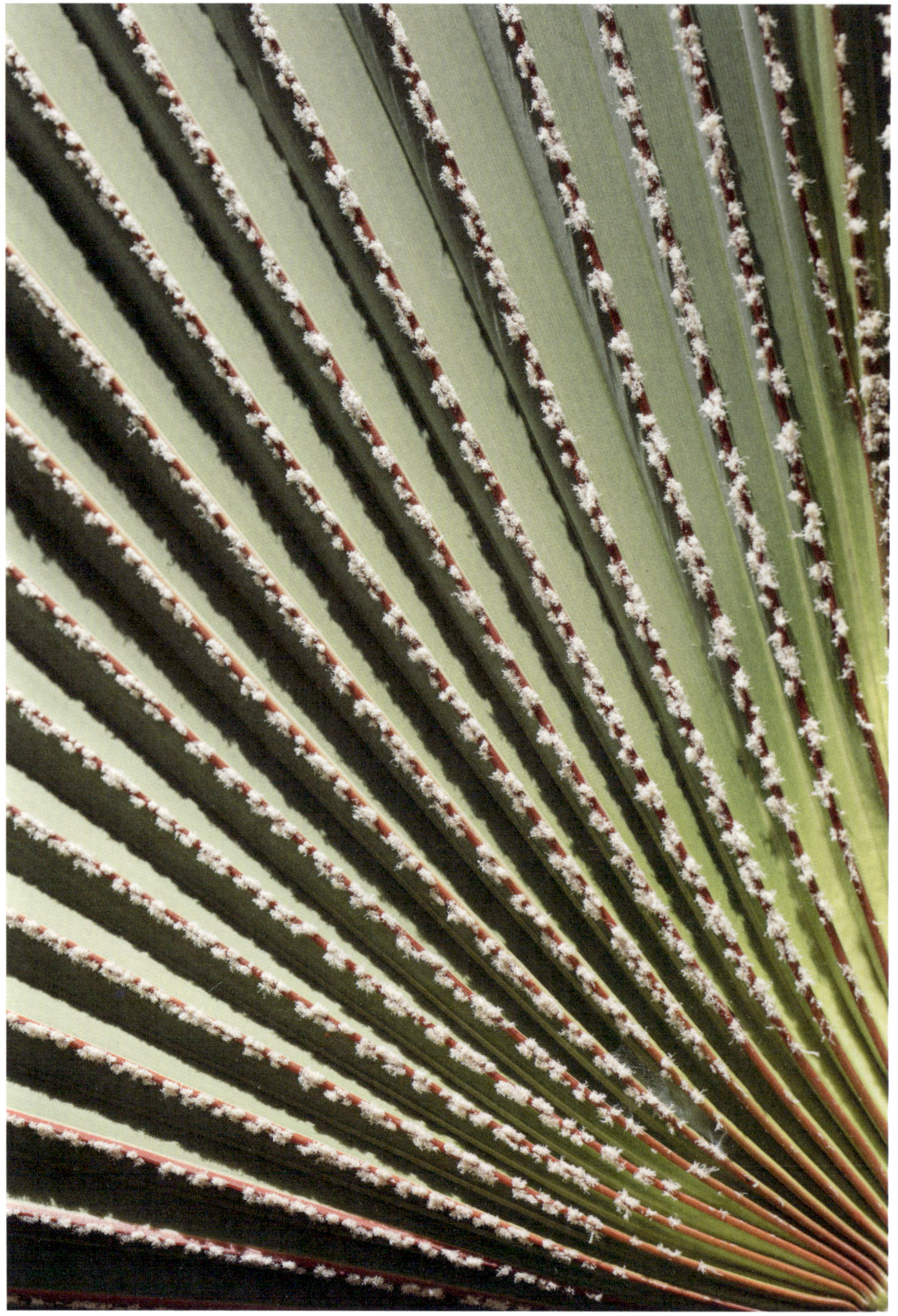

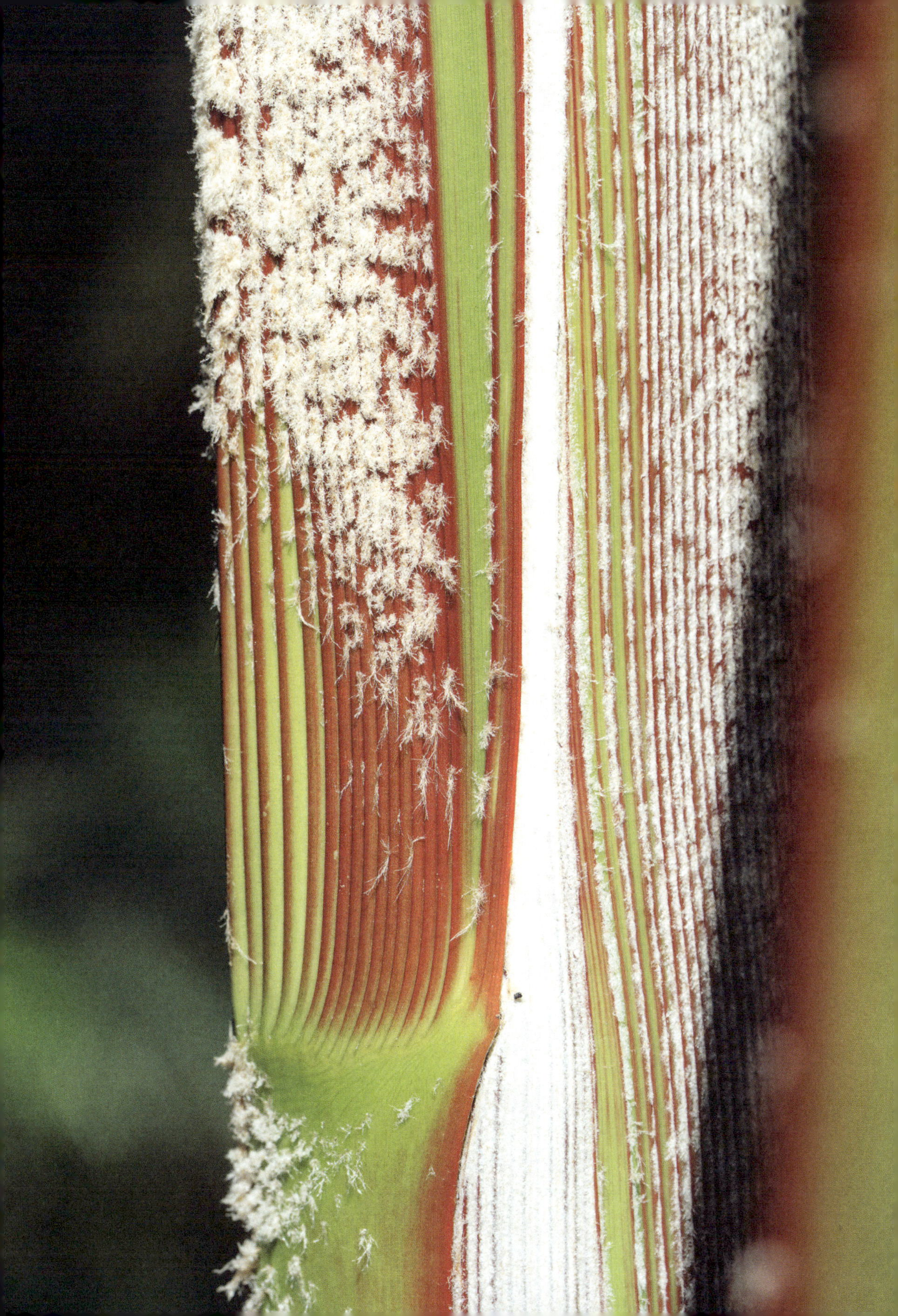

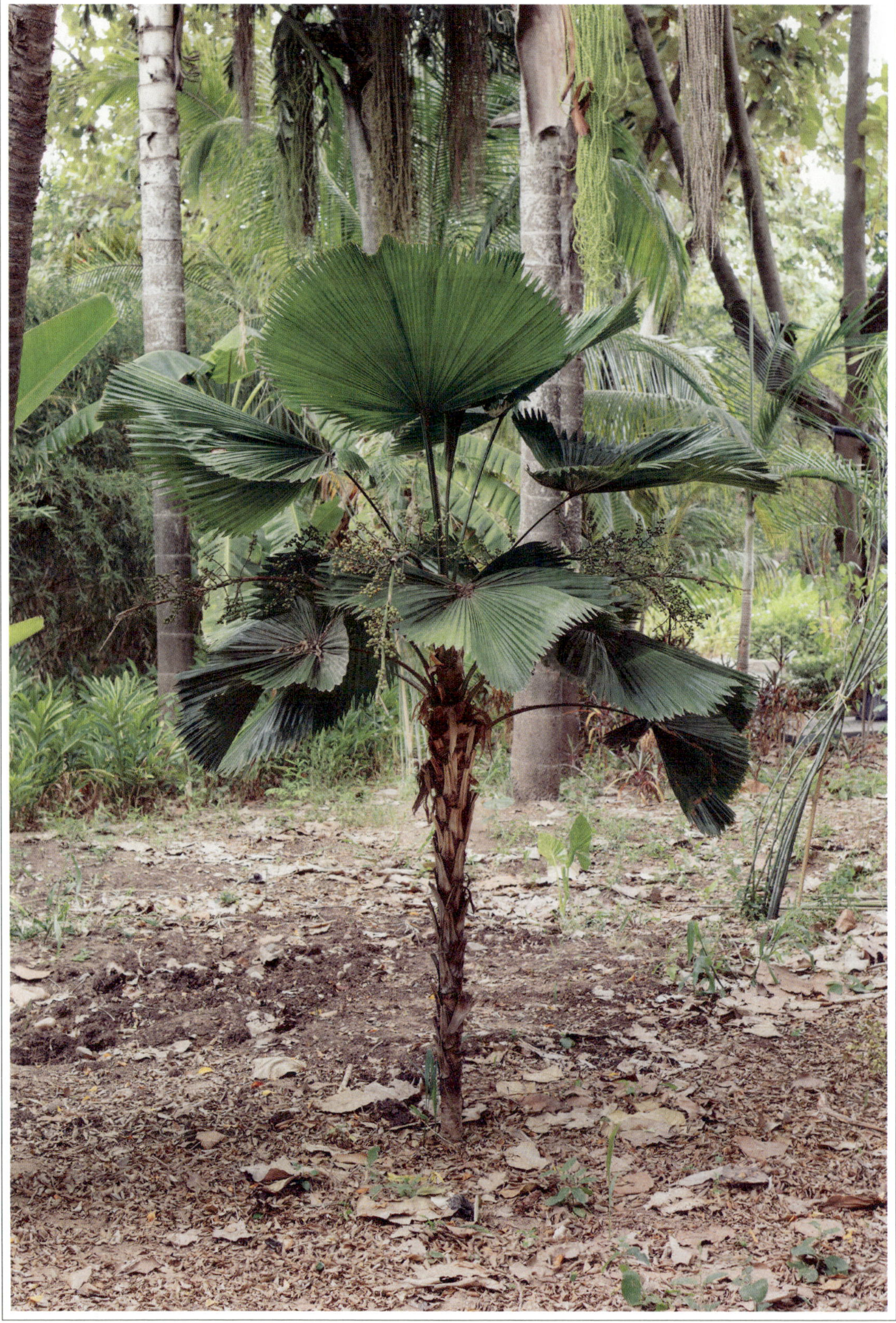

50

VANUATU FAN PALM, RUFFLED FAN PALM

Licuala grandis H. Wendl.

Status: Assessment of global conservation status required
Distribution: Solomon Islands, Vanuatu

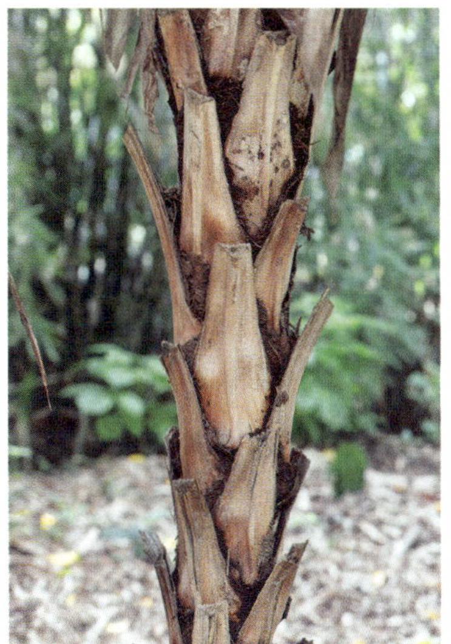

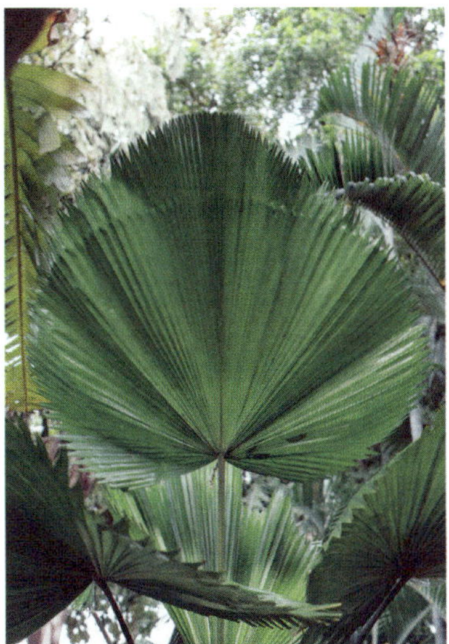

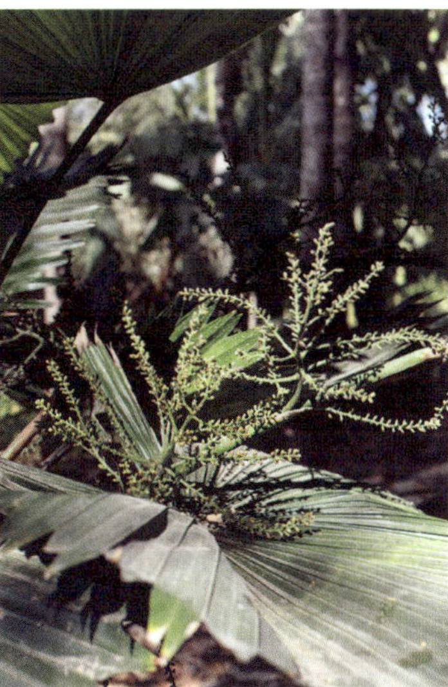

1. Trunk with leaf bases. 2. Leaf. 3. Inflorescence.

Licuala is a genus of over 130 species, all of which are confined to southern China, Southeast Asia, New Guinea, Australia, and the archipelagos of the western Pacific. *Licuala grandis*, native to tropical rainforests, is the most commonly cultivated species. It is prized by growers for its beautiful, nearly circular, fan-shaped leaves, borne on slender, solitary trunks up to 13 feet tall. Long flower stalks arch from the crown and bear inconspicuous light-yellow flowers. A group of scientists from Thailand and France analyzed the aroma of these little flowers and observed that they produce up to 76 different aromatic compounds, which may serve to attract pollinators. Scientists think the complexity of an aroma may be a clue to a very specific pollinator, rather than general ones like common bees. The fruits are bright orange-red at maturity. In Vanuatu, the leaves of this palm are specially used to waterproof the ridges of roofs thatched with the leaves of other palm species. Young ornamental plants like this palm require high humidity and lots of shade.

Licuala grandis plants are part of the original palm collection that Carlos Murillo Depraect started in the 1980s. There are few specimens in Jardín Botánico Culiacán, as the species is particularly difficult to grow from seeds.

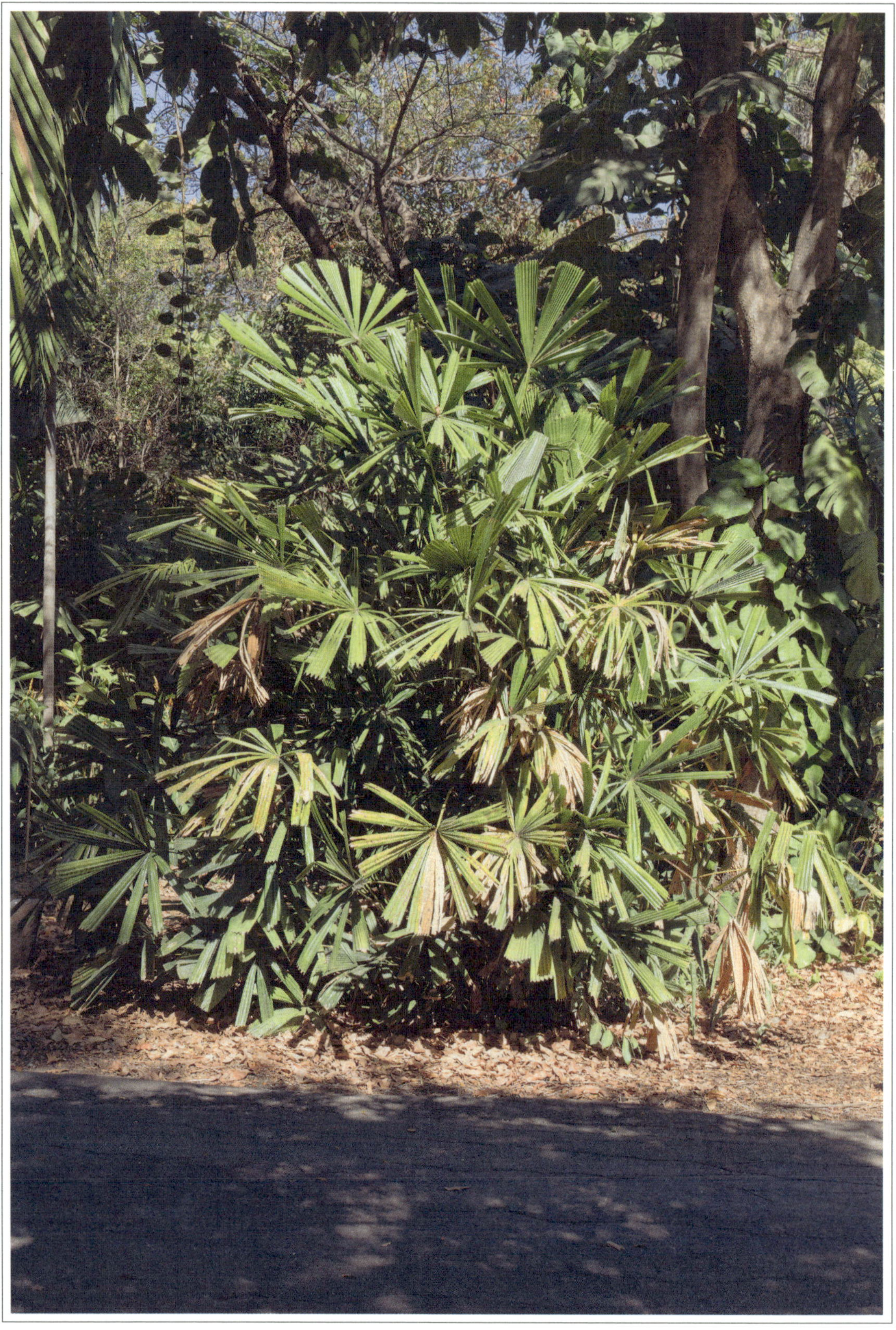

51
MANGROVE FAN PALM

Licuala spinosa Wurmb

Status: Assessment of global conservation status required
Distribution: Southeast Asia, Borneo, and the Philippines

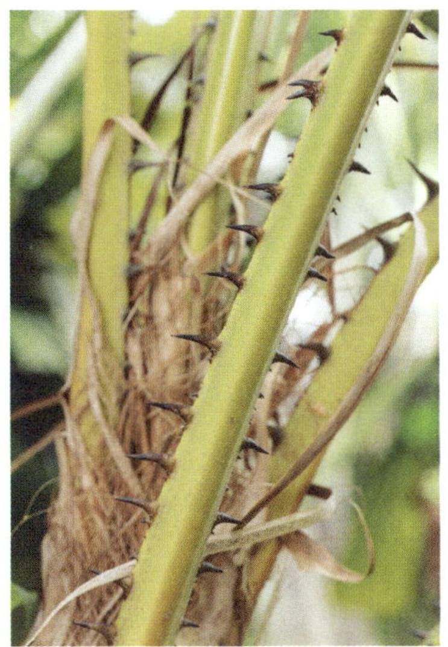
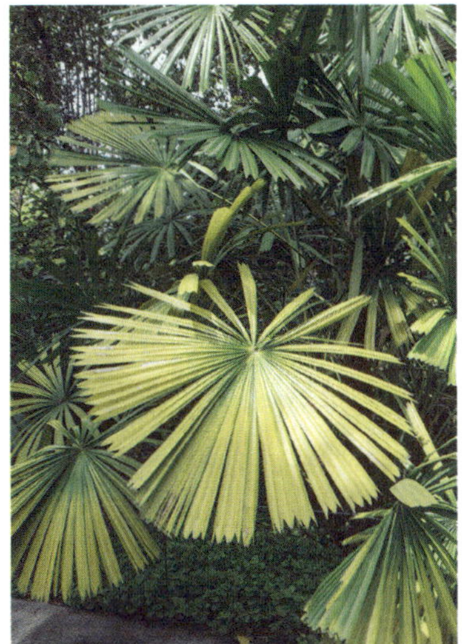
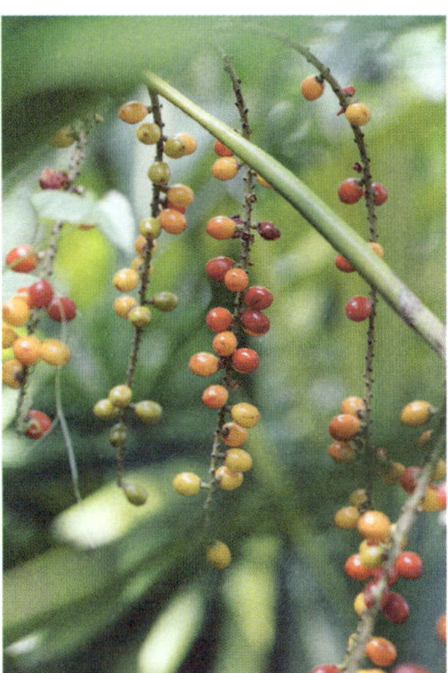

1. Petiole teeth. 2. Leaf. 3. Fruits.

Licuala spinosa is a clustering species, forming many stems up to 16 feet tall. Unlike other species of *Licuala*, which usually grow in shady forest habitats, *L. spinosa* grows in swamps, along beaches, and in mangroves. This is the only *Licuala* that can grow in open habitats, in full sunlight, so it is also amenable to sunny gardens. It forms large clusters of slender, erect stems that bear circular leaves divided into many thin wedges. The leaf stalks are armed with fearsome teeth. In Asia, the leaves are sometimes used to wrap up food.

There is no precise record of when Carlos Murillo Depraect first acquired specimens of *Licuala spinosa* for the Jardín Botánico Culiacán, but the gardeners believe it was around 1995. The gardeners call it the "windmill palm," owing to the shape of its leaves.

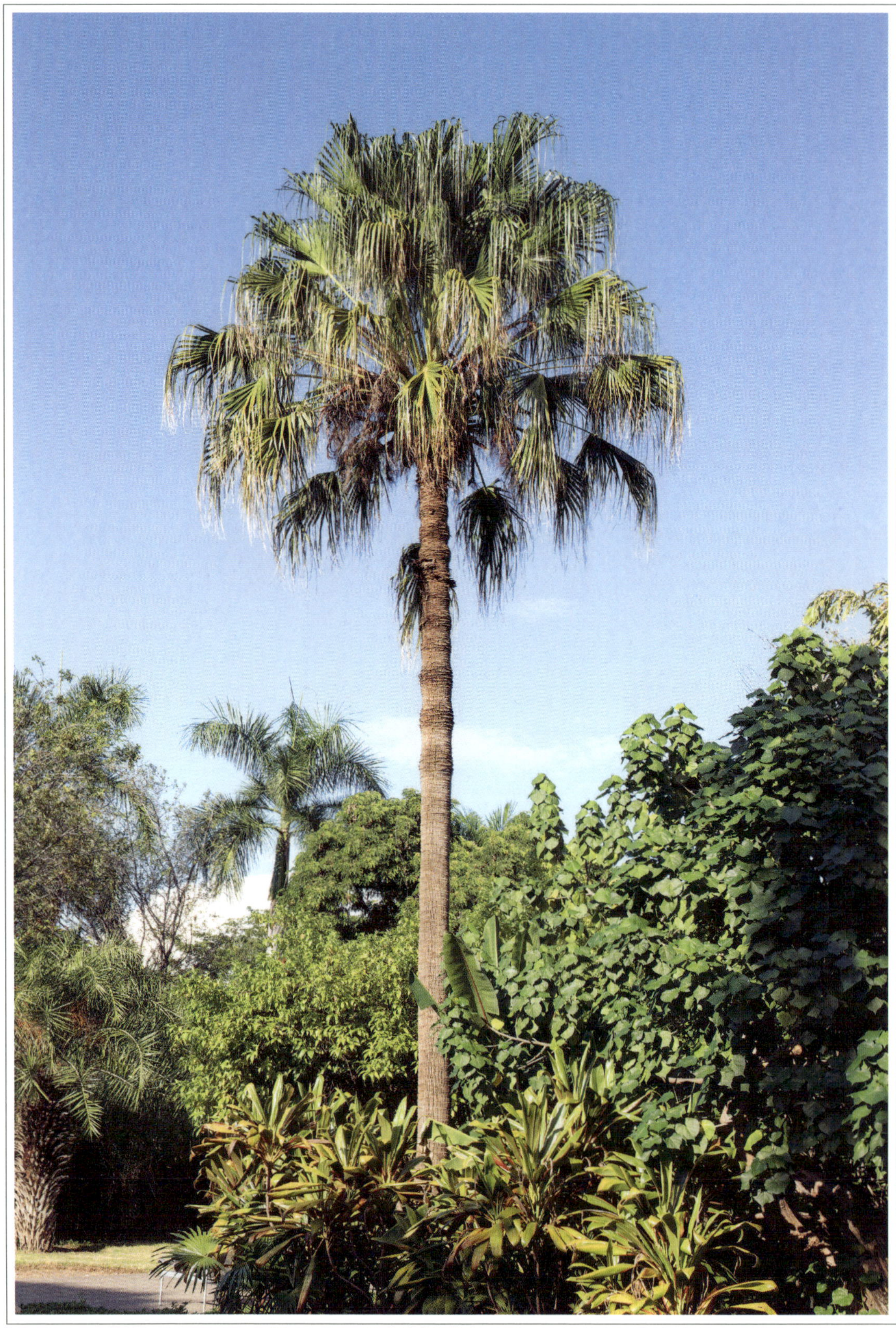

52

CABBAGE-TREE PALM

Livistona australis (R.Br.) Mart.

Status: Assessment of global conservation status required
Distribution: Endemic to eastern Australia

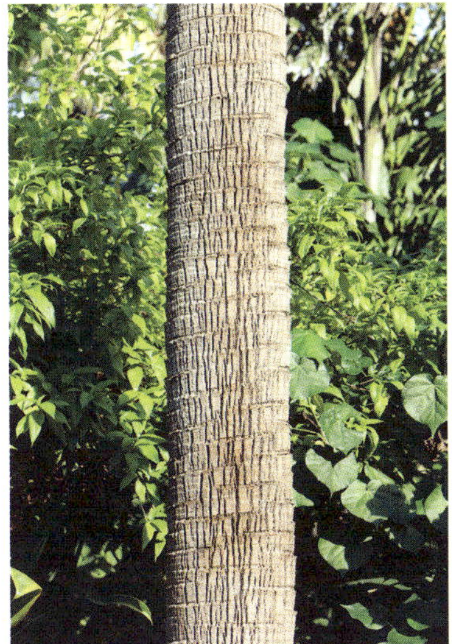

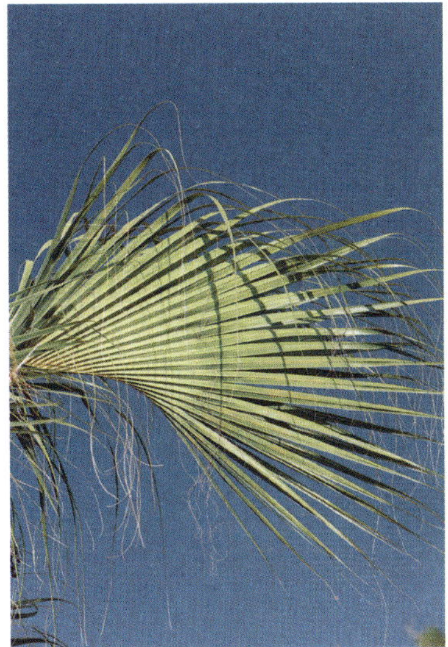

1. Trunk. 2. Leaf.

Livistona australis grows up to 80 feet tall, in colonies, in moist and wet forests. It is a solitary species, and the trunk has visible leaf scars, along with vertical fissures. The dark green leaves form a loose crown. The flowers are ivory white, and the fruits are a dull brownish black. Early settlers in Australia cut the palms to extract the edible, cabbage-like palm heart, so it is still called the cabbage palm in Australia, although it is no longer harvested for food. As an ornamental species, *Livistona australis* is hardy and easy to grow. Propagation is by seed.

Specimens of *Livistona australis* were acquired for the Jardín Botánico Culiacán through international exchanges arranged by Carlos Murillo Depraect. Workers at the garden call this species *palma repollo*, using the word for cabbage employed by people from Sinaloa. In other parts of Mexico, cabbage is called *col*. In the garden, bats use the leaves of these palms as daytime refuges.

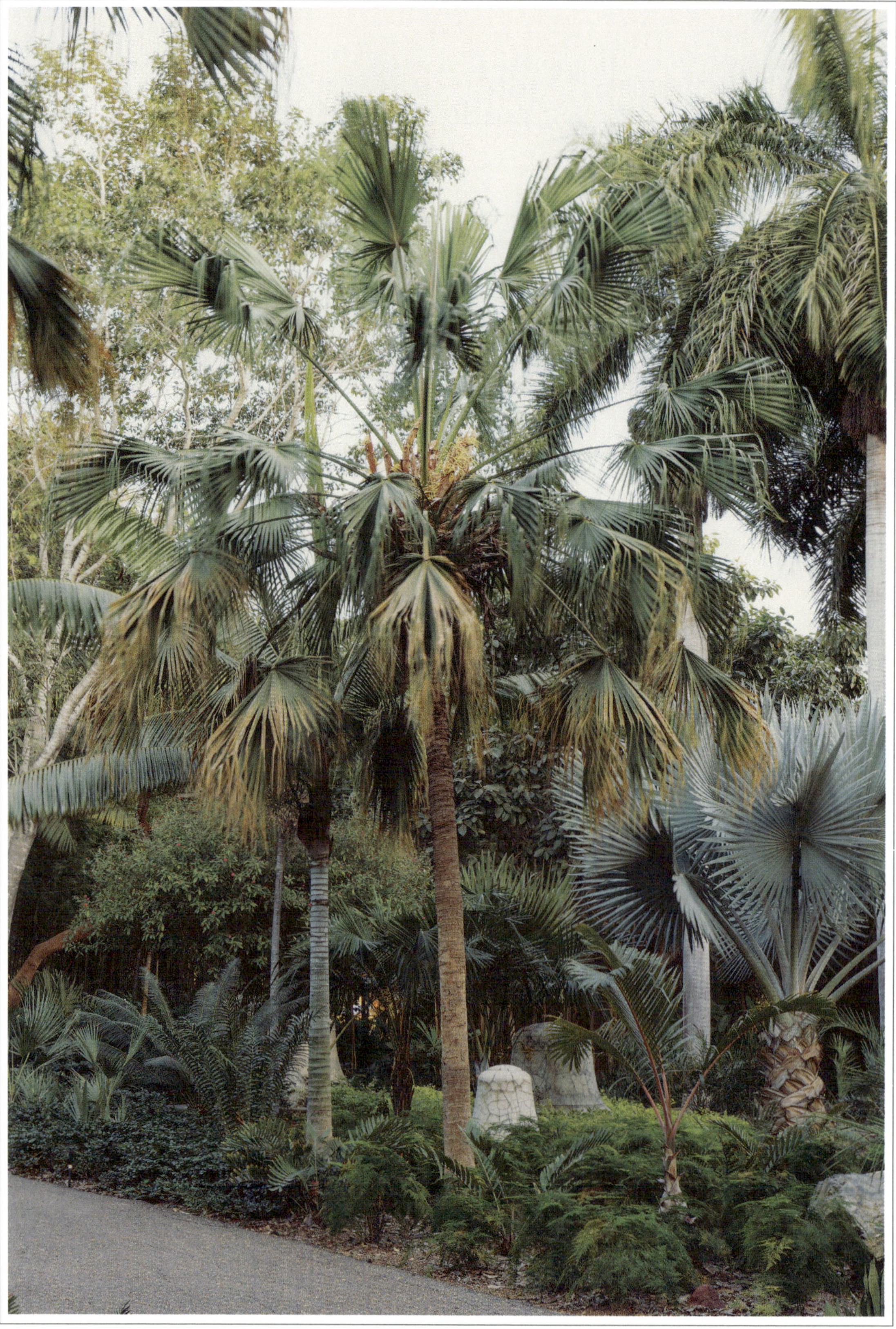

53
CHINESE FAN PALM

Livistona chinensis (Jacq.) R.Br. ex Mart.

Status: Assessment of global conservation status required
Distribution: Southern Japan, Taiwan, coastal China, and Micronesia

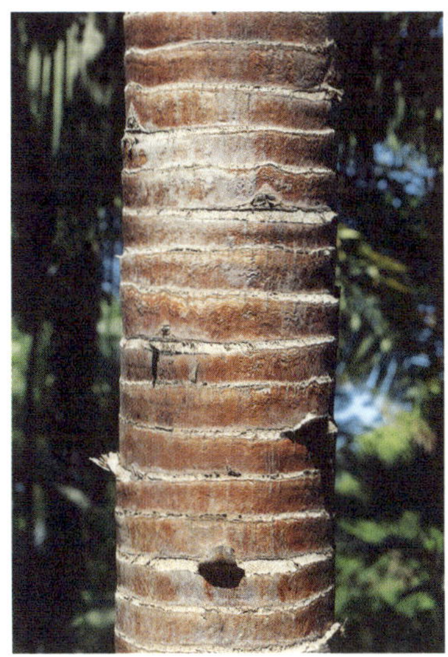
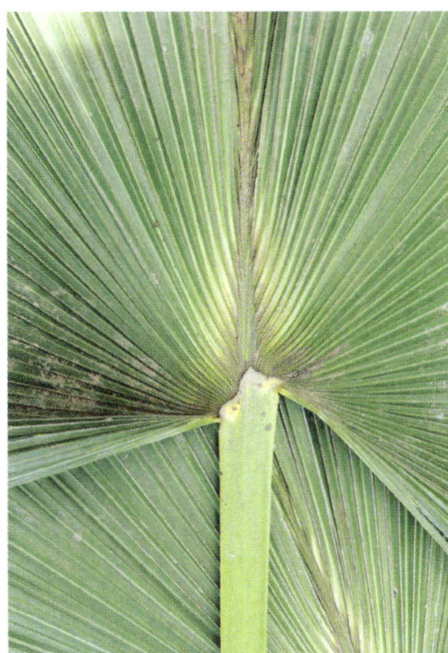
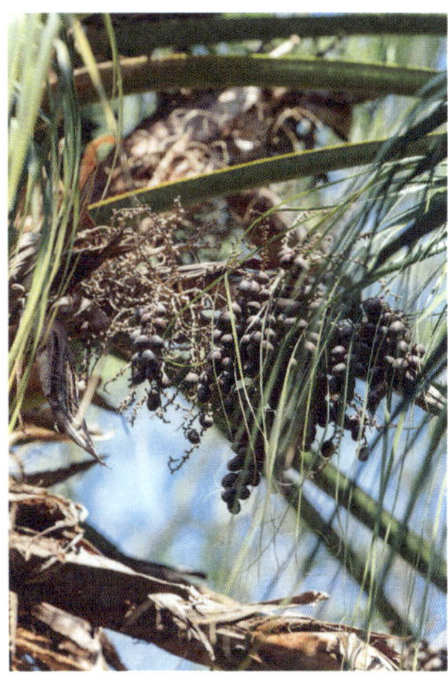

1. Trunk. 2. Leaf. 3. Fruits.

Livistona chinensis is a solitary palm that may reach up to 50 feet tall. It is cultivated in gardens throughout the world. Its bright green leaves have pendulous segment tips, and every year the palm bears long clusters of shiny blue fruits. *Livistona chinensis* is so adaptable and easy to grow that it has escaped cultivation, and it is now an introduced weed in Hawaii, Florida, Bermuda, New Caledonia, and the Mascarene Islands.

Livistona chinensis is one of the most common ornamental palms in the Culiacán region and one of the most abundant in the Jardín Botánico Culiacán. Most of the specimens in the collection are around thirty years old.

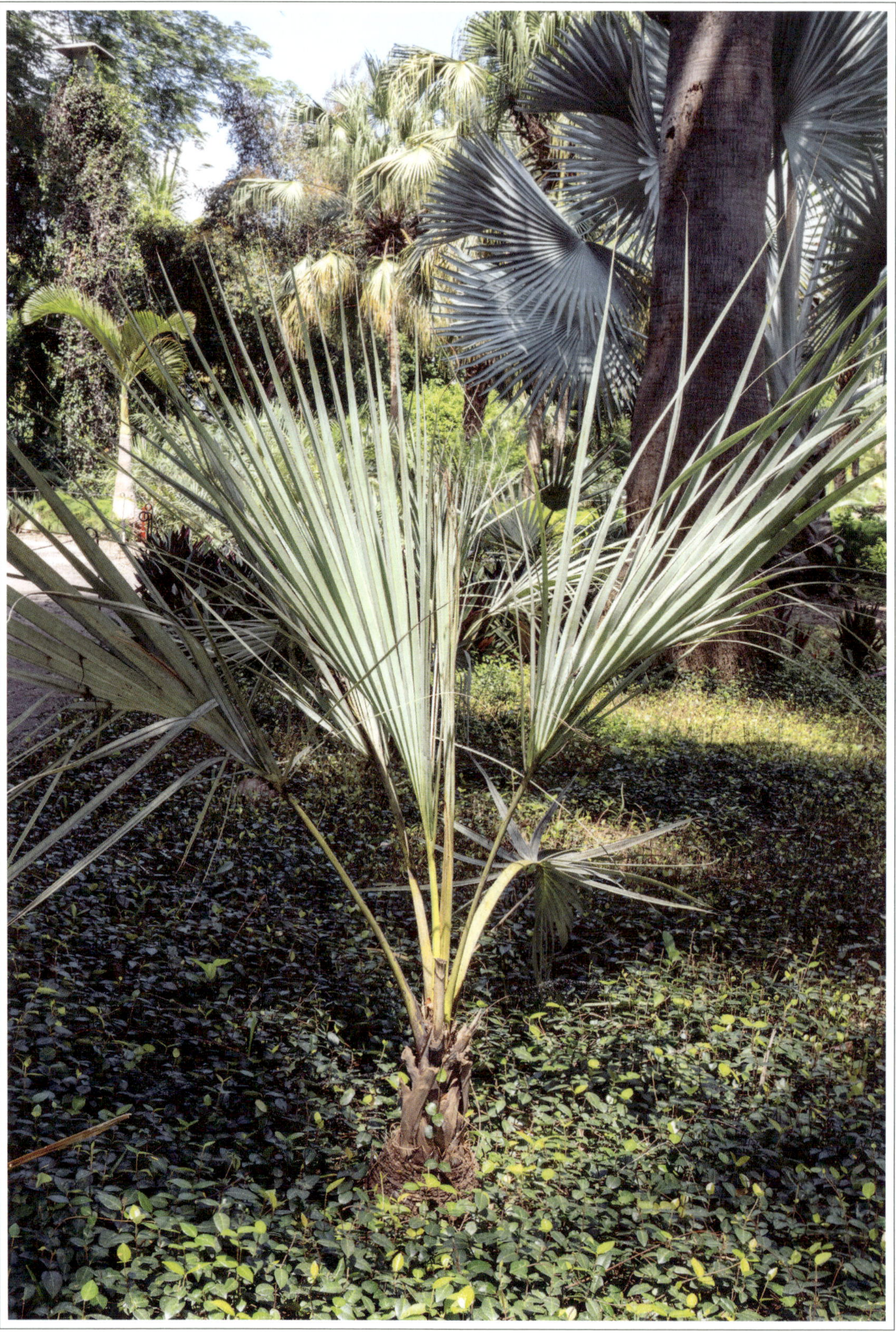

54
MEDEMIA PALM

Medemia argun (Mart.) Wurttenb. ex H. Wendl.

Status: Designated as Critically Endangered on the IUCN Red List
Distribution: Egypt and Sudan

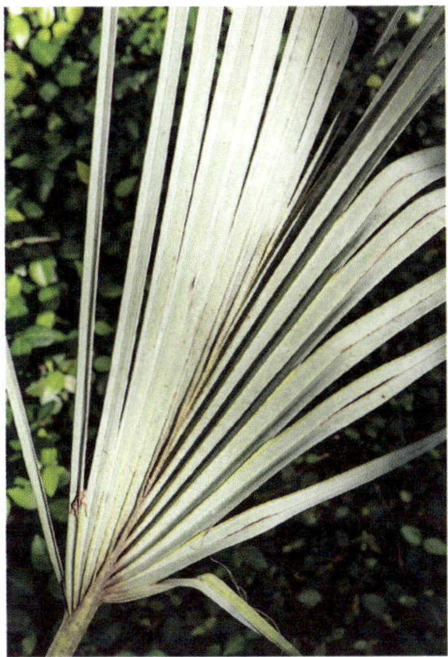

1. Leaf.

This palm forms a short stem from from 16 to 23 feet tall. Archeologists have found dried fruits of the palm in Egyptian tombs dating from as far back as 2500 BCE. In 1836, eleven years after these archaeological remains were first found, living palms with fruits matching those found in the tombs were discovered growing in oases in the Nubian Desert of southern Egypt and northern Sudan. Nineteenth century explorers occasionally encountered this palm while crossing the desert, but by the early twentieth century, as exploration declined, *Medemia argun* was nearly forgotten. Some wild plants were photographed by a botanist in 1965, but still the palm was known only from a few dried leaves and fruits and from the archaeological specimens. In 1995, two European nurserymen found populations of the palm alive in northern Sudan. They collected seeds and distributed them to botanical gardens and palm growers. *Medemia argun* has proven to be easy to grow and is now widely known, but the story of its discovery, loss, and rediscovery is a romantic adventure that continues to inspire amazement.

Specimens of this rare species were found in 2011 in a collector's nursery in the state of Yucatán. The climate of the area where those specimens came from and that of Culiacán are similar, so the palms adapted perfectly to environment of the Jardín Botánico Culiacán, where visitors can enjoy them in the Palmetum.

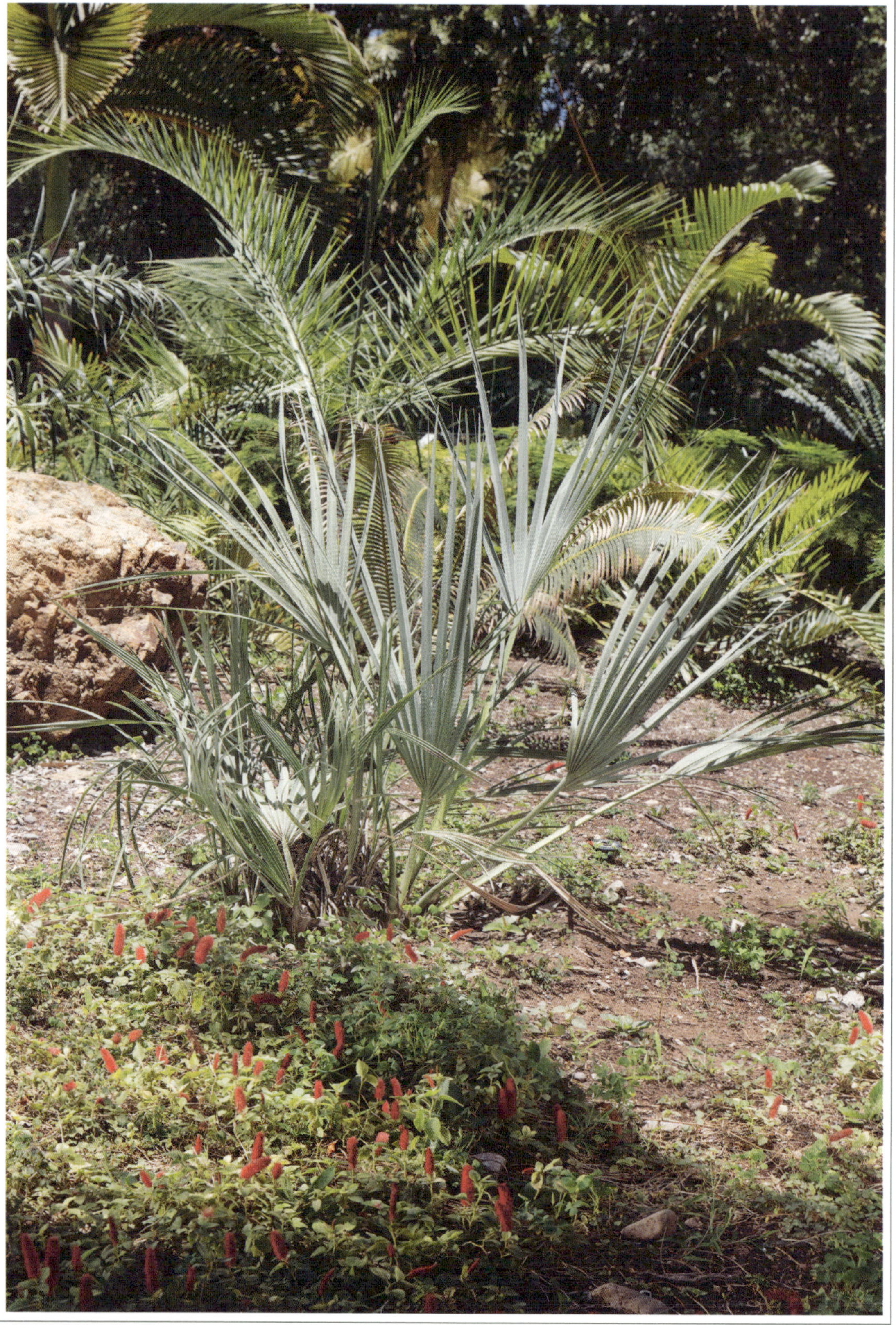

55

MAZARI PALM

Nannorrhops ritcheana (Griff.) Aitch.

Status: Assessment of global conservation status required
Distribution: From Pakistan to Iran and the Arabian Peninsula

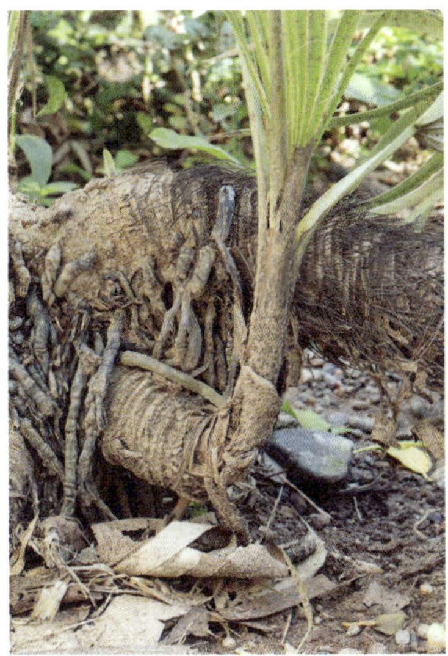

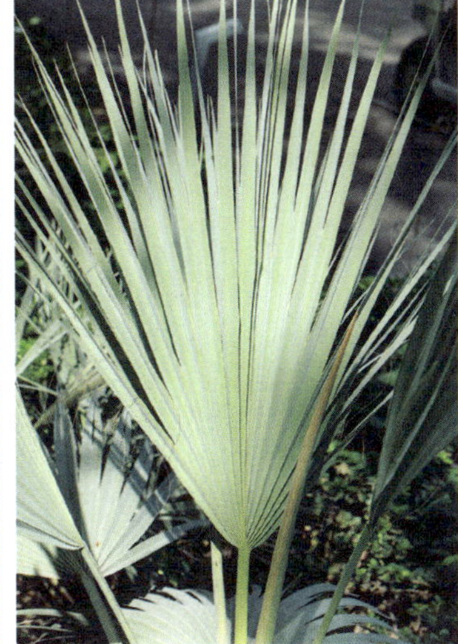

1. Stem. 2. Leaf.

The mazari palm is a medium-sized palm that reaches up to 35 feet in height. It is from a region and a habitat not often associated with palms. The species is also unusual for its unique growth form: the main stems are clustering, and each trunk branches into two equal stems, but one stem becomes a terminal flower stalk and then dies, while the other stem continues to grow and, eventually, to branch—commencing the flowering process again. The palm is tolerant of heat, thanks to its silvery leaves, while also able to endure periods of freezing weather. In its native range, the palm is heavily exploited for its leaves, which are used for basketry, matting, and rope. Without appropriate resource management, it may disappear from these areas.

Following a trip to Yucatán in 2011, the Jardín Botánico Culiacán team brought back this species, along with some other exotic ones, to enrich the Palmetum collection. It took a long time for the *Nannorrhops ritchiana* specimen to adapt to the garden's conditions, so it was not until 2017 that it was possible to make a place for it there. It is a palm that receives special horticultural attention, but even so, it may take years to see much growth.

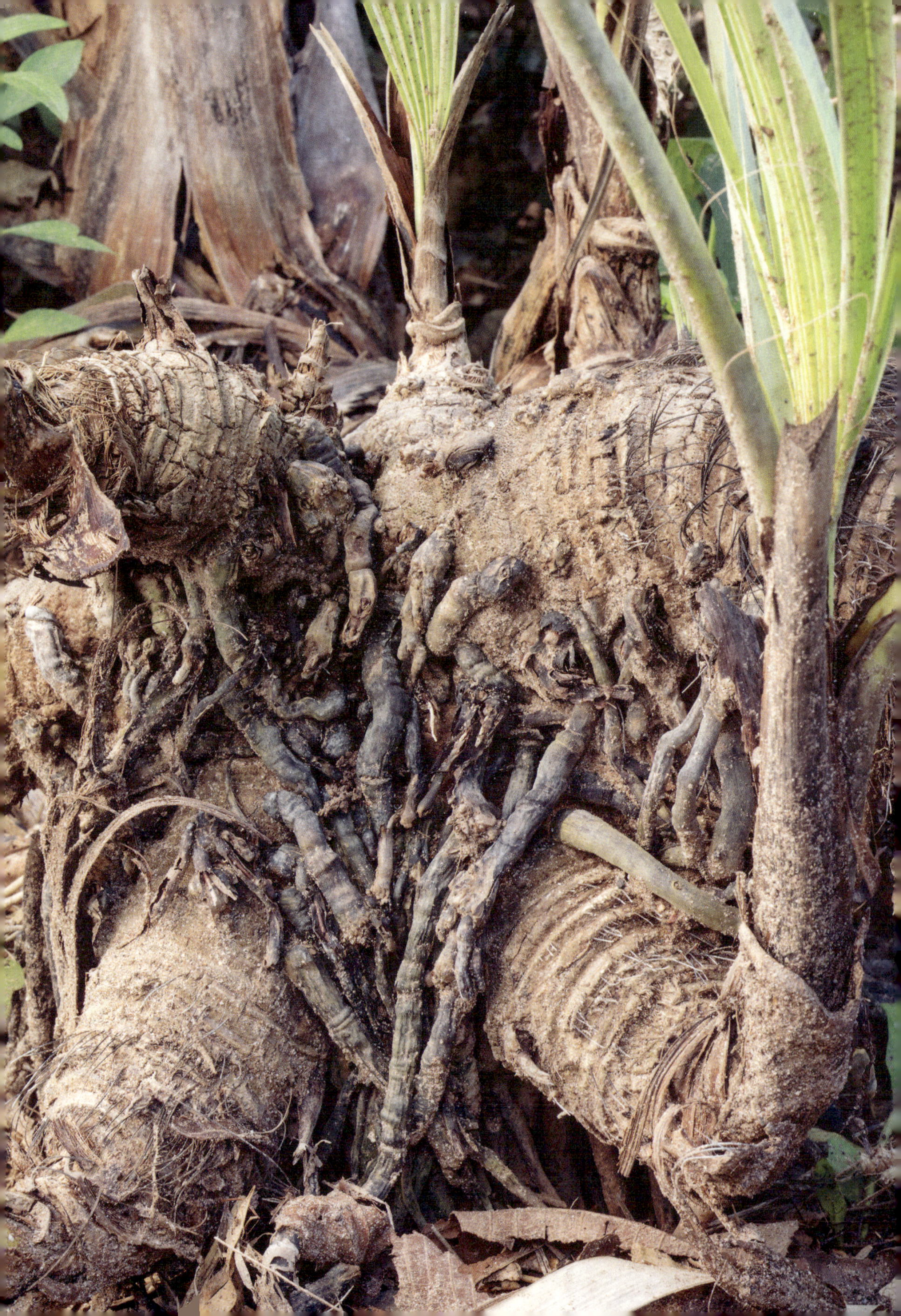

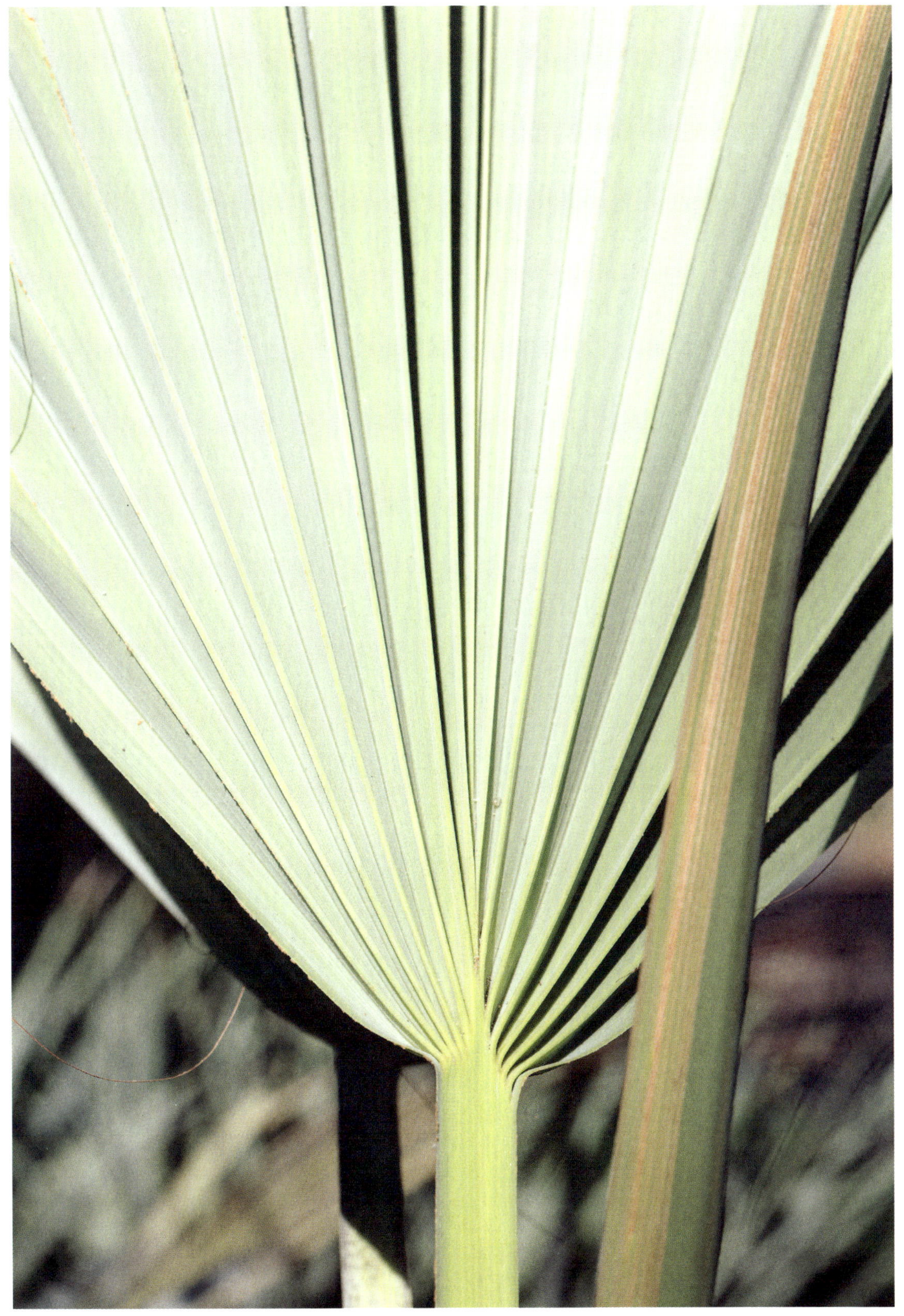

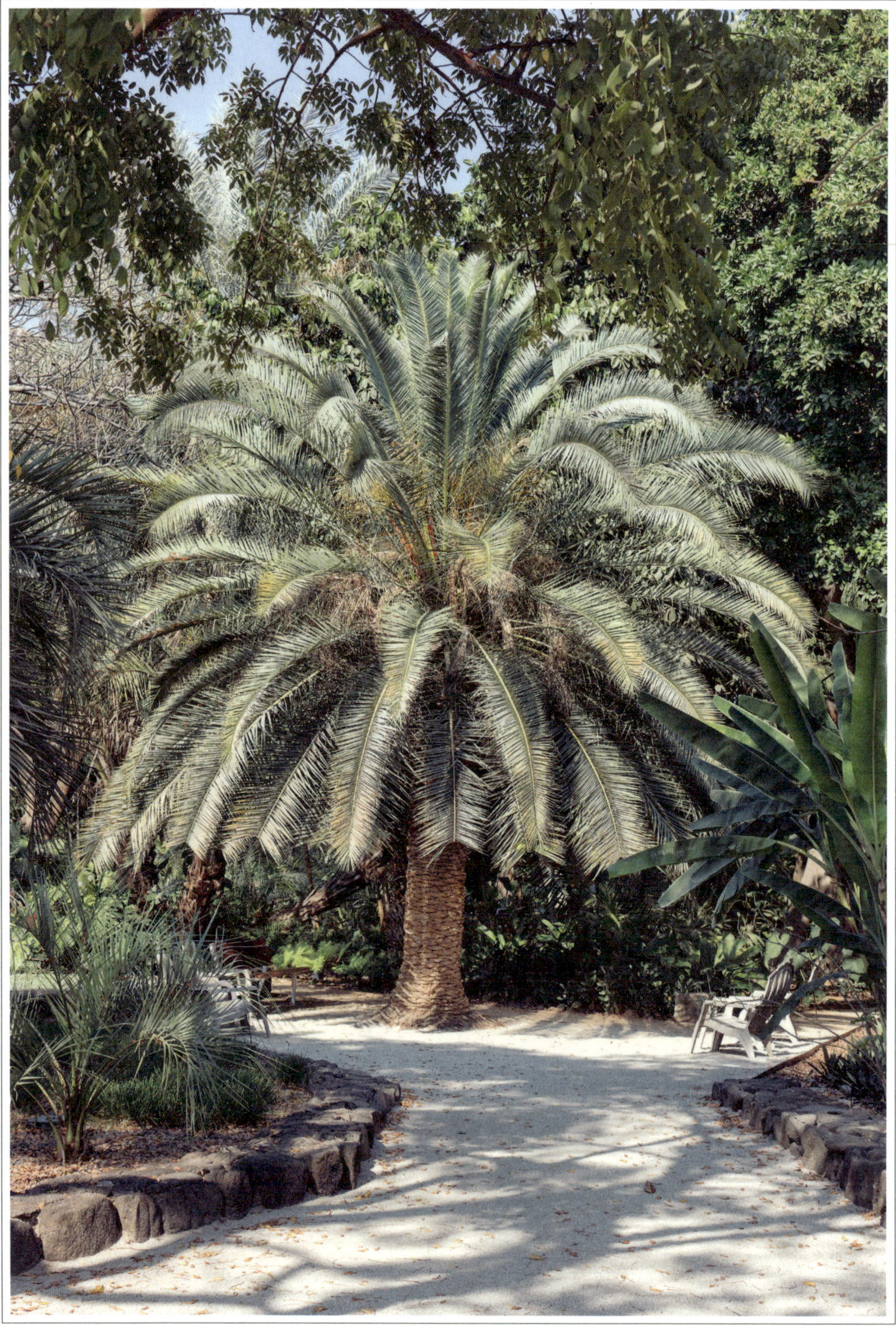

56

CANARY ISLAND DATE PALM

Phoenix canariensis Chabaud

Status: Designated as Least Concern on the IUCN Red List
Distribution: Canary Islands

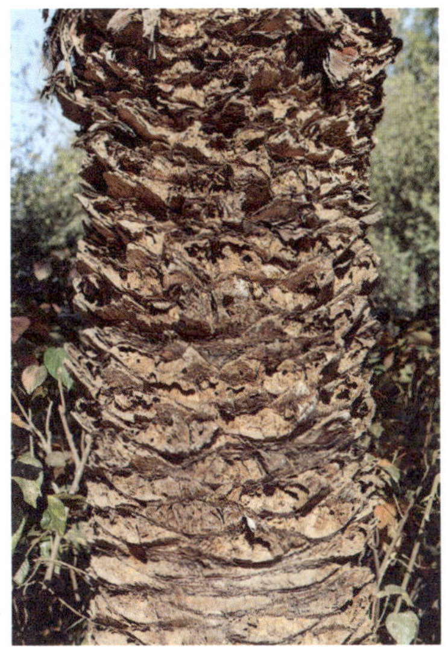
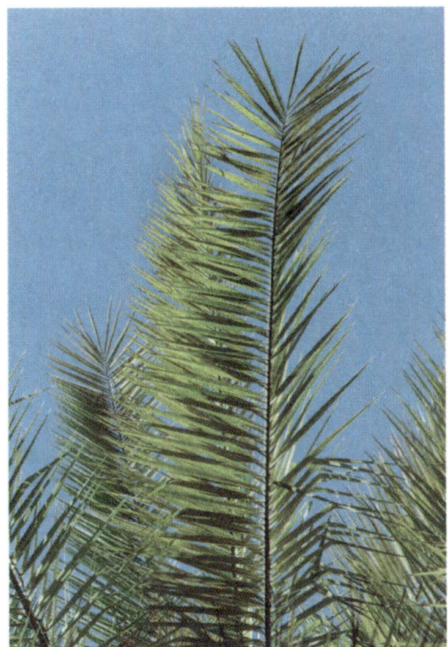
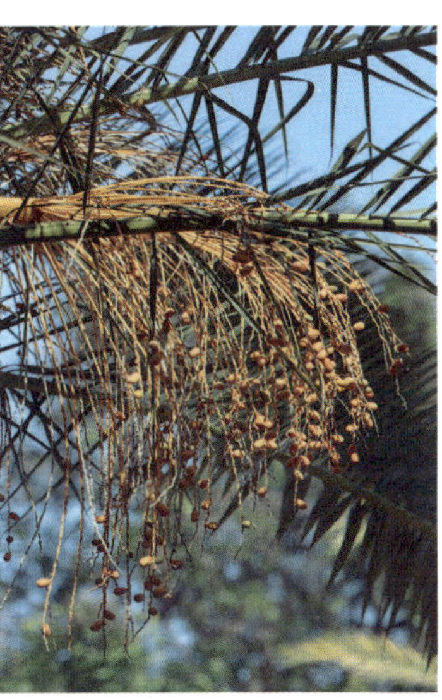

1. Trunk. 2. Leaf. 3. Fruits.

The Canary Island date palm is a tall, stately palm with a stout, solitary trunk from 65 to 100 feet tall and a large spherical crown of leaves. It is one of the most widely cultivated palms in the world, and yet it is found in nature only in the Canary Islands. Although it is used everywhere as an ornamental palm, in the Canary Islands it is used as a source of "palm honey," a syrup made from the palm sap. To extract the sap, the tapper climbs up into the crown (avoiding the sharp spines on the base of the leaf stalk) and cuts away the emerging leaves of the terminal bud. Great care must be taken not to cut too deeply into the bud, for that would kill the palm. The apex of the palm is scooped out to form a bowl, which slowly fills with sap. The sap is collected once or twice a day. After a few months, the bud begins to produce new leaves, and the palm is allowed to recover for a year or more before being tapped again. This kind of sustainable sap extraction has been practiced in the Canary Islands for centuries.

Gardeners at the Jardín Botánico Culiacán are not very fond of *Phoenix canariensis*, because of the aggressive spines at the base of the leaves. These spines make it very difficult to take care of the palm. The botanists know it is a very slow-growing palm, so they estimate that the few specimens found at the garden are around forty years old, probably planted toward the end of the 1970s.

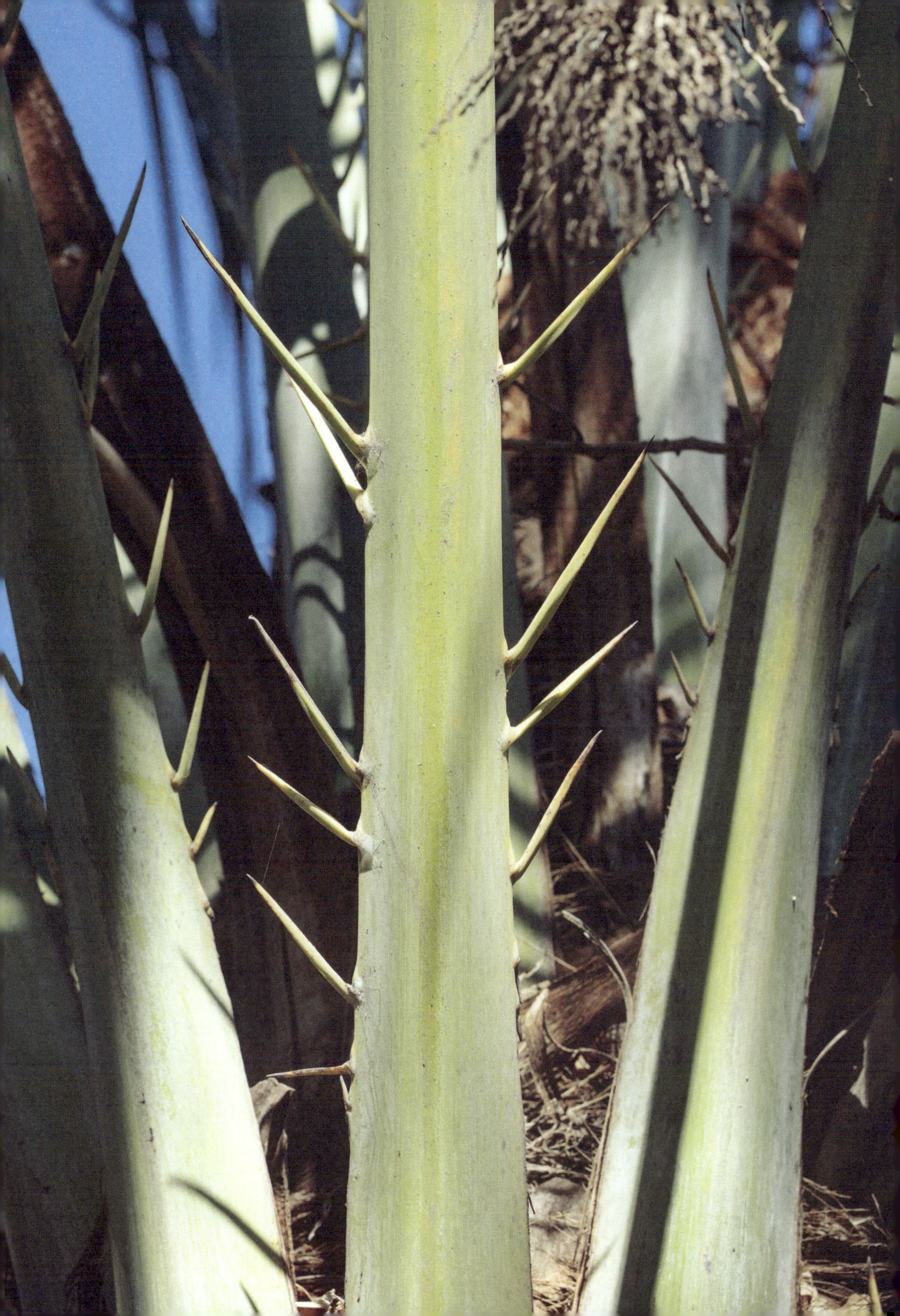

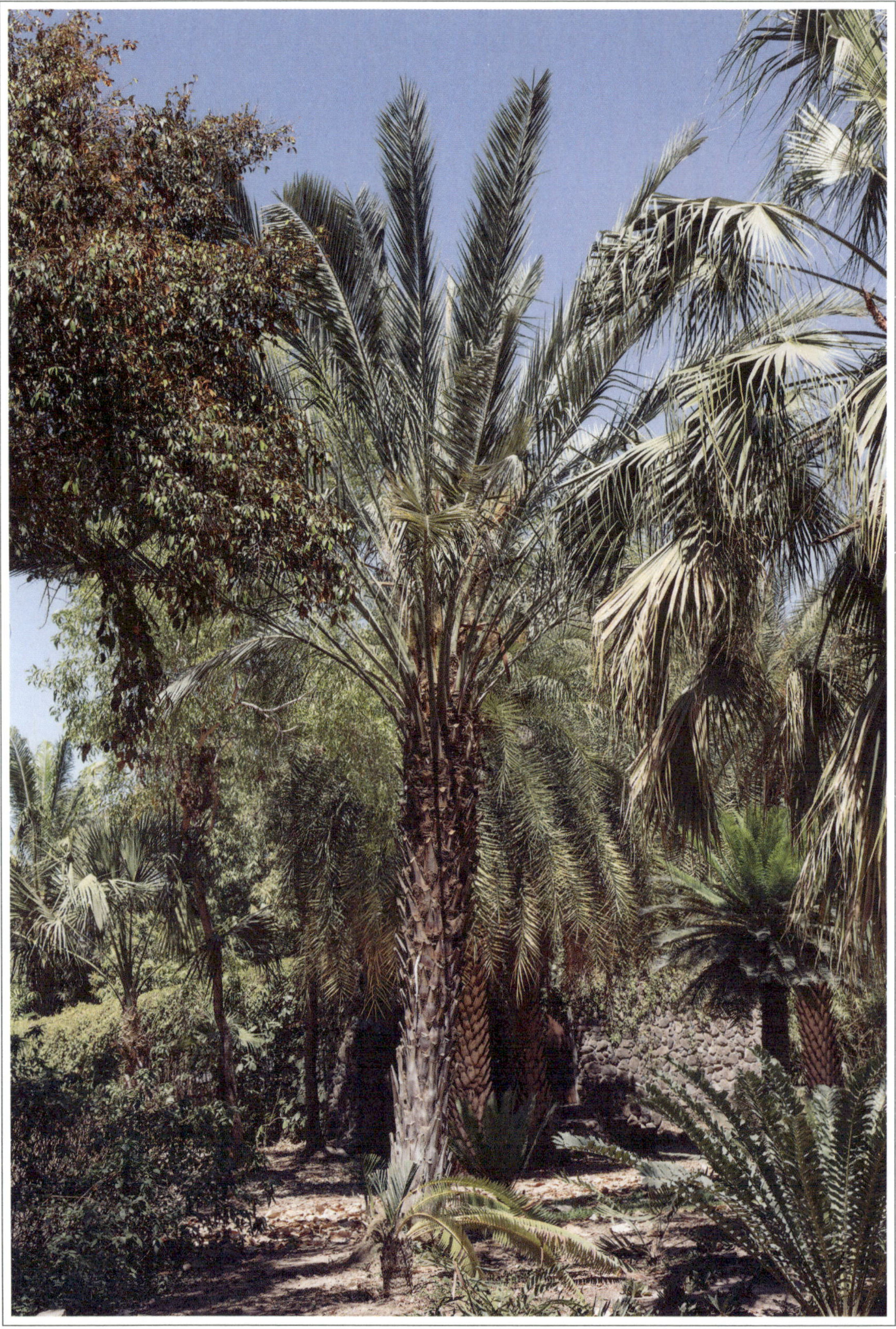

57
DATE PALM

Phoenix dactylifera L.

Status: Assessment of global conservation status required
Distribution: Cultivated worldwide

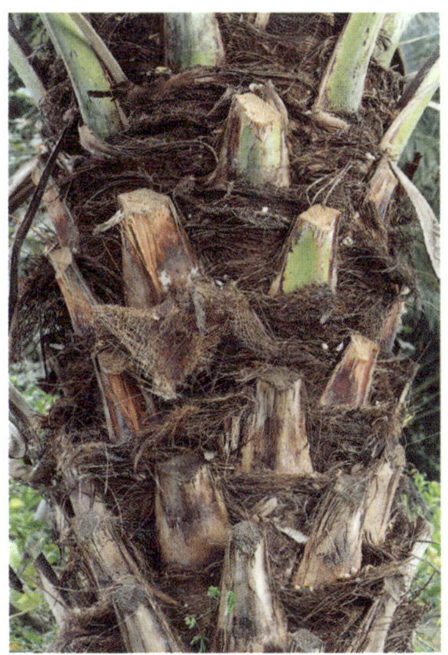
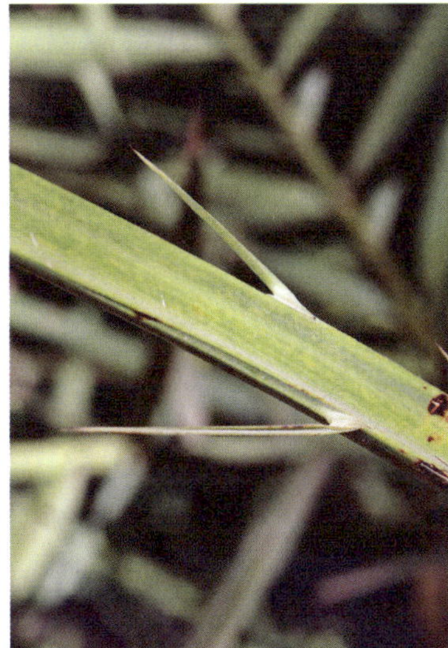
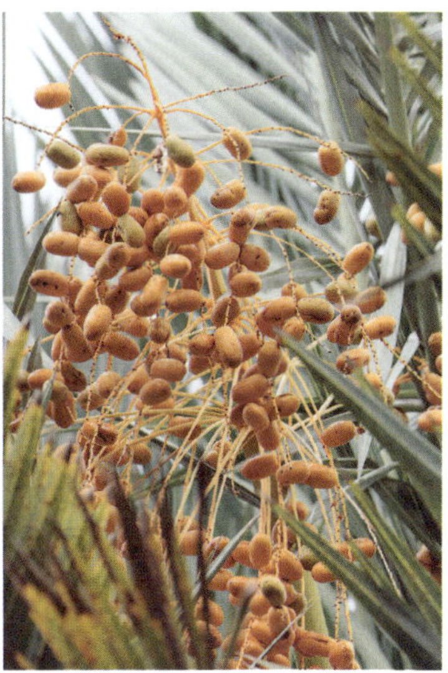

1. Trunk with retained leaf bases. 2. Spiny petiole. 3. Fruits.

Phoenix dactylifera is a robust clustering palm that can reach up to 80 feet in height. When young, the palm produces many clustering stems, but commercial farmers remove these and keep only one main stem. The date palm is not known to occur in the wild. It was domesticated in Mesopotamia in antiquity and its progenitor species is extinct. The date palm has had tremendous cultural and economic significance in the arid Middle East, both as a source of food and fiber and as a symbol of life, rebirth, and prosperity. Archeological remains of date seeds from the fourteenth century BCE have been found in Egypt. Depictions of the palm can be found on ancient tombs and temples and on coins, extending from Egypt to Iraq. Long before botanists understood the concept of sexuality in plants, ancient farmers discovered that pollen from male flowers had to be dusted onto female flowers in order to make fruits. Although it grows in deserts, it still requires irrigation, and ancient farmers used intricate systems of irrigation canals. Even today, farmers say that the "date palm grows with its feet in water and its head in fire."

This palm is one of the most beloved plants in the Jardín Botánico Culiacán, producing very sweet dates from March to May. The gardeners and the birds alike eat them a lot. Unfortunately, it is also one of the plants that gets sick very easily, so it requires constant care to protect it from fungi and mite attacks.

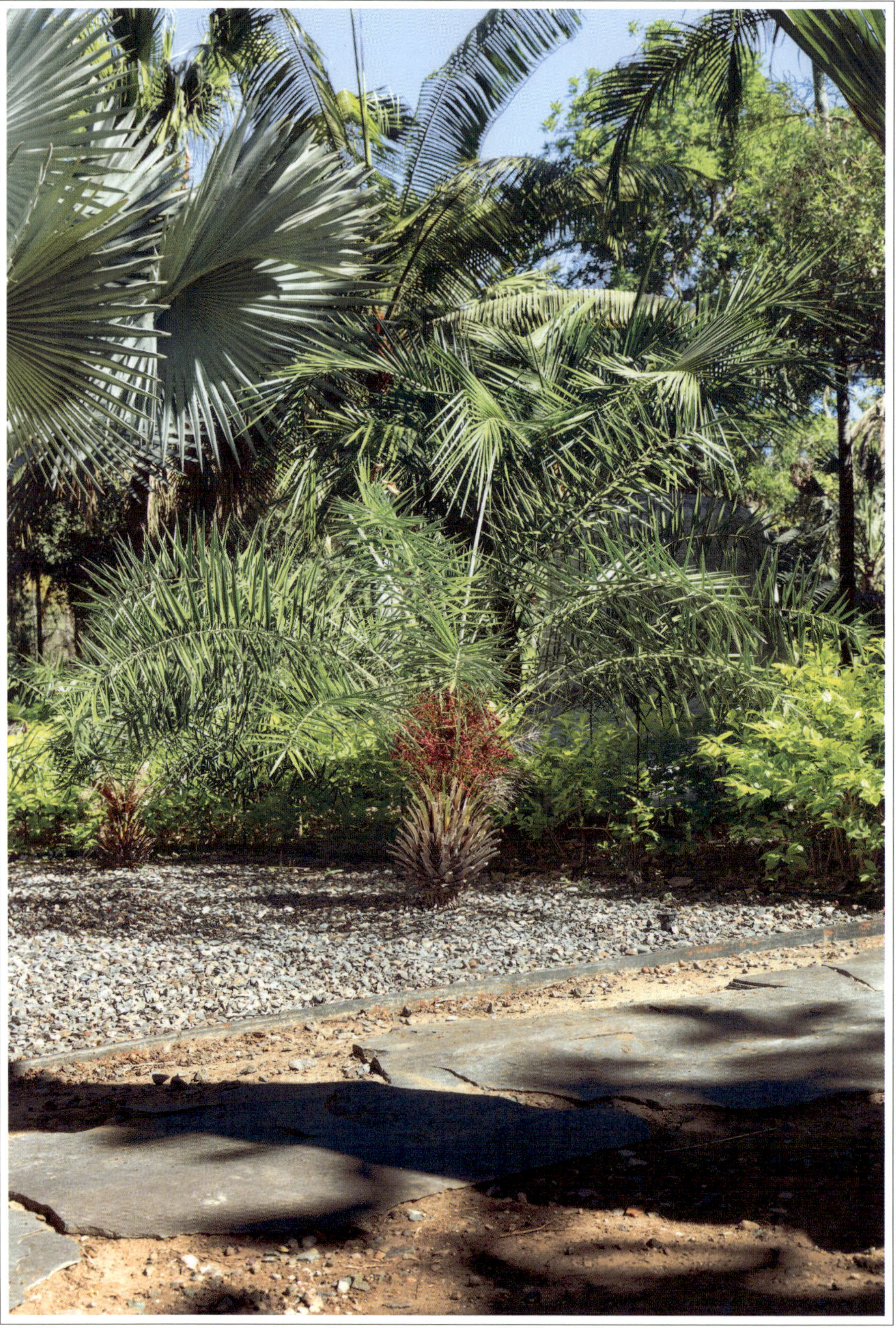

58

CEYLON DATE PALM

Phoenix pusilla Gaertn.

Status: Assessment of global conservation status required
Distribution: Southern India and Sri Lanka

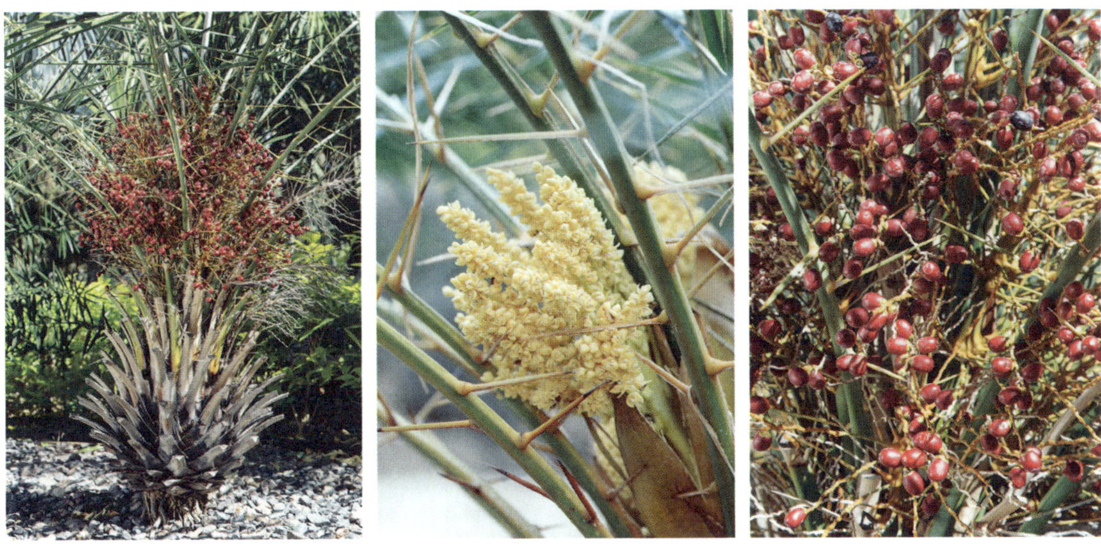

1. Trunk with retained leaf bases. 2. Flowers between the spiny petiole. 3. Fruits.

This small to medium-sized palm may grow up to 16 feet tall and can be solitary or clustering. Its native habitat is dry or wet forests. Like all species in the genus *Phoenix*, the lowermost leaflets are stiff and sharp, forming a phalanx of spines that protect the growing point of the stem. This distinctive leaflet formation is found in no other group of palms, so leaf fossils showing these spines can confidently be identified as *Phoenix*. The oldest such fossils are approximately 70 million years old. The spines on *Phoenix* leaves are the cause of many injuries to gardeners, especially when the spines penetrate bones, leading to persistent ailments that are difficult to diagnose. Great care must therefore be taken when working with any palms in this genus. The leaflets are used for weaving and the leaves for making brooms. The fruits are consumed by children in India and Sri Lanka and the carbonized stems are burned in brick ovens. In places where it has been introduced, *Phoenix pusilla* is used to prevent soil erosion. The popularity of the palm as a weaving material and for making charcoal is decimating its wild populations.

A specimen of this small palm was found in a collector's nursery in Yucatán in 2011. It was kept in the nursery of the Jardín Botánico Culiacán until 2016, when it had grown large enough for display, and was then placed in its exhibit spot for the opening of the art installation *Encounter*, by James Turrell.

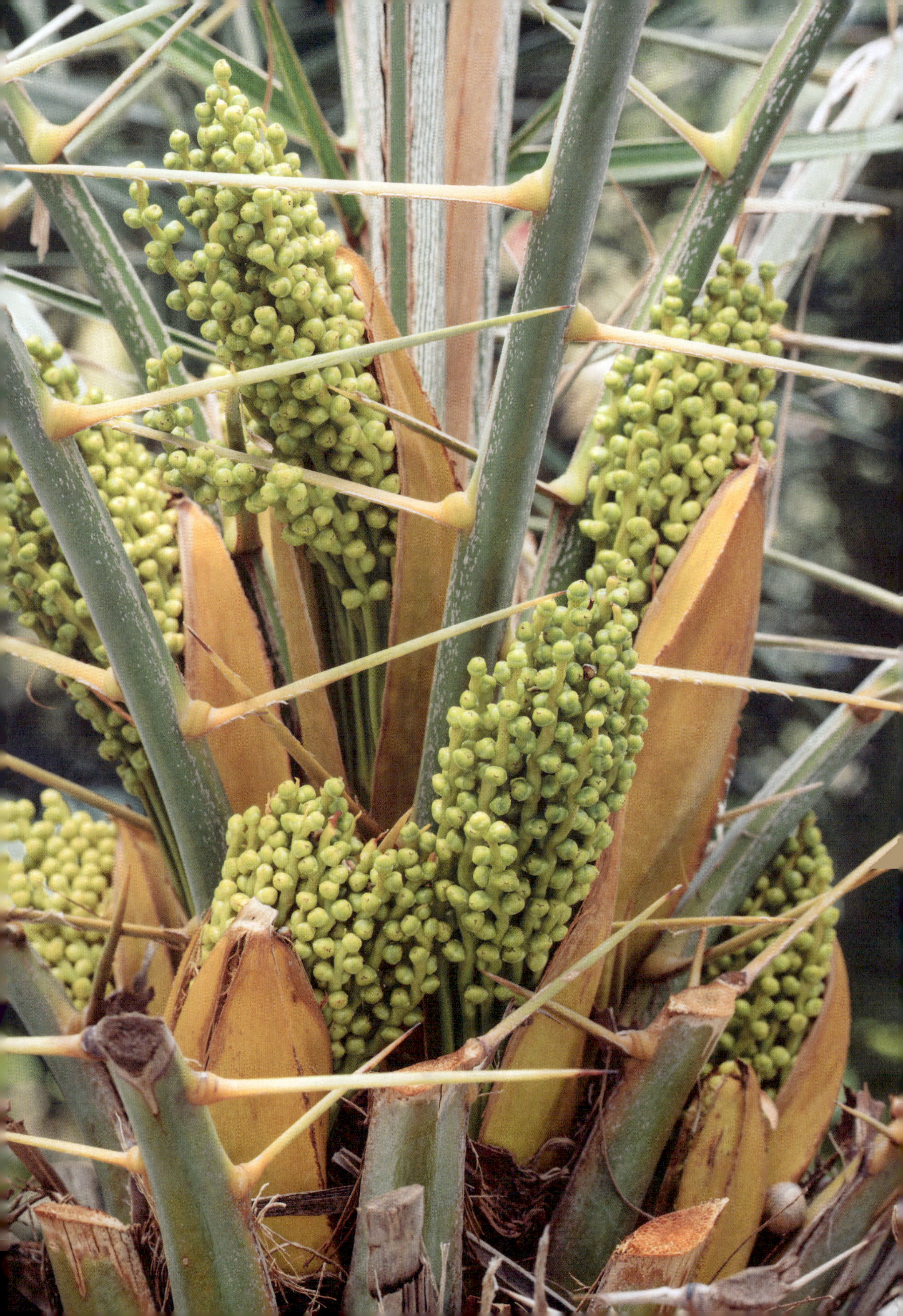

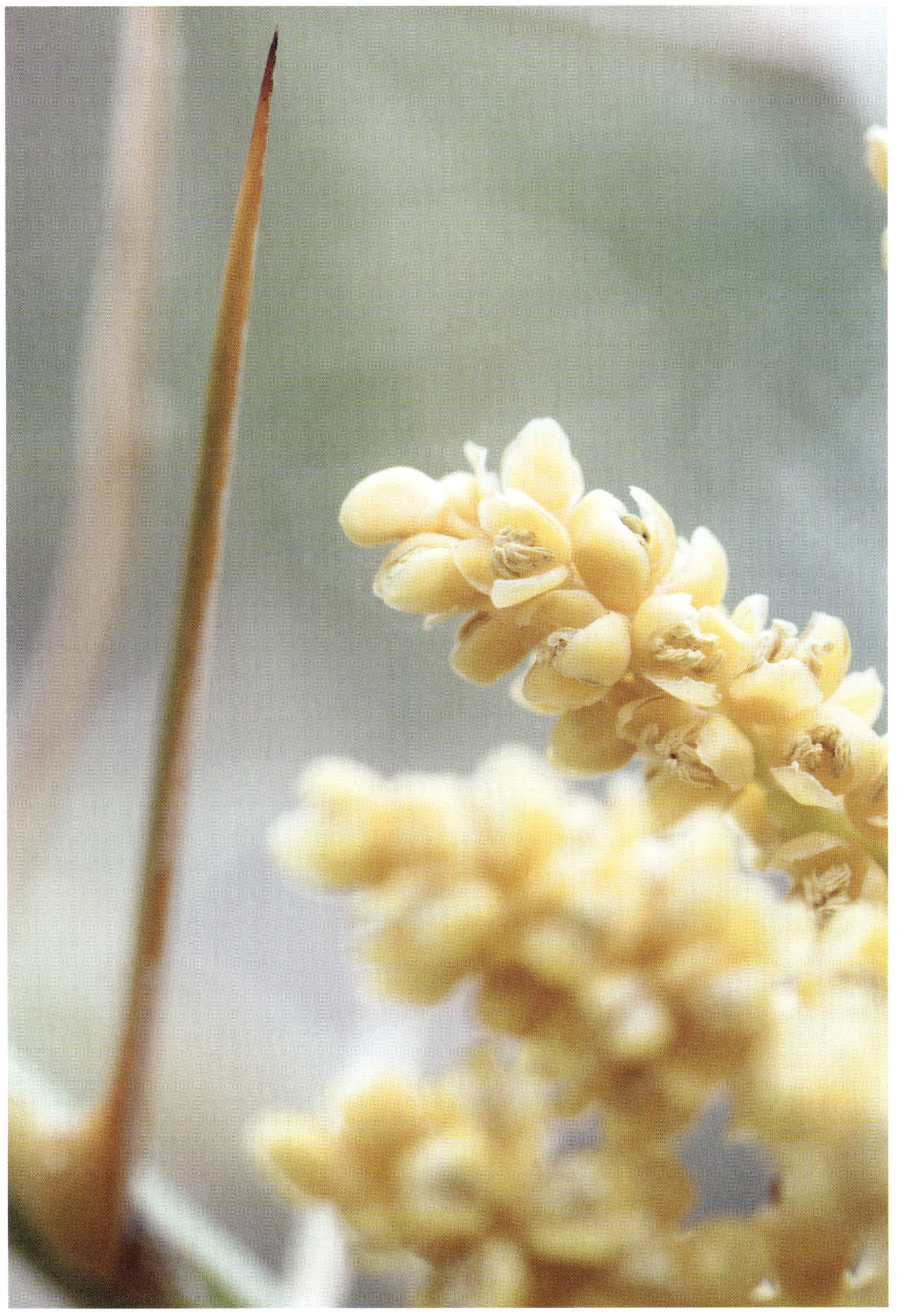

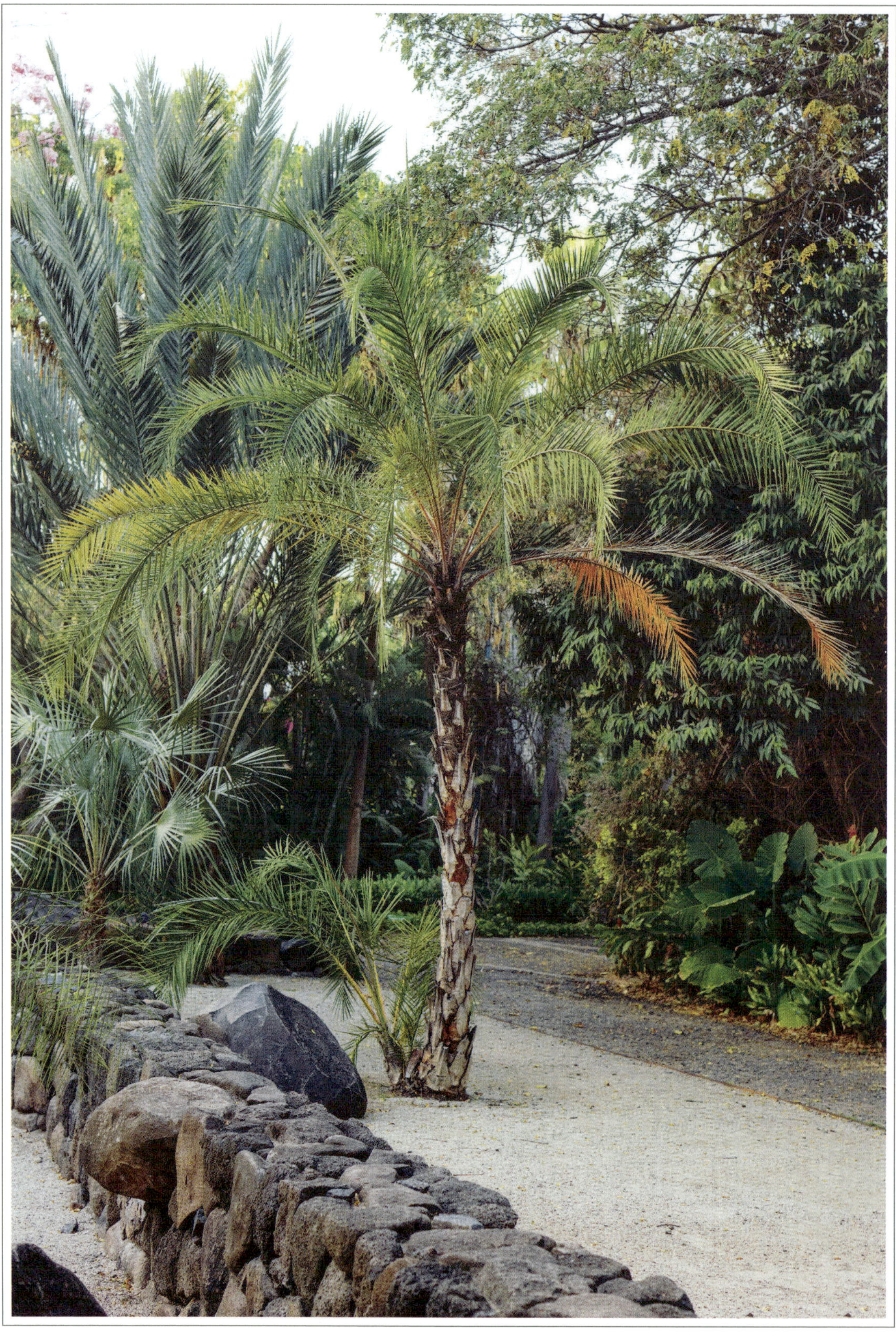

59
SENEGAL DATE PALM

Phoenix reclinata Jacq.

Status: Designated as Least Concern on the IUCN Red List
Distribution: Africa, Madagascar, and nearby islands

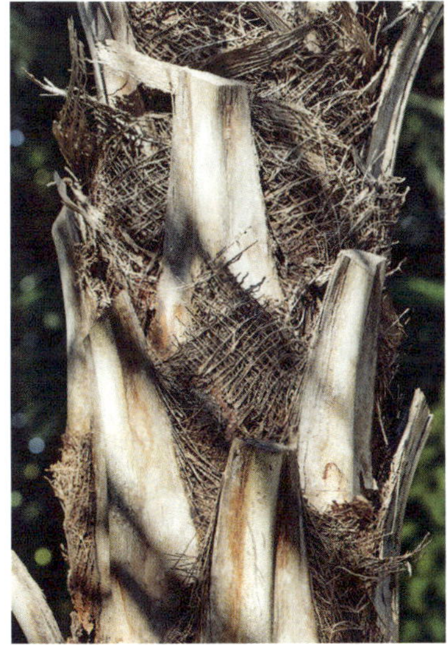
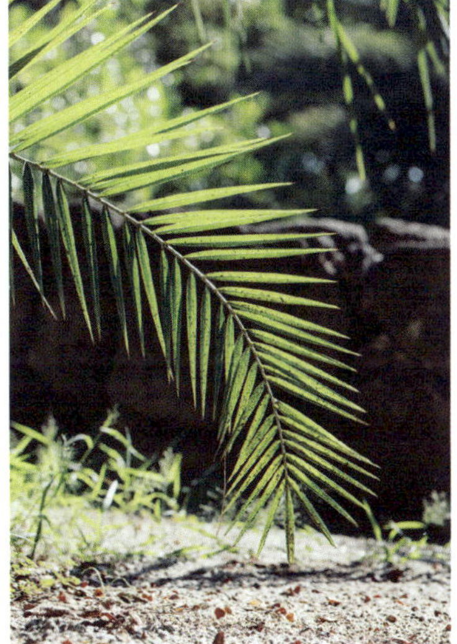

1. Trunk with retained leaf bases. 2. Leaf.

Phoenix reclinata is a medium-sized palm with slender stems that grow up to 35 feet tall and form large spreading clusters. It has the largest natural distribution of any palm in the *Phoenix* genus and it grows in a wide variety of habitats, from tropical rainforest to dry, rocky hillsides. Like all species of *Phoenix*, the base of the leaf is armed with leaflets that form bayonet-like spines. In nature, the shiny black fruits —similar to small, thin-fleshed dates—are consumed by birds, monkeys, and elephants. Humans harvest the edible fruits, while using the stems for construction and firewood and the leaves for weaving and in religious ceremonies. The sap is harvested from the terminal bud and fermented into wine.

Several specimens of *Phoenix reclinata* came in the 1990s to the Carlos Murillo Depraect's personal nursery from the Jardín Botánico Benjamin Francis Johnston in Los Mochis. Two of these survived and were placed on exhibit at the Jardín Botánico Culiacán. Today the garden has more specimens on display.

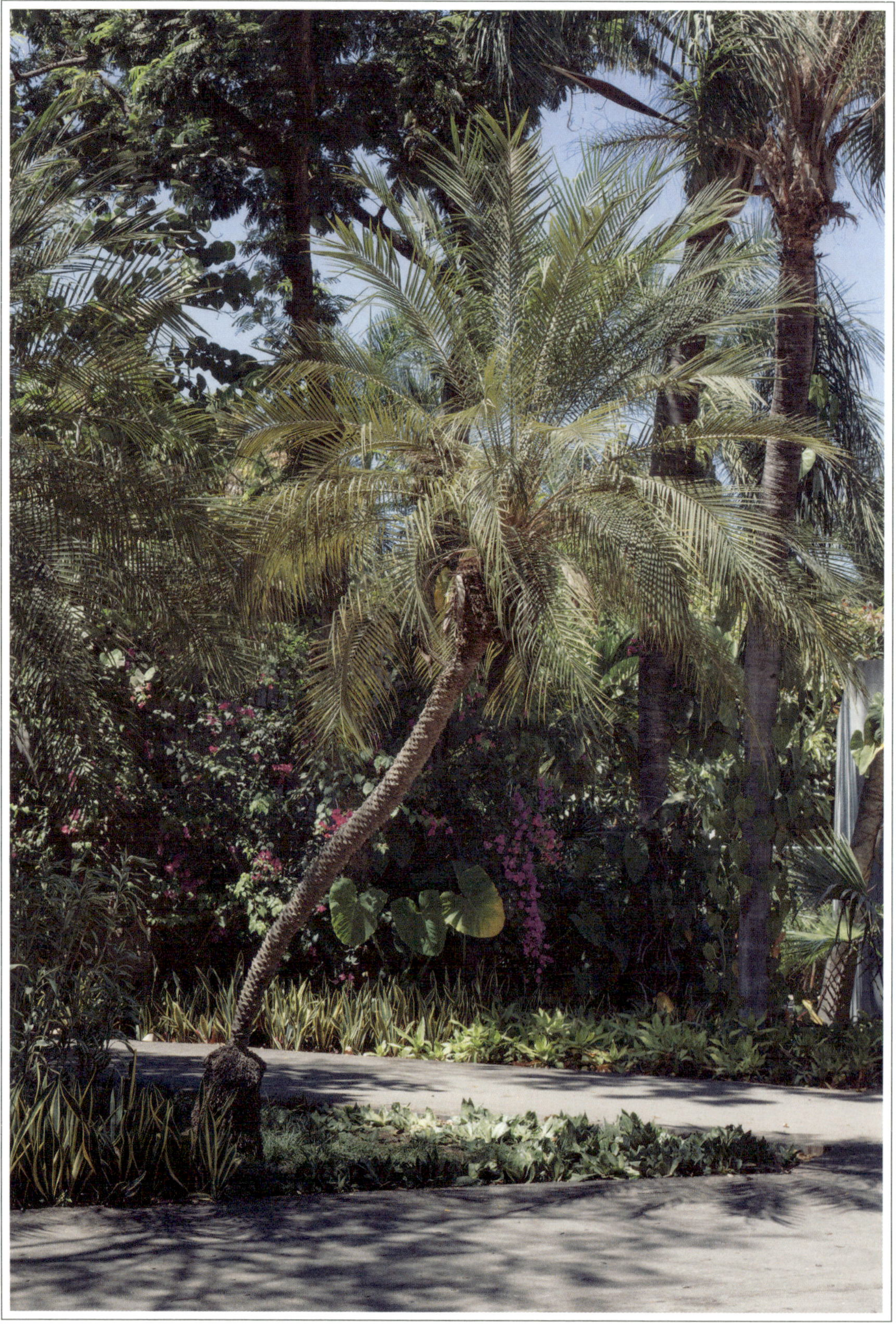

60

PYGMY DATE PALM

Phoenix roebelenii O'Brien

Status: Assessment of global conservation status required
Distribution: Southern China and Southeast Asia

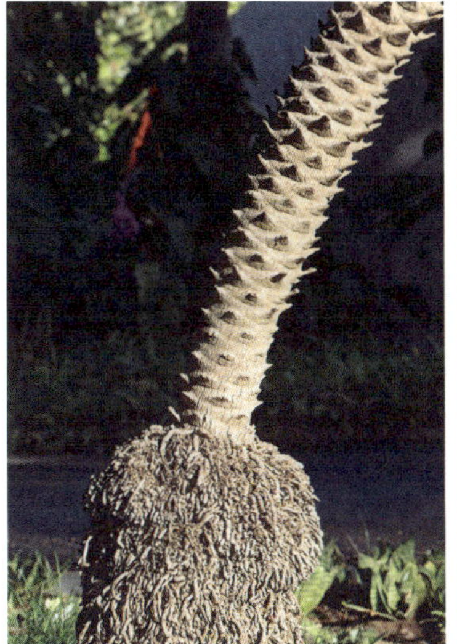

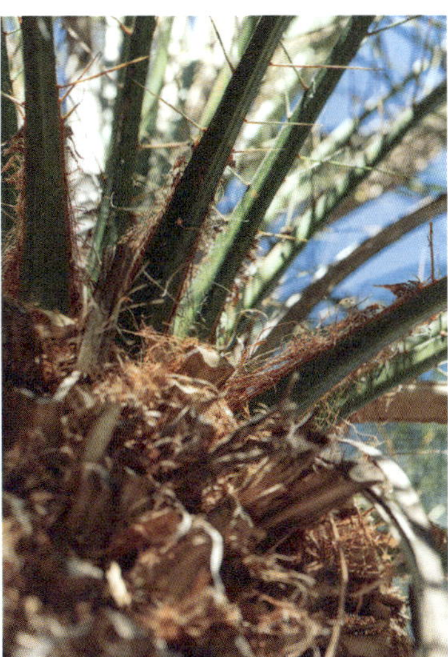

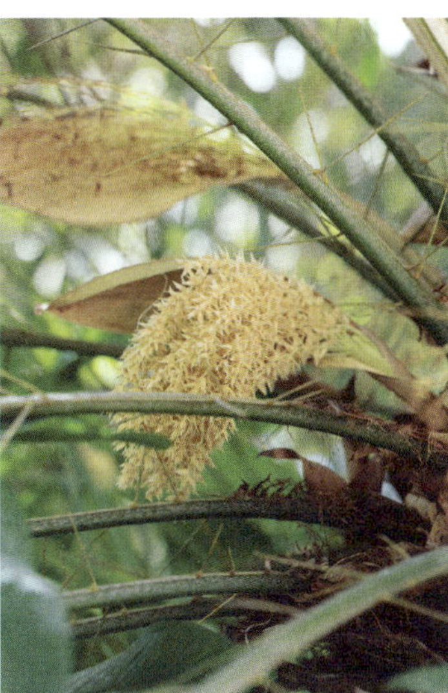

1. Trunk. 2. Spiny petiole. 3. Male flowers.

It is easy to see how the pygmy date palm got its name: it is like a date palm in miniature, growing up to 10 feet tall, and its small size and elegant growth habit make it perfect for gardens. This species is very popular and cultivated all over the world, as both a landscape plant and container plant. It is native to the upper basin of the Mekong River, which runs from southern China along the borders of Myanmar, Laos, Thailand, and Vietnam. The palm grows along the riverside, perched among giant boulders. Sadly, vast numbers of these palms have been poached from the wild to satisfy the landscape trade in Southeast Asia, and the species is no longer present along the river in Thailand. The species is a rheophytic palm, and some of its adaptations include flexible leaves and narrow leaflets. It also has naturally clustering stems, although in cultivation the stems are usually solitary, and growers often plant three or more palms together in one pot.

Records at the Jardín Botánico Culiacán show that the first specimen of *Phoenix roebelenii* arrived in 1986. Today it is a very common plant in nurseries around Culiacán, frequently seen in gardens designed by Carlos Murillo Depraect.

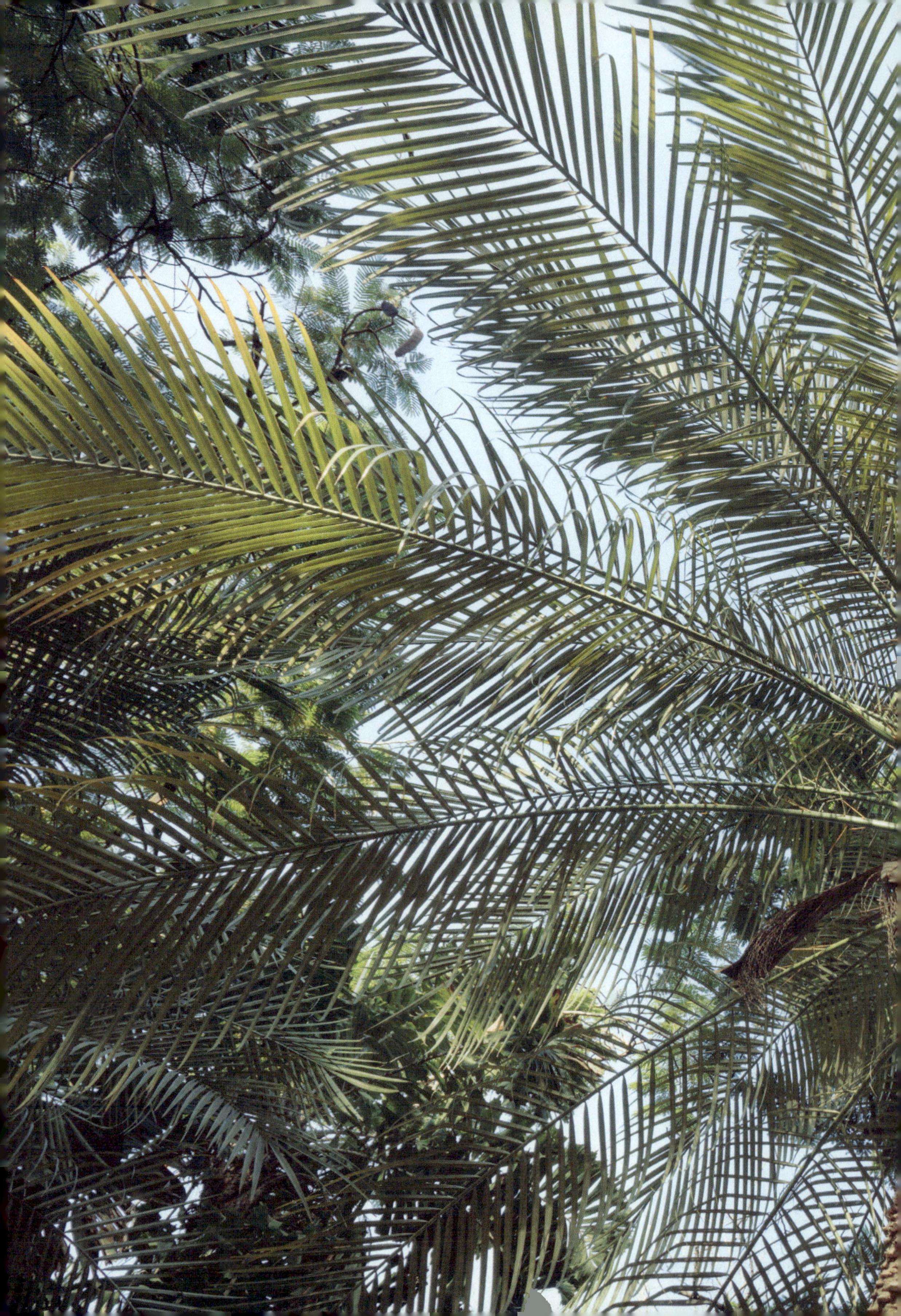

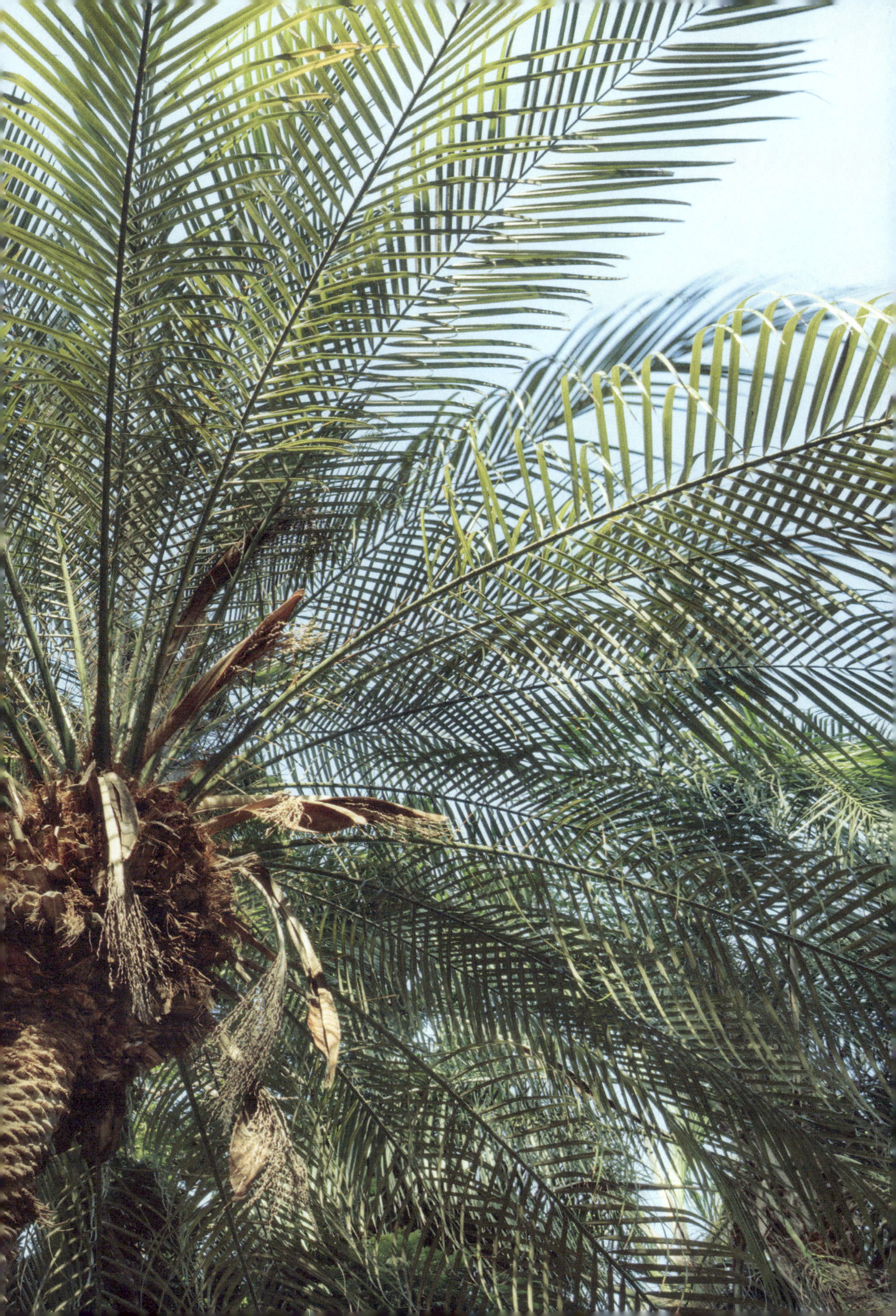

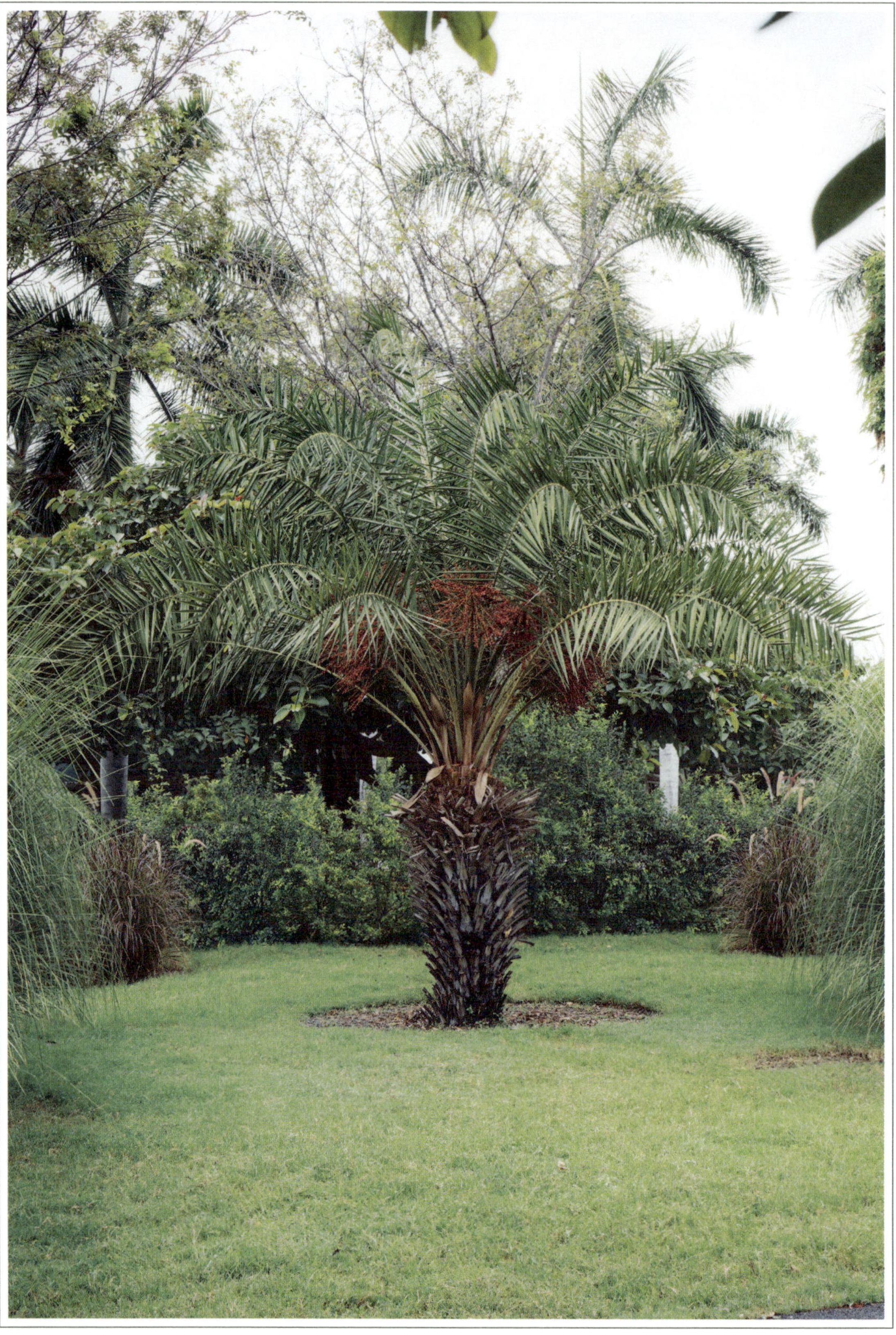

61

SILVER DATE PALM

Phoenix sylvestris (L.) Roxb.

Status: Assessment of global conservation status required
Distribution: India and Pakistan

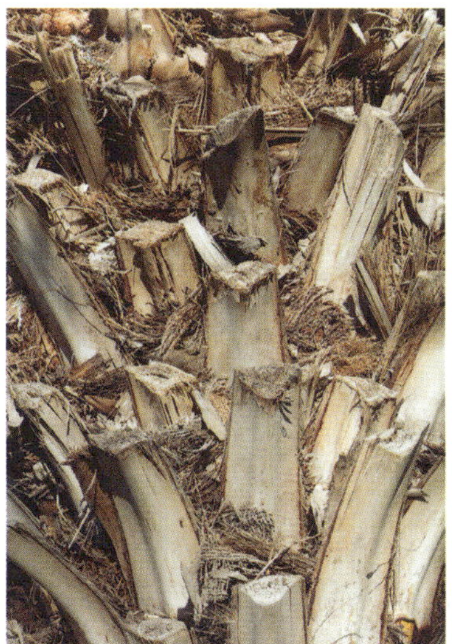

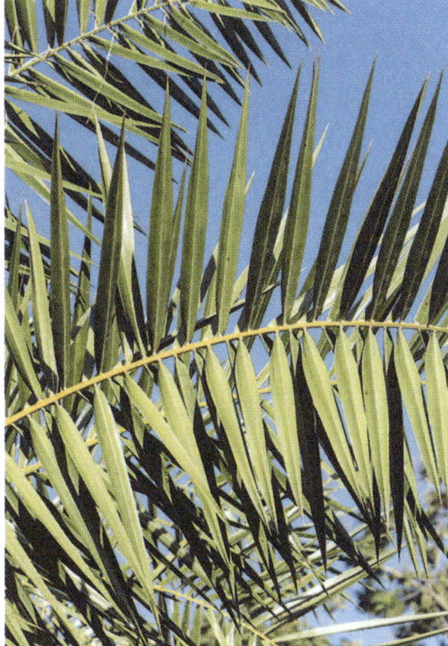

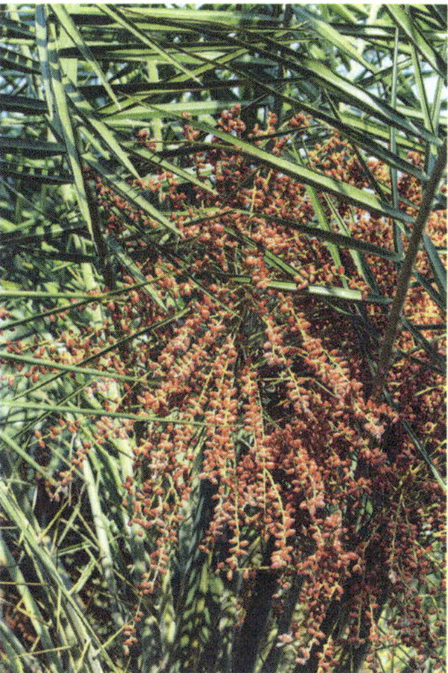

1. Trunk with retained leaf bases. 2. Leaf. 3. Fruits.

Phoenix sylvestris is a single-trunk palm that can grow up to 50 feet tall and bears a dense crown of silvery leaves. Throughout its range, it is an important source of sugar, not from its sweet fruits, but from the sap. The palms are climbed by skilled tappers, who carve a notch in the trunk just below the leaves. Sap flows from the wound and is collected in vessels tied to the tree. The sap can be consumed fresh, but it is more often boiled down to make sugar or allowed to ferment to make wine. This palm is found throughout the plains of Pakistan and India, but it is not known whether this distribution is natural or the result of humans, who may have carried the palm across the region in prehistoric times.

The Jardín Botánico Culiacán has numerous specimens, all of which were healthy until 2019. In that year, gardeners noticed a beetle attack in eight of the oldest specimens, three of them suffering irreparable damage. Green iguanas from the garden eat the fruits of this species.

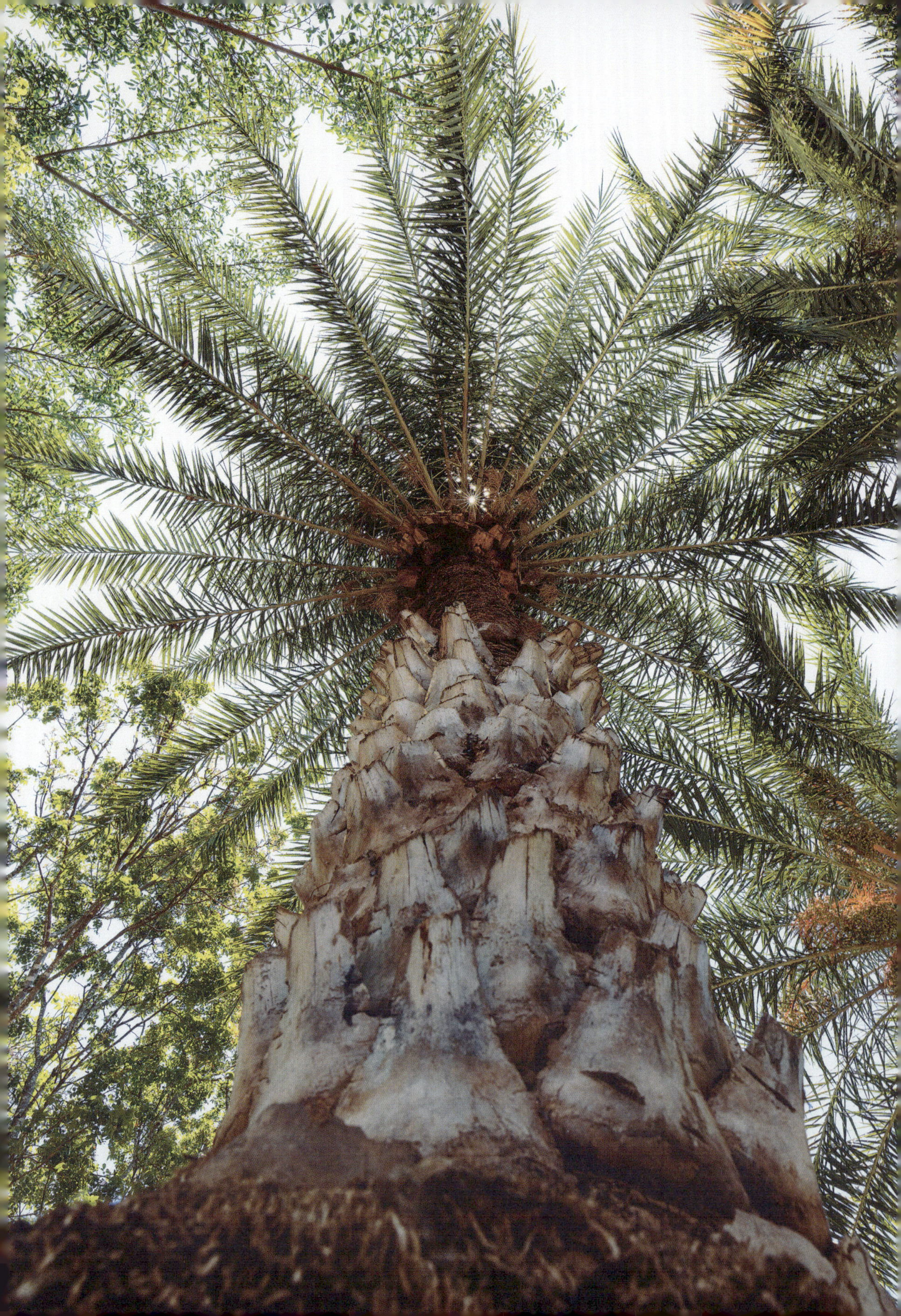

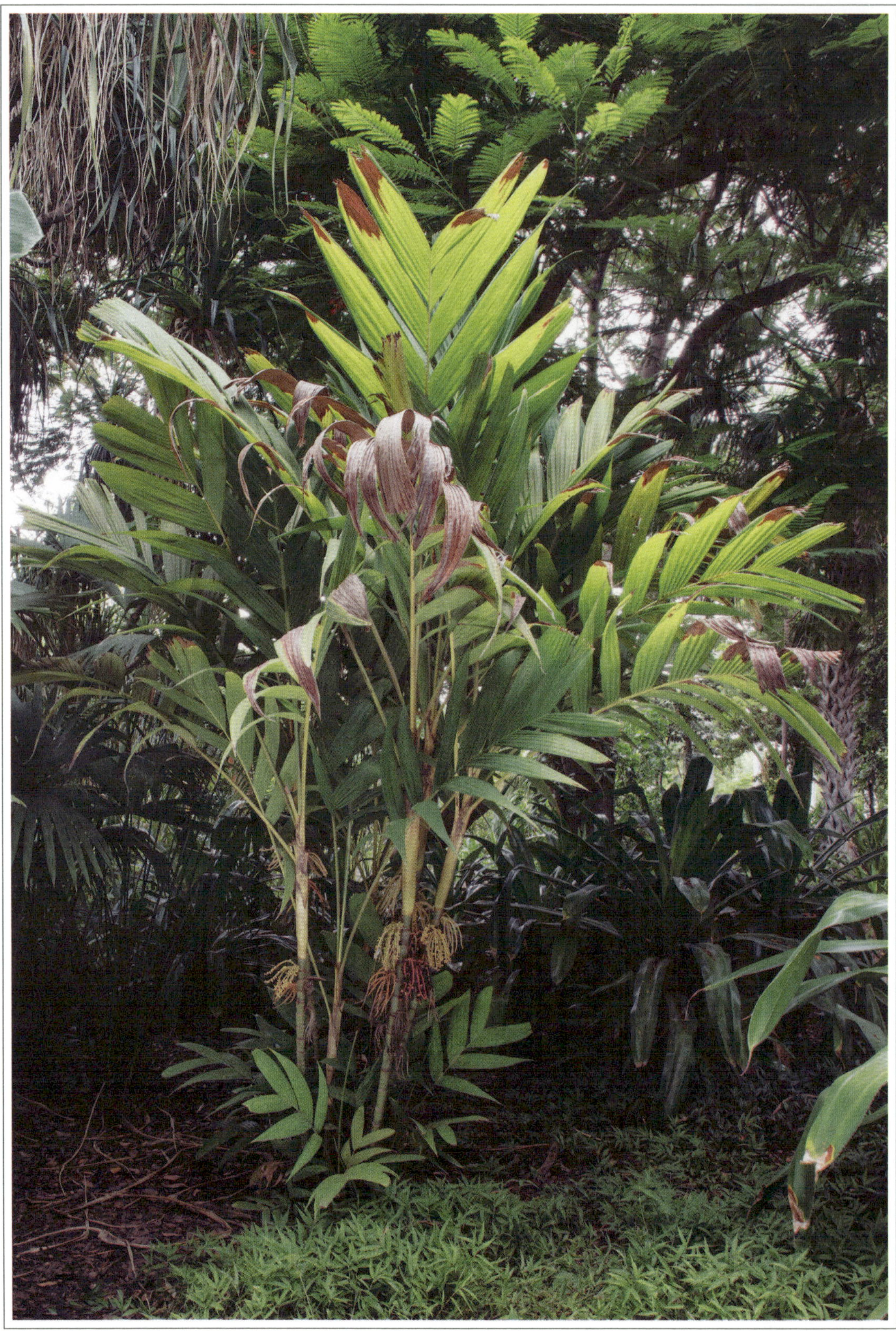

62
IVORY CANE PALM

Pinanga coronata (Blume ex Mart.) Blume

Status: Assessment of global conservation status required
Distribution: Indonesia and Malaysia

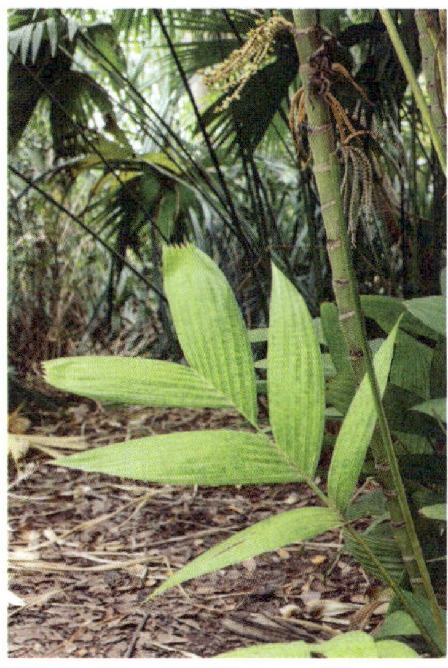
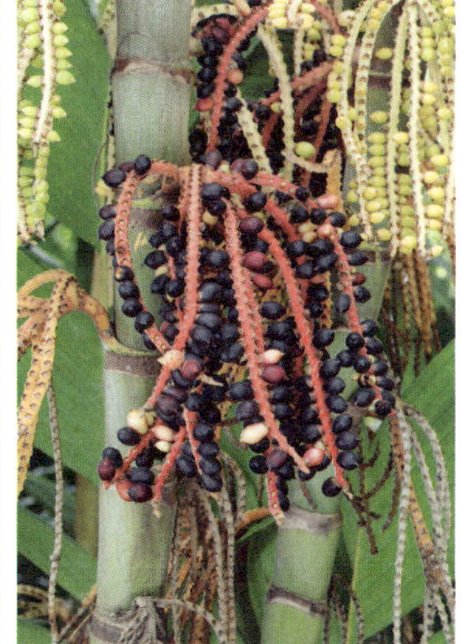

1. Leaf. 2. Ripe fruits.

A small palm that fits into any garden, *Pinanga coronata* is a popular palm in cultivation. The stems, from two to 10 feet tall, are tightly clustered, the leaves are irregularly divided, and the leaf bases are ivory-colored. The fruit clusters, which hang below the leaves, have bright pink branches and black fruits. The seeds are dispersed by several kinds of birds and by the Asian palm civet, an agile, nocturnal, cat-sized mammal of the weasel family that can easily climb palms to feed on their fruits.

Carlos Murillo Depraect appreciated this rare plant very much, but it was very difficult to acquire. Records at the Jardín Botánico Culiacán are not clear, but at least one seed probably arrived more than forty years ago, in the late 1970s, as a donation from the International Palm Society. At that time, it was common for members of the society to exchange seeds. This is no longer done today, and is sometimes even illegal, depending on the species.

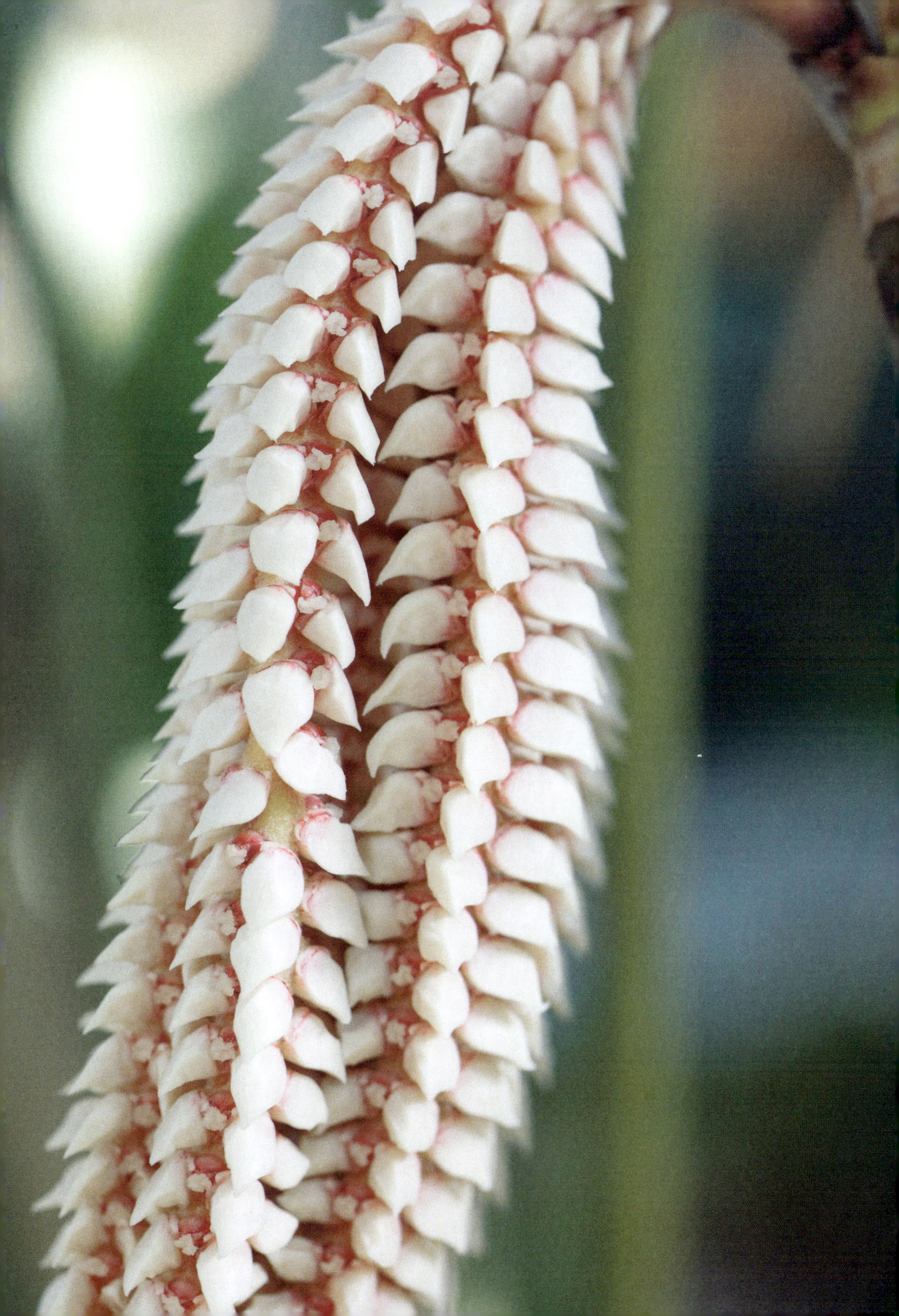

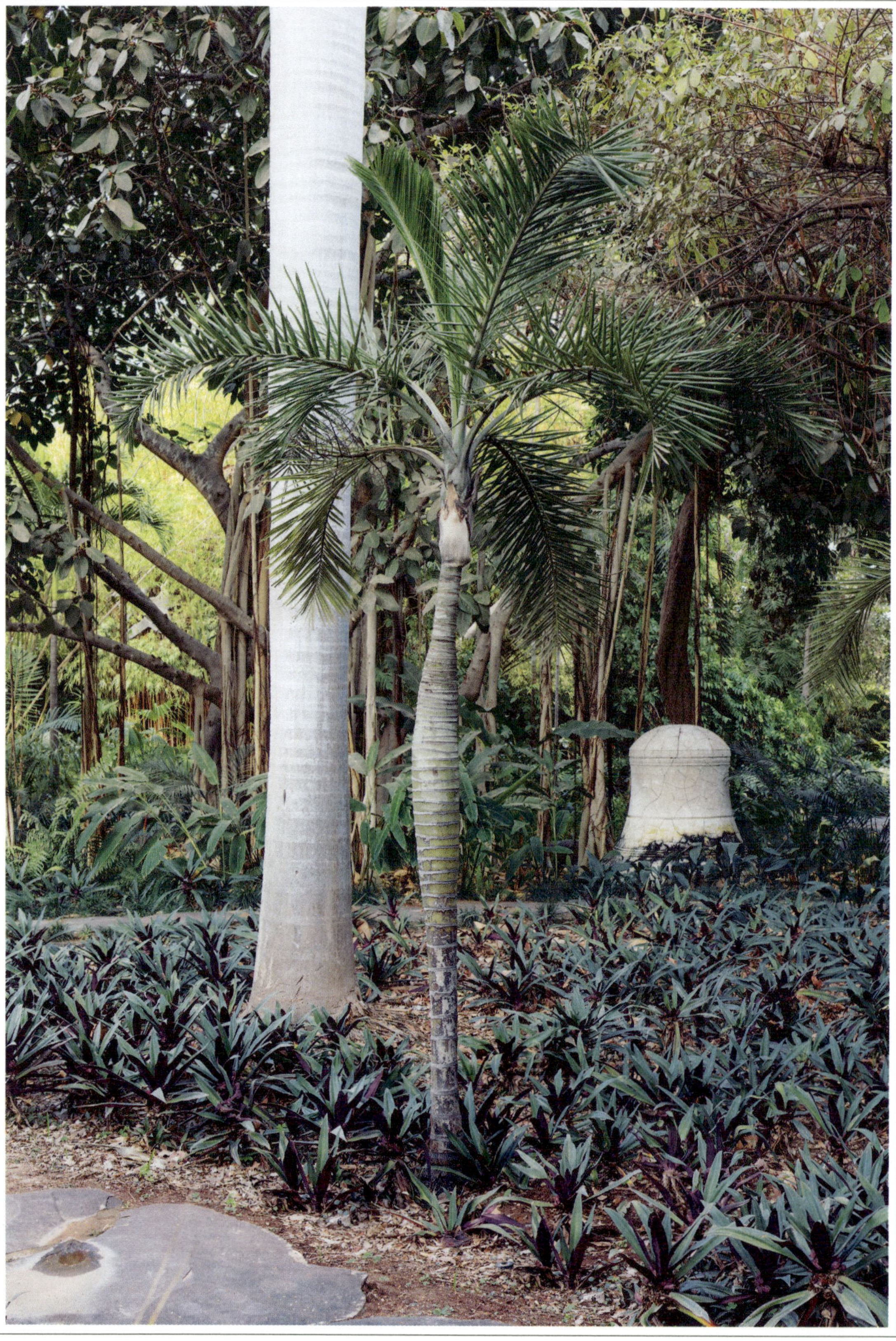

63

BUCCANEER PALM

Pseudophoenix sargentii H. Wendl. ex Sarg.

Status: Assessment of global conservation status required
Distribution: Yucatán Peninsula, Florida, the Bahamas, Cuba, the island of Hispaniola (Haiti and the Dominican Republic), and Dominica

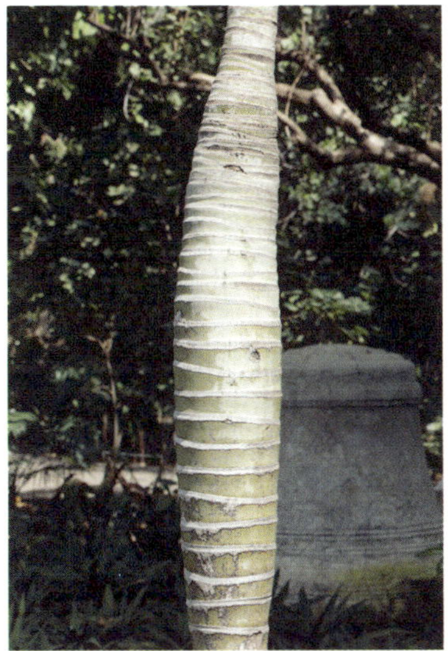

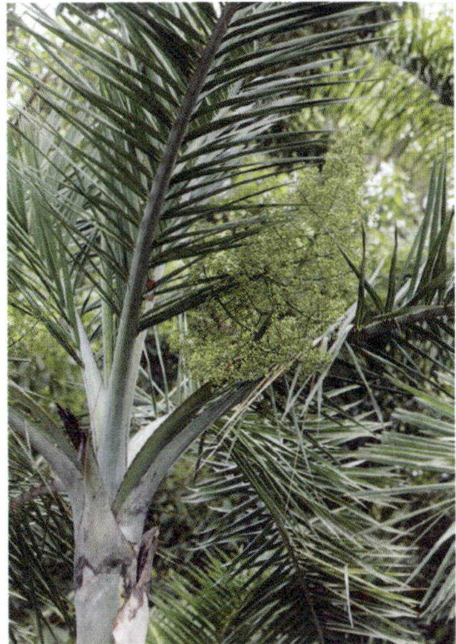

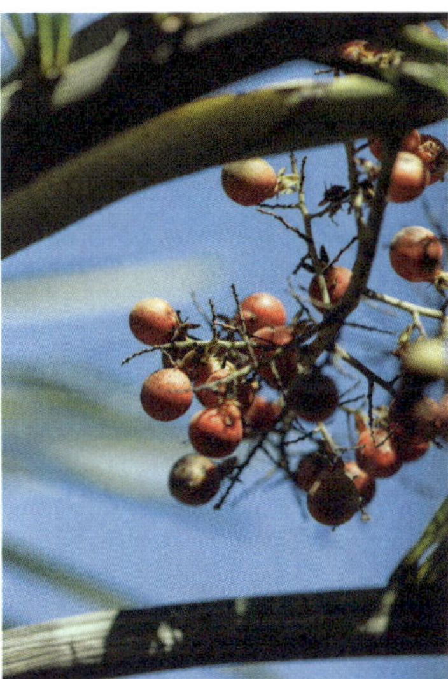

1. Trunk. 2. Leaves. 3. Ripe fruits.

This lovely medium-sized palm has a solitary, whitish trunk that grows up to 13 feet tall. In the wild, *Pseudophoenix sargentii* occurs naturally near a coastline, so it is a popular choice for dry, sandy, or beachfront gardens. It is tolerant of salt spray and drought, but will grow faster and more luxuriantly in good soil, with regular irrigation. This species bears a few stiff, slightly waxy leaves and large clusters of juicy red fruits. Unfortunately, in many areas, its coastal habitat has been destroyed to make room for tourist resorts, or the mature palms have been removed for use in landscaping.

The Jardín Botánico Culiacán has had a specimen of *Pseudophoenix sargentii* since 2004, but it is not known how it was acquired. Mexican palm expert Miguel Ángel García Bielma was able to observe this rare species in its natural habitat in the Yucatán—an estuary with flamingos—where he collected plants and seeds for the botanical garden.

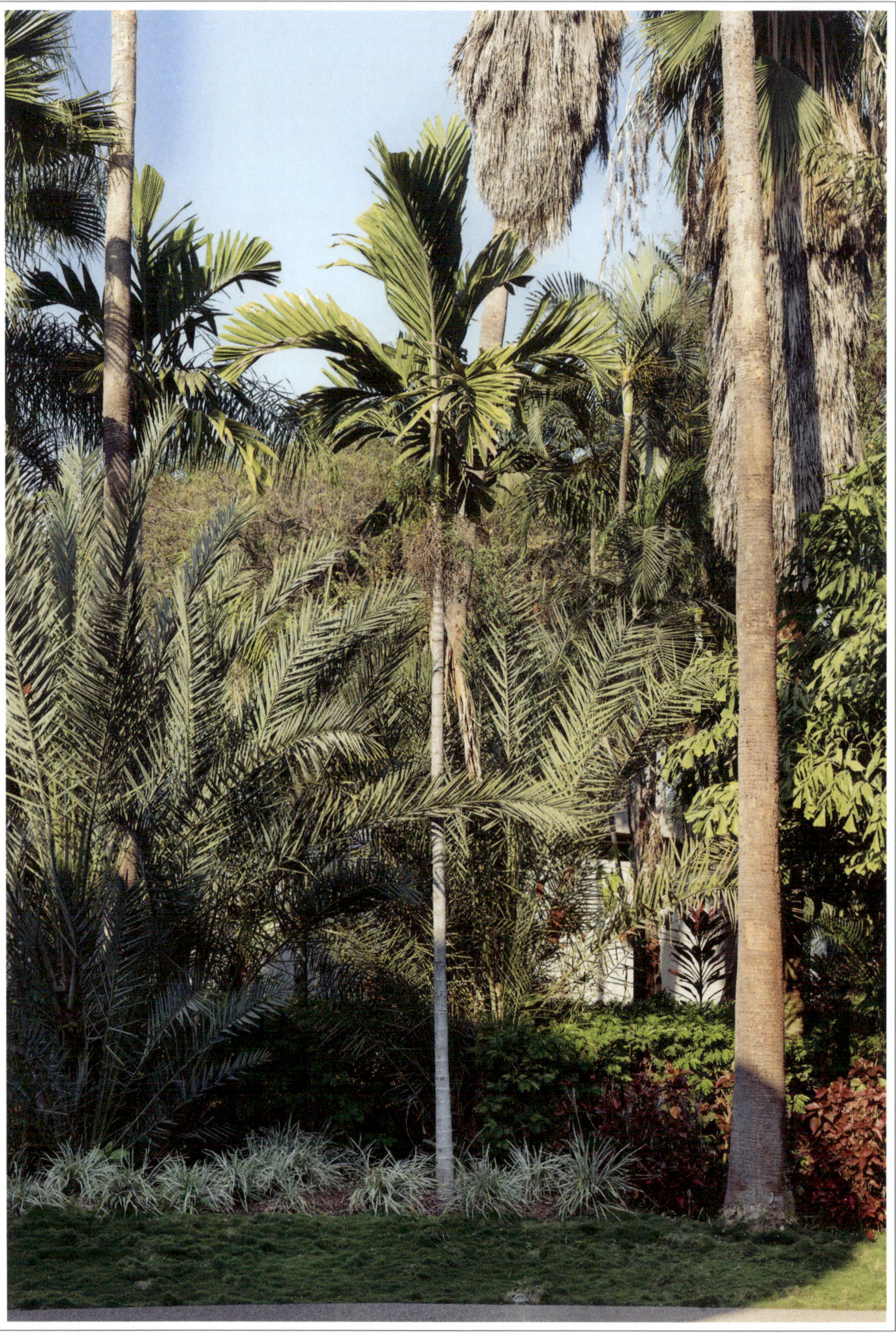

64

SOLITAIRE PALM

Ptychosperma elegans (R.Br.) Blume

Status: Assessment of global conservation status required
Distribution: Northern Australia

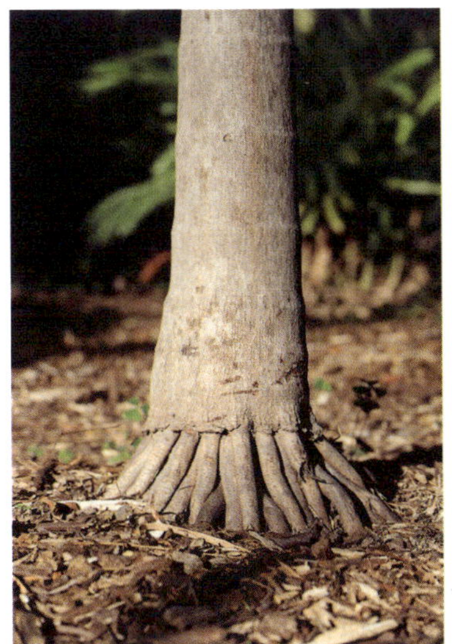
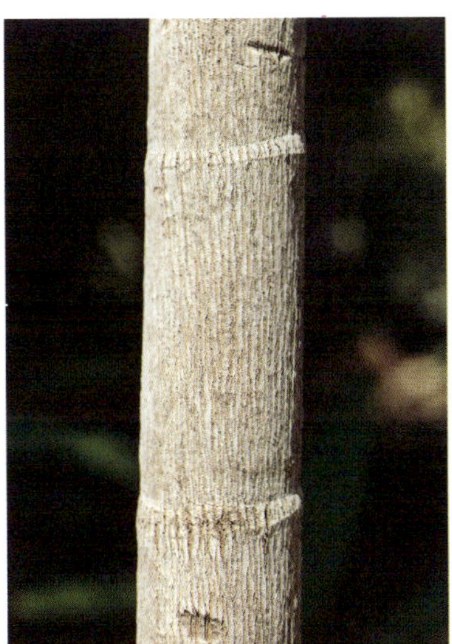
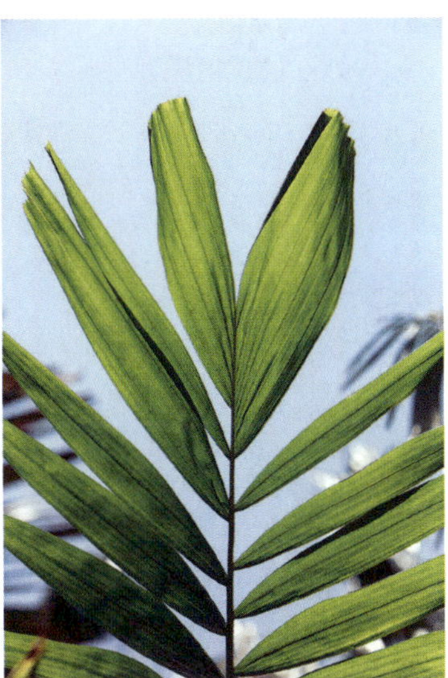

1. Emerging roots. 2. Trunk. 3. Detail of the leaf.

This palm can grow up to 35 feet tall, with a trunk no larger than four inches in diameter. The solitaire palm grows in coastal forests with moderate rainfall. It has been in cultivation since the mid-nineteenth century, prized for its elegant stature, slender trunk, and symmetry. Its trunk is whitish-gray, with very striking dark rings, called foliar scars, running along it. The leaves of *Ptychosperma elegans* are feathery and bright green. It is still a very popular landscape palm in warm areas of the world. The solitaire palm is fast-growing and tolerant of either sun or shade. It is often planted in groups of three, but in nature, the palm is always solitary, not clustering. Small white flowers grow in racemes and birds are fond of the small red fruits that hang below the leaves like large bunches of grapes. Because birds spread the seeds, the palm has become a weed in some parts of the world.

Fifteen years ago, Carlos Murillo Depraect started growing the specimens to be found in the Jardín Botánico Culiacán. Today the garden has more than 40 of them, on view at the Palmetum and the Tropical Rainforest collection.

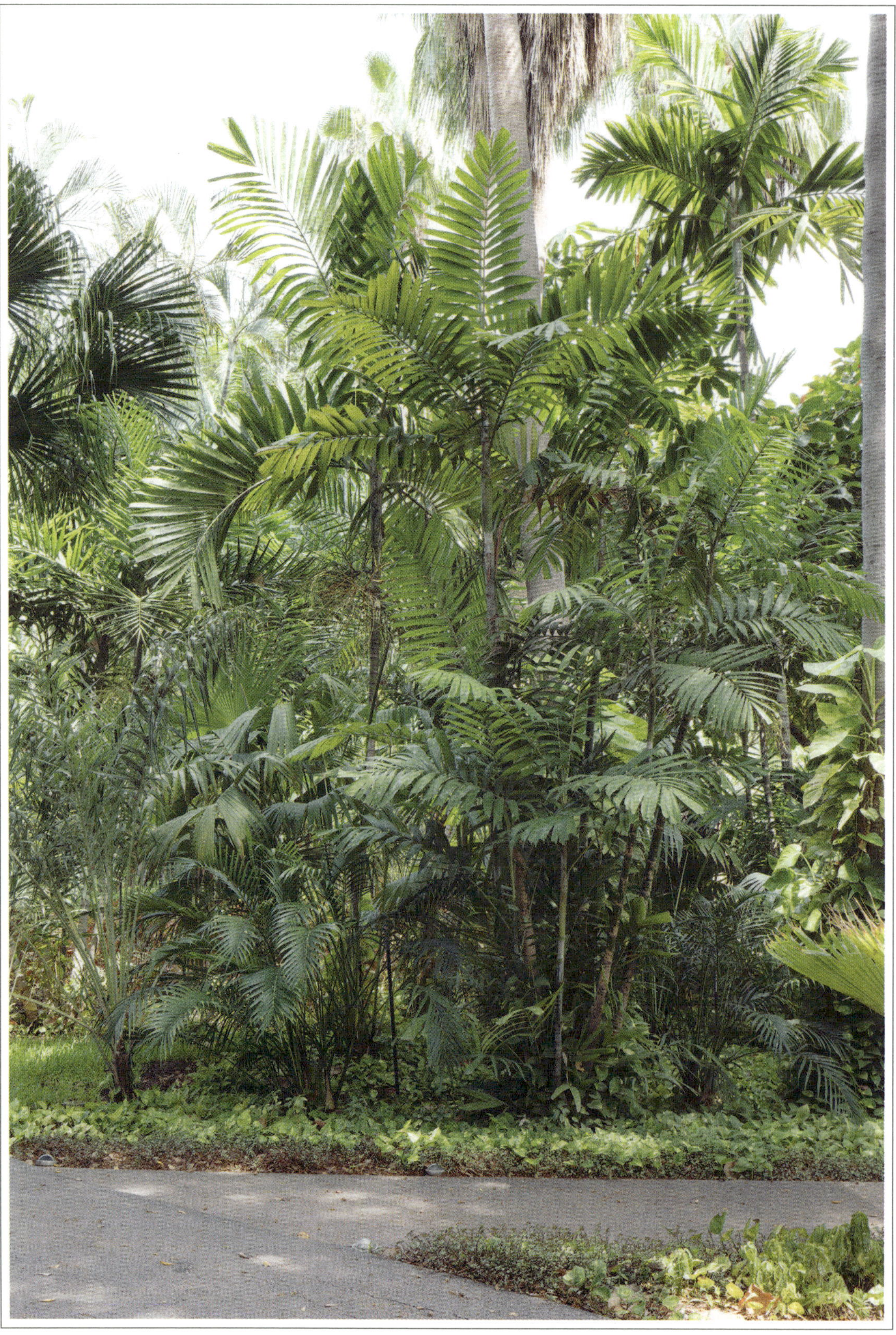

65

MACARTHUR PALM

Ptychosperma macarthurii (H. Wendl. Ex H.J. Veitch) H. Wendl. ex Hook.f.

Status: Assessment of global conservation status required
Distribution: Northern Australia and New Guinea

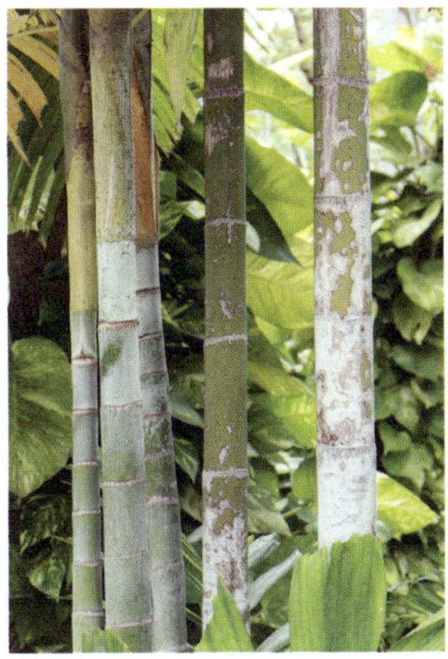

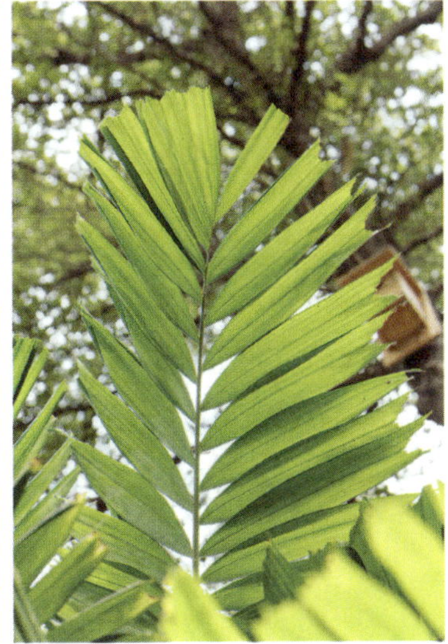

1. Stems. 2. Leaf.

The MacArthur palm is a clustering palm with stems up to 26 feet tall. This palm was introduced into gardens in the late nineteenth century and has been a popular palm ever since, for obvious reasons: it is a graceful palm, with numerous slender stems and clusters of bright red fruits. This palm is an asset to any garden, but it is intolerant of drought. It has escaped and become a weed in some parts of the tropics.

The species has been cultivated for more than 30 years at the Bachigualato ranch, originally under the care of Carlos Murillo Depraect. It was brought to the Jardín Botánico Culiacán in 1994. The palm is relatively new in landscape design, since it is expensive and difficult to acquire.

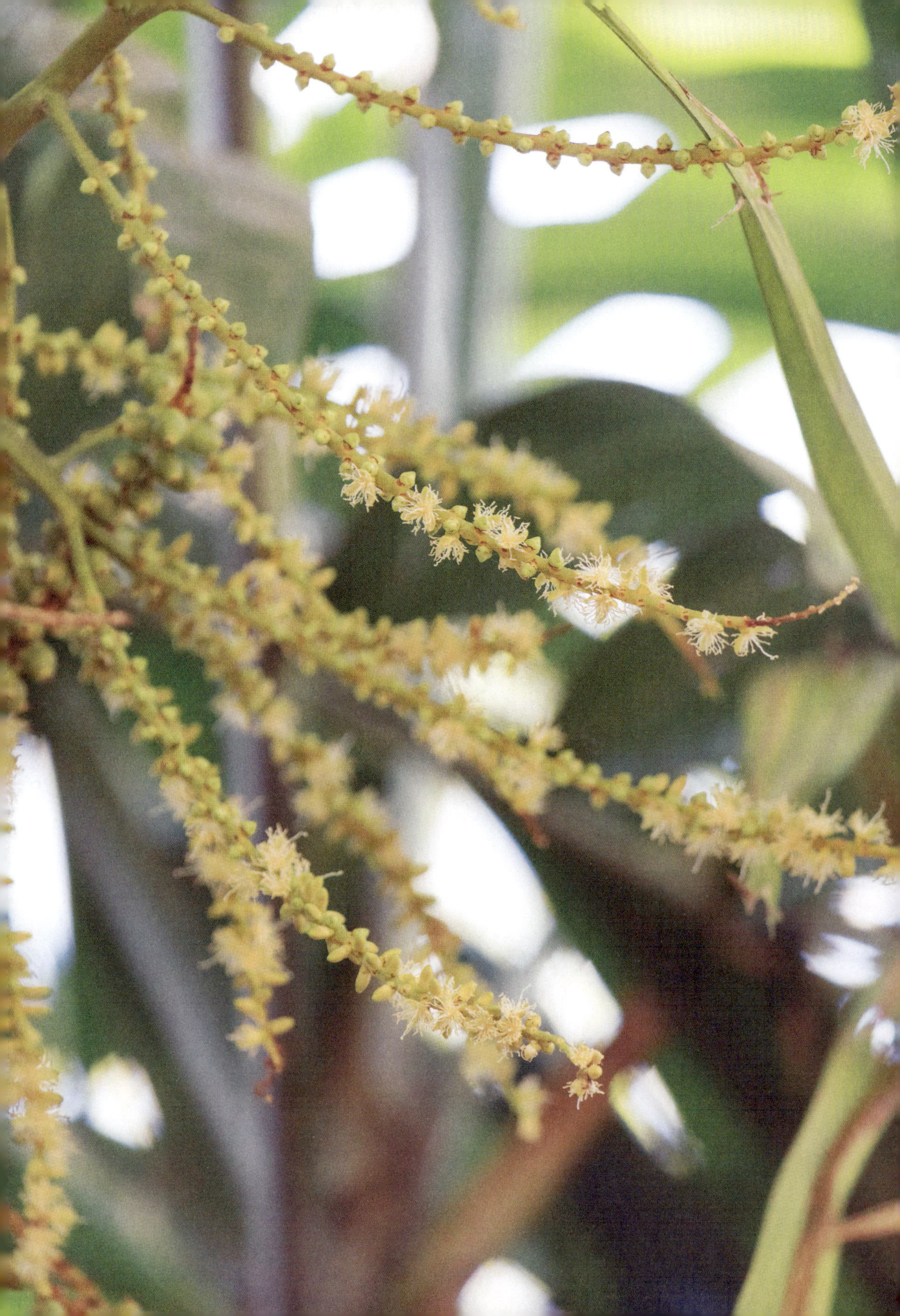

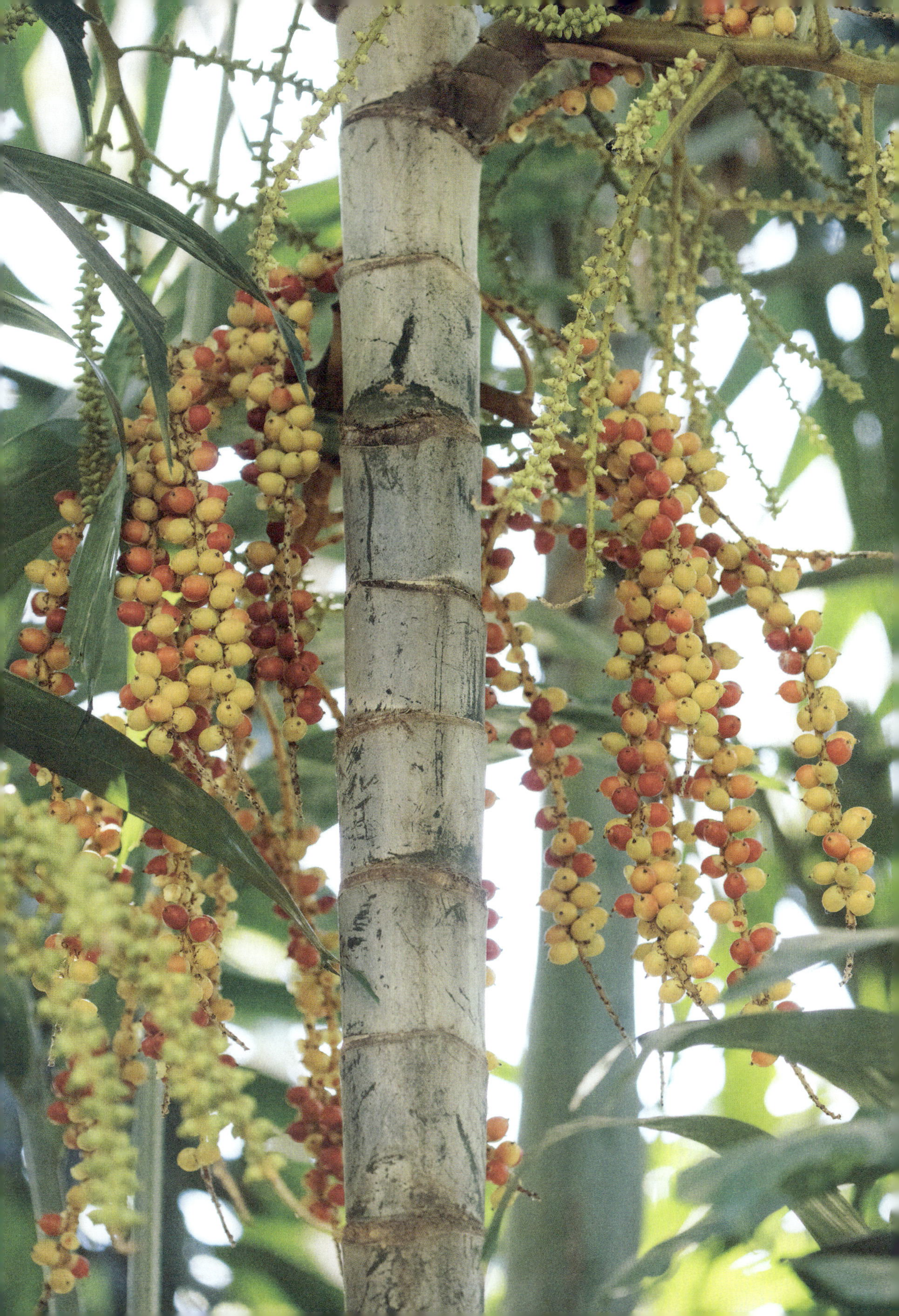

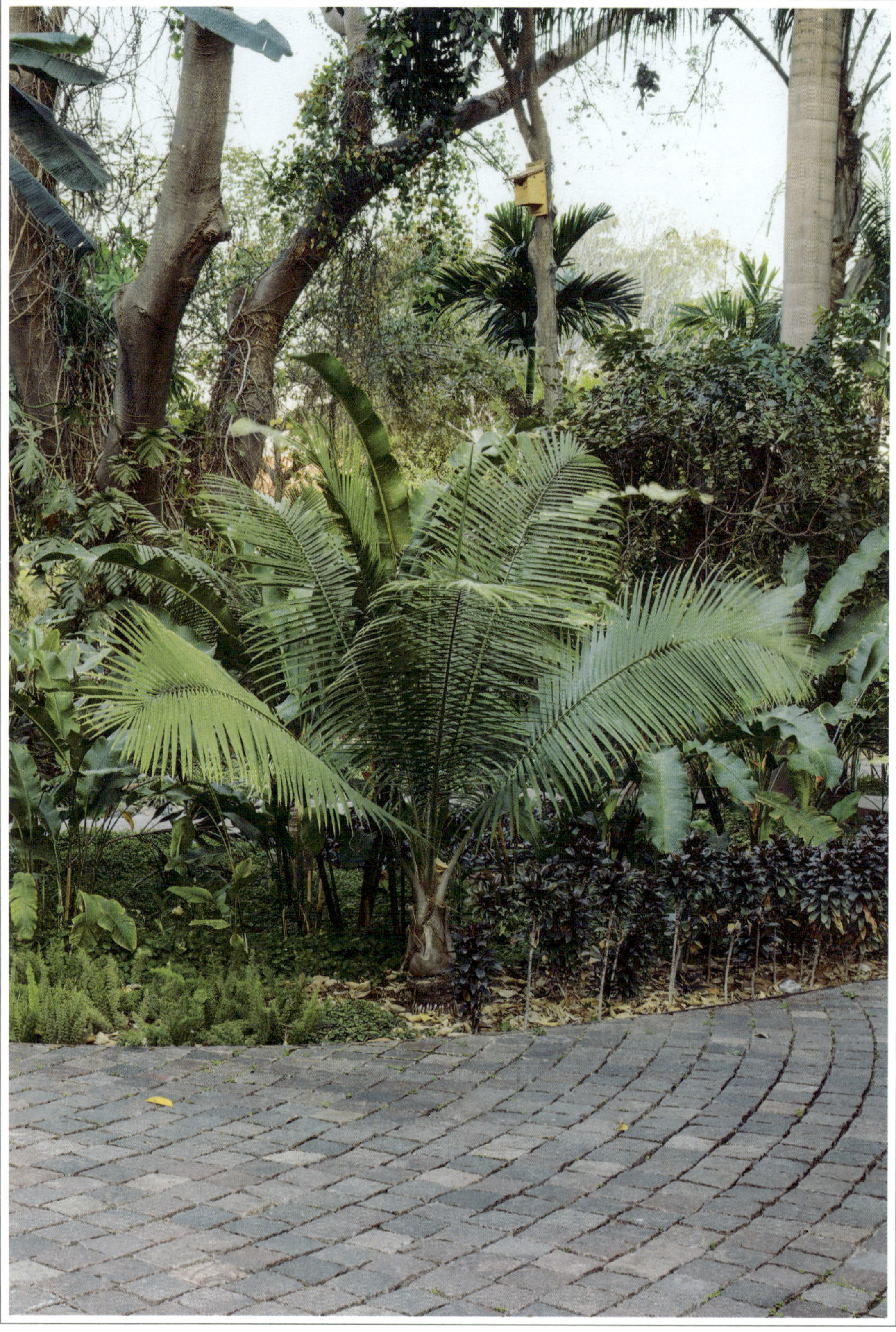

66

MAJESTIC PALM

Ravenea rivularis Jum. & H. Perrier

Status: Designated as Vulnerable on the IUCN Red List
Distribution: Endemic to Madagascar

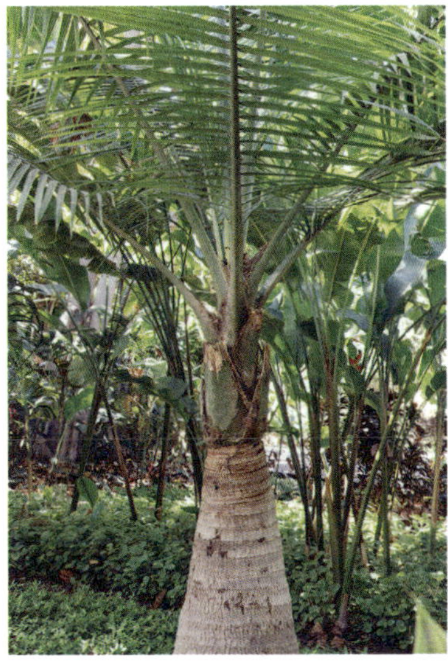

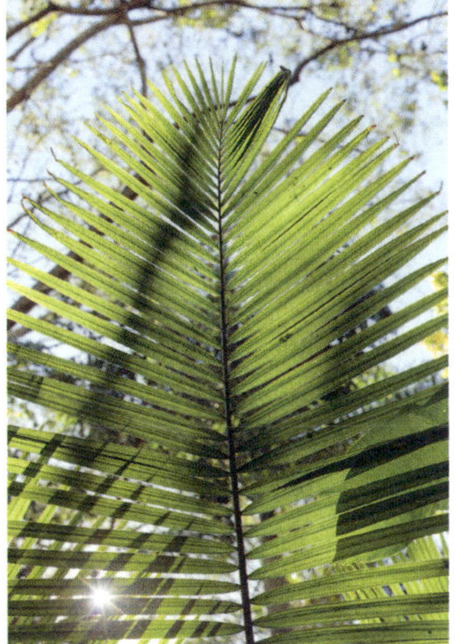

1. Trunk with leaf bases. 2. Leaf.

In its natural habitat, this species grows up to 65 feet tall, with a thick trunk and a full crown of graceful leaves. The fruits are small and red and borne on airy, branched stalks. The name *rivularis* means "of rivers" and offers a hint of this palm's natural habitat: wetlands, swamps, and river banks. *Ravenea rivularis* is grown by the tens of thousands all over the world. It is often sold as a potted houseplant, with no indication to the buyer that the palm is a giant that will outgrow its space.

The specimens of *Ravenea rivularis* at the Jardín Botánico Culiacán come from exchanges made with the seed bank of the International Palm Society around 1994. One of these palms, more than twenty-five years old at the time, died in 2013, during floods caused by Hurricane Manuel.

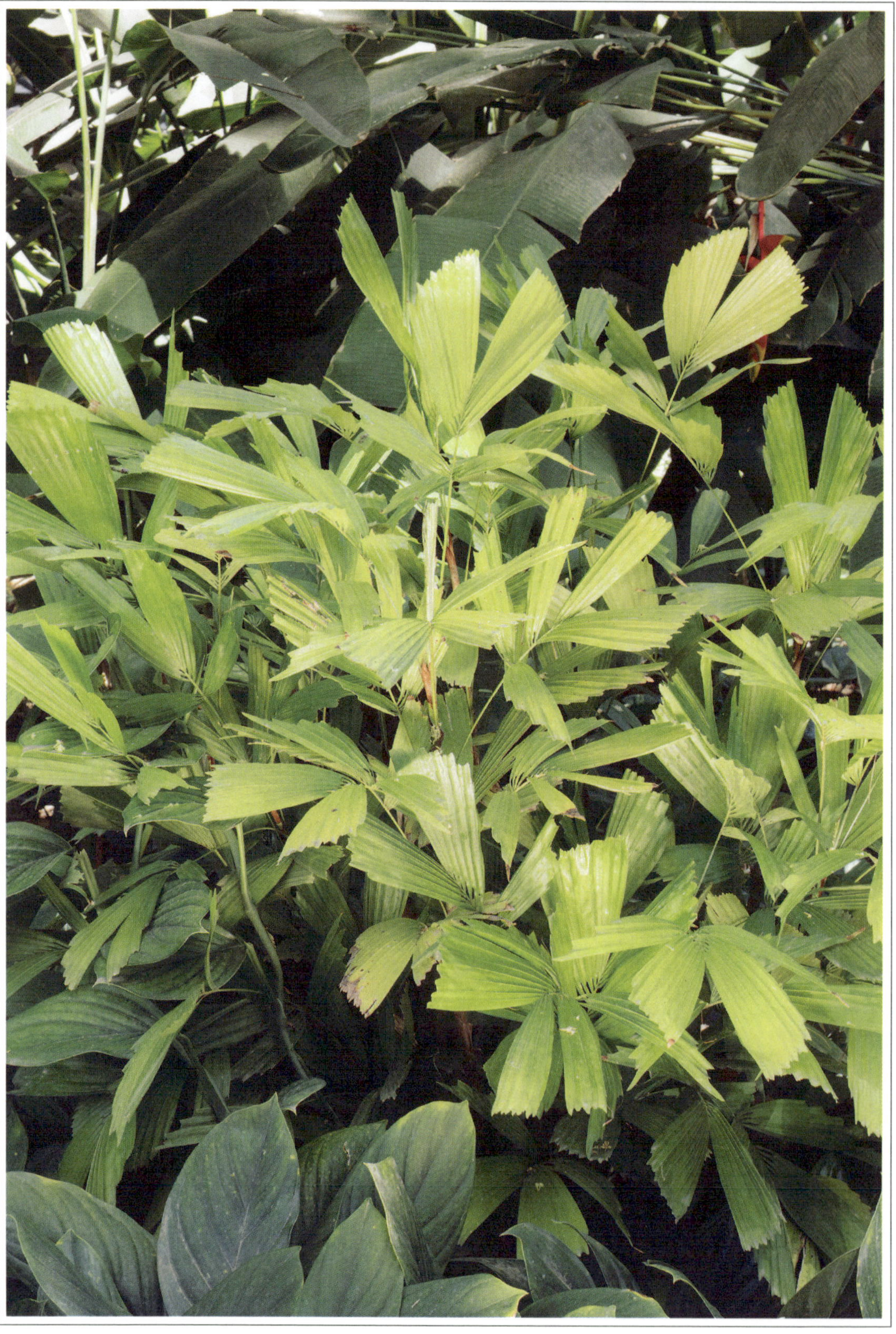

67

WINDOW PALM, WINDOWPANE PALM

Reinhardtia gracilis (H. Wendl.) Burret

Status: Assessment of global conservation status required
Distribution: Mexico, Central America, and Colombia

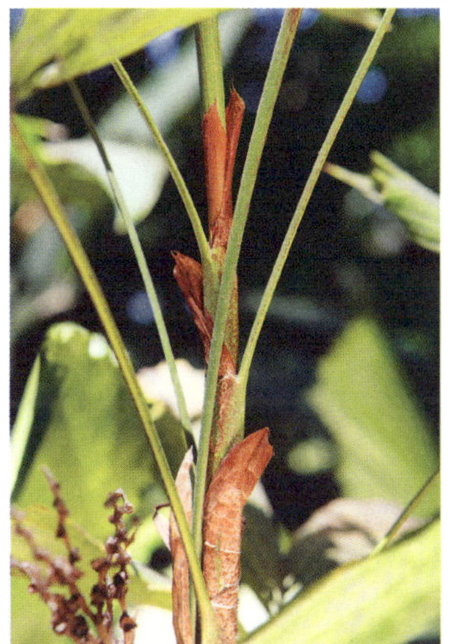
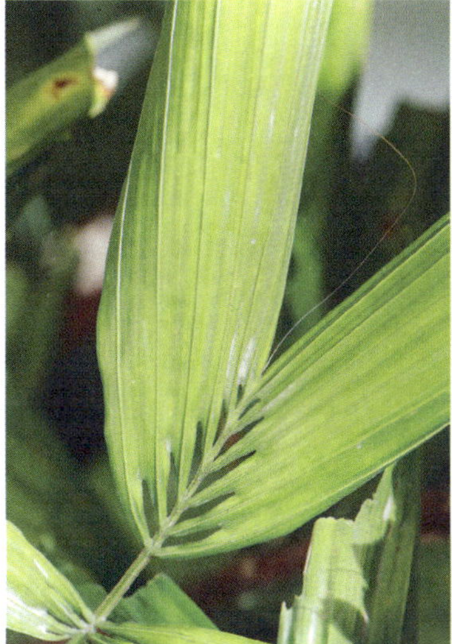
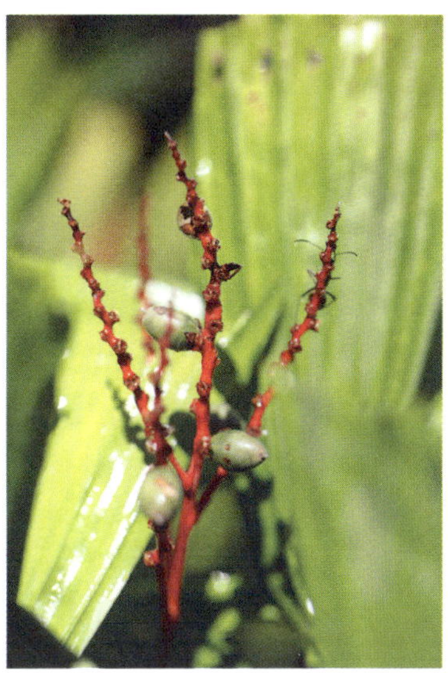

1. Petiole and leaf bases. 2. 'Windows' of the leaf. 3. Unripe fruits.

This delicate clustering palm has stems less than 6.5 feet tall. Although a perfect size for indoor cultivation, the palm rarely thrives outside of its rainforest home. It is uncommon in cultivation. *Reinhardtia gracilis* is best known for its unusual leaves, which are divided into large fishtail-shaped segments: at the base of these segments there are small perforations or "windows." No other palm has windows like these, and only two of the other five species of *Reinhardtia* have windows in their leaves, but they are smaller and less prominent. The function of the windows, if there is any, is unknown. The flower stalks are produced among the leaves. The fruits turn black when they are ripe, at which time the stalk turns bright pink. This contrast of black and pink (or red) is attractive to fruit-eating birds.

While searching for *Reinhardtia gracilis* specimens, botanists from the Jardín Botánico Culiacán had to travel to the tropical rainforests of Veracruz. It took them all day to find the species, and it was almost nightfall when they finally encountered the little palms. Conditions for collecting were difficult: with the deep fog and darkness, they had to be very careful not to lose them.

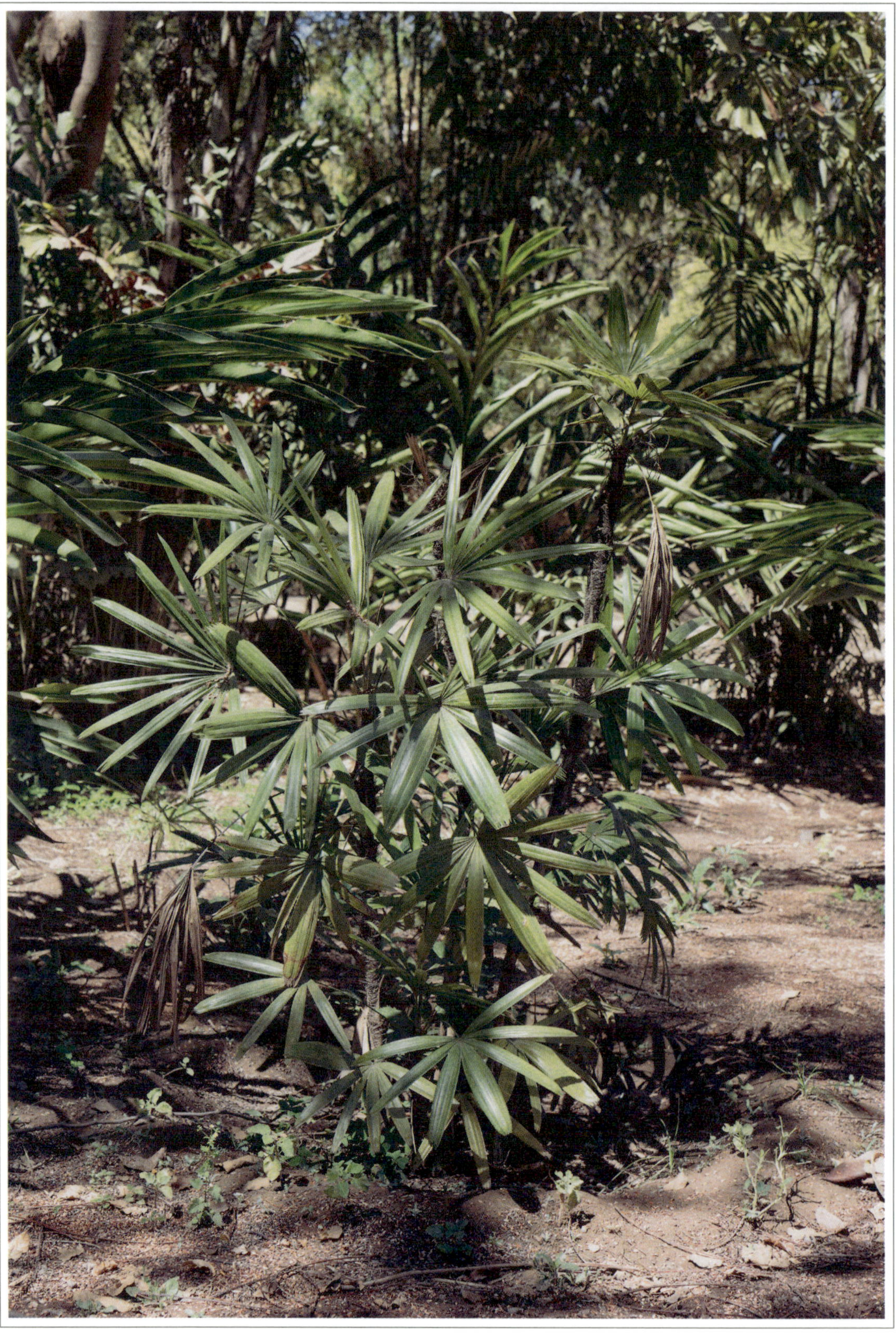

68

BROADLEAF LADY PALM

Rhapis excelsa (Thunb.) Henry

Status: Assessment of global conservation status required
Distribution: Southern China and Vietnam

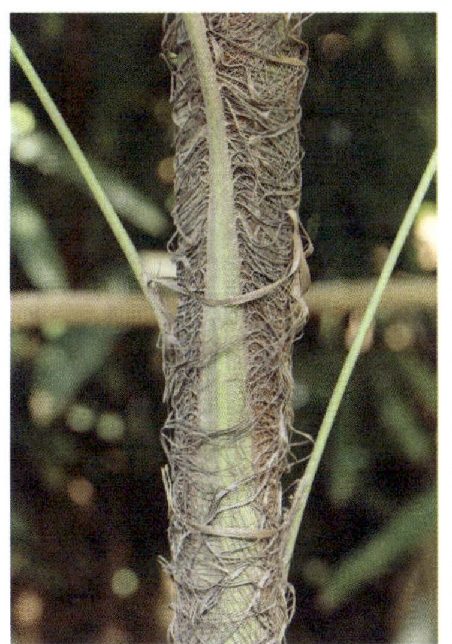

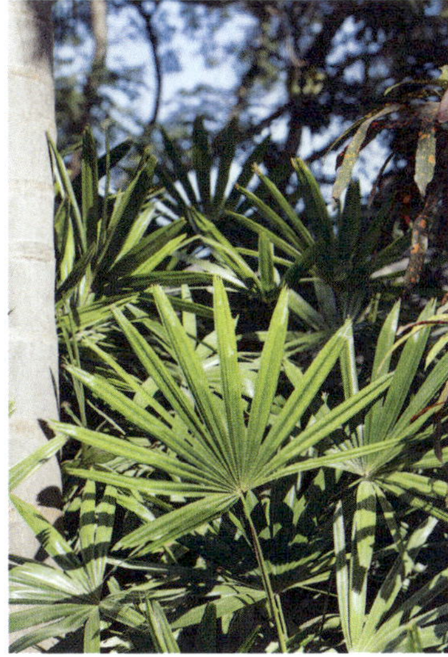

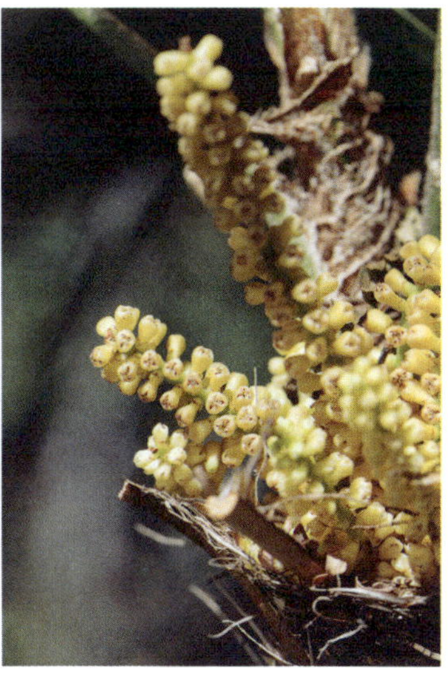

1. Petiole and leaf bases. 2. Leaf. 3. Flowers.

This small clustering palm, up to 13 feet tall, is cultivated all over the world. It has been a popular houseplant in Japan for many centuries, and the Japanese have given different names to cultivated varieties, many of which are variegated and dwarf. The name of the genus is from the Greek word for "rod" or "stick," in reference to the fact that the stems of these palms were used in China to make walking sticks and umbrella handles, which were exported to Europe in the nineteenth century.

Carlos Murillo Depraect has designed and built numerous houses and gardens since the 1960s. One of his favorite species was precisely *Rhapis excelsa*, because of volume and its tropical appearance. Today some of the specimens he planted still survive in the gardens he designed.

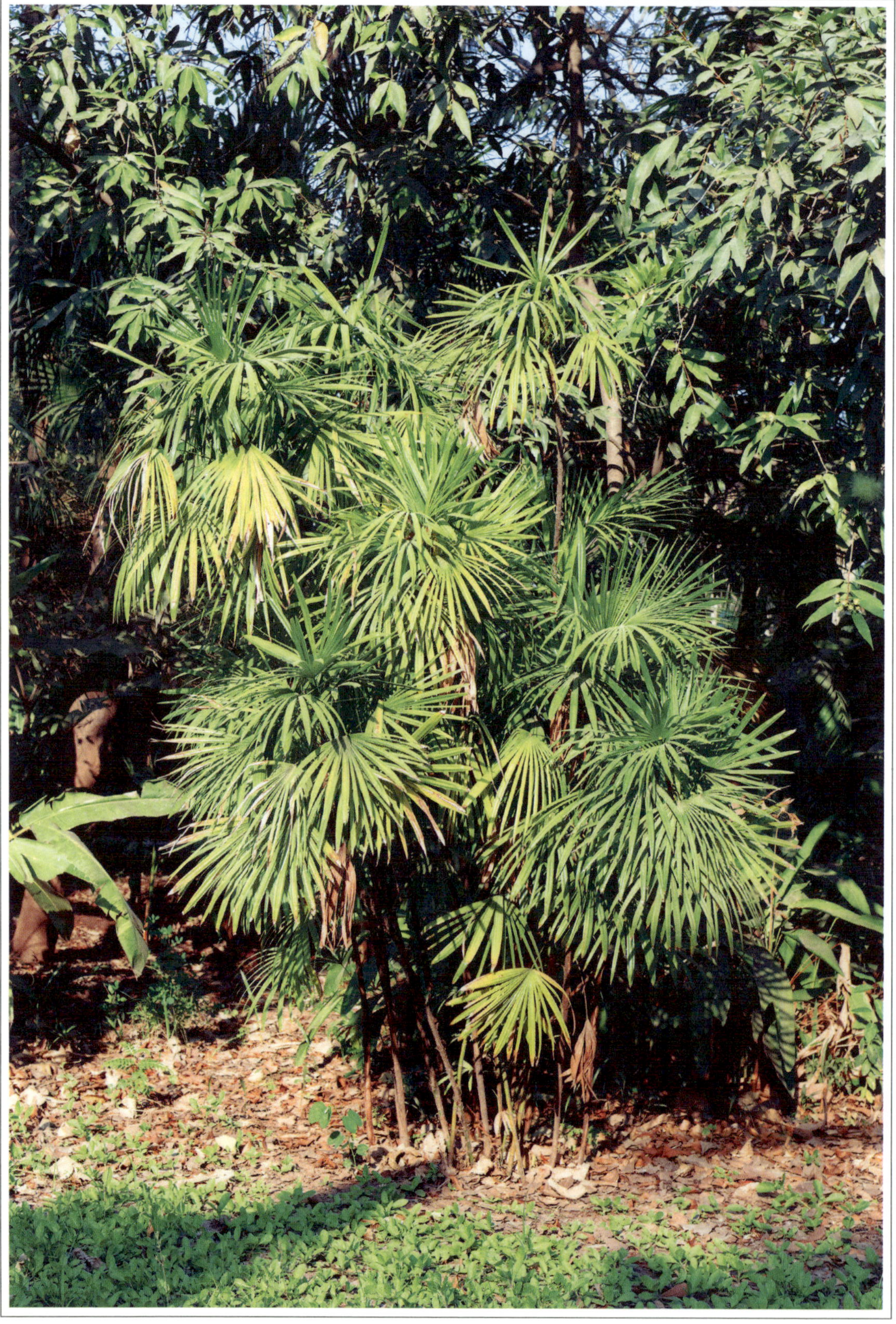

69

LADY PALM

Rhapis humilis Blume

Status: Assessment of global conservation status required
Distribution: Endemic to southern China

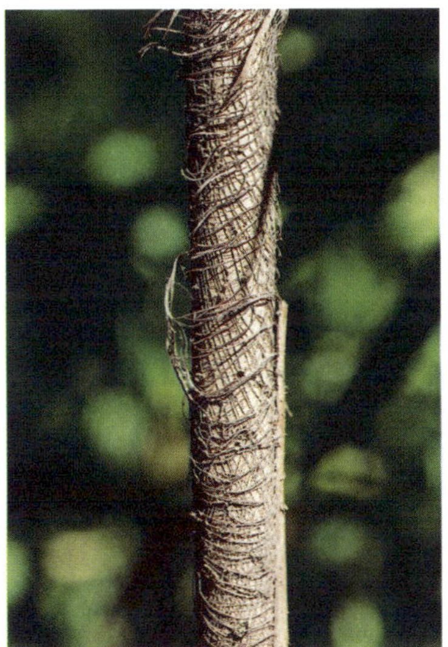

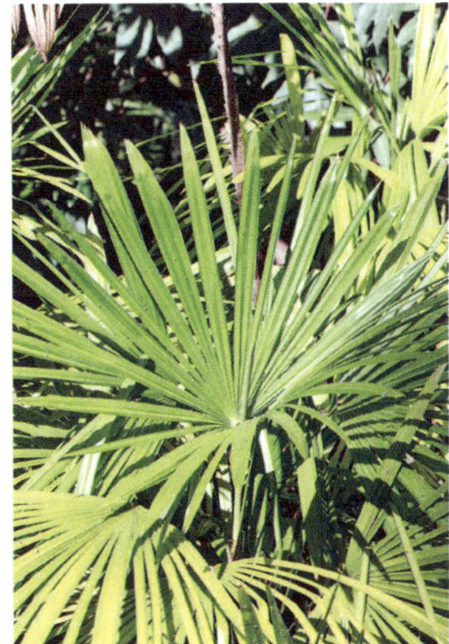

1. Trunk with leaf bases. 2. Leaves.

Somewhat larger than its cousin *Rhapis excelsa*, *Rhapis humilis* is still a small clustering palm that may reach up to 16 feet tall. It occurs in montane rainforests. *Rhapis humilis* is widely grown all over the world, often as a hedge or screen. The dried brown leaf sheaths remain attached to the stems for a long time, but eventually fall to reveal green, bamboo-like stems. The flowers are borne on short clusters among the leaves, and the fruits, seldom produced in cultivation, are pea-sized and pale yellow in color.

Records of how the first three specimens of *Rhapis humilis* were acquired by the Jardín Botánico Culiacán are not clear, but the personnel at the garden think that they may have arrived around the late 1990s. It is curious that, although the palm is native to China, more specimens came later from the Mexican state of Guerrero.

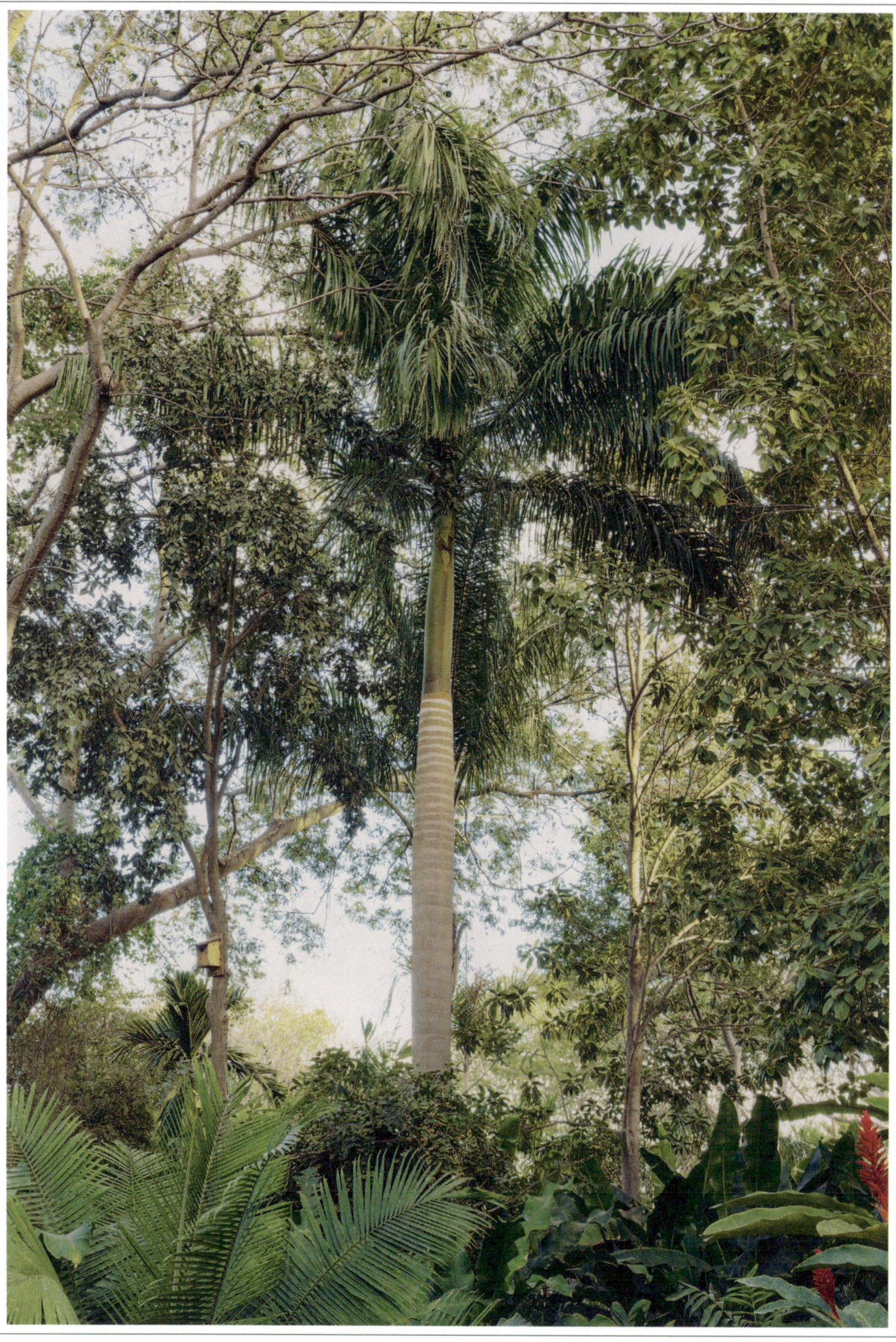

70

ROYAL PALM

Roystonea dunlapiana P.H. Allen

Status: Assessment of global conservation status required
Distribution: From Mexico to Central America

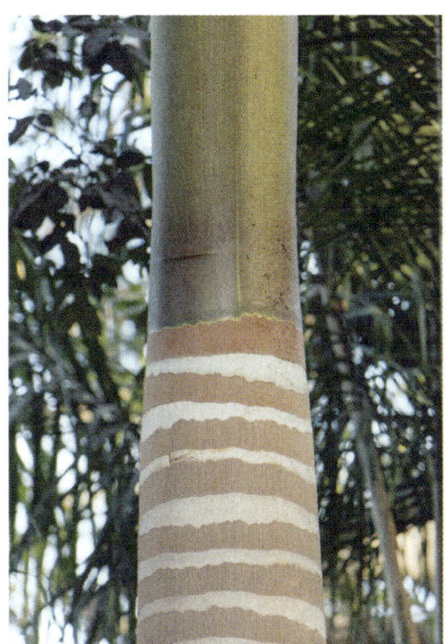

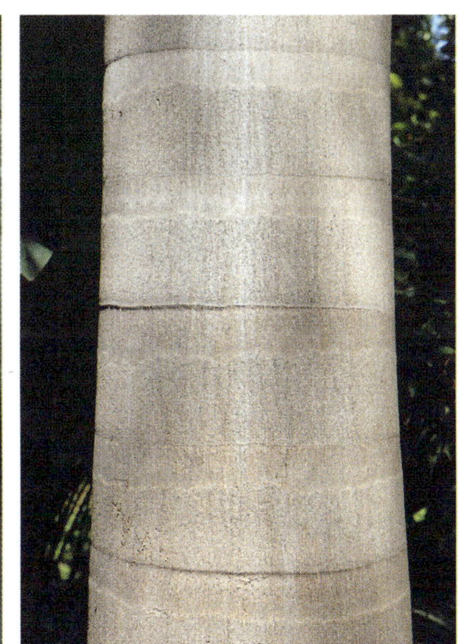

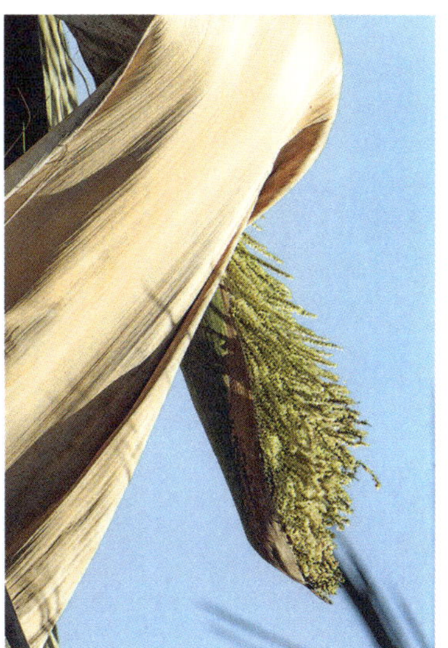

1. Trunk with leaf bases. 2. Trunk. 3. Inflorescence.

The royal palm grows to 65 feet tall in swamps and coastal estuaries along the Caribbean coast of the state of Quintana Roo in Mexico and in Central America. It is a single-stemmed palm with long pinnate leaves and large airy flower stalks. The small whitish flowers give way to purple fruits, which are widely consumed by birds, bats, and other mammals. It is seldom seen in cultivation.

Roystonea dunlapiana is very well represented in the Palmetum of the Jardín Botánico Culiacán, where there are more than 20 specimens. All of them come from a donation made in 2011 by the Centro de Investigación Científica de Yucatán (Scientific Research Center of Yucatán), so they had to be transported more than 1,550 miles, from Mérida, in the state of Yucatán, to Culiacán. This research center protects and reproduces this species for ornamental purposes.

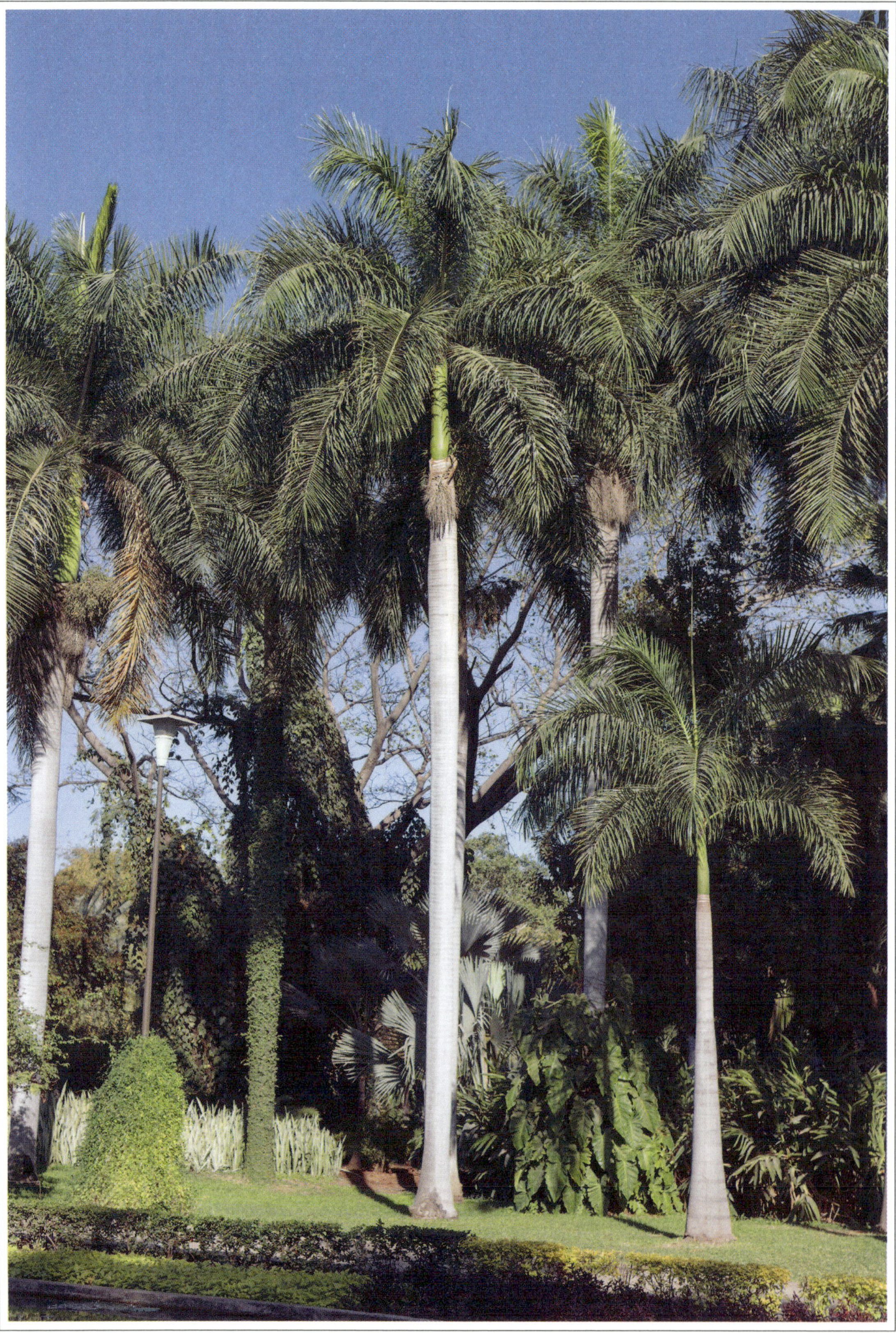

71

CUBAN ROYAL PALM

Roystonea regia (Kunth) O.F. Cook

Status: Assessment of global conservation status required
Distribution: Mexico, Cuba, the Cayman Islands, Florida, and the Bahamas

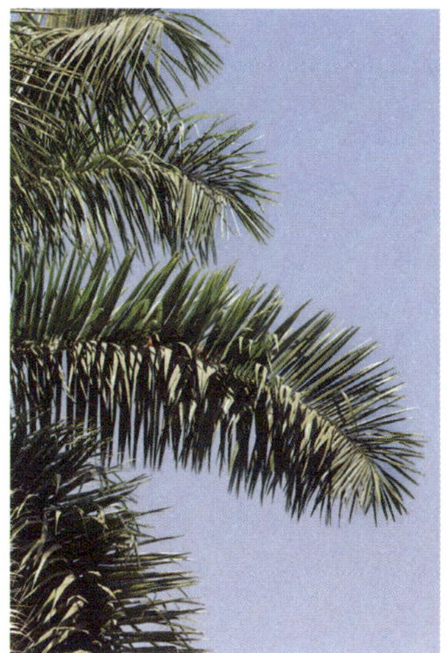

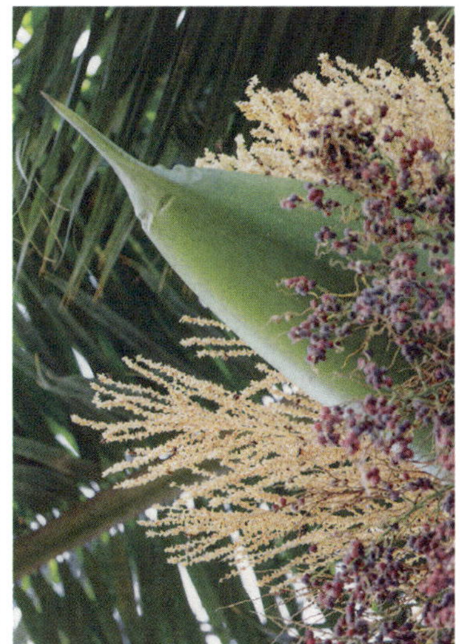

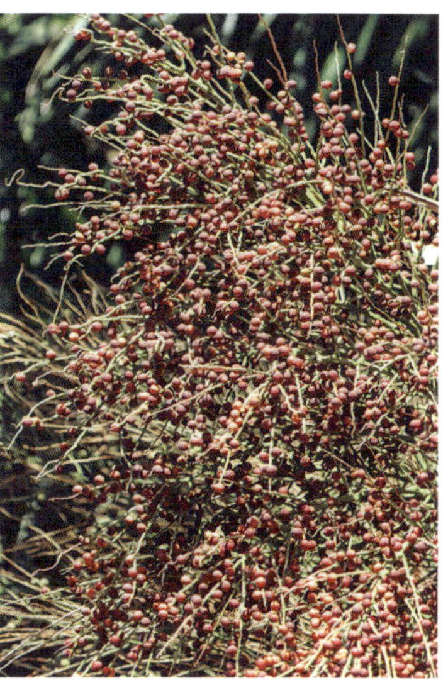

1. Leaf. 2. Bract revealing flowers. 3. Fruits.

This species occurs naturally in lowland forests, where it can grow up to 100 feet tall. It is widely used in landscaping throughout the tropics, being prized for its stately white columnar trunk and its long graceful leaves. It is the national tree of Cuba, and the Cubans make more use of this palm than of any other. The wood is used for constructing houses, as are the large leaf bases, which are also used as waterproof wrappers for bales of tobacco. The palm heart is edible and of the highest quality. The leaves are used for thatch roofing. Fresh fruits are cut from palms to use as food for pigs, and the pork from pigs fed on a diet of oily *Roystonea* fruits is said to be especially tasty.

Carlos Murillo Depraect used *Roystonea regia* specimens for the design of the main pond area at the Jardín Botánico Culiacán. He also used the species around the city of Culiacán, principally to embellish the gardens running along the middle of Boulevard Leyva Solano and adorning the main plaza, where the main buildings of the state and municipal governments are located. All of these palms are still alive.

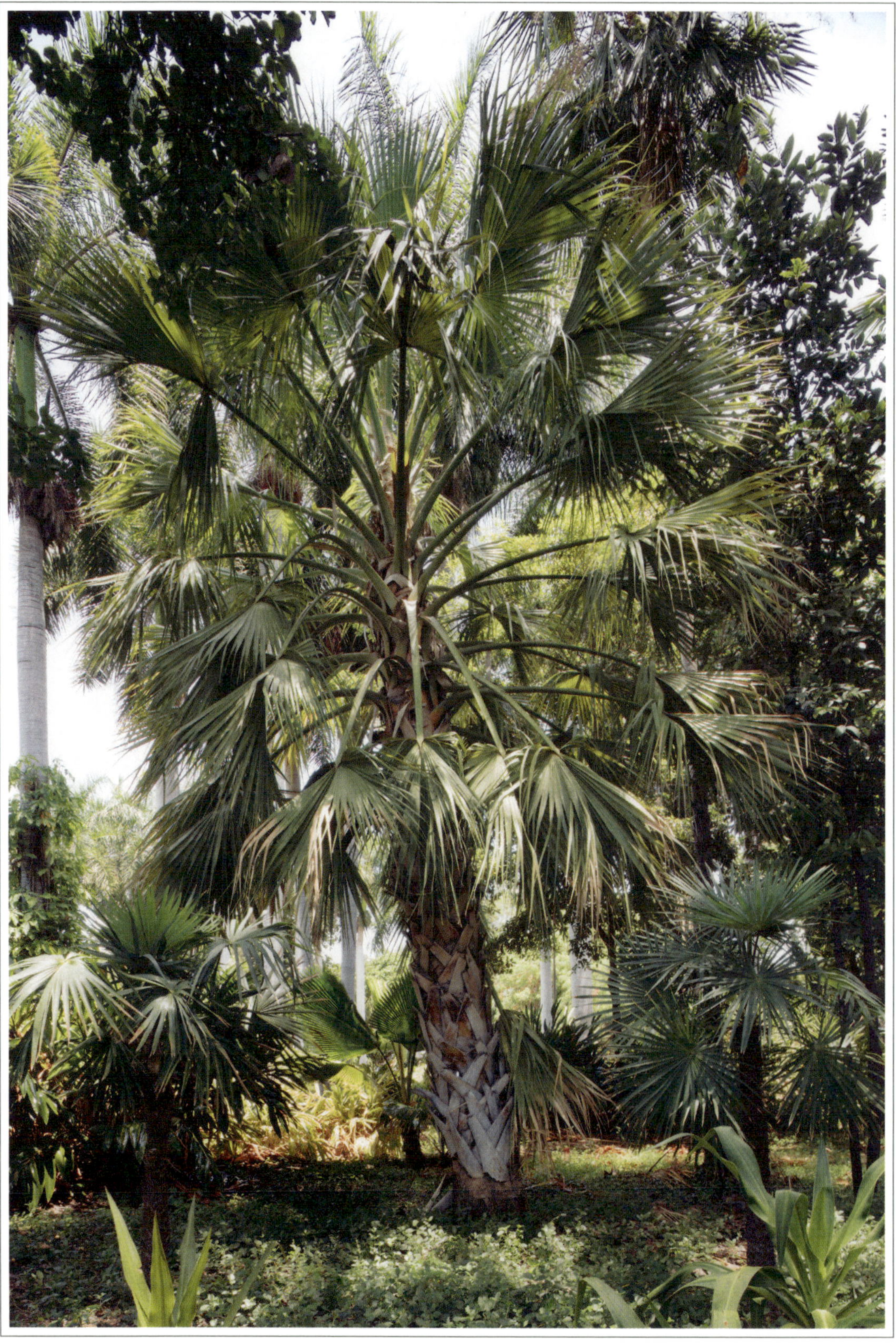

72

PUERTO RICAN HAT PALM

Sabal causiarum (O.F. Cook) Becc.

Status: Designated as Vulnerable on the IUCN Red List
Distribution: Island of Hispaniola (Haiti and the Dominican Republic) and Puerto Rico

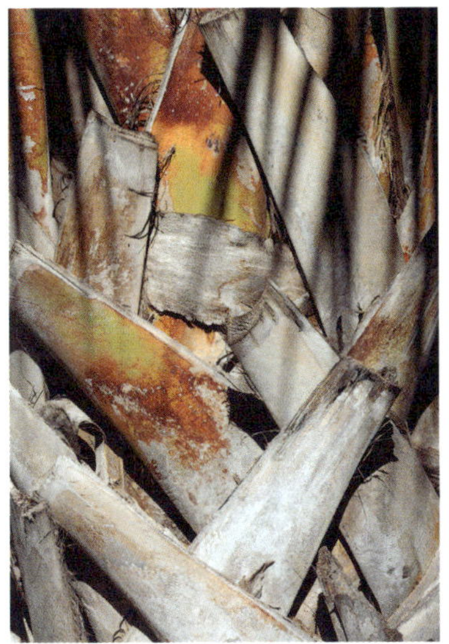

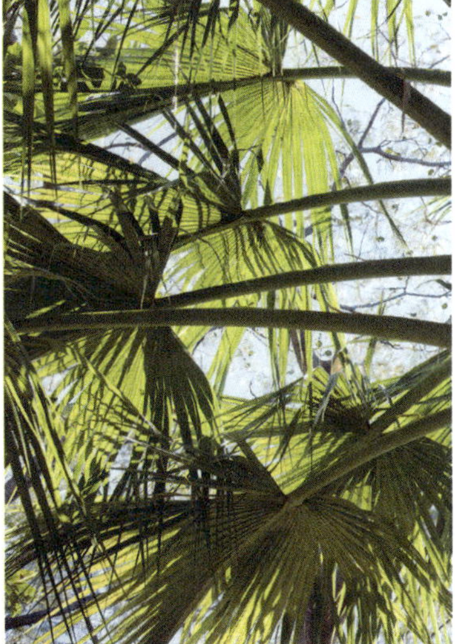

1. Trunk with retained leaf bases. 2. Leaves.

Sabal causiarum is one of the most massive species in the genus. It has a large trunk, which grows up to 24 inches in diameter and 35 feet tall. The leaves are grayish green and borne in a loose open crown. As with all species of *Sabal*, the leaves are used for weaving hats, baskets, and other objects, though ever fewer artisans still practice this traditional craft. The palm is threatened in some parts of its distribution range by land clearing and development, but fortunately it is also widely cultivated.

There is only one specimen of *Sabal causiarum* at the Jardín Botánico Culiacán, acquired in 1994. Botanists at the garden are working very hard to add more plants of this species. When there is only one specimen of a species in an important botanical collection, there is always the risk that it may be lost owing to disease or that it may never reproduce. This is why botanical gardens around the world make huge efforts to increase the size of their collections, often by means of exchanges with other gardens.

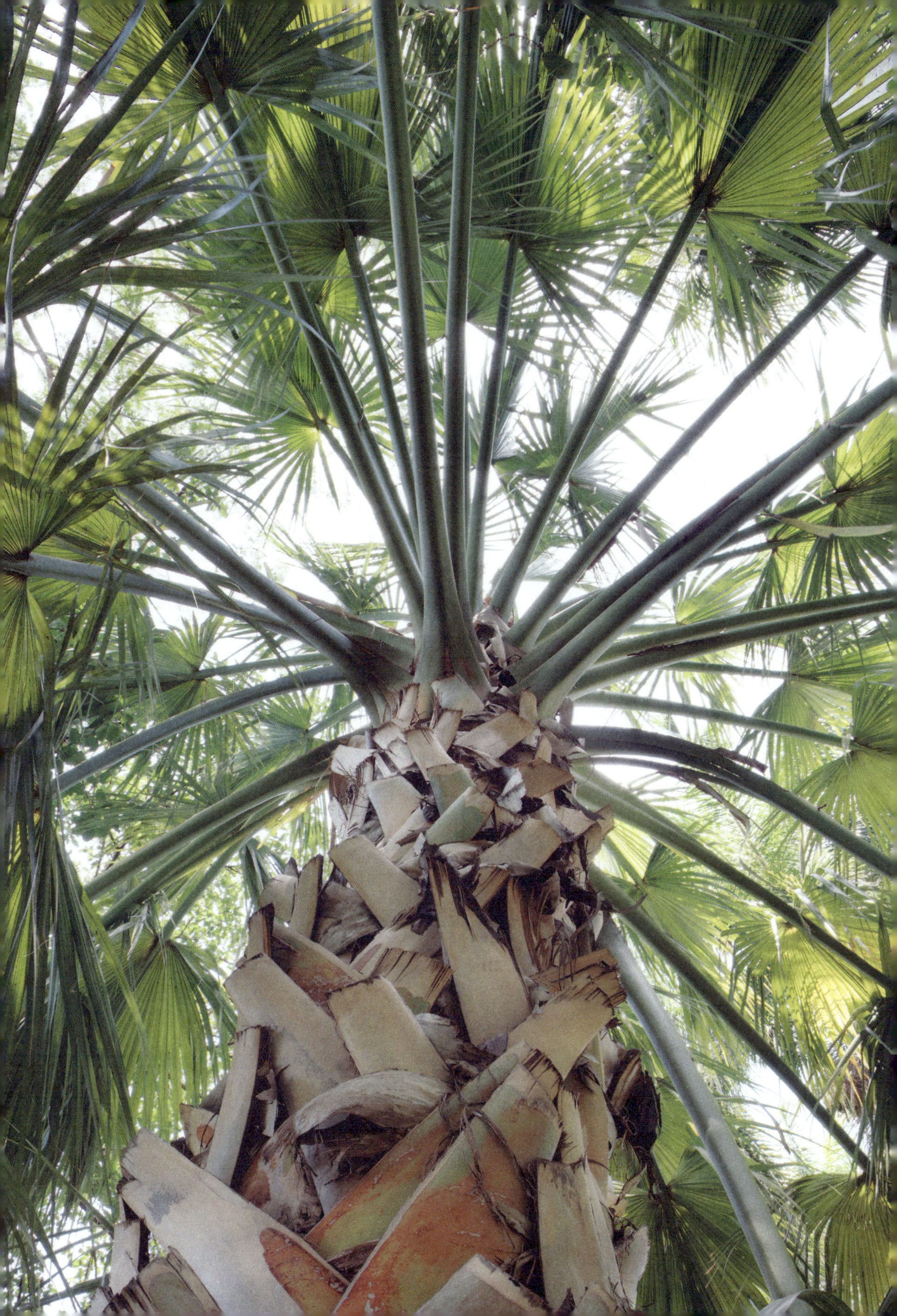

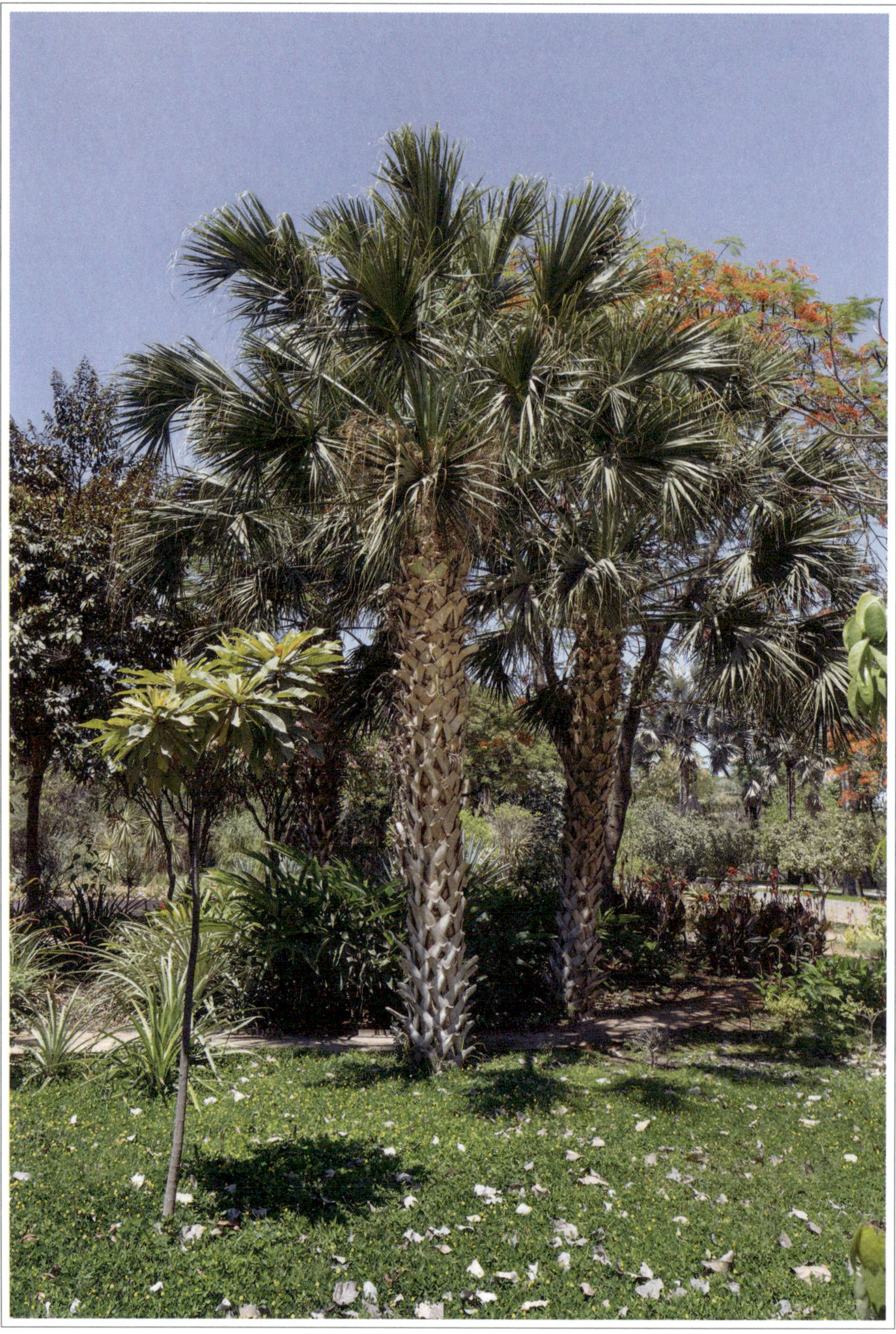

73

RIO GRANDE PALMETTO, TEXAS PALMETTO

Sabal mexicana Mart.

Status: Assessment of global conservation status required
Distribution: Texas, Mexico, and Guatemala

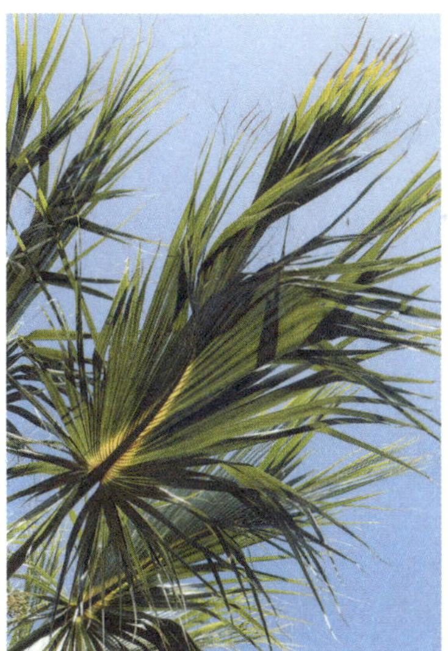

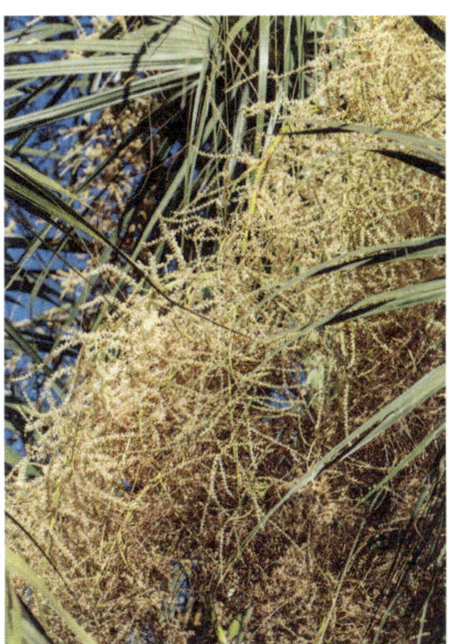

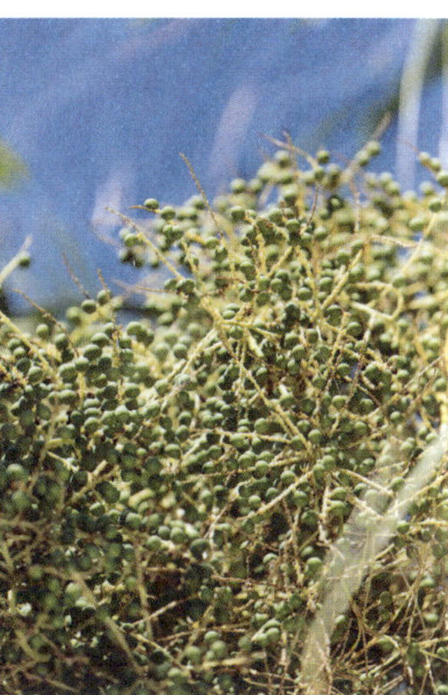

1. Leaf. 2. Flowers. 3. Unripe fruits.

This species grows from five to 35 feet in height, in semi-domesticated fields. Its leaves are prized for thatch. The Maya people have been harvesting leaves from this species for generations, using them for making roofs. The large black fruits are also sometimes eaten. In natural woodlands, the flowers and fruits of this species are an important resource for insects, birds, and other animals. The palms are important hosts for epiphytic plants, such as orchids and bromeliads, and for wild figs (*Ficus* species). The figs germinate and grow on the palms, eventually killing them, but they are an extremely important food source for a range of wildlife, including insects, birds, bats, monkeys, and other animals. *Sabal mexicana* is at the base of a food web that sustains the entire forest.

Specimens of *Sabal mexicana* have been growing successfully at the ranch of Carlos Murillo Depraect since 1989. Botanists at the Jardín Botánico Culiacán also acquired some wild specimens from the state of Oaxaca, thereby enriching the National Palm Collection. In Oaxaca, botanists have observed that the species grows in close proximity to the endemic Mexican palm *Chamaedora pochutlensis*.

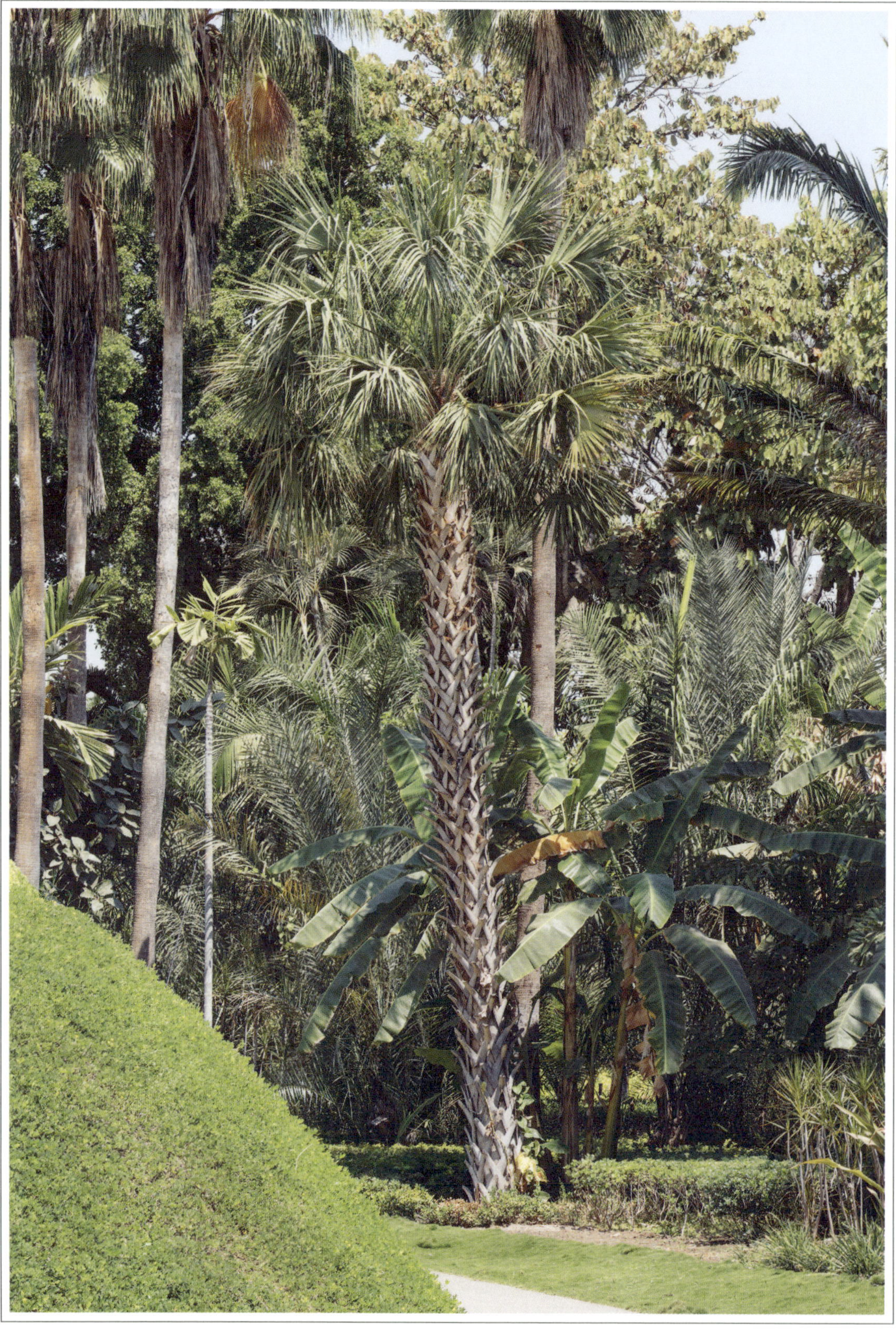

74
CABBAGE PALM

Sabal palmetto (Walter) Lodd. ex Schult. & Schult.f.

Status: Assessment of global conservation status required
Distribution: Southeastern United States, the Bahamas, and Cuba

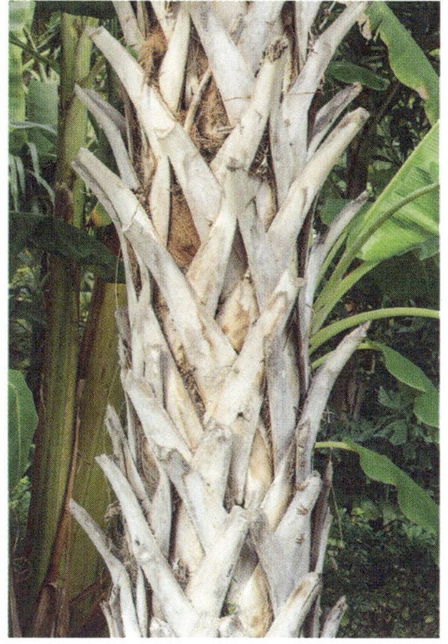
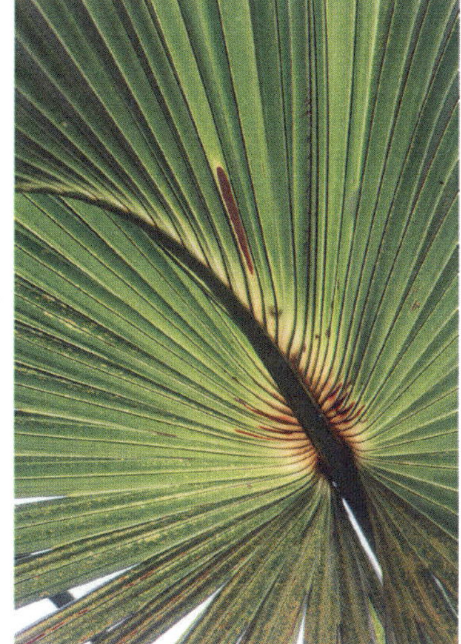

1. Trunk. 2. Leaf.

Sabal palmetto is a single-stemmed palm that grows to around 65 feet tall and bears a spherical crown of leaves. All across its range, it is an important resource for wildlife: bees and other insects are attracted to the flowers and many species of birds and bats feed on the fruits. Humans use the leaves for fiber and thatch. The terminal bud—the "heart" of the palm—is edible and delicious, tasting like crisp cabbage, but in order to harvest the bud, the palm must be killed. Other kinds of palms are also used for their edible cabbage or palm heart, such as *Bactris gasipaes* and *Euterpe oleracea*.

At the Jardín Botánico Culiacán, several birds and small mammals feed on the fruits of *Sabal palmetto*. One of the specimens of this palm was accidentally killed when a crane operator hit it while moving a tree. The botanists at the garden are working to increase the size of the *Sabal palmetto* seed collection at the garden's germplasm bank, in order to ensure the long-term availability of the species.

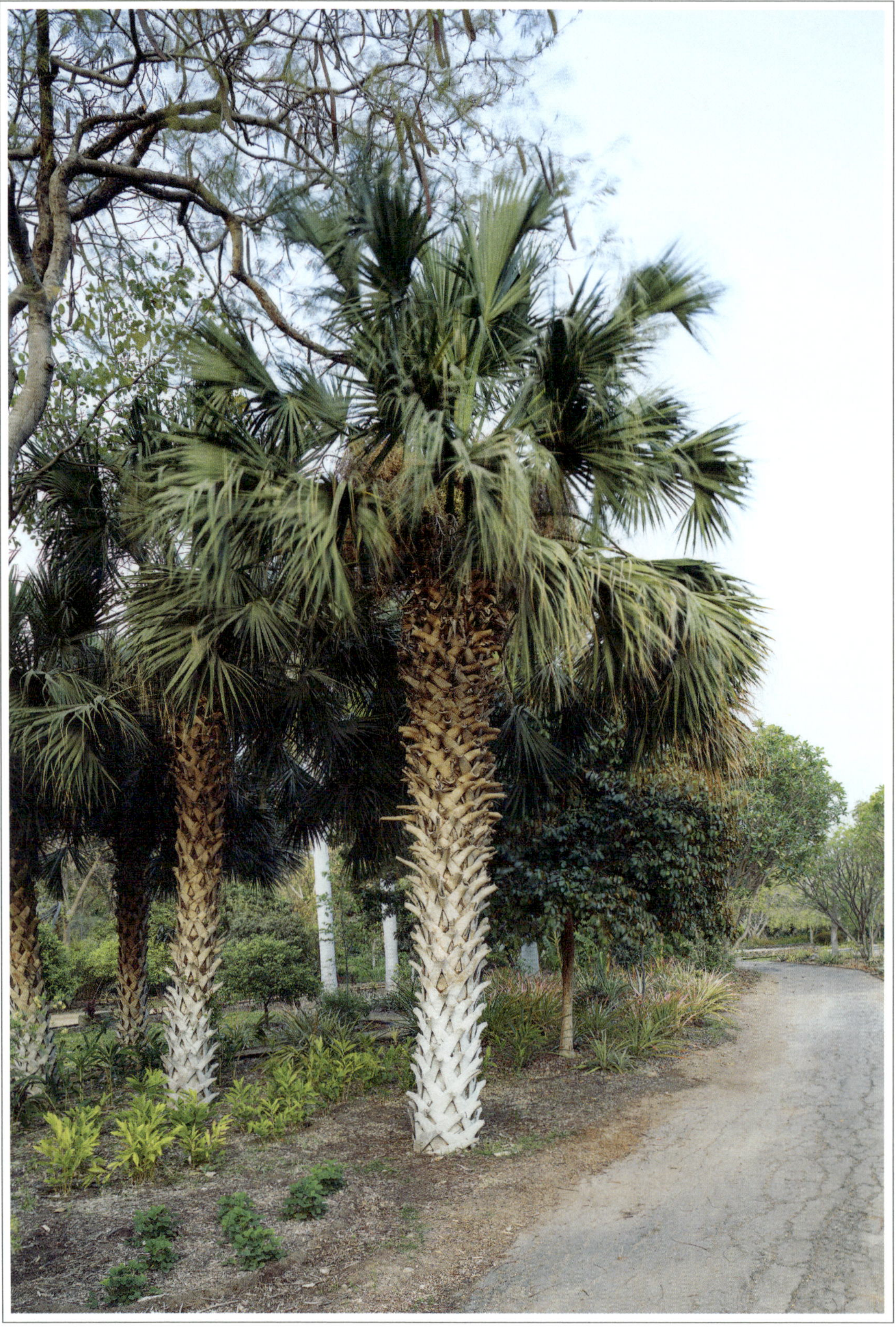

75
PUMOS PALM

Sabal pumos (Kunth) Burret

Status: Designated as Requiring Special Protection on the Mexican list of endangered species (NOM-059-SEMARNAT-2010) and as Vulnerable on the IUCN Red List
Distribution: Endemic to Mexico (Guanajuato, Guerrero, State of Mexico, Jalisco, Michoacán, Morelos, and Zacatecas)

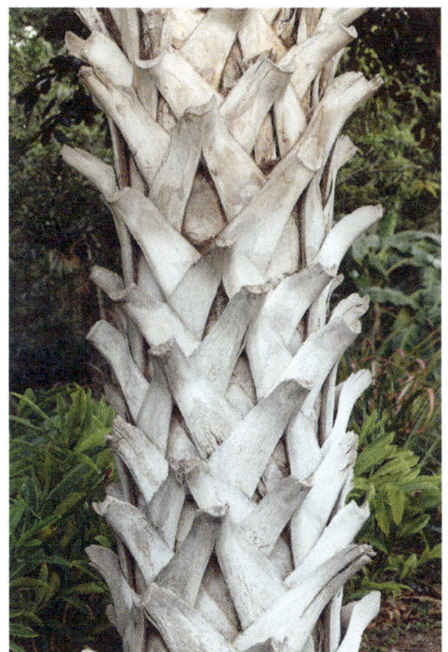
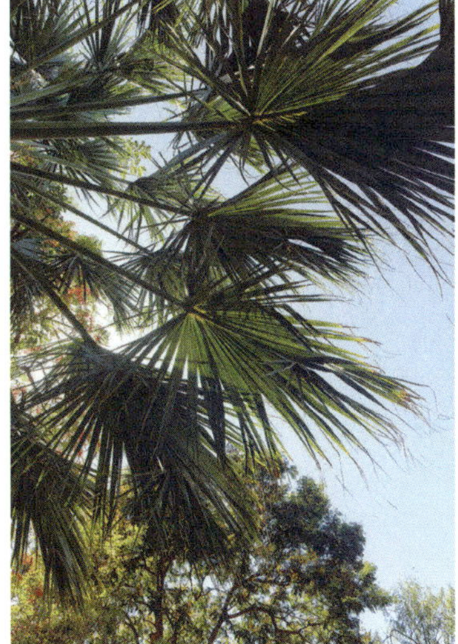
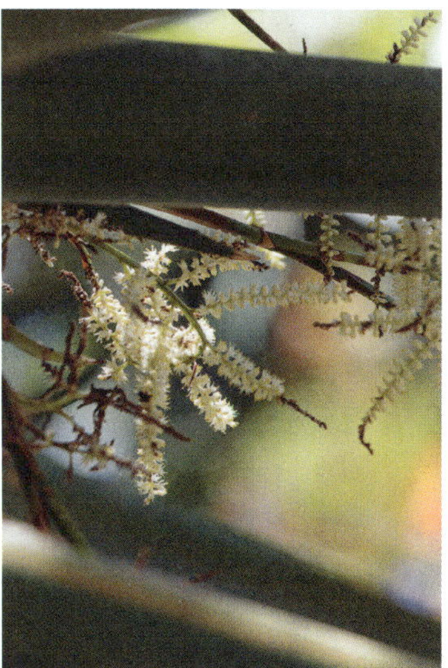

1. Trunk. 2. Leaves. 3. Flowers.

This species, which grows up to 50 feet tall, is native to hot dry habitats with sandy soils, especially in areas where tropical dry forest and oak forest meet. Amazingly, it is a palm that can tolerate orchids living on its crown. Its fan-shaped leaves are used for roofing and to make baskets, mats, brooms, hats, and ties, while the stem is used as a fuel and for building. The leaves and fruits are used to feed cattle. The species name comes from the fruit, known as *pumo*, the largest, fleshiest fruit of any of the *Sabal* species. This fruit is popular in the Huacana region of the state of Michoacán, where it is eaten fresh. For a long time, this palm was wrongly identified in the Jardín Botánico Culiacán as *Sabal uresana*, another species endemic to Mexico (specifically, to the northern states of Sinaloa and Sonora).

In early 2019, Miguel Ángel García Bielma, the Mexican botanist and palm specialist, visited the garden and identified it correctly, thus adding a new species to the National Palm Collection.

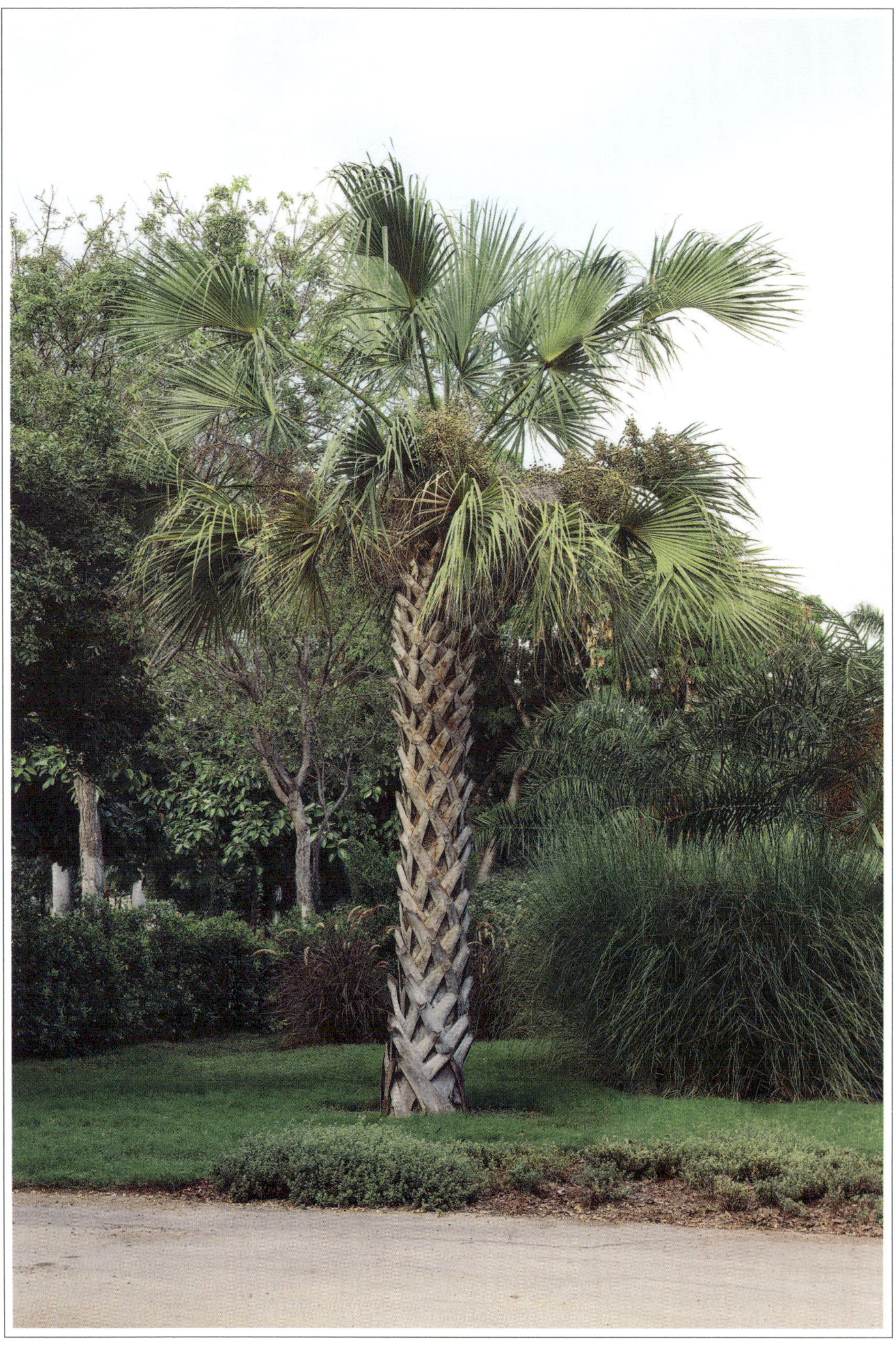

76

SAVANNAH PALMETTO

Sabal rosei (O.F. Cook) Becc.

Status: Assessment of global conservation status required
Distribution: Western Mexico

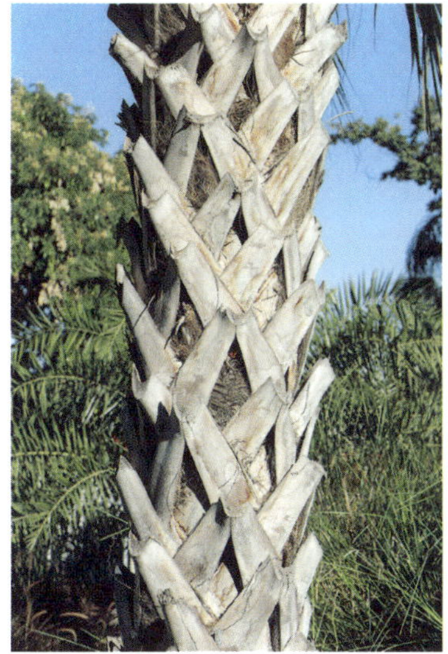
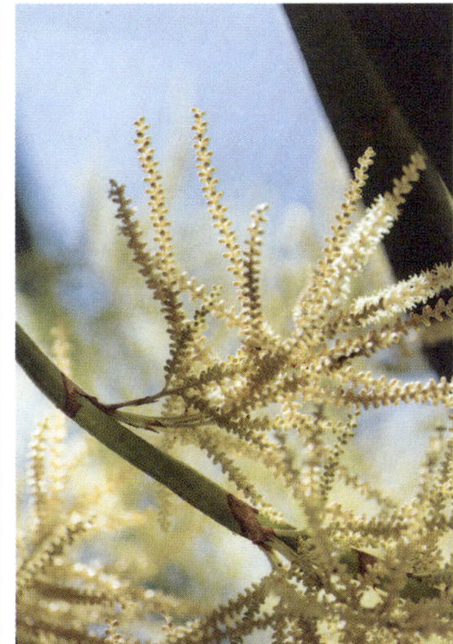
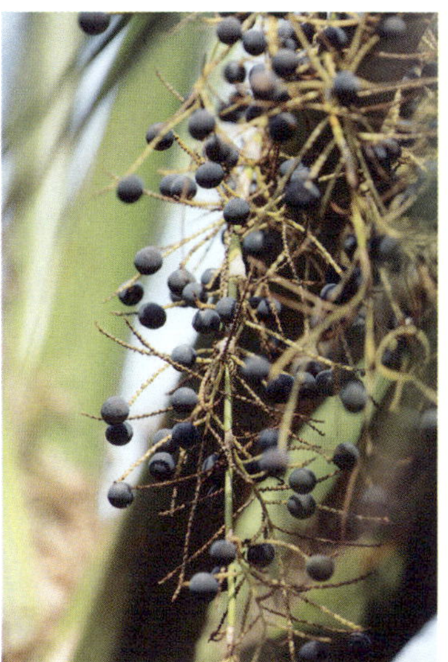

1. Trunk. 2. Flowers. 3. Ripe fruits.

Sabal rosei grows as a solitary palm to about 50 feet in height. This species occurs in the Mexican states of Jalisco, Nayarit, and Sinaloa, at low elevations in tropical deciduous forests, often in large populations. It is closely related to two other *Sabal* species, *Sabal uresana* (Sinaloa, Sonora, and Chihuahua) and *Sabal pumos* (Michoacán, Guerrero, and State of Mexico). It was named for Joseph Nelson Rose (1862–1928), a botanist from the United States who collected cacti and other plants in western Mexico in the early twentieth century. The species is occasionally used for roofing thatch and is not widely cultivated outside of Mexico.

In 2016, Erika Pagaza Calderón and Guillermo Millán, botanists from the Jardín Botánico Culiacán, collected new specimens of *Sabal rosei* from the wild. These palms are very fruitful: at the garden, the fruits are used mostly for workshops in which children make necklaces and bracelets from them, as a way of learning to appreciate and respect nature in a different way.

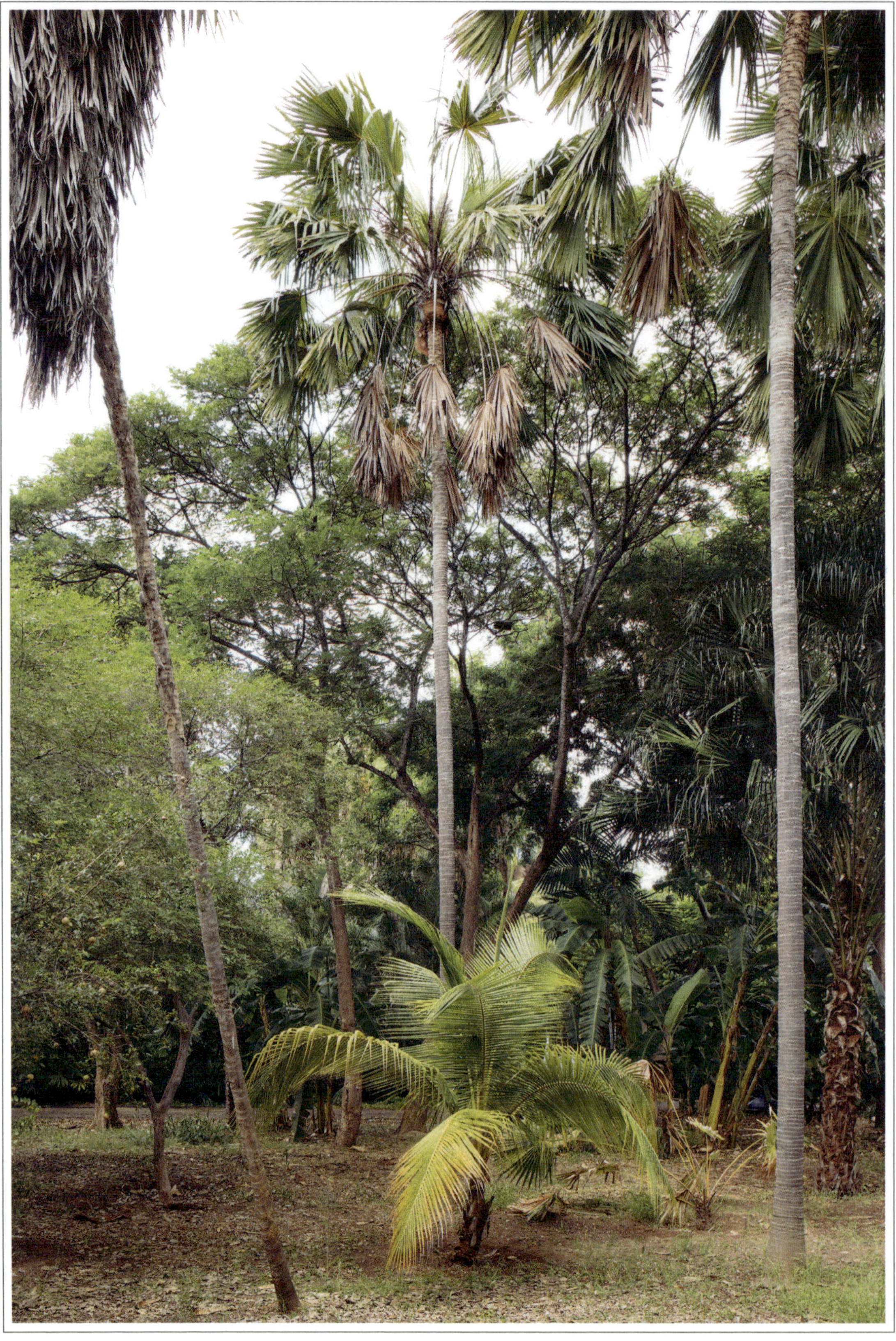

77
FOOTSTOOL PALM

Saribus rotundifolius (Lam.) Blume

Status: Assessment of global conservation status required
Distribution: Borneo, Sulawesi (Indonesia), New Guinea, and the Philippines

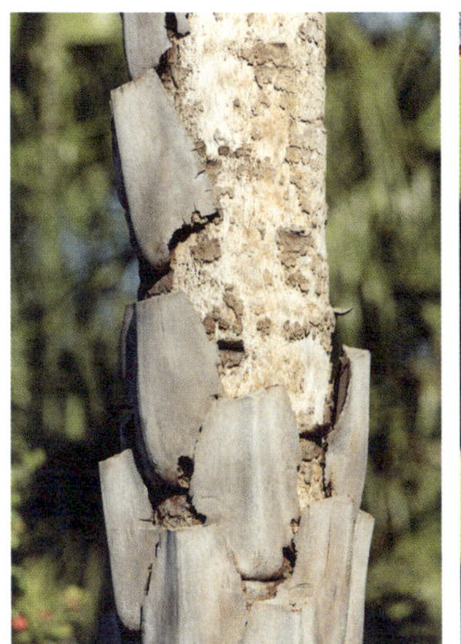
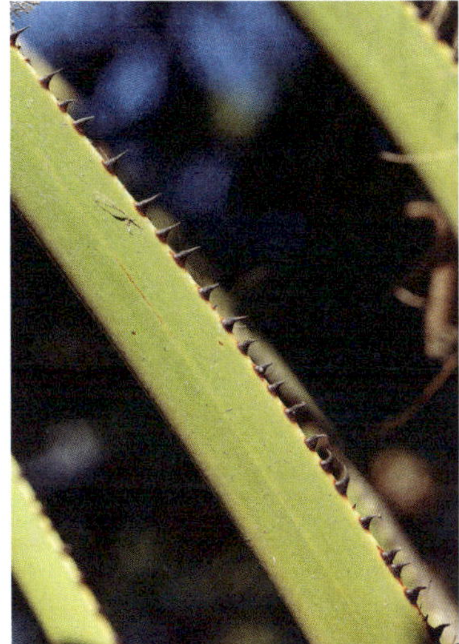
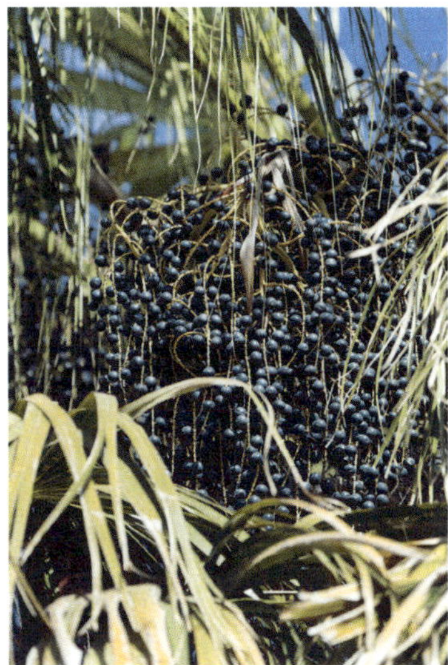

1. Trunk with retained leaf bases. 2. Petiole teeth. 3. Ripe fruits.

The footstool palm is a robust, single-stemmed palm that grows up to 150 feet tall. It can be found in swamp forests, mangrove forests, and rainforests near rivers. It is widely cultivated for its lush, round leaves (*rotundifolia* means "round leaf"), with their pendulous leaflet tips. When the plant is young, the leaves look like glossy, round footstools. In favorable conditions, it can rapidly grow into a tall, sturdy palm with a trunk ringed by prominent leaf scars. The leaf stalks are armed with large curved teeth. The flowers stalks are about as long as the leaf stalks and bear tiny pale-yellow flowers, which ripen into bright orange fruits measuring 0.39 inches–0.98 inches in diameter. *Saribus rotundifolius* is a preferred roosting palm for the bat *Scotophilus kuhli* in the Philippines. The bat bites through the main veins of the leaf segments, causing them to hang down and form a "tent" in which it can shelter itself from rain and predators. *Saribus rotundifolius* was previously classified (mistakenly) as *Livistona rotundifolia* and can be found in the older literature under that name.

The specimens of *Saribus rotundifolius* at the Jardín Botánico Culiacán are prolific and very attractive to birds at the garden. The first specimens arrived in 1995, grown from seeds from the US state of Florida and from the Philippines.

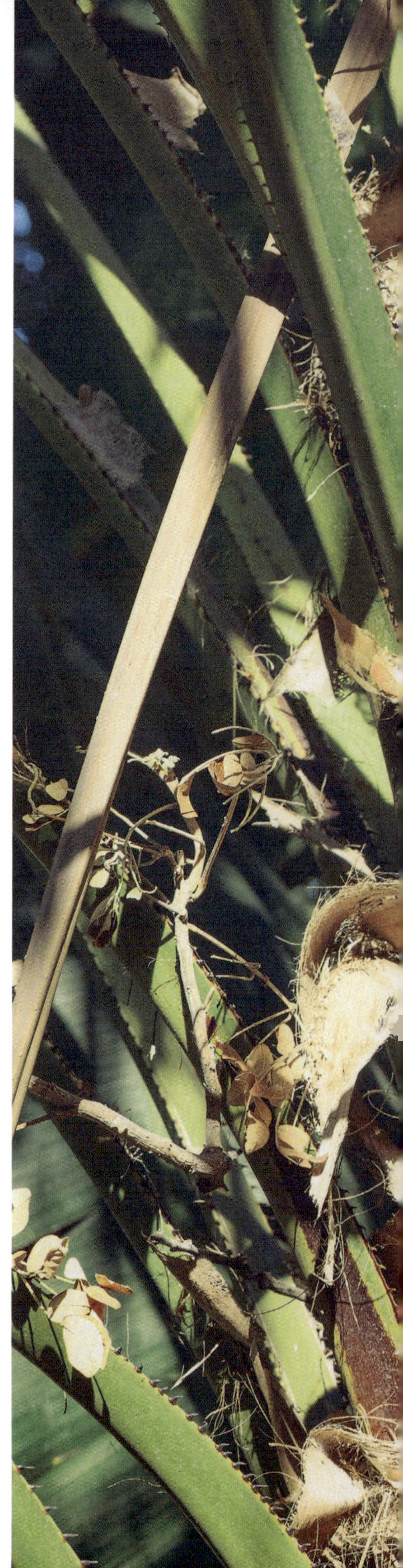

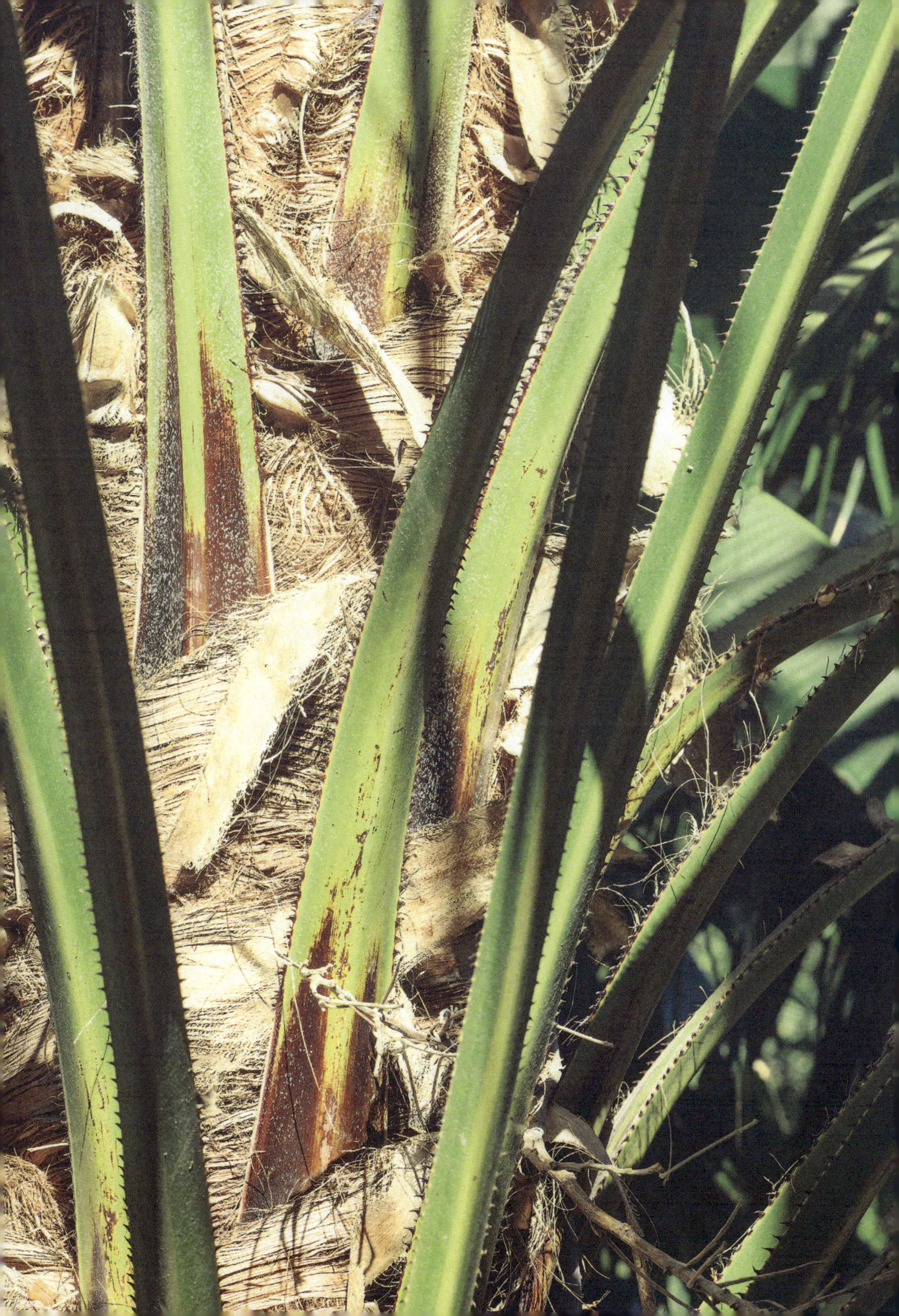

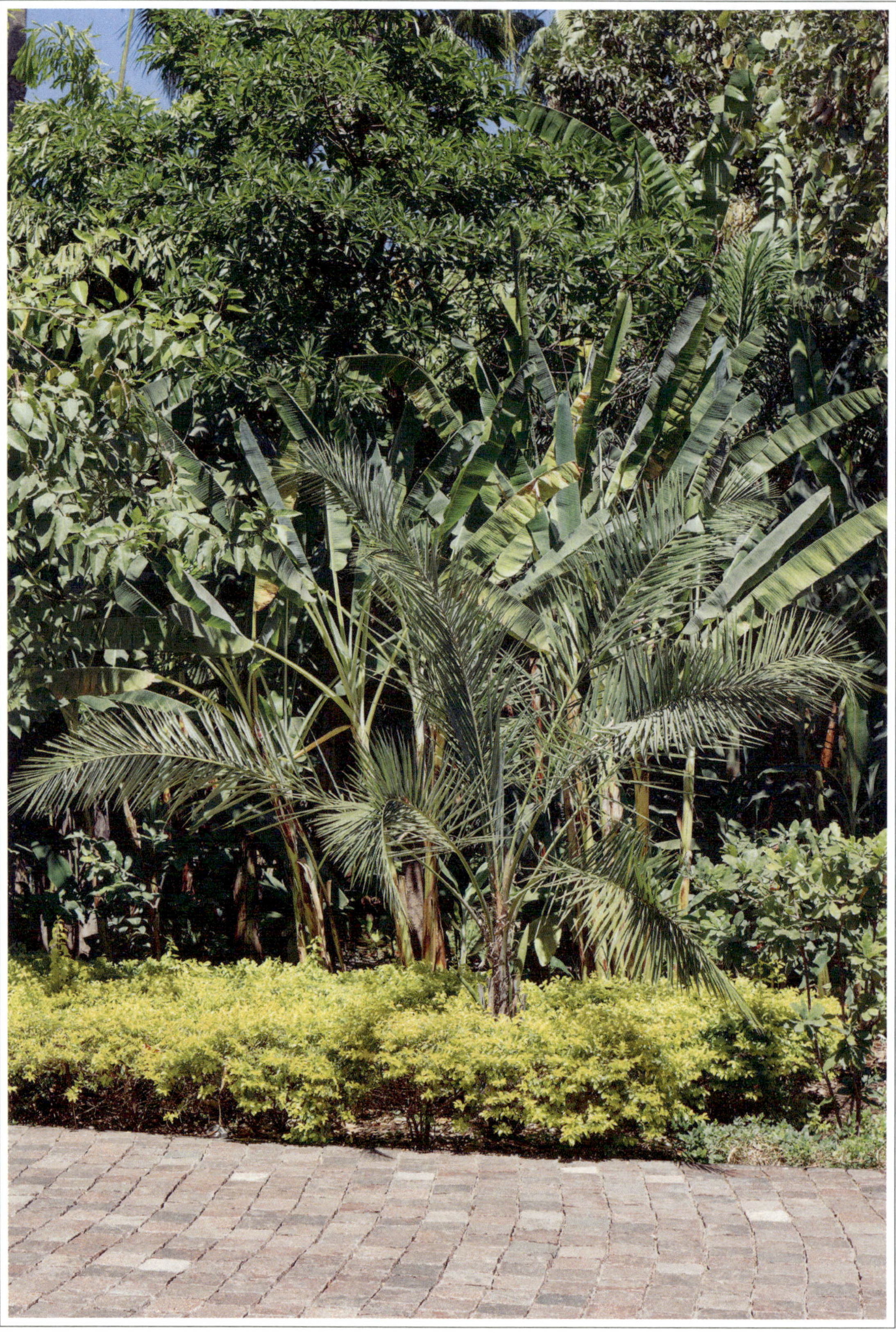

78

LICURI PALM

Syagrus coronata (Mart.) Becc.

Status: Assessment of global conservation status required
Distribution: Endemic to Brazil

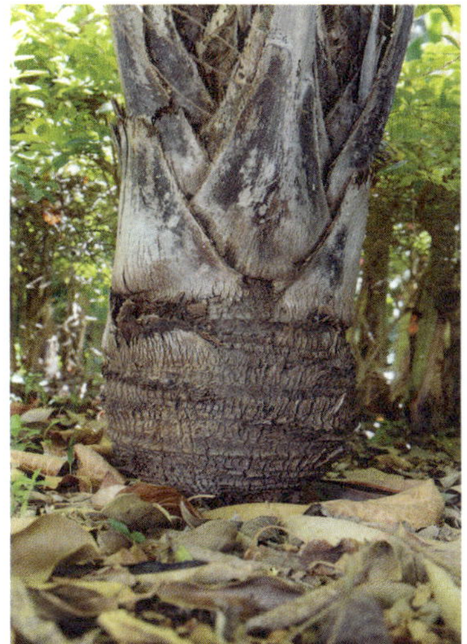

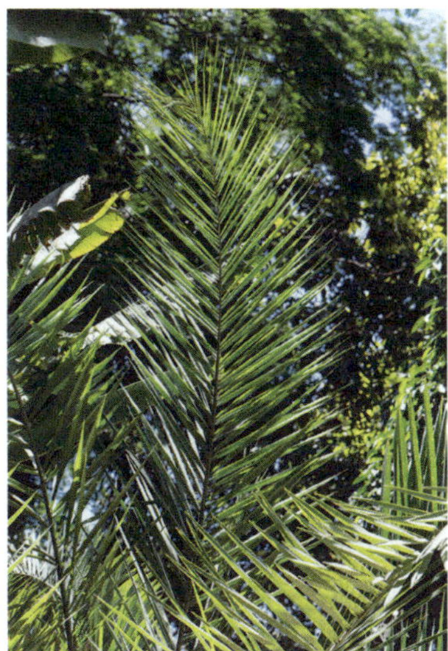

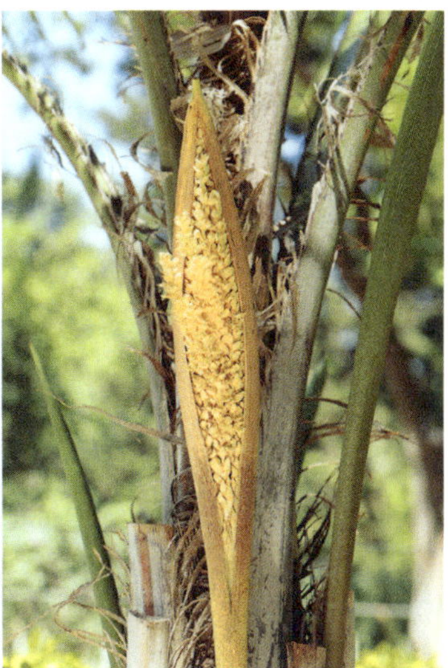

1. Trunk with retained leaf bases. 2. Leaf. 3. Bract revealing flowers.

The licuri palm is native to xeric shrub land and semi-deciduous forests, where it is a solitary palm that grows up to 35 feet tall. A beautiful medium-sized palm, tolerant of drought, it has become popular in gardens around the world. It is especially appealing because of the spiral pattern formed by the old retained leaf bases. In a population of this palm, variations can be observed in the patterning: some palms have tight spirals, while others have hardly any spirals at all, and the leaf bases are stacked one above the other. In its native habitat, the palm is used in many ways by the local indigenous people. The leaves are used for thatch and weaving, and also as torches. The wax from the surface of the leaflets can be harvested. The fruits and seeds are edible, and the oil from the seeds is used for cooking, lighting, and cosmetics.

Specimens of *Syagrus coronata* have been cared for in the nursery of the Jardín Botánico Culiacán for eight years. In the first half of 2019 they finally bloomed for the first time.

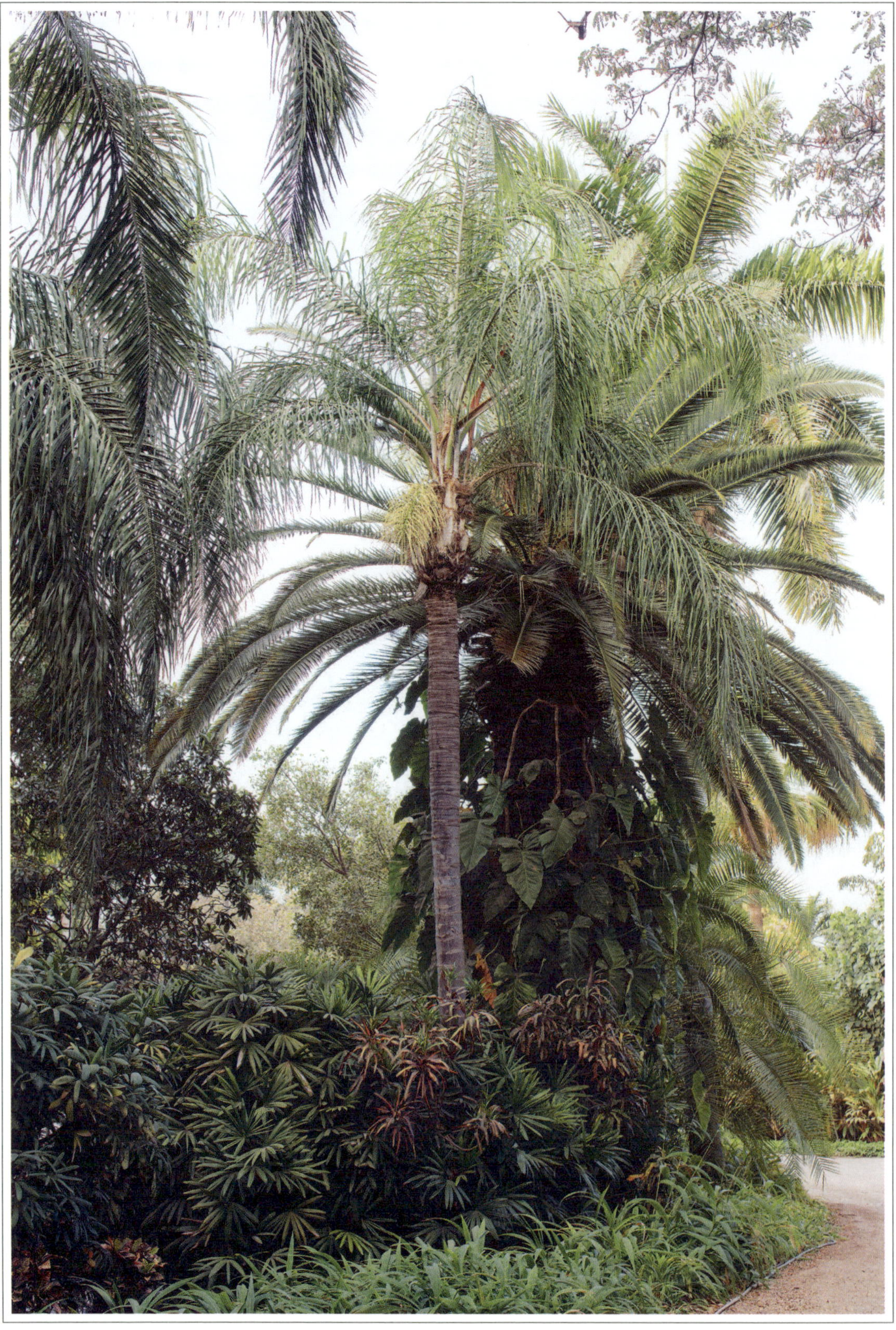

79

COCOS PALM

Syagrus romanzoffiana (Cham.) Glassman

Status: Assessment of global conservation status required
Distribution: Southern Brazil, Uruguay, Paraguay, and northern Argentina

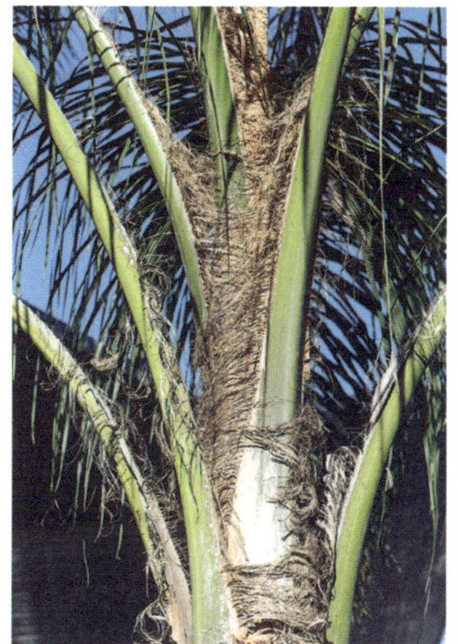
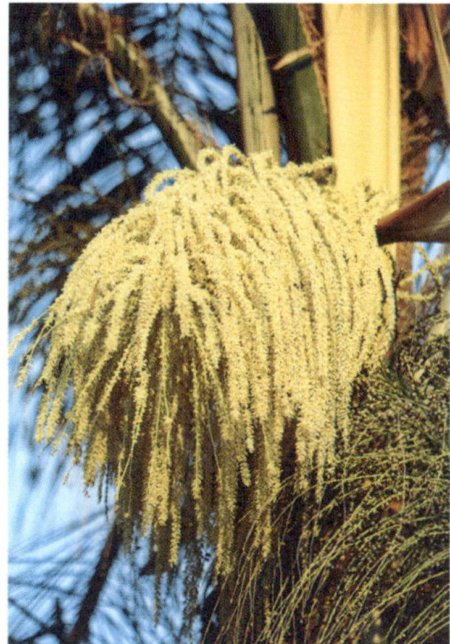
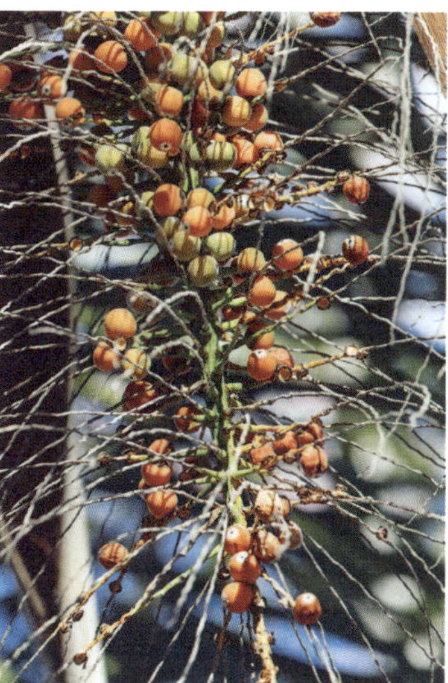

1. Leaf bases. 2. Inflorescence. 3. Ripe fruits.

Syagrus romanzoffiana is a medium to large-sized palm (up to 50 feet tall) that has become a popular garden palm all over the tropics and subtropics. It is a fast-growing species, easily propagated from seeds. The smooth trunk and unarmed, plumose leaves give the species an informal presence in the garden. In its native habitat, many animals rely on the juicy fruits for survival, and the palms depend on the animals to disperse the seeds. *Syagrus romanzoffiana* is a relative of the coconut (*Cocos nucifera*) and, like the coconut, its nut has three round depressions or pores at one end. One of these pores is where the seedling will emerge when the seed germinates.

In the 1990s, *Syagrus romanzoffiana* was one of the first species of palms that the landscape section of the Sociedad Botánica y Zoológica de Sinaloa started using for landscape design in the Culiacán area. It is commonly found in nurseries in the region and all over Mexico.

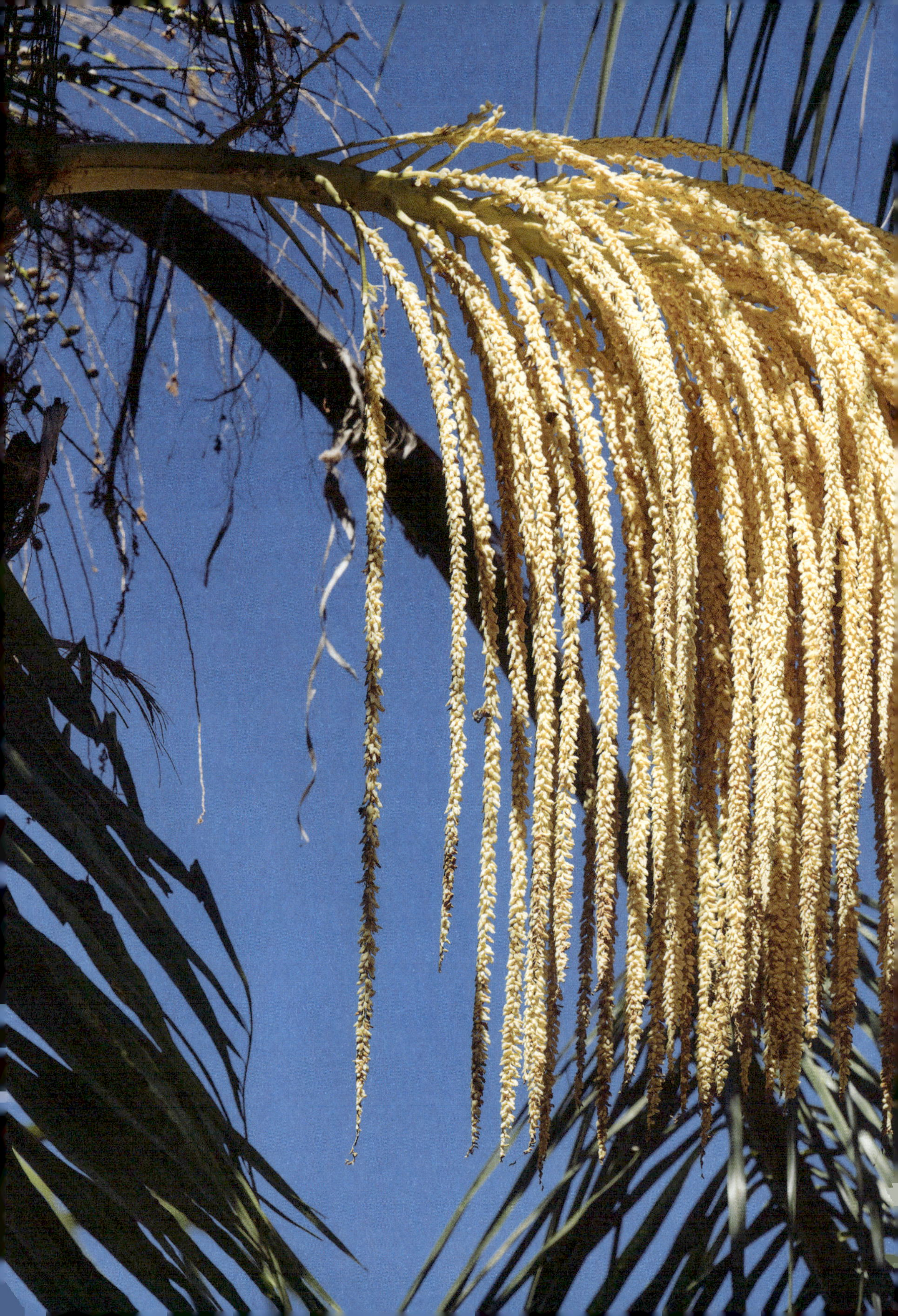

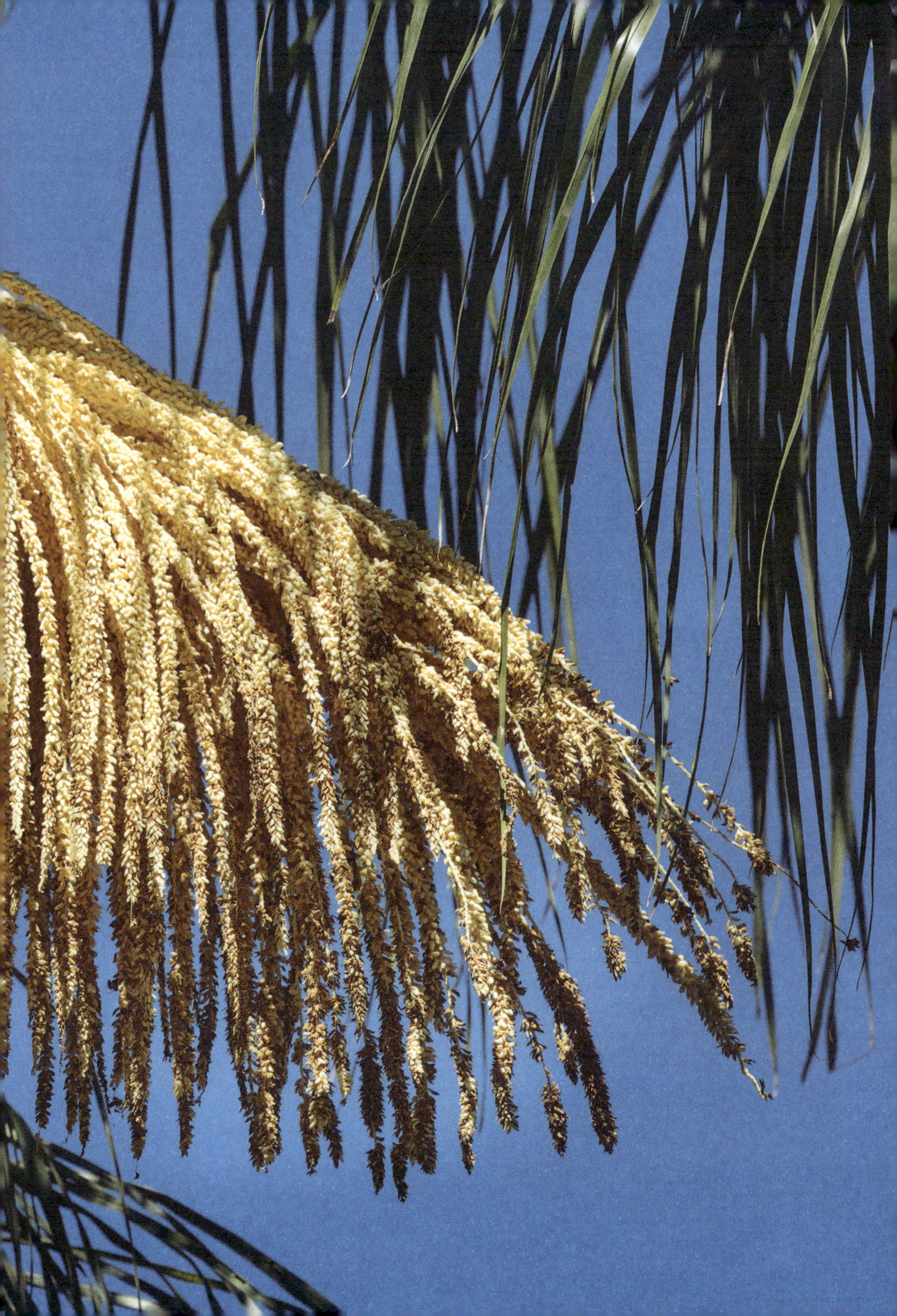

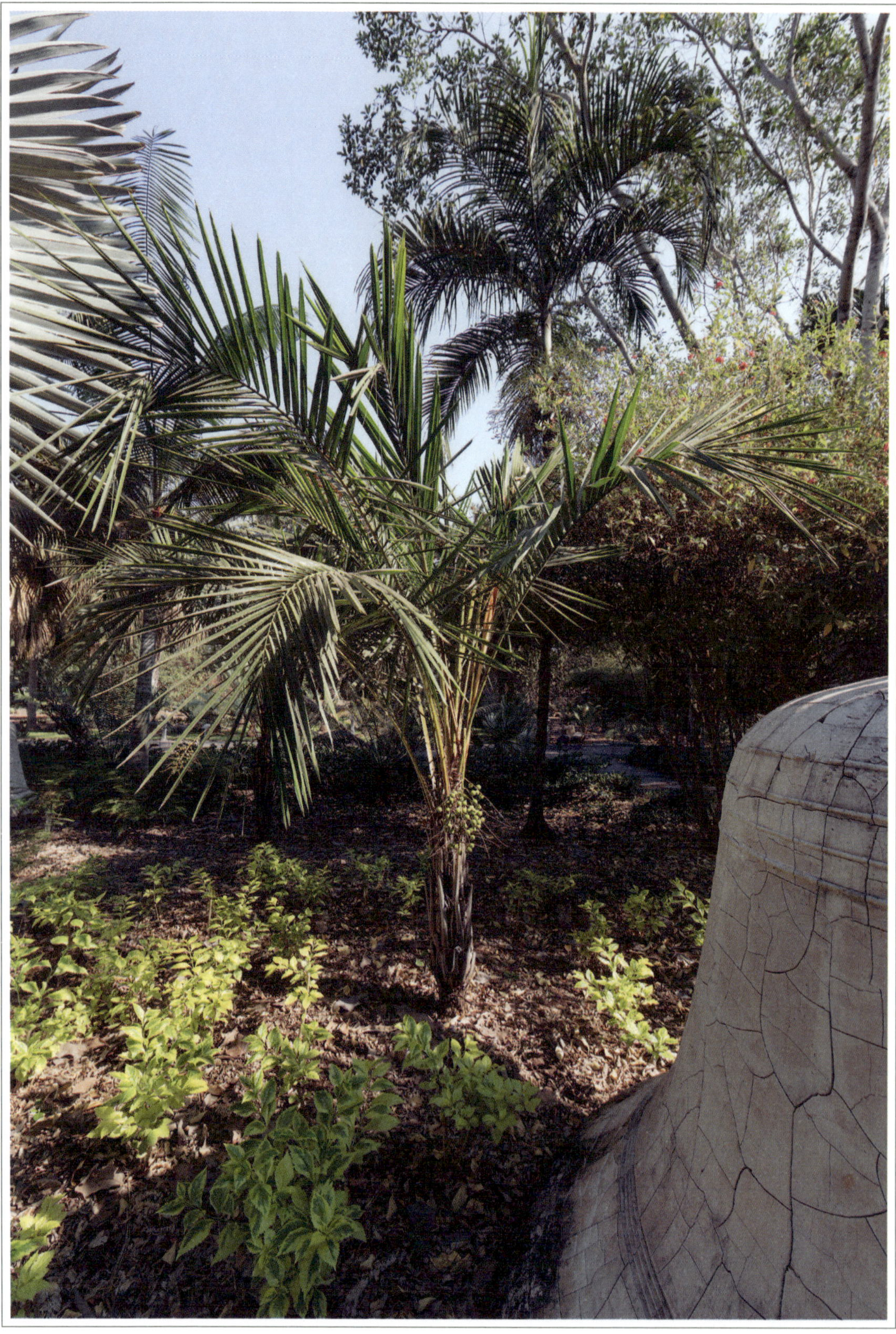

80

ARIKURY PALM

Syagrus schizophylla (Mart.) Glassman

Status: Assessment of global conservation status required
Distribution: Endemic to Brazil

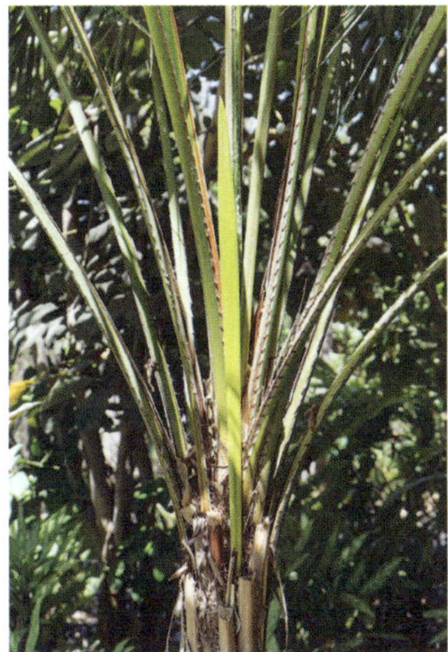

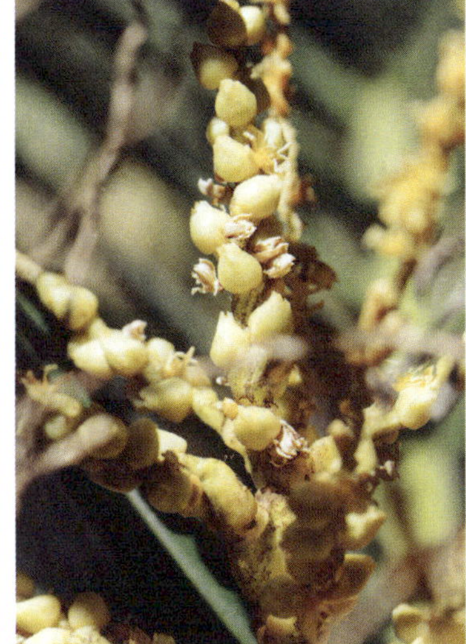

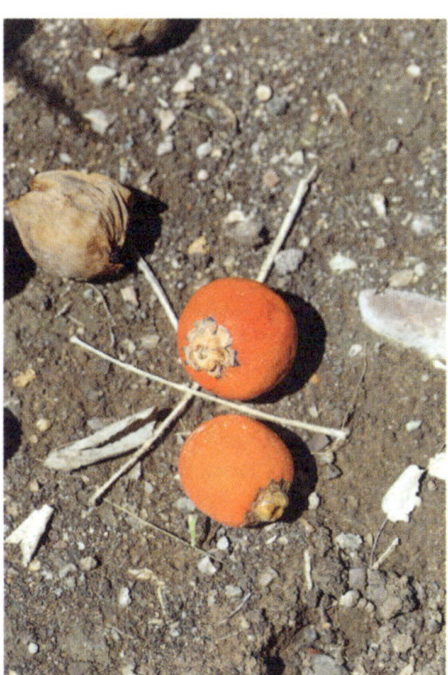

1. Petiole teeth. 2. Flowers. 3. Fruits.

This delightful small palm rarely grows to be more than 10 feet tall. It is therefore very popular in cultivation, in spite of the large teeth that arm the leaf stalk. The trunks are covered with the remains of the dead leaf stalks and the green leaves have an informal appearance. The palm has long sparsely-branched flower stalks that produce orange fruits. Both children and domestic animals are fond of the fruit, which is sweet but rather fibrous. The seeds, however, are bitter. The palm is native to coastal areas, often growing on sandy soil in moist broad-leaf forests. Such coastal areas are often subject to commercial development, so this species should be listed as Vulnerable. Unfortunately, it is not included on the IUCN Red List, although it needs to be widely protected.

Syagrus schizophylla is a relatively new species in the Jardín Botánico Culiacán, having been first acquired in 2011. Further specimens were later brought from Yucatán. The specimens in the garden bear abundant fruits, providing food for birds and the gardeners alike, who enjoy them because they are extremely sweet.

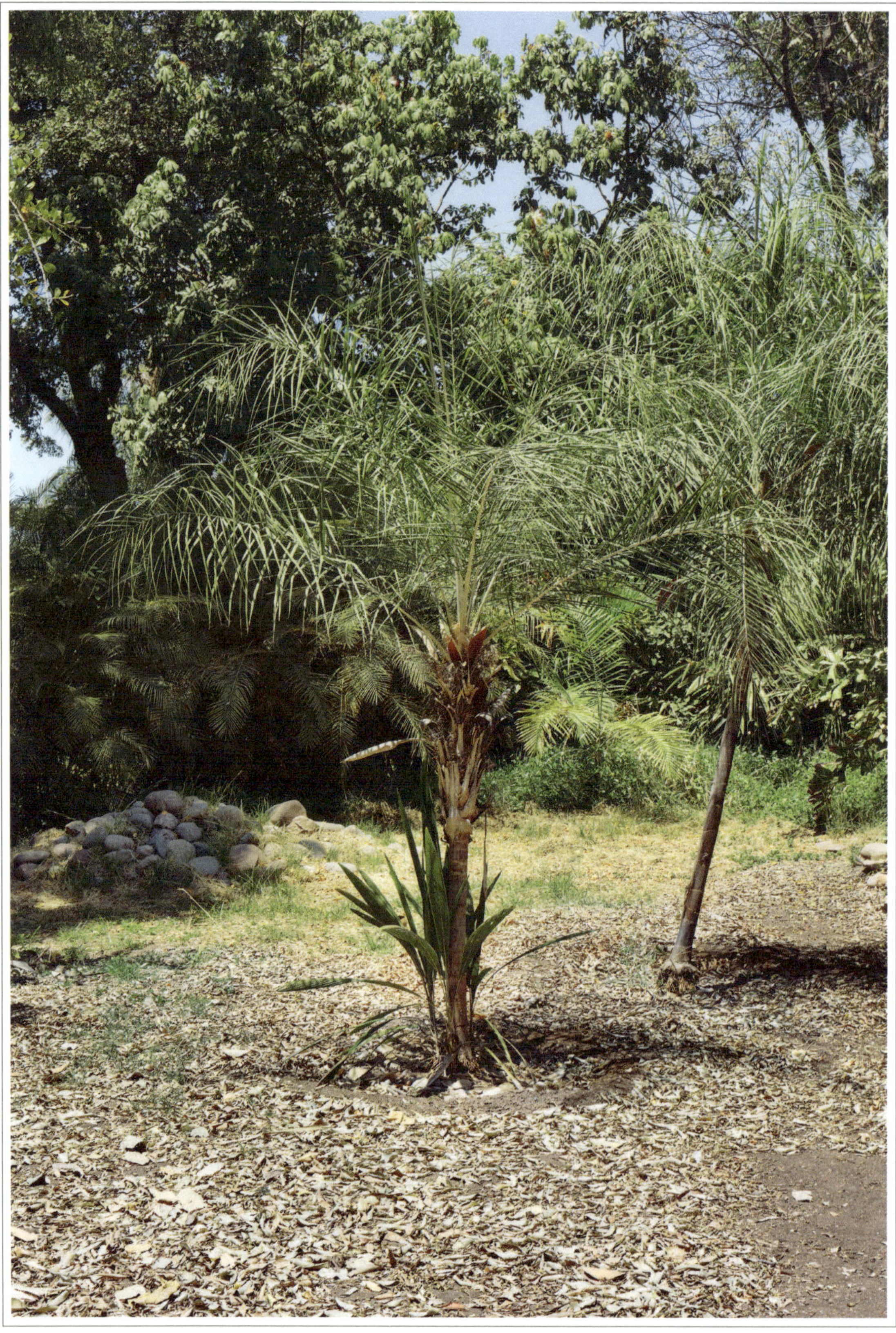

81

YUNGA PALM

Syagrus yungasensis M. Moraes

Status: Assessment of global conservation status required, but designated as Critically Endangered on the Bolivian Red List
Distribution: Endemic to the Yungas region of Bolivia

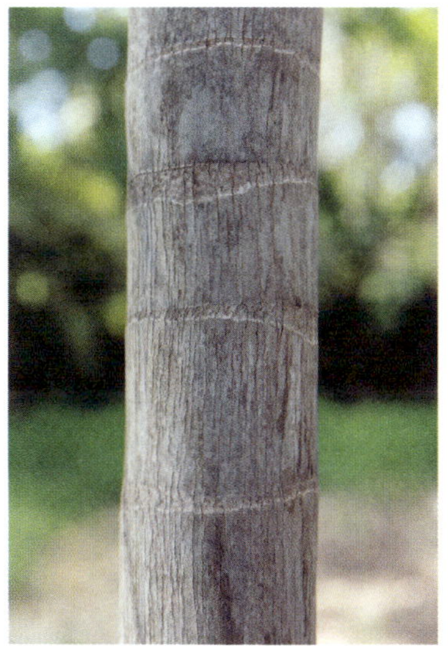
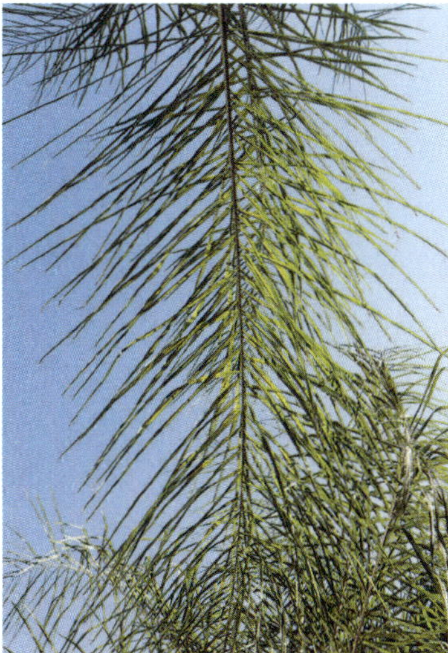
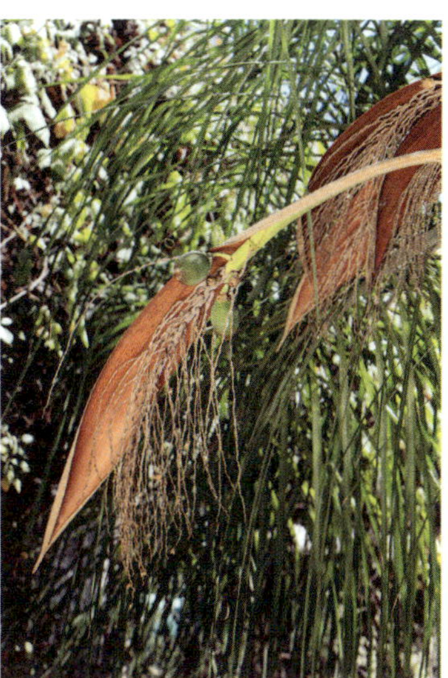

1. Trunk. 2. Leaf. 3. Unripe fruits.

Syagrus yungasensis is an attractive, medium-sized palm with plumose leaves, which grows up to 16 feet high. It deserves to be more widely cultivated, but is very seldom seen in gardens or landscapes. The habitat in which this species grows semi-deciduous forest is being increasingly cleared for agriculture, and only small fragments of the original vegetation remain. The palm's slim stem is very smooth and its feather-like leaves are around five feet long. It will produce up to eight inflorescences, each one around 3.2 feet long, with yellow flowers. The fruits are like small coconuts, the size of golf balls, consumed by squirrels and beetles, and even for their sweet juice. Like many seeds, the *Syagrus yungasensis* is very nutritious. The leaves are used for protecting seedbeds of coca plants and the trunks for building houses. This palm needs to be globally classified as Vulnerable to extinction.

The Jardín Botánico Culiacán has had specimens of *Syagrus yungasensis* since 2011. It is a plant with great ornamental value, but the garden propagates the species in the hope of preventing its extinction and perhaps of helping to reintroduce it into its original Yungas habitat in Bolivia.

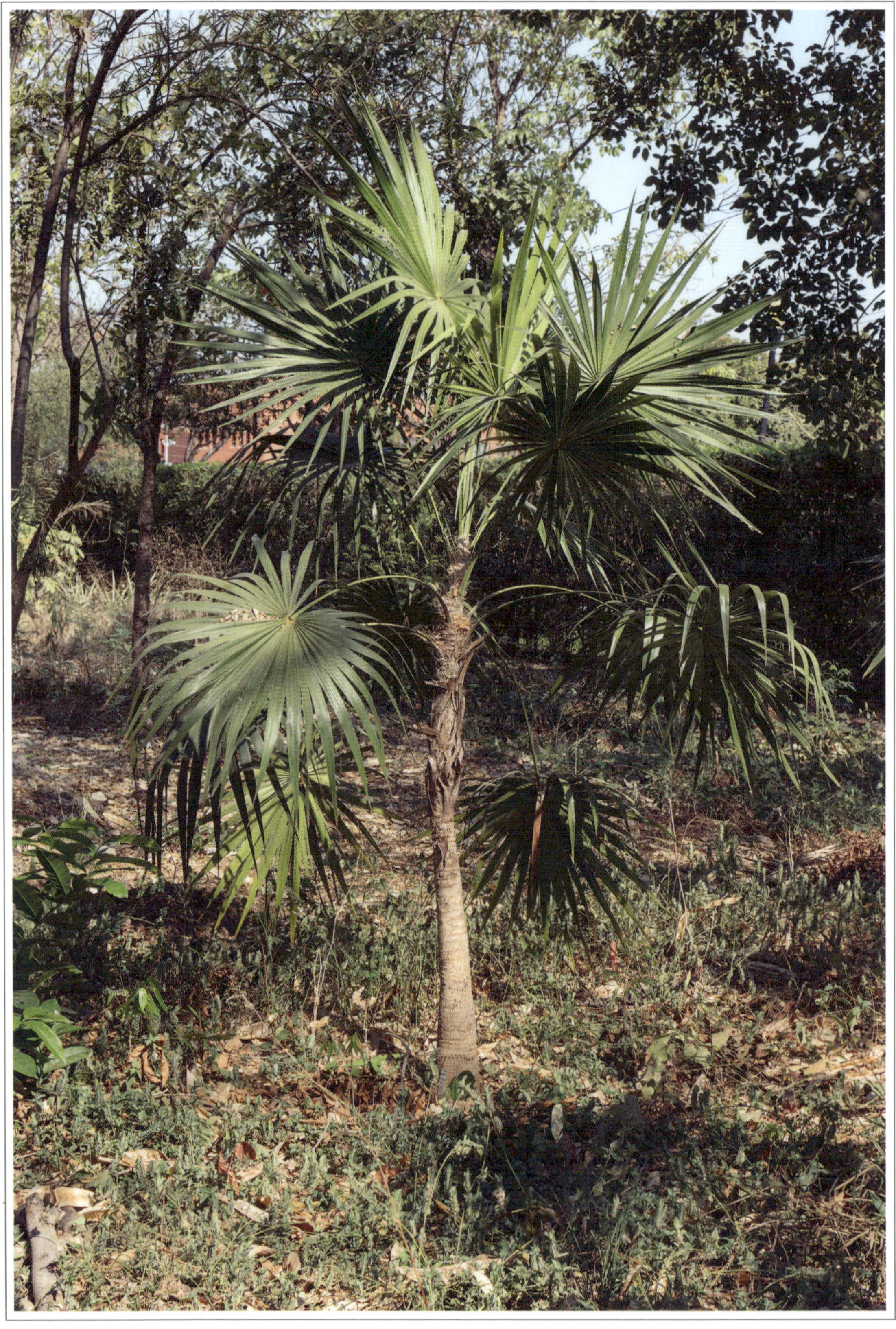

82
CHIT

Thrinax radiata Lodd. ex Schult. & Schult.f.

Status: Assessment of global conservation status required, but designated as Threatened on the Mexican list of endangered species (NOM-059-SEMARNAT-2010)
Distribution: Mexico, Central America, Cuba, Jamaica, the island of Hispaniola (Haiti and the Dominican Republic), Florida, and the Bahamas

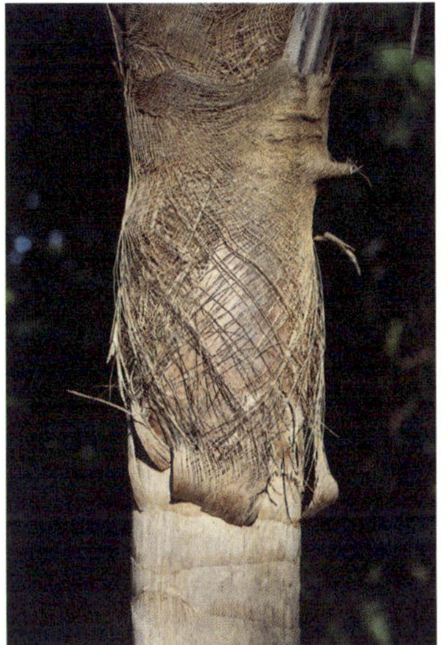
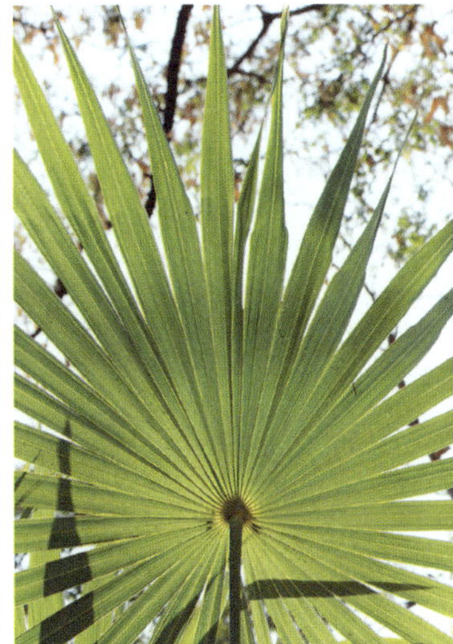
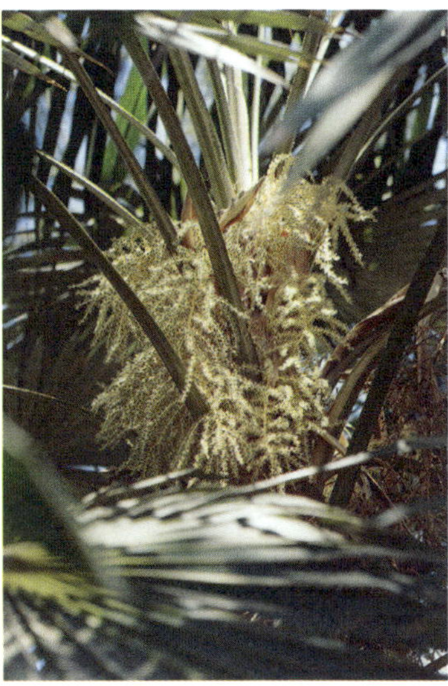

1. Trunk with leaf bases. 2. Leaf. 3. Flowers.

This single-stem palm has a slender trunk that grows to 20 feet in height and bears a spherical crown of bright green leaves. The chit is from the Yucatán Peninsula, where it grows in tropical rainforests. It can be found in areas of karst heavily eroded limestone, growing in pockets of soil or fissures in the rock. It can also grow on sandy quays near the sea. Both of these are difficult, taxing habitats. The palm grows very slowly in the wild, but rapidly in cultivation, with the help of rich soil and irrigation. The elegant trunk of *Thrinax radiata* has leaf scars that form a kind of mat of slender fibers. The large fan-shaped leaves (around 3.2 feet in diameter) give this palm a lush, tropical appearance that belies its adaptability and resilience. Creamy white flowers attract numerous kinds of insect pollinators, including melipone bees, although the pollen is also carried from palm to palm by the wind. The round white fruits are consumed by birds and bats, which disperse the seeds in the forest. People in the Yucatán Peninsula have traditionally used the trunk to make lobster traps and the leaves to make brooms and hats, as well as for roofing. These traditions are gradually being lost, owing to shrinking biodiversity.

The Jardín Botánico Culiacán has a population of around 30 individuals, which have been in the care of gardeners since 1986, around the time the garden was founded.

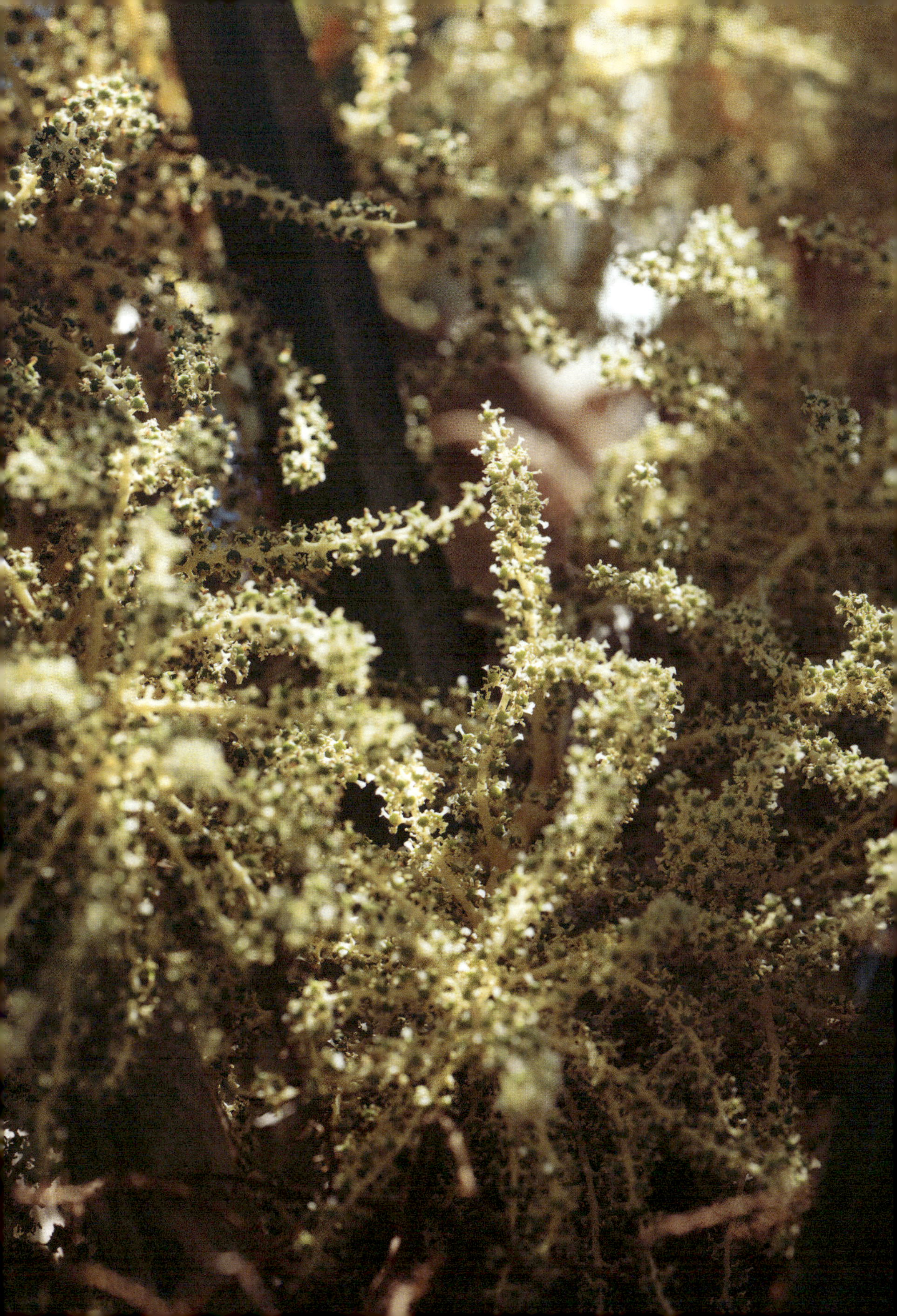

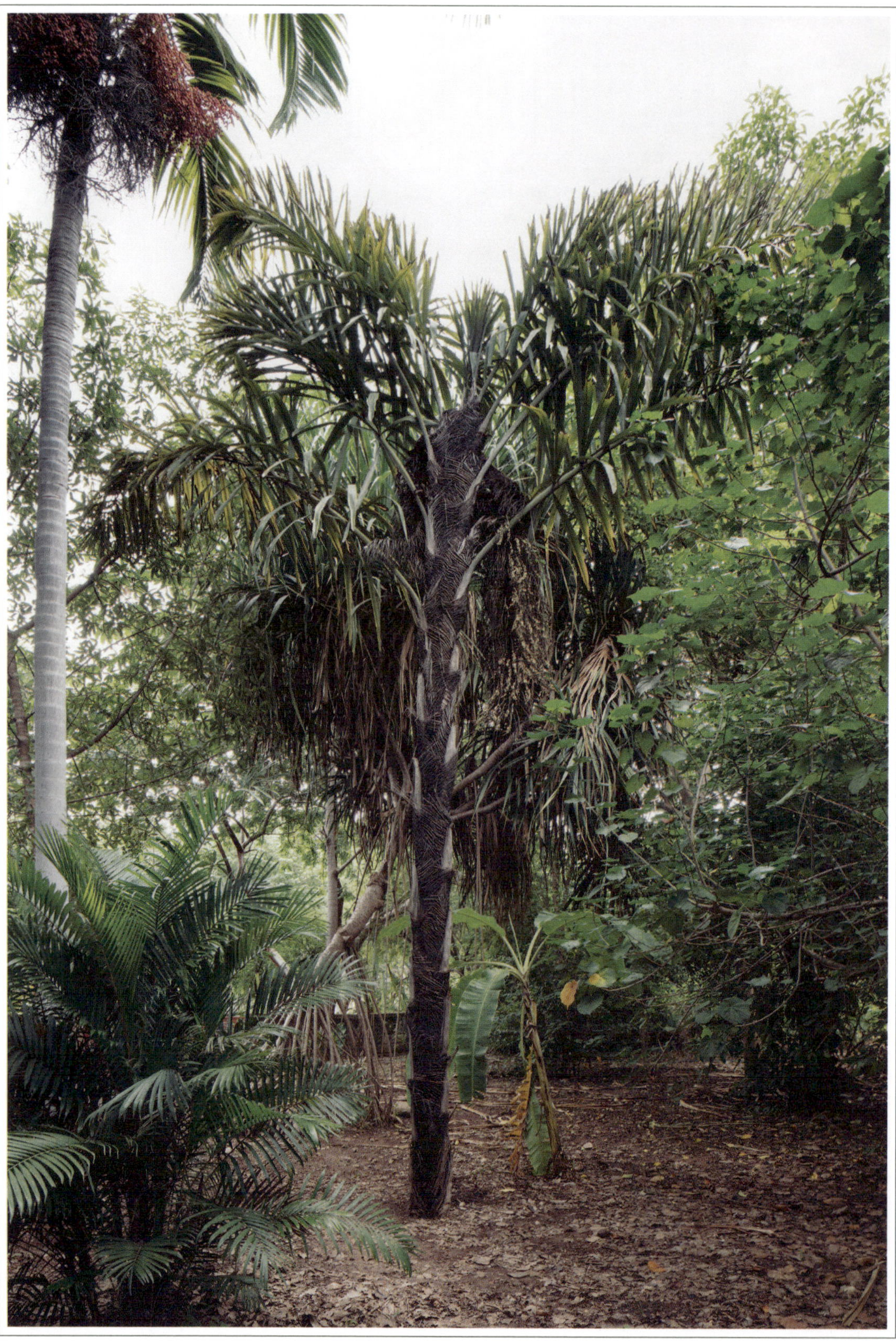

83
DISTICHOUS FISHTAIL PALM

Wallichia disticha T. Anderson

Status: Assessment of global conservation status required
Distribution: India, Bangladesh, southern China, Laos, Myanmar, and Thailand

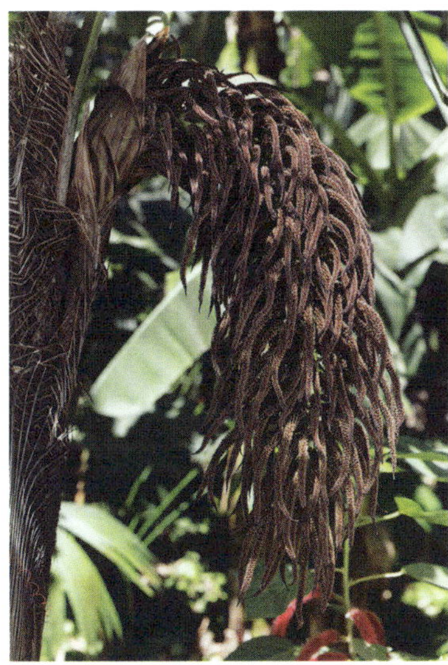
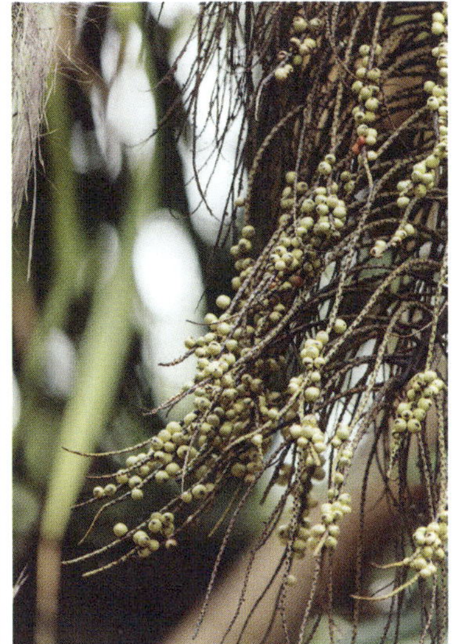

1. Inflorescence. 2. Fruits.

Wallichia disticha is a medium-sized palm that grows to about 13 feet before beginning to flower, but can eventually reach 26 feet in height. This palm's most distinctive feature is clearly visible: the long leaves are distichous, meaning that they are produced on either side of the trunk, so the palm is flat, as if it had been pressed between two enormous panes of glass. The trunk is covered in overlapping black fibers. This genus is closely related to *Arenga* and *Caryota*, and like the species in those genera, *Wallichia disticha* produces its flowers first at the top of the stem and subsequently at lower and lower points along the trunk. Once the lowermost flower stalks have been produced and the fruits have ripened, the palm dies. Since this species has a solitary stem, the individual dies completely. Reproduction is entirely by seed. The entire process, from first flowering to death, takes about two years. Its fruits are small and brownish-red; they have oxalate crystals that are very irritating to the skin and can cause renal problems if ingested. Before it flowers, the trunk of *Wallichia disticha* is very rich in starch and can be eaten in times of scarcity.

The Jardín Botánico Culiacán has only one specimen of *Wallichia disticha*. It is fifteen years old and began to flower during the first half of 2019.

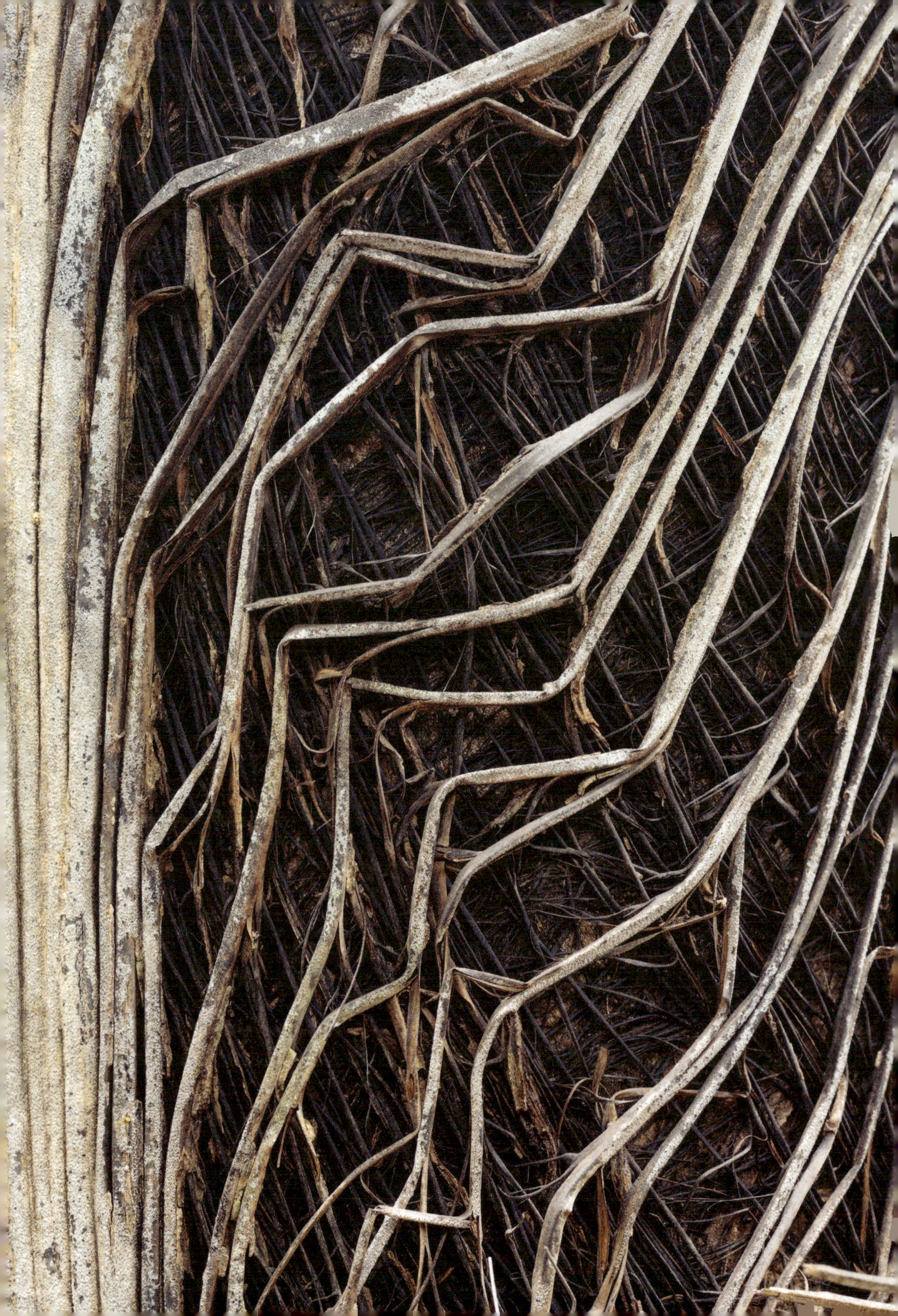

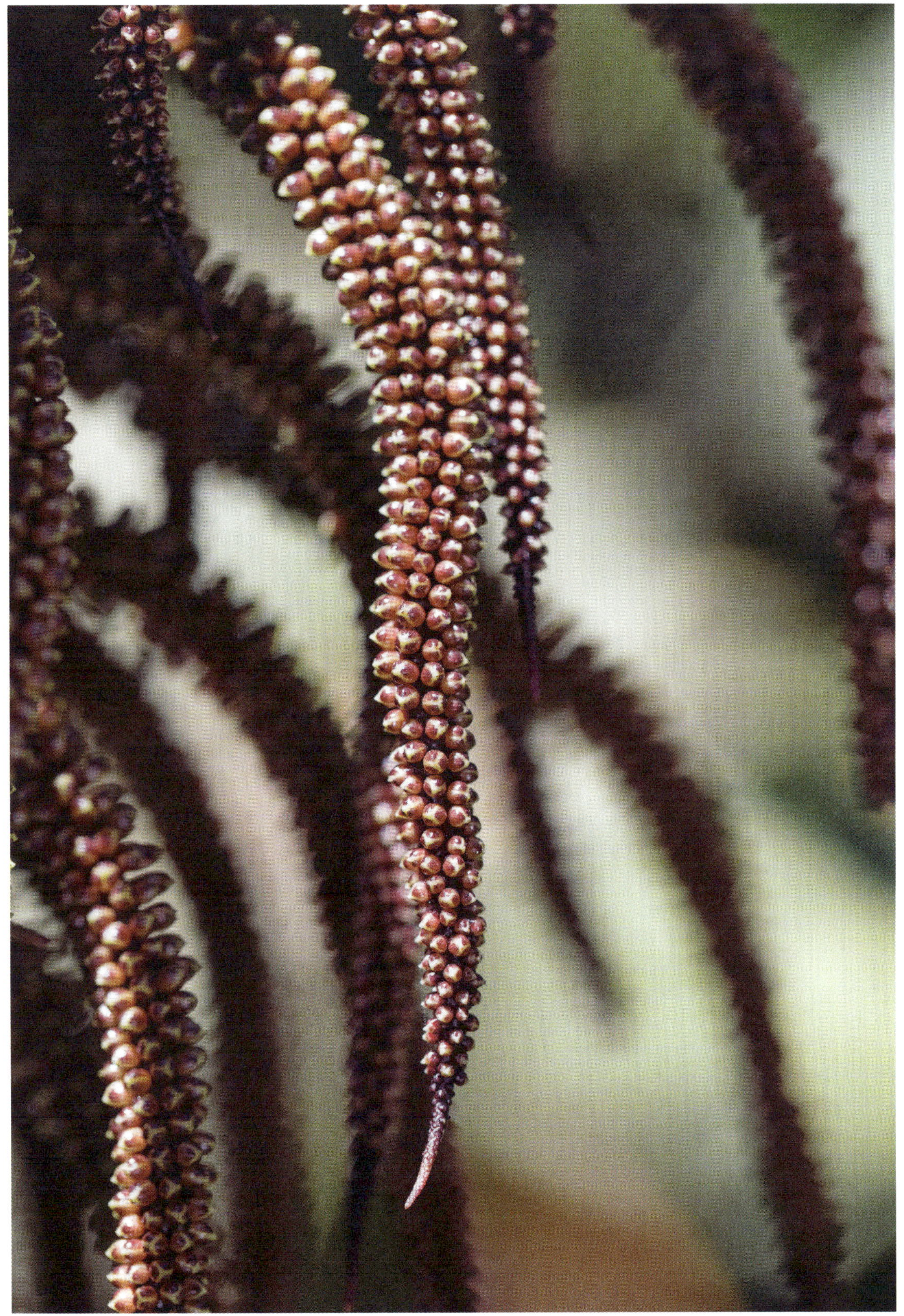

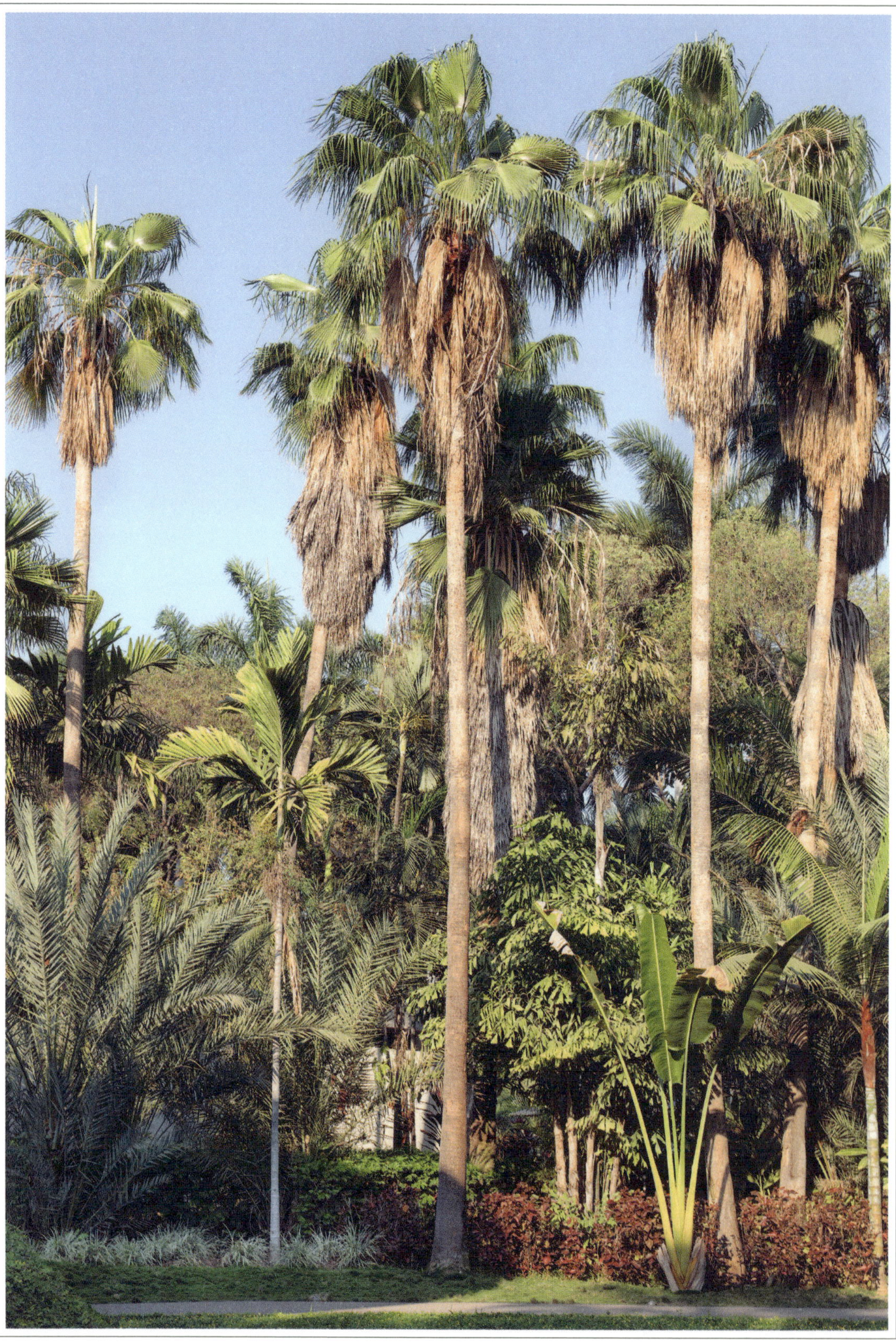

84

DESERT FAN PALM, PETTICOAT PALM

Washingtonia filifera (Linden ex André) H. Wendl. ex de Bary

Status: Designated as Near Threatened on the IUCN Red List
Distribution: Northwestern Mexico and the southwestern United States

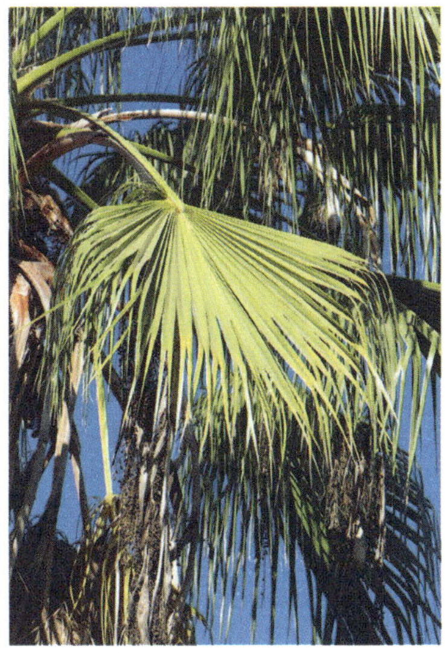

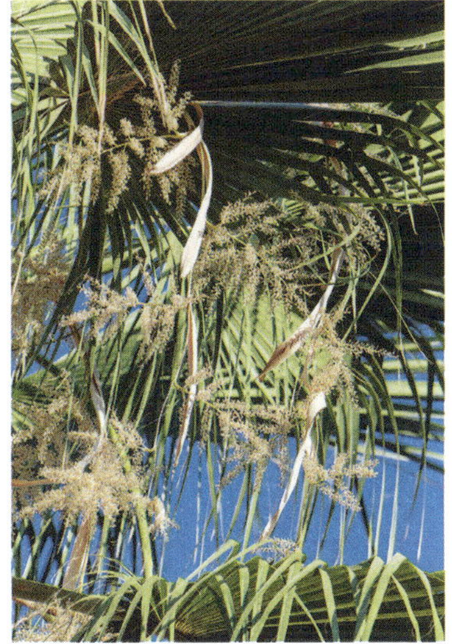

1. Leaf. 2. Inflorescence.

This species has a massive, very straight trunk, which grows to almost 65 feet tall. It is found in canyons and oases in the Sonoran Desert, where its roots have access to water throughout the year, but it can endure long spells of drought. Its common name, the desert fan palm, refers to the form of its gray-green leaves, which are wide and semicircular, with very thin filaments hanging from the tips. Its crown is very dense. The desert fan palm produces long pendulous stalks of creamy white flowers. Botanists believe that this species of palm can live for more than five hundred years. In the desert, where few food resources grow, both people and animals rely on the fruits of *Washingtonia filifera*. The fruits used to be eaten fresh or dried and stored for later use by the Cahuilla, a Native American people. The skirt of dead leaves was sometimes burned to stimulate flowering and fruiting. Birds, bats, and coyotes eat the fruits and disperse the seeds. Many species of birds, including owls and hooded orioles, nest in these palms.

Some of the specimens of *Washingtonia filifera* at the Jardín Botánico Culiacán come from the Jardín Botánico Benjamin Francis Johnston in Los Mochis in Sinaloa, where there are some palms more than a hundred years old, almost the same age as the city of Los Mochis itself.

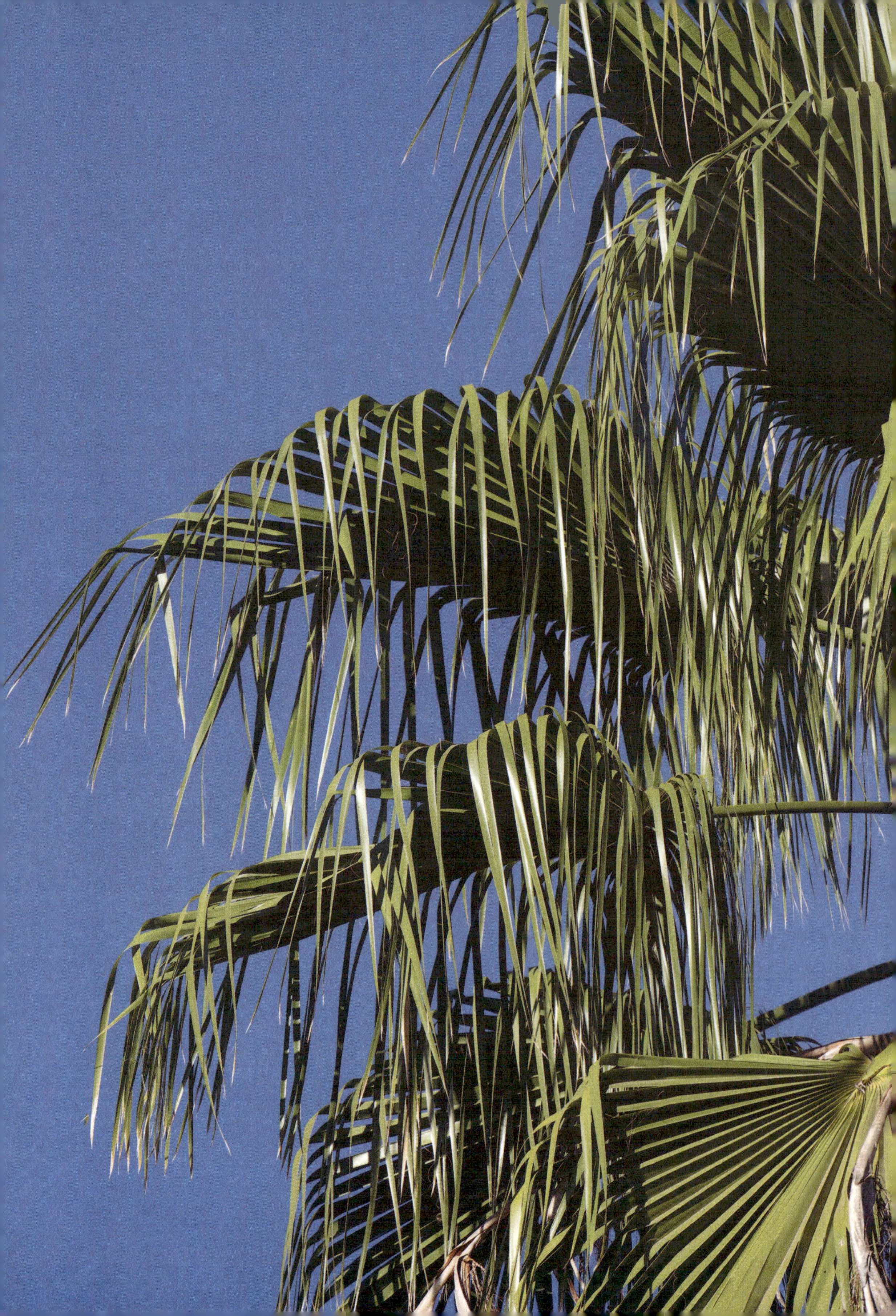

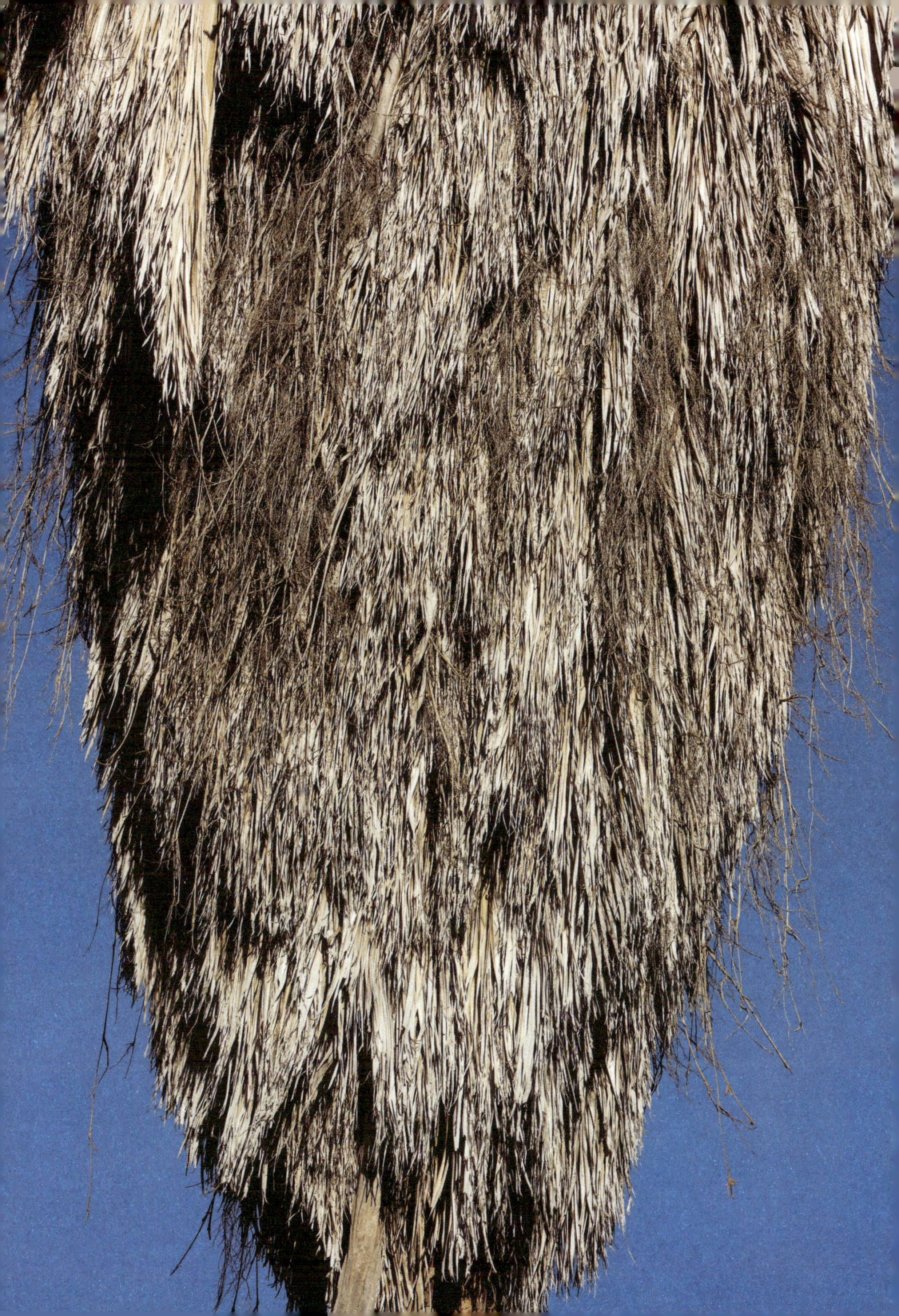

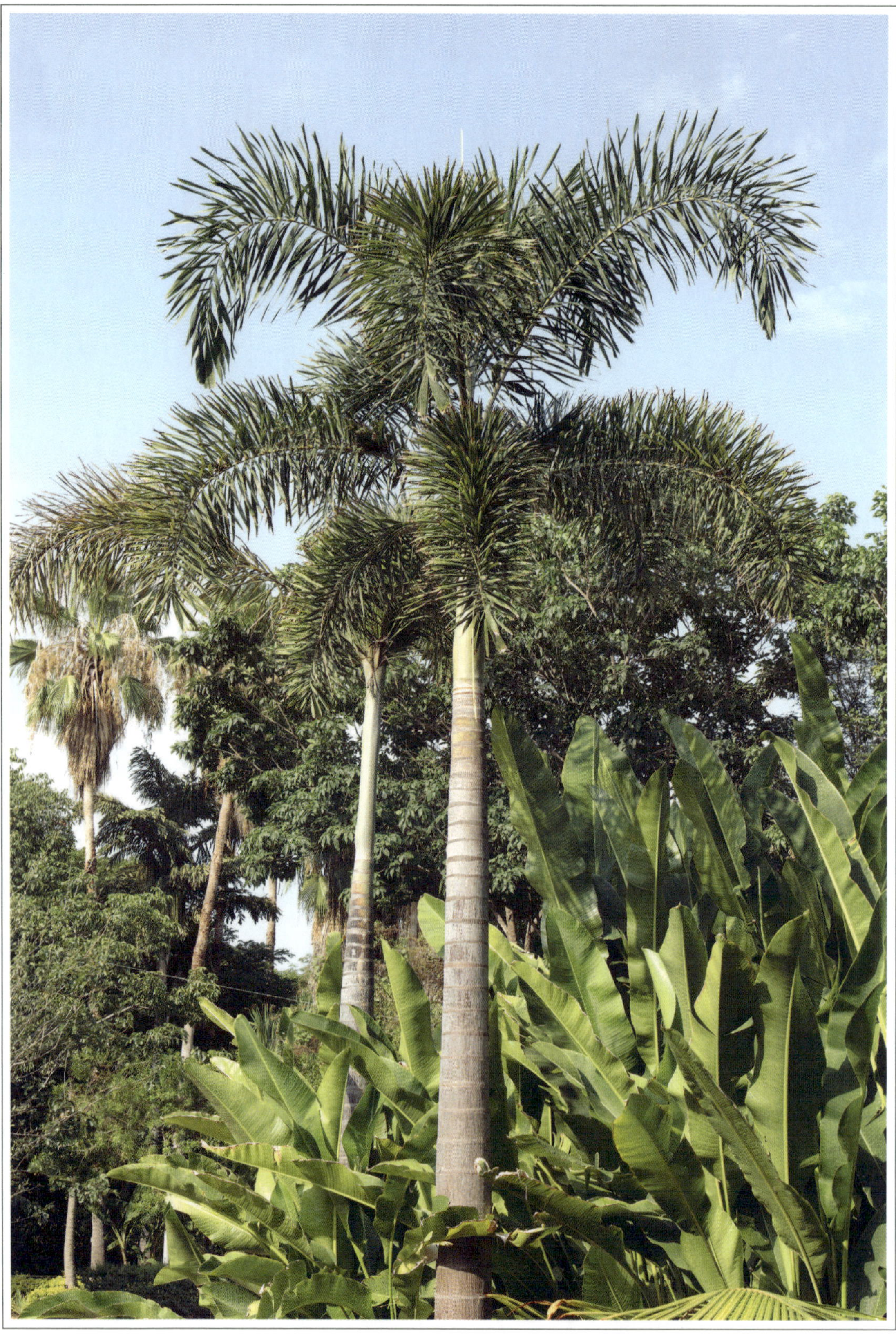

85

FOXTAIL PALM

Wodyetia bifurcata A.K. Irvine

Status: Designated as Conservation Dependent on the IUCN Red List, but an assessment of its global conservation status is required
Distribution: Northern Australia

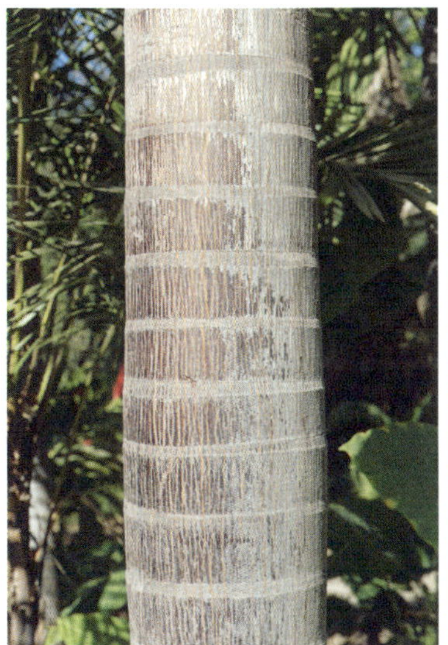

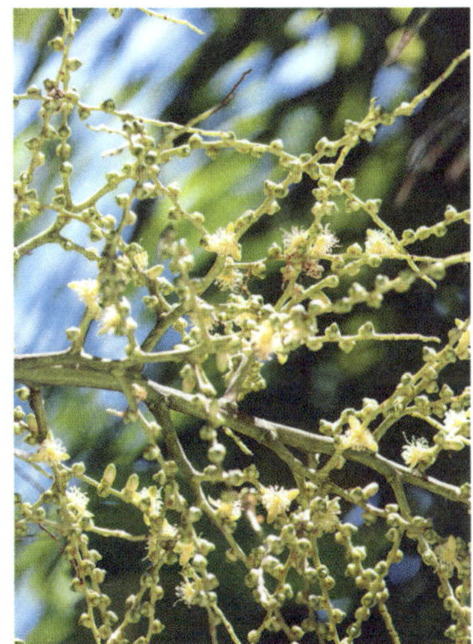

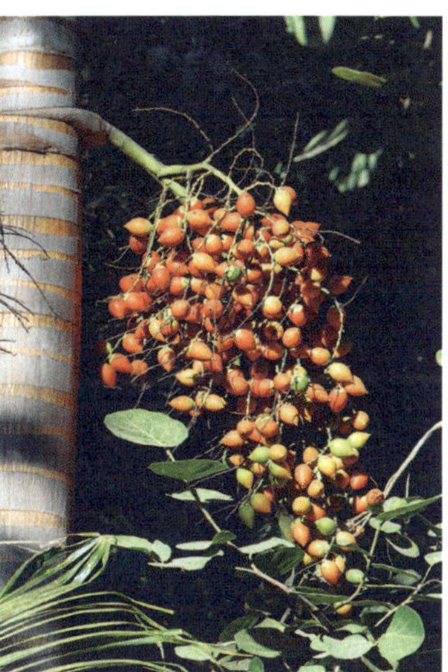

1. Trunk. 2. Flowers. 3. Fruits.

This attractive palm forms a tall trunk, up to 50 feet tall, often with a slight bulge in the middle. *Wodyetia bifurcata* occurs on hillsides strewn with large granite boulders. The habitat is hot and dry, and this species has several features that allow it to grow in such difficult conditions. The bulging trunk is like a huge water tank, storing up water during the rainy season and helping the palm survive the dry season. The leaflets are longitudinally divided and stick out in all directions, resembling the tail of a fox (hence the palm's common name). This feature prevents the surfaces of the leaflets from absorbing too much sunlight and overheating in hot, sunny weather. Each fleshy, orange-red fruit contains a single large seed enclosed by thick black fibers. The large, flightless cassowary bird probably eats the fruits and disperses the seeds. This palm is very popular in the horticultural trade.

Unfortunately, there is no record of the arrival of the first specimens of *Wodyetia bifurcata* at the Jardín Botánico Culiacán. Since 2015, however, a group of these palms emblazons the art installation *Encounter* by US artist James Turrell.

II

PALMS IN THE NURSERY

86

TEPEJILOTE

Chamaedorea alternans H. Wendl.

Status: Designated as Threatened on the Mexican list of endangered species (NOM -059- SEMARNAT -2010)
Distribution: Endemic to Mexico

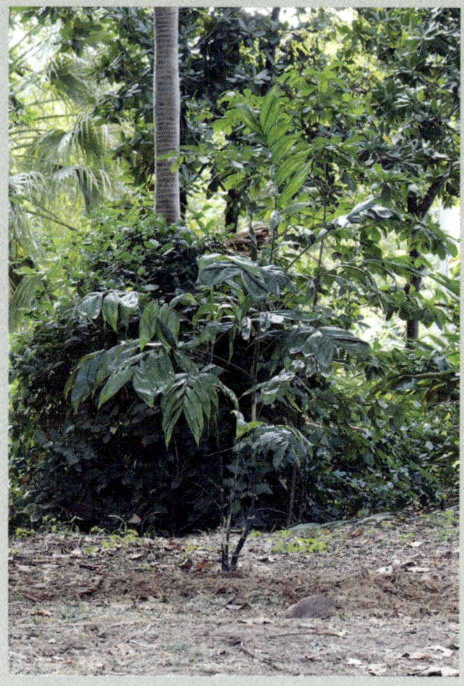

Chamaedorea alternans is a small palm, which grows up to 10 feet tall in the shade of tall trees. The common name of this species, the tepejilote, is the result of its similarity in appearance to *Chamaedorea tepejilote*. Both of these palms occur in the rainforests of southern Mexico and they have frequently been confused. In the past, some botanists recognized only one species, but there is now good evidence that there are two distinct, but related species. *Chamaedorea alternans* is found only in Veracruz, Chiapas, and Oaxaca and has larger fruits and seeds. It usually has multiple flower stalks at each node along the stem, although sometimes solitary flower stalks alternate with multiple ones (this alternation being the reason for its scientific name). The flower stalks are always solitary in the case of *Chamaedorea tepejilote*. The two species also produce flowers at different times during the year. In *Chamaedorea alternans* male (yellow) and female (greenish) flowers grow on different stalks, attracting insect pollinators such as wasps, flies, and mosquitoes, though they may be wind-pollinated as well. When fertilized, this palm produces oval fruits that ripen to a shiny black color and are dispersed by birds. Owing to deforestation, *Chamaedorea alternans* is now very scarce, and it is not cultivated, although it has great ornamental potential. The specimens in the Jardín Botánico Culiacán came from Los Tuxtlas in the state of Veracruz in 2016.

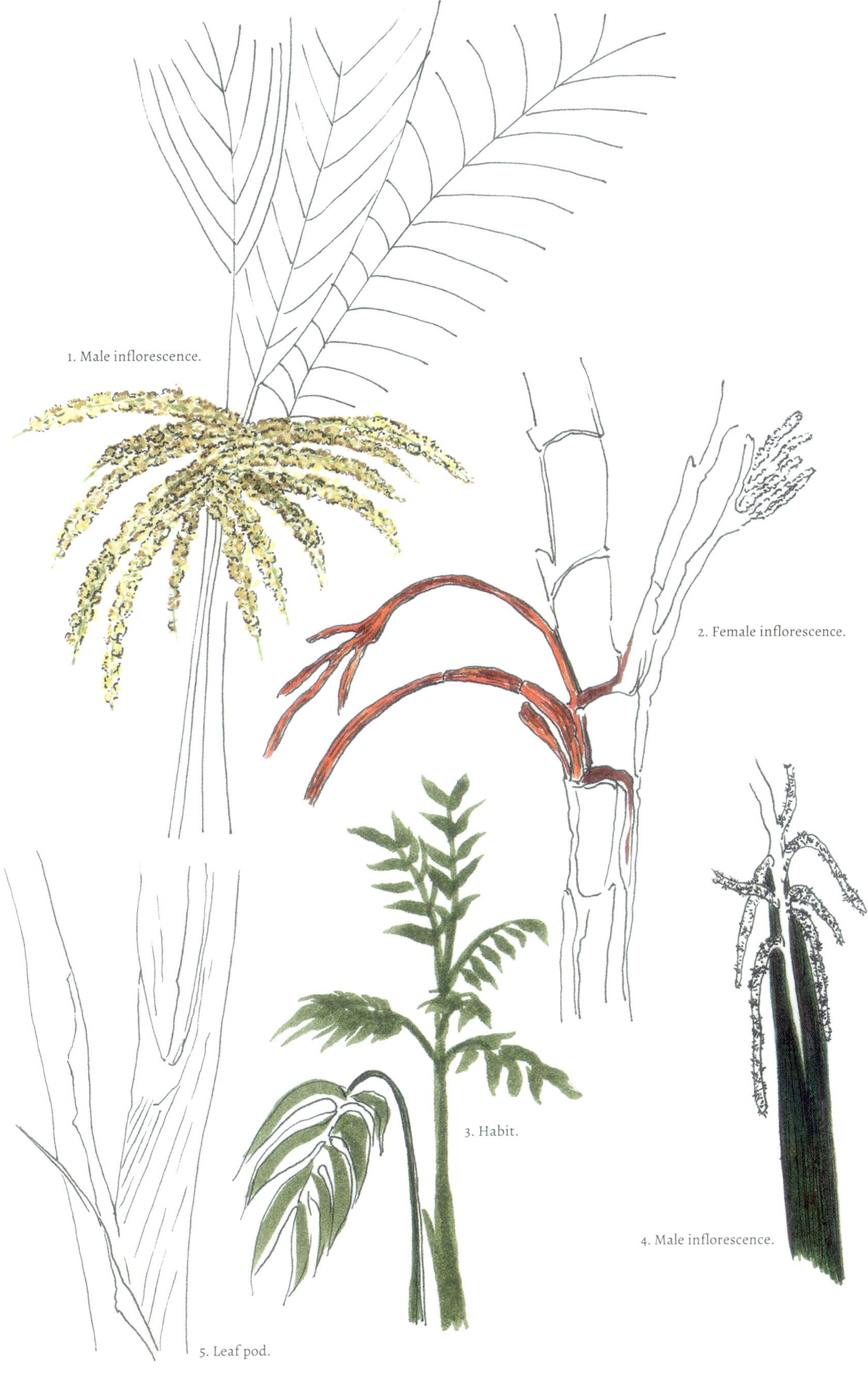
1. Male inflorescence.
2. Female inflorescence.
3. Habit.
4. Male inflorescence.
5. Leaf pod.

87

ARENBERGIA PALM

Chamaedorea arenbergiana H. Wendl.

Status: Designated as Threatened on the Mexican list of endangered species (NOM-059-SEMARNAT-2010)
Distribution: Southern Mexico, Guatemala, Honduras, and possibly Central America and Colombia

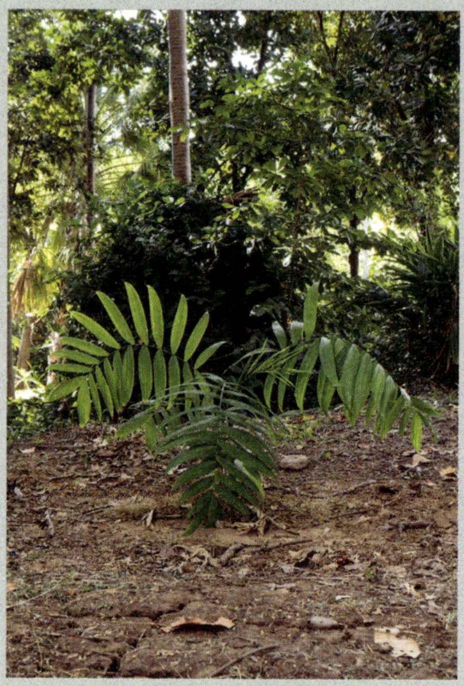

This small rainforest palm has solitary green stems that grow up to 10 feet long, handsome broad leaflets, and female flower spikes that resemble ears of corn. We know it occurs in southern Mexico, Guatemala, and Honduras, but—because the rainforests extend all the way to Colombia—*Chamaedorea arenbergiana* may also exist farther south, through Central America and into Colombia. In order to confirm this, more field work needs to be done. *Chamaedorea arenbergiana* resembles several other species, including *Chamaedorea tepejilote*, and the characteristics of the male flowers must be examined to confirm the identities of the different species. Unfortunately, male flowers are present on the plants for only a very brief time. Many specimens in palm collections lack male flowers, so reliable identification is not possible. For this reason, the complete native range of this species is still uncertain.

The Jardín Botánico Culiacán has a few specimens of *Chamaedorea tepejilote* that botanists rescued from a disturbed area. It was a difficult task to obtain them, because of the presence of poisonous snakes in the collecting area.

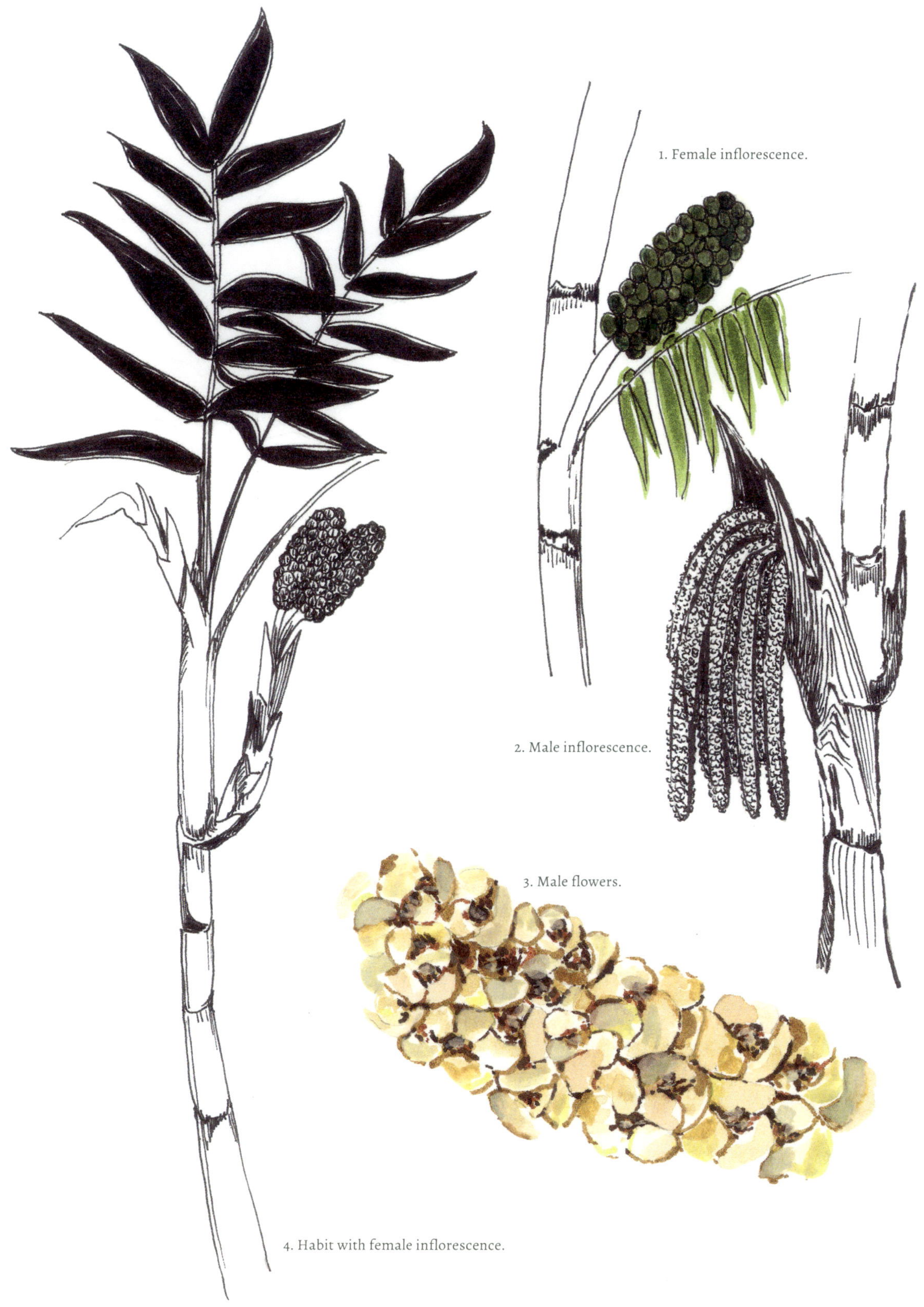
1. Female inflorescence.
2. Male inflorescence.
3. Male flowers.
4. Habit with female inflorescence.

88

SAN PABLO PALM

Chamaedorea pinnatifrons (Jacq.) Oerst.

Status: Designated as Least Concern on the IUCN Red List
Distribution: From Mexico to Bolivia

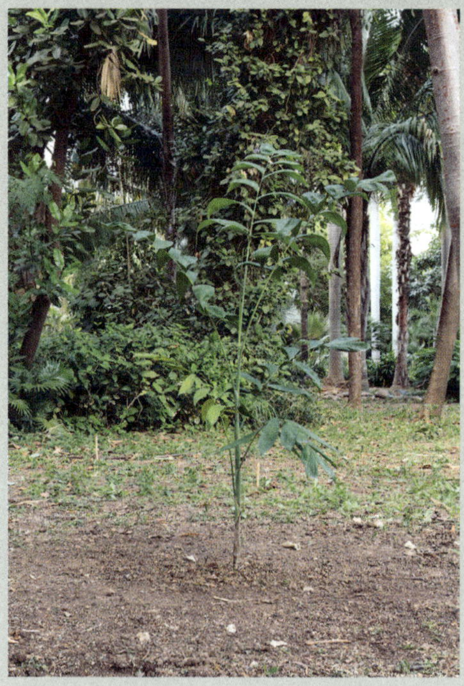

This is the most widespread species of *Chamaedorea*. It is a small palm, growing up to 10 feet tall and occurring in rainforests. Different forms of this species from distinct locations have confused botanists, who have given it over 25 different names. Further study may someday reveal that some forms should be recognized as distinct species, but for now botanists regard *Chamaedorea pinnatifrons* as the most variable of all *Chamaedorea* in the size and shape of its leaves, flowers, and fruits. The fruits are red or orange when ripe, which adds to this palm's ornamental qualities.

Some specimens of *Chamaedorea pinnatifrons* were collected in 2017 from the state of Oaxaca, but botanists observed that the palm was not particularly abundant in the areas they visited, so the Jardín Botánico Culiacán does not have many specimens. The specimens in the garden's nursery are carefully preserved, since the palm was so rare in the collecting zone.

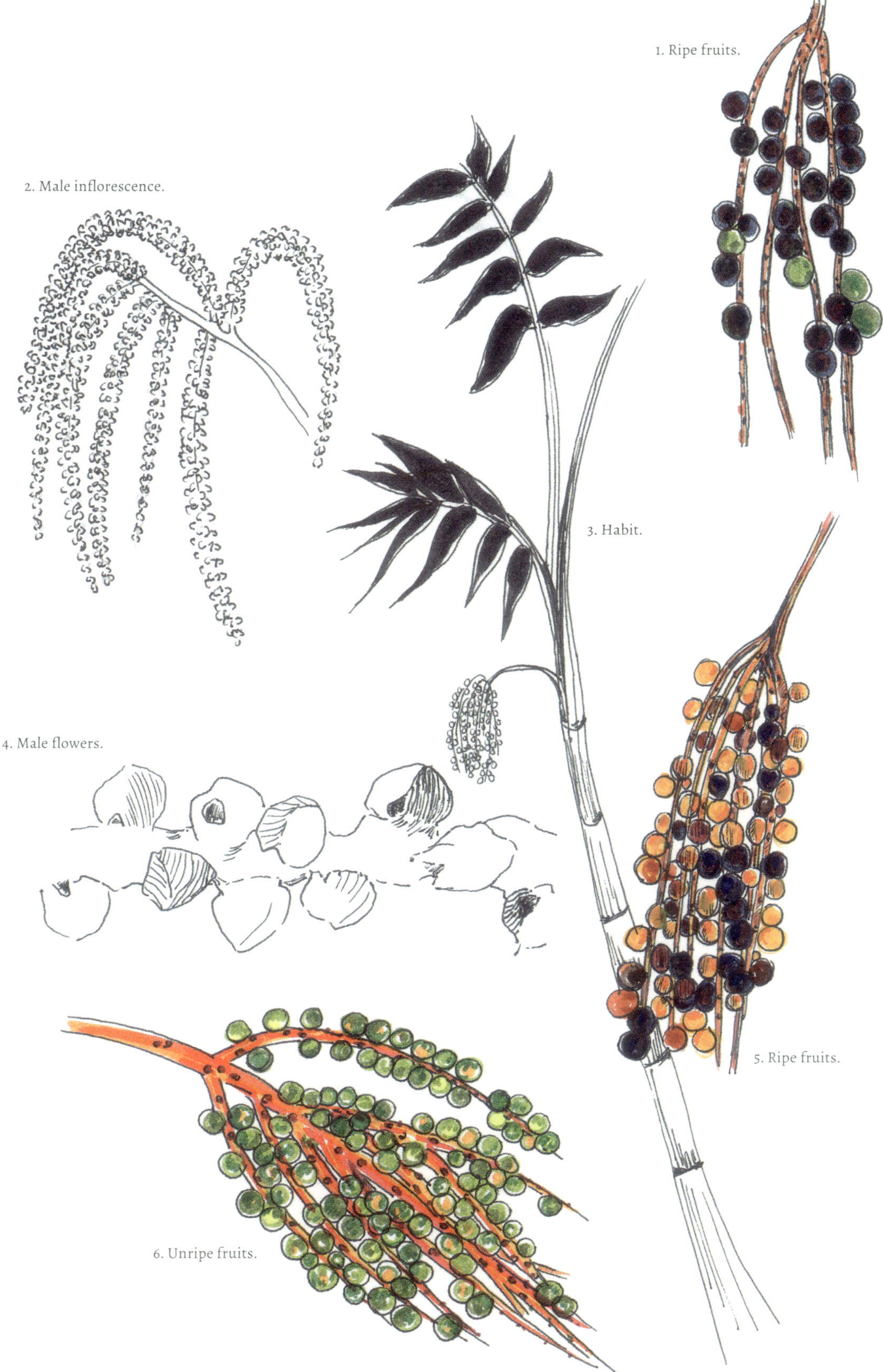
1. Ripe fruits.
2. Male inflorescence.
3. Habit.
4. Male flowers.
5. Ripe fruits.
6. Unripe fruits.

89
CLIMBING CHAMAEDOREA

Chamaedorea elatior Mart.

Status: Designated as Threatened on the Mexican list of endangered species (NOM-059-SEMARNAT-2010) and as Least Concern on the IUCN Red List
Distribution: Southern Mexico and Guatemala

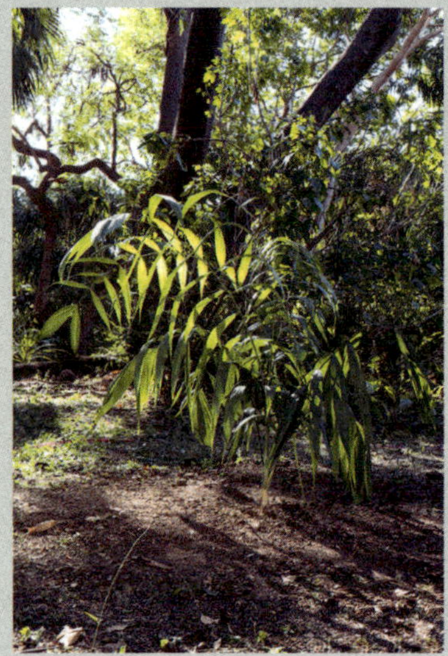

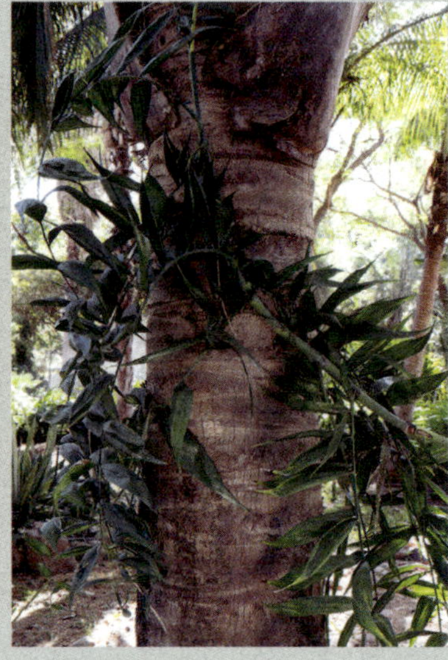

Although not greatly admired by palm growers, *Chamaedorea elatior* is a most remarkable species. It is the only species in the genus that is a climbing palm, with flexible stems up to 100 feet long. The climbing habit has evolved several times in the palm family, most famously in the ancestors to the genus *Calamus*, the rattan palms of Asia. In the Americas, the climbing habit evolved only twice: once in the ancestor to *Desmoncus*, which has several climbing species, and once in *Chamaedorea elatior*. Like its stems, the leaves of *Chamaedorea elatior* are also adapted for climbing. The upper leaflets are modified into backward-pointing hooks. They are weak hooks, but they help this palm to scramble up into trees, where it can gain access to light, or to sprawl across open ground. The name of the species comes from the Latin word *elatus*, which means "elongated," in reference to the stems. The male flowers are aromatic and so attract pollinators. The abundant fruits are dark and very small (less than half an inch in diameter). As in the case of many palms, this species is threatened by habitat destruction. The stems were commonly used to make little woven animals, but this artisanal tradition began to disappear as the palm became scarcer. If nurseries in villages cultivate it, artisans will have a sustainable source of raw material.

Several specimens were included in the National Palm Collection in 2016. They come from the state of Veracruz, where they were rescued from an abandoned nursery that was about to be burned. The species urgently requires human intervention, such as cultivation in nurseries, to protect it.

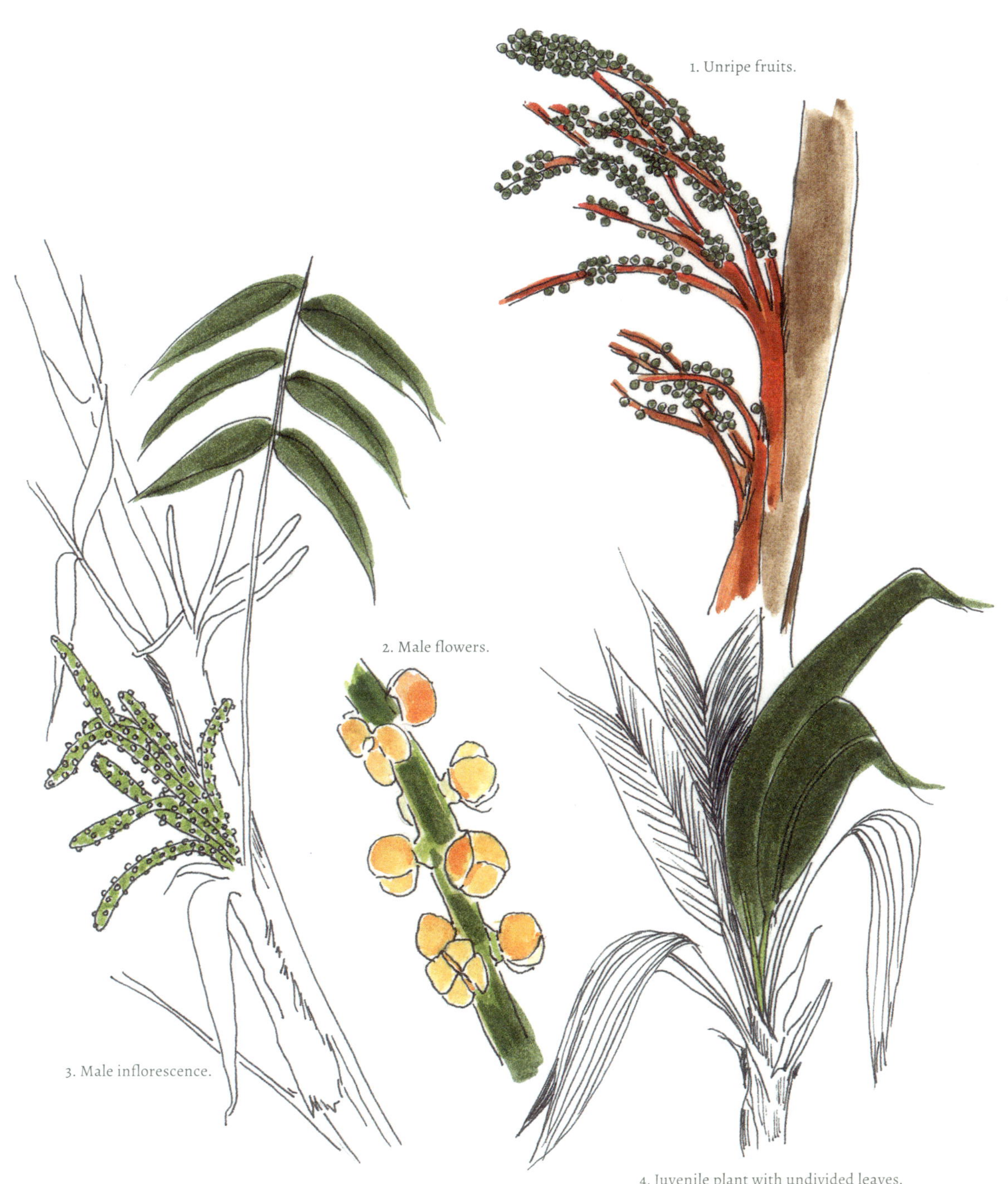

1. Unripe fruits.

2. Male flowers.

3. Male inflorescence.

4. Juvenile plant with undivided leaves.

90

PARLOR PALM, GOOD-LUCK PALM

Chamaedorea elegans Mart.

Status: Assessment of global conservation status required
Distribution: Southern Mexico, Belize, and Guatemala

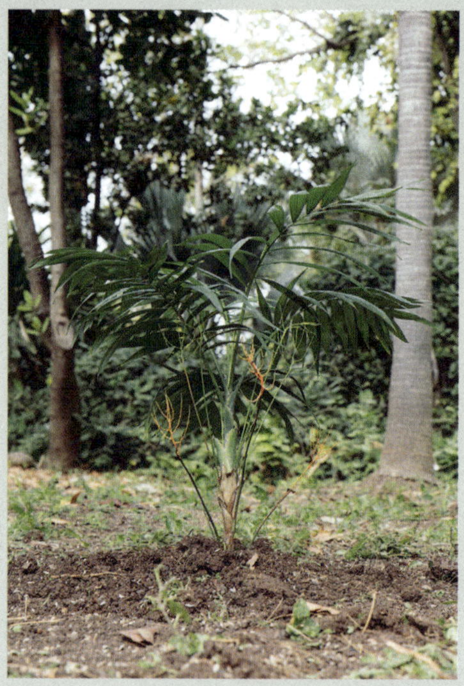

This charming little palm, which grows to only about 6.5 feet tall, occurs in the understory of wet tropical rainforests, in very nutrient-rich soils. *Chamaedorea elegans* was first discovered in Veracruz, Mexico, in the early part of the nineteenth century. Shortly thereafter, it became one of the most commonly cultivated palms in the homes and conservatories of Europe. Because of its diminutive size and ease of cultivation, the palm's popularity continues to this day, as commercial nurseries in Europe, North America, and Asia supply it to plant-lovers all over the world. In its places of origin, people use the leaves of *Chamaedorea elegans* for flower arrangements to honor the dead, on altars and in religious ceremonies, and in other non-liturgical situations (it is popular, for example, with street vendors). Today, around 400 million leaves are sold around the world, most of them produced in Mexico. The palm is solitary, but nurseries often put many seedlings in one pot in order to produce a fuller, leafier plant. When grown as a houseplant, the palm rarely produces fruits, which however are shiny and black, borne on branched orange stalks. *Chamaedorea elegans* flowers from May to October.

Decades ago, Carlos Murillo Depraect, while guiding visitors around the Jardín Botánico Culiacán, very much enjoyed telling the story that the green color of the US dollar bill came from the leaves of these palms. Although this is not actually true, it was very entertaining for people visiting the garden to hear.

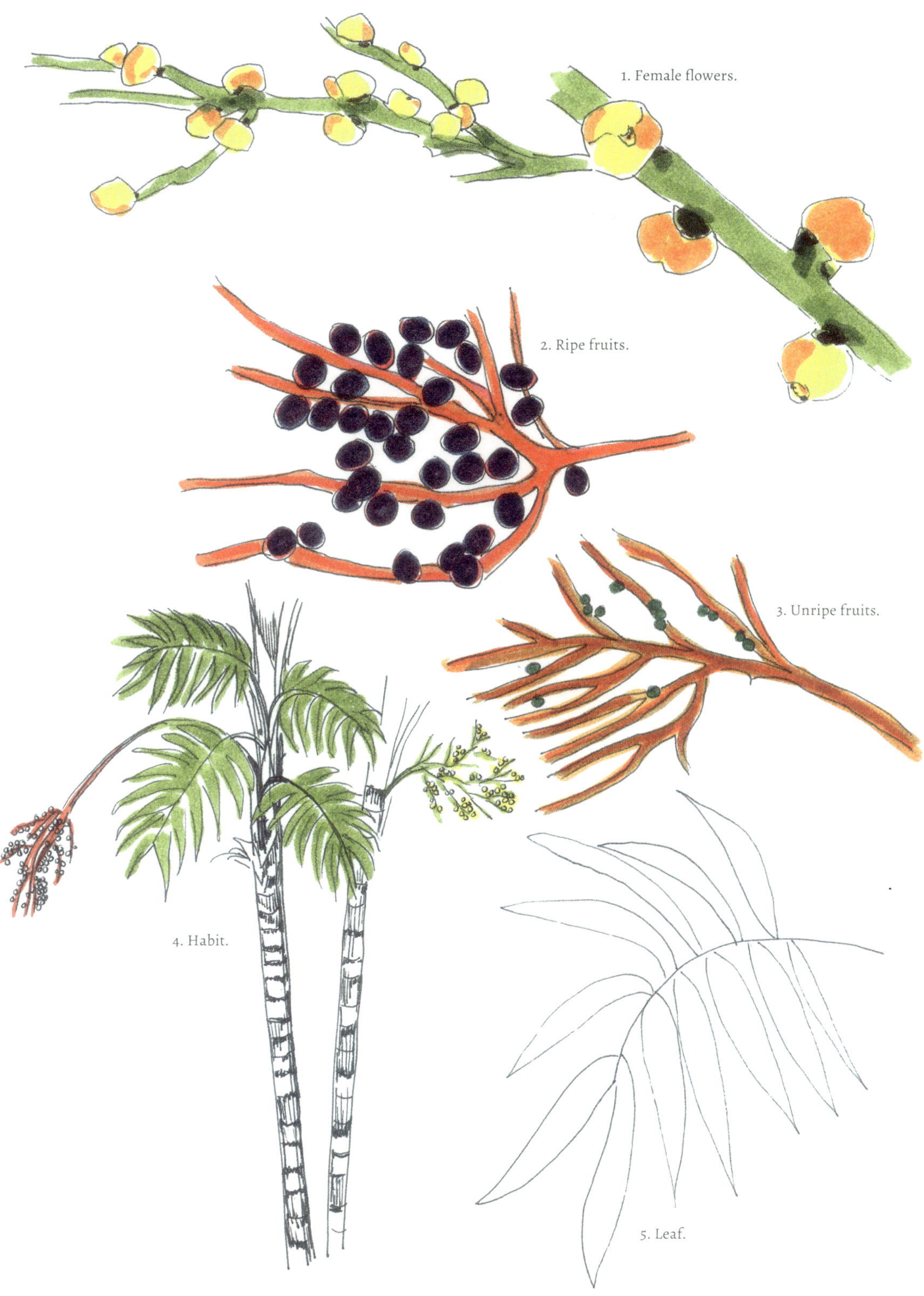
1. Female flowers.
2. Ripe fruits.
3. Unripe fruits.
4. Habit.
5. Leaf.

91

GRASS-LEAF PALM

Chamaedorea graminifolia H. Wendl.

Status: Designated as Threatened on the Mexican list of endangered species (NOM-059-SEMARNAT-2010)
Distribution: Mexico, Belize, Guatemala, Costa Rica, and Nicaragua

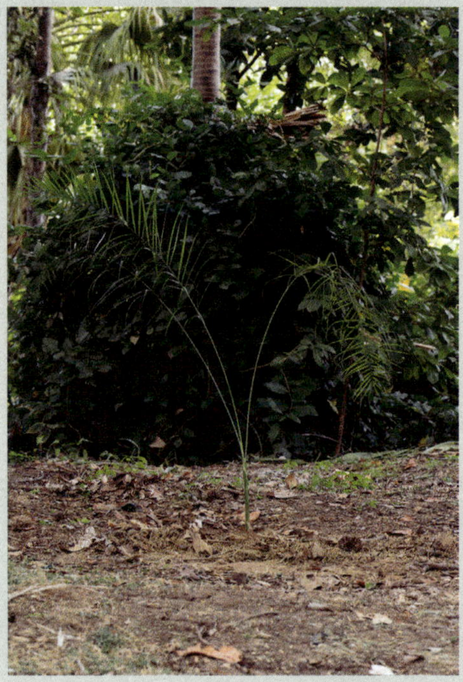

Chamaedorea graminifolia is a small rare solitary palm that grows up to 13 feet tall. It is found in transition areas between tropical rain forests and tropical dry forests, in calcium-rich soils. The palm has confused botanists for over a hundred years, only recently having been distinguished from *Chamaedorea schippii*. Both are from Costa Rica, but *Chamaedorea graminifolia* also occurs in Belize, Guatemala, and perhaps Mexico. *Chamaedorea graminifolia* gets its name from its narrow leaflets, which resemble blades of grass (*graminifolia* means "grass leaf" in Latin). It has a very narrow solitary stem resembling a bamboo (*Chamaedorea schippii* has clustered stems) and bright green leaflets with a single middle vein (they are gray-green and multi-veined in *Chamaedorea schippii*). Another characteristic that distinguishes the species is the male flowers. In its native region the species serves ornamental uses, but in spite of its beauty it is not widely cultivated. In Yucatán, the young flowers are eaten in salads and used for medicinal purposes.

The specimens at the Jardín Botánico Culiacán arrived in 2016, those from Ocozocoautla, Chiapas, having been donated by Prof. Miguel Ángel García Bielma.

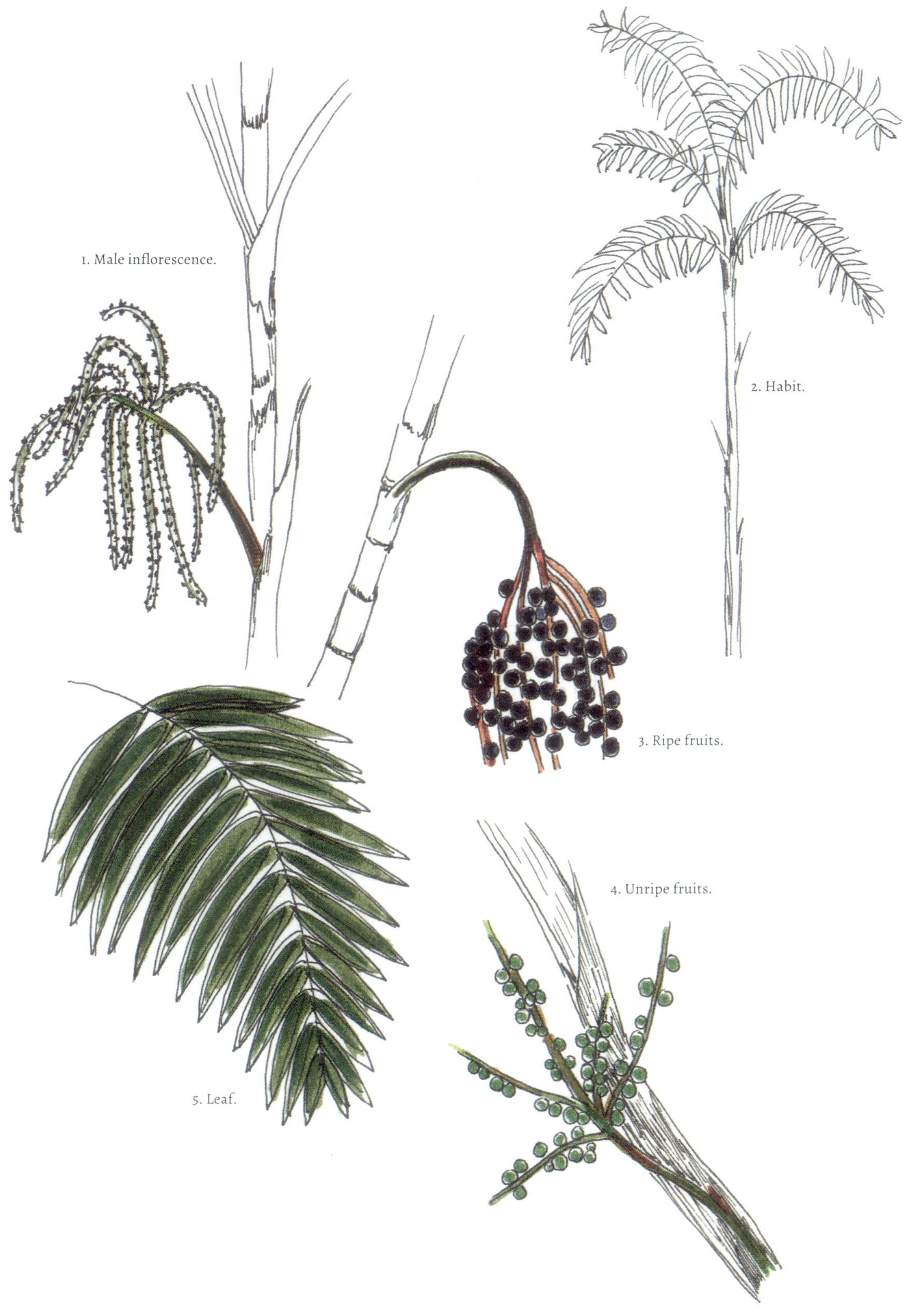
1. Male inflorescence.
2. Habit.
3. Ripe fruits.
4. Unripe fruits.
5. Leaf.

92

HOOPER'S PALM, SWOOPING BAMBOO PALM

Chamaedorea hooperiana Hodel

Status: Designated as Threatened on the Mexican list of endangered species (NOM-059-SEMARNAT-2010)
Distribution: Veracruz, Mexico

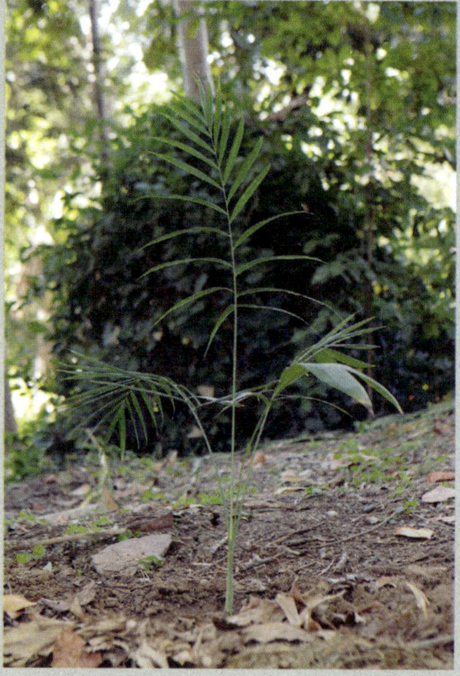

This species of *Chamaedorea* is from high elevation rainforests (3,280 feet above sea level) in Veracruz, where it grows to about 13 feet tall. It closely resembles *Chamaedorea graminifolia* in its narrow leaflets, but *Chamaedorea hooperiana* is a clustering palm, with new plants emerging close to the parent stem, often enclosed by the tough, persistent leaf base. It is also easily confused with *Chamaedorea pochutlensis*, but *Chamaedorea hooperiana* has thick, almost rubbery leaflets. *Chamaedorea hooperiana* is more adaptable to cultivation than either of the other two species, but it is still rarely seen in gardens.

Numerous specimens were collected for the Jardín Botánico Culiacán in Veracruz in 2016. One of the purposes of the National Palm Collection at the garden is to reproduce threatened species like this one, in order to prevent their extinction. If one day the natural ecosystem is restored, the species may be reintroduced into the wild.

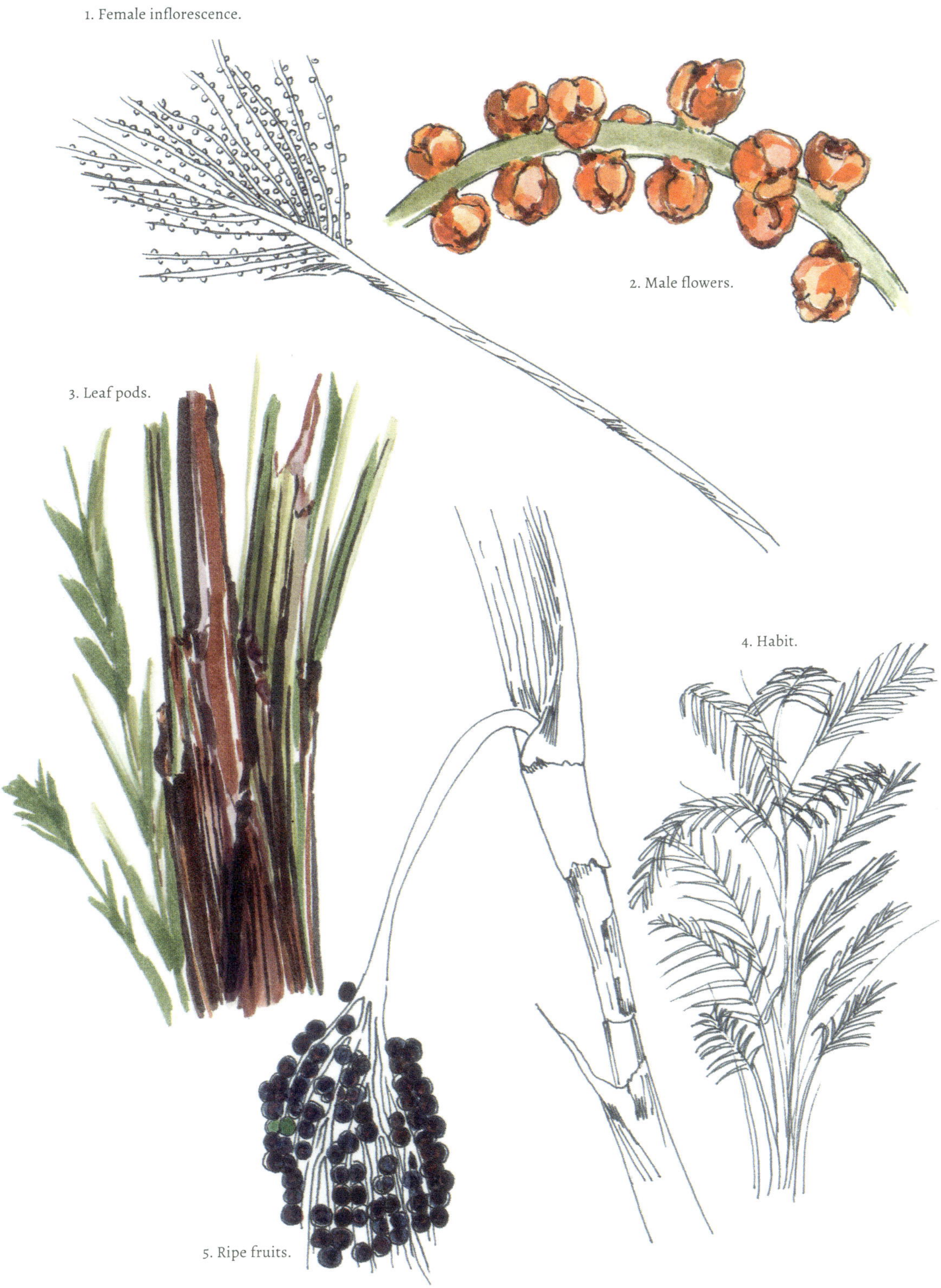

1. Female inflorescence.

2. Male flowers.

3. Leaf pods.

4. Habit.

5. Ripe fruits.

93
VERACRUZ PALM

Chamaedorea klotzschiana H. Wendl.

Status: Designated as Endangered by the IUCN Red List and as Requiring Special Protection on the Mexican list of endangered species (NOM-059-SEMARNAT-2010)
Distribution: Endemic to Veracruz, Mexico

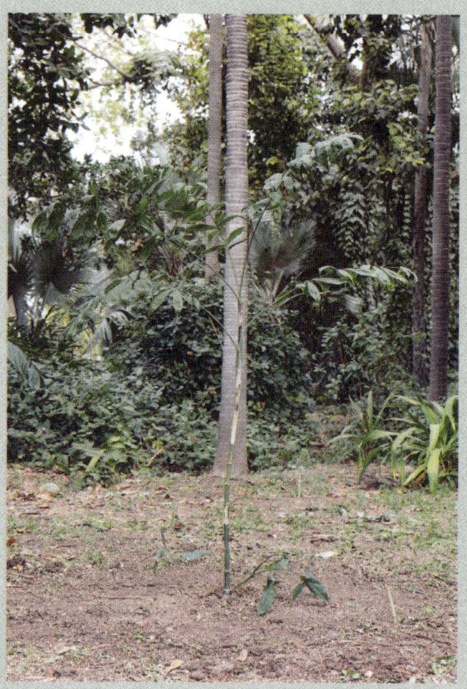

Chamaedorea klotzschiana is a solitary palm, about 10 feet tall, with distinctive leaves: the leaflets are bright green, elliptical, and grouped in clusters of from five to eight in number. The species is native to a small area of Veracruz consisting of tropical rainforest and oak forests, where it is threatened by deforestation and by collection for the horticulturist and florist trades. *Chamaedorea klotzschiana* has round fruits that ripen to shiny black; its seeds, when handled or eaten, can irritate the skin, owing to the presence of raphides. In some respects, this palm resembles *Chamaedorea glaucifolia*, but the latter has slender, gray-green leaflets. Because of its unusual foliage, the species is widely sought by growers and it has been in cultivation since the mid-nineteenth century.

The Jardín Botánico Culiacán has acquired seven specimens since 2016 and they are growing well. The garden is also working to conserve this species (as well as others) by developing techniques to produce healthy plants that can be reintroduced into the wild.

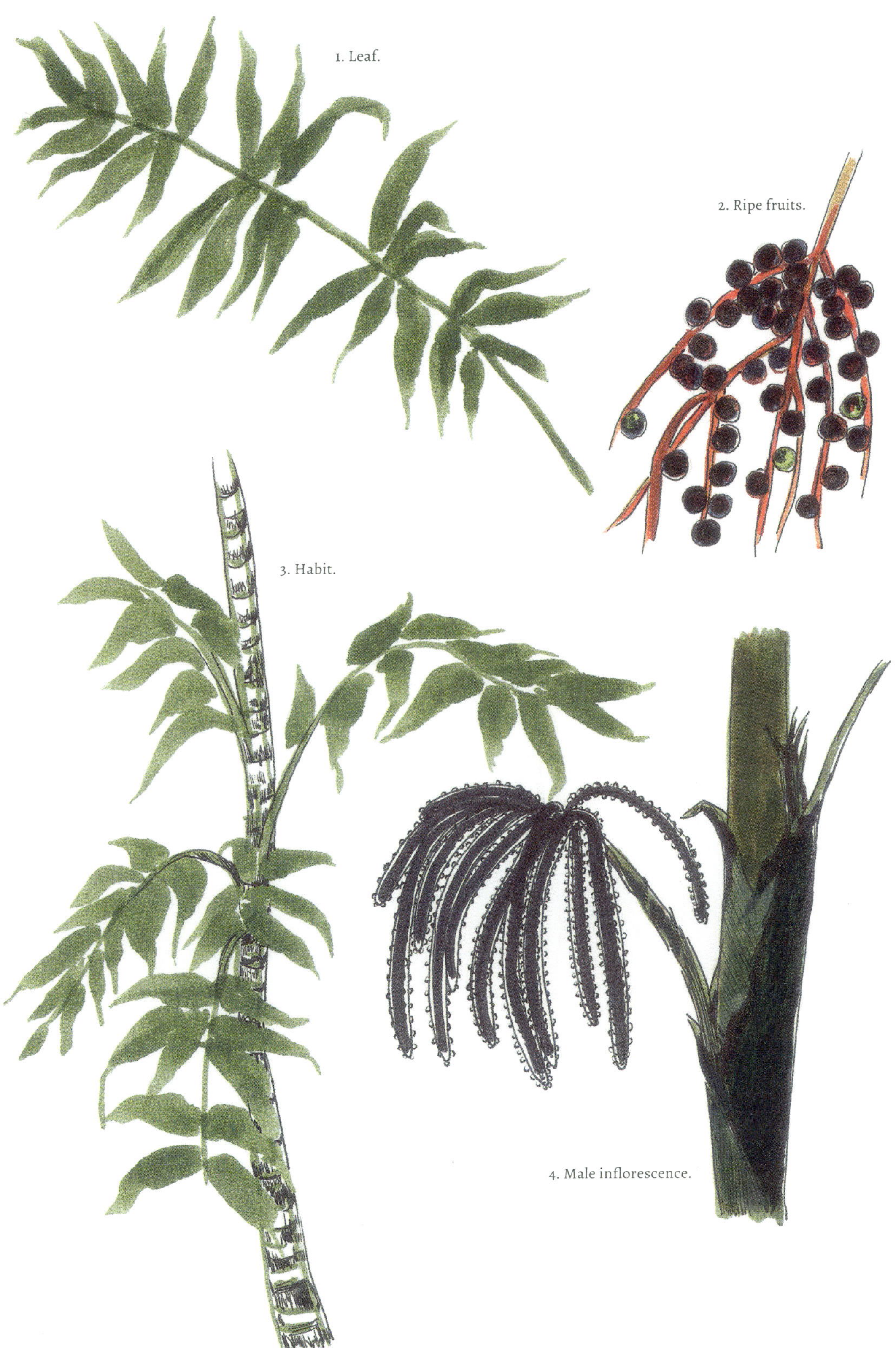
1. Leaf.
2. Ripe fruits.
3. Habit.
4. Male inflorescence.

94
LIEBMANN'S CHAMAEDOREA

Chamaedorea liebmannii Mart.

Status: Designated as Threatened on the Mexican list of endangered species (NOM-059-SEMARNAT-2010)
Distribution: Southern Mexico and Guatemala

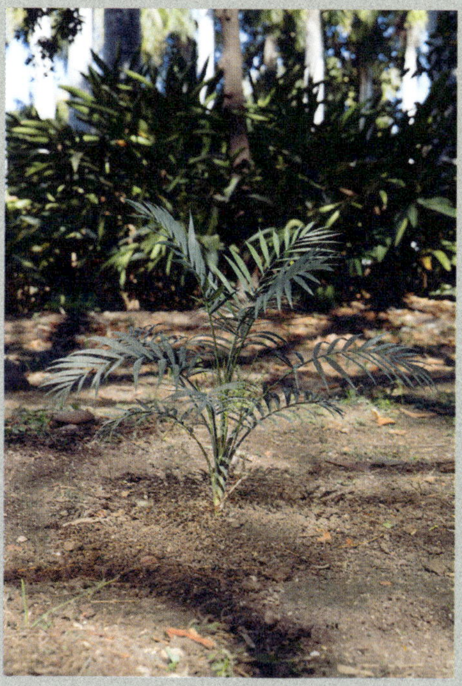

Another small *Chamaedorea* (about 13 feet tall) growing in cloud forests at high elevations in southern Mexico and Guatemala, this species was first discovered in Oaxaca and introduced into cultivation in Europe in the mid-nineteenth century. It has since fallen out of fashion and disappeared from cultivation. It is a solitary palm, with straight, narrow evenly, arranged leaflets. It is time perhaps to bring this attractive palm back into cultivation and thus help to rescue it from extinction.

Botanists from the Jardín Botánico Culiacán obtained seeds of *Chamaedorea liebmannii* while on an expedition in 2014, but they were unfortunately not successful. It was not until 2016 that the garden obtained a specimen from Veracruz.

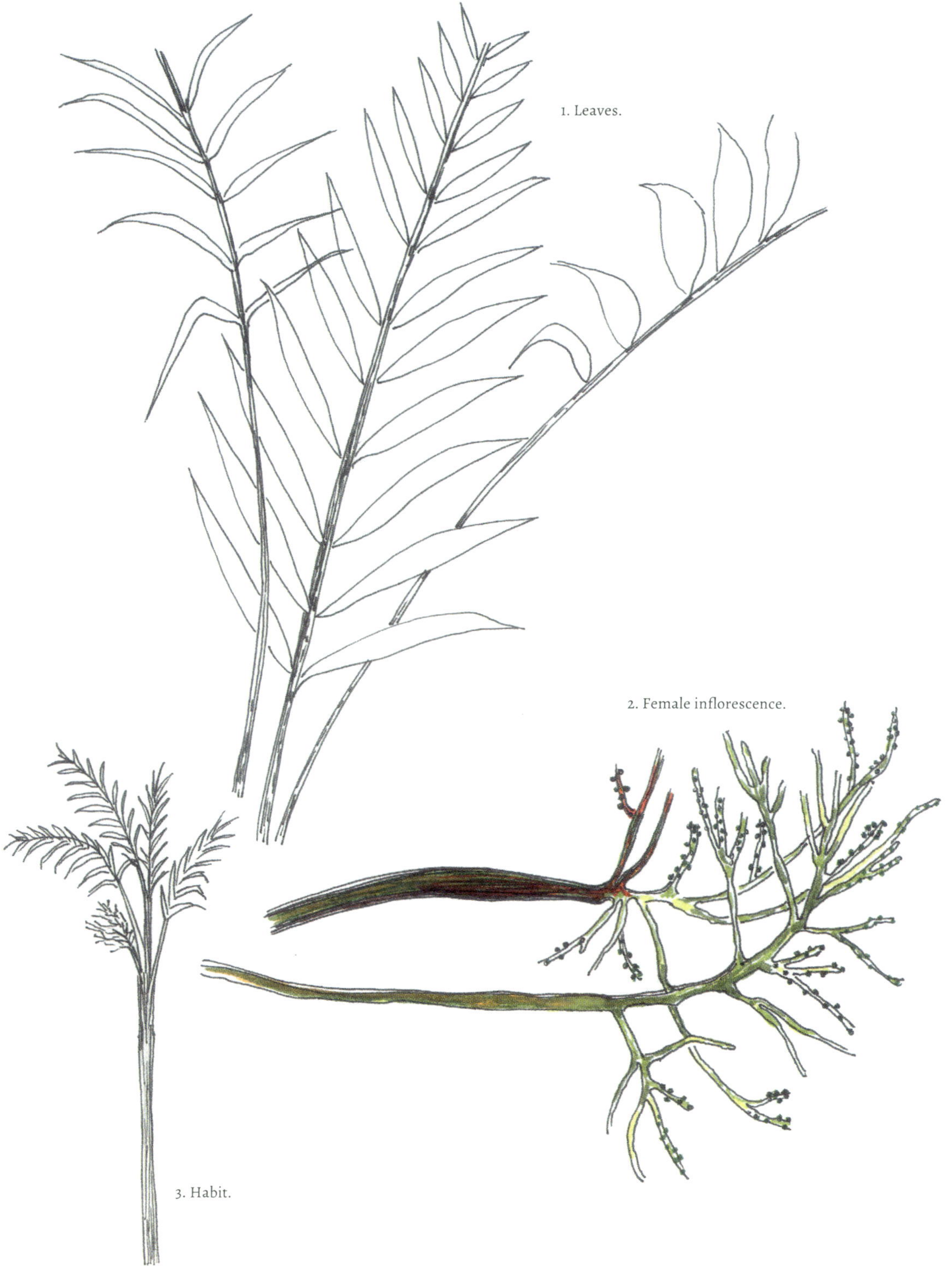
1. Leaves.
2. Female inflorescence.
3. Habit.

95

WHALE TAIL PALM, ST. PAUL'S CANE PALM

Chamaedorea linearis (Ruiz & Pav.) Mart.

Status: Assessment of global conservation status required
Distribution: Northwestern South America

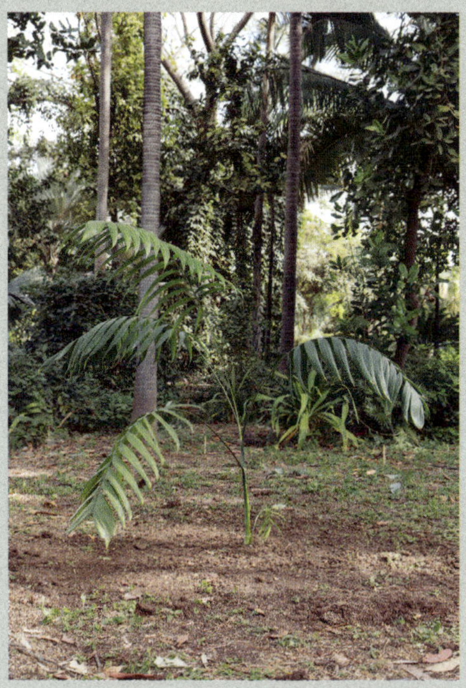

This solitary, erect palm from northwestern South America has a stem that grows up to 35 feet tall and three inches in diameter, extraordinary dimensions for a species of *Chamaedorea*, a genus known for small palms. It has a crown of regularly arranged linear leaflets (the inspiration for the scientific name) and its male or female flower stalks are branched and borne below the leaves. The size of the palm varies, as do the size and shape of its fruits, misleading botanists for over a century into thinking that more than one large species of *Chamaedorea* occurred in the area. As the area was better explored, however, and more specimens became available for study, the gaps between the different "species" were filled in. Now, only one large, variable species is recognized.

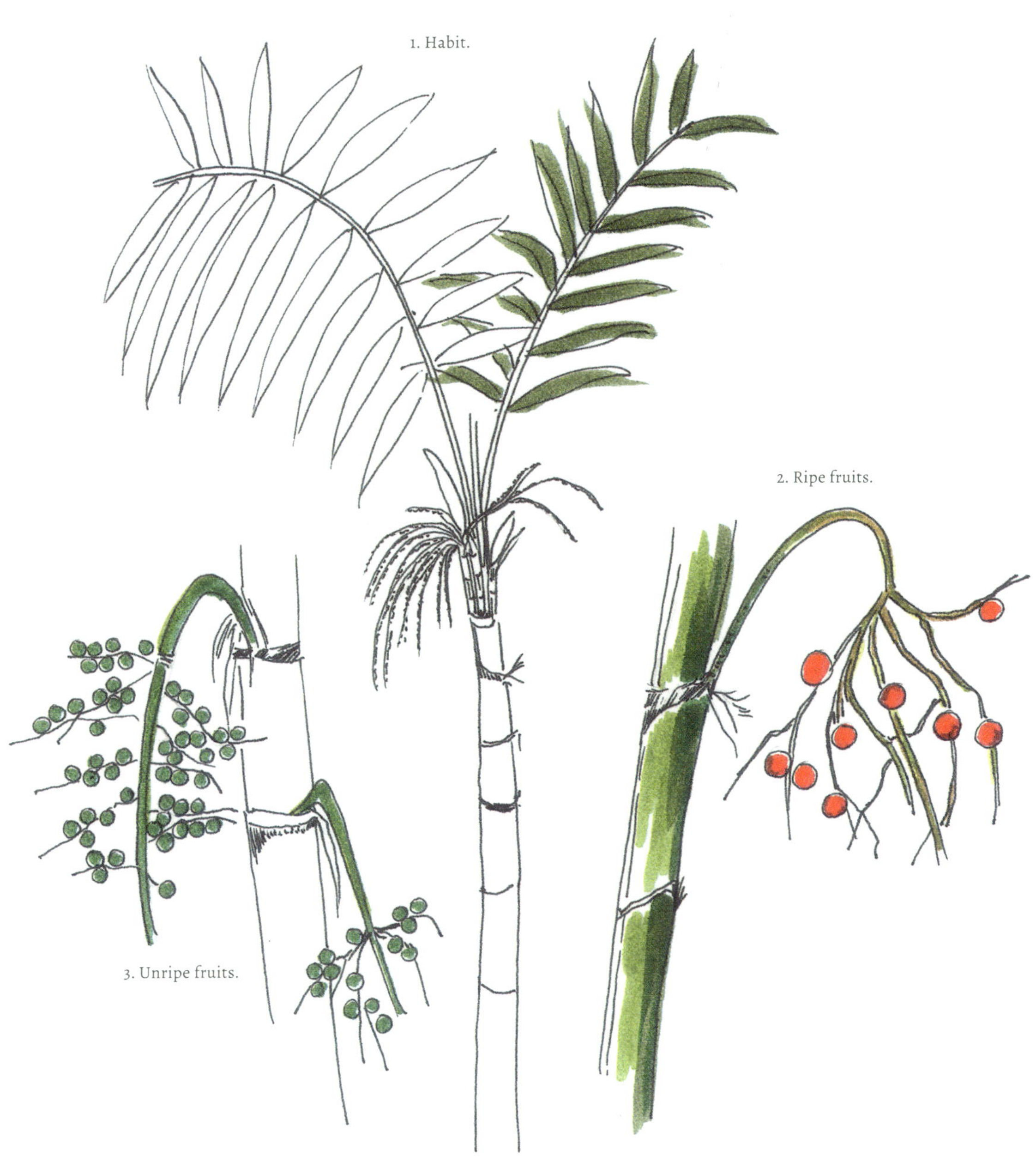
1. Habit.
2. Ripe fruits.
3. Unripe fruits.

96
MOUNTAIN CHAMAEDOREA

Chamaedorea oreophila Mart.

Status: Assessment of global conservation status required
Distribution: Endemic to southern Mexico

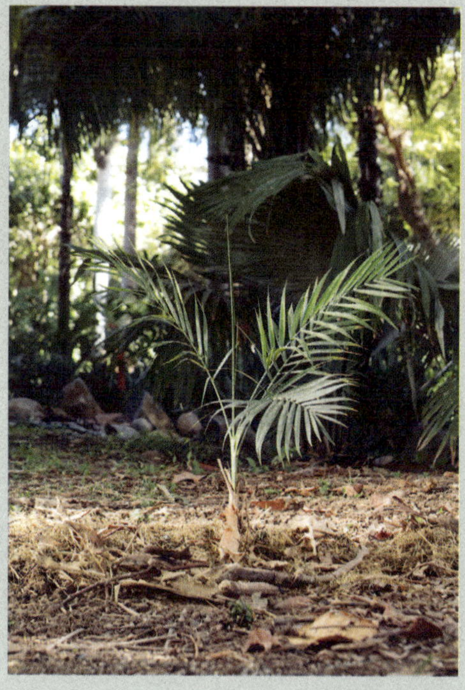

The species name means "mountain-lover" and accurately describes the natural habitat of this palm: high-elevation rainforest in southern Mexico. This single-stemmed species grows to 10 feet tall and has leaves with narrow, regularly-arranged leaflets, like *Chamaedorea elegans*. The male flower stalks are borne in groups of four to eight, and the flower-bearing portions are unbranched and pendulous. The female flower stalks, also unbranched and pendulous, bear bright orange fruits. This species is occasionally cultivated and makes an attractive addition to any garden.

Chamaedorea oreophila is a very delicate palm. Palm expert Miguel Ángel García Bielma collected a specimen during a botanical expedition for the National Palm Collection. He found it at the top of a mountain and had to cross a very dangerous cliff to collect it. This is just one of the reasons why the specimen of this palm is so valuable to the Jardín Botánico Culiacán and why everyone takes very good care of it.

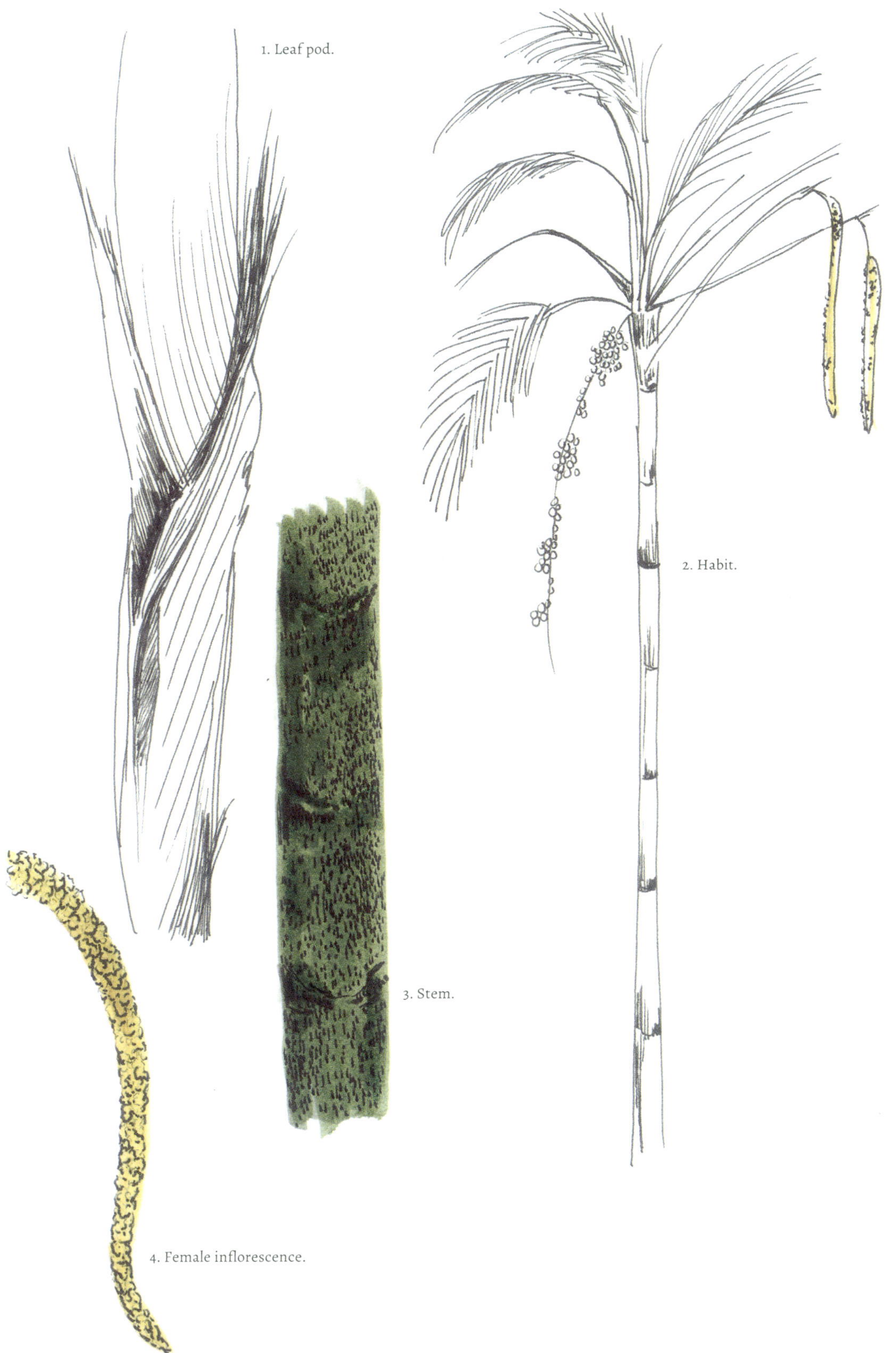
1. Leaf pod.
2. Habit.
3. Stem.
4. Female inflorescence.

97
CHILAC PALM

Chamaedorea neurochlamys Burret

Status: Assessment of global conservation status required
Distribution: Southern Mexico, Belize, Guatemala, and Honduras

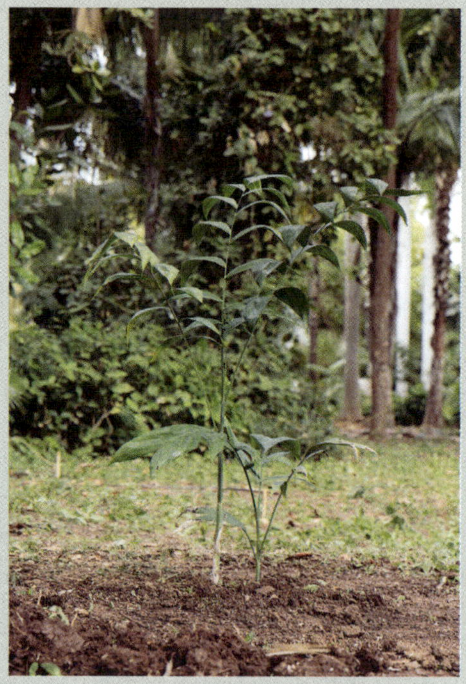

The trunk of this palm is solitary, about 13 feet tall, and the elliptical leaflets are regularly arranged. The top of the leaf sheath, just below the petiole, is white, a useful feature in distinguishing *Chamaedorea neuroclamys* from other similar species, such as *Chamaedorea falcifera* or *Chamaedorea pinnatifrons*. The fruits are kidney-shaped and orange-brown when ripe. The species ranges from Campeche and Quintana Roo through Chiapas in Mexico, then into Belize and on to Guatemala and Honduras, in lowland rainforest.

A specimen of *Chamaedorea neurochlamys* was found in 2017 in a very little-known area of the dense tropical rainforest between the states of Tabasco and Chiapas. Botanists at the Jardín Botánico Culiacán are doing a lot of research in order to understand its life cycle and so be able to cultivate and reproduce it in the garden.

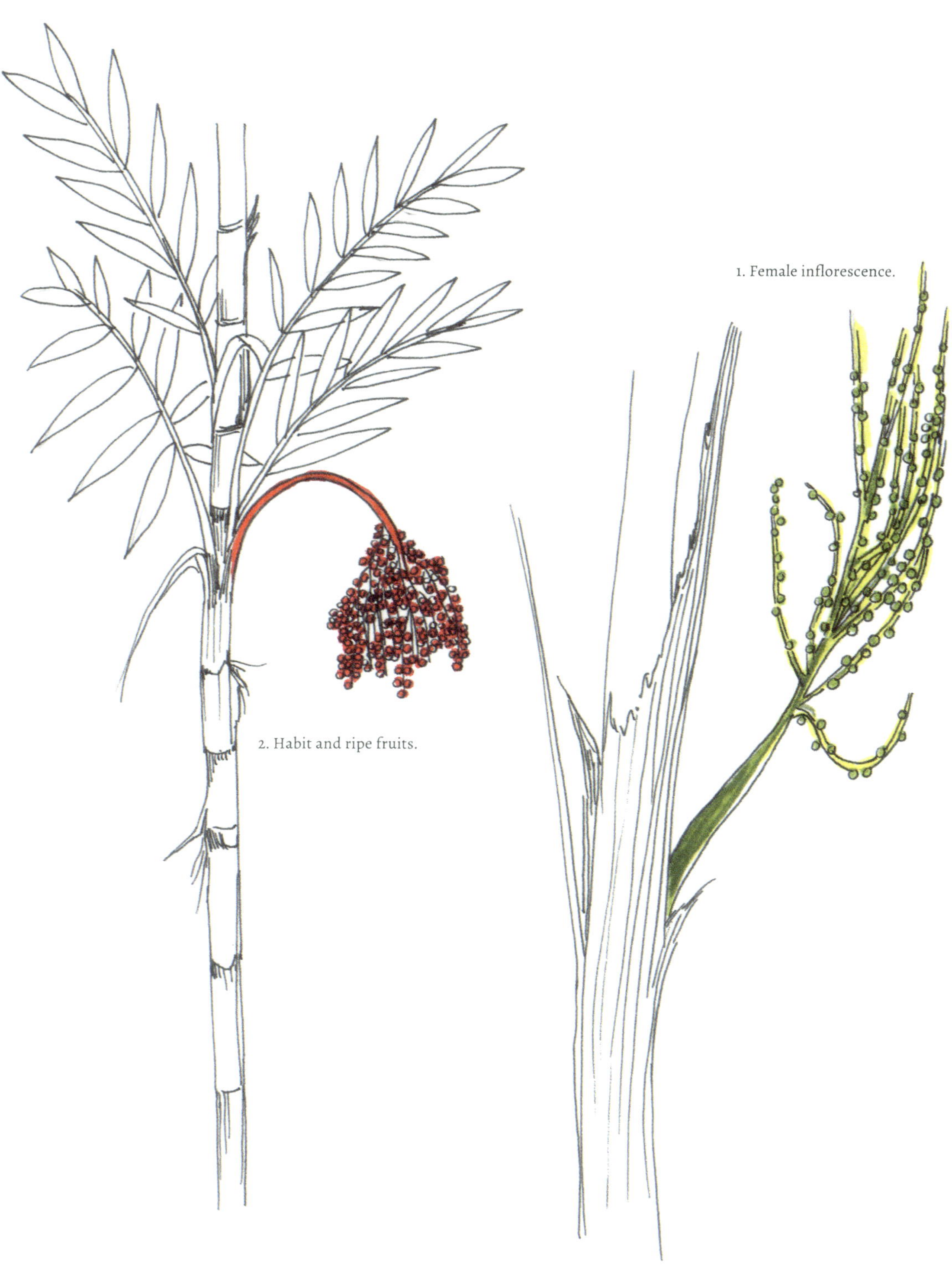
1. Female inflorescence.
2. Habit and ripe fruits.

98

CANNELILLA PALM

Chamaedorea pochutlensis Liebm.

Status: Designated as Threatened on the Mexican list of endangered species (NOM -059- SEMARNAT -2010)
Distribution: Endemic to Mexico

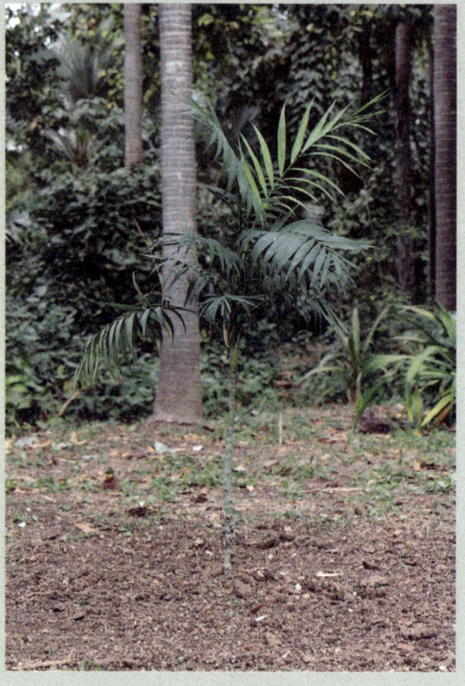

This small palm, growing to only three or 13 feet tall, is found in moist habitats, such as ravines and water courses, within the semi-deciduous forest of western Mexico, from Sinaloa to Oaxaca. It has multiple stems resembling bamboo and narrow, regularly-arranged leaflets. The species is named for the village of Pochutla in Oaxaca, where it was first discovered by botanists. It is seen occasionally in cultivation outside of Mexico, but it is then often misidentified as *Chamaedorea costaricana*. The two species can be distinguished by a feature of the sheathing leaf base, which bears triangular flaps of tissue at its apex in *Chamaedorea costaricana*, but is not so adorned in *Chamaedorea pochutlensis*. The latter species is more tolerant of cold and high light intensity than most others in the genus.

In 2017, botanists looking for *Chamaedorea pochutlensis* found one specimen by following a hunch. They discovered it on a coffee plantation whose owners had fortunately never eliminated it with the rest of the original vegetation.

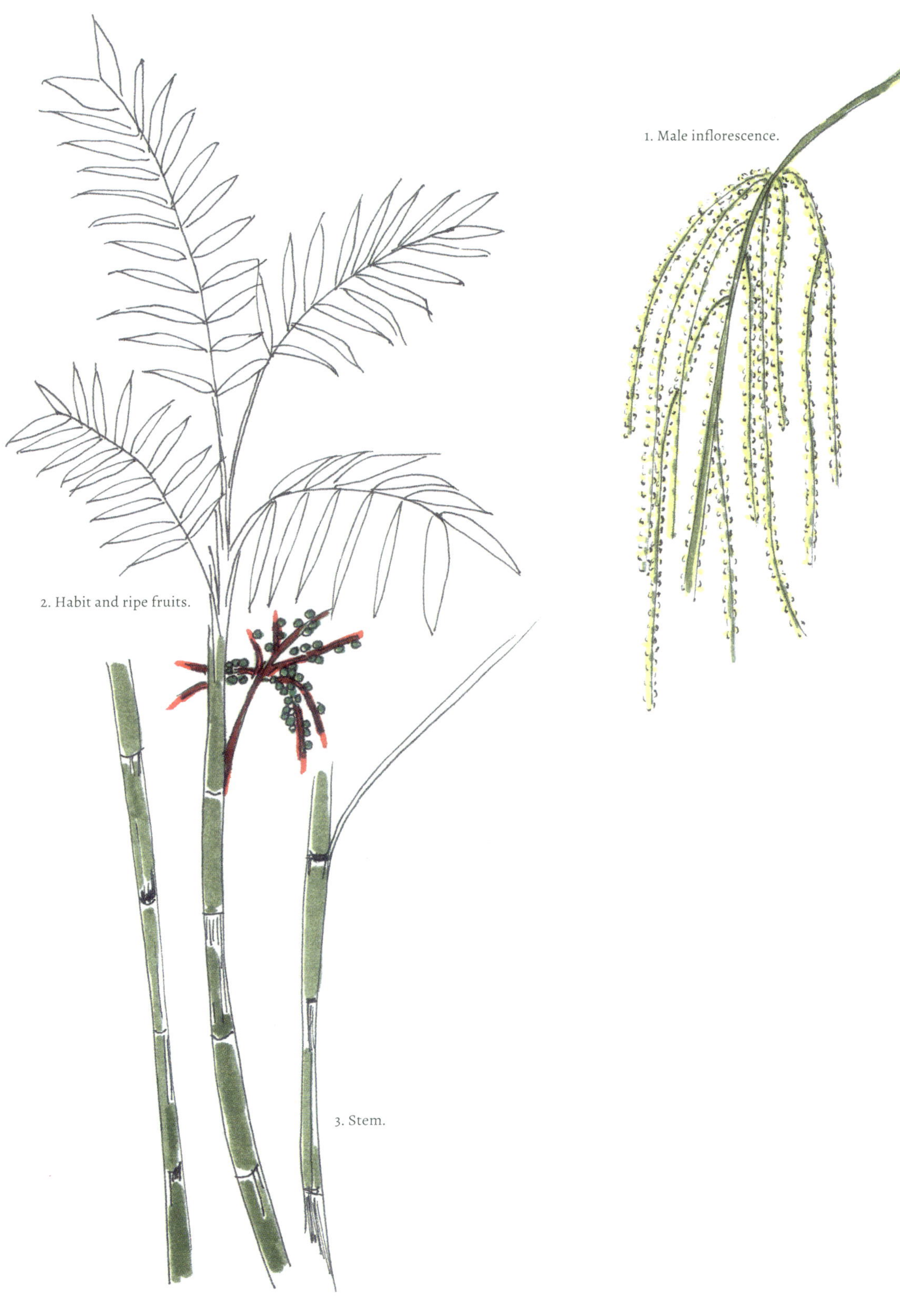
1. Male inflorescence.
2. Habit and ripe fruits.
3. Stem.

99

PACAYA PALM, COSTA RICAN BAMBOO PALM

Chamaedorea costaricana Oerst.

Status: Designated as Threatened on the Mexican list of endangered species (NOM-059- SEMARNAT -2010)
Distribution: Southern Mexico and Central America

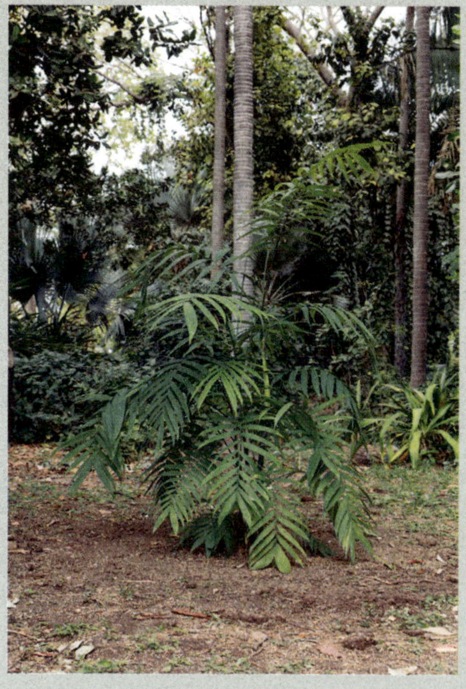

This handsome palm from Central America has multiple green ringed stems, two to 13 feet tall, which look like bamboo, and long dark green leaves with regularly-arranged leaflets. It is a beautiful palm, and for this reason now widespread in cultivation. It is one of the *Chamaedorea* species that is mass produced for commercial sales all over the world. It is sometimes confused with *Chamaedorea pochutlesis*, a species from western Mexico, but the two can be distinguished by the leaf base, where it sheaths the stem. In *Chamaedorea costaricana*, there are small triangular flaps of papery tissue (called ligules) on either side of the petiole; in *Chamaedorea pochutlensis*, these flaps of tissue are absent.

Botanists at the Jardín Botánico Culiacán have acquired a few specimens from the state of Veracruz, donated by palm specialist Miguel Ángel García Bielma.

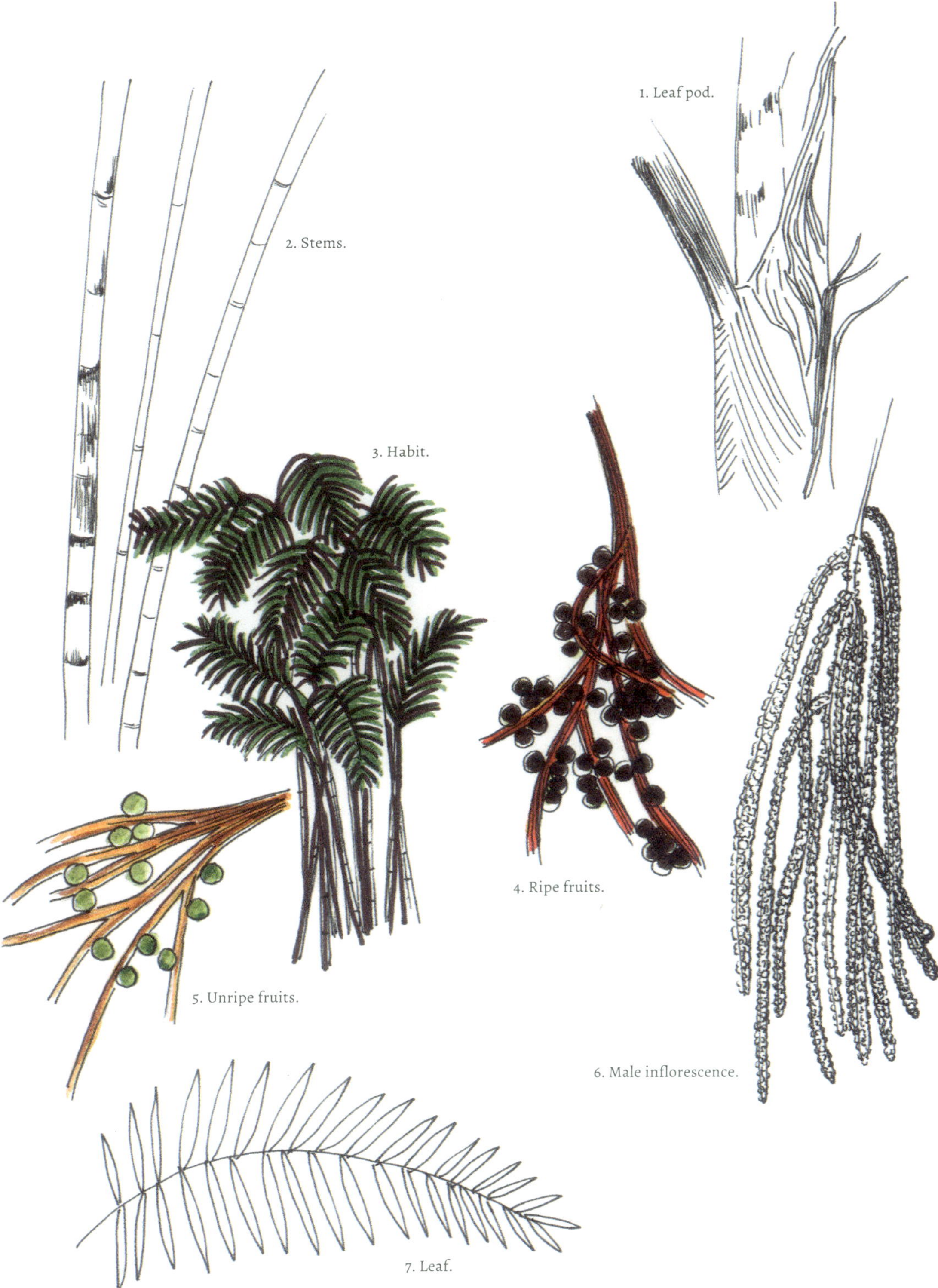
1. Leaf pod.
2. Stems.
3. Habit.
4. Ripe fruits.
5. Unripe fruits.
6. Male inflorescence.
7. Leaf.

100

NECKLACE CHAMAEDOREA

Chamaedorea geonomiformis H. Wendl.

Status: Designated as Threatened on the Mexican list of endangered species (NOM -059-SEMARNAT-2010)
Distribution: Southern Mexico, Guatemala, Honduras, and Costa Rica

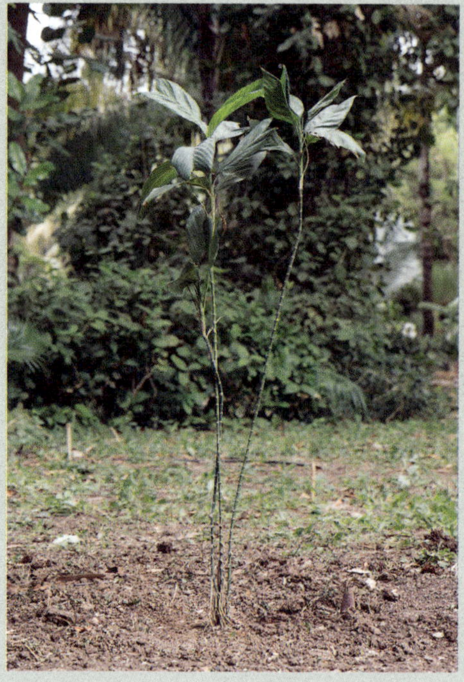

This attractive little palm, less than 3.2 feet tall, has been cultivated in gardens and greenhouses since the mid-nineteenth century. It is easy to see why it is so popular: it has small, solitary stems that bear just a few undivided, paddle-shaped leaves, each of which has a broad, V-shaped notch at its tip. The male and female flowers stalks are both sparsely branched, but the branches of the male are pendulous, while those of the female are erect. The distribution of this palm has a remarkable feature: it occurs in southern Mexico, Guatemala, and Honduras, and then again in Costa Rica. Botanists have no explanation of why it is not found in Nicaragua or El Salvador. Perhaps it has simply been overlooked. In Costa Rica, populations are endangered by people collecting wild plants for the horticulture trade.

The small specimen of *Chamaedorea geonomiformis* in the Jardín Botánico Culiacán was collected in 2016 in an area of Veracruz where venomous snakes are abundant. Collecting specimens in such conditions can be risky for a botanical team.

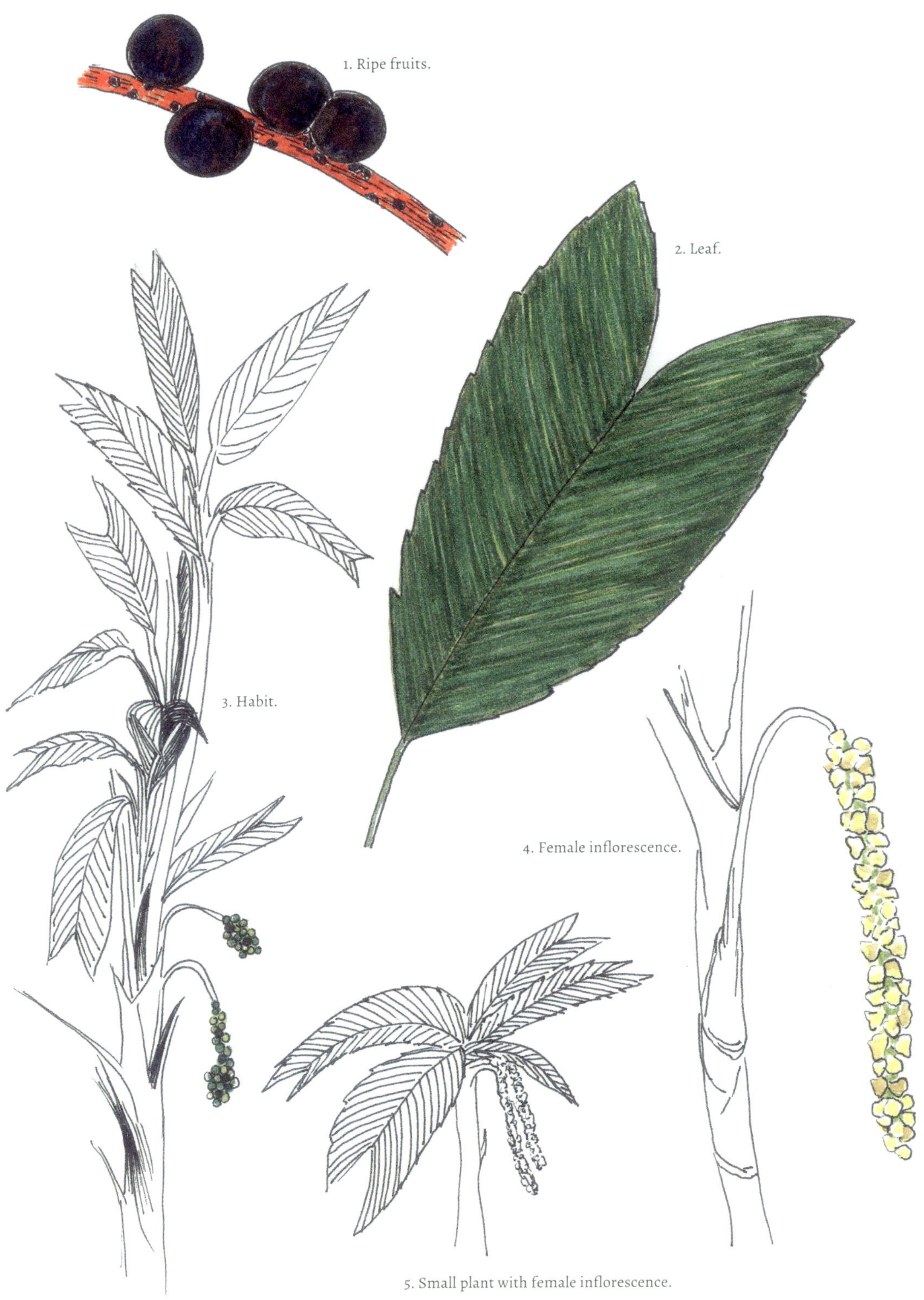
1. Ripe fruits.
2. Leaf.
3. Habit.
4. Female inflorescence.
5. Small plant with female inflorescence.

101

POTATO-CHIP PALM

Chamaedorea tuerckheimii (Dammer) Burret

Status: Designated as Endangered on the Mexican list of endangered species (NOM -059-SEMARNAT-2010), but not on the IUCN Red List or the CITES appendices. This species urgently requires protection.
Distribution: Mexico and Guatemala

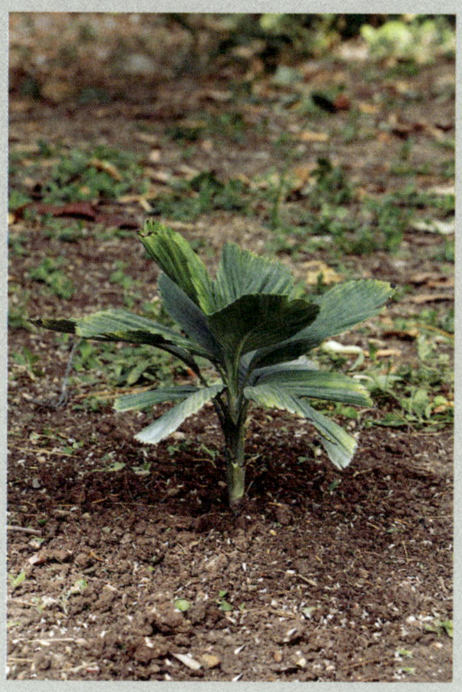

This is one of the most delightful and sought-after species of *Chamaedorea*. It is a diminutive palm, no more than 20 or 24 inches tall, with a full crown of undivided leaves no bigger than a human hand. The leaves are remarkably corrugated in appearance. It is a beautiful palm, but very delicate: it can quickly perish if growing conditions are less than perfect. Unfortunately, these two characteristics—its beauty and its fragility—may spell the doom of the species. In its native Veracruz and Guatemala, the palm cannot survive disturbance by agriculture or deforestation, and collectors have entirely removed some populations from their forest homes. The palm's needs are not easily met in cultivation, and most garden plants succumb to low temperatures, dry air, mineralized water, or pests.

For seven years the Jardín Botánico Culiacán looked for specimens in various places, mainly nurseries and botanical collections. This is a species that may become extinct in the wild very soon, so there is an urgent need to protect it. Botanists at the garden are very interested in contributing to the conservation of *Chamaedorea tuerckheimii*. Successful cultivation in the garden of species like this is one of the keys to preventing their extinction.

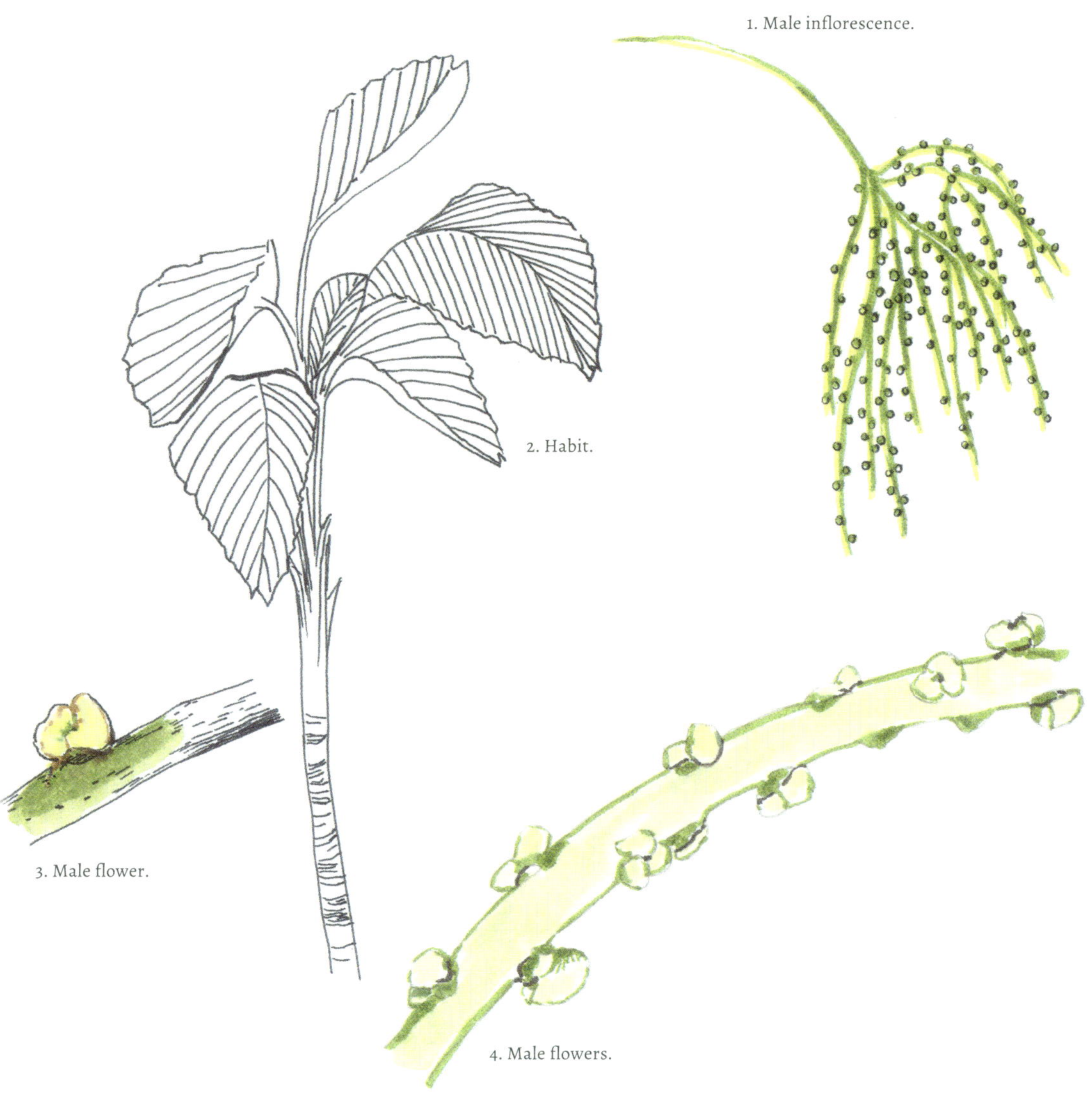
1. Male inflorescence.
2. Habit.
3. Male flower.
4. Male flowers.

102
ROOT SPINE PALM

Cryosophila stauracantha (Heynh.) R. J. Evans

Status: Assessment of global conservation status required
Distribution: Southern Mexico, Belize, and Guatemala

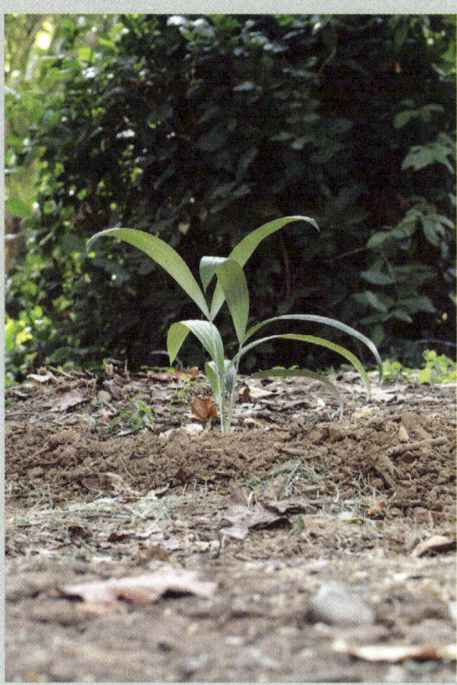

This attractive palm grows to about 35 feet tall and has fan-shaped leaves that are silvery on the undersides. The leaf segments are broad, grouped into twos or threes, and the leaf blade has a deep central split. The fruits are white. Like other *Cryosophila* species, the palm has root-spines that protect the stem and present a seemingly impenetrable barrier to climbing animals. As with other species, the leaves are used for brooms.

In 2016, Prof. Miguel Ángel García Bielma collected a specimen of *Cryosophila stauracantha* for the National Palm Collection at the Jardín Botánico Culiacán. While searching for a good botanical specimen, he discovered that people don't much like the palm for gardening purposes, because it is not very foliose. There is insufficient botanical information about this species and its conservation status, but deforestation in the rainforests of southern Mexico and Central America will probably soon lead to its becoming threatened. So far neither the Mexican authorities nor the IUCN have included it on any list of endangered species, but it is in urgent need of protection.

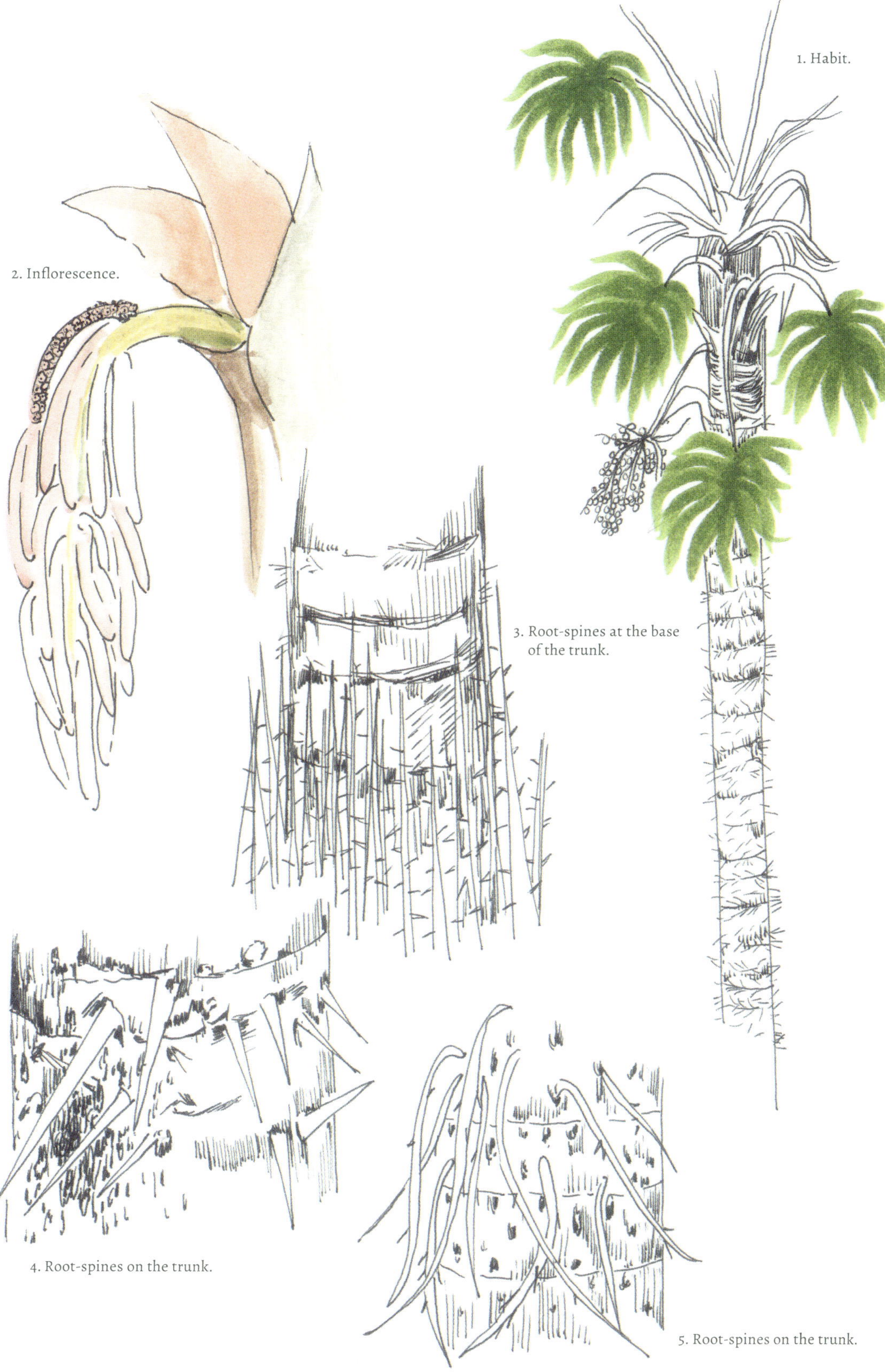
1. Habit.
2. Inflorescence.
3. Root-spines at the base of the trunk.
4. Root-spines on the trunk.
5. Root-spines on the trunk.

103

MEXICAN CLIMBING PALM

Desmoncus chinantlensis Liebm. ex Mart.

Status: Assessment of global conservation status required
Distribution: Mexico and Central America

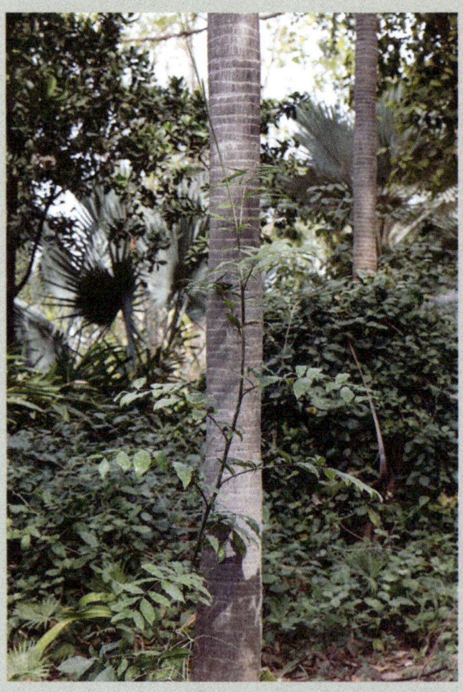

Most *Desmoncus* palms are climbers, a habit that is common among the rattan palms (*Calamus* spp.) of Asia but rare in the Americas, where only some species of *Desmoncus* and *Chamaedorea elatior* are high-climbing lianas. The stems are slender, only about an inch in diameter and around 35 feet long. *Desmoncus chinantlensis* climbs by means of its pinnate leaves, which are heavily armed with black, needle-like spines. The tip of the leaf stalk bears backward-pointing hooks, which are actually modified and stiffened leaflets. The leaves sway in the wind and catch onto nearby trees by means of those hooks. The hooks bear the weight of the palm, allowing it to grow up into the canopy. The stems are used for canes, baskets, and other handicrafts.

A specimen of this species arrived at the National Palm Collection in 2017. It was collected close to El Tigre, a little-known archeological site in the state of Campeche, and Estrella del Sur, a village near the border with Guatemala.

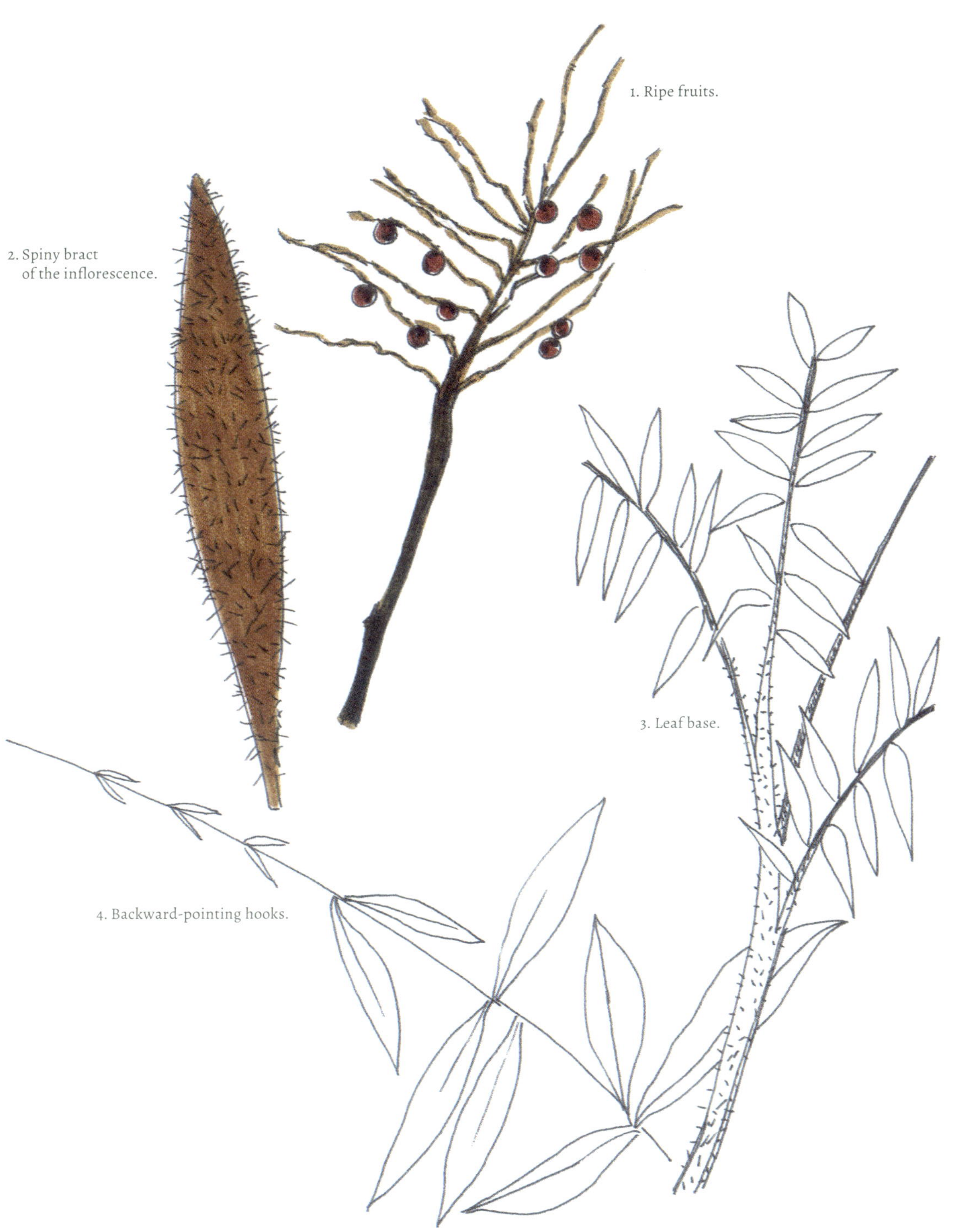
1. Ripe fruits.
2. Spiny bract
of the inflorescence.
3. Leaf base.
4. Backward-pointing hooks.

104

THATCH PALM

Geonoma pinnatifrons Willd.

Status: Designated as Threatened on the Mexican list of endangered species (NOM -059-SEMARNAT-2010)
Distribution: Southern Mexico, Central America, northern South America, the island of Hispaniola (Haiti and the Dominican Republic), and the Lesser Antilles

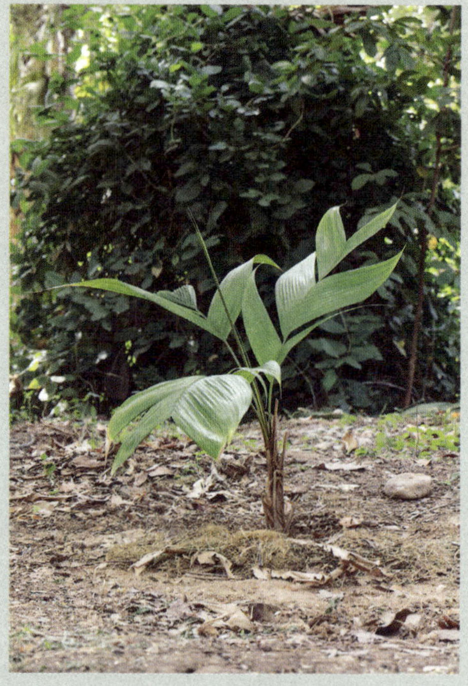

Geonoma pinnatifrons is a widespread rainforest species. This medium-sized palm has a solitary trunk from three to 26 feet tall and leaves from one to 6.5 feet long, irregularly divided into groups of leaflets. The leaves are sometimes used for thatch roofing. The flowers stalks are borne below the leaves and covered with fuzzy brown hairs. The flowers are small, white, and inconspicuous. The fruits are small, less than half an inch long, shiny black in color and ovoid in shape. They are consumed by birds and other animals that spread the seeds.

This is a very rare palm that is difficult to propagate. In 2016, a specimen from Veracruz was donated to the Jardín Botánico Culiacán by Prof. Miguel Ángel García Bielma, to form part of the National Palm Collection. It has been very difficult to grow the palm at the garden, because it is not adapting very well to environmental conditions in Culiacán.

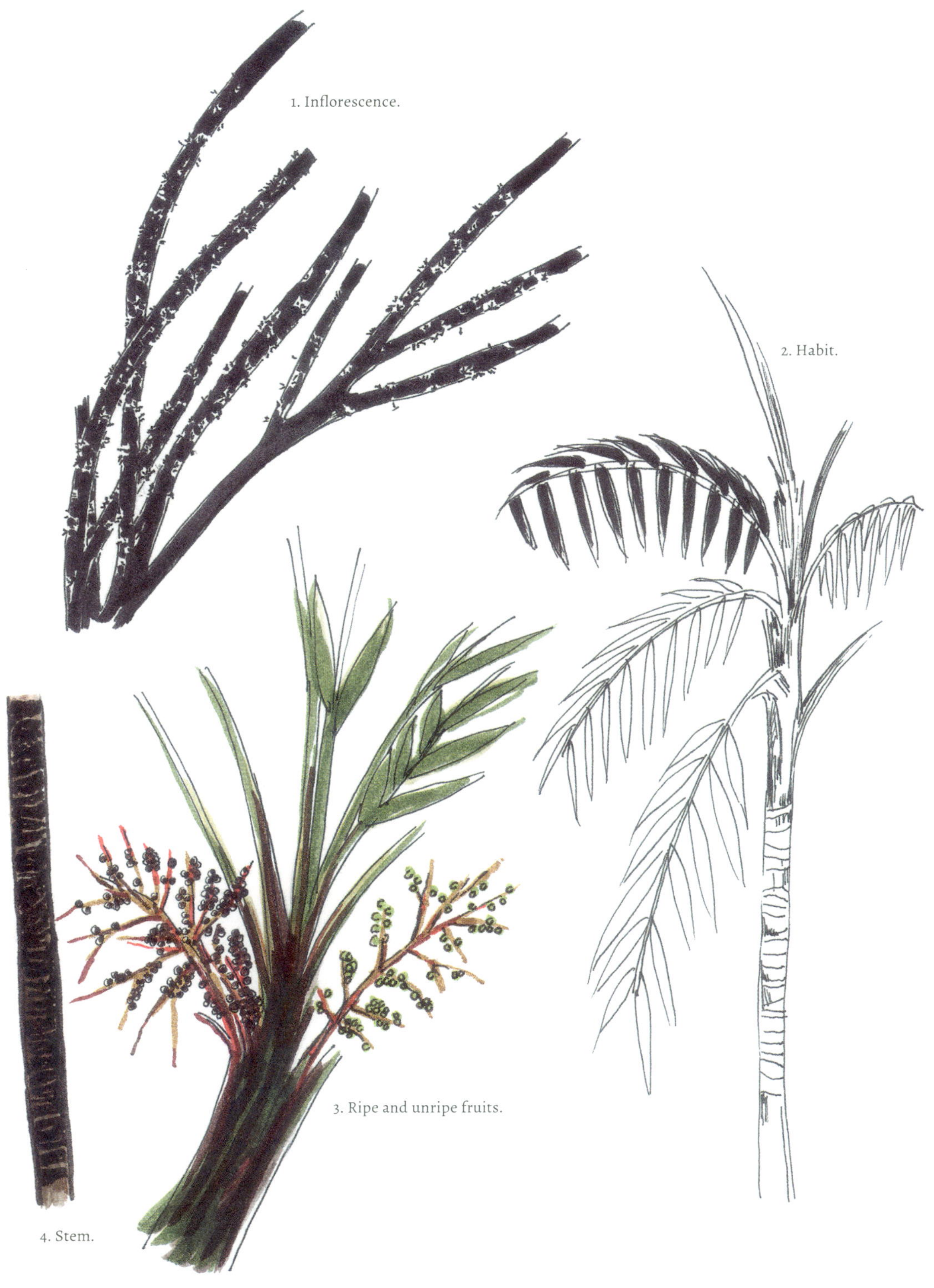
1. Inflorescence.
2. Habit.
3. Ripe and unripe fruits.
4. Stem.

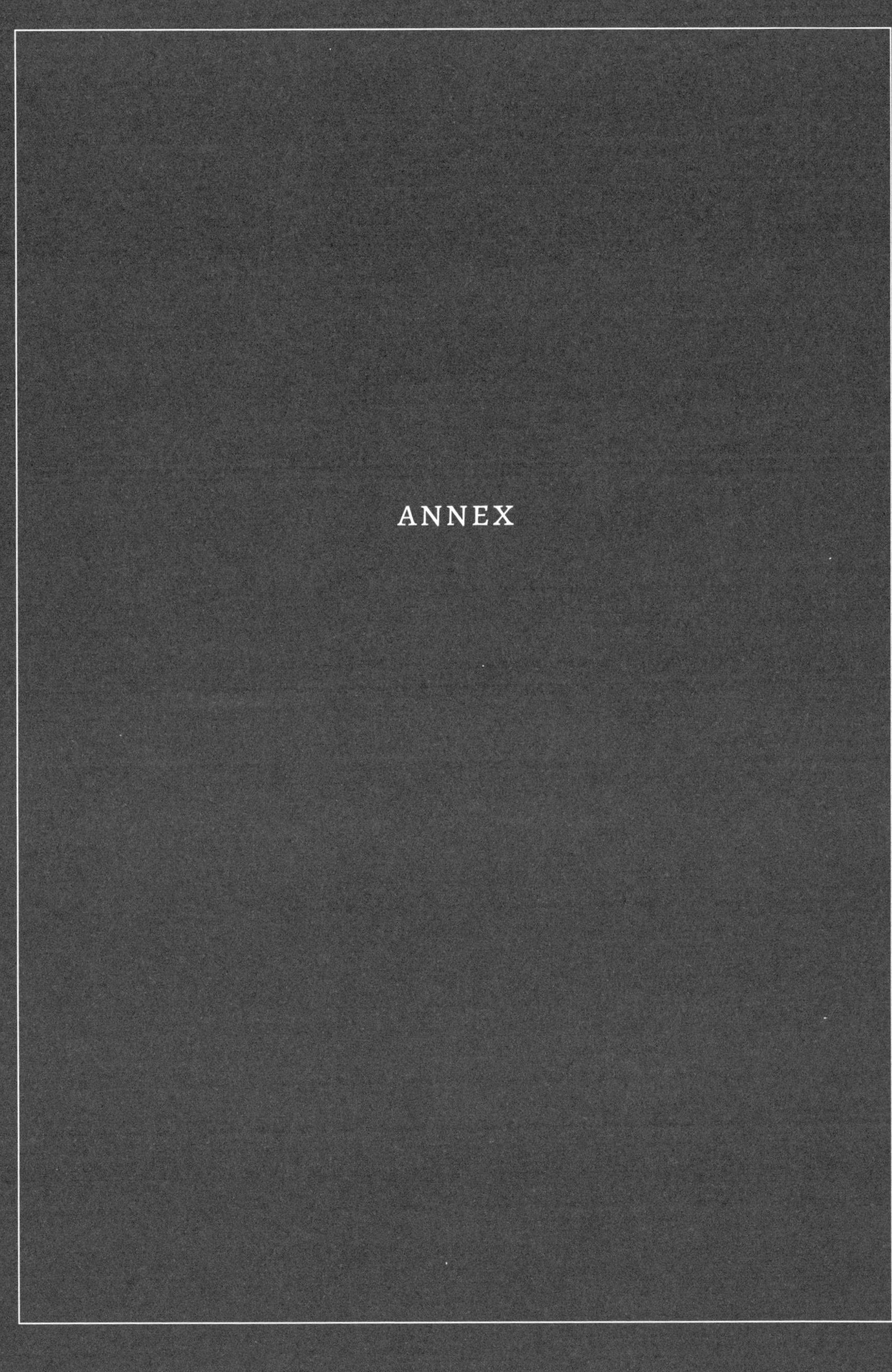

ANNEX

GLOSSARY

angiosperm "Enclosed seeds," a derivation from two Greek words: αγγειον (angion), a vase or amphora, and σπέρμα (sperma), seed. These are commonly flowering plants, whose ovules and seeds are encased by the fertile leaf that carries the ovules or carpel. In this way, to fertilize the ovule, the pollen grain must make contact with a surface of the carpel prepared to receive it, the stigma, instead of falling directly on the ovule as in gymnosperms. When the seeds ripen, they are enclosed inside the fruit. Members of this group are the main source of sustenance for humans—with only 15 species providing the bulk of the world's food—and provide many raw materials and natural products. Angiosperms are classified into monocotyledonous (liliopsida) and dicotyledonous (magnoliopsida) plants.

apex In botany, the growing point of a plant organ or body, usually accessory and of little importance.

Arecaceae Colloquially known as palm trees or palms, the *Arecaceae* are an important family of monocotyledonous plants, and the only family of the order Arecales. Individual members are easy to recognize: they are woody plants, without secondary stem growth, only primary. Despite being monocotyledonous, many of them are arborescent, with a large crown of leaves at the end of the stem, usually pinnate or webbed. Their flowers have three sepals and three petals, and are arranged in inflorescences provided with one or several spathes. The fruit is fleshy: a berry or a drupe. They are widely distributed in tropical to temperate regions, but mainly in warm climates.

Palm trees include economically important species such as the oil palm, coconut palm, date palm, and rattan, as well as ornamental ones such as the royal palm, common palm, and lounge palm.

asexual The formation of new individuals from the parent without the fusion of gametes. Such individuals have an identical genetic constitution to the parent.

basipetal Developing at the base of an axis, with the youngest structures at the point of attachment.

basipetal sequence Growing, maturing, or opening from the vertex towards the base in a sequence of leaves or flowers, where the development or opening of the sequence is from the base to the apex.

beta-carotene (or **β-carotene**) An intense orange-red organic pigment abundant in plants and fruits.

bipinnate One of the most complex types of composite leaves, consisting of a rachis or central axis from which two pairs of leaflets emerge sideways.

bracts A foliaceous organ found near flowers, usually green, and smaller than normal leaves. Its main function is to protect flowers or inflorescences.

canopy From the Latin *canopus*, an Egyptian city famous for its great luxuries. The habitat that includes the region of the tops and upper regions of the trees in a forest, especially in jungles. The tree canopy is the habitat of a unique, specialist flora and fauna not found in any other layer of the forest, and it acts as a protective shield. The canopy of an individual tree refers to the top layer of its leaves. It usually provides dense shade that blocks sunlight from reaching plants below.

carpels The transformed leaves that form flowers' gynoecia; several carpels can form a single pistil, with one or several cavities, or several independent pistils.

cellulose fibrils Cellulose fibrils or microfibrils are components of the cell wall of eukaryotic plant cells. This wall is formed by cellulose which is a polysaccharide whose molecules are linear glucose chains (linked by β 1-4 bonds) that can reach a length of four μm; it is rigid, insoluble in water, and contains from several hundred to several thousand units of β-glucose. The arrangement of cellulose microfibrils within the plant cell adds great strength to cell walls and therefore to the plant. Cellulose is the world's most abundant organic molecule, forming the majority of terrestrial biomass.

central rachis In plants, a rachis is the main axis of a compound structure. It can be the main stem of a compound leaf, such as in acacia or ferns.

clustering Plants of the same species, with new individuals emerging close to the parent stem, often enclosed by a persistent, tough leaf base.

crown The crown of a woody plant (palms, trees, shrubs) refers to the branches, leaves and reproductive structures that extend from the main trunk or stems. The main shapes of the crowns are excurrent, with cone-shaped branches and decurrent, more rounded shapes. Crowns are also characterized by their width, depth, surface area, volume, and density.

cyanide A highly reactive and toxic chemical, occurring naturally in some foods and in certain plants such as the *Dypsis lastelliana* palm. It can exist in several states: as a colorless gas, such as hydrogen cyanide (HCN), or in crystal form, for example sodium cyanide (NaCN).

dichotomously A type of branching in plants when the growing tip (the apical bud) forks into two equal growing points, which in turn divide similarly after a period of growth, and so on.

distichous A verticillate leaf arrangement where a leaf is inserted in each knot along two opposite sides of the stem.

Dracaenas There are two genera with at least 110 species of trees. Plants with an erect, more or less woody stem. Spirally arranged leaves, often in rosettes, have axillary inflorescences, in the form of a head or umbrella, the fruit is usually a red or orange berry, sometimes hard and woody, with up to three globular or elongated seeds. Most species are native to Africa and surrounding islands, with a few in southern Asia and only one in the tropics of Central America.

embryonic leaf In palms, the blades of new leaves undergo differential growth, with some areas growing faster than others, causing folds in the leaf blade. The leaf then develops divisions characteristic of palm leaves, programming cell death. This folding and division process is exclusive to palm trees.

endemism The biological term indicating that the distribution of a taxon is limited to a reduced geographical range and is not found naturally in any other part of the world. Therefore, when a species is said to be endemic to a certain region, it means that it is only possible to find it naturally in that place. Endemism applies to a very wide range of geographical scales. Thus, a species can be endemic to a mountain or a lake, an island, a country, or even a continent.

endosperm The nutritional tissue formed in the embryo sac in the seeds of most plants. It commonly surrounds the embryo and serves to nourish it during germination and early stages of life; nutrients are stored in the form of starch, although they are also found as oils and proteins.

epiphytic Derives from the Greek *epi*, envelope, and *phyton*, plant. These plants spend at least one phase of their life cycle growing non-parasitically on another plant, usually on trees. This guild constitutes about 10% of the world's flora. *Arecaceae*, *Bromeliacea*, *Cactacea* and *Orchidaceae* are among the many families with land lineages and epiphytes.

In the case of some species of the genus *Ficus* (matapalos), they are called strangling epiphytes, since as it grows, it wraps around the stem of the tree or palm (as in this case), emits roots that reach the ground and over the years strangles the palm and replaces it.

fan-shaped leaves Adjacent leaves or leaf segments that join laterally for a part or most of their length.

They originate from a single point at the tip of the petiole, which often includes a specialized expansion called a hastula.

feather-shaped leaves *See* **pinnate**

flower stalk The organ that supports the flowers and/or the erect, leafless flower stalk growing directly from the ground as in a tulip. *See* also **inflorescence**

foliage The set of leaves and branches on trees, shrubs, or plants.

foliar scars Some species of palm trees show prominent leaf scars at points where leaves were attached to the stem. The space between these leaf scars (internodes) is a function of the stem growth rate, as in the case of *Dypsis lutescens* and *Ptychosperma elegans*.

foliole One of the final segments of a composite leaf.

genus (plural, **genera**) A taxonomic category ranking between family and species, consisting of structurally or phylogenetically related species, or a single isolated species exhibiting unusual differentiation (monotypic genus). The name of the genus is the first word of a binomial scientific name (followed by the name of the species), and is always capitalized.

growth habits Each plant species has a different growth habit. Competition for water, space, light, and nutrients has influenced plants' evolution, allowing them to grow and adapt according to their environment. Water availability, particularly during the growing season, is one of the main environmental factors that affect the productivity and distribution of plants worldwide. In addition, interactions with animals have influenced plant growth habits. There are several different types of habits and descriptions of vegetation. Each one represents the type of plant and how it grows. For example, grass plants are vascular plants without woody tissue. Graminoids are grass, vines can be woody that are climbers with long stems. Finally, trees are woody plants with a single stem (or trunk) that can grow to different heights.

gynoecium (or **pistil**) A set of female organs, often bottle-shaped, in the center of the flower and consisting of one or more modified leaves or carpels that enclose the ovary, the location of the ovules that develop into the seeds.

gymnosperm Literally, bare seeds. They are those plants whose seeds in their maturity are not enclosed in a fruit and appear as scales distributed along an axis, forming a cone or pinecone. The largest and most important group from an economic perspective are conifers, such as pines, ginkos, and cycads.

habitat The place that offers the appropriate living conditions for an organism, species of animal, or plant community; a space in which a certain biological population inhabits and reproduces because it offers all the necessary conditions to do so.

inconspicuous A barely visible organ or set of organs.

inflorescence (floral stems) A system of spermatophyte branches from which flowers will develop, and usually more or less clearly defined in relation to the vegetative area. They are usually wrapped inside a protective bract called a prophyll. They consist of a main axis called a peduncle, with first and second-order branches called rachis. Flowers (dioecious palms) or partial inflorescences (monoecious palms) are usually born from the bracts' axils, and each flower is supported by the pedicel.

karst A form of relief caused by chemical weathering and erosion of rocks composed of water-soluble minerals such as limestone, dolomite, and plaster. Its name comes from one of the areas between Italy and Slovenia where it is best represented. This type of relief originated from the dragging or accumulation of soluble and disintegrated materials, such as those consisting of carbonates.

leaflets One of the ultimate segments of a compound leaf.

ligules A usually membranous appendix found at the line joining the leaf blade with the petiole of some leaves, and of certain petals at its base. It can also refer to the part of a flower's tongue-shaped corolla.

magnoliophyta The most extensive and varied group of plants with seeds, also known as angiosperms. The name derives from the genus *Magnolia*, necessarily a part of the group and chosen by some authors as its name because it was believed until recently that magnolias were the most similar flowers to the "ancestral angiosperm" (the first flowering plant with these characteristics, from which all the rest of the angiosperms would have descended).

mangrove A woody shrub or tree, belonging to the genus *Rhizophora*. It grows fruits and its long and extended branches with shoots descend until they touch the ground and take root. It has petiolate, opposing, whole, elliptical, obtuse, and thick leaves; axillary flowers with four yellowish petals; dried fruit of leathery peel; and small, almost round, and partly exposed roots. Mangroves form ecosystems, also called mangroves, which are a woody, dense, arboreal, and shrubby plant formations measuring from three to 100 feet high, composed of one or several mangrove species and with little presence of herbaceous and vines. It grows abundantly along coasts, on islets, and in marshlands of intertropical America.

mesocarp A botanical term for the intermediate layer of the pericarp—the fleshy part of the fruit located between the endocarp and the epicarp.

oxalate crystals Calcium oxalate crystals are mainly found in the protoplasm of specialized plant cells called idioblasts.

palm oil Obtained from the fruit of the African oil palm (*Elaeis guineensis*), this oil of vegetable origin is extracted from the palm fruit's mesocarp. The palm fruit is slightly red, as is the unrefined oil. The oil palm is native to West Africa, where the oil was already being obtained 5,000 years ago. It was then brought to America, introduced after the voyages of Columbus, and in more recent times it was introduced on a massive scale to Asia.

In addition to its uses in the food industry, palm oil derivatives are also used in the cosmetic industry. Its cultivation is of major economic importance for Malaysia, the world's largest provider of palm oil and derivatives (it is second only to soybean oil in terms of global production volume). In the Americas, the largest producers are Colombia and Ecuador.

panicle An inflorescence composed of clusters that decrease in size towards the apex. In other words, a branching cluster of flowers, in which the branches are in turn a subset. It is cataloged as a cluster of clusters, with a main rachis subdivided into secondary rachis, from which flowers with a pedicel are released. An example of a panicle is the vine.

pendulous A pendular or hanging inflorescence.

petals Often a colorful leaf, transformed to some extent, and part of a flower's corolla. In a "typical" flower, petals are striking and colored, and surround the reproductive parts. Their main function is to attract pollinators. The number of petals in a flower is indicative for botanical classification.

petiole From Latin *petiolus*, a diminutive form of *pes*, foot. The corner joining the blade of a leaf to its leaf base or stem. It helps to thicken and elongate, as well as to transport fluids between the stem and the leaf or leaf blade.

phalanx of spines In some palm species, thorns protect the surface of the stem.

pinnate A botanical term for feather-like leaves that derives from the Latin *pinnatus* (with wings or fins) used to designate foliaceous or laminar organs that have fairly numerous leaflets, completely separated from each other, and joined by a main axis, called the spine, an extension of the petiole to the leaf.

plicate leaves The leaves are the organs of the plant specialized in capturing the energy of sunlight through photosynthesis; the arrangement of some leaves in relation to others in the bud, before they unfurl, is called prefoliation. In one kind of prefoliation the leaf is folded, with the outer folder leaf containing another folded one, and in the other, the leaf is rolled up, with the rolled-up outer leaf containing another, rolled-up one.

pollinated A biotic agent (a bee, fly, wasp, beetle, butterfly, bird, or bat) that transports pollen from a flower's male organ (anther) to the female organ (stigma) allowing fertilization.

polysaccharides Biomolecules formed by the union of many monosaccharides. They carry out various functions, especially as energy and structural reserves. Polysaccharides such as starch and cellulose are chains, either branched or not, of more than 10 monosaccharides.

racemes A set of flowers or fruits supported by a common axis, and with pedicels of almost equal or greater length than the flowers themselves (for example, the vine).

rattan From Malay, *rotan*. The generic name for some 600 species of climbing palms, mainly of the genus *Calamus*. They are very thin and prickly-stemmed plants that climb several feet to the canopy of Old World rainforests (there are no genuine New World rattans). The thin stem can hardly withstand pressure, but it is very elastic, making it useful for basketry and furniture. The stems are usually extracted almost exclusively in the wild, from established jungles of trees that support rattan. Since the 1970s, wild rattan has declined due to loss of habitat and overharvesting.

ravines A landform characterized by craggy terrain. Ravines can be created by erosion caused by flowing water, the movement of tectonic plates, and they are always irregular. Their size can vary over time depending on how the riverbed or the water course has affected them.

rheophyte An aquatic plant that lives in fast-flowing water currents in environments where few other organisms can survive. Rheophytes tend to be found in currents that flow at rates of three to seven feet per second, and from three to 10 feet deep.

ringed stems *See* **foliar scars**

seedling The sporophyte growth stage that develops from an embryo and begins when the seed is longer dormant. Seedling development begins with the germination of the seed and ends when it develops its first mature leaves. A typical young seedling consists of three main parts: the radicle (embryonic root), the hypocotyl (embryonic bud), and the cotyledons (seed leaves).

semi-deciduous A botanical term referring to plants that lose their foliage for a very short period. This phenomenon occurs in tropical and sub-tropical woody species. Also known as semi-evergreen.

sepal The protection around a flower's angiosperms, wrapping the other floral parts in the early stages of development when the flower is still only a bud. They are generally a green or greenish cover to protect and enclose the floral parts.

serpentine soils A rare type of soil produced by eroded ultramafic rocks such as peridotite and its derivatives like serpentinite. Such soils have high levels of serpentine, especially antigorite, lizardite, and chrysotile, and has low calcium-to-magnesium ratios. This factor is important in explaining the particular biota for this soil type.

single midvein The distribution of the nerves that make up leaves' vascular tissue. Found in the leaf mesophyll, it provides sap and communicates the leaf with the rest of the plant. There are two types of venations: craspedodromous and camptodromous. In the case of *Chamaedorea graminifolia* a single vein exists in the leaflet.

solitary or clustered stems Palm trees can be single-stemmed or multi-stemmed (clustering) as a result of the growth of low axillary buds at the stem.

split Palm leaves have divisions due to programmed cell death. These divisions allow the leaf segment to separate at maturity, as happens with the segments of a coconut palm leaf, for example. The process of folding and then dividing is exclusive to the family of palm trees.

spreading leaves Open, wide foliage.

stamen A word of Latin derivation referring to the flower's male reproductive organ. Each stamen usually has a peduncle called a filament (again, from the Latin, *filum*), at the uppermost part of which there is an anther (from the Greek *anthera,* or flower), and pollen sacs, called microsporangia.

stem The organ responsible for supporting the leaves and flowers. It grows in the opposite direction to the root, helps transport sap through the xylem. It has three parts: the neck, the knot, and the buds. According to its consistency, the stem is classified as being herbaceous, woody, or suffruticose. Palm stems vary considerably in appearance and size, but they are generally cylindrical or slightly conical, and can occasionally be bulky.

stigma Located in the pistil, the stigma receives pollen, which will begin the fertilization process.

stolons A type of creeping stem that grows from the base of the main stems. They can develop either on or below the soil's surface (epigeal or underground stolons, respectively).

verticillate Where leaves are arranged in one or more whorls, in other words with several leaves arranged at the same point of the axis on the stem.

xeric shrubland An ecosystem formed by plant communities dominated by shrubs under 13 feet tall. Xerophilous vegetation (specifically adapted to dry environments) predominates in areas of low rainfall. The vegetation frequently consists of a type of hawthorn, low bushes, deciduous trees, and semi-desert grassland.

Acknowledgements

Agustín Coppel Luken
Isabel Gómez de Coppel
Julián Coppel Gómez

Bárbara Apodaca
América Ávalos
Ernesto Beltrán
Tatiana Bilbao
Alberto Bremermann
Martha Burgoa
Alba Cortés
All members of the CIAC team
Juan Cueto
Laura Estévez
Carlos Gandarilla
Magnolia de la Garza
Isabel Garcés
All members of the Jardín Botánico Culiacán team, especially the gardeners
kurimanzutto
Ana Maurer
Isabel Meza
Cuauhtémoc Niebla
Juan Rovalo
Paulina Sevilla
Simona Solórzano
Óscar Vélez

A collaboration between Colección Isabel y Agustín Coppel (CIAC A.C.), the Jardín Botánico Culiacán and Sociedad Botánica y Zoológica de Sinaloa, I.A.P.

Texts
Clementina Equihua Zamora
Miguel Ángel García Bielma
Carlos Murillo Michel
Erika Pagaza Calderón
Scott Zona

Research
Clementina Equihua Zamora
Erika Pagaza Calderón
Scott Zona

Research assistance
Fernando Colin
Carmelo Cortés
Samuel Ernesto Reyes Rodríguez

Photography
Enrique Macías Martínez

Art
Sofía Táboas

Editorial Coordination
Verana Codina
Mireya Escalante

Editorial Supervision
Turner

Translation
Pilar Villela
Mónica Galván

Copy Editing
Gregory Dechant
Quentin Pope

Design
David Kimura + Gabriela Varela

Image Processing and Prepress
Juan Carlos Almaguer Vega

Production
Turner

Typefaces
Alegreya and Alegreya Sans

Papers
Fedrigoni Arena White Rough 140 gsm

Print Run
750

First edition, 2020

ISBN 978-84-17866-29-7
Legal Deposit M-25733-2020

Distributed by
TURNER
www.turnerlibros.com

United States
DAP
orders@dapinc.com
www.artbook.com

Europe
ACC
sales@antique-acc.com
www.accdistribution.com/uk

SPANISH EDITION AVAILABLE

Spain
Machado Grupo de Distribución
machadolibros@machadolibros.com

Latin America
Océano
info@oceano.com
www.oceano.com

Made in Mexico
Printed in Spain

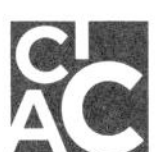

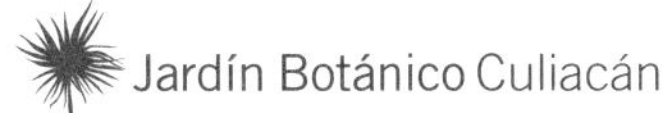

The Palm Collection at the Jardín Botánico Culiacán
was printed in December, 2020 in Madrid, Spain.
Typeset in Alegreya and Alegreya Sans,
designed by Juan Pablo del Peral. 750 copies were
printed for this edition.

* * *